CATO
HANDBOOK
FOR
CONGRESS

CATO HANDBOOK FOR CONGRESS

FOR

CONGRESS

POLICY RECOMMENDATIONS FOR THE 108TH CONGRESS

CATO INSTITUTE

Washington, D.C.

Library of Congress Cataloging-in-Publication Data

Cato Institute.
   Cato handbook for Congress : policy recommendations for the
      108th Congress.
      p. cm.
Edited by Edward H. Crane and David Boaz.
Includes bibliographical references.
ISBN 1-930865-39-2 (pbk : alk. paper)
   1. Political planning—United States. 2. United States—Politics and
government--2001- 3. United States—Economic policy--2001- 4.
United States--Social policy--1993- 5. United States--Foreign
relations--2001- I. Crane, Edward H., 1944- II. Boaz, David, 1953-
III. Title.

JK468.P64C38 2003
320'.6'0973090511—dc21   2002041509

Printed in the United States of America.

CATO INSTITUTE
1000 Massachusetts Ave., N.W.
Washington, D.C. 20001

Contents

MONEY AND BANKING

DOMESTIC POLICY

REGULATION

ENERGY AND ENVIRONMENT

FOREIGN AND DEFENSE POLICY

INTERNATIONAL ECONOMIC POLICY

1. Introduction

Seven years ago, President Bill Clinton informed the nation in his State of the Union address that the "era of big government" was over. It now appears that his pronouncement may have been premature. Turning Clinton's statement on its head, Sen. Charles Schumer (D-N.Y.) wrote in December 2001, "The era of a shrinking federal government has come to a close." Schumer was hardly alone. Well before the wreckage of the World Trade Center had stopped smoldering, such pundits as Francis Fukuyama and George Will were eagerly heralding the "fall" of libertarianism and the "death" of small-government conservatism. September 11 had proven—had it not?—the necessity of a muscular central government with sweeping powers. The wave of corporate scandals beginning with Enron's collapse had proven it again by demonstrating the need for robust regulation to comfort increasingly skittish investors.

In light of this new conventional wisdom, it might seem anachronistic, even quaint, to echo President Reagan's famous claim that "government is not the solution to our problem; government *is* the problem." Who, in these chaotic times, could seriously suggest that we need, not larger and more flexible government, but fewer federal programs, less spending, fewer regulations?

Well, the Cato Institute. Not merely because we have been committed to the principles of limited government, respect for individual rights, and open markets since our inception, but because the new orthodoxy is grossly at variance with reality. Our military and intelligence forces must, of course, focus their full energies on dismantling the al-Qaeda terrorist network and preventing any future attacks against the homeland. But neither public sentiment nor the public good demands a wider scope for government in general. If anything, the great challenges the United States now faces require, more than ever, that its government respect the boundaries set by the Constitution, so that it may focus more vigorously on its core functions.

As poll watchers well know, there was a paradoxical surge of public trust in government following the attacks of September 11, 2001, just

1

when the failure of government to carry out its most central obligation—the protection of the homeland—had been made terrifyingly clear. Perhaps the rise in trust can best be interpreted as a sort of prospective vote of confidence, a reflection, not of our belief in what government had been doing, but in our expectation of its capabilities when put to the test. Optimism has its limits, however, and the most recent data show that long-term trends toward lower public trust in government, and policy preferences favoring smaller government, are beginning to reassert themselves.

Plus Ça Change: The Public Mood

The 1960s and 1970s saw a continual decline in public support for more government activism, a trend that bottomed out in 1980. Support for activism then climbed throughout the 1980s, perhaps because of the prosperity of the era and the perceived success of the Reagan administration. Since 1990, however, the overall trend has been away from support for government activism; in recent years, the policy mood measure has declined steadily and about as steeply as it did during the 1970s. The Washington establishment seems not to realize that, as the 108th Congress convenes, the political mood of Americans is every bit as skeptical as it was in 1981 at the start of the Reagan revolution.

Conventional wisdom notwithstanding, data compiled by University of North Carolina political scientist James Stimson reveal no perceptible shift in this trend as a result of the 2001 terror attacks. Stimson's latest data, from 2002, indicate a continued move away from support for expansive government. The evidence also indicates a renewed decline in public trust in the federal government. For many years survey researchers have asked citizens how much they trusted the federal government to do the right thing. The proportion that answered "just about always" or "most of the time" provides a rough measure of public trust in the federal government. Trust has declined most of the time since its historic high point in the 1960s.

About a month after September 11, Princeton Survey Research Associates posed the trust question to a sample of Americans. They found 57 percent of those polled trusted the federal government to do the right thing "just about always" or "most of the time"—strikingly higher than the recent trend. But this trust soon faded: the same question posed in May 2002 showed that only 40 percent of respondents trusted the federal government. This fits well with a public mood skeptical of expanded federal power. After all, a public that trusts government less and less will hardly demand that it do more and more.

The willingness of a frightened polity to sacrifice civil liberties for the sake of increased security has also ebbed. Early in 2002, a Gallup/CNN/USA Today poll found that 47 percent of those polled thought the government should take all necessary steps to prevent terrorism even if the respondent's civil liberties suffered; 49 percent opposed such steps if the price included their basic civil liberties. By June 2002, 56 percent opposed preventing terrorism at the cost of civil liberties, and 40 percent supported "all necessary steps" against terrorism. Americans seem to be moving back toward their pre–September 11 views on civil liberties.

On a wide variety of issues, citizens are increasingly willing to seek innovative private-sector solutions to problems government has failed to ameliorate. An annual Phi Delta Kappa/Gallup poll on school choice found a dramatic leap in support for vouchers: a majority of those polled would now support a proposal to "allow parents to send their school-age children to any public, private, or church-related school they choose," with government paying part or all of the tuition. Perhaps most surprising, a Cato Institute/Zogby International poll conducted during the stock market slump in the summer of 2002, mere weeks after news of the WorldCom scandal broke, found that more than 68 percent of likely voters favored "changing the Social Security system to give younger workers the choice to invest a portion of their Social Security taxes through individual accounts." Clearly, the prophets of a new "era of big government" are less skilled at gauging voter opinion than they are at projecting their own policy preferences onto the electorate.

The Beltway Cocoon

What explains this massive disparity between what the public wants and what pundits and elected officials seem to think the public wants? In part, it may simply be that the panicked call to "do something" and the resurgence of faith in government following the attacks on New York and Washington, D.C., understandably made a more palpable impression on most observers than the cooling off that followed. The more troublesome explanation, though, is that there exists in Congress a systemic bias toward seeing the expansion of government as a solution to almost every problem. That bias is not a fluke but a direct consequence of the current structure of American electoral politics.

3

Whereas the Founders of the American republic envisioned a government of citizen legislators for whom public service would be a solemn but *temporary* charge, we now see a regime composed almost exclusively of professional politicians. It was not always this way: average congressional tenure has risen steeply over the past century. Chief among the culprits responsible for this change is the huge and growing advantage enjoyed by House incumbents, who in recent years have seen reelection rates rise above 98 percent. In addition to all the traditional privileges afforded incumbents—a staff devoted to constituent service, the power of franking, access to Congress's television studio, to say nothing of the ability to name hospitals and highways after oneself—sitting legislators are now protected by increasingly stringent campaign finance laws, which limit the ability of challengers to overcome those advantages through vigorous political speech. Even redistricting, which historically led to dozens of more competitive congressional races, has deteriorated into a bipartisan, computer-driven process of incumbent protection.

Incumbent advantage leads to a vicious cycle, wherein the most competent potential challengers are deterred from entering contests, except those for open seats, further tightening the incumbent's hold on power. As incumbent protection drives up average tenure, the amount of time one must be willing to commit to politics in order to build support or secure an influential committee chair also increases. Decades of this process have transformed politics into a game worth playing only for those determined to make a career of it.

This may not be entirely bad: some such people may just be unusually committed to public service. But whatever their motives, those who find the prospect of spending their lives in government attractive are also likely to have an inflated view of the role and importance of the state in American life. An old story about the chess genius Bobby Fischer has him interrupting a conversation about politics between some fellow players with the demand, "What's that got to do with chess?" Entrenched political classes are afflicted with a parallel sort of myopia. For them, discussion of any public benefit bubbling up from civil society or the private sector provokes the response, "What has that got to do with a new federal program?" To promote real political leadership, it will probably be necessary to change the institutional constraints that give rise to that kind of tunnel vision. In the meantime, however, legislators who sincerely desire to serve the public trust must force themselves to notice this pervasive bias and to overcome it.

Terror and Scandal

The two developments most frequently cited as evidence for the necessity of enlarging government power are the War on Terror and the spate of corporate accounting scandals that began with Enron's collapse. Legislators have been eager to propose new laws intended to combat both terror and corporate malfeasance, but there has been far less examination of how existing laws contributed to both problems. While new laws may in some instances be both necessary and proper, we should put first things first. Before we contemplate what else we can do to make things better, we ought to ask what we may already be doing to make things worse.

Crooked CEOs are wholly responsible for defrauding investors, but as William Niskanen observes in Chapter 22, legal incentives increased both the likelihood of the bankruptcies that fraud was intended to cover and the lack of managerial accountability that made the fraud itself possible. Biases in the tax code encourage corporations to take on excessive debt and to compensate CEOs in the form of stock options. Since option holders can win big on a dramatic rise in the price of their companies' stock, but lose nothing if it drops further below the exercise price, options encourage them to take larger risks than they otherwise might. Moreover, corporate governance rules—an inscrutable tangle of federal securities laws, state regulations, and policies particular to each company—have left managers increasingly insulated from the shareholder scrutiny and control that might check unsound business practices. In the long term, fixing these structural imbalances will do more to prevent future scandals than will parading a few handcuffed CEOs before the evening news cameras.

Of course, when malfeasance does occur, there is surely a place for government in punishing deception. However, instead of asking why the Securities and Exchange Commission failed to use its already ample powers to catch that deception earlier on, Congress, eager to demonstrate its "toughness," tipped the balance too far in the other direction by effectively criminalizing corporate risk taking and created a redundant Accounting Oversight Board of dubious constitutionality.

The government's response to terror has in many ways been equally unreflective. There has been no serious examination of how government failed on September 11. We have not yet had an independent investigation of intelligence and other failures. But we know that poor communication between intelligence agencies led to the neglect of numerous warning signs that an attack was imminent. We know that the Immigration and Naturalization Service was not keeping track of people who entered on temporary visas. We know that for more than a year, both before and after September 11, the FBI kept 10 agents employed conducting a full-time wiretap of a New Orleans brothel. We know that at the moment the planes crashed into the World Trade Center, the president of the United States was in an elementary school classroom in Florida—a striking example of the federal government's loss of focus on its essential functions in an endless and diffuse morass of programs.

It would be natural to conclude that federal law enforcement has used its existing powers ineffectively—perhaps because it has been forced to squander its energies on prying in the bedrooms of adults, breaking down the doors of sick people who smoke marijuana, and carrying out police functions that both intelligent policy and constitutional fidelity demand be left to the states. Instead, Congress's response has been to fiddle a bit with the Federal Emergency Management Agency and the INS and create new layers of bureaucracy—apparently on the theory that nothing speeds along the smooth flow of information like more red tape—while leaving the major structural problems unaddressed. Instead of finding ways to make better use of existing police and intelligence powers, it has recklessly added to those powers. It is almost as though endless discussions of the "tradeoffs between liberty and security" have led us to infer that constricting liberty automatically increases security. Yet as Robert Levy and Timothy Lynch argue in their analyses of current threats to civil liberties in Chapters 12 and 13, proposals to introduce a national ID or to try "enemy combatants," as determined via executive fiat, by military tribunal would do little to make Americans safer. They would, in fact, have only one absolutely certain effect: the evisceration of citizens' rights to privacy and due process.

No less troubling is our newly bellicose approach to foreign affairs. The kind of hysterical overreaction to hypothetical worst-case scenarios that was once the exclusive province of the most radical fringe of the environmental movement has apparently found a home at the heart of the current administration. At a time when we have more than enough proven threats with which to cope, advocates of "preemption" would have us swing erratically from perceived enemy to perceived enemy. This disastrous prescription would blur our collective focus, undermining our efforts to break the back of the terrorist networks that are our most pressing concern, and, indeed, swelling their ranks. Osama bin Laden would surely like nothing better than an American attempt to establish an imperial caliphate in the heart of the Muslim world; the administration's reasons for sharing his eagerness are opaque.

Conclusion

Fidelity to our founding principles of respect for civil liberties and limited government is easy when times are easy, as they were through much of the tech boom of the 1990s. The true test of our faith in those principles comes now, when we are beset by diabolical assaults from without and economic turmoil within, when public anxiety may temporarily make it seem expedient to put those principles aside.

We know that the Constitution is functioning properly when it frustrates us. Bland and innocuous speech has little need of constitutional protections; the First Amendment exists to safeguard the contentious, provocative, and even offensive speech that stirs censorious impulses. By the same token, the importance of paying scrupulous deference to the Constitution's limits on federal power, of respecting its careful system of checks and balances, is greatest precisely when the temptation to flout them is strongest. The enemies of freedom have made their horrifying statement already. By demonstrating a commitment to the core ideals of a constitutional republic, the defenders of freedom now have an opportunity to make theirs. This *Handbook* provides the policy vocabulary from which that statement can be constructed. In these pages, our scholars survey the major issues confronting the 108th Congress and provide concrete recommendations with the goal of preserving both the security to which Americans are entitled and the freedom that serves as a beacon to the world and a reproach to our enemies.

Suggested Readings

Bastiat, Frederic. *The Law.* 1850. Irvington, N.Y.: Foundation for Economic Education, 1998.

Boaz, David. *Libertarianism: A Primer.* New York: Free Press, 1997.

Brooks, David L., ed. *From Magna Carta to the Constitution: Documents in the Struggle for Liberty.* San Francisco: Fox & Wilkes, 1993.

Constitution of the United States of America.

Crane, Edward H. *Defending Civil Society.* Cato's Letter no. 8. Washington: Cato Institute, 1994.

Epstein, Richard. *Simple Rules for a Complex World.* Cambridge, Mass.: Harvard University Press, 1995.

Friedman, Milton. *Capitalism and Freedom.* Chicago: University of Chicago Press, 1962.

Friedman, Milton, and Rose D. Friedman. *The Tyranny of the Status Quo.* San Diego: Harcourt Brace, 1984.

Higgs, Robert. *Crisis and Leviathan: Critical Episodes in the Growth of American Government.* Oxford: Oxford University Press, 1987.

Murray, Charles. *In Pursuit: Of Happiness and Good Government.* New York: Simon & Schuster, 1988.

—Prepared by Edward H. Crane and David Boaz

2. Limited Government and the Rule of Law

> **Congress should**
>
> - live up to its constitutional obligations and cease the practice of delegating legislative powers to administrative agencies; legislation should be passed by Congress, not by unelected administration officials;
> - before voting on any proposed act, ask whether that exercise of power is authorized by the Constitution, which enumerates the powers of Congress;
> - exercise its constitutional authority to approve only those appointees to federal judgeships who will take seriously the constitutional limitations on the powers of both states and the federal government; and
> - pass and send to the states for their approval a constitutional amendment limiting senators to two terms in office and representatives to three terms, in order to return the legislature to citizen legislators.

Limited government is one of the greatest accomplishments of humanity. It is imperfectly enjoyed by only a portion of the human race, and, where it is enjoyed, its tenure is ever precarious. The experience of the 20th century is surely witness to the insecurity of constitutional government and to the need for courage in achieving it and vigilance in maintaining it.

Advocates of limited government are not anti-government per se, as some people would charge. Rather, they are hostile to concentrations of coercive power and to the arbitrary use of power against right. With a deep appreciation for the lessons of history and the dangers of unconstrained government, they are for constitutionally limited government, with the delegated authority and means to protect our rights, but not so powerful as to destroy or negate them.

The American system was established to provide limited government. The independent existence of the United States was based on certain truths:

> that all Men are created equal, that they are endowed by their Creator with certain unalienable Rights, that among these are Life, Liberty, and the Pursuit of Happiness—That to secure these Rights, Governments are instituted among Men, deriving their just Powers from the Consent of the Governed, that whenever any Form of Government becomes destructive of these Ends, it is the Right of the People to alter or to abolish it, and to institute new Government, laying its Foundation on such Principles, and organizing its Powers in such Form, as to them shall seem most likely to effect their Safety and Happiness.

On this foundation the American Founders established a system of government based on delegated, enumerated, and thus limited powers.

The American Founders did not pluck these truths out of thin air, nor did they simply invent the principles of American government. They drew from their knowledge of thousands of years of human history, during which many peoples struggled for liberty and limited government. There were both defeats and victories along the way. The results were distilled in the founding documents of the American experiment in limited government: the Declaration of Independence, the Articles of Confederation, the state constitutions, and the Constitution of the United States.

The American Founders were careful students of history. It was Thomas Jefferson, in his influential *A Summary View of the Rights of British America*, prepared in 1774, who noted that "history has informed us that bodies of men as well as individuals are susceptible of the spirit of tyranny." Another Founder, Patrick Henry, devoted great attention to the study of history. He summed up the importance of history thus: "I have but one lamp by which my feet are guided, and that is the lamp of experience. I know of no way of judging the future but by the past." History—the lamp of experience—is indispensable to understanding and defending the liberty of the individual under constitutionally limited, representative government.

Through the study of history the Americans learned about the division of power among judicial, legislative, and executive branches; about federalism; about checks and balances among divided powers; about redress and representation; and about the right of resistance, made effective by the legal right to bear arms, an ancient right of free persons. Liberty and limited government were not invented in 1776; they were reaffirmed and strengthened. The American Revolution set the stage for the benefits of liberty and limited government to be extended to all. As John Figgis, professor of modern history at Cambridge University, noted at the beginning of the 20th century:

> The sonorous phrases of the Declaration of Independence . . . are not an original discovery, they are the heirs of all the ages, the depository of the emotions and the thoughts of seventy generations of culture.

The roots of the history of limited government stretch far back, to the establishment of the principle of the higher law by the ancient Hebrews and by the Greek philosophers. The story of the Golden Calf in the Book of Exodus and the investigations of nature by Aristotle both established— in very different ways—the principle of the higher law. Law is not merely an expression of will or power; it is based on transcendent principles. The legislator is as bound by law as is the subject or citizen; no one is above the law.

Many strands have been entwined to form the fabric of liberty:

- The struggle between church and state, which was put into high gear in the Latin West by Pope Gregory VII in the 11th century under the motto, "freedom of the church." That movement, which created an institutional distinction between the church and the secular authorities, was the first major "privatization" of a previously state-owned industry (the church) and provided the foundation for such important institutions as the rule of law and legal accountability, federalism, and the independent and self-governing associations that make up civil society.
- The growth of civil society in the self-governing chartered towns of Europe, in which the guiding principle was "city air makes one free." The independent cities of Europe were the seedbeds of modern civil society—of the market economy, of personal liberty, and of the security of person and property.
- The fixing of limits on the powers of monarchs and executives through written constitutions. The Magna Carta of 1215 is the most memorable of those documents to inheritors of the Anglo-Saxon political tradition. It included the requirement that taxes could not be imposed without the consent of the "general council of the realm," which provided the origin of the English parliament, as well as other very specific limitations on the king's power, including the stipulations that no

one be imprisoned or outlawed or exiled or his estate seized "except by the lawful judgment of his peers or the law of the land" and that "merchants shall have safe conduct in and out of England." That was the precursor of the Petition of Right of 1628, the Bill of Rights of 1689, the American Declaration of Independence, and the American Constitution and Bill of Rights.

Those various movements reinforced each other in a multitude of ways. The assertion of the freedom of the church and even of its supremacy over the secular powers was bound up with the idea of the higher law, by which all are judged—emperor, pope, and peasant alike. As legal scholar Henry Bracton, a judge during the reign of Henry III, noted of the royal authority, "The law makes him king. Let the king therefore give to the law what the law gives to him, dominion and power; for there is no king where will, and not law, bears rule." Were the king to consider himself above the law, it was the job of the king's council—the precursor of parliament—to rein him in: "if the king were without a bridle, that is, the law, they ought to put a bridle upon him." Not only was the nascent parliament above the king; the law was above the parliament, as Sir Edward Coke noted in the 17th century:

> when an act of Parliament is against common right and reason, or repugnant, or impossible to be performed, the common law will controul it, and adjudge such Act to be void.

The supremacy of the law over the exercise of power is a hallmark of the Western legal tradition. The rule of law is not satisfied by merely formal or ceremonial exercises, such as the publication of edicts in barely understandable form, whether in the archaic "Law French" of the king's courts or the pages of the *Federal Register*, the laws must be understandable and actually capable of being followed.

There was also widespread recognition of the principle of reciprocity between the holders of power and the general populace. Rights were spelled out in contractual form in constitutions and charters. Those rights were not gifts from the powerful, which could be taken away on a whim, but something on which one could take a stand. Tied up in the notion of a chartered right was the ancillary right to defend that right, even to the point of resistance with force of arms. The higher law, reciprocity and mutuality of obligations, written charters of rights, the right to be consulted on policy and to grant or refuse one's consent, and the right of resistance in defense of those rights are the foundations of constitutionally limited government. They were won over many centuries at great sacrifice.

Just how precious that heritage is can be gleaned from comparing it with the history of Russia, where, until very recently, there was no reciprocity between rulers and ruled and no independent power able to challenge the rulers. The principality of Muscovy and its successors were despotic to a high degree, with no charters of liberty, no power higher than the tsar (or his successor, the Communist Party), no limits on power—in effect, no law. As Harvard University historian Richard Pipes noted in his book *Russia under the Old Regime*, ''There is no evidence in medieval Russia of mutual obligations binding prince and his servitor, and, therefore, also nothing resembling legal and moral 'rights' of subjects, and little need for law and courts.'' The immense difficulties in establishing the rule of law, a system of well-defined and legally secure property, and a market economy are testimony to the great and vital importance of building on a tradition of stable, constitutionally limited government. They also remind us how important it is for us to maintain our heritage of limited government and the rule of law.

The struggle for limited government was a struggle of liberty against power. The demands for religious liberty and the protection of property were fused in the heroic resistance of the Netherlands to the Empire of Spain in their great revolt. The Dutch inspired the English to rise up against the Stuart kings, who sought to fasten upon the English the absolutism that had made such headway on the Continent. The American Revolution was one link in a long chain of revolutions for liberty. The historian John Lothrop Motley opened his magisterial history *The Rise of the Dutch Republic* by connecting the Dutch Republic with the United States of America:

> The rise of the Dutch Republic must ever be regarded as one of the leading events of modern times. . . . The maintenance of the right by the little provinces of Holland and Zealand in the sixteenth, by Holland and England united in the seventeenth, and by the United States of America in the eighteenth centuries, forms but a single chapter in the great volume of human fate; for the so-called revolutions of Holland, England, and America, are all links of one chain.

Motley continued:

> For America the spectacle is one of still deeper import. The Dutch Republic originated in the opposition of the rational elements of human nature to

13

sacerdotal dogmatism and persecution—in the courageous resistance of historical and chartered liberty to foreign despotism.

The Dutch, like the British and the Americans after them, became a shining example of what was possible when people were free: prosperity was possible without the guiding hand of the king and his bureaucrats; social harmony was possible without enforced religious conformity; law and government were possible without an unlimited and absolute sovereign.

The story of the attempts to institute absolutism in the Netherlands and in England was well known by the American Founders, who were, after all, British colonists. One cannot understand the American attempt to institute limited, representative government without understanding the history of England. What they were struggling against was the principle that the powers of the state are "plenary," that they fill up the whole space of power. King James I of England (then King James VI of Scotland) had written in 1598 that "the King is above the law, as both the author and giver of strength thereto." In 1610 James made *A Speech to the Lords and Commons of the Parliament at White-Hall* in which he railed against the notions of popular consent and the rule of law and stated that "as to dispute what God may do is blasphemy . . . so it is sedition in subjects to dispute what a king may do in the height of his power."

In other words, there are no limits to power. Distinct echoes of that view are still heard today. For example, the solicitor general of the United States, Drew Days, arguing in the case of *United States v. Lopez* before the Supreme Court, was unable to identify a single act of Congress, other than those expressly prohibited by the Constitution, that would be impermissible under the Clinton administration's expansive view of the Commerce Clause. Solicitor Days contended that the powers of Congress are plenary, that is, unlimited, unless, perhaps, specifically prohibited. That all-too-common view turns the notion of limited government on its head. Limited government means that government is limited both to the exercise of its delegated powers and in the means it can employ, which must be both "necessary and proper." The English Revolution of 1640, the Glorious Revolution of 1688, and the American Revolution of 1776 were fought precisely to combat unlimited government. What Americans need is not unlimited government, as Days proposed, but limited government under law, exercising delegated and enumerated powers. That is how the equal liberties of citizens are protected. As the philosopher John Locke, himself an active participant in the struggles for limited government in Britain and the primary inspiration of the American revolutionaries, argued in his *Second Treatise on Government*:

> *The end of Law* is not to abolish or restrain, but *to preserve and enlarge Freedom*: For in all the states of created beings capable of Laws, where *there is no Law, there is no Freedom.* For *Liberty* is to be free from restraint and violence from others, which cannot be, where there is no Law: But Freedom is not, as we are told, *A Liberty for every Man to do what he lists*: (For who could be free, when every other Man's Humour might domineer over him?) But a *Liberty* to dispose, and order, as he lists, his Person, Actions, Possessions, and his whole Property, within the Allowance of those Laws under which he is; and therein not to be subject to the arbitrary Will of another, but freely follow his own.

The American experiment in limited government generated a degree of liberty and prosperity that was virtually unimaginable only a few centuries before. That experiment revealed flaws, of course, none of which was more striking and repugnant than the toleration of slavery, or "man-stealing," as it was called by its libertarian opponents, for it deprived an individual of his property in his own person. That particular evil was eliminated by the Thirteenth Amendment to the Constitution, showing the self-correcting nature and basic resilience of the American constitutional system, which could survive such a cataclysm as the Civil War.

Other flaws, however, have been revealed or have surfaced since. Among them are the following:

- An erosion of the basic principles of federalism, as the federal government has consistently encroached on the authority of the states. Federal criminalization of acts that are already criminalized by the states, for example, usurps state authority (as well as circumventing—opinions of the Supreme Court notwithstanding—the prohibition of double jeopardy in the Fifth Amendment to Constitution: "nor shall any person be subject for the same offense to be twice put in jeopardy of life or limb"). An even more striking contemporary example of the overreach of federal law is the continued exercise of federal controls over marijuana use in the nine states that have broken with federal law and allow medical use of that drug. The Tenth Amendment is quite explicit on this point: "The powers not delegated to the United States by the Constitution, nor prohibited by it to the States, are reserved to the States respectively, or to the people."
- Violation of the separation of powers between the various branches of government. In Article I, section 8, for example, the Constitution

15

explicitly reserves the power to declare war to the Congress, a power that the Congress has allowed to be usurped by the executive branch and which it should retake to itself.

- Failure of the legislative branch to fulfill its responsibilities when it delegates its legislative powers to administrative agencies of the executive branch, such as the Food and Drug Administration and the Federal Trade Commission. In addition to violating the Constitution, that has led to the erosion of the rule of law, as such administrative agencies have burdened the population with an unimaginably complex welter of edicts; the *Federal Register* ran 64,431 pages in 2001, reflecting a degree of minute regulation that is unreasonable and burdensome and that virtually guarantees that any citizen involved in a commercial transaction, for example, will run afoul of some part of it, no matter how well intentioned or scrupulous he or she may be. Such a situation is an invitation to the arbitrary exercise of power, rather than the application of law. That illegal delegation of powers is an abdication of the representative function described in the *Federalist Papers* and elsewhere by the Founders. Members of Congress are thereby converted from representatives of their constituents into "fixers," who offer to intercede on behalf of constituents with the agencies that are illegally exercising the authority of the legislative branch. Thus, members of Congress can avoid responsibility for onerous laws but can take credit for gaining special treatment for their constituents. That system may be thoroughly congenial to the interests of the existing officeholders of both the executive and the legislative branches, but it is directly contrary to the doctrine of the separation of powers and to the very concept of representative government.

- Inattention to the important role of the federal judiciary as a check on arbitrary and unauthorized exercises of power. Especially since the Court-packing "constitutional revolution of 1937," there has been too little attention by the federal judiciary—and by the Congress in ratifying judicial nominees—to fulfilling the role of the courts in enforcing constitutional restraints on both the federal and the state governments, as set out in Article III, section 2, of the Constitution. Sections of the Constitution that have suffered from relative neglect include Article I, section 1 ("All legislative Powers herein granted shall be vested in a Congress of the United States"); Article I, section 8 (enumerating and thus limiting the powers of Congress); Article I, section 10 ("No state shall ... pass any ... Law impairing the Obligation of Contracts"); the Fifth Amendment ("No person shall be ... deprived of life, liberty, or property, without due process of law; nor shall private property be taken for public use without just compensation"); the Ninth Amendment ("The enumeration in the Constitution of certain rights shall not be construed to deny or disparage others retained by the people"); the Tenth Amendment ("The powers not delegated to the United States by the Constitution, nor prohibited by it to the States, are reserved to the States respectively, or to the people"); and the Fourteenth Amendment ("No state shall make or enforce any law which shall abridge the privileges or immunities of citizens of the United States"). Although the First and Fourteenth Amendments have indeed been the source of significant judicial activity, the Court has not consistently applied the prohibitions of the First Amendment to either commercial speech or political speech (the latter in the context of campaign finance), nor has the Court rectified the novel (and specious) distinction between personal liberties and economic liberties drawn by Justice Harlan F. Stone in *United States v. Carolene Products Co.* (1938).

- The failure to pass a constitutional amendment limiting members of the Senate to two terms and members of the House of Representatives to three terms. Just as the president is limited in the number of terms he or she can serve, so should be the other elected branch of government, to guarantee the rotation in office that the Founders believed essential to popular government.

Those flaws can, however, be corrected. What is needed is the courage to place the health of the constitutional order and the future of the American system above short-term political gain. The original American Founders were willing "to mutually pledge to each other our Lives, our Fortunes, and our sacred Honor." Nothing even remotely approaching that would be necessary for today's members of Congress to renew and restore the American system of constitutionally limited government.

In defending the separation of powers established by the Constitution, James Madison clearly tied the arrangement to the goal of limiting government power:

> It may be a reflection on human nature that such devices should be necessary to control the abuses of government. But what is government itself but the greatest of all reflections on human nature? If men were angels, no govern-

17

ment would be necessary. If angels were to govern men, neither external nor internal controls would be necessary. In framing a government which is to be administered by men over men, the great difficulty lies in this: you must first enable the government to control the governed; and in the next instance oblige it to control itself. A dependence on the people is, no doubt, the primary control on the government; but experience has taught mankind the necessity of auxiliary precautions.

What is needed for the survival of limited government is a renewal of both of the forces described by Madison as controls on government: dependence on the people, in the form of an informed citizenry jealous of its rights and ever vigilant against unconstitutional or otherwise unwarranted exercises of power, and officeholders who take seriously their oaths of office and accept the responsibilities they entail.

Suggested Readings

Berman, Harold. *Law and Revolution: The Formation of the Western Legal Tradition.* Cambridge, Mass.: Harvard University Press, 1983.

Boaz, David. *Libertarianism: A Primer.* New York: Free Press, 1997.

Boaz, David, ed. *The Libertarian Reader: Classic and Contemporary Readings from Lao-tzu to Milton Friedman.* New York: Free Press, 1997.

Bramsted, E. K., and K. J. Melhuish, eds. *Western Liberalism: A History in Documents from Locke to Croce.* New York: Longman, 1978.

Brooks, David L., ed. *From Magna Carta to the Constitution: Documents in the Struggle for Liberty.* San Francisco: Fox & Wilkes, 1993.

Ely, James W. Jr. *The Guardian of Every Other Right: A Constitutional History of Property Rights.* New York: Oxford University Press, 1998.

Epstein, Richard A. *Simple Rules for a Complex World.* Cambridge, Mass.: Harvard University Press, 1997.

————. *Takings: Private Property and the Right of Eminent Domain.* Cambridge, Mass.: Harvard University Press, 1985.

Hamilton, Alexander, James Madison, and John Jay, *The Federalist Papers.* New York: Mentor, 1961.

Hayek, F. A. *The Constitution of Liberty.* Chicago: University of Chicago Press, 1960.

Higgs, Robert. *Crisis and Leviathan: Critical Episodes in the Growth of American Government.* New York: Oxford University Press, 1987.

Jefferson, Thomas. "A Summary View of the Rights of British North America." In *The Portable Jefferson.* New York: Penguin Books, 1977.

Locke, John. *Two Treatises of Government.* 1690. Cambridge: Cambridge University Press, 1988.

Spencer, Herbert. *Political Writings.* Cambridge: Cambridge University Press, 1994.

Storing, Herbert, ed. *The Anti-Federalist.* Chicago: University of Chicago Press, 1985.

—Prepared by Tom G. Palmer

3. Congress, the Courts, and the Constitution

Congress should

- encourage constitutional debate in the nation by engaging in constitutional debate in Congress, as was urged by the House Constitutional Caucus during the 104th Congress;
- enact nothing without first consulting the Constitution for proper authority and then debating that question on the floors of the House and the Senate;
- move toward restoring constitutional government by carefully returning power wrongly taken over the years from the states and the people; and
- reject the nomination of judicial candidates who do not appreciate that the Constitution is a document of delegated, enumerated, and thus limited powers.

Introduction

In a chapter devoted to advising members of Congress about their responsibilities under the Constitution, one hardly knows where to begin—so far has Congress taken us, over the 20th century, from constitutional government. James Madison, the principal author of the Constitution, assured us in *Federalist* no. 45 that the powers of the federal government under that document were "few and defined." No one believes that describes Washington's powers today. That raises fundamental questions about the constitutional legitimacy of modern American government.

For a while at century's end, after the realigning election of 1994, it looked like Congress was at last going to rethink its seemingly inexorable push toward ever-larger government. In fact, the 104th Congress saw the creation in the House of a 100-strong Constitutional Caucus dedicated to promoting the restoration of limited constitutional government. And shortly thereafter, President Clinton announced that the era of big government was over. But the spirit of that Congress has waned over time. By the 107th Congress, respect for constitutional limits on congressional power was all but gone.

The principles of the matter have not gone away, however; nor of course has the Constitution itself. It is still the law of the land, however little Congress heeds it. And the moral, political, and economic implications of limited constitutional government have not changed either. That kind of government is the foundation for liberty, prosperity, and the vision of equality that most people cherish. Indeed, that insight has been gaining ground around the world as the Leviathans of the 20th century have aged or crumbled. Yet all too many members of Congress seem still to believe that the good life is brought about primarily by government programs, not by individuals acting in their private capacities. And they believe equally that the Constitution authorizes them to enact such programs.

In growing numbers, however, Americans know better. Below the level that polling usually reaches, they have come to see that government rarely solves the problems it purports to solve; in fact, it usually makes those problems worse. More deeply, they have come to understand that a life dependent on government is too often not only impoverishing but impoverished. It is no accident, therefore, that the electoral trends of the past quarter of a century have been in the direction of less government, even if Washington has been slow to appreciate that message.

In moving from a world in which government is expected to solve our problems to a world in which individuals, families, and communities assume that responsibility—indeed, take up that challenge—the basic questions are how much and how fast to reduce government. Those are not questions about how to make government run better—government will always be plagued by waste, fraud, and abuse—but about the fundamental role of government in this nation.

How Much to Reduce Government

The first of those questions—how much to reduce government—would seem on first impression to be a matter of policy; yet in America, if we take the Constitution seriously, it is not for the most part a policy question, a question about what we may or may not want to do. For the Founding Fathers thought long and hard about the proper role of government in our lives, and they set forth their thoughts in a document that explicitly enumerates the powers of the federal government.

Thus, setting aside for the moment all practical concerns, the Constitution tells us as a matter of first principle how much to reduce government by telling us, first, what powers the federal government in fact has and, second, how governments at all levels must exercise their powers—by respecting the rights of the people.

That means that if a federal power or federal program is not authorized by the Constitution, it is illegitimate. Given the present size of government, that is a stark conclusion, to be sure. But it flows quite naturally from the Tenth Amendment, the final statement in the Bill of Rights, which says, "The powers not delegated to the United States by the Constitution, nor prohibited by it to the States, are reserved to the States respectively, or to the people." In a nutshell, the Constitution establishes a government of delegated, enumerated, and thus limited powers. As the *Federalist Papers* make clear, the Constitution was written not simply to empower the federal government but to limit it as well.

Since the Progressive Era, however, the politics of government as problem solver has dominated our public discourse. And since the collapse of the Supreme Court during the New Deal, following President Roosevelt's notorious Court-packing scheme, the Court has abetted that view by standing the Constitution on its head, turning it into a document of effectively unenumerated and hence unlimited powers. (For a fuller discussion of the Constitution and the history of its interpretation, see Chapter 3 of the *Cato Handbook for Congress: 104th Congress*.)

Indeed, limits on government today come largely from political and budgetary rather than from constitutional considerations. Thus, it has not been because of any perceived lack of constitutional authority that government in recent years has failed to undertake a program, when that has happened, but because of practical limits on the power of government to tax and borrow—and even those limits have failed in times of economic prosperity. That is not the mark of a limited, constitutional republic. It is the mark of a parliamentary system, limited only by periodic elections.

The Founding Fathers could have established such a system, of course. They did not. But we have allowed those marks of a parliamentary system to supplant the system they gave us. To restore truly limited government, therefore, we have to do more than define the issues as political or budgetary. We have to go to the heart of the matter and raise the underlying constitutional questions. In a word, we have to ask the most fundamental question of all: does the government have the authority, the constitutional authority, to do what it is doing?

How Fast to Reduce Government

As a practical matter, however, before Congress or the courts can relimit government as it was meant to be limited by the Constitution, they need to take seriously the problems posed by the present state of public debate on the subject. It surely counts for something that a substantial number of Americans—to say nothing of the organs of public opinion—have little apprehension of or appreciation for the constitutional limits on activist government. Thus, in addressing the question of how fast to reduce government, we have to recognize that the Supreme Court, after more than 65 years of arguing otherwise, is hardly in a position, by itself, to relimit government in the far-reaching way a properly applied Constitution requires. But neither does Congress at this point have sufficient moral authority, even if it wanted to, to end tomorrow the vast array of programs it has enacted over the years with insufficient constitutional authority.

For either Congress or the Court to be able to do fully what should be done, therefore, a proper foundation must first be laid. In essence, the climate of opinion must be such that a sufficiently large portion of the American public stands behind the changes that are undertaken. When enough people come forward to ask—indeed, to demand—that government limit itself to the powers it is given in the Constitution, thereby freeing individuals, families, and communities to solve their own problems, we will know we are on the right track.

Fortunately, a change in the climate of opinion on such basic questions has been under way for some time now. The debate today is very different than it was only a decade ago, much less a quarter of a century ago. But there is a good deal more to be done before Congress and the courts are able to move in the right direction in any far-reaching way, much less say that they have restored constitutional government in America. To continue the process, then, Congress should take the lead in the following ways.

Encourage Constitutional Debate in the Nation by Engaging in Constitutional Debate in Congress, As Was Urged by the House Constitutional Caucus during the 104th Congress

Under the leadership of House freshmen like J. D. Hayworth and John Shadegg of Arizona, Sam Brownback of Kansas, and Bob Barr of Georgia, together with a few senior congressmen like Richard Pombo of California, an informal Constitutional Caucus was established in the "radical" 104th Congress. Its purpose was to encourage constitutional debate in Congress and the nation and, in time, to restore constitutional government. Unfortunately, the caucus has been moribund since then. It needs to be revived—along with the spirit of the 104th Congress—and its work needs to be expanded.

The caucus was created in response to the belief that the nation had strayed very far from its constitutional roots and that Congress, absent leadership from elsewhere in government, should begin addressing the problem. By itself, of course, neither the caucus nor the entire Congress can solve the problem. To be sure, in a reversal of all human experience, Congress in a day could agree to limit itself to its enumerated powers and then roll back the countless programs it has enacted by exceeding that authority. But it would take authoritative opinions from the Supreme Court, reversing a substantial body of largely post–New Deal decisions, to embed those restraints in "constitutional law"—even if they have been embedded in the Constitution from the outset, the Court's modern readings of the document notwithstanding.

The Goals of the Constitutional Caucus

The ultimate goal of the caucus and Congress, then, should be to encourage the Court to reach such decisions. But history teaches, as noted above, that the Court does not operate entirely in a vacuum, that to some degree public opinion is the precursor and seedbed of its decisions. Thus, the more immediate goal of the caucus should be to influence the debate in the nation by influencing the debate in Congress. To do that, it is not necessary or even desirable, in the present climate, that every member of Congress be a member of the caucus—however worthy that end might ultimately be—but it is necessary that those who join the caucus be committed to its basic ends. And it is necessary that members establish a clear agenda for reaching those ends.

To reduce the problem to its essence, every day members of Congress are besieged by requests to enact countless measures to solve endless problems. Indeed, listening to much of the recent campaign debate, one might conclude that no problem is too personal or too trivial to warrant the attention of the federal government. Yet most of the "problems" Congress spends most of its time addressing—from health care to day care to retirement security to economic competition—are simply the personal and economic problems of life that individuals, families, and firms, not governments, should be addressing. What is more, as a basic point of constitutional doctrine, under a constitution like ours, interpreted as ours was meant to be interpreted, there is little authority for government at any level to address such problems.

Properly understood and used, then, the Constitution can be a valuable ally in the efforts of the caucus and Congress to reduce the size and scope of government. For in the minds and hearts of most Americans, it remains a revered document, however little it may be understood by a substantial number of them.

The Constitutional Vision

If the Constitution is to be thus used, however, the principal misunderstanding that surrounds it must be recognized and addressed. In particular, the modern idea that the Constitution, without further amendment, is an infinitely elastic document that allows government to grow to meet public demands of whatever kind must be challenged. More Americans than presently do must come to appreciate that the Founding Fathers, who were keenly aware of the expansive tendencies of government, wrote the Constitution precisely to check that kind of thinking and that possibility. To be sure, the Founders meant for government to be our servant, not our master, but they meant it to serve us in a very limited way—by securing our rights, as the Declaration of Independence says, and by doing those few other things that government does best, as spelled out in the Constitution.

In all else, we were meant to be free—to plan and live our own lives, to solve our own problems, which is what freedom is all about. Some may characterize that vision as tantamount to saying, "You're on your own," but that kind of response simply misses the point. In America individuals, families, and organizations have never been "on their own" in the most important sense. They have always been members of communities, of civil society, where they could live their lives and solve their problems by following a few simple rules about individual initiative and responsibility, respect for property and promise, and charity toward the few who need help from others. Massive government planning and programs have upset that natural order of things—less so in America than elsewhere, but very deeply all the same.

Those are the issues that need to be discussed, both in human and in constitutional terms. We need, as a people, to rethink our relationship to government. We need to ask not what government can do for us but what we can do for ourselves and, where necessary, for others—not through government but apart from government, as private citizens and organizations. That is what the Constitution was written to enable. It empowers government in a very limited way. It empowers people—by leaving them free—in every other way.

To proclaim and eventually secure that vision of a free people, the Constitutional Caucus should reconstitute itself and rededicate itself to that end at the beginning of the 108th Congress and the beginning of every Congress thereafter. Standing apart from Congress, the caucus should nonetheless be both of and above Congress—as the constitutional conscience of Congress. Every member of Congress, before taking office, swears to support the Constitution—hardly a constraining oath, given the modern Court's open-ended reading of the document. Members of the caucus should dedicate themselves to the deeper meaning of that oath. They should support the Constitution the Framers gave us, as amended by subsequent generations, not as "amended" by the Court's expansive interpretations.

Encouraging Debate

Acting together, the members of the caucus could have a major impact on the course of public debate in this nation—not least, by virtue of their numbers. What is more, there is political safety in those numbers. As Benjamin Franklin might have said, no single member of Congress is likely to be able to undertake the task of restoring constitutional government on his own, for in the present climate he would surely be hanged, politically, for doing so. But if the caucus hangs together, the task will be made more bearable and enjoyable—and a propitious outcome made more likely.

On the agenda of the caucus, then, should be those specific undertakings that will best stir debate and thereby move the climate of opinion. Drawn together by shared understandings, and unrestrained by the need for serious compromise, the members of the caucus are free to chart a principled course and employ principled means, which they should do.

They might begin, for example, by surveying opportunities for constitutional debate in Congress, then making plans to seize those opportunities. Clearly, when new bills are introduced, or old ones are up for reauthorization, an opportunity is presented to debate constitutional questions. But even before that, when plans are discussed in party sessions, members should raise constitutional issues. Again, the caucus might study the costs and benefits of eliminating clearly unconstitutional programs, the better to determine which can be eliminated most easily and quickly.

Above all, the caucus should look for strategic opportunities to employ constitutional arguments. Too often, members of Congress fail to appreciate that if they take a principled stand against a seemingly popular program—and state their case well—they can seize the moral high ground and prevail ultimately over those who are seen in the end to be more politically craven.

All of that will stir constitutional debate—which is just the point. For too long in Congress that debate has been dead, replaced by the often dreary budget debate. This nation was not established by men with green eyeshades. It was established by men who understood the basic character of government and the basic right to be free. That debate needs to be revived. It needs to be heard not simply in the courts—where it is twisted through modern "constitutional law"—but in Congress as well.

Enact Nothing without First Consulting the Constitution for Proper Authority and Then Debating That Question on the Floors of the House and the Senate

It would hardly seem necessary to ask Congress, before it enacts any measure, to cite its constitutional authority for doing so. After all, is that not simply part of what it means, as a member of Congress, to swear to support the Constitution? And if Congress's powers are limited by virtue of being enumerated, presumably there are many things Congress has no authority to do, however worthy those things might otherwise be. Yet so far have we strayed from constitutional thinking that such a requirement is today treated perfunctorily—when it is not ignored altogether.

The most common perfunctory citations—captured ordinarily in constitutional boilerplate—are to the General Welfare and Commerce Clauses of the Constitution. It is no small irony that both those clauses were written as shields against overweening government; yet today they are swords of federal power.

The General Welfare Clause

The General Welfare Clause of Article I, section 8, of the Constitution was meant to serve as a brake on the power of Congress to tax and spend in furtherance of its enumerated powers or ends: the spending that attended the exercise of an enumerated power had to be for the *general* welfare, not for the welfare of particular parties or sections of the nation.

That view, held by Madison, Jefferson, and most others, stands in marked contrast to the view of Hamilton—that the Constitution established an *independent* power to tax and spend for the general welfare. But as South Carolina's William Drayton observed on the floor of the House in 1828, Hamilton's view would make a mockery of the doctrine of enumerated powers, the centerpiece of the Constitution, rendering the enumeration of Congress's other powers superfluous: whenever Congress wanted to do something it was barred from doing by the absence of a power to do it, it could simply declare the act to be serving the "general welfare" and get out from under the limits imposed by enumeration.

That, unfortunately, is what happens today. In 1936 the Court came down, almost in passing, on Hamilton's side, declaring that there is an independent power to tax and spend for the general welfare. Then in 1937, in upholding the constitutionality of the new Social Security program, the Court completed the job when it stated the Hamiltonian view not as dicta but as doctrine, then reminded Congress of the constraints imposed by the word "general," but added that the Court would not police that restraint; rather, Congress would be left to police itself, the very Congress that was distributing money from the Treasury with ever greater particularity. Since that time the relatively modest redistributive schemes that preceded the New Deal have grown exponentially until today they are everywhere.

The Commerce Clause

The Commerce Clause of the Constitution, which grants Congress the power to regulate "commerce among the states," was also written primarily as a shield—against overweening *state* power. Under the Articles of Confederation, states had erected tariffs and other protectionist measures that impeded the free flow of commerce among the states. Indeed, the need to break the logjam that resulted was one of the principal reasons for the call for a convention in Philadelphia in 1787. To address the problem, the Framers gave *Congress* the power to regulate—or "make regular"—commerce among the states. It was thus meant to be a power primarily to facilitate free trade.

That functional account of the commerce power is consistent with the original understanding of the power, the 18th-century meaning of "regulate," and the structural limits entailed by the doctrine of enumerated powers. Yet today the functional account is all but unknown. Following decisions by the Court in 1937 and 1942, Congress has been able to regulate

27

anything that even "affects" interstate commerce, which in principle is everything. Far from regulating to ensure the free flow of commerce among the states, much of that regulation, for all manner of social and economic purposes, actually frustrates the free flow of commerce.

As the explosive growth of the modern redistributive state has taken place almost entirely under the General Welfare Clause, so, too, the growth of the modern regulatory state has occurred almost entirely under the Commerce Clause. That raises a fundamental question, of course: if the Framers had meant for Congress to be able to do virtually anything it wanted under those two simple clauses alone, why did they bother to enumerate Congress's other powers, or bother to defend the doctrine of enumerated powers throughout the *Federalist Papers*? Had they meant that, those efforts would have been pointless.

Lopez *and Its Aftermath*

Today, as noted above, congressional citations to the General Welfare and Commerce Clauses usually take the form of perfunctory boilerplate. When it wants to regulate some activity, Congress makes a bow to the doctrine of enumerated powers by claiming that it has made findings that the activity at issue "affects" interstate commerce—say, by preventing interstate travel. Given those findings, Congress then claims it has authority to regulate the activity under its power to regulate commerce among the states.

Thus, when the 104th Congress was pressed in the summer of 1996 to do something about what looked at the time like a wave of church arsons in the South, it sought to broaden the already doubtful authority of the federal government to prosecute such acts by determining that church arsons "hinder interstate commerce" and "impede individuals in moving interstate." Never mind that the prosecution of arson has traditionally been a state responsibility, there being no general federal police power in the Constitution. Never mind that church arsons have virtually nothing to do with interstate commerce, much less with the free flow of goods and services among the states. The Commerce Clause rationale, set forth in boilerplate language, was thought by Congress to be sufficient to enable it to move forward and enact the Church Arson Prevention Act of 1996—unanimously, no less.

Yet only a year earlier, in the celebrated *Lopez* case, the Supreme Court had declared, for the first time in nearly 60 years, that Congress's power under the Commerce Clause has limits. To be sure, the Court raised the bar against federal regulation only slightly: Congress would have to show that the activity it wanted to regulate "substantially" affected interstate commerce, leading Justice Thomas to note in his concurrence that the Court was still a good distance from a proper reading of the clause. Nevertheless, the decision was widely heralded as a shot across the bow of Congress. And many in Congress saw it as confirming at last their own view that the body in which they served was simply out of control, constitutionally. Indeed, when it passed the act at issue in *Lopez*, the Gun-Free School Zones Act of 1990, Congress had not even bothered to cite any authority under the Constitution. In what must surely be a stroke of consummate hubris—and disregard for the Constitution—Congress simply assumed that authority.

But to make matters worse, despite the *Lopez* ruling—which the Court reinforced in May 2000 when it found parts of the Violence Against Women Act unconstitutional on similar grounds—Congress in September 1996 passed the Gun-Free School Zones Act again. This time, of course, the boilerplate was included—even as Sen. Fred Thompson of Tennessee was reminding his colleagues from the floor of the Senate that the Supreme Court had recently told them that they "cannot just have some theoretical basis, some attenuated basis" under the Commerce Clause for such an act. The prosecution of gun possession near schools—like the prosecution of church arsons, crimes against women, and much else—is very popular, as state prosecutors well know. But governments can address problems only if they have authority to do so, not from good intentions alone. Indeed, the road to constitutional destruction is paved with good intentions.

Congressional debate on these matters is thus imperative: it is not enough for Congress simply to say the magic words—"General Welfare Clause" or "Commerce Clause"—to be home free, constitutionally. Not every debate will yield satisfying results, as the examples above illustrate. But if the Constitution is to be kept alive, there must at least be debate. Over time, good ideas tend to prevail over bad ideas, but only if they are given voice. The constitutional debate must again be heard in the Congress of the United States as it was over much of our nation's history, and it must be heard before bills are enacted. The American people can hardly be expected to take the Constitution and its limits on government seriously if their elected representatives do not.

Move toward Restoring Constitutional Government by Carefully Returning Power Wrongly Taken over the Years from the States and the People

If Congress should enact no new legislation without grounding its authority to do so securely in the Constitution, so too should it begin repealing legislation not so grounded, legislation that arose by assuming power that rightly rests with the states or the people. To appreciate how daunting a task that will be, simply reflect again on Madison's observation that the powers of the federal government under the Constitution are "few and defined."

But the magnitude of the task is only one dimension of its difficulty. Let us be candid: there are many in Congress who will oppose any efforts to restore constitutional government for any number of reasons, ranging from the practical to the theoretical. Some see their job as one primarily of representing the interests of their constituents, especially the short-term interests reflected in the phrase "bringing home the bacon." Others simply like big government, whether because of an "enlightened" Progressive Era view of the world or because of a narrower, more cynical interest in the perquisites of enhanced power. Still others believe sincerely in a "living constitution," one extreme form of which—the "democratic" form—imposes no limit whatsoever on government save for periodic elections. Finally, there are those who understand the unconstitutional and hence illegitimate character of much of what government does today but believe it is too late in the day to do anything about it. All of those people and others will find reasons to resist the discrete measures that are necessary to begin restoring constitutional government. Yet, where necessary, their views will have to be accommodated as the process unfolds.

Maintaining Support for Limited Government

Given the magnitude of the problem, then, and the practical implications of repealing federal programs, a fair measure of caution is in order. As the nations of Eastern Europe and the former Soviet Union have learned, it is relatively easy to get into socialism—just seize all property and labor and place it under state control—but much harder to get out of it. It is not simply a matter of returning what was taken, for much has changed as a result of the taking. People have died and new people have come along. Public law has replaced private law. And new expectations and dependencies have arisen and become settled over time. The transition to freedom that many of those nations are experiencing is what we and many other nations around the world today are facing, to a lesser extent, as we too try to reduce the size and scope of our governments.

As programs are reduced or eliminated, then, care must be taken to do as little harm as possible—for two reasons at least. First, there is some sense in which the federal government today, vastly overextended though it is, stands in a contractual relationship with the American people. That is a very difficult idea to pin down, however, for once the genuine contract—the Constitution—has broken down, the "legislative contracts" that arise to take its place invariably reduce, when parsed, to programs under which some people have become dependent upon others, although neither side had a great deal to say directly about the matter at the outset. Whatever its merits, that contractual view is held by a good part of the public, especially in the case of so-called middle-class entitlements.

That leads to the second reason why care must be taken in restoring power to the states and the people, namely, that the task must be undertaken, as noted earlier, with the support of a substantial portion of the people— ideally, at the urging of those people. Given the difficulty of convincing people—including legislators—to act against their relatively short-term interests, it will take sound congressional judgment about where and when to move. More important, it will take keen leadership, leadership that is able to frame the issues in a way that will communicate both the rightness and the soundness of the decisions that are required.

In exercising that leadership, there is no substitute for keeping "on message" and for keeping the message simple, direct, and clear. The aim, again, is both freedom and the good society. We need to appreciate how the vast government programs we have created over the years have actually reduced the freedom and well-being of all of us—and have undermined the Constitution besides. Not that the ends served by those programs are unworthy—few government programs are undertaken for worthless ends. But individuals, families, private firms, and communities could bring about most of those ends, voluntarily and at far less cost, if only they were free to do so—especially if they were free to keep the wherewithal that is necessary to do so. If individual freedom and individual responsibility are values we cherish—indeed, are the foundations of the good society—we must come to appreciate how our massive government programs have undermined those values and, with that, the good society itself.

Redistributive Programs

Examples of the kinds of programs that should be returned to the states and the people are detailed elsewhere in this *Handbook*, but a few are in order here. Without question, the most important example of devolution to come from the "radical" 104th Congress was in the area of welfare. However flawed the final legislation may have been from both a constitutional and a policy perspective, it was still a step in the right direction. Ultimately, as will be noted below in a more general way, welfare should not be even a state program. Rather, it should be a matter of private responsibility, as it was for years in this nation. But the process of getting the federal government out of the business of charity, for which there is no authority in the Constitution, has at least begun.

Eventually, that process should be repeated in every other "entitlement" area, from individual to institutional to corporate, from Social Security and Medicare to the National Endowment for the Arts to the Department of Agriculture's Market Access Program and on and on. Each of those programs was started for a good reason, to be sure, yet each involves taking from some to give to others—means that are both wrong and unconstitutional, to say nothing of monumentally inefficient. Taken together, they put us all on welfare in one way or another, and we are all the poorer for it.

Some of those programs will be harder to reduce, phase out, or eliminate than others, of course. Entitlement programs with large numbers of beneficiaries, for example, will require transition phases to ensure that harm is minimized and public support is maintained. Other programs, however, could be eliminated with relatively little harm. Does anyone seriously doubt that there would be art in America without the National Endowment for the Arts? Indeed, without the heavy hand of government grant making, the arts would likely flourish as they did long before the advent of the NEA—and no one would be made to pay, through his taxes, for art he abhorred.

It is the transfer programs in the "symbolic" area, in fact, that may be the most important to eliminate first, for they have multiplier effects reaching well beyond their raw numbers, and those effects are hardly neutral on the question of reducing the size and scope of government. The National Endowment for the Arts, the National Endowment for the Humanities, the Corporation for Public Broadcasting, the Legal Services Corporation, and the Department of Education have all proceeded without constitutional authority—but with serious implications for free speech and for the cause of limiting government. Not a few critics have pointed to the heavy hand of government in those symbolic areas. Of equal importance, however, is the problem of compelled speech: as Jefferson wrote, "To compel a man to furnish contributions of money for the propagation of opinions which he disbelieves is sinful and tyrannical.'' But on a more practical note, if Congress is serious about addressing the climate of opinion in the nation, it will end such programs not simply because they are without constitutional authority but because they have demonstrated a relentless tendency over the years in only one direction—toward even more government. Indeed, one should hardly expect those institutions to be underwriting programs that advocate less government when they themselves exist through government.

Regulatory Redistribution

If the redistributive programs that constitute the modern welfare state are candidates for elimination, so too are many of the regulatory programs that have arisen under the Commerce Clause. Here, however, care must be taken not simply from a practical perspective but from a constitutional perspective as well, for some of those programs may be constitutionally justified. When read functionally, recall, the Commerce Clause was meant to enable Congress to ensure that commerce among the states is regular, and especially to counter state actions that might upset that regularity. Think of the Commerce Clause as an early North American Free Trade Agreement, without the heavy hand of ''managed trade'' that often accompanies the modern counterpart.

Thus conceived, the Commerce Clause clearly empowers Congress, through regulation, to override state measures that may frustrate the free flow of commerce among the states. But it also enables Congress to take such affirmative measures as may be necessary and proper for facilitating free trade, such as clarifying rights of trade in uncertain contexts or regulating the interstate transport of dangerous goods. What the clause does not authorize, however, is regulation for reasons other than to ensure the free flow of commerce—the kind of ''managed trade'' that is little but a thinly disguised transfer program designed to benefit one party at the expense of another.

Unfortunately, most modern federal regulation falls into that final category, whether it concerns employment or health care or insurance or whatever. In fact, given budgetary constraints on the ability of government to tax and spend—to take money from some, run it through the Treasury, then give it to others—the preferred form of transfer today is through regulation. That puts it ''off budget.'' Thus, when an employer, an insurer, a lender, or a landlord is required by regulation to do something he would otherwise have a right not to do, or not do something he would otherwise have a right to do, he serves the party benefited by that regulation every bit as much as if he were taxed to do so, but no tax increase is ever registered on any public record.

The temptation for Congress to resort to such "cost-free" regulatory redistribution is of course substantial, and the effects are both far-reaching and perverse. Natural markets are upset as incentives are changed; economies of scale are skewed as large businesses, better able to absorb the regulatory burdens, are advantaged over small ones; defensive measures, inefficient from the larger perspective, are encouraged; and general uncertainty, anathema to efficient markets, is the order of the day. Far from facilitating free trade, redistributive regulation frustrates it. Far from being justified by the Commerce Clause, it undermines the very purpose of the clause.

Federal Crimes

In addition to misusing the commerce power for the purpose of regulatory redistribution, Congress has misused that power to create federal crimes. Thus, a great deal of "regulation" has arisen in recent years under the commerce power that is nothing but a disguised exercise of a police power that Congress otherwise lacks. As noted earlier, the Gun-Free School Zones Act, the Church Arson Prevention Act, and the Violence Against Women Act are examples of legislation passed nominally under the power of Congress to regulate commerce among the states; but the actions subject to federal prosecution under those statutes—gun possession, church arson, and gender-motivated violence, respectively—are ordinarily regulated under *state* police power, the power of states, in essence, to "police" or secure our rights. The ruse of regulating them under Congress's commerce power is made necessary because there is no federal police power enumerated in the Constitution—except as an implication of federal sovereignty over federal territory or an incidence of some enumerated power.

That ruse should be candidly recognized. Indeed, it is a mark of the decline of respect for the Constitution that when we sought to fight a war on liquor earlier in the century we felt it necessary to do so by first amending the Constitution—there being no power otherwise for such a federal undertaking. Today, however, when we engage in a war on drugs— with as much success as we enjoyed in the earlier war—we do so without as much as a nod to the Constitution.

The Constitution lists three federal crimes: treason, piracy, and counterfeiting. Yet today there are more than 3,000 federal crimes and perhaps

300,000 regulations that carry criminal sanctions. Over the years, no faction in Congress has been immune, especially in an election year, from the propensity to criminalize all manner of activities, utterly oblivious to the lack of any constitutional authority for doing so. We should hardly imagine that the Founders fought a war to free us from a distant tyranny only to establish a tyranny in Washington, in some ways even more distant from the citizens it was meant to serve.

Policing the States

If the federal government has often intruded upon the police power of the states, so too has it often failed in its responsibility under the Fourteenth Amendment to police the states. Here is an area where federal regulation has been, if anything, too restrained—yet also unprincipled, oftentimes, when undertaken.

The Civil War Amendments to the Constitution changed fundamentally the relationship between the federal government and the states, giving citizens an additional level of protection, not against federal but against state oppression—the oppression of slavery, obviously, but much else besides. Thus, the Fourteenth Amendment prohibits states from abridging the privileges or immunities of citizens of the United States; from depriving any person of life, liberty, or property without due process of law; and from denying any person the equal protection of the laws. By implication, section 1 of the amendment gives the courts the power to secure those guarantees. Section 5 gives Congress the "power to enforce, by appropriate legislation, the provisions of this article."

As the debate that surrounded the adoption of those amendments makes clear, the Privileges or Immunities Clause was meant to be the principal source of substantive rights in the Fourteenth Amendment, and those rights were meant to include the rights of property, contract, and personal security—in short, our "natural liberties," as Blackstone had earlier understood that phrase. Unfortunately, in 1873, in the notorious *Slaughterhouse Cases,* a bitterly divided Supreme Court essentially eviscerated the Privileges or Immunities Clause. There followed, for nearly a century, the era of Jim Crow in the South and, for a period stretching to the present, a Fourteenth Amendment jurisprudence that is as contentious as it is confused.

Modern liberals have urged that the amendment be used as it was meant to be used—against state oppression; but they have also urged that it be used to recognize all manner of "rights" that are no part of the theory of rights that stands behind the amendment as understood at the time of ratification. Modern conservatives, partly in reaction, have urged that the amendment be used far more narrowly than it was meant to be used—for fear that it might be misused, as it has been.

The role of the judiciary under section 1 of the Fourteenth Amendment will be discussed below. As for Congress, its authority under section 5—"to enforce, by appropriate legislation, the provisions of this article"—is clear, provided Congress is clear about those provisions. And on that, we may look, again, to the debates that surrounded not only the adoption of the Fourteenth Amendment but the enactment of the Civil Rights Act of 1866, which Congress reenacted in 1868, just after the amendment was ratified.

Those debates give us a fairly clear idea of what it was that the American people thought they were ratifying. In particular, all citizens, the Civil Rights Act declared, "have the right to make and enforce contracts, to sue, be parties and give evidence; to inherit, purchase, lease, sell, hold, and convey real personal property, and to full and equal benefit of all laws and proceedings for the security of persons and property." Such were the privileges and immunities the Fourteenth Amendment was meant to secure.

Clearly, those basic common law rights, drawn from the reason-based classical theory of rights, are the stuff of ordinary state law. Just as clearly, however, states have been known to violate them, either directly or by failure to secure them against private violations. When that happens, appeal can be made to the courts, under section 1, or to Congress, under section 5. The Fourteenth Amendment gives no power, of course, to secure the modern "entitlements" that are no part of the common law tradition of life, liberty, and property: the power it grants, that is, is limited by the rights it is meant to secure. But it does give a power to reach even intrastate matters when states are violating the provisions of the amendment. The claim of "states' rights," in short, is no defense for state violations of individual rights.

Thus, if the facts had warranted it, something like the Church Arson Prevention Act of 1996, depending on its particulars, might have been authorized not on Commerce Clause grounds but on Fourteenth Amendment grounds. If, for example, the facts had shown that arsons of white churches were being prosecuted by state officials whereas arsons of black churches were not, then we would have had a classic case of the denial of the equal protection of the laws. With those findings, Congress would have had ample authority under section 5 of the Fourteenth Amendment "to enforce, by appropriate legislation, the provisions of this article."

Unfortunately, in the final version of the act, Congress removed citations to the Fourteenth Amendment, choosing instead to rest its authority entirely on the Commerce Clause. Not only is that a misuse of the Commerce Clause, inviting further misuse; but, assuming the facts had warranted it, it is a failure to use the Fourteenth Amendment as it was meant to be used, inviting further failures. To be sure, the Fourteenth Amendment has itself been misused, both by Congress and by the courts. But that is no reason to ignore it. Rather, it is a reason to correct the misuses.

In its efforts to return power to the states and the people, then, Congress must be careful not to misunderstand its role in our federal system. Over the 20th century, Congress assumed vast powers that were never its to assume, powers that belong properly to the states and the people. Those need to be returned. But at the same time, Congress and the courts do have authority under the Fourteenth Amendment to ensure that citizens are free from state oppression. However much that authority may have been underused or overused, it is there to be used; and if it is properly used, objections by states about federal interference in their "internal affairs" are without merit.

Reject the Nomination of Judicial Candidates Who Do Not Appreciate That the Constitution Is a Document of Delegated, Enumerated, and Thus Limited Powers

As noted earlier, Congress can relimit government on its own initiative simply by restricting its future actions to those that are authorized by the Constitution and repealing those past actions that were taken without such authority; but for those limits to become "constitutional law," they would have to be recognized as such by the Supreme Court, which essentially abandoned that view of limited government during the New Deal. Thus, for the Court to play its part in the job of relimiting government constitutionally, it must recognize the mistakes it has made over the years, especially following Roosevelt's Court-packing threat in 1937, and rediscover the Constitution—a process it began in *Lopez*, however tentatively, when it returned explicitly to "first principles."

But Congress is not powerless to influence the Court in that direction: as vacancies arise on the Court and on lower courts, it has a substantial say about who sits there through its power to advise and consent. To exercise that power well, however, Congress must have a better grasp of the basic issues than it has shown in recent years during Senate confirmation hearings for nominees for the Court. In particular, the Senate's obsession with questions about "judicial activism" and "judicial restraint," terms that in themselves are largely vacuous, only distracts it from the real issue—the nominee's philosophy of the Constitution. To appreciate those points more fully, however, a bit of background is in order.

From Powers to Rights

The most important matter to grasp is the fundamental change that took place in our constitutional jurisprudence during the New Deal and the implications of that change for the modern debate. The debate today is focused almost entirely on rights, not powers. Indeed, until the 107th Congress and its focus on ideology, the principal concern during Senate confirmation hearings had been with a nominee's views about what rights are "in" the Constitution. That is an important question, to be sure, but it must be addressed within a much larger constitutional framework, a framework too often missing from recent hearings.

Clearly, the American debate began with rights—with the protests that led eventually to the Declaration of Independence. And in that seminal document, Jefferson made rights the centerpiece of the American vision: rights to life, liberty, and the pursuit of happiness, derived from a premise of moral equality, itself grounded in a higher law discoverable by reason— all to be secured by a government of powers made legitimate through consent.

But when they set out to draft a constitution, the Framers focused on powers, not rights, for two main reasons. First, their initial task was to create and empower a government, which the Constitution did once it was ratified. But their second task, of equal importance, was to limit that government. Here, there were two main options. The Framers could have listed a set of rights that the new government would be forbidden to violate. Or they could have limited the government's powers by enumerating them, then pitting one against the other through a system of checks and balances—the idea being that where there is no power there is, by implication, a right, belonging to the states or the people. They chose the second option, for they could hardly have enumerated all of our rights, but they *could* enumerate the new government's powers, which were meant from the outset to be, again, "few and defined." Thus, the doctrine of enumerated powers became our principal defense against overweening government.

Only later, during the course of ratification, did it become necessary to add a Bill of Rights—as a secondary defense. But in so doing, the Framers were still faced with a pair of objections that had been posed from the start. First, it was impossible to enumerate all of our rights, which in principle are infinite in number. Second, given that problem, the enumeration of only certain rights would be construed, by ordinary methods of legal construction, as denying the existence of others. To overcome those objections, therefore, the Framers wrote the Ninth Amendment: "The enumeration in the Constitution of certain rights shall not be construed to deny or disparage others retained by the people."

Constitutional Visions

Thus, with the Ninth Amendment making it clear that we have both enumerated and unenumerated rights, the Tenth Amendment making it clear that the federal government has only enumerated powers, and the Fourteenth Amendment later making it clear that our rights are good against the states as well, what emerges is an altogether libertarian picture. Individuals, families, firms, and the infinite variety of institutions that constitute civil society are free to pursue happiness however they wish, in accord with whatever values they wish, provided only that in the process they respect the equal rights of others to do the same; and governments are instituted to secure that liberty and do the few other things their constitutions make clear they are empowered to do.

That picture is a far cry from the modern liberal's vision, rooted in the Progressive Era, which would have government empowered to manage all manner of economic affairs. But it is a far cry as well from the modern conservative's vision, which would have government empowered to manage all manner of social affairs. Neither vision reflects the true constitutional scheme. Both camps want to use the Constitution to promote their own substantive agendas. Repeatedly, liberals invoke democratic power for ends that are nowhere in the Constitution; at other times they invoke "rights" that are no part of the plan, requiring government programs that are nowhere authorized. For their agenda, conservatives rely largely on expansive readings of democratic power that were never envisioned, thereby running roughshod over rights that were meant to be protected.

From Liberty to Democracy

The great change in constitutional vision took place during the New Deal, when the idea that galvanized the Progressive Era—that the basic

39

purpose of government is to solve social and economic problems—was finally instituted in law through the Court's radical reinterpretation of the Constitution. As noted earlier, following the 1937 Court-packing threat, the Court eviscerated our first line of defense, the doctrine of enumerated powers, when it converted the General Welfare and Commerce Clauses from shields against power into swords of power. Then in 1938 a cowed Court undermined the second line of defense, our enumerated and unenumerated rights, when it declared that henceforth it would defer to the political branches and the states when their actions implicated ''nonfundamental'' rights like property and contract—the rights associated with ''ordinary commercial affairs.'' Legislation implicating such rights, the Court said, would be given ''minimal scrutiny'' by the Court, which is tantamount to no scrutiny at all. By contrast, when legislation implicated ''fundamental'' rights like voting, speech, and, later, certain ''personal'' liberties, the Court would apply ''strict scrutiny'' to that legislation, probably finding it unconstitutional.

With that, the Constitution was converted, without benefit of amendment, from a libertarian to a largely democratic document. The floodgates were now open to majoritarian tyranny, which very quickly became special-interest tyranny, as public-choice economic theory amply demonstrates should be expected. Once those floodgates were opened, the programs that poured through led inevitably to claims from many quarters that rights were being violated. Thus, the Court in time would have to try to determine whether those rights were ''in'' the Constitution—a question the Constitution had spoken to indirectly, for the most part, through the now-discredited doctrine of enumerated powers; and if it found the rights in question, the Court would then have to try to make sense of its distinction between ''fundamental'' and ''nonfundamental'' rights.

Judicial "Activism" and "Restraint"

It is no accident, therefore, that until very recently the modern debate has been focused on rights, not powers. With the doctrine of enumerated powers effectively dead, with government's power essentially plenary, the only issues left for the Court to decide, for the most part, are whether there might be any rights that would limit that power and whether those rights are or are not ''fundamental.''

Both liberals and conservatives today have largely bought into this jurisprudence. As noted above, both camps believe the Constitution gives a wide berth to democratic decisionmaking. Neither side any longer asks the first question, the fundamental question: do we have authority, constitutional authority, to pursue this end? Instead, they simply assume that authority, take a policy vote on some end before them, then battle in court over whether there are any rights that might restrict their power.

Modern liberals, fond of government programs, call upon the Court to be "restrained" in finding rights that might limit their redistributive and regulatory schemes, especially "nonfundamental" rights like property and contract. At the same time, even as they ignore those rights, liberals ask the Court to be "active" in finding other "rights" that were never meant to be among even our unenumerated rights.

But modern conservatives are often little better. Reacting to the abuses of liberal "activism," many conservatives call for judicial "restraint" across the board. Thus, if liberal programs have run roughshod over the rights of individuals to use their property or freely contract, the remedy, conservatives say, is not for the Court to invoke the doctrine of enumerated powers—that battle was lost during the New Deal—nor even to invoke the rights of property and contract that are plainly in the Constitution— that might encourage judicial activism—but to turn to the democratic process to overturn those programs. Oblivious to the fact that restraint in finding rights is tantamount to activism in finding powers, and ignoring the fact that it was the democratic process that gave us the problem in the first place, too many conservatives offer us a counsel of despair amounting to a denial of constitutional protection.

No one doubts that in recent decades the Court has discovered "rights" in the Constitution that are no part of either the enumerated or unenumerated rights that were meant to be protected by that document. But it is no answer to that problem to ask the Court to defer wholesale to the political branches, thereby encouraging it, by implication, to sanction unenumerated *powers* that are no part of the document either. Indeed, if the Tenth Amendment means anything, it means that there are no such powers. Again, if the Framers had wanted to establish a simple democracy, they could have. Instead, they established a limited, constitutional republic, a republic with islands of democratic power in a sea of liberty, not a sea of democratic power surrounding islands of liberty.

Thus, it is not the proper role of the Court to find rights that are no part of the enumerated or unenumerated rights meant to be protected by the Constitution, thereby frustrating authorized democratic decisions. But neither is it the proper role of the Court to refrain from asking whether those decisions are in fact authorized and, if authorized, whether their implementation is in violation of the rights guaranteed by the Constitution, enumerated and unenumerated alike.

The role of the judge in our constitutional republic is thus profoundly important and oftentimes profoundly complex. "Activism" is no proper posture for a judge, but neither is "restraint." Judges must apply the Constitution to cases or controversies before them, neither making it up nor ignoring it. They must appreciate especially that the Constitution is a document of delegated, enumerated, and thus limited powers. That will get the judge started on the question of what rights are protected by the document; for where there is no power there is, again, a right, belonging either to the states or to the people: indeed, we should hardly imagine that, before the addition of the Bill of Rights, the Constitution failed to protect most rights simply because most were not "in" it. But reviving the doctrine of enumerated powers is only part of the task before the Court; it must also revive the classical theory of rights if the restoration of constitutional government is to be completed correctly.

Those are the two sides—powers and rights—that need to be examined in the course of Senate confirmation hearings for nominees for the courts of the United States. More important than knowing a nominee's "judicial philosophy" is knowing his philosophy of the Constitution. For the Constitution, in the end, is what defines us as a nation.

If a nominee does not have a deep and thorough appreciation for the basic principles of the Constitution—for the doctrine of enumerated powers and for the classical theory of rights that stands behind the Constitution—then his candidacy should be rejected. In recent years, Senate confirmation hearings have become extraordinary opportunities for constitutional debate throughout the nation. Those debates need to move from the ethereal realm of "constitutional law" to the real realm of the Constitution. They are extraordinary opportunities not simply for constitutional debate but for constitutional renewal.

Alarmingly, however, in the 107th Congress we saw the debate move not from "constitutional law" to the Constitution but in the very opposite direction—to raw politics. The demand that judicial nominees pass an "ideological litmus test"—that they reflect and apply the "mainstream values" of the American people, whatever those may be—is tantamount to expecting and asking judges not to *apply* the law, which is what judging is all about, but to *make* the law according to those values, whatever the actual law may require. The duty of judges under the Constitution is to decide cases according to the law, not according to whatever values or ideology may be in fashion. For that, the only ideology that matters is the ideology of the Constitution.

Conclusion

America is a democracy in the most fundamental sense of that idea: authority, or legitimate power, rests ultimately with the people. But the people have no more right to tyrannize each other through democratic government than government itself has to tyrannize the people. When they constituted us as a nation by ratifying the Constitution and the amendments that have followed, our ancestors gave up only certain of their powers, enumerating them in a written constitution. We have allowed those powers to expand beyond all moral and legal bounds—at the price of our liberty and our well-being. The time has come to return those powers to their proper bounds, to reclaim our liberty, and to enjoy the fruits that follow.

Suggested Readings

Bailyn, Bernard. *The Ideological Origins of the American Revolution.* Cambridge, Mass.: Belknap, 1967.

Barnett, Randy E. *The Structure of Liberty: Justice and the Rule of Law.* New York: Oxford University Press, 1998.

Barnett, Randy E., ed. *The Rights Retained by the People: The History and Meaning of the Ninth Amendment.* Fairfax, Va.: George Mason University Press, 1989.

Corwin, Edward S. *The "Higher Law" Background of American Constitutional Law.* Ithaca, N.Y.: Cornell University Press, 1955.

Dorn, James A., and Henry G. Manne, eds. *Economic Liberties and the Judiciary.* Fairfax, Va.: George Mason University Press, 1987.

Epstein, Richard A. *Principles for a Free Society: Reconciling Individual Liberty with the Common Good.* Reading, Mass.: Perseus Books, 1998.

————. "The Proper Scope of the Commerce Power." *Virginia Law Review* 73 (1987).

————. *Simple Rules for a Complex World.* Cambridge, Mass.: Harvard University Press, 1995.

————. *Takings: Private Property and the Power of Eminent Domain.* Cambridge, Mass.: Harvard University Press, 1985.

Hamilton, Alexander, James Madison, and John Jay. *The Federalist Papers.* New York: Mentor, 1961.

Lawson, Gary. "The Rise and Rise of the Administrative State." *Harvard Law Review* 107 (1994).

Lawson, Gary, and Patricia B. Granger. "The 'Proper' Scope of Federal Power: A Jurisdictional Interpretation of the Sweeping Clause." *Duke Law Journal* 43 (1993).

Locke, John. "Second Treatise of Government." In *Two Treatises of Government.* Edited by Peter Laslett. New York: Mentor, 1965.

Miller, Geoffrey P. "The True Story of Carolene Products." *Supreme Court Review* (1987).

Pilon, Roger. "Freedom, Responsibility, and the Constitution: On Recovering Our Founding Principles." *Notre Dame Law Review* 68 (1993).

———. "How Constitutional Corruption Has Led to Ideological Litmus Tests for Judicial Nominees." Cato Institute Policy Analysis no. 446, August 8, 2002.

———. "The Purpose and Limits of Government." *Cato's Letter,* no. 13 (1999).

———. "Restoring Constitutional Government." *Cato's Letter,* no. 9 (1995).

Reinstein, Robert J. "Completing the Constitution: The Declaration of Independence, Bill of Rights and Fourteenth Amendment." *Temple Law Review* 66 (1993).

Shankman, Kimberly C., and Roger Pilon. "Reviving the Privileges or Immunities Clause to Redress the Balance among States, Individuals, and the Federal Government." Cato Institute Policy Analysis no. 326, November 23, 1998.

Siegan, Bernard H. *Economic Liberties and the Constitution.* Chicago: University of Chicago Press, 1980.

Sorenson, Leonard R. *Madison on the "General Welfare" of America.* Lanham, Md.: Rowman & Littlefield, 1995.

Warren, Charles. *Congress as Santa Claus: Or National Donations and the General Welfare Clause of the Constitution.* 1932. Reprint, New York: Arno Press, 1978.

Yoo, John Choon. "Our Declaratory Ninth Amendment." *Emory Law Journal* 42 (1993).

—Prepared by Roger Pilon

CONFRONTING TERROR

4. Clearing the Decks for War

The U.S. government should

- promptly eliminate the foreign aid budget devoted to developmental aid,
- withdraw all U.S. military personnel from Bosnia and Kosovo within one year,
- withdraw all U.S. troops stationed in Western Europe by 2005,
- withdraw all U.S. troops stationed in South Korea by 2005,
- withdraw all U.S. troops stationed in Japan by 2007,
- transfer some of the funding and personnel involved in the above withdrawals to units and tasks relevant to the war on terrorism, and
- demobilize all surplus forces.

President Bush has emphasized that the war against terrorism will be lengthy and difficult, despite the gratifying initial successes in Afghanistan. He is right. Even if the war is confined (as it should be) to campaigns against those organizations responsible for the September 11, 2001, attacks or any future attacks instead of becoming an amorphous crusade against evil in the world, the conflict will not be over quickly. That's why it is imperative that the United States promptly clear the decks for war. America must jettison obsolete or unnecessary commitments and expenditures.

When a family suffers an unexpected hardship or tragedy, it does not continue with business as usual, leaving its priorities and spending patterns unaltered. Likewise, a nation must alter its priorities when facing difficulties. For America, the war against the terrorists who committed the September 11 outrages will be the top priority for the foreseeable future. Yet, instead of reducing or eliminating less essential commitments, Washington seems inclined to pile the new commitments on top of the old.

45

Barely a year into the war on terrorism, the failure to trim other commitments is already creating strains on the military. Gen. Tommy Franks, the commander of U.S. forces in Afghanistan, and other military leaders have complained that the deployment is creating overburdened and stressed-out personnel. That is a most troubling development. The United States has fewer than 10,000 troops in Afghanistan and only a few thousand more deployed in Pakistan and some of the Central Asian republics near Afghanistan. As military deployments go, the campaign against al-Qaeda and the Taliban to this point has not been an especially large one. Yet even this modest effort is creating significant strains. One has to wonder how severe the strain will become if a substantially larger deployment in the war on terrorism is ever required.

There are numerous commitments that should be candidates for elimination, including a plethora of wasteful and unnecessary domestic spending programs. The United States should also make significant cuts in the realm of international affairs, starting with the elimination of the $10.9 billion of developmental aid in the foreign aid budget. Numerous scholars have documented the dismal record of developmental aid over the past half century (see Chapter 66). U.S. developmental aid programs have subsidized counterproductive economic policies in recipient countries and helped entrench corrupt political elites. Such aid was a foolish expenditure the United States could ill afford even before September 11. In a post–September 11 environment, it should be one of the first programs on the chopping block.

But developmental aid is not the only arena in which the U.S. government needs to reorder its priorities in international affairs. There are also a number of obsolete or unnecessary security commitments that should be terminated. Four such candidates for elimination stand out.

Terminate the Nation-Building Missions in the Balkans

The nation-building missions in Bosnia and Kosovo were foolish and unnecessary from the outset. Despite the exertions of America and its NATO allies, Bosnia is no closer to being a viable country today than it was when the Dayton Peace Agreement was signed more than seven years ago. The NATO intervention in Kosovo is even worse. It merely strengthened the hand of Albanian nationalists who want to create a Greater Albania and who have recently stirred up trouble across the border in Macedonia.

The missions in Bosnia and Kosovo cost the United States nearly $6 billion a year. More than 3,000 U.S. troops are tied down in Bosnia in glorified police work. More than 6,000 troops are stationed in Kosovo performing similar tedious tasks. U.S. leaders should immediately inform the European members of NATO that we will be withdrawing all of our forces over the next year.

The European allies would then have to decide whether to continue the Balkan peacekeeping missions without U.S. participation or withdraw their own forces as well. U.S. leaders should not especially care which option the Europeans select. The Balkans have never been an arena in which vital American interests were at stake. The region is more important to the nations of the European Union, and they should decide whether a peacekeeping venture is worth the expense and bother. It is absurd to argue that the prosperous nations of the European Union cannot police the Balkans if they wish to do so. American money, as well as the U.S. military personnel tied down in useless peacekeeping tasks, could be used far more effectively to prosecute the war against terrorism.

Withdraw the 100,000 U.S. Troops Stationed in Western Europe

The U.S. troop presence in Western Europe is an utterly obsolete commitment inherited from the Cold War. As noted in Chapter 51, the original concept of NATO did not include the permanent stationing of U.S. troops in Europe. Since the Cold War has been over for more than a decade, the time is long overdue for the withdrawal of all such personnel still deployed on the Continent.

Even the most creative defenders of the deployment would have difficulty explaining just why the troops are still there. The U.S. forces are apparently on duty to prevent an invasion of Western Europe by a Warsaw Pact that no longer exists led by a Soviet Union that no longer exists. How tank divisions stationed in Germany benefit the security of the United States in the 21st century is truly a mystery.

The Europeans clearly can provide for their own security without relying on U.S. troops. There is no serious security threat in Europe, nor is one likely to emerge in the foreseeable future. The security problems that do exist are small-scale, with the disorders in the Balkans being the primary examples. The nations of the European Union should certainly be able to manage their own defense and deal with such minor security contingencies. Collectively, the European Union has a population larger than that of the

United States as well as a larger gross domestic product. That is true even without taking into account the new nations that will be added to the EU within the next two years.

True, the European nations (especially the major states in the EU) might have to raise their military budgets slightly to offset the withdrawal of U.S. forces, but that action would hardly result in an onerous burden. Besides, it is appropriate that the Europeans pay the full cost of their own defense. Giving the prosperous European allies a de facto defense subsidy made no sense even before September 11. It is a luxury the United States simply cannot afford in a post–September 11 setting.

The U.S. military units stationed in Europe should be withdrawn by the beginning of 2005 and demobilized. Some of the personnel should then be reassigned to lighter, more mobile units that would be relevant in the fight against terrorism. The military commitment to NATO costs the United States nearly $40 billion a year. Even a partial demobilization would save American taxpayers several billion dollars.

Withdraw the 37,000 U.S. Troops Stationed in South Korea

The U.S. troop presence in South Korea is another obsolete, Cold War–era obligation. U.S. troops stayed in that country after the end of the Korean War in 1953. At that time, a plausible argument could be made for the commitment. U.S. leaders worried that a new war on the peninsula would be merely one phase of an overall communist offensive to dominate all of East Asia—a development that would have threatened important American interests. Moreover, South Korea was a poor, war-torn country incapable of defending itself. Not only did it face a hostile, well-armed communist North Korea, but it faced a North Korea backed by both Moscow and Beijing.

That is clearly no longer the case. Today, South Korea faces only one adversary: a desperately poor and increasingly isolated North Korea. The last thing either Moscow or Beijing desires is another war on the Korean peninsula. Indeed, in recent years both Russia and China have distanced their policies from those of their ostensible North Korean ally and forged close political and economic ties with South Korea. Moreover, South Korea now has enormous advantages in the contest with North Korea. The South has twice the population and an economy nearly 40 times larger than that of its adversary. A nation with those characteristics should certainly be able to defend itself.

Unfortunately, U.S. officials seem to have adopted an American version of the Brezhnev Doctrine when it comes to the military tie to South Korea. That doctrine, articulated by Soviet leader Leonid Brezhnev, asserted that once a nation became a member of the communist camp it must always remain in the communist camp. The U.S. version seems to be "Once a security dependent of the United States, always a security dependent of the United States."

Instead of taking responsibility for its own security, South Korea chooses to underinvest in defense and remain dependent on the United States for major portions of its military needs. Despite being next door to one of the more bizarre and unpredictable regimes in the world, Seoul actually spends a *lower* percentage of its gross domestic product on defense than does the United States. Moreover, one of South Korea's first responses to the East Asian financial crisis in the late 1990s was to cut its already anemic defense budget.

U.S. leaders should inform their South Korean counterparts that the days of free riding on the U.S. security guarantee are over. America has its own war to wage, and it can no longer afford to subsidize prosperous security clients. The security commitment to South Korea costs the United States approximately $15 billion a year. Even if some of the forces withdrawn were subsequently redeployed to wage the war on terrorism, American taxpayers would realize substantial savings.

Withdraw the Nearly 50,000 Troops Stationed in Japan

The U.S. military presence in Japan is yet another obsolete commitment. In the decades following World War II, U.S. officials wanted to keep Japanese rearmament to a minimum. Indeed, Article 9 of Japan's constitution, placed in the document in response to intense pressure from the United States, renounced war and seemed to preclude the existence of any armed forces. Because Washington soon wanted some Japanese assistance in the struggle against the Soviet Union, however, U.S. leaders endorsed a more flexible interpretation of Article 9, and Japan developed modest ground, air, and naval "self-defense forces."

Nevertheless, the United States has never fully trusted Japan and has shown no support for Japan's playing a vigorous security role—much less an independent security role—in East Asia. Even the much-touted changes in the defense guidelines for the U.S.-Japanese alliance, adopted in 1997, authorize Japan merely to provide nonlethal logistical support for U.S. military operations in East Asia unless Japan itself is attacked.

U.S. officials seem content to keep Japan as a barely trusted junior security helper. The tradeoff for that limitation is that Tokyo expects the United States to keep military forces in Japan and take primary responsibility for Japan's security.

That policy needs to change. Some of the U.S. forces stationed in Japan sit as uselessly as the troops stationed in Western Europe. The more than 18,000 Marines stationed on Okinawa fall into that category. The air and naval units deployed in Japan arguably contribute to the overall stability of East Asia, but they also provide a de facto defense subsidy to Japan.

It is time for Japan to step forward and assume its rightful role as the principal stabilizing power in East Asia. Japan has the world's second largest economy, and its military forces—although relatively small—are modern and capable. A modest increase in defense spending would enable Japan to offset the withdrawal of U.S. forces in a few years. Although the security environment in East Asia is not as benign as the environment in Europe, there is no need for a large U.S. military presence. It should be humiliating for Japan, with all its capabilities, to still be dependent on the United States for its security.

The Marines on Okinawa should be withdrawn over the next two years, and the air and naval units should depart gradually thereafter. Some of the latter units probably would be redeployed to assist in the war on terrorism, but even so, much of the nearly $20 billion a year cost of the U.S. military commitment to Japan could be saved.

It is uncertain whether the United States would need to redirect all of the money saved from terminating the foreign aid budget and ending obsolete or unnecessary overseas military commitments to the war on terrorism. Clearly, some additional resources ought to be devoted to beefing up our special forces units and intelligence gathering and evaluation capabilities. They have both been shortchanged for years, and yet they are the front-line forces in the fight against terrorism.

But there may well be some money left over. That is not a bad thing. At the very least, such savings might head off the looming prospect of a return to large federal budget deficits. The savings might even be enough to give the beleaguered American taxpayer a modest break. But however the money is used, it would be better than the current wasteful situation.

Recommended Readings

Bandow, Doug. "Korean Detente: A Threat to Washington's Anachronistic Military Presence?" Cato Institute Foreign Policy Briefing no. 59, August 17, 2000.

———. "Okinawa: Liberating America's East Asian Military Colony." Cato Institute Policy Analysis no. 344, May 18, 1999.

————. *Tripwire: Korea and U.S. Foreign Policy in a Changed World.* Washington: Cato Institute, 1996.

Carpenter, Ted Galen. "Fixing U.S. Foreign Policy." *Reason,* October 2002.

————. *NATO's Empty Victory: A Postmortem on the Balkan War.* Washington: Cato Institute, 2000.

Carpenter, Ted Galen, ed. *NATO Enters the 21st Century.* London: Frank Cass, 2001.

Dempsey, Gary, ed. *Exiting the Balkan Thicket.* Washington: Cato Institute, 2002.

Eland, Ivan. *Putting "Defense" Back into U.S. Defense Policy.* Westport, Conn.: Praeger, 2001.

Harrison, Selig S. *Korean Endgame: A Strategy for Reunification and U.S. Disengagement.* Princeton, N.J.: Princeton University Press, 2002.

Layne, Christopher. "Death Knell for NATO? The Bush Administration Confronts the European Security and Defense Policy." Cato Institute Policy Analysis no. 394, April 4, 2001.

Olsen, Edward A. "A Northeast Asian Peace Dividend." *Strategic Review* (Summer 1998).

————. *U.S. National Defense for the Twenty-First Century: The Grand Exit Strategy.* London: Frank Cass, 2002.

—Prepared by Ted Galen Carpenter

5. Waging an Effective War

Congress should

- stress to the administration that the joint resolution approved by the Senate and House of Representatives authorized the president "to use all necessary and appropriate force against those nations, organizations, or persons he determines planned, authorized, committed, or aided the terrorist attacks that occurred on September 11, 2001," not to wage an amorphous war on "evil";
- urge the administration to focus the war on terrorism only on the al-Qaeda terrorist network and not expand it to other terrorist groups or countries that have not attacked the United States;
- urge the administration to reduce military operations in Afghanistan and expand military operations into the Peshawar border region in Pakistan to root out al-Qaeda and Taliban forces; and
- recognize that much of the war against terrorism will not involve military action but will emphasize diplomatic, intelligence, and law enforcement cooperation with other countries.

The war on terrorism is unlike any other war the United States has waged. The enemy is not a traditional nation-state with armed forces. Instead, it is a dispersed terrorist network operating in more than 60 countries around the world. As demonstrated on September 11, terrorists are unlikely to attack using conventional military means—and they are willing to sacrifice themselves in suicide operations. Also unlike traditional wars, the war on terrorism does not have a geographical front where battle lines are clearly drawn. The terrorists will choose where they will attack (either in the United States or U.S. targets abroad), but the United States may not know where to direct retaliatory action. This war is likely to be long (if the English experience with the Irish Republican Army and the Israeli experience with Palestinian terrorist groups are any indication). The mere absence of terrorist violence against the United States or U.S. targets overseas will not be a reliable standard for determining if the war is being won. There could be long lulls between terrorist attacks. And there is not likely to be a clearly and easily defined victory—the terrorists will probably not surrender. Realistically, the United States may not be able to win the war in the traditional sense of "winning" and "losing." Recognizing and accepting that the strategic outcome may be ambiguous can help effective engagement with the enemy.

Focus on al-Qaeda

To begin, the United States must clearly define the terrorist enemy, and in this instance the enemy is the al-Qaeda terrorist network, which is the group responsible for the September 11 attacks against the World Trade Center towers and the Pentagon. Indeed, the joint resolution of Congress after the attacks authorized the president "to use all necessary and appropriate force against those nations, organizations, or persons he determines planned, authorized, committed, or aided the terrorists attacks that occurred on September 11, 2001." Therefore, the focus of the war and our efforts must be on al-Qaeda, not a more expansive and nebulous war against terrorism in general. That means avoiding distractions (which use up scarce resources and could potentially lead to getting bogged down) that are tenuous and tangential to al-Qaeda, such as the Abu Sayef in the Philippines and Muslim Chechen rebels in the Republic of Georgia. Both of those are internal problems best left to their respective governments. Similarly, the United States needs to avoid making false linkages between the war on terrorism and the war on drugs by including the Colombian FARC as a target. And the United States must avoid needlessly stirring the hornets' nest by trying to connect al-Qaeda to other terrorist groups, such as Hamas and Hezbollah, which do not focus their attacks against the United States, without clear proof that such groups are collaborating against the United States. It also means understanding that—unless hard evidence proves otherwise—except for the Taliban regime in Afghanistan, al-Qaeda is not linked to, does not receive support from, and has not been given safe haven by other countries. In other words, the war on terrorism should not be expanded to include military operations against any of the countries of the "axis of evil."

It is also important to understand that military operations—such as Operation Enduring Freedom in Afghanistan—are likely to be the exception rather than the rule in the war on terrorism. Intelligence and law enforcement operations will probably be more important to the successful prosecution of the war. Thus, even calling this a "war" on terrorism is somewhat misleading, given traditional thinking about wars and how they are waged.

Afghanistan

Operation Anaconda and subsequent military operations in the wake of Operation Enduring Freedom have demonstrated that only tattered remnants of the Taliban and al-Qaeda remain in Afghanistan. Furthermore, the U.S. bombing of a wedding party in the Uruzgan province in July 2002 demonstrates that the continued use of airpower for military operations inside Afghanistan may be counterproductive. Therefore, if there is a requirement for "mop-up" operations against al-Qaeda and the Taliban inside Afghanistan, the United States should rely more on ground forces— in particular special operations forces.

That said, given the post-Taliban political maneuvering by various regional and local actors in Afghanistan, the United States needs to be extremely careful and wary about intelligence received from Afghan sources about al-Qaeda and Taliban in hiding. There is evidence to suggest that ulterior motives may have been behind intelligence information that prompted several U.S. military actions against the wrong targets or the killing of innocent civilians in Afghanistan. The U.S. military can ill afford too many of those episodes. The biggest mistake the United States can make in Afghanistan is to have the Afghan people view the U.S. military presence as an invading and occupying military force rather than the force that liberated them from oppressive Taliban rule. History shows that while the various factions inside Afghanistan often fight among themselves, they tend to unite against any invading power.

The other "traps" that U.S. military forces need to avoid in Afghanistan are peacekeeping and nation building. Both are nonessential to the successful prosecution of the war on terrorism. The United States needs to recognize that domestic opposition to the Karzai government does not automatically mean the opponents are al-Qaeda or Taliban supporters who are a threat to the United States. Furthermore, the U.S. military should not be used (or be perceived) to prop up the Karzai government. That government must be able to sustain itself on its own merits. That the Karzai government might fall does not necessarily mean the return of Taliban rule and a safe haven for al-Qaeda. Rather, the country would likely revert to its traditional form of governance—a highly decentralized system with a nominal national government and most power held by tribal leaders and so-called regional warlords. That may not be either efficient or democratic by Western standards, but U.S. interests in the war on terrorism demand only that whatever government is in power in Afghanistan not provide safe haven and support for al-Qaeda terrorists. That the United States is serious and willing to take all necessary action to realize this objective is certainly the single most important lesson learned by the Afghans from Operation Enduring Freedom.

Pakistan

Ultimately, Afghanistan becomes less important as a place to conduct military operations in the war on terrorism and more important as a place from which to launch military operations. And those operations should be directed across the border into neighboring Pakistan, which is where al-Qaeda and the Taliban are known to have fled.

Such operations will not be easy. The lessons learned in Afghanistan suggest that the United States should expect to have to rely more heavily on ground forces to find, engage, and destroy al-Qaeda and Taliban forces. In other words, military victories in Pakistan will not be won with airpower and precision-guided munitions, which means that U.S. forces are likely to experience casualties. Given that al-Qaeda and the Taliban have apparently found shelter in the western Pakistan border area, U.S. military forces cannot reasonably expect support from the population in the region. Indeed, in some instances, the inhabitants may put up fierce resistance. And because of the political situation in Pakistan, the United States cannot count on significant support from Pakistan's army and other military forces. President Pervez Musharraf of Pakistan is conducting a high-wire balancing act that will make it difficult enough for him to condone U.S. military action inside his country, let alone actively participate in such action. But if Pakistan is to claim to be an ally of the United States in the war on terrorism, the United States must prevail and persuade Musharraf to allow the U.S. military to expand operations in Pakistan to finish the job it started in Afghanistan.

Weak States

It is apparent that weak states are potential breeding grounds and hiding places for terrorists. Therefore, the Middle East and Africa are areas that require careful attention. Certainly, the United States must be prepared to use military force when and where necessary. But first and foremost, the United States should work to convince the governments of countries that are likely to be hiding places and bases of reconstitution for al-Qaeda—for example, Sudan, Somalia, and Yemen—to take action themselves. Only if such countries refuse or are unable to take action against a significant al-Qaeda presence should the United States consider conducting military operations (in all likelihood with special forces) to hunt down and capture or kill al-Qaeda members.

Saudi Arabia

The United States also needs to put political and diplomatic pressure on friendly Arab countries to cooperate and assist with hunting down al-Qaeda inside their borders. Most notably, 15 of the 19 hijackers involved in the September 11 attacks against the World Trade Center towers and the Pentagon were Saudi nationals. Yet—as was the case after the 1996 bomb attack on the Khobar Towers in Dharan that killed 19 Americans—the Saudi government has been less than cooperative and remains reluctant to take any meaningful action against potential terrorists. Given the U.S. military presence in Saudi Arabia (at the request of the House of Saud and itself a contributing factor to making the United States a target for terrorism), such behavior is unacceptable. Just as President Musharraf must ultimately be convinced to give the U.S. military freedom of action in western Pakistan if he is to continue to claim to be an ally in the war on terrorism, the Saudis must also cooperate. If they don't, the United States should sever its ties with the House of Saud.

Indonesia

Another area of the world that bears watching is Indonesia, which has the world's largest Muslim population and is just emerging from years of political, social, and economic turmoil. Various claims have been made about an al-Qaeda presence, including terrorist training camps, in Indonesia. Therefore, the United States needs to determine carefully whether there is a direct al-Qaeda presence in Indonesia or the situation involves an indigenous insurgency with tenuous and tangential links to al-Qaeda (in the Philippines, for example). The mere presence of radical Muslims does not necessarily signify a direct threat from al-Qaeda. And if a stable, democratic government in Indonesia is crucial to preventing future terrorism, the United States needs to be careful about placing undue strains on Indonesia's fledging democracy. The presence of U.S. troops in the country, for example, could fuel the anger of Muslim extremists. As is the case with Sudan, Somalia, and Yemen, the United States needs to coax and cajole the Indonesian government to take necessary actions and precautions. But use of U.S. military force should be resorted to only if there is direct evidence of a significant al-Qaeda presence and all other options for dealing with the threat have been exhausted.

Allies and Friendly Countries

The rest of the war on terrorism will be waged against al-Qaeda cells operating in countries that are either allies of or friendly to the United States. The task will be to ferret out and capture al-Qaeda members. The war will not be military in nature. Rather, it will be the hard (and sometimes mundane) work of intelligence and law enforcement agencies. That will require unprecedented cooperation between such U.S. agencies and those in foreign countries. (Cooperation should be limited to intelligence and law enforcement; the U.S. military should not become involved in fighting other nations' wars for them.) The United States needs to improve relations with foreign intelligence agencies in order to be able to share information about suspected al-Qaeda operatives. Foreign law enforcement and internal security agencies will have primary responsibility for apprehending suspected al-Qaeda terrorists. And the hurdles of extradition will have to be overcome so that foreign governments hand over the terrorists who are caught. Again, the United States will need to exert political and diplomatic skill to elicit such cooperation. The threat of military force (let alone its actual use) is not a viable option.

In the final analysis, the United States will not be able to go it alone in the war on terrorism. The United States will need to convince other countries to take actions that are in U.S. interests. Diplomacy and statecraft may ultimately be the most important tools for achieving success against al-Qaeda.

Suggested Readings

Bandow, Doug. "Befriending Saudi Princes: A High Price for a Dubious Alliance." Cato Institute Policy Analysis no. 428, March 20, 2002.

Bergen, Peter L. *Holy War, Inc.* New York: Free Press, 2001.

Carr, Caleb. *The Lessons of Terror*. New York: Random House, 2002.

Doran, Michael Scott. "Somebody Else's Civil War." *Foreign Affairs* 81, no. 1 (January–February 2002).

Eland, Ivan. "Robust Response to 9/11 Is Needed but Poking the Hornets' Nest Is Ill-Advised." Cato Institute Foreign Policy Briefing no. 69, December 18, 2001.

Hadar, Leon T. "Pakistan in America's War against Terrorism: Strategic Ally or Unreliable Client?" Cato Institute Policy Analysis no. 436, May 8, 2002.

Hoffman, Bruce. *Inside Terrorism*. New York: Columbia University Press, 1998.

Peña, Charles V. "The Anti-Terrorism Coalition: Don't Pay an Excessive Price." Cato Institute Foreign Policy Briefing no. 68, December 11, 2001.

Vlahos, Michael. "Terror's Mask: Insurgency within Islam." Johns Hopkins University, Applied Physics Laboratory, May 2002.

—Prepared by Charles V. Peña

6. Homeland Security

Congress should

- monitor closely the implementation of the new Department of Homeland Security and instruct the president to trim and stream-line the disparate bureaucracies incorporated into it so that the department can be effective in fighting agile terrorist groups;
- prune and then consolidate the agencies of the intelligence community to reduce the coordination problems that led to the events of September 11, 2001;
- abolish the Office of Homeland Security and the Homeland Security Council and the position of the homeland security adviser (now that a Department of Homeland Security has been established) and use the existing National Security Council and national security adviser to coordinate homeland security issues among agencies; and
- ensure that the new department does not undertake measures that improve homeland security only at the margins, while undermining America's unique and cherished civil liberties.

In the largest open society in the world, improving homeland security is a daunting task. Among other vulnerable targets, the United States has thousands of miles of borders; thousands of bridges, sports stadiums, and shopping malls; and hundreds of skyscrapers and nuclear power plants. Defending against terrorist attacks perpetrated with weapons of mass destruction or disruption may be even more challenging. According to the 1997 Defense Science Board report, *DoD Responses to Transnational Threats*, "There are a number of challenges that have been regarded as 'too hard' to solve: the nuclear terrorism challenge, defense against biological and chemical warfare threat, and defense against the information warfare threat." Yet the September 11, 2001, attacks on the Pentagon and

World Trade Center put intense pressures on Congress and the Bush administration to show that security against future attacks is being enhanced. The key question is whether rearranging boxes on the government's organizational chart and adding new bureaucracy will make the average American safer from terrorist attacks. Unless the agencies being incorporated into the new Department of Homeland Security are trimmed and streamlined in order to fight agile terrorists, the answer is no.

Adding New Bureaucracy May Reduce Security Rather Than Enhance It

Originally, the Bush administration opposed the Democratic proposal to create a new department charged with homeland security. Then revelations about the existence of intelligence information that might have helped uncover the September 11 attacks before they occurred and about the lack of coordination in and among government agencies—within the Federal Bureau of Investigation and between the FBI and the Central Intelligence Agency—which led to failure to piece the information together and act on it, caused the administration to reverse its opposition to the creation of a new security bureaucracy.

As usual, Washington's response to a crisis is a reorganization of government, and this one is the largest since 1947. Bits and pieces of disparate departments and agencies will be pasted together to form the new department. For example, among other federal entities, the Federal Emergency Management Agency, the Customs Service and Secret Service (from the Treasury Department), the Coast Guard and Transportation Security Administration (from the Transportation Department), the Animal and Plant Health Inspection Service (from the Agriculture Department), and the Border Patrol and Immigration and Naturalization Service (from the Justice Department) will be included in the new department.

The threat from al-Qaeda and other terrorist groups is one of agile, nonbureaucratic adversaries who have the great advantage of being on the offense—knowing where, when, and how they will attack. Terrorists take advantage of the sluggishness of and the poor coordination among military, intelligence, law enforcement, and domestic response bureaucracies to attack gaps in the defenses. Yet the Bush administration rushed—before the congressional intelligence panels had completed their work to determine the exact nature of the government lapses prior to September 11—to propose a solution that did not seem to deal with preliminary indications of what the major problem seems to have been: a lack of coordination between and within the intelligence agencies that make up the vast U.S. intelligence bureaucracy. Instead, the president has proposed reorganizing other government agencies into a new super bureaucracy, leaving out the CIA and FBI. Furthermore, although seeming to consolidate federal efforts at homeland defense, the new department may actually reduce U.S. security by adding bureaucracy rather than reducing it. More bureaucracy means more coordination problems of the kind that seem to have been prevalent in the intelligence community prior to September 11.

The intelligence community and other agencies involved in security have traditionally battled nation-states. Fortunately, those states have governments with bureaucracies that are often more sluggish than our own government's agencies. In contrast, terrorist groups have always been nimble opponents that were difficult to stop, but they were not a strategic threat to the U.S. homeland. As dramatically illustrated by the attacks of September 11, terrorists willing to engage in mass slaughter (with conventional weapons or weapons of mass destruction) and commit suicide now pose a strategic threat to the U.S. territory and population.

No security threat to the United States matches this one. To fight this nontraditional threat, the U.S. government must think outside the box and try to be as nimble as the opponent (a difficult task). The Bush administration is correct that the current U.S. government structure—with more than 100 federal entities involved in homeland security—is not optimal for defending the nation against the new strategic threat. Although consolidating federal efforts is not a bad idea in itself, creating a new department does not ensure that the bureaucracy will be more streamlined, experience fewer coordination problems, or be more effective in the fight against terrorism.

In fact, the reorganization will add yet another layer of bureaucracy to the fight against terrorism. In his message to Congress urging the passage of his proposal to create the new department, the president made a favorable reference to the National Security Act of 1947, which merged the Departments of War and the Navy to create the Department of Defense and created an Office of the Secretary of Defense to oversee the military services. But today, 55 years after the act's passage, that office is a bloated bureaucracy that exercises comparatively weak oversight of military services whose failure to coordinate and cooperate even during wartime is legendary. Even Secretary of Defense Donald Rumsfeld has compared the efficiency and responsiveness of the DoD bureaucracy to Soviet central planning.

The proposed new department is similar to DoD because it will bring together agencies with very different missions and methods of operation and create a large new departmental bureaucracy to try to rein them all in. As was the case when DoD was created, consolidation of the government's efforts is laudable, but it may be unhelpful or even counterproductive to establish another layer of bureaucracy without cutting out layers of management from the agencies being merged or removing some agencies entirely from the homeland security arena and giving their functions to other agencies. Interagency coordination problems may become intra-agency coordination problems.

Consolidation of agencies would have been fine had cutting come before pasting rather than vice versa. In other words, agencies should have been trimmed and reformed (and some totally eliminated) before they were consolidated. Instead, the agencies will be consolidated, with cuts or savings to come later. That promise is not likely to be fulfilled. Once the new, large, consolidated department is created—it will be one of the largest departments in the government—the new department head will be a powerful advocate for more money and people rather than the opposite.

Although the Bush administration did promise some efficiencies from consolidation, the administration did not project overall net savings from the reorganization. At best, policymakers in the administration promised that a consolidated department would not increase costs. But it is telling that the president's plan had no cost estimates accompanying it. Historically, mergers of government agencies have increased costs rather than decreased them. Although some longer-term savings from consolidation of payroll and computer systems may occur, creating the new secretary's bureaucracy to ride herd on all of the agencies will likely increase net costs. The president's proposal for the department calls for adding one deputy secretary, five under secretaries, and up to 16 assistant secretaries. According to the Congressional Budget Office, the new department could cost as much as $4.5 billion more (from 2003 to 2007) than operating the disparate agencies separately.

So the president's plan is likely to cost more rather than less. Following the money is important; if costs are not going down, the plan is unlikely to streamline the government's efforts at counterterrorism and homeland defense. With too many federal entities already involved in homeland security, more government is not better than less. With so many agencies involved, if a catastrophic attack with weapons of mass destruction occurred, administrative chaos would be the probable outcome. After creation of the new department, there will be fewer organizational entities but probably more government. A stealthy and nimble enemy is at the gates, and there is not much time to put the government on a diet. Instead, the government may be headed to the pastry shop. More bureaucracy means more coordination problems and more opportunities for terrorists.

Bush's Plan Does Not Solve the Problem with Intelligence and May Make It Worse

The president's plan for a new department does not solve what seems to be the primary problem—the lack of coordination within and between U.S. intelligence agencies, specifically the FBI and the CIA. Those agencies are conspicuously missing from the new department.

Yet, for enhanced homeland security, intelligence is the key ingredient. The U.S. government has infinitely more resources for use against al-Qaeda and other terrorist groups than they do against it. If the U.S. government can discover plots or the location of targets and terrorists in time to take action, the overwhelming U.S. superiority in military and law enforcement resources can be brought to bear to foil the plot. Mitigating the effects of the attack after it happens is important, but, in many cases, the government may be able to only marginally help reduce casualties. Without good intelligence, that may be the government's only role. The United States already has an unparalleled ability to collect vast amounts of raw intelligence data—the pieces of the jigsaw puzzle—but the already too numerous agencies in the U.S. intelligence community have had trouble fusing it into a complete picture.

Regrettably, in intelligence, as in the overall homeland security realm, the reorganization will make the government even less likely to put the jigsaw puzzle together and even more ungainly and sluggish in combating terrorists. A new intelligence analysis center will be created in the new Department of Homeland Security to analyze threats to the U.S. homeland. However, the FBI, the CIA, and other intelligence agencies already analyze such threats. Thus, the new agency will be analyzing the analyses of other agencies. If the new analysis center is supposed to be fusing the analyses of those agencies, it would seem to be usurping the role of the intelligence community staff under the director of central intelligence. Furthermore, if the FBI and the CIA fail to fully cooperate or coordinate with each other because of turf jealousies, excessive secrecy, or burdensome bureaucratic rules for interagency coordination, the problem is likely to get worse as another competing bureaucracy is added.

The Government Already Had the Machinery to Coordinate Homeland Security

The National Security Council includes the heads of the major departments and agencies that are responsible for the nation's security. The president's powerful national security adviser officially only coordinates policy among the agencies but in reality is a potent independent voice in the policymaking process. It would seem logical that catastrophic terrorism against the U.S. homeland would affect national security and thus fit under the purview of the NSC and the national security adviser. But apparently not.

Before proposing the new Department of Homeland Security, the president created a White House Office of Homeland Security, a homeland security adviser, and a Homeland Security Council. Even with the creation of the new department, all of this bureaucracy remains. The president maintains that protecting America from terrorism will remain a multidepartmental issue and will continue to require those entities to oversee interagency coordination. But the roles of the homeland security adviser and the Homeland Security Council appear to be redundant with those of the national security adviser and the NSC. For 55 years, the NSC existed to provide for the national security, but as soon as the nation was attacked at home, a new security bureaucracy was thought to be needed. By creating a new cabinet department, U.S. policymakers appear to subscribe to the strange notion that the NSC should provide for security only overseas.

Piling new bureaucracy on new bureaucracy is not the way to fight nimble terrorists. Sen. Richard Shelby (R-Ala.), vice chairman of the Senate Select Committee on Intelligence, noted that the FBI and the CIA are not very agile, and the General Accounting Office has recommended reducing the layers, levels, and units within the FBI. That recommendation should apply to all agencies that remain in the homeland security arena. Many of the more than 100 federal entities involved in homeland security need to be removed from performing the mission. To reduce the chances of lapses in intelligence coordination and chaos in domestic crisis response, there should be fewer government entities in need of coordination. Although reducing the number of people and the amount of bureaucracy seems to go against the tide in the present crisis atmosphere, preliminary indications are that the main problem is coordination among governmental entities, not a lack of raw information or insufficient resources. In short, Congress should not be afraid to streamline or even eliminate agencies involved in homeland security—both within and outside the new department.

Homeland Security and Civil Liberties

Congress should carefully scrutinize any new security measures to make sure they really enhance security and do not merely erode the civil liberties that make America unique. Osama bin Laden is a sophisticated operative who has stated that one of his major goals is to change the U.S. system. If America's civil liberties are eroded needlessly, bin Laden may achieve an even bigger victory than he did with the horrific attacks of September 11.

In a crisis, the government has an incentive to take measures designed to show progress in dealing with it. In the wake of the September 11 attacks, many of the measures proposed or implemented by the Justice Department to restrict civil liberties seemed to be "for show," with little hope of effectively fighting terrorism—for example, the Terrorism Information and Prevention System program that would have inundated law enforcement agencies with dead-end leads from postal and utility workers spying on private residences and businesses. Congress needs to make sure the new department avoids such fiascos. In short, Congress needs to make sure that any new security measures are needed and effective and do not unduly restrict civil liberties.

Suggested Readings

Congressional Budget Office. "Congressional Budget Office Cost Estimate: H.R. 2005—Homeland Security Act of 2002." July 23, 2002.

Eland, Ivan. "Homeland Security: Calibrating Calamity." *Washington Times,* July 25, 2002.

———. Testimony before the Subcommittee on Technology, Terrorism, and Government Information of the Senate Judiciary Committee. June 25, 2002.

Lynch, Timothy. "Breaking the Vicious Cycle: Preserving Our Liberties While Fighting Terrorism." Cato Institute Policy Analysis no. 443, June 26, 2002.

Office of the Secretary of Defense. *Final Report.* Vol. 1 of *The Defense Science Board 1997 Summer Study Task Force on DoD Responses to Transnational Threats.* October 1997.

Taylor, Eric R. "Are We Prepared for Terrorism Using Weapons of Mass Destruction? Government's Half Measures." Cato Institute Policy Analysis no. 387, November 27, 2000.

———. "The New Homeland Security Apparatus: Impeding the Fight against Agile Terrorists." Cato Institute Foreign Policy Briefing no. 70, June 26, 2002.

—Prepared by Ivan Eland

7. Reducing the "Lightning Rod" Problem

Congress should support a decisive, but narrowly focused, war on terrorism to eradicate the terrorists who perpetrated the September 11, 2001, attacks. In the long term, Congress should refuse to provide funds for U.S. military presence and military and political interventions overseas that are not required to defend vital U.S. interests and could result in catastrophic retaliatory attacks by terrorists on U.S. targets, including the American homeland. Most urgently, Congress should

- direct that U.S. military forces be withdrawn from Saudi Arabia;
- adopt a more even-handed approach to the Israeli-Palestinian conflict by removing U.S. military and economic support for Israel and ending active mediation of the Israeli-Palestinian conflict;
- end the comprehensive economic sanctions against Iraq; and
- end support for despotic Arab governments, such as those in Egypt and Saudi Arabia.

Current U.S. policies are unnecessary for U.S. security and incite radical Islamist terrorists to attack U.S targets.

The U.S. Government Has Endangered Citizens

Compared with other nations, the United States is disproportionately attacked by terrorists—in terms of both number of attacks and casualties. In 2001, according to the U.S. State Department's *Patterns of Global Terrorism 2001*, anti-U.S. attacks accounted for 63 percent of terrorist incidents worldwide. During the same year, attacks in North America alone (the vast majority of the casualties were American citizens) accounted for 71 percent of the world's casualties caused by terrorist attacks. Why do terrorists single out the United States?

Some observers argue that the United States is a lightning rod for terrorists because it is a large, rich, capitalist nation; because it is a constitutional republic whose citizens enjoy many freedoms; or because American culture is pervasive and perceived as decadent by some groups. Although those factors no doubt have some effect, a deeper analysis should raise suspicions about them as significant causes for anti-U.S. terrorism. Many other countries are large, rich, capitalist nations with republican forms of government (for example, Germany and Japan), but they do not experience the magnitude of terrorism that afflicts the United States. True, American culture is pervasive, but American economic and political values (that is, civil society) are the envy of the world. Absent the element of U.S. government–driven military power, those values do not usually have coercive or ill effects on other countries and are not generally resented.

Many analysts focus on perceived Islamic hatred of decadent American culture. Yet more than one Zogby poll of numerous Islamic and Arab countries has shown that majorities in those countries liked American freedom, democracy, technology, and culture—including movies and television. Conversely, overwhelming majorities disliked U.S. government policies toward the Middle East. More important, if the goal is to uncover the motivations of the radical Islamists who attack the United States (and it should be, because that task is vital to both fighting and avoiding terrorism but has been neglected because of its sensitivity), the best place to start is with what Islamists say and write. For example, Peter Bergen, the CNN correspondent who interviewed Osama bin Laden and wrote *Holy War, Inc.*, notes that bin Laden has never railed against the decadence of American or Western culture. His hatred of America is generated by U.S. foreign policy—his biggest bone of contention is the unnecessary U.S. military presence in Saudi Arabia, which he believes desecrates Islam's holiest sites located there.

Although some pundits have claimed that America is targeted by terrorists for ''who it is'' rather than ''what it does,'' even high-level U.S. government sources admit a link between interventionist U.S. foreign policy (that is, being the world's policeman) and retaliatory terrorist attacks on U.S. targets.

That link was recognized in the upper levels of the U.S. government long before the September 11 terrorist attacks. According to a study completed in 1997 by the Defense Science Board, a panel of experts that advises the secretary of defense:

As part of its global power position, the United States is called upon frequently to respond to international causes and deploy forces around the world. America's position in the world invites attacks simply because of its presence. *Historical data show a strong correlation between U.S. involvement in international situations and an increase in terrorist attacks against the United States* [emphasis added].

In an August 8, 1998, radio address justifying cruise missile attacks on Afghanistan and Sudan in response to bin Laden's earlier bombings of two U.S. embassies, President Bill Clinton admitted as much but put a positive spin on it with political hyperbole: "Americans are targets of terrorism in part because we have unique leadership responsibilities in the world, because we act to advance peace and democracy, and because we stand united against terrorism."

Most striking of all is the post–September 11 "National Strategy for Homeland Security" issued by the Bush White House's Office of Homeland Security in July 2002:

> For more than six decades, America has sought to protect its own sovereignty and independence through a strategy of global presence and engagement. In so doing, America has helped many other countries and peoples advance along the path of democracy, open markets, individual liberty, and peace with their neighbors. Yet there are those who oppose America's role in the world, and who are willing to use violence against us and our friends. Our great power leaves these enemies with few conventional options for doing us harm. One such option is to take advantage of our freedom and openness by secretly inserting terrorists into our country to attack our homeland. Homeland security seeks to deny this avenue of attack to our enemies and thus to provide a secure foundation for America's ongoing global engagement.

What is astonishing is that after 60 years the aberration in American history of acting as the world's policeman has become an end in itself. It is even a higher goal than that which should be any government's primary function—to make its territory and citizens safe and secure. Profligate intervention in the affairs of other nations (the United States is the only country in the world that regularly intervenes in every region of the world) is not a national security policy—in fact, it is quite the opposite. The Office of Homeland Security periodically issues "duck and cover" warnings to U.S. citizens at home, and the State Department does so to U.S. tourists, expatriates, and business people abroad. But the U.S. government's own actions are responsible for the disproportionate bull's-eye that is being drawn around Americans.

Extended Defense Perimeter Actually Increases the Vulnerability of the Homeland

During the Cold War the military paradigm of defending forward to keep the adversary far away from the homeland made some sense. The United States faced a foe with conventional military forces and reaped advantages from ensuring that its opponent did not make inroads in certain key strategic areas of the world. Although both superpowers possessed nuclear weapons, the disadvantages of U.S. intervention overseas were limited by the "managed competition" between the two behemoths that avoided direct interventions in the other's regions of core concern. Now, however, the disadvantages vastly outweigh any advantages gained from profligate U.S. interventions in remote parts of the world that are no longer strategic (if they ever were). The United States no longer has to check the advances of another superpower and now faces an unconventional foe in a war that has no front line. All of the layers of the extended U.S. defense perimeter did not prevent al-Qaeda from carrying out a catastrophic attack on the U.S. homeland and actually reduced U.S. security by generating much of the hatred that led to the attack. In short, the nontraditional interventionist foreign policy on a grand scale—initiated during the Cold War but abhorrent to U.S. policymakers for the prior 170 years—is now out of date and profoundly dangerous.

What the United States Should Do about Terrorism

The U.S. government has several options for dealing with terrorism. The possibilities include improving intelligence, enhancing homeland security measures, increasing military and covert action against terrorists, and reducing military and covert action. Even U.S. intelligence professionals reach the disquieting conclusion that there will be more terrorist attacks and that U.S. intelligence will not be able to detect some of them before they happen. That conclusion is especially unnerving now that terrorists are clearly willing to inflict mass casualties and are willing to give their lives in the attack. It should be noted that the conventional means used in the September 11 attacks are not the worst possibility; attacks with chemical, biological, or nuclear weapons could be far more deadly.

The United States certainly should take measures to enhance homeland security, but the public should not be lulled by all the official activity into thinking that the U.S. government can do more than catch some of the attackers before they attack or reduce casualties at the margins after an attack. The United States is one of the largest and most open societies in the world—both in population and in area. The nation has thousands of miles of borders, countless skyscrapers and sports stadiums, vulnerable infrastructure, and a political system that prevents law enforcement's behaving too aggressively in the fight against terrorism. Moreover, according to the Defense Science Board, the problems of nuclear terrorism, defense against the threat of biological and chemical weapons, and defense against information warfare have historically been regarded as "too hard" to solve. Yet the U.S. government is now inculcating the American public with a false sense that government can solve those problems.

Finally, the question of military and covert action needs to be addressed. In the short term, the United States has no choice but to try to eradicate bin Laden and the al-Qaeda terrorist network by using intelligence, law enforcement, and, if necessary, military assets. In most nations (for example, Yemen and Pakistan), the United States should first rely on supporting local governments in their efforts to eradicate terrorists within their borders and, if that proves insufficient or ineffective, then take direct military action. But the United States should not get dangerously distracted in this war against the enemy at the gates by military or covert actions against terrorist groups that do not normally focus their attacks on the United States (for example, Hezbollah or Hamas) or against rogue states that cannot be linked to the September 11 attacks. Many foreign terrorist organizations on the State Department's terrorism list do not focus their attacks on the United States. Attacking them militarily or using covert action (which the Bush administration has authorized) is simply stirring the hornets' nest unnecessarily. The United States can continue to engage in lower-profile regional cooperation in intelligence and law enforcement with other nations to combat such groups.

Although narrowly focused military action will be needed in the short term to expunge the threat from al-Qaeda, a policy of military restraint should be adopted in the long term. Because improvements in intelligence capabilities (particularly intelligence from human sources) and homeland security measures will provide positive results only at the margins in the detection, prevention, and mitigation of terrorist attacks, it is vital that the United States lower its target profile vis-à-vis terrorists. That goal can be achieved by reducing the U.S. military presence abroad and intervening militarily or politically only on the rare occasions when vital U.S. interests are threatened.

Specific Recommendations to Lessen U.S. Vulnerability to Terrorist Attacks

Remove the U.S. Military Presence from Saudi Arabia

The withdrawal of U.S. forces from the land of Islam's most holy sites would remove an irritant that inflames Islamic terrorists to strike U.S. targets but would not adversely affect other U.S. security interests. Even if it were necessary to use the U.S. military to defend Persian Gulf oil— and economists from across the political spectrum attest that it is not— the United States did so successfully during the Gulf War in 1991 without having a prior peacetime military presence in Saudi Arabia. Furthermore, a substantial portion of U.S. military assets has already been moved to surrounding countries because of restrictions on their use imposed by the Saudi regime. Anonymously, even senior U.S. military officials have expressed to the *Washington Post* a desire to withdraw U.S. forces from Saudi territory.

Furthermore, it is ethically questionable to use U.S. forces to defend a despotic regime with an abysmal human rights record that indirectly supported al-Qaeda terrorists and directly supported the radical religious schools in Pakistan that spawned those terrorists and the repressive Taliban regime in Afghanistan that harbored them. The Saudi government also makes the lives of American service personnel miserable by putting heavy restrictions on their personal lives and their mingling with Saudi citizens.

Some observers would argue that withdrawing from Saudi Arabia would hand bin Laden a victory by fulfilling his desire for a U.S. withdrawal. That argument can be nullified as long as the United States neutralizes most of the al-Qaeda network as U.S. forces pull back from Saudi Arabia. In addition, according to the *Washington Post*, because of fears that the American presence was destabilizing their regime by stirring up Islamic militants, the Saudis have been on the verge of asking U.S. forces to leave. The United States should take advantage of those sentiments as a cover and quietly pull out its forces if asked to do so.

Develop a More Even-Handed Approach to the Israeli-Palestinian Conflict by Cutting Off Military and Economic Aid to Israel

Unbalanced U.S. involvement in the Israeli-Palestinian conflict inflames the Islamic world and is a principal motive behind terrorist attacks by Islamists on U.S. targets worldwide. The desire to assist a nation inclined toward democracy is understandable, but doing so is no longer advisable given the possibility of retaliatory mass terrorist attacks, including the use of nuclear, chemical, and biological weapons, on the U.S. homeland.

In attempting to mediate the negotiation of a settlement to an intractable conflict, the United States is perceived by Arabs to be pushing the Palestinians to end violence more than they are prodding Israel to do so. But both sides in the struggle have used excessive violence against civilians. Those excesses have made it even less likely that either side would be willing to end the conflict. The United States should discontinue futile efforts to pressure the parties to reach a settlement that neither wants and therefore has little chance of succeeding. Both sides must indicate a strong willingness to reach a settlement before the United States resumes mediation. When the United States does so, its role should be strictly limited and neutral. A much more modest and disinterested U.S. mediation role would lower the U.S. target profile to Islamic terrorism.

End Comprehensive Economic Sanctions against Iraq

The most grinding and complete sanctions in world history should come to an end. When economic sanctions are imposed, the target regime— usually a despotic government that tightly controls its nation's political and economic systems—usually transfers the pain of sanctions to the poorest members of society and earns enormous profits from smuggling. In addition, the sanctions create a strong "rally-around-the-flag" effect for the regime against the nations that imposed the strictures. The embargo also takes the blame for economic problems that are caused by the regime's poor policies. In those ways, economic sanctions have the perverse effect of actually strengthening the despotic government's hold on power. Although counterintuitive, the best way to weaken a despotic regime is to get Western products, services, and investment, and the ideas that go with them, into the target nation. But that strategy will work only over the long term.

In the case of Iraq, the bone-crushing U.S.-led embargo has devastated the Iraqi poor but made Saddam Hussein's regime stronger. The sanctions' ill effects on Iraqi society have provoked radical Islamic elements all over the world. The United States should break with conventional wisdom and lead the world in scrapping the sanctions. By doing so, the United States would lower the probability of retaliatory catastrophic terrorist attacks on U.S. targets.

Stop Supporting Despotic Regimes in the Middle East

The Cold War is over, and supporting "friendly" authoritarian regimes, such as Saudi Arabia and Egypt, is no longer necessary (if it ever was).

As noted before, other strategic reasons for supporting them—for example, the great oil reserves in Saudi Arabia—are questionable. Saudi Arabia and the other authoritarian Persian Gulf oil producers—which obtain the vast bulk of their export earnings and foreign currency from the sale of oil—are more desperate to sell the oil than the United States is to buy it. The corruption of those regimes generates the hatred of radical Islamists, as does U.S. support for those governments. As would implementing the other three recommendations, ending support for such authoritarian nations would lower the U.S. profile as a target for Islamic radicals.

Suggested Readings

Carpenter, Ted Galen. *America Entangled: The Persian Gulf Crisis and Its Consequences.* Washington: Cato Institute, 1991.

Carr, Caleb. *Lessons of Terror: A History of Warfare against Civilians: Why It Has Always Failed and Why It Will Fail Again.* New York: Random House, 2002.

Eland, Ivan. "Does U.S. Intervention Overseas Breed Terrorism? The Historical Record." Cato Institute Foreign Policy Briefing no. 50, December 17, 1998.

————. "Protecting the Homeland: The Best Defense Is to Give No Offense." Cato Institute Policy Analysis no. 306, May 5, 1998.

————. "Robust Response to 9/11 Is Needed but Poking the Hornets' Nest Is Ill-Advised." Cato Institute Foreign Policy Briefing no. 69, December 18, 2001.

Hoffman, Bruce. *Inside Terrorism.* New York: Columbia University Press, 1998.

Hoge, James F. Jr., and Gideon Rose, eds. *How Did This Happen?: Terrorism and the New Year.* New York: Public Affairs, 2001.

Smith, James M., and William C. Thomas, eds. *The Terrorism Threat and U.S. Government Response: Operational and Organizational Factors.* U.S. Air Force Institute for National Security Studies, March 2001.

U.S. Department of State. *Patterns of Global Terrorism 2001.* Washington: U.S. Department of State, May 2002.

—Prepared by Ivan Eland

GOVERNMENT REFORM

8. The Delegation of Legislative Powers

Congress should

- require all "lawmaking" regulations to be affirmatively approved by Congress and signed into law by the president, as the Constitution requires for all laws; and
- establish a mechanism to force the legislative consideration of existing regulations during the reauthorization process.

Separation of Powers: The Bulwark of Liberty

When the legislative and executive powers are united in the same person, or in the same body of magistrates, there can be no liberty.
—Montesquieu, *The Spirit of the Laws*

Article I, section 1, of the U.S. Constitution stipulates, "All legislative powers herein granted shall be vested in the Congress of the United States, which shall consist of a Senate and House of Representatives." Article II, section 3, stipulates that the president "shall take care that the laws be faithfully executed." Thus, as we all learned in high school civics, the Constitution clearly provides for the separation of powers between the various branches of government.

The alternative design—concentration of power within a single governmental body—was thought to be inimical to a free society. John Adams wrote in 1776 that "a single assembly, possessed of all the powers of government, would make arbitrary laws for their own interest, and adjudge all controversies in their own favor." James Madison in *Federalist* no. 47 justified the Constitution's separation of powers by noting that it was a necessary prerequisite for "a government of laws and not of men." Further, he wrote, "The accumulation of all powers, legislative, executive, and judiciary, in the same hands, whether of one, a few, or many, and whether hereditary, self-appointed, or elective, may justly be pronounced the very definition of tyranny.''

For the first 150 years of the American Republic, the Supreme Court largely upheld the original constitutional design, requiring that Congress rather than administrators make the law. The suggestion that Congress could broadly delegate its lawmaking powers to others—particularly the executive branch—was generally rejected by the courts. And for good reasons. First, the Constitution was understood to be a document of enumerated and thus limited powers, and nowhere was Congress either explicitly or even implicitly given the power to delegate. Second, the fear of power concentrated in any one branch still animated both the Supreme Court and the legislature. Third, Americans believed that those who make the law should be directly accountable at the ballot box.

The upshot was that the separation of powers effectively restrained federal power, just as the Founders had intended. As Alexis de Tocqueville observed, ''The nation participates in the making of its laws by the choice of its legislators, and in the execution of them by the choice of agents of the executive government.'' He also observed that ''it may also be said to govern itself, so feeble and so restricted is the share left to the administrators, so little do the authorities forget their popular origins and the power from which they emanate.''

The New Deal: "Delegation Running Riot"

The sense of political crisis that permeated the 1930s effectively buried the nondelegation doctrine. In his first inaugural address, Franklin Roosevelt compared the impact of the ongoing economic depression to a foreign invasion and argued that Congress should grant him sweeping powers to fight it.

Shortly after taking office, Congress in 1933 granted Roosevelt virtually unlimited power to regulate commerce through passage of the Agricultural Adjustment Act (which authorized the president to increase agricultural prices via administrative production controls) and the National Industrial Recovery Act (known as the NIRA), which authorized the president to issue industrial codes to regulate all aspects of the industries they covered.

The Supreme Court, however, temporarily arrested the tide in 1935 in its unanimous opinion in *A.L.A. Schechter Poultry Corp. v. United States.* The Court overturned the industrial code provisions of the NIRA, and, in a separate opinion, Justice Benjamin Cardozo termed the NIRA—and thus the New Deal—''delegation running riot.'' That same year, the Court struck down additional NIRA delegations of power in *Panama Refining Co. v. Ryan.*

Largely because of the *Schechter* and *Panama Refining* decisions, President Roosevelt decried the Court's interference with his political agenda and proposed legislation enlarging the size of the Court so that he could appoint additional justices—the so-called Court-packing plan. He lost that battle but won the war. Although the Court never explicitly reversed its 1935 decisions and continues to articulate essentially the same verbal formulas defining the scope of permissible delegation—indeed, *Schechter* and *Panama Refining* theoretically are good law today—it would be nearly 40 years before the Court again struck down business regulation on delegation grounds.

As long as Congress articulates some intelligible standard (no matter how vague or arbitrary) to govern executive lawmaking, courts today are prepared to allow delegation, in the words of Justice Cardozo, to run riot. John Locke's admonition that the legislature "cannot transfer the power of making laws to any other hands, for it being but a delegated power from the people, they who have it cannot pass it over to others," is a forgotten vestige of an era when individual liberty mattered more than administrative convenience. As Federal District Judge Roger Vinson wrote in *United States v. Mills* in 1989, "A delegation doctrine which essentially allows Congress to abdicate its power to define the elements of a criminal offense, in favor of an un-elected administrative agency such as the [Army] Corps of Engineers, does violence to this time-honored principle.... Deferent and minimal judicial review of Congress' transfer of its criminal lawmaking function to other bodies, in other branches, calls into question the vitality of the tripartite system established by our Constitution. It also calls into question the nexus that must exist between the law so applied and simple logic and common sense. Yet that seems to be the state of the law."

Delegation: The Corrosive Agent of Democracy

The concern over congressional delegation of power is not simply theoretical and abstract, for delegation does violence, not only to the ideal construct of a free society, but also to the day-to-day practice of democracy itself. Ironically, delegation does not help to secure "good government"; it helps to destroy it.

Delegation Breeds Political Irresponsibility

Congress delegates power for much the same reason that Congress ran budget deficits for decades. With deficit spending, members of Congress can claim credit for the benefits of their expenditures yet escape blame for the costs. The public must pay ultimately, of course, but through taxes levied at some future time by some other officials. Likewise, delegation allows legislators to claim credit for the benefits that a regulatory statute airily promises yet escape the blame for the burdens it will impose, because they do not issue the laws needed to achieve those high-sounding benefits. The public inevitably must suffer regulatory costs to realize regulatory benefits, but the laws will come from an agency that legislators can then criticize for imposing excessive burdens on their constituents.

Just as deficit spending allows legislators to appear to deliver money to some people without taking it from others, delegation allows them to appear to deliver regulatory benefits without imposing regulatory costs. It provides, in the words of former Environmental Protection Agency deputy administrator John Quarles, "a handy set of mirrors—so useful in Washington—by which politicians can appear to kiss both sides of the apple."

Delegation Is a Political Steroid for Organized Special Interests

As University of Miami law professor John Hart Ely has noted, "One reason we have broadly based representative assemblies is to await something approaching a consensus before government intervenes." The Constitution was intentionally designed to curb the "facility and excess of law-making" (in the words of James Madison) by requiring that statutes go through a bicameral legislature and the president.

Differences in the size and nature of the constituencies of representatives, senators, and the president—and the different lengths of their terms in office—increase the probability that the actions of each will reflect a different balance of interests. That diversity of viewpoint, plus the greater difficulty of prevailing in three forums rather than one, makes it far more difficult for special-interest groups or bare majorities to impose their will on the totality of the American people. Hence, the original design effectively required a supermajority to make law as a means of discouraging the selfish exercise of power by well-organized but narrow interests.

Delegation shifts the power to make law from a Congress of all interests to subgovernments typically representative of only a small subset of all interests. The obstacles intentionally placed in the path of lawmaking disappear, and the power of organized interests is magnified.

That is largely because diffuse interests typically find it even more difficult to press their case before an agency than before a legislature. They often have no direct representation in the administrative process, and effective representation typically requires special legal counsel, expert witnesses, and the capacity to reward or to punish top officials through political organization, press coverage, and close working relationships with members of the appropriate congressional subcommittee. As a result, the general public rarely qualifies as a "stakeholder" in agency proceedings and is largely locked out of the decisionmaking process. Madison's desired check on the "facility and excess of law-making" is thus smashed.

Delegation Breeds the Leviathan State

Perhaps the ultimate check on the growth of government rests in the fact that there is only so much time in a day. No matter how many laws Congress would like to pass, there are only so many hours in a session to do so. Delegation, however, dramatically expands the realm of the possible by effectively "deputizing" tens of thousands of bureaucrats, often with broad and imprecise missions to "go forth and legislate." Thus, as Jacob Weisberg has noted in the *New Republic*, "As a labor-saving device, delegation did for legislators what the washing machine did for the 1950s housewife. Government could now penetrate every nook and cranny of American life in a way that was simply impossible before."

The Threadbare Case for Delegation

Although delegation has become so deeply embedded in the political landscape that few public officials even recognize the phenomenon or the issues raised by the practice, political observers are becoming increasingly aware of the failure of delegation to deliver its promised bounty of good government.

The Myth of Technical Expertise

It was once maintained that delegation produces more sensible laws by transferring lawmaking from elected officials, who are beholden to concentrated interests, to experts, who can base their decisions solely on a cool appraisal of the public interest. Yet most agency heads are not scientists, engineers, economists, or other kinds of technical experts; they are political operatives. Since the Environmental Protection Agency's

inception in 1970, for example, the overwhelming majority of its administrators and assistant administrators have been lawyers. As MIT professor
Michael Golay wrote in *Science*, "Environmental protection policy disagreements are not about what to conclude from the available scientific
knowledge; they represent a struggle for political power among groups
having vastly differing interests and visions for society. In this struggle,
science is used as a means of legitimizing the various positions . . . science
is a pawn, cynically abused as may suit the interests of a particular
protagonist despite great ignorance concerning the problems being
addressed." Perhaps that's why the EPA's own Science Advisory Board
was forced to concede in a 1992 report that the agency's science "is
perceived by many people both inside and outside the agency to be adjusted
to fit policy."

We should not necessarily bemoan the lack of agency expertise, for it
is not entirely clear that government by experts is superior to government
by elected officials. There is no reason to believe that experts possess
superior moral knowledge or a better sense of what constitutes the public
good. Indeed, specialization often impairs the capacity for moral judgment
and often breeds professional zealotry. Likewise, specialized expertise
provides too narrow a base for the balanced judgments that intelligent
policy requires.

Although both agency administrators and legislators often lack the
expertise to evaluate technical arguments by themselves, they can get help
from agency and committee staff, government institutes (like the Centers
for Disease Control or the General Accounting Office), and private sources
such as medical associations, think tanks, and university scientists. After
all, that is what the hearings process is supposed to be about.

And only someone naive about modern government would seriously
claim today that the winds of politics blow any less fiercely in administrative meeting rooms than they do in the halls of Congress. As Nobel
laureate economist James Buchanan and others have observed, public
officials have many incentives to pursue both private and political ends
that often have little to do with their ostensible missions.

Is Congress Too Busy?

New Dealers once argued that "time spent on details [by Congress]
must be at the sacrifice of time spent on matters of the broad public
policy." But Congress today spends little time on "matters of broad public
policy," largely because delegation forces Congress to spend a large chunk

of its time constructing the legislative architecture—sometimes over a thousand pages of it—detailing exactly how various agencies are to decide important matters of policy. Once that architecture is in place, members of Congress find that a large part of their job entails navigating through those bureaucratic mazes for special interests jockeying to influence the final nature of the law. Writing such instructions and performing agency oversight to ensure that they are carried out would be unnecessary if Congress made the rules in the first place.

Moreover, delegation often works to prolong disputes and keep standards of conduct murky because pressures from legislators and the complicated procedures imposed upon agencies turn lawmaking into an excruciatingly slow process. Agencies typically report that they have issued only a small fraction of the laws that their long-standing statutory mandates require. Competing interests devote large sums of money and many of their best minds to this seemingly interminable process. For example, it took the EPA 16 years to ban lead in gasoline despite the fact that the 1970 Clean Air Act explicitly gave them the authority to do so. Simply making the rules the first time around in the legislative process would take less time than the multiyear regulatory sausage machine requires to issue standards.

Complex Rules for a Complex World

Perhaps the most widely accepted justification for some degree of delegation is the complex and technical nature of the world we live in today. As the Supreme Court opined in 1989, "Our jurisprudence has been driven by a practical understanding that in our increasingly complex society, replete with ever changing and more technical problems, Congress simply cannot do its job absent an ability to delegate power under broad general directives."

Yet the vast majority of decisions delegated to the executive branch are not particularly technical in nature. They are instead hotly political, for the reasons mentioned above. If Congress must regulate, it could (and probably should) jettison micromanagerial command-and-control regulations that make up the bulk of the *Federal Register* and instead adopt regulations that are less prescriptive and more performance based or market oriented. Most regulatory analysts on both the left and the right agree that this would also have the happy consequences of decreasing regulatory costs, increasing regulatory efficiency, and decreasing the burden on regulators. In addition, a Congress not skewed toward regulation by delegation would rediscover practical reasons for allowing many matters to be left to state and local regulators.

Conclusion

Forcing Congress to vote on each and every administrative regulation that establishes a rule of private conduct would prove the most revolutionary change in government since the Civil War—not because the idea is particularly radical, but because we are today a nation governed, not by elected officials, but by unelected bureaucrats. The central political issues of the 108th Congress—the complex and heavy-handed array of regulations that entangle virtually all manner of private conduct, the perceived inability of elections to affect the direction of government, the disturbing political power of special interests, the lack of popular respect for the law, the sometimes tyrannical and self-aggrandizing exercise of power by government, and populist resentment of an increasingly unaccountable political elite—are but symptoms of a disease largely caused by delegation.

"No regulation without representation!" would be a fitting battle cry for the 108th Congress if it is truly interested in fundamental reform of government. It is a standard that both the left and the right could comfortably rally around, given that many prominent constitutional scholars, policy analysts, and journalists—from Nadine Strossen, president of the American Civil Liberties Union, to former judge Robert Bork—have expressed support for the end of delegation.

Some observers complain that voting on all regulations would overwhelm Congress. Certainly, federal agencies do issue thousands of regulations every year. However, the flow of new rules is no argument against congressional responsibility. Congress could bundle relatively minor regulations together and vote on the whole package. Both houses could then give major regulations—those that impose costs of more than $100 million annually—close scrutiny.

Of course, forcing Congress to take full and direct responsibility for the law would not prove a panacea. The legislature, after all, has shown itself to be fully capable of violating individual rights, subsidizing special interests, writing complex and virtually indecipherable law, and generally making a hash of things. But delegation has helped to make such phenomena, not the exception, but the rule of modern government. No more crucial—and potentially popular—reform awaits the attention of the 108th Congress.

Suggested Readings

Anthony, Robert. "Unlegislative Compulson: How Federal Agency Guidelines Threaten Your Liberty." Cato Policy Analysis no. 312, August 11, 1998.

Breyer, Stephen. "The Legislative Veto after Chadha." Thomas F. Ryan lecture. *Georgetown Law Journal* 72 (1984).

DeLong, James. *Out of Bounds—Out of Control: Regulatory Enforcement at the EPA.* Washington: Cato Institute, 2002.

Lawson, Gary. "Delegation and the Constitution." *Regulation* 22, no. 2 (1999).

Lowi, Theodore. *The End of Liberalism: The Second Republic of the United States.* 2d ed. New York: W. W. Norton, 1979.

Schoenbrod, David. *Power without Responsibility: How Congress Abuses the People through Delegation.* New Haven, Conn.: Yale University Press, 1993.

Smith, Nick. "Restoration of Congressional Authority and Responsibility over the Regulatory Process." *Harvard Journal on Legislation* 33 (1996).

—Prepared by David Schoenbrod and Jerry Taylor

9. Term Limits and the Need for a Citizen Legislature

Each member of Congress should

- pledge to be a citizen legislator by limiting his or her time in office to no more than three additional terms in the House of Representatives and no more than two additional terms in the Senate and
- keep that pledge.

Americans are dissatisfied with Washington. For more than a generation, polls have found a steady decline in the proportion of citizens who believe Washington can be trusted to do what is right. Most people believe that politics has nothing to do with their lives or that it is run for the benefit of a few. Not surprisingly, a poll by Princeton Survey Research Associates revealed that only 12 percent of the electorate have a great deal of confidence in Congress as an institution.

Americans can reclaim their democracy. They can have a government that is accountable to their will, a government for and by the people. They can have a citizen legislature in Washington and in every statehouse in America. Citizen legislators will make laws that make sense to ordinary people and revive our national faith in representative government.

How can we have citizen legislatures? The power of office has virtually put incumbents beyond the reach of the people. Restoring democracy requires term limits for incumbents. All members of Congress should pledge to limit their stay on Capitol Hill.

The People Support Term Limits

Members of Congress should listen to the good sense of the American people on this issue. For years, national polls have found that three of four voters support term limits. In a June 2000 poll by Diversified Research,

Inc., 69 percent of Californians said that they still approved of the original (1990) term limits initiative. In March 2002, a ballot initiative designed to weaken California's term limits law was soundly defeated at the polls. According to Paul Jacob, executive director of U.S. Term Limits, ''If the people of this country got a chance tomorrow to vote on term limits for members of Congress, you would see them rush to the nearest polling place.''

Indeed, the people have spoken loudly and clearly on term limits in virtually all of the states that provide an opportunity to do so. Twenty-two states representing nearly half of Congress had term limited their delegations by 1994. The great majority of those states had opted to limit their representatives to three terms, and all of those states had limited their senators to two terms. Only 2 of the 22 states chose six terms for the House.

In November 2000, Nebraska became the 19th state to limit the terms of state legislators. By 2001, term limits had affected more than 700 legislative seats. The first 19 states passed term limits by an average of 67 percent of the vote (Table 9.1). Moreover, every effort by incumbents to roll back term limits has been defeated by voters.

Despite the overwhelming support of the American people for term limits, the incumbent establishment has made it extremely difficult for the will of the people to be translated into law. When the Supreme Court declared that states could not limit the terms of their representatives in Washington, advocates of term limits petitioned the new Republican Congress—which had put term limits in its Contract with America— to pass a constitutional amendment to impose nationwide term limits. Incumbent members of Congress had an obvious conflict of interest on the issue, and they did not pass an amendment.

Take the Pledge

Americans believe term limits will make Congress a citizen legislature. But a Congress controlled by career politicians will never pass a term limits amendment. So the term limits movement, one of the most successful grassroots political efforts in U.S. history, has set out to change Congress from a bastion of careerism into a citizen legislature the best way it can— district by district.

George Washington set the standard. Perhaps the most popular and powerful American in history, Washington nevertheless stepped down after two terms as president. He handed back to the people the immense

Table 9.1
State Legislative Term Limits
Making a Difference One State at a Time

State	Year	Limited: Terms (total years allowed)	Year Law Takes Effect	Percentage Voting Yes
Arizona	1992	House: 4 terms (8 years) Senate: 4 terms (8 years)	House: 2000 Senate: 2000	74%
Arkansas	1992	House: 3 terms (6 years) Senate: 2 terms (8 years)	House: 1998 Senate: 2000	60%
California	1990	Assembly: 3 terms (6 years) Senate: 2 terms (8 years)	House: 1996 Senate: 1998	52%
Colorado	1990	House: 4 terms (8 years) Senate: 2 terms (8 years)	House: 1998 Senate: 1998	71%
Florida	1992	House: 4 terms (8 years) Senate: 2 terms (8 years)	House: 2000 Senate: 2000	77%
Louisiana**	1995	House: 3 terms (12 years) Senate: 3 terms (12 years)	House: 2007 Senate: 2007	76%
*Maine**	1993	House: 4 terms (8 years) Senate: 4 terms (8 years)	House: 1996 Senate: 1996	68%
Michigan	1992	House: 3 terms (6 years) Senate: 2 terms (8 years)	House: 1998 Senate: 2002	59%
Missouri	1992	House: 4 terms (8 years) Senate: 2 terms (8 years)	House: 2002 Senate: 2002	75%
Montana	1992	House: 4 terms (8 years) Senate: 2 terms (8 years)	House: 2000 Senate: 2000	67%
Nebraska	2000	Unicameral: 2 terms (8 years)	2008	56%
Nevada	1994	Assembly: 6 terms (12 years) Senate: 3 terms (12 years)	House: 2006 Senate: 2006	70%
Ohio	1992	House: 4 terms (8 years) Senate: 2 terms (8 years)	House: 2000 Senate: 2000	66%
Oklahoma	1990	12-year combined total for both houses	2002	67%
South Dakota	1992	House: 4 terms (8 years) Senate: 2 terms (8 years)	House: 2000 Senate: 2000	64%

(continued)

Table 9.1
(continued)

State	Year	Limited: Terms (total years allowed)	Year Law Takes Effect	Percentage Voting Yes
*Utah***	1994	House: 6 terms (12 years)	House: 2006	
		Senate: 3 terms (12 years)	Senate: 2006	n/a
*Wyoming****	1992	House: 6 terms (12 years)	House: 2004	
		Senate: 3 terms (12 years)	Senate: 2004	77%
Average Percentage of Vote				67%

SOURCE: U.S. Term Limits, www.termlimits.org/Current_Info/State_TL/Index.html.
Note: Italics indicate states limited by statute. All others are limited by state constitutional amendment.
*Maine's law is retroactive.
**Louisiana's and Utah's laws were passed by the state legislatures.
***Wyoming's law was originally passed by initiative in 1994. The legislature amended the law to allow members of the House to serve 12 years. A referendum to return to the original 6-year House limits garnered 54% of the vote but failed to get 50% plus 1 of all voters to veto the legislature.

power and trust they had given to him—dramatically making the case that no one should monopolize a seat of power.

The tradition of a two-term limit for the president lasted uninterrupted for almost a century and a half. When Franklin D. Roosevelt broke the tradition, Congress moved to codify the term limit by proposing the Twenty-Second Amendment to the Constitution, which the states ratified in just 12 short months. The presidential term limit remains tremendously popular.

We can establish such a tradition in Congress. Since 1994, several dozen new faces have entered the halls of Congress serious about changing the culture of Washington and after pledging to limit themselves to three terms in the House or two terms in the Senate. Those pledges have resonated with the voters who understand that a lawmaker's career interests do not always coincide with the interests of the people back home. A poll by Fabrizio-McLaughlin and Associates asked, "Would you be more likely to vote for a candidate who pledges to serve no more than three terms in the House, or a candidate who refuses to self limit?" Seventy-two percent of respondents said they would be more likely to vote for the self-limiter.

Self-limiters serve their constituents well. Rep. Matt Salmon of Arizona, in reaffirming the pledge he made in 1994 to serve only three terms in the House, said:

The independence that comes from limiting my terms has enabled me to vote against the bloated budget deal of 1997, and to challenge my own party's leadership when I feel it would be best for the people of Arizona. Instead of looking ahead to my own career in the House, I am able to put my Arizona constituents first.

Self-limiters also resist Washington's culture of spending. They are able to vote for spending limits because of the freedom of conscience afforded by their term limit pledge. The self-limiters' collective experience suggests that self-limitation helps to discipline a politician's legislative behavior. Self-limiters exercise greater independence than their non-term-limited peers and appear less fearful of incurring the wrath of either party power brokers or special interest groups. During the past several years, many self-limiters stood out as the most fiscally conservative members of Congress.

Not surprisingly, self-limiters have spearheaded opposition to pork-barrel spending and committee budget increases. They have demanded honest accounting and pioneered the political push for real reform of flawed government programs such as Social Security and Medicare—so often used by professional politicians as political footballs.

Term Limits on Committee Chairs

Most laws begin life in congressional committees led by powerful chairs who act as gatekeepers for floor votes on legislation. For decades, the average tenure of a committee chair was about 20 years. The seniority system allowed entrenched politicians from the least competitive districts to wield power over other members, not on the basis of merit, but because of their longevity. In the past, the only way to lose a chair was by death, resignation, retirement, or electoral defeat.

The seniority system increased the level of pork-barrel spending and blocked much needed change. For example, in a Cato Institute Policy Analysis, "Term Limits and the Republican Congress," Aaron Steelman examined 31 key tax and spending proposals in the 104th and 105th Congresses. He found that junior Republicans in Congress were "more than twice as likely to vote for spending or tax cuts as were senior Republicans." Steelman pointed out that "veteran Republican legislators have proven they are comfortable with big government. It is unlikely that fundamental change in Washington will occur while they continue to control legislative debate and action."

For those reasons, in 1995 the Speaker of the House decided to limit the terms of House committee chairs to three terms, totaling six years. Those limits are an important dent in a corrupt system. Term limits on those powerful positions make the House more responsible and open the way for newer members to influence policy. In 1996, the Republican caucus imposed six-year limits on GOP committee chairs. As a consequence, some changes have occurred on the traditional Senate leadership career path. But the pace of change should be quickened, not slowed. The 108th Congress should retain term limits on committee chairs in the House and extend them to Senate committee chairs.

Why We Need a Citizen Legislature

Why are term limits so popular? Americans believe that career legislators and professional politicians have created a gaping chasm between themselves and their government. For democracy to work, it must be representative—a government of, by, and for the people. Democracy in America requires a citizen legislature.

To be a citizen legislator, a member of Congress should not be far removed from the private sector. The members of the House of Representatives, in particular, should be close to the people they represent. As Rhode Island's Roger Sherman wrote at the time of our nation's founding: "Representatives ought to return home and mix with the people. By remaining at the seat of government, they would acquire the habits of the place, which might differ from those of their constituents." In the era of year-round legislative sessions, the only way to achieve that objective is through term limits.

What should be the limit on terms? Some observers have proposed as many as six terms (or 12 years) for the House. Three terms for the House is better for several reasons. America is best served by a Congress whose members are there out of a sense of civic duty but who would rather live their lives in the private sector, holding productive jobs in civil society, far removed from government and politics. Such individuals might be willing to spend two, four, or even six years in Washington, but not if the legislative agenda is being set by others who have gained their authority through seniority. Twelve-year "limits," which amount to a mini-career, do little to remove this major obstacle to a more diverse and representative group of Americans seeking office.

We have solid evidence that short, three-term limits enhance the democratic process: Proposition 140 in California, which was passed by the voters there in 1990 and limited the state assembly to three two-year terms. The 1992 assembly elections witnessed a sharp increase in the number of citizens seeking office, with a remarkable 27 freshmen elected to the 80-member lower house of the California legislature. In an article on that freshman class, the *Los Angeles Times* said:

> Among the things making the group unusual is that most of them are true outsiders. For the first time in years, the freshman class does not include an abundance of former legislative aides who moved up the ladder to become members. . . . Among the 27 are a former U.S. Air Force fighter pilot, a former sheriff-coroner, a paralegal, a retired teacher, a video store owner, a businesswoman-homemaker, a children's advocate, an interior designer, a retired sheriff's lieutenant, and a number of businessmen, lawyers, and former city council members.

A scholarly study of the California legislature by Mark Petracca of the University of California at Irvine found that the strict term limits Californians passed in 1990 had had the following consequences:

- Turnover in both legislative chambers had increased markedly.
- The number of incumbents seeking reelection had dropped sharply.
- The percentage of elections in which incumbents won reelection had dropped significantly.
- The number of women in both houses had increased.
- The number of uncontested races had declined.
- The number of candidates seeking office in both chambers had increased.
- The winning margin of incumbents had declined.

While perhaps not attractive to people seeking to be career politicians, all those developments please the great majority of Americans who favor a return to citizen legislatures.

Similarly, a three-term limit for the U.S. House of Representatives will return control of the House—not just through voting, but also through participation—to the people. We must make the possibility of serving in Congress a more attractive option for millions more Americans.

A second reason for shorter term limits is that the longer one is in Congress, the more one is exposed to and influenced by the "culture of ruling" that permeates life inside the Beltway. Groups like the National Taxpayers Union have shown that the longer people serve in Congress, the bigger spenders, taxers, and regulators they become. That is just as true of conservatives as it is of liberals. It is also understandable. Members of Congress are surrounded at work and socially by people who spend other people's money and regulate their lives. It is the unusual individual—although such people do exist—who is not subtly but surely affected by that culture.

Three terms rather than six would better serve as an antidote to the growing "professionalization" of the legislative process. As Mark Petracca has written:

> Whereas representative government aspires to maintain a proximity of sympathy and interests between representative and represented, professionalism creates authority, autonomy, and hierarchy, distancing the expert from the client. Though this distance may be necessary and functional for lawyers, nurses, physicians, accountants, and social scientists, the qualities and characteristics associated with being a "professional" legislator run counter to the supposed goals of a representative democracy. Professionalism encourages an independence of ambition, judgment, and behavior that is squarely at odds with the inherently dependent nature of representative government.

Finally, shorter limits for the House would enhance the competitiveness of elections and, as previously noted, increase the number and diversity of Americans choosing to run for Congress. The most competitive races (and the ones that bring out the largest number of primary candidates) are for open seats.

At least a third of all House seats would be open each election under three-term limits, and it is probable that as many as half would not feature an incumbent seeking reelection. We also know from past experience that women and minorities have greater electoral success in races for open seats.

The members of a true citizen legislature literally view their time in office as a leave of absence from their real careers. Their larger ambitions lie in the private sector and not in expanding the ambit of government. Citizen legislators are true public servants, not the new masters of the political class.

State Legislative Term Limits Are Working

Term limits are taking effect all over the country in state legislatures—and they are working. Term limits were intended to end careerism among legislators. Scholarly research on the effects of term limits suggests that they have substantially attained that goal. Congress should take note:

- Term limits remain popular with state electorates long after their introduction.

- Term limits stimulate electoral competition in state legislative elections.
- Term limits enable nontraditional candidates to run for seats in state legislatures. Female, Hispanic, and Asian candidates find it easier to enter term-limited legislatures than non-term-limited bodies.
- Term limits weaken seniority systems in state legislatures.
- Term limits have not strengthened interest groups, state bureaucracies, or legislative staffs as predicted by critics of term limits.
- Term limits foster public policies that serve to halt, or at least reduce, the growth in the size and scope of government. Term-limited politicians demonstrate greater respect than their non-term-limited colleagues for taxpayers' money.

Clearly, term limits are working. Congress can't hold out forever.

Conclusion

The term limits movement is not motivated by disdain for the institution of Congress. It is motivated by a sincere desire on the part of the American people to regain control of the most representative part of the federal government. Resistance to this movement on the part of elected federal legislators only underscores the image of an Imperial Congress.

Those who sign the Term Limits Declaration are on the record as citizen legislators. Increasingly, that pledge will make the difference in winning competitive seats in Congress. The seniority system, rotten at its core, cannot survive a Congress where more and more members are under term limits. Nor can wrong-headed policies and wasteful spending projects survive a Congress with so many citizen legislators.

Term limits remain an issue to be reckoned with. Public support is even stronger and deeper for candidates making personal term limits commitments than for a term limits amendment. Voters seek to replace career politicians with dedicated citizen legislators as the best solution to what ails us in Washington. Political leaders who understand the problems created by a permanent ruling elite in Washington—or who simply want to abide by the overwhelming will of their constituents—will pledge to serve no more than three additional terms in the House or two in the Senate.

Suggested Readings

Crane, Edward H., and Roger Pilon, eds. *The Politics and Law of Term Limits*. Washington: Cato Institute, 1994.

Bandow, Doug. "The Political Revolution That Wasn't: Why Term Limits Are Needed Now More Than Ever." Cato Institute Policy Analysis no. 259, September 5, 1996.

Basham, Patrick, "Assessing the Term Limits Experiment: California and Beyond," Cato Institute Policy Analysis no. 413, August 31, 2001.

Carey, John M., Richard G. Niemi, and Lynda W. Powell. *Term Limits in the State Legislatures*. Ann Arbor: University of Michigan Press, 2000.

Elhauge, Einer. "What Term Limits Do That Ordinary Voting Cannot." Cato Institute Policy Analysis no. 328, December 16, 1998.

O'Keefe, Eric. *Who Rules America? The People vs. the Political Class*. Spring Green, Wis.: Citizen Government Foundation, 1999.

O'Keefe, Eric, and Aaron Steelman. "The End of Representation: How Congress Stifles Electoral Competition." Cato Institute Policy Analysis no. 279, August 20, 1997.

Owings, Stephanie, and Rainald Borck. "Legislative Professionalism and Government Spending: Do Citizen Legislators Really Spend Less?" *Public Finance Review* 23 (2000).

Steelman, Aaron. "Term Limits and the Republican Congress." Cato Institute Briefing Paper no. 41, October 27, 1998.

—Prepared by Edward H. Crane and Patrick Basham

10. Campaign Finance, Corruption, and the Oath of Office

> **Congress should**
>
> - repeal the Bipartisan Campaign Reform Act of 2002,
> - reject proposals to mandate electoral advertising paid for by the owners of the television networks,
> - reform the Federal Election Commission to bring it under the rule of law, and
> - deregulate the current campaign finance system.

The 107th Congress passed the most sweeping new restrictions on campaign finance in a generation, the Bipartisan Campaign Reform Act of 2002, marking them to take effect at the conclusion of the 2002 elections. During much of the 108th Congress, the new law, challenged the day it was signed, will be working its way through the judicial system. Meanwhile, proponents of even more restrictions will be urging Congress to mandate "free" political advertising for candidates and to replace the current Federal Election Commission with a new agency modeled on the Federal Bureau of Investigation.

The new law and the proposed changes in current law reflect the mistaken assumptions of the so-called reformers. We begin by exposing those flawed assumptions about corruption and American politics.

Freedom and Corruption

We begin, as we must, with the Constitution, which prohibits the government from abridging freedom of speech. In the seminal case of *Buckley v. Valeo* (1976), the Supreme Court recognized that restrictions on political spending are restrictions on political speech:

A restriction on the amount of money a person or group can spend on political communication during a campaign necessarily reduces the quantity of expression by restricting the number of issues discussed, the depth of their exploration, and the size of the audience reached. This is because virtually every means of communicating ideas in today's mass society requires the expenditure of money.

Note that the Court did not say, "Money equals speech." It said that money is necessarily tied to speech in a society in which candidates communicate to the voters through the mass media. Restricting political spending thus restricts political speech just as surely as throttling the speaker on the proverbial street corner soapbox limits speech. Both spending ceilings and strangulation shut off the medium of political expression and thus the protected speech itself.

Unfortunately, contributions to campaigns do not enjoy the same constitutional protections. In 1974, Congress imposed limits on campaign contributions for the purpose of preventing "corruption or the appearance of corruption." Until recently those ceilings have governed American elections without being adjusted for inflation. BCRA raised the limits on "hard money" contributions, but their real value remains well below the ceilings enacted in 1974.

The lower protection provided for contributions makes little sense. Political candidates spend money to obtain the means (often television time) to get their messages across to voters; such spending, as noted earlier, is properly protected speech. But contributors give to candidates for the same reason—to enable candidates to obtain the means to advance their views to the electorate. Thus, limiting contributions inevitably "reduces the quantity of expression by restricting the number of issues discussed, the depth of their exploration, and the size of the audience reached" by the candidate.

What about corruption? Campaign finance reformers claim to be driven by the desire to end corruption or its appearance. But what is the nature of the corruption that concerns reformers? And just how much corruption is there to be rooted out?

Clean government requires that public office not be sold—not for money, not for personal gain, not even for elective office. Thus, money is not the real issue, even if cases of corruption often involve money. The issue, rather, is trust. Public office is a trust, solemnized by the oath of office, through which officeholders swear to support the Constitution. That oath obligates public officials to serve the general good, the good of all, as spelled out in the Constitution, a document intended to serve all the people. When an officeholder sells his vote to a special interest for any narrower reason, he appears, at least, to be breaching the trust he assumed when he swore to support the Constitution. His oath entails an obligation to avoid even the appearance of doing so.

As a practical matter, however, corruption requires us to distinguish between appearance and reality. A member of Congress who votes for a bill in exchange for some payoff is said to be corrupt. But if that same member votes the same way because he believes he is serving the general good, he is not thought to be corrupt. The same act may or may not be corrupt depending on the reasons behind it. Yet reasons or motives, being subjective, are notoriously difficult for others to determine, especially when they are mixed. What are we to say when a member accepts a campaign contribution from a special interest, votes as the interest wishes, but does so because he genuinely believes he is voting for the general good? After all, a particular good and the general good may coincide.

Until the federal law of 1974, we recognized the difficulties of discerning corruption and chose to enact only limited rules addressing fairly clear cases of favors granted for cash, what the Supreme Court has called quid pro quo corruption. Judged by that standard, our legal system has found rather less corruption in politics than the reformers would have us believe exists. Social scientists also report scant evidence of corruption of the legislature. One proponent of public financing concludes, "Various studies have failed to produce the sort of evidence of a strong correlation between campaign donations and a representative's public actions needed to back up suspicions of general quid pro quo understandings." Thus, the basic premise of the campaign finance reform movement—that money corrupts and more money corrupts even more—comes up short on the evidence.

Congressional Conflicts of Interest

The intense interest in the campaign finance regulation shown by members of Congress—substantially greater than the interest shown by most Americans—should hardly surprise. For no other issue today affects members more directly—not taxes, not spending, not war or peace. Indeed, campaign finance law bears directly on the ability of members to remain in office. All the talk of good government aside, for many it is a matter of job security. Thus, the high correlation between past campaign finance legislation and reelection rates is no accident, for the temptation to write the law to favor incumbents is palpable and inescapable.

There, in stark relief, is the conflict of interest that every member of Congress faces when considering proposals to reform our campaign finance law. Campaign finance regulation brings every member face to face with the problem of self-dealing—not only the self-dealing the regulations are supposed to prevent but, more immediately, the self-dealing that is inherent in writing regulations not simply for oneself but for those who would challenge one's power to write such regulations in the first place.

Figure 10.1 graphically suggests the electoral consequences of having the winners write the rules for financing congressional campaigns.

Only one congressional election since 1974 has seen an incumbent reelection rate lower than 90 percent. Even the "revolution" of 1994, which changed control of the House of Representatives, saw 90 percent of incumbents reelected. The last three elections have seen reelection rates of over 98 percent.

Campaign finance restrictions may not fully explain the lack of competition in American politics. But those restrictions encumber entry into the political market and thus discourage credible challenges to incumbents. A challenger needs large sums to mount a campaign for public office, especially at the federal level. He needs big money to overcome the manifest advantages of incumbency—name recognition, the power of

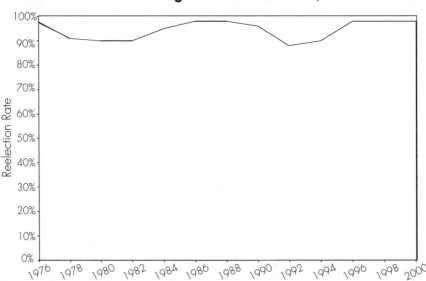

Figure 10.1
Reelection Rates of Congressional Incumbents, 1976–2000

SOURCES: Norman J. Ornstein, Thomas E. Mann, and Michael J. Malbin, *Vital Statistics on Congress: 1999–2000* (Washington: AEI Press, 2000), p. 57; and Cato calculations.

office, the franking privilege, a knowledgeable staff, campaign experience, and, perhaps most important, easy access to the media. Yet current law limits the supply of campaign dollars: in any given election cycle, an individual can give no more than $1,000 to a candidate, and a political party or a political action committee (PAC) can give no more than $5,000. BCRA did raise the limit for individuals to $2,000. But again that remains far less in real dollars than was allowed by the original 1974 law.

In a free and open political system, challengers would be able to do what they used to be able to do—find a few "deep pockets" to get themselves started, then build support from there, unrestrained by any restrictions save for the traditional prohibitions on vote selling and vote buying. That is how liberal Eugene McCarthy challenged an incumbent president in 1968. It is how conservative James Buckley challenged an incumbent senator and a major party challenger in 1970. Today, neither would be able to do that—thanks to the "reforms" of 1974. Both would incur massive compliance costs, including the risk of future litigation and prosecution. Both would be discouraged, in all likelihood, from mounting a challenge. That is not healthy for democracy.

BCRA makes things worse. By banning "soft money"—unregulated contributions given to the political parties—Congress has complicated the lives of challengers. Parties have traditionally directed soft money contributions to races in which challengers might have a chance. A Cato Institute study found, not surprisingly, that state restrictions on giving to parties (regulations similar to BCRA's soft money ban) reduce the overall competitiveness of elections. At the same time, BCRA does not affect donations by PACs, most of which go to incumbents. BCRA does loosen federal contribution limits for incumbents running against self-funding individuals. Apparently, contributions over $2,000 corrupt politics—unless an incumbent faces a self-funding millionaire. That strains credulity. In the end, BCRA seems little more than an incumbent protection law, a monument to the dangers of self-dealing.

But conflict of interest does not end with the ban on soft money. For several years now, interest groups have underwritten aggressive issue ads criticizing members of Congress during their reelection campaigns. To be sure, some of those ads have been unfair or inaccurate, but the Constitution protects the right to be both. With the passage of BCRA, however, Congress decided to regulate such issue advertising by redefining it as "express advocacy" and hence as subject to federal election law, including contribution limits. In effect, Congress has decided to complicate the lives of its critics. Making issue ads subject to election law means the next election will have fewer issue ads, less debate of public matters, and less criticism of elected officials. Many experts think the Supreme Court will strike down those restrictions on political speech. Congress might save the Court the trouble by reconsidering its regulations.

Taxpayer Financing of Campaigns

Many people have argued that our system could preclude corruption or its appearance by prohibiting all private contributions, whether designated as campaign contributions or not, and moving to a system of taxpayer-financed campaigns. As a practical matter, how would a system of public campaign financing work? Would incumbents and challengers receive equal amounts of money? Given the extraordinary advantages of incumbency noted above, that would hardly level the playing field or respect the democratic process. Then what is the right ratio? When Congress last seriously debated taxpayer financing in 1997, the funding levels proposed were not adequate. Law professor Bradley Smith, now a federal election commissioner, assessed the 1997 proposal:

> Every challenger spending less than the proposed limit in Senate campaigns had lost in each of the 1994 and 1996 elections, whereas every incumbent spending less than the limit had won. Similarly, only 3 percent of challengers spending less than the proposed limit for House races had won in 1996, whereas 40 percent of challengers spending more than that limit had won.

Taxpayer financing of congressional campaigns would only exacerbate the conflict of interest faced by every member in writing campaign finance regulations.

Proponents of campaign finance reform will likely propose that the 108th Congress enact mandatory political advertising paid for by the owners of the television networks. Over the years, such proposals have taken several forms; the latest would make the networks "donate" air time, which would then be given to the political parties in the form of vouchers. Thus, the shareholders of the companies that own the networks effectively would be taxed to pay for this advertising. Proponents justify such taxes as a fair price for the use of public property, the airwaves. In fact, economist Thomas Hazlett has shown that government's claim to "ownership" of the airwaves amounts to nothing more than imposing political control over the media of radio and television. Even if we grant for purposes of argument that the airwaves belong to the public, we might ask why the broadcasters have to pay for political advertising. After all, trucking companies pay taxes for the upkeep of roads, but they are not required to haul freight for members of Congress.

The Federal Election Commission

Not content to have passed BCRA, reformers now argue that the Federal Election Commission has failed to enforce the old law, that the FEC will undermine BCRA, and that Congress should replace the FEC with a stronger agency—one with a law enforcement mission, a kind of Federal Bureau of Investigation for elections and political campaigns.

The juxtaposition of the FBI and political campaigns should give immediate pause. Do we want a federal law enforcement agency investigating the campaigns of members of Congress and those who challenge them for office? That is an invitation for political or partisan abuse. The late, unlamented Independent Counsel statute comes immediately to mind. Do members of Congress really want every detail of their last campaigns subject to investigation by an agency controlled either by their political enemies or the reformers themselves?

This does not mean the FEC should continue to exist. Congress should get rid of the FEC as part of a broader deregulation of political speech and electoral campaigns. Absent that, Congress should move to reform the FEC to make its procedures comport with the rule of law.

Defendants before the FEC have few due process safeguards. When a complaint comes before the commission, its general counsel makes the case against the alleged lawbreaker, who has no right to appear before the commission. The general counsel provides the commission with a report that summarizes and criticizes the legal arguments of the accused and is present to answer questions from the commissioners. Those reports are not given to the accused even though they may contain new arguments or information.

The FEC also sends out discovery subpoenas on the recommendation of its general counsel. To contest a subpoena, a citizen must appeal to the FEC itself, which turns the matter over to its Office of General Counsel. Need we mention that the commission rarely grants motions to quash its own subpoenas? Beyond that, the commission often will not provide the accused with documents that might aid the defendant. How could all of this accord with the rule of law?

The FEC has hardly been a pussycat in enforcing federal restrictions on campaign finance. Like most burgeoning bureaucratic empires, it has continually tried to extend its regulatory authority. Consider issue advocacy. In *Buckley v. Valeo* the Supreme Court said that the government could regulate only those ads that expressly advocated the election or defeat of a candidate. The First Amendment protects all other advocacy about political issues.

The FEC has tried through most of its history to expand the meaning of "express advocacy" beyond explicit words advocating the election or defeat of a candidate. Time and again courts have rejected those grabs for more power. Thus, in 1997 a federal court struck down an FEC regulation redefining express advocacy, concluding that the commission's argument that "no words of advocacy are necessary to expressly advocate the election of a candidate" could not have been offered in good faith. Far from weak, the FEC's stance on express advocacy has defied judicial authority and tended toward lawlessness.

The FEC has attacked political speech in other ways as well. Thus, the government can constitutionally regulate "political committees." Some people on the FEC argue that spending on issue advocacy, a protected freedom, makes a group a political committee and thus subjects it to regulation. In the Orwellian world of the FEC, a constitutional freedom justifies government coercion. Federal law also regulates electoral activities if they are coordinated with a candidate. The FEC has always pushed a broad concept of coordination, the better to bring more political activity under its control.

Not surprisingly those aggressive FEC attacks have chilled political activities at the grassroots. After all, individuals and small groups hardly have the resources to take on a bevy of specialized, zealous lawyers supported by taxpayers. The FEC represents yet another expansive federal bureaucracy that should be reined in by Congress in the near term and eliminated over the long term.

The Real Problem

The laws we now have on the books have made our politics less competitive by favoring incumbents over challengers, thereby striking at the very heart of democratic government. The whole point of democracy, after all, is to enable the people, through the ballot box, to select and thereby control those who govern. To the extent that campaign finance law undermines that power, it undermines democracy. Moreover, as we will now see, to the extent that incumbency is correlated with ever-larger government, as studies repeatedly show, our present law exacerbates the very problem it was meant to reduce—corruption.

We come, then, to the heart of the matter. The focus on campaign finance reform is a distraction from the real issue, the ultimate source of the potential for corruption—ubiquitous government. Government today is a magnet for corruption of every form because it exercises vast powers over virtually every aspect of life. Given that reality, is it any wonder that special interests—indeed that every interest but the general—should be trying either to take advantage of that or to protect themselves from it?

The Founders understood the problem of what they called "factions." They understood that interests would be tempted to capture government for their own ends. To reduce that temptation, they wrote a constitution that granted government only limited powers. They understood that the best way to reduce corruption is to reduce the *opportunities* for corruption.

Far from forcing everyone to contribute to campaigns, the Founders left individuals free to decide the matter for themselves—and free also to decide how much to contribute. The Founders were mindful of the potential for real corruption, which they left to traditional legal means to ferret out. They had a pair of better ideas about how to handle the various forms of corruption. The first was to rely on competition, to construct a system that enabled interest to be pitted against interest. There is no shortage, after all, of special interests. But if you fetter them all, through some grand regulatory scheme, you stifle the natural forces that are necessary for the health of the system. No individual, no committee of Congress, no blue-ribbon committee of elders, can fine-tune the system of political competition. It has to be free to seek its own equilibrium.

The second idea was equally simple, yet equally profound: limit power in the first place, the better to limit the opportunities for corruption. After all, if a member of Congress has only limited power to sell, there will be limited opportunities to buy. That will not eliminate all corruption, of course, but it will greatly reduce it.

Once we recognize the essential character of corruption—that it is a breach of the trust that is grounded in the oath of office and, ultimately, in the Constitution—it becomes clear that the problem is much broader than is ordinarily thought, even if most such corruption should not be the subject of regulation and prosecution. In fact, people who try to reduce the issue to one of money—big money buying access—miss the larger picture entirely. Money may induce a member to vote for an interest narrower than the general good—the evidence notwithstanding—but when we ratified the Constitution we gave members the opportunity to do so only to a very limited degree. In fact, it was because we understood, as Lord Acton would later put it, that power tends to corrupt and absolute power corrupts absolutely, that we so limited our officials. And we realized that they would be tempted to breach their oaths of office not only for money but for power as well—indeed, for the office itself. Thus, it was not "special interests" alone that the Founders feared but the people too: The Founders wanted to protect against the capture of government by that ever-changing special interest known as "the majority." For that reason too—no, especially—they limited government's powers.

The problem with post–New Deal government, with its all but unlimited power to redistribute and regulate at will, is that it virtually ensures that members of Congress will act not for the general good, the good of all, but for some narrower interest. Indeed, the modern state is premised on "corruption," for when it takes from some to give to others, it does not serve the *general* good—and cannot, *by definition*. Thus, candidates find themselves selling their office right from the start. When they promise "free" goods and services from government, in exchange for votes, they are selling their office, plain and simple: "Vote for me and I'll vote to give you these goods." That is where corruption begins. It begins with the corruption—or death (the root of "corruption"}—of the oath of office. For not remotely does our Constitution authorize the kind of redistributive state we have in this nation today (see Chapter 3 of this *Handbook* for a detailed discussion).

To root out the kind of generalized corruption that is endemic to modern government, then, one should begin not with more campaign finance regulations but with the Constitution and the oath of office. The Constitution establishes a government of delegated, enumerated, and thus limited powers. It sets forth powers that are, as Madison put it in *Federalist* no. 45, "few and defined." Thus, it addresses the problem of self-dealing by limiting the opportunities for self-dealing. If Congress has only limited power to control citizens' lives—if citizens are otherwise free to plan and live their own lives—there is little power for members of Congress to sell, whether for cash, for perquisites, or for votes.

Before they take the solemn oath of office, therefore, members of Congress should reflect on whether they are swearing to support the Constitution as written and understood by those who wrote and ratified it or the Constitution the New Deal Court discovered in 1937. The contrast between the two could not be greater. One was written for limited government; the other was crafted for potentially unlimited government. As that potential has materialized, the opportunities for corruption of every kind have become ever more manifest, as members know only too well. Indeed, to appreciate the point, we need only notice the corruption that is endemic to totalitarian systems—the ultimate redistributive states—despite draconian sanctions against it. It goes with ubiquitous government.

Conclusion

In most cases, therefore, the answer to the corruption that is thought to attend our system of private campaign financing is not more campaign finance regulations but fewer such regulations. The limits on campaign contributions, in particular, should be removed, for they are the source of many of our present problems. More generally, however, the opportunities for corruption that were so expanded when we abandoned constitutionally limited government need to be radically reduced. Members of Congress can do that by taking the Constitution and their oaths of office more seriously.

Suggested Readings

Basham, Patrick. "It's the Spending, Stupid! Understanding Campaign Finance in the Big Government Era." Cato Institute Briefing Paper no. 64, July 18, 2001.

BeVier, Lillian R. "Campaign Finance 'Reform' Proposals: A First Amendment Analysis." Cato Institute Policy Analysis no. 282, September 4, 1997.

Hazlett, Thomas W. "The Rationality of U.S. Regulation of the Broadcast Spectrum." *Journal of Law and Economics* 33 (April 1990): 133–75.

LaRaja, Ray, and Thad Kousser. "The Effect of Campaign Finance Laws on Electoral Competition: Evidence from the States." Cato Institute Policy Analysis no. 426, February 14, 2002.

Pilon, Roger. "Freedom, Responsibility, and the Constitution: On Recovering Our Founding Principles." *Notre Dame Law Review* 68 (1993).

Smith, Bradley A. "Campaign Finance Regulation: Faulty Assumptions and Undemocratic Consequences." Cato Institute Policy Analysis no. 238, September 13, 1995.

———. *Unfree Speech: The Folly of Campaign Finance Reform.* Princeton, N.J.: Princeton University Press, 2001.

Smith, Bradley A., and Stephen M. Hoersting. "A Toothless Anaconda: Innovation, Impotence and Overenforcement at the Federal Election Commission." *Election Law Journal* 1 (2002): 145–71.

—Prepared by Roger Pilon and John Samples

11. Reclaiming the War Power

The horror of September 11, 2001, changed many things: it ended a certain American innocence and sense of invincibility; it taught Americans that those who hate us could strike at us on our own soil; and it provided ample justification for defending ourselves by waging war on al-Qaeda and its nation-state allies. It did not, however, amend the Constitution. Indeed, President Bush has repeatedly made it clear that the fight against terrorists is a fight to maintain our free institutions and the way of life they sustain. Six days after the destruction of the World Trade Center and the attack on the Pentagon, President Bush issued a proclamation in honor of our Constitution. In it, he declared that "today, in the face of the terrorist attacks of September 11, 2001, we must call upon, more than ever, the Constitutional principles that make our country great."

No constitutional principle is more important than the principle that the war power belongs to Congress. In affairs of state, no more momentous decision can be made than the decision to go to war. For that reason, in a democratic republic it is essential that that decision be made by the most broadly representative body: the legislature. As James Madison put it: "In

109

no part of the constitution is more wisdom to be found, than in the clause which confides the question of war or peace to the legislature, and not to the executive department.''

The Constitutional Framework

Under the Constitution as Madison and the other Framers designed it, the president lacks the authority to initiate military action. In the Framers' view, absent prior authorization by Congress, the president's war powers were purely reactive; if the territory of the United States or U.S. forces were attacked, the president could respond. But he could not undertake aggressive actions without prior congressional authorization.

On August 17, 1787, the Constitutional Convention considered the recommendation of the Committee of Detail that the legislature should have sole power "to make war." Only one delegate, South Carolina's Pierce Butler, spoke in favor of granting that authority to the executive. As Madison's notes from the convention tell us, Butler's proposal was not warmly received. "Mr. [Elbridge] Gerry [of Massachusetts said he] never expected to hear in a republic a motion to empower the Executive alone to declare war." For his part, George Mason of Virginia "was agst. giving the power of war to the Executive, because not to be trusted with it. . . . He was for clogging rather than facilitating war."

However, the delegates did take seriously the objection, raised by Charles Pinckney of South Carolina, that the House of Representatives was too large and unwieldy, and met too infrequently, to supervise all the details attendant to the conduct of a war. For that reason, "Mr. M[adison] and Mr. Gerry moved to insert '*declare*,' striking out '*make*' war; leaving to the Executive the power to repel sudden attacks." Roger Sherman of Connecticut "thought [the proposal] stood very well. The Executive shd. be able to repel and not to commence war." The motion passed.

The document that emerged from the convention vests with Congress the bulk of the powers associated with military action, among them the powers "to declare War, [and] grant Letters of Marque and Reprisal." Other important war-making powers include the power "to raise and support Armies, but no Appropriation of Money to that Use shall be for a longer Term than two years," and "to provide for calling forth the Militia to execute the Laws of the Union, suppress Insurrections and repel invasions."

Significantly, several of the enumerated powers allocated to Congress involve the decision to initiate military action. Viewed in this light, Congress's power to issue letters of marque and reprisal and its power to call out the militia inform our understanding of Congress's authority to declare war. A letter of marque and reprisal is a legal device (long fallen into disuse) empowering private citizens to take offensive action against citizens of foreign countries, usually privateers attacking ships. Since military attacks carried out by American citizens might well be considered acts of war by foreign powers, and accordingly embroil the United States in hostilities, the Constitution vests the important decision to grant this power in the most deliberative body: the legislature. Similarly, Article I, section 8, gives Congress power over the militia, allowing Congress to decide when domestic unrest has reached the point where military action is required.

In contrast, the authority granted to the executive as commander in chief of U.S. Armed Forces is entirely supervisory and reactive. The president commands the Army and Navy, should Congress choose to create them, and leads them into battle, should Congress choose to declare war. He commands the militia to suppress rebellions, should the militia be "called into the actual Service of the United States." In this, as Hamilton noted in *Federalist* no. 69, the president acts as no more than the "first General" of the United States. And generals, it should go without saying, are not empowered to decide with whom we go to war. The Constitution leaves that decision to Congress. As Constitutional Convention delegate James Wilson explained to the Pennsylvania ratifying convention: "This system will not hurry us into war; it is calculated to guard against it. It will not be in the power of a single man, or a single body of men, to involve us in such distress; for the important power in declaring war is vested in the legislature at large."

War with Iraq

Given that constitutional framework, the yearlong debate about war with Iraq left a lot to be desired. Bush administration officials proceeded as if no authorization were necessary. Then, in August 2002, the White House Counsel's Office brazenly insisted that the administration already had congressional authorization for Gulf War II, in the form of the 1991 joint resolution that authorized the first Persian Gulf War. How could a resolution passed in 1991 to give a previous president authority to expel Saddam Hussein from Kuwait authorize another president to take Baghdad 11 years later? A good question, the answer to which was not at all apparent in the 1991 resolution. Such tendentious stretching of legal authority might have been appropriate for a trial lawyer zealously pressing his client's

111

interest. But for a president sworn to uphold the Constitution, and seeking legal justification to lead troops into battle, something more than clever "lawyering" was required: new and independent authorization for a new war.

To its credit, the administration eventually sought, and secured, congressional authorization for use of force against Iraq. It did so despite the fact that some prominent members of Congress did not want to be burdened with the vast responsibility the Constitution places on their shoulders. Senate Minority Leader Trent Lott (R-Miss.), for instance, treated the Democrats' push for congressional authorization as a partisan annoyance rather than a solemn constitutional duty, calling it "a blatant political move that's not helpful."

In some ways, this is nothing new. Throughout the 20th century, congressional control of the war power eroded, not simply as a result of executive branch aggrandizement, but also because of congressional complicity. The imperial presidency continues to grow, largely because many legislators want to duck their responsibility to decide the question of war and peace; delegate that responsibility to the president; and reserve their right to criticize him, should military action go badly.

Indeed, even in authorizing the president to use force, Congress attempted to shirk its responsibility to decide on war. After voting for the resolution, which gave the president all the authority he needs to attack Iraq should he choose to do so, prominent members of Congress insisted they hadn't really voted to use force. That was for the president to decide. As Senate Majority Leader Tom Daschle (D-S.D.) put it: "Regardless of how one may have voted on the resolution last night, I think there is an overwhelming consensus . . . that while [war] may be necessary, we're not there yet."

It is not for the president to decide whether we are "there yet." The Constitution leaves that question to Congress. Thus far in the war on terror, though, Congress has dodged that responsibility, delegating it to the president. The use-of-force resolution Congress passed immediately after September 11, 2001, contains an even broader delegation of authority to the president, authorizing him to make war on "those nations, organizations, or persons *he determines* planned, authorized, committed, or aided the terrorist attacks that occurred on Sept. 11, 2001, or harbored such organizations or persons" [emphasis added]. By its plain terms, the resolution leaves it to the president to decide when the evidence that a target nation has cooperated with al-Qaeda justifies war. President Bush has exercised that authority in good faith so far, declining to argue that the flimsy evidence of a Saddam–al-Qaeda connection permits him to attack Iraq under the September 14, 2001, resolution. But if Congress wants a say on whether we should go to war with Iran, Syria, Lebanon, or any number of other nations the president may target in the future, it will have a difficult case to make.

Such broad delegations of legislative authority are constitutionally suspect in the domestic arena; surely they are no less so when it comes to questions of war and peace. As Madison put it:

> Those who are to *conduct* a war cannot in the nature of things, be proper or safe judges, whether *a war ought to be commenced, continued, or concluded.* They are barred from the latter functions by a great principle in free government, analogous to that which separates the sword from the purse, or the power of executing from the power of enacting laws [emphasis in original].

Preemptive Wars

The administration's new security doctrine, which emphasizes preemptive military strikes, may have equally troubling consequences for congressional control over the war power. Under the new doctrine, rogue nations in the process of developing nuclear, chemical, or biological weapons will be vulnerable at any time to sudden attack by the United States. In a graduation speech given at West Point on June 1, 2002, President Bush discussed the new strategy: "The war on terror will not be won on the defensive," he said, "we must take the battle to the enemy . . . [and] be ready for preemptive action when necessary." The administration formalized the policy in the National Security Strategy of the United States of America, released in September. That document does not discuss whether preemptive wars will be conducted pursuant to congressional authorization or launched unilaterally as surprise attacks by the president. In the case of Iraq, which may be the administration's first preemptive war, the president has not used the doctrine as an excuse to bypass the constitutional requirement of congressional authorization. But the development of the doctrine must be carefully monitored by this Congress and future ones, lest it become a pretext for unilateral presidential war making.

Granted, the Constitution does not categorically rule out unilateral military action by the president. No one would argue that, when missiles are in the air or enemy troops are landing on our shores, the president is obliged to call Congress into session before he can respond. As Madison's notes from the Constitutional Convention make clear, the constitutional consensus about war powers was that, though Congress had the power to "commence war," the president would have "the power to repel sudden attacks." Within that power, there's some latitude for preemptive strikes. If a rogue state plans a nerve gas attack on the New York subway system, the president need not and should not wait until enemy agents are ashore to order military action.

But if the preemptive strike doctrine morphs into a freestanding justification for presidential wars, that will have grave consequences for the constitutional balance of power. The doctrine applies whether or not any specific attack on the United States is planned and whether or not U.S. intelligence can establish with any certainty that the target has weapons of mass destruction (WMD). It could be used by this administration or future ones to avoid the inconvenient task of securing authority from Congress. That would change the president's constitutional power to repel sudden attacks into a dangerous and unconstitutional power to *launch* sudden attacks.

Moreover, such a power would be ripe for abuse. Firm evidence of WMD capability is very hard to come by—indeed, in the case of Iraq, Secretary of Defense Donald Rumsfeld doubts that even an intensive, on-the-ground inspection regime, such as the United Nations operated in Iraq until December 1998, could determine with any degree of certainty what Saddam's WMD capabilities are. Justifications for preemptive wars will necessarily be speculative and susceptible to manipulation. The potential for politically driven attacks would be enormous.

Public opinion polls indicate that Americans view President Bush as a person of integrity and reward him with a high level of public trust. But Bush will not be the last president to wield the broad new powers his administration is forging in the domestic and foreign affairs arenas. As Rumsfeld has noted, the war on terror will take years, and if and when victory is achieved, we may not know with any certainty that we've won.

Our entire constitutional system repudiates the notion that electing good men is a sufficient check on abuse of power. As President Bush himself noted in his September 17 proclamation: "In creating our Nation's Constitutional framework, the Convention's delegates recognized the dangers inherent in concentrating too much power in one person, branch, or institution." It's imperative that the 108th Congress resist the tendency to concentrate power and the further growth of the imperial presidency.

Suggested Readings

Fisher, Louis. *Congressional Abdication on War and Spending.* College Station: Texas A&M University Press, 2000.

———. *Presidential War Power.* Lawrence: University Press of Kansas, 1995.

Healy, Gene. ''Arrogance of Power Reborn: The Imperial Presidency and Foreign Policy in the Clinton Years.'' Cato Institute Policy Analysis no. 389, December 13, 2000.

Levy, Leonard W. *Original Intent and the Framers' Constitution.* New York: Macmillan, 1988.

Schlesinger, Arthur. *The Imperial Presidency.* Boston: Houghton-Mifflin, 1973.

Wormuth, Francis D., and Edwin B. Firmage. *To Chain the Dog of War.* Dallas: Southern Methodist University Press, 1986.

—Prepared by Gene Healy

THREATS TO CIVIL LIBERTIES

12. USA PATRIOT Act and Domestic Detention Policy

Congress should

- tighten the PATRIOT Act's requirements for advance judicial approval and judicial review;
- impose a shorter-term sunset clause on all provisions of the PATRIOT Act;
- exclude ordinary criminal activities from coverage of the PATRIOT Act;
- establish rules that govern detention of citizens and noncitizens suspected of terrorist links; and
- ensure that domestic detainees have access to counsel and judicial review.

USA PATRIOT Act

Government is legitimately charged with defending life, liberty, and property against both domestic and foreign predators. First among those obligations is to protect life. With America under attack, and lives at risk, civil liberties cannot remain inviolable. But that does not mean civil liberties can be arbitrarily flouted without establishing, first, that national security interests are compelling and, second, that those interests can be vindicated only by encroaching on individual rights. Some parts of the PATRIOT Act do not pass that test.

Proponents of the new bill surely understood that many of its provisions were incompatible with civil liberties. Yet rather than modify the offending provisions, the president and Congress decided to promote the bill as an expression of patriotism. Hence the acronym—USA PATRIOT—and its bloated title, Uniting and Strengthening America by Providing Appropriate

Tools Required to Intercept and Obstruct Terrorism. The sales pitch worked. Fearful of being labeled disloyal after the atrocities of September 11, 2001, the House endorsed the bill 357 to 66, followed by a 98-to-1 romp through the Senate, with only Russ Feingold (D-Wis.) in opposition.

From its initial draft to its final adoption, the PATRIOT Act zipped through in six weeks—less time than Congress typically spends on routine bills that raise no constitutional concerns. Congress's so-called deliberative process was reduced to this: closed-door negotiations, no conference committee, no committee reports, no final hearing at which opponents could testify, not even an opportunity for most of the legislators to read the 131 single-spaced pages about to become law. Indeed, for part of the time, both the House and Senate were closed because of the anthrax scare; congressional staffers weren't able to retrieve their working papers.

The negligible legislative record will make it difficult for courts to determine the intent of Congress. And because legislative intent matters to some judges—for example, Supreme Court Justices Stephen Breyer and David Souter—the PATRIOT Act might ultimately be invalidated as unconstitutionally vague. Ironically, Congress's rush job, which facilitated passage of the bill, could be the cause of the bill's downfall. The same law that was promoted as an act of patriotism might even provide a rationale for releasing madmen who committed horrific acts against the United States.

Yet the more acute objections to the new statute are substantive, not procedural. They fall into three main categories. First, any law with the potential to dramatically alter conventional notions of individual freedom should fastidiously guard against abuse. The doctrine of separation of powers has been a traditional buffer against such abuse. Requiring advance judicial authorization of executive actions, followed by judicial review to ensure that those actions have been properly performed, shields our liberties from excessive concentrations of power in a single branch of government.

Under the PATRIOT Act, however, the locus of power is unmistakably the executive branch. In some cases, law enforcement officials have access to business and personal records without advance judicial notice or subsequent judicial review. In other cases—voicemail retrieval is an example—advance approval is necessary, but the requisite court order can be obtained with a minimal showing of relevancy. That same low standard governs traces of Internet surfing and e-mail. Equally objectionable, under sec. 213 of the act, secret "sneak and peek" searches of physical property can be conducted without knowledge of the property owner until a "reasonable'' time after the search has occurred. No knowledge means no opportunity to contest the validity of the search, including such obvious infractions as rummaging through office drawers when the warrant authorizes a garage search, or even searching the wrong address.

Second, the new rules are defended as a necessary instrument of antiterrorism. If so, why do many of the provisions apply not only to suspected terrorist acts but also to everyday national security investigations and even ordinary criminal matters? In effect, our government has used the events of September 11 to impose national police powers that skirt time-honored constraints on the state. The executive branch will not always wield its new powers in the service of ends that Americans find congenial.

To illustrate, the PATRIOT Act expands the Foreign Intelligence Surveillance Act (FISA)—a Carter-administration program that created a special federal court to approve electronic surveillance of citizens and resident aliens alleged to be acting on behalf of a foreign power. Previously, the FISA court granted surveillance authority if foreign intelligence was the primary purpose of an investigation. No longer. Under sec. 218 of the PATRIOT Act, foreign intelligence need only be a "significant" purpose of an investigation. That sounds like a trivial change, but it isn't. Because the standard for FISA approval is lower than "probable cause," and because FISA now applies to ordinary criminal matters if they are dressed up as national security inquiries, the new rules could open the door to circumvention of the Fourth Amendment's warrant requirements. The result: rubber-stamp judicial consent to phone and Internet surveillance, even in regular criminal cases, and FBI access to medical, educational, business, and other records that conceivably relate to foreign intelligence probes.

Third, laws that compromise civil liberties must be revisited periodically to ensure that temporary measures, undertaken in response to a national security emergency, do not endure longer than necessary. Such laws must contain sunset clauses; that is, the law should expire automatically within a short time of enactment—thus imposing on government the continuing obligation to justify its intrusions. In this instance, the Bush administration rejected any sunset provision whatsoever. Congress demurred and insisted on including such a provision, but it applied only to new wiretap and surveillance powers, not to the whole bill. Moreover, the sunset date was fixed at December 31, 2005—more than four years after passage of the legislation. Plainly, a shorter time frame—say, two years—would have been appropriate. If the emergency persisted, Congress and the president could reenact the law.

Detention of Noncitizens in the United States

The PATRIOT Act also raises questions about detention of noncitizens in the United States. Under sec. 412 of the act, the attorney general can detain, for seven days, noncitizens suspected of terrorism. After seven days, deportation proceedings must commence or criminal charges must be filed. Originally, the Justice Department had asked for authority to detain suspects indefinitely without charge. Congress could not be persuaded to go along. But the final bill, for all practical purposes, allows expanded detention simply by charging the detainee with a technical immigration violation. If a suspect cannot be deported, he can still be detained if the attorney general certifies every six months that national security is at stake.

Underlining the magnitude and scope of that problem, the *Wall Street Journal* reported on November 1, 2001, that seven Democrats had filed Freedom of Information Act requests for a detailed accounting from Attorney General John Ashcroft on the status of roughly 1,200 detainees, mainly in New York and New Jersey. The lawmakers mentioned that some detainees had reportedly "been denied access to their attorneys, proper food, or protection from . . . physical assault." Some of them were allegedly being held in solitary confinement even though they hadn't been charged with any criminal offense. According to a representative of the New York Legal Aid Society, several Arab detainees had been limited to one phone call per week to a lawyer and, if the line was busy, they had to wait another week. On November 25, the *New York Times* cited a senior law enforcement official who said that just 10 to 15 of 1,200 detainees were suspected al-Qaeda sympathizers. The government had not found evidence linking a single one of them to the September 11 attacks.

Whether or not those reports proved accurate, it was time for the government to supply some answers. Here's what the *Washington Post* had to say in an October 31, 2001, editorial criticizing the Justice Department for resisting legitimate requests for information on the detainees: "The questions are pretty basic. How many of the 1,000-plus are still in custody? Who are they? What are the charges against them? What is the status of their cases? Where and under what circumstances are they being held? The department refuses not only to provide the answers but also to give a serious explanation of why it won't provide them."

Eight months later, the Justice Department still had not identified the remaining detainees. A department spokesman said only that fewer than 400 were still in custody—74 for immigration violations, 100 who had been criminally charged, 24 held as material witnesses, and 175 awaiting deportation. They had been denied legal counsel, access to their families, and details of pending charges, if any. In effect, nearly 400 detainees remained in legal limbo as the first anniversary of September 11 rapidly approached.

Ultimately, the Supreme Court may have to clarify how the civil liberties/national security tradeoff will unfold. Two terms ago, in *Zadvydas v. Davis*, the Court held that immigrants who have committed crimes cannot be detained indefinitely; they must be deported within a reasonable period or released. Moreover, said the Court, temporary and even illegal immigrants, not just U.S. citizens, are entitled to due process. Still, the Court noted that different rules may apply to immigrants who are suspected of terrorism or considered national security risks.

Thus, the law is murky, and the legislation passed in the aftermath of September 11 adds new elements of uncertainty. Nonetheless, the controlling principle is unambiguous. Any attempt by government to chip away at constitutionally guaranteed rights must be subjected to the most painstaking scrutiny to determine whether less invasive means could accomplish the same ends.

Detention of U.S. Citizens

Yaser Esam Hamdi is also in legal limbo. He was raised in Saudi Arabia, captured in Afghanistan, sent to Guantanamo, then transferred to a Norfolk, Virginia, military brig after the Defense Department learned that he was a U.S. citizen, born in Louisiana. Hamdi is being detained indefinitely, without seeing an attorney, even though he hasn't been charged with any crime. José Padilla, who allegedly plotted to build a radiological "dirty bomb," is a U.S. citizen too. He was arrested at Chicago's O'Hare airport after a flight from Pakistan, then transferred from civilian to military custody in Charleston, South Carolina. Like Hamdi, Padilla is being detained by the military—indefinitely, without seeing an attorney, even though he hasn't been charged with any crime. Meanwhile, Zacarias Moussaoui, purportedly the 20th hijacker, is not a U.S. citizen. Neither is Richard Reid, the alleged shoe bomber. Both have attorneys. Both have been charged before federal civilian courts.

What gives? Four men: two citizens and two noncitizens. Is it possible that constitutional rights—like habeas corpus, which requires the government to justify continued detentions, and the Sixth Amendment, which ensures a speedy and public jury trial with assistance of counsel—can be denied to citizens yet extended to noncitizens? That's what the Bush administration would have us believe. Citizen Hamdi's treatment is legitimate, insists Attorney General John Ashcroft, because Hamdi is an "enemy combatant" and there is "clear Supreme Court precedent" to handle those persons differently, even if they are citizens.

Ashcroft's so-called clear precedent is a 1942 Supreme Court case, *Ex Parte Quirin*, which dealt with Nazi saboteurs, at least one of whom was a U.S. citizen. "Enemy combatants," said the Court, are either lawful— for example, the regular army of a belligerent country—or unlawful— for example, terrorists. When *lawful* combatants are captured, they are POWs. As POWs, they cannot be tried (except for war crimes); they must be repatriated after hostilities are over; and they have to provide only their name, rank, and serial number if interrogated. Clearly, that's not what the Justice Department had in mind for Hamdi.

Unlawful combatants are different. When unlawful combatants are captured, they can be tried by a military tribunal. That's what happened to the Nazi saboteurs in *Quirin*. But Hamdi has not been charged, much less tried. Indeed, the president's executive order of November 2001 excludes U.S. citizens from the purview of military tribunals. If the president were to modify his order, the *Quirin* decision might provide legal authority for the military to try Hamdi. But the decision provides no legal authority for detaining a citizen without an attorney solely for purposes of aggressive interrogation.

Moreover, the Constitution does not distinguish between the protections extended to ordinary citizens on one hand and unlawful-combatant citizens on the other. Nor does the Constitution distinguish between crimes covered by the Fifth and Sixth Amendments and terrorist acts. Still, the *Quirin* Court justified those distinctions—noting that Congress had formally declared war and thereby invoked articles of war that expressly authorized the trial of unlawful combatants by military tribunal. Today, the situation is different. We've had virtually no input from Congress: no declaration of war, no authorization of tribunals, and no suspension of habeas corpus.

Yet those functions are explicitly assigned to Congress by Article I of the Constitution. It is Congress, not the executive branch, which has the power "To declare War" and "To constitute Tribunals inferior to the supreme Court." Only Congress can suspend the "Privilege of the Writ of Habeas Corpus . . . when in Cases of Rebellion or Invasion the public Safety may require it." Congress has not spoken—except by enacting the PATRIOT Act. And there, we do find authorization for detention of persons suspected of terrorism—but only *noncitizens* and only for *seven days*, after which they must be released unless criminal charges are filed or deportation proceedings commenced.

No charges were filed in Hamdi's case. That's why a federal public defender sued on his behalf in May 2002, demanding that he be charged or released. A district court judge in Norfolk ordered the Justice Department to explain Hamdi's detention and agreed that he had a right to counsel. Predictably, the Justice Department appealed. In its legal brief to the U.S. Court of Appeals for the Fourth Circuit, the government insisted, "There is no right under the laws and customs of war for an enemy combatant to meet with counsel concerning his detention." Moreover, asserted the Justice Department, "The court may not second-guess the military's enemy combatant determination. Going beyond that determination would ... intrude upon the Constitutional prerogative of the Commander in Chief."

That astonishing statement amounts to an explicit declaration by the executive branch that it may unilaterally abrogate habeas corpus, even for a U.S. citizen. Furthermore, the Justice Department announced that it would extend its new doctrine to "enemy combatants ... captured ... on the battlefield in a foreign land; ... captured overseas and brought to the United States [or] captured and detained in this country." In July 2002 the Fourth Circuit remanded the Hamdi case to the district court to reconsider "the implications [including] what effect petitioner's unmonitored access to counsel might have on the government's ongoing gathering of intelligence." The chief judge of the Fourth Circuit, J. Harvie Wilkinson, ordered the lower court to be deferential when considering the Justice Department's position. Still, Wilkinson affirmed the need for judicial review. He warned, "With no meaningful judicial review, any American citizen alleged to be an enemy combatant could be detained indefinitely without charges or counsel."

Perhaps that warning will persuade the administration that it may not set the rules, prosecute infractions, determine guilt or innocence, then review the results of its own actions—unless of course the administration has statutory or constitutional authority. Even persons convinced that President Bush cherishes civil liberties and understands that the Constitution is not mere scrap paper must be unsettled by the prospect that an unknown and less honorable successor could exploit some of the dangerous precedents that the Bush administration is attempting to put in place.

Conclusion

If civil libertarians have a single overriding concern about the PATRIOT Act and our detention policies, it is this: the Bush administration has concentrated too much unchecked authority in the hands of the executive branch—making a mockery of the doctrine of separation of powers that has been a cornerstone of our Constitution for two and a quarter centuries. We cannot, for example, permit the executive branch to declare unilaterally that a U.S. citizen may be characterized as an enemy combatant, whisked away, detained indefinitely without charges, denied legal counsel, and prevented from arguing to a judge that he is wholly innocent.

That does not mean the Justice Department must set people free to unleash weapons of mass destruction. But it does mean, at a minimum, that Congress must get involved, exercising its responsibility to enact a new legal regimen for detainees in time of national emergency. That regimen must respect our rights under the Constitution, including the right to judicial review of executive branch decisions. Constitutional rights are not absolute. But they do establish a strong presumption of liberty, which can be overridden only if government demonstrates, first, that its restrictions are essential and, second, that the goals it seeks to accomplish cannot be accomplished in a less invasive manner. When the executive, legislative, and judicial branches agree on the framework, the potential for abuse is diminished. When only the executive has acted, the foundation of a free society can too easily erode.

Suggested Readings

Lynch, Timothy. "Breaking the Vicious Cycle: Preserving Our Liberties While Fighting Terrorism." Cato Institute Policy Analysis no. 443, June 26, 2002.

Quirin, Ex Parte. 317 U.S. 1 (1942).

Shapiro, Stephen J., et al. "*Inter Arma Silent Leges*: In Times of Armed Conflict, *Should the Laws Be Silent?*" Association of the Bar of the City of New York, Committee on Military Affairs and Justice, December 2001.

Sonnett, Neal R., et al. "Preliminary Report: Task Force on Treatment of Enemy Combatants." American Bar Association, August 8, 2002.

Taylor, Stuart. "Jailed with No Key." *Legal Times*, July 22, 2002.

—Prepared by Robert A. Levy

13. National ID Cards and Military Tribunals

> **Congress should**
> - resist the establishment of a national identification card and
> - resist the establishment of military tribunals for civilians.

In the wake of a calamitous terrorist attack, such as the one that America experienced on September 11, 2001, it is prudent for Congress to review our laws, policies, and customs with an eye to changes that would enhance our safety and security. Each policy proposal, however, should be carefully examined. Congress should not hastily enact any proposal simply because it is packaged as an "anti-terrorism" measure. Every proposal should be vetted for its necessity, efficacy, and constitutionality.

National ID Cards

It was only a matter of days after the attack of September 11 before some members of Congress proposed the implementation of a national ID card system as a way of thwarting additional terrorist attacks. The national ID card has been proposed in the past as a way of stopping illegal immigration. Since September 11 the policy proposal has been repackaged as a "security" measure.

The national ID card proposal would be a very bad deal for America because it would require some 250 million people to surrender some of their freedom and some of their privacy for something that is not going to make the country safe from terrorist attack. An ID card with biometric identifiers may seem "foolproof," but there are several ways that terrorists will be able to get around such a system. If terrorists are determined to attack America, they can bribe the employees who issue the cards or the employees who check the cards. Terrorists could also recruit people who possess valid cards—U.S. citizens or lawful permanent residents—to carry out attacks.

Proponents of the card point to countries in Europe, such as France, that already have national ID card systems. But the experience of those countries is nothing to brag about. The people in those countries have surrendered their privacy and their liberty, yet they continue to experience terrorist attacks. National ID cards simply do not deliver the security that is promised.

Moreover, the establishment of a national ID card system will dilute civil liberties. The Fourth Amendment to the Constitution protects Americans against unreasonable searches and seizures. The quintessential "seizure" under the Fourth Amendment is to be arrested or detained by the police. The police can seize or arrest a person when they have an arrest warrant or when they have "probable cause" to believe that the suspect has just committed a crime in their presence. But the police cannot stop people on the street and demand an ID, at least not under current law. The police can *request* an ID; they can *request* that people answer their questions. But the key point is that Americans get to decide whether or not they wish to cooperate. The legal presumption right now is on the side of the individual citizen. The people do not have to justify themselves to the police. The police have to justify their interference with individual liberty.

A national ID card system will turn that important legal principle upside down. After the enactment of the system, pressure will begin to build to enact laws that will require citizens to produce an ID whenever a government official demands it. This is very likely to happen for two reasons. First, in the countries that already have national ID card systems, the police have acquired such powers. Second, in this country there already are cases in which the police have arrested Americans for failure to produce IDs. Thus far, however, courts have thrown out such arrests, ruling that such a refusal does not constitute "disorderly conduct" or "resisting an officer." And yet, if Congress passes a law that says people must produce IDs, the courts may well yield on that point.

It is important to note that many of the proponents of the national ID card—such as Alan Dershowitz of Harvard Law School and Larry Ellison from Oracle—present the idea in its most innocuous form. The proponents say the card will be "voluntary" and that people will have to present it only at airports. They say there will be no legal duty to produce an ID card. But, over time, the amount of information on the card will surely expand. The number of places where one will have to present an ID card will also expand, and it will eventually become compulsory. And, sooner or later, a legal duty to produce an ID whenever a government official demands it will be created.

Secretary of Defense Donald Rumsfeld has already warned us to expect more terrorist attacks, so it is a safe bet that more anti-terrorism proposals will emerge in Congress in the wake of such attacks. Perhaps there will be an attack a year from now, and a limited national ID card will be proposed and enacted. Maybe five years later, America will be attacked again; people will die, and law enforcement will go to Congress and say, "We have a national ID card, but the problem is that it is voluntary, not compulsory." Thus, by increments, America will get the full-blown national ID card system that is now in place in other countries. Congress should avoid this slippery slope by focusing its attention on more meritorious proposals. A national ID card expands the power of government over law-abiding citizens, but it will not really enhance security.

Military Tribunals

In November 2001, President Bush issued a "military order" that said that suspected terrorists could, on his command, be tried before specially designated military tribunals instead of civilian courts. That order immediately came under fire because of its disregard for constitutional norms.

Article III, section 2, of the Constitution provides, "The Trial of all Crimes, except in Cases of Impeachment; shall be by Jury." The Sixth Amendment to the Constitution provides, "In all criminal prosecutions, the accused shall enjoy the right to a speedy and public trial, by an impartial jury." To limit the awesome powers of government, the Framers of the Constitution designed a system in which citizen juries would stand between the apparatus of the state and the accused. If the government prosecutor can convince a jury that the accused has committed a crime and belongs in prison, the accused will lose his liberty and perhaps his life. If the government cannot convince the jury with its evidence, the prisoner will go free. In America, an acquittal by a jury is final and unreviewable by state functionaries.

The federal government did try people before military commissions during the Civil War. To facilitate that process, President Abraham Lincoln suspended the writ of habeas corpus—so that the prisoners could not challenge the legality of their arrest or conviction. The one case that did reach the Supreme Court, *Ex Parte Milligan* (1866), deserves careful attention.

127

In *Milligan*, the attorney general of the United States maintained that the legal guarantees set forth in the Bill of Rights were "peace provisions." During wartime, he argued, the federal government can suspend the Bill of Rights and impose martial law. If the government chooses to exercise that option, the commanding military officer becomes "the supreme legislator, supreme judge, and supreme executive." Under that legal theory, many American citizens were arrested, imprisoned, and executed without the benefit of the legal procedure set forth in the Constitution—trial by jury.

The Supreme Court ultimately rejected the position advanced by the attorney general. Here is one passage from the *Milligan* ruling:

> The great minds of the country have differed on the correct interpretation to be given to various provisions of the Federal Constitution; and judicial decision has been often invoked to settle their true meaning; but until recently no one ever doubted that the right to trial by jury was fortified in the organic law against the power of attack. It is *now* assailed; but if ideas can be expressed in words and language has any meaning, *this right*—one of the most valuable in a free country—is preserved to every one accused of crime who is not attached to the army, or navy, or militia in actual service. The sixth amendment affirms that "in all criminal prosecutions the accused shall enjoy the right to a speedy and public trial by an impartial jury," language broad enough to embrace all persons and cases.

The *Milligan* ruling is sound. While the Constitution empowers the Congress "To make Rules for the Government and Regulation of the land and naval Forces" and "To provide for organizing, arming, and disciplining, the Militia," the Supreme Court ruled that the jurisdiction of the military courts could not extend beyond those people who were actually serving in the army, navy, and militia. That is an eminently sensible reading of the constitutional text.

President Bush and his lawyers maintain that terrorists are "unlawful combatants" and that unlawful combatants are not entitled to the protections of the Bill of Rights. The defect in the president's claim is circularity. A primary function of the trial process is to sort through conflicting evidence in order to find the truth. Anyone who *assumes* that a person who has merely been accused of being an unlawful combatant is, in fact, an unlawful combatant can understandably maintain that such a person is not entitled to the protection of our constitutional safeguards. The flaw, however, is that that argument begs the very question under consideration.

To take a concrete example, suppose that the president accuses a lawful permanent resident of the United States of aiding and abetting terrorism.

The person accused responds by denying the charge and by insisting on a trial by jury so that he can establish his innocence. The president responds by saying that "terrorists are unlawful combatants and unlawful combatants are not entitled to jury trials." The president also says that the prisoner is not entitled to any access to the civilian court system to allege any violations of his constitutional rights. With the writ of habeas corpus suspended, the prisoner and his attorney can only file legal appeals with the president—the very person who ordered the prisoner's arrest in the first instance!

The Constitution's jury trial clause is not a "peace provision" that can be suspended during wartime. Reasonable people can disagree about how to prosecute war criminals who are captured overseas in a theater of war, but the president cannot make himself the policeman, prosecutor, and judge of people on U.S. soil. In America, the president's power is "checked" by the judiciary and by citizen juries.

Conclusion

It is very important that policymakers not lose sight of what we are fighting for in the war on terrorism. The goal should be to fight the terrorists within the framework of a free society. The federal government should be taking the battle to the terrorists, to their base camps, and killing the terrorist leadership; it should not be transforming our free society into a surveillance state.

Suggested Readings

Crews, Clyde Wayne. "Human Bar Code: Monitoring Biometric Technologies in a Free Society." Cato Institute Policy Analysis no. 452, September 17, 2002.

Kopel, David. "You've Got Identity: Why a National ID Is a Bad Idea." *National Review Online*, February 5, 2002.

Levy, Robert A. "Don't Shred the Constitution to Fight Terror." *Wall Street Journal*, November 20, 2001.

Lynch, Timothy. "Breaking the Vicious Cycle: Preserving Our Liberties While Fighting Terrorism." Cato Institute Policy Analysis no. 443, June 26, 2002.

———. "Executive Branch Arrests and Trials." Testimony before the Senate Judiciary Committee on Military Tribunals. December 4, 2001, www.cato.org/testimony/ct_tl120401.html.

Twight, Charlotte. "Watching You: Systematic Federal Surveillance of Ordinary Americans." Cato Institute Briefing Paper no. 69, October 17, 2001.

—Prepared by Timothy Lynch

14. Regulation of Electronic Speech and Commerce

Congress should

- resist the urge to regulate offensive content on the Web,
- allow the market to address privacy and marketing concerns,
- not undercut individuals' efforts to maintain anonymity on the Internet,
- not attempt to regulate adult behavior such as online gambling,
- reject attempts to impose new restrictions on encryption and new surveillance on American citizens,
- avoid replacing true diversity and democracy on the Internet with politically motivated "Internet commons" or "public spaces,"
- avoid online protectionism by refusing to allow incumbent businesspeople to undercut electronic trade on the Internet, and
- avoid imposing burdensome and unconstitutional tax collection schemes on the Internet.

It seems that everybody's got a plan to tame the freewheeling Internet these days. The technology and telecommunications sectors of the American economy are increasingly under assault at the local, state, federal, and international levels. Republicans and Democrats alike are looking for ways to regulate everything from privacy to porn, while simultaneously seeking ways to subsidize access. The Progressive Policy Institute describes a "failure of cyber-libertarianism" that leads, naturally enough, to its "Strategic National E-Commerce Policy" framework. Ralph Nader would establish a World Consumer Protection Organization to counter the Internet's libertarian streak, which he finds intolerable. Countless other special interests are clamoring for increased government activism.

But policymakers must resist intervention. Whether the government acts as regulator or facilitator of the high-tech economy and the Internet, there will be unintended consequences. Industry should find self-regulatory solutions instead of looking to Washington for answers or assistance.

Protecting Kids Online

The Communications Decency Act, passed to ban pornography on the Internet, was struck down by the Supreme Court in 1997. But Washington continues efforts to regulate Internet content. In 2002 the Supreme Court upheld a portion of the Child Online Protection Act, passed by Congress in 1998 to shield children from online pornography by requiring that website operators verify the age of visitors. The Court held that free speech is not necessarily violated by the imposition of community standards on a national scale.

Although the Supreme Court does not reject the notion of ''contemporary community standards,'' the lower court got it right when it noted that the community standard notion lets the most squeamish dictate what all others can see on the Web. In the name of protecting children, the law interferes with content that adults should have the right to see under the First Amendment.

On an Internet that is increasingly capable of direct peer-to-peer communication and broadcast, individual choices and behavior replace ''community standards.'' And laws like COPA can have unintended consequences: barriers to those who seek porn voluntarily will likely increase e-mail solicitations for porn (spam), which COPA wouldn't regulate.

The best and least restrictive defense is parental supervision, and helpful tools, including filtering software and filtered online services, are available in the private sector. Filtered online services can limit the receipt of unwanted salacious e-mail, for which COPA is no use. Another tool at parents' disposal is tracking software that lets them monitor everything a child does or has done on the Internet.

Online Marketing and Privacy

Websites, as is well known, frequently collect information about visitors and often sell it. Some legislators want to require online and even main street firms to reveal what information they collect and share, and to allow customers to ''opt out.'' Others would require a much more restrictive opt-in standard for "sensitive" consumer information; under that standard no information could be used until a consumer granted permission.

But is all the fuss over information-age marketing justified? Free-flowing information means more and cheaper stuff. Certainly, business use of personal information to move merchandise may sometimes be irritating, but federal regulation, which will hurt e-commerce and consumers, isn't the answer. Small businesses will suffer more than larger companies that have already assembled databases.

As businesses respond to consumer preferences, more stringent privacy protections are emerging. The notice and choice sought in privacy legislation already exist. Most highly trafficked sites already feature privacy policies. Users can set their Web browsers to reject information gathering. Software tools that provide for anonymous surfing or warn when information is being collected further empower consumers. The marketplace increasingly forces sites to develop online privacy policies as ever-more-efficient browser technology alerts users to the level of security provided.

Moreover, Washington itself can be the leading privacy offender. September 11, 2001, brought renewed government surveillance, authorized by the PATRIOT Act, that raises serious constitutional issues and should be the focus of any serious congressional privacy debate. We don't get to "opt out" of government information collection. Washington does not have a track record that inspires confidence in it as a protector of personal information.

Unsolicited E-Mail (spam) Policy

One legitimate purpose of limited government is to stop the use of force and fraud. That extends to fraudulent e-mail solicitations, the prosecution of which is the job of the Federal Trade Commission.

Peddling fraudulent merchandise or impersonating somebody else in the e-mail's header information should be punished, as should breaking a contract made with an Internet service provider (ISP) that prohibits bulk mailing. But in the debate over the outpouring of spam, it's important to avoid unintentionally stifling beneficial e-commerce. Sometimes, commercial e-mail, even if unsolicited, may be welcome if the sender is a business selling legal and legitimate products in a nonabusive manner.

Increasingly, legitimate companies are embracing permission-based, "opt-in" e-mail standards, which enable people to receive e-mail only from senders they have chosen. If legislation merely sends the most egregious offenders offshore, that may simply create legal and regulatory hassles for small businesses trying to make a go of legitimate e-commerce or for mainstream companies that are not spammers. Unwise legislation could also create headaches for noncommercial e-mailers.

A smarter approach is e-mail filtering, such as setting the owner's screen to receive only from recognized and approved e-mail addresses. That standard is particularly appropriate for children's e-mail accounts. Emerging "handshake" or "challenge and response" systems capable of totally blocking spam show promise: since the most offensive spam is sent by automatic bulk mailing programs that aren't capable of receiving a reply, spam no longer appears in the inbox. Identifiers or "seals" for trusted commercial e-mail could be another means of helping ISPs block unwanted e-mail.

As the market works to shift costs of commercial e-mail back to the sender, we must be on guard against legislative confusion: How might the definition of "spam" expand beyond "unsolicited" and "commercial" e-mail, and would such expansion be a good thing? What about unsolicited political or nonprofit bulk e-mailings, or press releases, resume blasts, and charitable solicitations? What about newsletters that contain embedded ads or link back to for-profit websites? Would pop-up ads become suspect in the aftermath of spam legislation? They're not e-mail, but they are unsolicited and commercial.

Another piece of proposed legislation would grant ISPs the power to decide what is spam and to unilaterally block it with "good faith" immunity and sue the spammer. It is appropriate for consumers and ISPs to effect complete blackouts of spammers if they like; computers, wires, servers, and routers are private property. But it's not necessary to federalize such contracts.

Finally, legislative bans on false e-mail return addresses, as well as bans on software capable of hiding such information, have worrisome implications for free speech and anonymity for individuals—not just misbehaving businesses. Individuals can use "spamware" to create contemporary versions of the anonymous flyers that have played such an important role in our history. Individuals must retain the ability to safeguard their anonymity even in (or perhaps especially in) a mass communications tool like e-mail. In an era in which so many people are concerned about online privacy, legislation that impedes a technology that can protect privacy would be strange indeed.

Given the perfectly understandable desire to stop unsolicited mail, it is all too easy for Congress to undermine legitimate commerce, communications, and free speech. And crippling Internet commerce would be especially pointless if spam continued pouring in from overseas.

The Internet and Anonymity

Anonymous speech is as old as America. Gentlemen calling themselves ''Publius'' wrote the *Federalist Papers.* Thomas Paine's *Common Sense* was signed by ''An Englishman.'' Today, e-mail encryption is an important example of the tradition of speaking freely and anonymously.

But encryption technology in the hands of people bent on destruction can be deadly. Some observers believe that the terrorists who attacked America communicated via encrypted messages. Fear of this indisputable threat led to renewed proposals to give government a ''back door key'' to encryption products. Similarly, calls for a national ID card exemplify new urges to shine a federal light on individuals. But calls for prohibitions on encryption products are a nonstarter in the sense that trying to prohibit bad actors from acquiring hardware or software is futile in today's global, integrated marketplace.

Government's job is to restrict the liberty of dangerous criminals and enemies—not that of innocent citizens, or to treat everyone as a suspect. The USA PATRIOT Act has set up a new law enforcement infrastructure that can easily increase surveillance of nonterrorists, but that is clearly beyond the stated intent of combating terrorism. New powers should apply only to terrorism, not to routine criminal investigations. While surveillance can and likely will be enhanced to respond to the new realities of instant electronic communications, the Fourth Amendment's protections against unreasonable and warrantless searches must not suffer.

Proposals to reregulate encryption are the digital equivalent of seizing grandma's nail clippers at the airport; terrorists would simply resort to illegal encryption. Congress decided in the mid-1990s that the benefits of readily available access to encryption technology are significant. Like proposals to mandate that everyone carry a national ID card, reregulation of encryption is a needless undermining of anonymity and privacy.

It's important to remember that the root of the terrorist threat America faces does not lie entirely in cyberspace, so fighting encryption is a misplaced priority. Despite the intense Internet privacy debate of recent years, the real dispute isn't about whether such privacy is achievable; it's about whether government will allow it where the capability finally exists. Encryption is essential, not just for keeping intact a pure version of the principle of free speech, but for such ''mundane'' needs as private communication, secure online commerce, and business-to-business exchanges. Restrictions would damage the security of America's financial systems, making it easier for the everyday hacker, not to mention the terrorist, to invade personal information and tinker with the financial infrastructure. One of the imperatives in combating terrorism is to secure sensitive and critical systems from attack. Since encryption is essential for self-protection of companies and individuals, misguided legislation undermining it hampers sensible, private security measures.

The encryption genie is out of the bottle. Not only can malevolent programmers create their own strings of ones and zeros capable of encrypting communications, so can legitimate companies overseas. And requiring the deposit of an encryption "key" at a central governmental location creates a "honey pot" for hackers to attack, reducing our security. Encryption legislation to deliberately reduce our privacy would have been unthinkable only recently, given widespread concerns about privacy. As Rep. Bob Goodlatte (R-Va.) has pointed out, we need more encryption, not less. New encryption techniques are critical to the protection of intellectual property, such as digital distribution of books, movies, and music, on which a rising share of America's wealth creation depends.

Moreover, encryption plays a key role in the struggle for human liberty itself. It has aided political dissidents shielding themselves from brutal governments, helping democracy and individual liberty flourish overseas. Regulating encryption could encumber us far more than the terrorists, who can still encrypt as well as use other means of communication. Legal encryption may not be essential for terror, but it is essential for our advanced economy.

Internet Gambling

Some members of Congress want to stop online gambling by banning the acceptance of credit cards or other instruments for processing gambling transactions. It's understandable that politicians would be concerned about gambling operations being used as tools for terrorist money laundering.

But in this privacy-sensitive era, the question arises: if you were gambling on the Internet, how would the government ever know about it? For the government to know about such personal, consensual behavior requires spying. But to impose federal surveillance of consumer financial transactions before consumers have even widely embraced Internet banking and commerce has serious implications for people's willingness to welcome online finance.

Banks and ISPs would be drafted as snoops to sift all financial transactions. Not surprisingly, credit card companies don't want to be held responsible for ensuring that companies for which they process card services are not involved in gambling operations.

Other rationales for gambling restrictions are to target shady dealers who run phony, fraudulent operations and to protect people from addiction to gambling. That is paternalism: Consumers should screen any gambling operations with which they transact and avoid fly-by-night operators. And gambling adults are responsible for their own behavior.

What constitutes "gambling" is often in the eye of the legislator. Fantasy sports get a limited exemption in proposed legislation, as do horseracing and jai alai. And investing in certain technical financial instruments can be a "gamble" in the sense that "the opportunity to win is predominantly subject to chance"—as proposed legislation defines gambling. Yet the anti-gambling proposals exempt "any over-the-counter derivative instrument," though these clearly are not for the squeamish.

Once we travel down the road of regulating behavior on the Internet, there's basically no limit to government's ability to regulate voluntary speech and interaction and to substitute its moral vision for that of individuals.

Protecting an Internet "Commons"

Some scholars and organizations are clamoring for creation of "public spaces" on the Internet. For example, University of Chicago law professor Cass Sunstein worries that the individual's habit of personalizing or filtering his Web experiences thwarts the "unanticipated encounters" and "common experiences" that should unite us as a democracy. Where the private sector doesn't come through, he wants the government to "pick up the slack," requiring sites to disclose their biases and link to opposing views. And he wants popular sites to act as a "public sidewalk," providing links "designed to ensure more exposure to substantive questions." Presumably the government would decide if a site is guilty of "failure to attend to public issues." According to this view, free speech doesn't mean saying what you want but providing a platform for other views.

Acting on similar beliefs, former leaders of the Public Broadcasting System and the Federal Communications Commission set up the Digital Promise project to "halt the encroachment of purely market values" on the Internet. They propose the establishment of a Digital Opportunity Investment Trust fund program, or "DO IT," to fund "the development of online courses, training materials, archives, software, civic information, quality arts and cultural programs, and other digital resources and services of the highest standards to meet the needs of all citizens and help them gain access to the best minds and talents in our society.''

DO IT might best be thought of as a sort of ministry of cyber culture, the fusion of the National Endowment for the Arts, PBS, and the "E-Rate" program (or Gore tax). The $18 billion program would be funded by revenues from wireless spectrum auctions. Legislation has already been introduced to make DO IT a reality.

Despite those worries, a torrent of "shared experiences" bombards us despite personalization and filtering. As one critic put it, given Sunstein's view, "these sort[s] of chance encounters should be happening to me less and less on the Internet. Instead, they seem to be happening more and more." Sources of exposure have ranged from the early bulletin boards of the 1980s to the peer-to-peer networks of today. And in between they encompass Web pages, search engines, chat rooms, e-mail, auctions, Internet phones, instant messaging, and more.

The Internet is already a public space, in the proper sense of the term. The public shouldn't be compelled to subsidize content deemed appropriate for cyber citizenship. Nothing in government's legitimate scope qualifies it as a fountain of superior, purer information or a source of social cohesion. Governments are well-known for censorship and control, such as the mandating of library filters and ratings for movies, music, and videogames.

Most fundamentally, the public spaces premise fails because it rests on the notion that capitalism and freedom are inimical to, rather than prerequisites for, civil society and the diffusion of ideas. We cherish a free press, dissent, and debate because governments can threaten those values. We need markets to maximize output, including that of true and useful "public" information.

In practice, a public spaces regime would simply deteriorate into congressional mandates and funding of "approved" sites. But funding is the role of venture capitalists, who have learned that not every Internet venture makes sense. Government programs would be failure proof in the sense that politics rather than competition for eyeballs would matter. Whereas the unalloyed Internet constitutes a real free press, a potpourri of information people seek (or that the unpopular post on their own dime), public spaces will consist of "worthy" things people are forced to pay for or link to.

Online Free Speech and the Rising Threat of Global Internet Regulation

As countries across the globe become more aware of the power of the Internet as a communications medium and channel for global commerce, they grow more interested in regulating what takes place online.

The most prominent example of such international regulatory mischief so far has been the efforts by the French courts to force the American-based Web portal company Yahoo! to remove, or at least block from the view of French citizens, those portions of its website where Nazi memorabilia are for sale. Although a lower district court in California held in November 2001 that the French ruling could not be extraterritorially enforced here in America, the Paris Criminal Court held in February 2002 that the case could go forward. Many other countries also have extraterritorial speech regulations. If such parochial speech controls were enforceable across the globe, it would obviously force content providers and network operators to restrict their speech so as to avoid potential liability or penalties.

But can parochial standards really be applied to the Web? Or is the Web truly a borderless medium that cannot be regulated in any workable sense by local authorities? Many important legal issues are at play, especially when you expand the discussion beyond free speech to include commercial regulation of the Internet. Some scholars have suggested that international treaties could be the answer. Others are calling for a "UN for the Internet," or some sort of global regulatory body to resolve such questions. Still others suggest that the best answer is to do nothing, since anarchy, at least so far, has the advantage of broadening the range of free speech globally.

Although Americans have good reason to ignore the French ruling in the Yahoo! case, the question remains: how will these disputes be decided in the future? As Net connectivity across the globe grows, and human communication and interaction bridge the geographic divides between countries and continents, governments will attempt to force this new technology into old regulatory paradigms. Defenders of free speech would be wise to start thinking about ways to convince them to do otherwise.

State and Local Restraints of Electronic Trade

New York Times reporter John Markoff noted in a December 2000 column, "In a remarkably short period, the World Wide Web has touched or has promised to alter—some would say threaten—virtually every aspect of modern life.'' Of course, not everyone has enthusiastically embraced the changes the Internet has brought, *especially* those who feel threatened by it.

This is particularly true in the business marketplace where many well-established industries and older institutions fear that the Net is displacing their businesses or perhaps entire industry sectors by bringing consumers and producers closer together.

That older industries fear newer ones is nothing new, of course. Any new and disruptive technology will attract its fair share of skeptics and opponents. Steamboat operators feared the railroads; railroaders feared truckers; truckers feared air shippers; and undoubtedly horse and buggy drivers feared the first automobiles that crossed their path.

Fear of technological change is to be expected; the problem is that older industries often have significantly more clout in the political market-place and can convince policymakers to act on their behalf. State licensing or franchising laws are often the favored club for entrenched industries that are looking for a way to beat back their new competitors. Demanding that producers comply with a crazy-quilt of state and local regulations will often be enough to foreclose new market entry altogether.

That is simply old-fashioned industrial protectionism. But requiring national or even global commercial vendors—as is clearly the case with e-commerce and Internet sellers—to comply with parochial laws and regulations is antithetical to the interests of consumers and the economy in general. Consumers clearly benefit from the development of online commercial websites and value the flexibility such sites give them to do business directly with producers and distributors. More important, the development of a vibrant online commercial sector provides important benefits for the economy as a whole in terms of increased productivity. The Progressive Policy Institute has estimated that protectionist laws and regulations could cost consumers more than $15 billion in the aggregate.

Lawmakers must be flexible in crafting public policies so as to not upset the vibrant, dynamic nature of this marketplace and be willing to change existing structures, laws, or political norms to accommodate or foster the expansion of new technologies and industry sectors. The fact that some Old Economy, Manufacturing Age interests may not like the emergence of the New Economy, Information Age sectors and technologies does not mean policymakers should seek to accommodate older interests by stifling the development of the cyber sector. Such a Luddite solution will hurt consumers and further set back the development of the online marketplace. Congress must exercise its powers under the Commerce Clause of the Constitution to protect interstate electronic commerce when it is seriously threatened by state and local meddling.

Internet Taxation

A remarkably contentious battle has taken place in recent years over the Internet Tax Freedom Act of 1998 and the federally imposed moratorium on state and local taxation of the Internet. The ITFA moratorium does not prohibit states or localities from attempting to collect sales or use taxes on goods purchased over the Internet; it merely prohibits state and local government from imposing "multiple or discriminatory" taxation of the Internet or special taxes on Internet access.

What pro-tax state and local officials are really at war with is not the ITFA but 30 years of Supreme Court jurisprudence that has not come down in their favor. The Court has ruled that states can require only firms with a physical presence, or "nexus," in their states to collect taxes on their behalf.

The effort to tax the Internet is a classic case of misplaced blame. In their zeal to find a way to collect taxes on electronic transactions to supposedly "level the (sales tax) playing field," most state and local officials conveniently ignore the fact that the current sales tax system is perhaps the most unlevel playing field anyone could possibly have designed. Several politically favored industries and politically sensitive products receive generous exemptions from sales tax collection obligations or even from the taxes themselves.

Sales tax collection was fairly effective in the post–World War II period when a sizable portion of the American economy was still goods based and subject to the tax.

But as America began a gradual shift to a service-based economy in subsequent decades, serious strains were placed on the sales tax system since sales taxes had traditionally not been collected on services. Therefore, the vast majority of "service-sector" industries and professions receive a blanket exemption from sales tax obligations.

So, as the service sector became a larger portion of the American economy, the overall sales tax base shrank accordingly. Limited efforts have been made by some states to expand sales tax coverage to include services, but those efforts have met with staunch corporate and consumer opposition. Regardless, the combined effect of the service-sector exemptions and exemptions for "special" goods-producing industries, such as agriculture and clothing, has been the gradual diminution of the sales tax base in America.

In fact, in a December 2000 study in the *National Tax Journal,* economists Donald Bruce and William F. Fox of the University of Tennessee Center for Business and Economic Research estimated that the sales tax base as a percentage of personal income has fallen from roughly 52 percent in the late 1970s to less than 42 percent today. Worse yet, evidence suggests that, as the sales tax base has been gradually eroding in recent decades, average sales tax rates have been going up. In other words, we now have a rising average tax rate over a shrinking tax base. That is the textbook definition of an inefficient tax. Optimally, economists want a low tax rate over a very broad tax base.

Citizens should be cognizant of the deficiencies of the current system and not allow state and local policymakers to trick them into thinking that the Internet is to blame for the holes in their sales tax bases. Electronic commerce sales constituted a surprisingly low 1.1 percent of aggregate retail sales in 2001 according to U.S. Department of Commerce data. In light of this, it's hard to see how the Internet is to blame for the declining sales tax base.

Before state or local officials beg Congress to save them from the massive sales tax drain brought on by the Internet, they need to clean up the mess they've created. And if they really want to find a way to "level the playing field" and tax Internet transactions, an origin-based sales tax system would allow them to do so in an economically efficient and constitutionally sensible way. In the meantime, however, Congress would be wise to permanently extend the existing ITFA moratorium on multiple and discriminatory taxes, as well as Internet access taxes, and let Supreme Court precedents continue to govern the interstate marketplace for electronic commerce transactions.

Suggested Readings

Bell, Tom W. "Internet Gambling: Popular, Inexorable, and (Eventually) Legal." Cato Institute Policy Analysis no. 336, March 8, 1999, www.cato.org/pubs/pas/pa-336es.html.

———. "Internet Privacy and Self-Regulation: Lessons from the Porn Wars." Cato Institute Briefing Paper no. 65, August 9, 2001, www.cato.org/pubs/briefs/bp-065es.html.

Corn-Revere, Robert. "Caught in the Seamless Web: Does the Internet's Global Reach Justify Less Freedom of Speech?" Cato Institute Briefing Paper no. 71, July 24, 2002, www.cato.org/pubs/briefs/bp-071es.html.

Crews, Clyde Wayne Jr. "Why Canning 'Spam' Is a Bad Idea." Cato Institute Policy Analysis no. 408, July 26, 2001, www.cato.org/pubs/pas/pa-408es.html.

Lukas, Aaron. "Tax Bytes: A Primer on the Taxation of Electronic Commerce." Cato Institute Trade Policy Analysis no. 9, www.freetrade.org/pubs/pas/tpa-009es.html.

Singleton, Solveig. "Privacy as Censorship: A Skeptical View of Proposals to Regulate Privacy in the Private Sector." Cato Institute Policy Analysis no. 295, January 22, 1998, www.cato.org/pubs/pas/pa-295.html.

———. "Will the Net Turn Car Dealers into Dinosaurs? State Limits on Auto Sales Online." Cato Institute Briefing Paper no. 58, July 25, 2000, www.cato.org/pubs/briefs/bp-058es.html.

Wallace, Jonathan D. "Nameless in Cyberspace: Anonymity on the Internet." Cato Institute Briefing Paper no. 54, December 8, 1999, www.cato.org/pubs/briefs/bp-054es.html.

—Prepared by Clyde Wayne Crews Jr. and Adam Thierer

15. Property Rights and Regulatory Takings

Congress should

- enact legislation that specifies the constitutional rights of property owners under the Fifth Amendment's Just Compensation Clause;
- follow the traditional common law in defining "private property," "public use," and "just compensation";
- treat property taken through regulation the same as property taken through physical seizure; and
- provide a single forum in which property owners may seek injunctive relief and just compensation promptly.

America's Founders understood clearly that private property is the foundation not only of prosperity but of freedom itself. Thus, through the common law and the Constitution, they protected property rights—the rights of people to freely acquire and use property. With the growth of the modern regulatory state, however, governments at all levels today are eliminating those rights through so-called regulatory takings—regulatory restraints that take property rights, reducing the value of the property, but leave title with the owner. And courts are doing little to protect such owners because the Supreme Court has yet to develop a principled, much less comprehensive, theory of property rights. That failure has led to the birth of the property rights movement in state after state. It is time now for Congress to step in—to correct its own violations and to give guidance to the courts as they adjudicate complaints about state violations.

When government condemns property outright, taking title from the owner, courts require it to compensate the owner for his losses under the Fifth Amendment's Takings or Just Compensation Clause: "nor shall private property be taken for public use without just compensation." The modern problem is not there—provided the compensation is just—but with regulatory takings that provide goods for the public at the expense of owners, who are often left with worthless titles. Courts have been reluctant to award compensation in such cases because they have failed to grasp the principles of the matter—due in part to an unwarranted deference to the regulatory state. As a result, owners sometimes lose their entire investment in their property, and they can do nothing about it. Meanwhile, governments are only encouraged to further regulation since the goods that are thus provided are cost free to the public.

Over the past decade, however, the Supreme Court has chipped away at the problem and begun to require compensation in some cases—even if its decisions are largely ad hoc, leaving most owners to bear the losses themselves. Thus, owners today can get compensation when title is actually taken, as just noted; when their property is physically invaded by government order, either permanently or temporarily; when regulation for other than health or safety reasons takes all or nearly all of the value of the property; and when government attaches conditions that are unreasonable or disproportionate when it grants a permit to use property. Even if that final category of takings were clear, however, those categories would not constitute anything like a comprehensive theory of the matter, much less a comprehensive solution to the problem. For that, Congress (or the Court) is going to have to turn to first principles, much as the old common law judges did. The place to begin, then, is not with the public law of the Constitution but with the private law of property.

Property: The Foundation of All Rights

It is no accident that a nation conceived in liberty and dedicated to justice for all protects property rights. Property is the foundation of every right we have, including the right to be free. Every legal claim, after all, is a claim to something—either a defensive claim to keep what one is holding or an offensive claim to something someone else is holding. John Locke, the philosophical father of the American Revolution and the inspiration for Thomas Jefferson when he drafted the Declaration of Independence, stated the issue simply: "Lives, Liberties, and Estates, which I call by the general Name, *Property.*" And James Madison, the principal author of the Constitution, echoed those thoughts when he wrote that "as a man is said to have a right to his property, he may be equally said to have a property in his rights."

146

Much moral confusion would be avoided if we understood that all of our rights—all of the things to which we are "entitled"—can be reduced to property. That would enable us to separate genuine rights—things to which we hold title—from specious "rights"—things to which other people hold title, which we may want. It was the genius of the old common law, grounded in reason, that it grasped that point. And the common law judges understood a pair of corollaries as well: that property, broadly conceived, separates one individual from another and that individuals are independent or free to the extent that they have sole or exclusive dominion over what they hold. Indeed, Americans go to work every day to acquire property just so they can be independent.

Legal Protection for Property Rights

It would be to no avail, however, if property, once acquired, could not be used and enjoyed—if rights of acquisition, enjoyment, and disposal were not legally protected. Recognizing that, common law judges, charged over the years with settling disputes between neighbors, have drawn upon principles of reason and efficiency, and upon custom as well, to craft a law of property that respects, by and large, the equal rights of all.

In a nutshell, the basic rights they have recognized, after the rights of acquisition and disposal, are the right of sole dominion—or the right to exclude others, the right against trespass; the right of quiet enjoyment— a right everyone can exercise equally, at the same time and in the same respect; and the right of active use—at least to the point where such use violates the rights of others to quiet enjoyment. Just where that point is, of course, is often fact dependent—and is the business of courts to decide. But the point to notice, in the modern context, is that the presumption of the common law is on the side of free use. At common law, that is, people are not required to obtain a permit before they can use their property— no more than people today are required to obtain a permit before they can speak freely. Rather, the burden is upon those who object to a given use to show how it violates their right of quiet enjoyment. That amounts to having to show that their neighbor's use takes something they own free and clear. If they fail, the use may continue.

Thus, the common law limits the right of free use only when a use encroaches on the property rights of others, as in the classic law of nuisance. The implications of that limit, however, should not go unnoticed, especially in the context of such modern concerns as environmental protection. Indeed, it is so far from the case that property rights are opposed to

147

environmental protection—a common belief today—as to be just the opposite: the right against environmental degradation is a *property* right. Under common law, properly applied, people cannot use their property in ways that damage their neighbors' property—defined, again, as taking things those neighbors hold free and clear. Properly conceived and applied, then, property rights are self-limiting: they constitute a judicially crafted and enforced regulatory scheme in which rights of active use end when they encroach on the property rights of others.

The Police Power and the Power of Eminent Domain

But if the common law of property defines and protects private rights— the rights of owners with respect to each other—it also serves as a guide for the proper scope and limits of public law—defining the rights of owners and the public with respect to each other. For public law, at least at the federal level, flows from the Constitution; and the Constitution flows from the principles articulated in the Declaration—which reflect, largely, the common law. The justification of public law begins, then, with our rights, as the Declaration makes clear. Government then follows, not to give us rights through positive law, but to recognize and secure the rights we already have. Thus, to be legitimate, government's powers must be derived from and consistent with those rights.

The two public powers that are at issue in the property rights debate are the police power—the power of government to secure rights—and the power of eminent domain—the power to take property for public use upon payment of just compensation, as set forth, by implication, in the Fifth Amendment.

The police power—the first great power of government—is derived from what Locke called the Executive Power, the power each of us has in the state of nature to secure his rights. Thus, as such, it is legitimate, since it is nothing more than a power we already have, by right, which we gave to government, when we constituted ourselves as a nation, to exercise on our behalf. Its exercise is legitimate, however, only insofar as it is used to secure rights, and only insofar as its use respects the rights of others. Thus, while our rights give rise to the police power, they also limit it. We cannot use the police power for non-police-power purposes. It is a power to secure rights, through restraints or sanctions, not some general power to provide public goods.

A complication arises with respect to the federal government, however, for it is not a government of general powers. Thus, there is no general federal police power, despite modern developments to the contrary (which essentially ignore the principle). Rather, the Constitution establishes a government of delegated, enumerated, and thus limited powers, leaving most powers, including the police power, with the states or the people, as the Tenth Amendment makes clear. (See Chapter 3 of this *Handbook* for greater detail on this point.) If we are to abide by constitutional principle, then, we have to recognize that whatever power the federal government has to secure rights is limited to federal territory, by implication, or is incidental to the exercise of one of the federal government's enumerated powers.

But if the police power is thus limited to securing rights, and the federal government's police power is far more restricted, then any effort to provide public goods must be accomplished under some other power—under some enumerated power, in the case of the federal government. Yet any such effort will be constrained by the Just Compensation Clause, which requires that any provision of public goods that entails taking private property— whether in whole or in part is irrelevant—must be accompanied by just compensation for the owner of the property. Otherwise the costs of the benefit to the public would fall entirely on the owner. Not to put too fine a point on it, that would amount to plain theft. Indeed, it was to prohibit that kind of thing that the Founders wrote the Just Compensation Clause in the first place.

Thus, the power of eminent domain—which is not enumerated in the Constitution but is implicit in the Just Compensation Clause—is an instrumental power: it is a means through which government, acting under some other power, pursues other ends—building roads, for example, or saving wildlife. Moreover, unlike the police power, the eminent domain power is not inherently legitimate: indeed, in a state of nature, none of us would have a right to condemn a neighbor's property, however worthy our purpose, however much we compensated him. Thus, it is not for nothing that eminent domain was known in the 17th and 18th centuries as "the despotic power." It exists from practical considerations alone— to enable public projects to go forward without being held hostage to lone holdouts in a position to extract monopoly charges. As for its justification, the best that can be said for eminent domain is this: the power was ratified by those who were in the original position; and it is "Pareto superior," as economists say, meaning that at least one party (the public) is made better off by its use while no one is made worse off—provided the owner does indeed receive just compensation.

When Is Compensation Required?

We come then to the basic question: When does government have to compensate owners for the losses they suffer when regulations reduce the value of their property? The answers are as follows.

First, when government acts to secure rights—when it stops someone from polluting on his neighbor or on the public, for example—it is acting under its police power and no compensation is due the owner, whatever his financial losses, because the use prohibited or "taken" was wrong to begin with. Since there is no right to pollute, we do not have to pay polluters not to pollute. Thus, the question is not whether value was taken by a regulation but whether a *right* was taken. Proper uses of the police power take no rights. To the contrary, they protect rights.

Second, when government acts not to secure rights but to provide the public with some good—wildlife habitat, for example, or a viewshed or historic preservation—and in doing so prohibits or "takes" some otherwise *legitimate* use, then it is acting, in part, under the eminent domain power and it does have to compensate the owner for any financial losses he may suffer. The principle here is quite simple: the public has to pay for the goods it wants, just like any private person would have to. Bad enough that the public can take what it wants by condemnation; at least it should pay rather than ask the owner to bear the full cost of its appetite. It is here, of course, that modern regulatory takings abuses are most common as governments at all levels try to provide the public with all manner of amenities, especially environmental amenities, "off budget." As noted above, there is an old-fashioned word for that practice: it is "theft," and no amount of rationalization about "good reasons" will change that. Even thieves, after all, have "good reasons" for what they do.

Finally, when government acts to provide the public with some good and that act results in financial loss to an owner but takes no right of the owner, no compensation is due because nothing the owner holds free and clear is taken. If the government closes a military base, for example, and neighboring property values decline as a result, no compensation is due those owners because the government's action took nothing they owned. They own their property and all the uses that go with it that are consistent with their neighbors' equal rights. They do not own the value in their property.

Some Implications of a Principled Approach

Starting from first principles, then, we can derive principled answers to the regulatory takings question. And we can see, in the process, that there is no difference in principle between an "ordinary" taking and a regulatory taking, between taking full title and taking partial title—a distinction that critics of property rights repeatedly urge, claiming that the Just Compensation Clause requires compensation only for "full" takings. If we take the text seriously, as we should, the clause speaks simply of "private property." As the quote above from Madison suggests, "property" denotes not just some "underlying estate" but all the estates—all the uses—that can rightly be made of a holding. In fact, in every area of property law except takings we recognize that property is a "bundle of sticks," any one of which can be bought, sold, rented, bequeathed, what have you. Yet takings law has clung to the idea that only if the entire bundle is taken does government have to pay compensation.

That view enables government to extinguish nearly all uses through regulation—and hence to regulate nearly all value out of property—yet escape the compensation requirement because the all but empty title remains with the owner. And it would allow a government to take 90 percent of the value in year one, then come back a year later and take title for a dime on the dollar. Not only is that wrong, it is unconstitutional. It cannot be what the Just Compensation Clause stands for. The principle, rather, is that property is indeed a bundle of sticks: take one of those sticks and you take something that belongs to the owner. The only question then is how much his loss is worth.

Thus, when the Court a few years ago crafted what is in effect a 100 percent rule, whereby owners are entitled to compensation only if regulations restrict uses to a point where all value is lost, it went about the matter backwards. It measured the loss to determine whether there was a taking. As a matter of first principle, the Court should first have determined whether there was a taking, then measured the loss. It should first have asked whether otherwise legitimate uses were prohibited by the regulation. That addresses the principle of the matter. It then remains simply to measure the loss in value and hence the compensation that is due. The place to start, in short, is with the first stick, not the last dollar.

The principled approach requires, of course, that the Court have a basic understanding of the theory of the matter and a basic grasp of how to resolve conflicting claims about use in a way that respects the equal rights of all. That is hardly a daunting task, as the old common law judges demonstrated. In general, the presumption is on the side of active use, as noted earlier, until some plaintiff demonstrates that such use takes the

151

quiet enjoyment that is his by right—and the defendant's right as well. At that point the burden shifts to the defendant to justify his use: absent some defense like the prior consent of the plaintiff, the defendant may have to cease his use—or, if his activity is worth it, offer to buy an easement or buy out the plaintiff. Thus, a principled approach respects equal rights of quiet enjoyment—and hence environmental integrity. But it also enables active uses to go forward—though not at the expense of private or public rights. Users can be as active as they wish, provided they handle the "externalities" they create in a way that respects the rights of others.

What Congress Should Do

The application of such principles is often fact dependent, as noted earlier, and so is best done by courts. But until the courts develop a more principled and systematic approach to takings, it will fall to Congress to draw at least the broad outlines of the matter, both as a guide for the courts and as a start toward getting its own house in order.

In this last connection, however, the first thing Congress should do is recognize candidly that the problem of regulatory takings begins with regulation. Doubtless the Founders did not think to specify that regulatory takings are takings too, and thus are subject to the Just Compensation Clause, because they did not imagine the modern regulatory state: they did not envision our obsession with regulating every conceivable human activity and our insistence that such activity—residential, business, what have you—take place only after a grant of official permission. In some areas of business today we have almost reached the point at which it can truly be said that everything that is not permitted is prohibited. That is the opposite, of course, of our founding principle: everything that is not prohibited is permitted—where "permitted," means "freely allowed," not allowed "by permit."

Home owners, developers, farmers and ranchers, mining and timber companies, businesses large and small, profit making and not for profit, all have horror stories about regulatory hurdles they confront when they want to do something, particularly with real property. Many of those regulations are legitimate, of course, especially if they are aimed, preemptively, at securing genuine rights. But many more are aimed at providing some citizens with benefits at the expense of other citizens. They take rights from some to benefit others. At the federal level, such transfers are not likely to find authorization under any enumerated power. But even if constitutionally authorized, they need to be undertaken in conformity with the Just Compensation Clause. Some endangered species, to take a prominent modern example, may indeed be worth saving, even if the authority for doing so belongs to states, and even if the impetus comes from a relatively small group of people. We should not expect a few property owners to bear all the costs of that undertaking, however. If the public truly wants the habitat for such species left undisturbed, let it buy that habitat or, failing that, pay the costs to the relevant owners of their leaving their property unused.

In general, then, Congress should review the government's many regulations to determine which are and are not authorized by the Constitution. If not authorized, they should be rescinded, which would end quickly a large body of regulatory takings now in place. But if authorized under some enumerated power of Congress, the costs now imposed on owners, for benefits conferred on the public generally, should be placed "on budget." Critics of doing that are often heard to say that if we did go on budget, we couldn't afford all the regulations we want. What they are really saying, of course, is that taxpayers would be unwilling to pay for all the regulations the critics want. Indeed, the great fear of those who oppose taking a principled approach to regulatory takings is that once the public has to pay for the benefits it now receives "free," it will demand fewer of them. It should hardly surprise that when people have to pay for something they demand less of it.

It is sheer pretense, of course, to suppose that such benefits are now free, that they are not already being paid for. Isolated owners are paying for them, not the public. As a matter of simple justice, then, Congress needs to shift the burden to the public that is demanding and enjoying the benefits. Among the virtues of doing so is this: once we have an honest, public accounting, we will be in a better position to determine whether the benefits thus produced are worth the costs. Today, we have no idea about that because all the costs are hidden. When regulatory benefits are thus "free," the demand for them, as we see, is all but unbounded.

But in addition to eliminating, reducing, or correcting its own regulatory takings—in addition to getting its own house in order—Congress needs to enact general legislation on the subject of takings that might help to restore respect for property rights and reorient the nation toward its own first principles. To that end, Congress should

Enact Legislation That Specifies the Constitutional Rights of Property Owners under the Fifth Amendment's Just Compensation Clause

As already noted, legislation of the kind here recommended would be unnecessary if the courts were doing their job correctly and reading the Just Compensation Clause properly. Because they are not, it falls to Congress to step in. Still, there is a certain anomaly in asking Congress to do the job. Under our system, after all, the political branches and the states represent and pursue the interests of the people within the constraints established by the Constitution; and it falls to the courts, and the Supreme Court in particular, to ensure that those constraints are respected. To do that, the Court interprets and applies the Constitution as it decides cases brought before it—cases often brought against the political branches or a state, as here, where an owner seeks either to enjoin a government action on the ground that it violates his rights or to obtain compensation under the Just Compensation Clause, or both. Thus, it is somewhat anomalous to ask or expect Congress to right wrongs that Congress itself may be perpetrating. After all, is not Congress, in its effort to carry out the public's will, simply doing its job?

The answer, of course, is yes, Congress is doing its job, and thus this call for reform—against the "natural" inclination of Congress, if you will—is somewhat anomalous. But that is not the whole answer. For members of Congress take an oath to uphold the Constitution, which requires them to exercise independent judgment about the meaning of its terms. In doing that, they need to recognize that we do not live in anything like a pure democracy. The Constitution sets powerful and far-reaching restraints on the powers of all three branches of the federal government and, since ratification of the Civil War Amendments, on the states as well. Thus, the simple-minded majoritarian view of our system—whereby Congress simply enacts whatever some transient majority of the population wants enacted, leaving it to the Court to determine the constitutionality of the act—must be resisted as a matter of the oath of office. The oath is taken on behalf of the people, to be sure, but through and in conformity with the Constitution. When the Court fails to secure the liberties of the people, there is nothing in the Constitution to prevent Congress from exercising the responsibility entailed by the oath of office. In fact, that oath requires Congress to step into the breach.

There is no guarantee, of course, that Congress will do a better job of interpreting the Constitution than the Court. In fact, given that Congress is an "interested" party, it could very well do a worse job, which is why the Founders placed "the judicial Power"—entailing, presumably, the power ultimately to say what the law is—with the Court. But that is no reason for Congress to ignore its responsibility to make its judgment known, especially when the Court is clearly wrong, as it is here. Although nonpolitical in principle, the Court does not operate in a political vacuum—as it demonstrated in 1937, unfortunately, after Franklin Roosevelt's notorious Court-packing threat. If the Court can be persuaded to undo the centerpiece of the Constitution, the doctrine of enumerated powers, one imagines it can be persuaded to restore property rights to their proper constitutional status.

Thus, in addition to rescinding or correcting legislation that now results in uncompensated regulatory takings, and enacting no such legislation in the future, Congress should also enact a more general statute that specifies the constitutional rights of property owners under the Fifth Amendment's Just Compensation Clause, drawing upon common law principles to do so. That means that Congress should

Follow the Traditional Common Law in Defining "Private Property," "Public Use," and "Just Compensation"

As we saw above, property rights in America are not simply a matter of the Fifth Amendment—of positive law. Indeed, during the more than two years between the time the Constitution was ratified and took effect and the time the Bill of Rights was ratified, property rights were protected not only against private but against public invasion as well. That protection stemmed, therefore, not from any explicit constitutional guarantee but from the common law. Thus, the Just Compensation Clause was meant simply to make explicit, against the new federal government, the guarantees that were already recognized under the common law. (Those guarantees were implicit in the new Constitution, of course, through the doctrine of enumerated powers; for no uncompensated takings were therein authorized.) With the ratification of the Civil War Amendments—and the Fourteenth Amendment's Privileges or Immunities Clause in particular—the common law guarantees against the states were constitutionalized as well. Thus, because the Just Compensation Clause takes its inspiration and meaning from the common law of property, it is there that we must look to understand its terms.

Those terms begin with "private property": "nor shall private property be taken for public use without just compensation." As every first-year law student learns, "private property" means far more than a piece of real estate. Were that not the case, property law would be an impoverished subject indeed. Instead, the common law reveals the many significations of the concept "property" and the rich variety of arrangements that human imagination and enterprise have made of the basic idea of private ownership. As outlined above, however, those arrangements all come down to three basic ideas—acquisition, exclusive use, and disposal—the three basic property rights, from which more specifically described rights may be derived.

With regard to regulatory takings, however, the crucial thing to notice is that, absent contractual arrangements to the contrary, the right to acquire and hold property entails the right to use and dispose of it as well. As Madison said, people have "a property" in their rights. If the right to property did not entail the right of use, it would be an empty promise. People acquire property, after all, only because doing so enables them to use it, which is what gives it its value. Indeed, the fundamental complaint about uncompensated regulatory takings is that, by thus eliminating the uses from property, government makes the title itself meaningless, which is why it is worthless. Who would buy "property" that cannot be used?

The very concept of "property," therefore, entails all the legitimate uses that go with it, giving it value. And the uses that are legitimate are those that can be exercised consistent with the rights of others, private and public alike, as defined by the traditional common law. As outlined above, however, the rights of others that limit the rights of an owner are often fact dependent. Thus, legislation can state only the principle of the matter, not its application in particular contexts. Still, the broad outlines should be made clear in any congressional enactment: the term "private property" includes all the uses that can be made of property consistent with the common law rights of others, and those uses can be restricted without compensating the owner only to secure such rights, not to secure public goods or benefits.

The "public use" requirement also needs to be tightened, not least because it is a source of private-public collusion against private rights. As noted above, eminent domain was known in the 17th and 18th centuries as "the despotic power" because no private person would have the power to condemn, even if he had a worthy reason and did pay just compensation. Yet we know that public agencies often do condemn private property for such private uses as railroad rights-of-way, auto plant construction, and casino parking lots. Those are rank abuses of the public use principle: they amount to grants of private eminent domain—and invitations to public graft and corruption. Every private use has spillover benefits for the public, of course. But if that were the standard for defining "public use," then every time someone wanted to expand his business over his neighbor's property, he could go to the relevant public agency and ask that the neighbor's property be condemned since the expansion would benefit the public through increased jobs, business, taxes, what have you. He would no longer need to bargain with his neighbor but could simply ask—or "pay"—the agency to condemn the property "for the public good."

Because it is a despotic power, even when just compensation is paid, eminent domain should be used sparingly and only for a truly *public* use. That means for a use that is broadly enjoyed by the public, rather than by some narrow part of the public; and in the case of the federal government it means for a constitutionally authorized use. More precisely, it means for a use that is owned and controlled by the public. Condemnation, after all, transfers title—either in part, for a regulatory taking, or in whole, for a full taking. If the condemnation transfers title from one private party to another, it is simply illegitimate.

Thus, condemnation for building a sports stadium may be authorized under some state's constitution, but if the stadium is then owned and managed by and for the benefit of private parties, the "public use" standard has been abused, whatever the spill-over "public" benefits may be. Here again it is the title that settles the matter. Yet even if the public keeps the title, but the effect of the transfer is to benefit a small portion of the public rather than the public generally, the condemnation is also likely to be illegitimate because it is not truly for a "public" use. If some small group wants the benefits provided by the condemnation, private markets provide ample opportunities for obtaining them—the right way. To avoid abuse and the potential for corruption, then, Congress needs to define "public use" rigorously, with reference to titles and use.

Finally, Congress should define "just compensation" with reference to its function: it is a remedy for the wrong of taking someone's property. That the Constitution implicitly authorizes that wrong does not change the character of the act, of course. As noted above, eminent domain is "justified" for practical reasons—and because "we" authorized it originally, although none of us today, of course, was there to do so. Given the character of the act, then, the least the public can do is make the victim whole. That too will be a fact-dependent determination. But Congress should at least make it clear that "just" compensation means compensation for all losses that arise from the taking, plus an added measure to acknowledge the fact that the losses arise not by mere accident, as with a tort, but from a deliberate decision by the public to force the owner to give up his property.

It should be noted, however, that not every regulatory taking will require compensation for an owner. Minimal losses, for example, may be difficult to prove and not worth the effort. Moreover, some regulatory restrictions may actually enhance the value of property or of particular pieces of property—say, if an entire neighborhood is declared "historic." Finally, "just compensation" should always reflect market value before, and with no anticipation of, regulatory restrictions. Given the modern penchant for regulation, that may not always be easy. But in general, given the nature of condemnation as a forced taking, any doubt should be resolved to the benefit of the owner forced to give up his property.

If Congress enacts general legislation that specifies the constitutional rights of property owners by following the common law in defining the terms of the Just Compensation Clause, it will abolish, in effect, any real distinction between full and partial takings. Nevertheless, Congress should be explicit about what it is doing. Any legislation it enacts should

Treat Property Taken through Regulation the Same As Property Taken through Physical Seizure

The importance of enacting a unified and uniform takings law cannot be overstated. Today, we have one law for "full takings," "physical seizures," "condemnations"—call them what you will—and another for "partial takings," "regulatory seizures," or "condemnations of uses." Yet there is overlap, too: thus, as noted above, the Court recently said that if regulations take all uses, compensation is due—perhaps because eliminating all uses comes to the same thing, in effect, as a "physical seizure," whereas eliminating most uses seems not to come to the same thing.

That appearance is deceptive, of course. In fact, the truth is much simpler—but only if we go about discovering it from first principles. If we start with an owner and his property, then define "property," as above, as including all legitimate uses, it follows that any action by government that takes any property is, by definition, a taking—requiring compensation for any financial losses the owner may suffer as a result. The issue is really no more complicated than that. There is no need to distinguish "full" from "partial" takings: *every* condemnation, whether "full" or "partial," is a taking. Indeed, the use taken is taken "in full." Imagine that the property were converted to dollars—100 dollars, say. Would we say that if the government took all 100 dollars there was a taking, but if it took only 50 of the 100 dollars there was not a taking? Of course not. Yet that is what we say under the Court's modern takings doctrine because, as one justice recently put it, "takings law is full of these 'all-or-nothing' situations."

That confusion must be ended. Through legislation specifying the rights of property owners, Congress needs to make it clear that compensation is required whenever government eliminates common law property rights and an owner suffers a financial loss as a result—whether the elimination results from regulation or from outright condemnation.

The promise of the common law and the Constitution will be realized, however, only through procedures that enable aggrieved parties to press their complaints. Some of the greatest abuses today are taking place because owners are frustrated at every turn in their efforts to reach the merits of their claims. Accordingly, Congress should

Provide a Single Forum in Which Property Owners May Seek Injunctive Relief and Just Compensation Promptly

In its 1998 term the Supreme Court decided a takings case that began 17 years before, in 1981, when owners applied to a local planning commission for permission to develop their land. After having submitted numerous proposals, all rejected, yet each satisfying the commission's recommendations following a previously rejected proposal, the owners finally sued, at which point they faced the hurdles the courts put before them. Most owners, of course, cannot afford to go through such a long and expensive process, at the end of which the odds are still against them. But that process today confronts property owners across the nation as they seek to enjoy and then to vindicate their rights. If it were speech or voting or any number of other rights, the path to vindication would be smooth by comparison. But property rights today have been relegated to a kind of second-class status.

The first problem, as noted above, is the modern permitting regime. We would not stand for speech or religion or most other rights to be enjoyed only by permit. Yet that is what we do today with property rights, which places enormous, often arbitrary power in the hands of federal, state, and local "planners." Driven by political goals and considerations—notwithstanding their pretense to "smart growth"—planning commissions open the application forum not only to those whose *rights* might be at stake but to those with *interests* in the matter. Thus is the common law distinction between rights and interests blurred and eventually lost. Thus is the matter transformed from one of protecting rights to one of deciding whose "interests" should prevail. Thus are property rights effectively politicized. And that is the end of the matter for most owners because that is as far as they can afford to take it.

When an owner does take it further, however, he finds the courts are no more inclined to hear his complaint than was the planning commission. Federal courts routinely abstain from hearing federal claims brought against state and local governments, requiring owners to litigate their claims in state courts before they can even set foot in a federal court on their federal claims. Moreover, the Supreme Court has held that an owner's claim is not ripe for adjudication unless (1) he obtains a final, definitive agency decision regarding the application of the regulation in question, and (2) he exhausts all available state compensation remedies. Needless to say, planners, disinclined to approve applications to begin with, treat those standards as invitations to stall until the "problem" goes away. Finally, when an owner does get into federal court with a claim against the federal government, he faces the so-called Tucker Act Shuffle: he cannot get injunctive relief and compensation from the same court but must instead go to a federal district court for an injunction and to the Federal Court of Claims for compensation.

The 105th and 106th Congresses tried to address those procedural hurdles through several measures, none of which passed both houses. They must be revived and enacted if the unconscionable way we treat owners, trying simply to vindicate their constitutional rights, is to be brought to an end. This is not a matter of "intruding" on state and local governments. Under the Fourteenth Amendment, properly understood and applied, those governments have no more right to violate the constitutional rights of citizens than the federal government has to intrude on the legitimate powers of state and local governments. Federalism is not a shield for local tyranny. It is a brake on tyranny, whatever its source.

Conclusion

The Founders would be appalled to see what we have done to property rights over the course of the 20th century. One would never know that their status, in the Bill of Rights, was equal to that of any other right. The time has come to restore respect for these most basic of rights, the foundation of all of our rights. Indeed, despotic governments have long understood that if you control property, you control the media, the churches, the political process itself. We are not at that point yet. But if regulations that provide the public with benefits continue to grow, unchecked by the need to compensate those from whom they take, we will gradually slide to that point—and in the process will pay an increasingly heavy price for the uncertainty and inefficiency we create. The most important price, however, will be to our system of law and justice. Owners are asking simply that their government obey the law—the common law and the law of the Constitution. Reduced to its essence, they are saying simply this: Stop stealing our property; if you must take it, do it the right way—pay for it. That hardly seems too much to ask.

Suggested Readings

Bethell, Tom. *The Noblest Triumph: Property and Prosperity through the Ages.* New York: St. Martin's, 1998.

Coyle, Dennis J. *Property Rights and the Constitution: Shaping Society through Land Use Regulation.* Albany, N.Y.: State University of New York Press, 1993.

DeLong, James V. *Property Matters: How Property Rights Are under Assault—And Why You Should Care.* New York: Free Press, 1997.

Eagle, Steven J. *Regulatory Takings.* Charlottesville, Va.: Michie Law Publishers, 1996.

Ely, James W. Jr. *The Guardian of Every Other Right: A Constitutional History of Property Rights.* 2d ed. New York: Oxford University Press, 1998.

Epstein, Richard A. *Takings: Private Property and the Power of Eminent Domain.* Cambridge, Mass.: Harvard University Press, 1985.

Farah, Joseph, and Richard Pombo. *This Land Is Our Land: How to End the War on Private Property.* New York: St. Martin's, 1996.

Locke, John. "Second Treatise of Government." In *Two Treatises of Government.* Edited by Peter Laslett. New York: Mentor, 1965.

Madison, James. "Property." In *National Gazette*, March 29, 1792. Reprinted in *The Papers of James Madison*, vol. 14, *6 April 1791–16 March 1793.* Edited by Robert A. Rutland et al. Charlottesville: University Press of Virginia, 1983.

Pilon, Roger. "Are Property Rights Opposed to Environmental Protection?" In *The Moral High Ground: An Anthology of Speeches from the First Annual New York State Conference on Private Property Rights.* Edited by Carol W. LaGrasse. Stony Creek, N.Y.: Property Rights Foundation of America, 1995.

———. "Property Rights, Takings, and a Free Society." *Harvard Journal of Law and Public Policy* 6 (1983).

Pipes, Richard. *Property and Freedom: How through the Centuries Private Ownership Has Promoted Liberty and the Rule of Law.* New York: Alfred A. Knopf, 1999.

Siegan, Bernard H. *Property and Freedom: The Constitution, the Courts, and Land-Use Regulation.* New Brunswick, N.J.: Transaction Press, 1997.

Siegan, Bernard H., editor. *Planning without Prices: The Takings Clause As It Relates to Land Use Regulation without Just Compensation.* Lexington, Mass.: Lexington Books, 1977.

—Prepared by Roger Pilon

161

16. Tobacco and the Rule of Law

Congress should

- deny funding for the Justice Department's racketeering suit against cigarette makers,
- enact legislation to abrogate the multistate tobacco settlement, and
- reject proposed legislation to regulate cigarette manufacturing and advertising.

Introduction

Ten months after tobacco companies and 46 state attorneys general settled their differences for a quarter of a trillion dollars, the U.S. Department of Justice decided that it wanted a share of the plunder. DOJ's complaint alleged that cigarette companies had been conspiring since the 1950s to defraud the American public and conceal information about the effects of smoking. Specifically, the government contended that industry executives knowingly made false and misleading statements about whether smoking causes disease and whether nicotine is addictive.

On the one hand, DOJ promoted its novel lawsuit against cigarette makers. On the other hand, the same watchdog agency stood idly by while tobacco companies and state attorneys general teamed up to violate the antitrust laws. The multistate tobacco settlement, a cunning and deceitful bargain between the industry and the states, allows the tobacco giants to monopolize cigarette sales and foist the cost onto smokers.

Congress can take affirmative steps to counteract those abuses of executive power: first, by denying funds for DOJ's ongoing lawsuit and, second, by enacting legislation that abrogates the multistate tobacco settlement.

At the same time, Congress should reject any attempt to regulate cigarette advertising or the content of tobacco products.

Deny Funding for DOJ's Racketeering Suit against Cigarette Makers

In its litigation against the tobacco industry, the federal government demanded billions of dollars to pay for health care expenditures—mostly Medicare outlays—related to smoking. DOJ's legal theory was modeled after the states' lawsuits, which were designed to replenish depleted Medicaid coffers. Like the states, the federal government argued that it could sue tobacco companies without stepping into the shoes of each smoker. That way, so the theory goes, DOJ would not be subject to the "assumption-of-risk" defense that had been a consistent winner for the industry over four decades of litigation.

As you would expect, government officials understood the assumption-of-risk principle perfectly well. Indeed, former veterans affairs secretary Jesse Brown invoked it when the government itself was threatened with liability for having provided soldiers with cigarettes over many years. It would be "borderline absurdity" to pay for "veterans' personal choice to engage in conduct damaging to their health," he said. "If you choose to smoke, you are responsible for the consequences."

Evidently that principle applied only if the defendant was a government agency. When private companies were sued, DOJ asserted that it could recover from the tobacco industry merely because smoking injured someone covered by Medicare—even if that person, having voluntarily assumed the risk of smoking, could not recover on his own. The same tobacco company selling the same cigarettes to the same smoker, resulting in the same injury, would be liable only if the smoker was a Medicare recipient and the government was the plaintiff. Otherwise, the assumption-of-risk defense would apply. Liability hinged on the injured party's Medicare status, a happenstance unrelated to any misconduct by the industry.

The federal government also wanted the court to ignore the traditional tort law requirement that causation be demonstrated on a smoker-by-smoker basis. Instead, DOJ wanted to adduce only aggregate statistics, indicating a higher incidence of certain diseases among smokers than among nonsmokers. For example, statistics showed that smokers are more likely than nonsmokers to suffer burn injuries. So tobacco companies would have to pay for many careless persons who fell asleep with a lit cigarette. Similarly, the industry would have to shell out for persons who had heart attacks and other "smoking-related" diseases but who never smoked. Without individualized corroborating evidence, aggregate statistics might suggest liability. Only common sense would dictate otherwise.

To reinforce and supplement its bizarre tort theories, DOJ relied on three statutes: the Medical Care Recovery Act, the Medicare Secondary Payer Act, and the civil provisions of the Racketeer Influenced and Corrupt Organizations Act. Federal judge Gladys Kessler dismissed both the MCRA and MSPA claims out of hand. She allowed the RICO claim to go forward, although she expressed some reservations about the government's ability to prove damages.

Nowadays, RICO is used as a standard bullying tactic by plaintiffs' attorneys, even though the act was supposed to be invoked against organized crime. This time, however, DOJ had to deal with an embarrassing admission, tucked away in the final sentence of the press release that announced its lawsuit: "There are no pending Criminal Division investigations of the tobacco industry."

Two dozen prosecutors and FBI agents had conducted a five-year, multi-million-dollar inquiry during which they dissected allegations and plowed through documents for evidence that tobacco executives perjured themselves and manipulated nicotine levels. Whistleblowers and company scientists testified before grand juries. The outcome: not a single indictment of a tobacco company or industry executive.

Nonetheless, then–attorney general Janet Reno somehow conjured up a RICO claim that accused the industry of the very same infractions for which grand juries could not find probable cause. Here's just one example, count number three: In November 1959, the industry "did knowingly cause a press release to be sent and delivered by the U.S. mails to newspapers and news outlets. This press release contained statements attacking an article written by then–U.S. Surgeon General Leroy Burney about the hazards of smoking." There you have it—racketeering, in all its sordid detail.

Clinton administration insiders knew that the charges were trumped up. Former Clinton aide Rahm Emanuel put it this way: "If the White House hadn't asked, [Reno] would never have looked at it again." So it's politics, not law, that's driving this litigation. The American public needs to know that our tort system is rapidly becoming a tool for extortion. Sometimes opportunistic politicians seek money; sometimes they pursue policy goals; often they abuse their power. When Clinton was unable to persuade Congress to enact another tax on smokers, he simply bypassed the legislature and asked a federal court to impose damages in lieu of taxes. Evidently, anything goes—and the rule of law goes out the window. But Congress can do better. Call off the government's anti-tobacco crusade. Put an immediate stop to DOJ's power grab by denying funds to continue its lawsuit.

Enact Legislation to Abrogate the Multistate Tobacco Settlement

While DOJ presses its campaign to extort money from hapless tobacco companies, the Antitrust Division looks the other way as those same companies, in collaboration with state attorneys general, commit what is arguably the most egregious antitrust violation of our generation—a collusive tobacco settlement that is bilking 45 million smokers out of a quarter of a trillion dollars.

The Master Settlement Agreement, signed in November 1998 by the major tobacco companies and 46 state attorneys general, transforms a competitive industry into a cartel, then guards against destabilization of the cartel by erecting barriers to entry that preserve the dominant market share of the tobacco giants. Far from being victims, the big four tobacco companies are at the very center of the plot. They managed to carve out a protected market for themselves—at the expense of smokers and tobacco companies that did not sign the agreement.

To be sure, the industry would have preferred that the settlement had not been necessary. But given the perverse legal rules under which the state Medicaid recovery suits were unfolding, the major tobacco companies were effectively bludgeoned into negotiating with the states and the trial lawyers. Finding itself in that perilous position, the industry shrewdly bargained for something pretty close to a sweetheart deal.

The MSA forces all tobacco companies—even new companies and companies that were not part of the settlement—to pay "damages," thus foreclosing meaningful price competition. Essentially, the tobacco giants have purchased (at virtually no cost to themselves) the ability to exclude competitors. The deal works like this: Philip Morris, Reynolds, Lorillard, and Brown & Williamson knew they would have to raise prices substantially to cover their MSA obligations. Accordingly, they were concerned that smaller domestic manufacturers, importers, and new tobacco companies that didn't sign the agreement would gain market share by underpricing cigarettes. To guard against that likelihood, the big four and their state collaborators added three provisions to the MSA:

First, if the aggregate market share of the four majors were to decline by more than two percentage points, then their "damages" payments would decline by three times the excess over the two-percentage-point threshold. Any reduction would be charged against only those states that did not adopt a "Qualifying Statute," attached as an exhibit to the MSA. Naturally, because of the risk of losing enormous sums of money, all of the states have enacted the statute.

Second, the Qualifying Statute requires all tobacco companies that did not sign the MSA to post pro rata damages—based on cigarette sales— in escrow for 25 years to offset any liability that might hereafter be assessed! That's right—no evidence, no trial, no verdict, no injury, just damages. That was the stick. Then came the carrot.

Third, if a nonsettling tobacco company agreed to participate in the MSA, the Qualifying Statute would not apply. In fact, the new participant would be allowed to increase its market share by 25 percent of its 1997 level. Bear in mind that no nonsettling company in 1997 had more than 1 percent of the market, which, under the MSA, could grow to a whopping 1.25 percent. Essentially, the dominant companies guaranteed themselves virtually all of the market in perpetuity.

Perhaps as troubling, the settlement has led to massive and continuing shifts of wealth from millions of smokers to concentrated pockets of the bar. Predictably, part of that multi-billion-dollar booty has started its roundtrip back into the political process—to influence state legislators, judges, attorneys general, governors, city mayors, maybe some federal officials. With all that money in hand, trial lawyers have seen their political influence grow exponentially. Every day that passes more firmly entrenches the MSA as a fait accompli, and more tightly cements the insidious relationship between trial attorneys and their allies in the public sector. The billion-dollar spigot must be turned off before its corrupting effect on the rule of law is irreversible.

An obvious way to turn off the spigot is to abrogate the MSA. If it is allowed to stand, the MSA will create and finance a rich and powerful industry of lawyers who know how to manipulate the system and are not averse to violating the antitrust laws. Congress should dismantle the MSA to restore competition. That's a tall order, but the stakes are immense.

Reject Proposed Legislation to Regulate Cigarette Manufacturing and Advertising

Under legislation introduced in June 2002 by Sens. Edward Kennedy (D-Mass.), Mike DeWine (R-Ohio), and Richard Durbin (D-Ill.), the Food and Drug Administration would be authorized to regulate cigarette ads and ingredients, including nicotine—or to ban nicotine altogether. Lamentably, Philip Morris—the industry leader with the most to gain from restrictions on would-be competitors—quickly chimed in to support many of the proposals. Yet, if tobacco is to be regulated as a drug, Congress will simply be guaranteeing a pervasive black market in tobacco products. FDA regulation that makes cigarettes taste like tree bark, coupled with higher prices, will inevitably foment illegal dealings dominated by criminal gangs hooking underage smokers on an adulterated product freed of all the constraints on quality that competitive markets usually afford.

The war on cigarettes, like other crusades, may have been well-intentioned at the beginning; but as zealotry takes hold, the regulations become foolish and ultimately destructive. Consider the current attempt to control tobacco advertising. Not only are the public policy implications harmful, but there are obvious First Amendment violations that should concern every American who values free expression. Our Constitution protects Klan speech, flag burning, and gangsta rap, which, by the way, directly targets teenagers. But if Tiger Woods showed up in an ad for Camel cigarettes, the anti-tobacco crowd would bring the boot of government down hard on the neck of R.J. Reynolds.

Industry critics point to the impact of tobacco ads on uninformed and innocent teenagers. But the debate is not about whether teens smoke; they do. It's not about whether smoking is bad for them; it is. The real question is whether tobacco advertising can be linked to increases in aggregate consumption. There's no evidence for that link. The primary purpose of cigarette ads, like automobile ads, is to persuade consumers to switch from one manufacturer to another. Six European countries that banned all tobacco ads have seen overall sales *increase*—probably because health risks are no longer documented in the banned ads.

In 1983, the Supreme Court held that government may not "reduce the adult population . . . to reading only what is fit for children." Thirteen years later, the Court affirmed that even vice products like alcoholic beverages are entitled to commercial speech protection. Most recently, the Court threw out Massachusetts regulations banning selected cigar and smokeless tobacco ads. Those ads are not the problem. Kids smoke because of peer pressure, because their parents smoke, and because they are rebelling against authority.

If advertising were deregulated, newer and smaller tobacco companies would vigorously seek to carve out a bigger market share by emphasizing health claims that might bolster brand preference. In 1950, however, the Federal Trade Commission foreclosed health claims—such as "less smoker's cough"—as well as tar and nicotine comparisons for *existing* brands. To get around that prohibition, aggressive companies created *new* brands, which they supported with an avalanche of health claims. Filter cigarettes grew from roughly 1 percent to 10 percent of domestic sales within four years.

Then in 1954, the FTC tightened its restrictions by requiring scientific proof of health claims, even for new brands. The industry returned to promoting taste and pleasure; aggregate sales expanded. By 1957, scientists had confirmed the benefit of low-tar cigarettes. A new campaign of "Tar Derby" ads quickly emerged, and tar and nicotine levels collapsed 40 percent in two years. To shut down the flow of health claims, the FTC next demanded that they be accompanied by epidemiological evidence, of which none existed. The commission then negotiated a "voluntary" ban on tar and nicotine comparisons.

Not surprisingly, the steep decline in tar and nicotine ended in 1959. Seven years later, apparently alerted to the bad news, the FTC reauthorized tar and nicotine data but continued to proscribe associated health claims. Finally, in 1970 Congress banned all radio and television ads. Overall consumption has declined slowly since that time. In today's climate, the potential gains from health-related ads are undoubtedly greater than ever— for both aggressive companies and health-conscious consumers. If, however, government regulation expands, those gains will not be realized. Instead of "healthy" competition for market share, we will be treated to more imagery and personal endorsements—the very ads that anti-tobacco partisans decry.

If the imperative is to reduce smoking among children, the remedy lies with state governments, not the U.S. Congress. The sale of tobacco products to youngsters is illegal in every state. Those laws need to be vigorously enforced. Retailers who violate the law must be prosecuted. Proof of age requirements are appropriate if administered objectively and reasonably. Vending machine sales should be prohibited in areas such as arcades and schools where children are the main clientele. And if a minor is caught smoking or attempting to acquire cigarettes, his parents should be notified. Parenting is, after all, primarily the responsibility of fathers and mothers, not the government.

Instead, government has expanded its war on tobacco far beyond any legitimate concern with children's health. Mired in regulations, laws, taxes, and litigation, we look to Congress to extricate us from the mess it helped create. Yet if Congress authorizes the FDA to regulate cigarette ads and control the content of tobacco products, it will exacerbate the problem. Equally important, Congress will have delegated excessive and ill-advised legislative authority to an unelected administrative agency, and set the stage for significant intrusions on commercial free speech.

Suggested Readings

Bulow, Jeremy, and Paul Klemperer. "The Tobacco Deal." In *Brookings Papers on Economic Activity: Microeconomics 1998.* Washington: Brookings Institution, 1998.

Calfee, John E. "The Ghost of Cigarette Advertising Past." *Regulation*, November–December 1986.

Levy, Robert A. "Tobacco-Free FDA." *Administrative Law & Regulation News* 2, no. 3 (Winter 1998).

———. "Tobacco Medicaid Litigation: Snuffing Out the Rule of Law." Cato Institute Policy Analysis no. 275, June 20, 1997.

O'Brien, Thomas C. "Constitutional and Antitrust Violations of the Multistate Tobacco Settlement." Cato Institute Policy Analysis no. 371, May 18, 2000.

—Prepared by Robert A. Levy

17. The War on Drugs

Congress should

- repeal the Controlled Substances Act of 1970,
- repeal the federal mandatory minimum sentences and the mandatory sentencing guidelines,
- direct the administration not to interfere with the implementation of state initiatives that allow for the medical use of marijuana, and
- shut down the Drug Enforcement Administration.

Ours is a federal republic. The federal government has only the powers granted to it in the Constitution. And the United States has a tradition of individual liberty, vigorous civil society, and limited government. Identification of a problem does not mean that the government ought to undertake to solve it, and the fact that a problem occurs in more than one state does not mean that it is a proper subject for federal policy.

Perhaps no area more clearly demonstrates the bad consequences of not following such rules than does drug prohibition. The long federal experiment in prohibition of marijuana, cocaine, heroin, and other drugs has given us crime and corruption combined with a manifest failure to stop the use of drugs or reduce their availability to children.

In the 1920s Congress experimented with the prohibition of alcohol. On February 20, 1933, a new Congress acknowledged the failure of alcohol prohibition and sent the Twenty-First Amendment to the states. Congress recognized that Prohibition had failed to stop drinking and had increased prison populations and violent crime. By the end of 1933, national Prohibition was history, though many states continued to outlaw or severely restrict the sale of liquor.

Today Congress confronts a similarly failed prohibition policy. Futile efforts to enforce prohibition have been pursued even more vigorously in the 1980s and 1990s than they were in the 1920s. Total federal expenditures for the first 10 years of Prohibition amounted to $88 million—about $733 million in 1993 dollars. Drug enforcement costs about $19 billion a year now in federal spending alone.

Those billions have had some effect. Total drug arrests are now more than 1.5 million a year. Since 1989 more people have been incarcerated for drug offenses than for all violent crimes combined. There are now about 400,000 drug offenders in jails and prisons, and more than 60 percent of the federal prison population consists of drug offenders.

Yet, as was the case during Prohibition, all the arrests and incarcerations haven't stopped the use and abuse of drugs, or the drug trade, or the crime associated with black-market transactions. Cocaine and heroin supplies are up; the more our Customs agents interdict, the more smugglers import. And most tragic, the crime rate has soared. Despite the good news about crime in the past few years, crime rates remain at unprecedented levels.

As for discouraging young people from using drugs, the massive federal effort has largely been a dud. Despite the soaring expenditures on anti-drug efforts, about half the students in the United States in 1995 tried an illegal drug before they graduated from high school. Every year from 1975 to 1995, at least 82 percent of high school seniors said they found marijuana "fairly easy" or "very easy" to obtain. During that same period, according to federal statistics of dubious reliability, teenage marijuana use fell dramatically and then rose significantly, suggesting that cultural factors have more effect than the "war on drugs."

The manifest failure of drug prohibition explains why more and more people—from Nobel laureate Milton Friedman to conservative columnist William F. Buckley Jr., former secretary of state George Shultz, Minnesota governor Jesse Ventura, and New Mexico governor Gary Johnson—have argued that drug prohibition actually causes more crime and other harms than it prevents.

Repeal the Controlled Substances Act

The United States is a federal republic, and Congress should deal with drug prohibition the way it dealt with alcohol prohibition. The Twenty-First Amendment did not actually legalize the sale of alcohol; it simply repealed the federal prohibition and returned to the several states the authority to set alcohol policy. States took the opportunity to design diverse liquor policies that were in tune with the preferences of their citizens.

After 1933 three states and hundreds of counties continued to practice prohibition. Other states chose various forms of alcohol legalization.

The single most important law that Congress must repeal is the Controlled Substances Act of 1970. That law is probably the most far-reaching federal statute in American history, since it asserts federal jurisdiction over every drug offense in the United States, no matter how small or local in scope. Once that law is removed from the statute books, Congress should move to abolish the Drug Enforcement Administration and repeal all of the other federal drug laws.

There are a number of reasons why Congress should end the federal government's war on drugs. First and foremost, the federal drug laws are constitutionally dubious. As previously noted, the federal government can exercise only the powers that have been delegated to it. The Tenth Amendment reserves all other powers to the states or to the people. However misguided the alcohol prohibitionists turned out to have been, they deserve credit for honoring our constitutional system by seeking a constitutional amendment that would explicitly authorize a national policy on the sale of alcohol. Congress never asked the American people for additional constitutional powers to declare a war on drug consumers. That usurpation of power is something that few politicians or their court intellectuals wish to discuss.

Second, drug prohibition creates high levels of crime. Addicts commit crimes to pay for a habit that would be easily affordable if it were legal. Police sources have estimated that as much as half the property crime in some major cities is committed by drug users. More dramatic, because drugs are illegal, participants in the drug trade cannot go to court to settle disputes, whether between buyer and seller or between rival sellers. When black-market contracts are breached, the result is often some form of violent sanction, which usually leads to retaliation and then open warfare in the streets.

Our capital city, Washington, D.C., has become known as the "murder capital" even though it is the most heavily policed city in the United States. Make no mistake about it, the annual carnage that accounts for America's still shockingly high murder rates has little to do with the mind-altering effects of a marijuana cigarette or a crack pipe. It is instead one of the grim and bitter consequences of an ideological crusade whose proponents will not yet admit defeat.

Third, since the calamity of September 11, 2001, U.S. intelligence officials have repeatedly warned us of further terrorist attacks. Given that danger, it is a gross misallocation of law enforcement resources to have federal police agents surveilling marijuana clubs in California when they could be helping to discover sleeper cells of terrorists on U.S. territory. The Drug Enforcement Agency has 9,000 agents, intelligence analysts, and support staff. Their skills would be much better used if those people were redeployed to full-time counterterrorism investigations.

Fourth, drug prohibition is a classic example of throwing money at a problem. The federal government spends some $19 billion to enforce the drug laws every year—all to no avail. For years drug war bureaucrats have been tailoring their budget requests to the latest news reports. When drug use goes up, taxpayers are told the government needs more money so that it can redouble its efforts against a rising drug scourge. When drug use goes down, taxpayers are told that it would be a big mistake to curtail spending just when progress is being made. Good news or bad, spending levels must be maintained or increased.

Fifth, drug prohibition channels more than $40 billion a year into the criminal underworld occupied by an assortment of criminals, corrupt politicians, and, yes, terrorists. Alcohol prohibition drove reputable companies into other industries or out of business altogether, which paved the way for mobsters to make millions in the black market. If drugs were legal, organized crime would stand to lose billions of dollars, and drugs would be sold by legitimate businesses in an open marketplace.

Drug prohibition has created a criminal subculture in our inner cities. The immense profits to be had from a black-market business make drug dealing the most lucrative endeavor for many people, especially those who care least about getting on the wrong side of the law.

Drug dealers become the most visibly successful people in inner-city communities, the ones with money and clothes and cars. Social order is turned upside down when the most successful people in a community are criminals. The drug war makes peace and prosperity virtually impossible in inner cities.

Students of American history will someday ponder the question of how today's elected officials could readily admit to the mistaken policy of alcohol prohibition in the 1920s but recklessly pursue a policy of drug prohibition. Indeed, the only historical lesson that recent presidents and Congresses seem to have drawn from Prohibition is that government should not try to outlaw the sale of booze. One of the broader lessons that they should have learned is this: prohibition laws should be judged according to their real-world effects, not their promised benefits. If the

108th Congress will subject the federal drug laws to that standard, it will recognize that the drug war is not the answer to problems associated with drug use.

Respect State Initiatives

The failures of drug prohibition are becoming obvious to more and more Americans. A particularly tragic consequence of the stepped-up war on drugs is the refusal to allow sick people to use marijuana as medicine. Prohibitionists insist that marijuana is not good medicine, or at least that there are legal alternatives to marijuana that are equally good. Those who believe that individuals should make their own decisions, not have their decisions made for them by Washington bureaucracies, would simply say that that's a decision for patients and their doctors to make. But in fact there is good medical evidence of the therapeutic value of marijuana— despite the difficulty of doing adequate research on an illegal drug. A National Institutes of Health panel concluded that smoking marijuana may help treat a number of conditions, including nausea and pain. It can be particularly effective in improving the appetite of AIDS and cancer patients. The drug could also assist people who fail to respond to traditional remedies.

More than 70 percent of U.S. cancer specialists in one survey said they would prescribe marijuana if it were legal; nearly half said they had urged their patients to break the law to acquire the drug. The British Medical Association reports that nearly 70 percent of its members believe marijuana should be available for therapeutic use. Even President George Bush's Office of National Drug Control Policy criticized the Department of Health and Human Services for closing its special medical marijuana program.

Whatever the actual value of medical marijuana, the relevant fact for federal policymakers is that in 1996 the voters of California and Arizona authorized physicians licensed in those states to recommend the use of medical marijuana to seriously ill and terminally ill patients residing in the states, without being subject to civil and criminal penalties.

It came as no surprise when the Clinton administration responded to the California and Arizona initiatives by threatening to bring federal criminal charges against any doctor who recommended medicinal marijuana or any patient who used such marijuana. After all, President Clinton and his lawyers repeatedly maintained that no subject was beyond the purview of federal officialdom.

175

President Bush, on the other hand, has spoken of the importance of the constitutional principle of federalism. Shortly after his inauguration, Bush said, "I'm going to make respect for federalism a priority in this administration." Unfortunately, the president's actions have not matched his words. Federal police agents and prosecutors continue to raid medical marijuana clubs in California and Arizona. And both of the president's drug policy officials, Drug Czar John Walters and DEA Chief Asa Hutchinson, have been using their offices to meddle in state and local politics. If it is inappropriate for governors and mayors to entangle themselves in foreign policy—and it is—it is also inappropriate for federal officials to entangle themselves in state and local politics. In the 107th Congress, Reps. Barney Frank (D-Mass.), Dana Rohrabacher (R-Calif.), and Ron Paul (R-Tex.) jointly proposed the States' Rights to Medical Marijuana Act, which would have prohibited federal interference with any state that chose to enact a medical marijuana policy. The 108th Congress should enact a similar bill without delay.

One of the benefits of a federal republic is that different policies may be tried in different states. One of the benefits of our Constitution is that it limits the power of the federal government to impose one policy on the several states.

Repeal Mandatory Minimums

The common law in England and America has always relied on judges and juries to decide cases and set punishments. Under our modern system, of course, many crimes are defined by the legislature, and appropriate penalties are defined by statute. However, mandatory minimum sentences and rigid sentencing guidelines shift too much power to legislators and regulators who are not involved in particular cases. They turn judges into clerks and prevent judges from weighing all the facts and circumstances in setting appropriate sentences. In addition, mandatory minimums for nonviolent first-time drug offenders result in sentences grotesquely disproportionate to the gravity of the offenses.

Rather than extend mandatory minimum sentences to further crimes, Congress should repeal mandatory minimums and let judges perform their traditional function of weighing the facts and setting appropriate sentences.

Conclusion

Drug abuse is a problem for those involved in it and for their families and friends. But it is better dealt with as a moral and medical than as a criminal problem—"a problem for the surgeon general, not the attorney general," as former Baltimore mayor Kurt Schmoke puts it.

The United States is a federal republic, and Congress should deal with drug prohibition the way it dealt with alcohol prohibition. The Twenty-First Amendment did not actually legalize the sale of alcohol; it simply repealed the federal prohibition and returned to the several states the authority to set alcohol policy. States took the opportunity to design diverse liquor policies that were in tune with the preferences of their citizens. After 1933 three states and hundreds of counties continued to practice prohibition. Other states chose various forms of alcohol legalization.

Congress should repeal the Controlled Substances Act of 1970, shut down the Drug Enforcement Administration, and let the states set their own policies with regard to currently illegal drugs. They would do well to treat marijuana, cocaine, and heroin the way most states now treat alcohol: It should be legal for stores to sell such drugs to adults. Drug sales to children, like alcohol sales to children, should remain illegal. Driving under the influence of drugs should be illegal.

With such a policy, Congress would acknowledge that our current drug policies have failed. It would restore authority to the states, as the Founders envisioned. It would save taxpayers' money. And it would give the states the power to experiment with drug policies and perhaps devise more successful rules.

Repeal of prohibition would take the astronomical profits out of the drug business and destroy the drug kingpins who terrorize parts of our cities. It would reduce crime even more dramatically than did the repeal of alcohol prohibition. Not only would there be less crime; reform would also free federal agents to concentrate on terrorism and espionage and free local police agents to concentrate on robbery, burglary, and violent crime.

The war on drugs has lasted longer than Prohibition, longer than the Vietnam War. But there is no light at the end of this tunnel. Prohibition has failed, again, and should be repealed, again.

Suggested Readings

Benjamin, Daniel K., and Roger Leroy Miller. *Undoing Drugs: Beyond Legalization.* New York: Basic Books, 1991.

Boaz, David. "A Drug-Free America—Or a Free America?" *U.C. Davis Law Review* 24 (1991).

Boaz, David, ed. *The Crisis in Drug Prohibition.* Washington: Cato Institute, 1991.

Buckley, William F. Jr., et al. "The War on Drugs Is Lost." *National Review,* February 12, 1996.

Luna, Erik. "The Misguided Guidelines: A Critique of Federal Sentencing." Cato Institute Policy Analysis, no. 458, November 1, 2002.

Lynch, Timothy, ed. *After Prohibition: An Adult Approach to Drug Policies in the 21st Century.* Washington, Cato Institute, 2000.

Masters, Bill. *Drug War Addiction.* St. Louis: Accurate Press, 2002.

McNamara, Joseph. "The Defensive Front Line." *Regulation* (Winter 2001): 19–21.

Ostrowski, James. "The Moral and Practical Case for Drug Legalization." *Hofstra Law Review* 18 (1990).

Pilon, Roger. "The Medical Marihuana Referendum Movement in America: Federalism Implications." Testimony before the House Crime Subcommittee, October 1, 1997.

—Prepared by David Boaz and Timothy Lynch

18. Restoring the Right to Bear Arms

Congress should

- use its constitutional authority over the District of Columbia to overturn D.C.'s handgun ban and enact a "shall issue" concealed carry licensing statute,
- repeal the Gun Control Act of 1968, and
- enact legislation that would authorize airlines to arm pilots who volunteer and complete appropriate training.

For decades, the Second Amendment was consigned to constitutional exile, all but erased from constitutional law textbooks and effectively banished from the nation's courts. But no more. Recent developments in the law and in political culture have begun the process of returning the amendment to its proper place in our constitutional pantheon. The 108th Congress now has a historic opportunity, not simply to stave off new gun-control proposals, but to begin restoring Americans' right to keep and bear arms.

Emergence from Exile

Ideas have consequences, and so does constitutional text. Though elite opinion reduced the Second Amendment to a constitutional inkblot for a good part of the 20th century, gun enthusiasts and grassroots activists continued to insist that the amendment meant what it said. And slowly, often reluctantly, legal scholars began to realize that the activists were right. Liberal law professor Sanford Levinson conceded as much in a 1989 *Yale Law Review* article titled "The Embarrassing Second Amendment." UCLA Law School's Eugene Volokh took a similar intellectual journey. After a 1990 argument with a nonlawyer acquaintance who loudly maintained that the Second Amendment protected an individual right, Volokh concluded that his opponent was a "blowhard and even a bit of a kook."

But several years later, as he researched the subject, he discovered to his "surprise and mild chagrin, that this supposed kook was entirely right": the amendment secures the individual's right to keep and bear arms.

That's also what the Fifth Circuit Court of Appeals concluded in October 2001 when it decided *United States v. Emerson*. It held that the Constitution "protects the right of individuals, including those not then actually a member of any militia . . . to privately possess and bear their own firearms . . . that are suitable as personal individual weapons."

U.S. Attorney General John Ashcroft has endorsed the *Emerson* court's reading of the amendment. First, in a letter to the National Rifle Association, Ashcroft stated his belief that "the text and the original intent of the Second Amendment clearly protect the right of individuals to keep and bear firearms." That letter was followed by Justice Department briefs before the Supreme Court in the *Emerson* case and in *United States v. Haney*. For the first time, the federal government argued in formal court papers that the "Second Amendment . . . protects the rights of individuals, including persons who are not members of any militia . . . to possess and bear their own firearms, subject to reasonable restrictions designed to prevent possession by unfit persons or . . . firearms that are particularly suited to criminal misuse."

The Right of the People

What's driving the new consensus? Let's look at the amendment's text: "A well regulated Militia, being necessary to the security of a free State, the right of the people to keep and bear Arms, shall not be infringed."

The operative clause ("the right of the people to keep and bear Arms, shall not be infringed") secures the right. The explanatory clause ("A well regulated Militia, being necessary to the security of a free State") justifies the right. That syntax was not unusual for the times. For example, Article I, section 8, of the Constitution gives Congress the power to grant copyrights in order to "Promote the Progress of Science and useful Arts." Yet copyrights are also granted to *Hustler*, to racist publications, even to literature that expressly seeks to retard science and the arts. The proper understanding of the copyright provision is that promoting science and the arts is one justification—but not the only justification—for the copyright power. Analogously, the militia clause helps explain why we have a right to bear arms, but it's not necessary to the exercise of that right.

As George Mason University law professor Nelson Lund puts it, imagine if the Second Amendment said, "A well-educated Electorate, being necessary to self-governance in a free state, the right of the people to keep and read Books shall not be infringed." Surely, no rational person would suggest that only registered voters have a right to read. Yet that is precisely the effect if the text is interpreted to apply only to a well-educated electorate. Analogously, the Second Amendment cannot be read to apply only to members of the militia.

The Second Amendment, like the First and the Fourth, refers explicitly to "the right of the people." Consider the placement of the amendment within the Bill of Rights, the part of the Constitution that deals exclusively with rights of individuals, not powers of the state. No one can doubt that First Amendment rights (speech, religion, assembly) belong to us as individuals. Similarly, Fourth Amendment protections against unreasonable searches and seizures are individual rights. In the context of the Second Amendment, we secure "the right of the people" by guaranteeing the right of each person. Second Amendment protections are not *for* the state but for each individual *against* the state—a deterrent to government tyranny.

And not just against government tyranny. The Second Amendment also secures our right to protect ourselves from criminal predators. After all, in 1791 there were no organized, professional police forces to speak of in America. Self-defense was the responsibility of the individual and the community, and not, in the first instance, of the state. Armed citizens, responsibly exercising their right of self-defense, are an effective deterrent to crime.

Today, states' incompetence at defending citizens against criminals is a more palpable threat to our liberties than is tyranny by the state. But that incompetence coupled with a disarmed citizenry could well create the conditions that lead to tyranny. The demand for police to defend us increases in proportion to our inability to defend ourselves. That's why disarmed societies tend to become police states. Witness law-abiding inner-city residents, many of whom have been disarmed by gun control, begging for police protection against drug gangs—despite the terrible violations of civil liberties that such protection entails, such as curfews and anti-loitering laws. The right to bear arms is thus preventive—it reduces the demand for a police state. George Washington University law professor Robert Cottrol put it this way: "A people incapable of protecting themselves will lose their rights as a free people, becoming either servile dependents of the state or of the criminal predators."

Over the years, our elected representatives have adopted a dangerously court-centric view of the Constitution: a view that decisions about constitutionality are properly left to the judiciary. But members of Congress also swear an oath to uphold the Constitution. Congress can make good on that oath by taking legislative action to restore our right to keep and bear arms. To that end, Congress should take the following steps.

Repeal D.C.'s Handgun Ban and Enact Concealed Carry

No jurisdiction in the United States works as doggedly to disarm citizens as does the District of Columbia, our nation's capital and on-again, off-again murder capital. Yes, the city council grudgingly legalized pepper spray in 1993 (provided, of course, that it's properly registered), but that brief concession to self-defense hasn't led to any revision of the District's gun laws, which are still among the most restrictive in America. D.C. bans the possession of unregistered handguns and prohibits, with very few exceptions, the registration of any handgun not validly registered in the District prior to 1976.

In the wake of the *Emerson* decision and Attorney General Ashcroft's endorsement of the individual right to keep and bear arms, the District's federal public defender decided that D.C.'s sweeping gun ban was vulnerable. In May 2002, the *Washington Post* reported that D.C.'s federal defender had filed motions challenging the gun ban on behalf of several clients accused of violating the ban and the District's law against carrying firearms. In all, roughly three dozen challenges to the D.C. law have been filed thus far.

Because the District is not a state, felonies under D.C. law are prosecuted by the U.S. attorney for the District of Columbia, an employee of the Justice Department—the same Justice Department that is now on record as favoring an individual rights theory of the Second Amendment. To be sure, Ashcroft had declared in an internal memorandum that the Justice Department "will continue to defend the constitutionality of all existing federal firearms laws." But D.C. law, although enacted pursuant to congressional delegation, is not federal law. Therefore, the U.S. attorney might have been expected to support a motion to drop the handgun possession charges pending in these cases.

Instead, the U.S. attorney argued that the D.C. handgun ban must be upheld in light of binding precedent from the D.C. Court of Appeals in a 1987 case, *Sandidge v. United States*. That case flatly repudiates the individual right to bear arms. The *Sandidge* court stated baldly that "the right to keep and bear arms is not a right conferred upon the people by the federal constitution"—a statement that's rather hard to square with the Second Amendment, which speaks of the "right" of the "people" to "keep and bear arms."

It's one thing for Attorney General Ashcroft to endorse the individual right to bear arms in a letter to a friendly interest group, or to affirm it in a footnote in a legal brief. It's quite another to follow up words with action. As Julie Leighton of the District's Public Defender Service puts it, Ashcroft's Justice Department "is currently prosecuting individuals solely for 'bearing' a pistol, even though many of those individuals have no prior convictions and are adult citizens of full mental capacity. Thus the United States persists in prosecuting District of Columbia residents for conduct that the Attorney General has expressly deemed protected by the United States Constitution."

Whatever the reasons for Attorney General Ashcroft's perplexing decision to continue prosecuting gun-ban violations, Congress has the constitutional authority to protect District residents' right to bear arms. Article I, section 8, clause 17, of the Constitution gives Congress the power "to exercise exclusive legislation in all cases whatsoever" over the District of Columbia. Congress can and should use that authority to repeal the District's gun ban and enact a "shall-issue" concealed carry licensing statute. Such statutes mandate that handgun permits be issued to citizens who satisfy certain objective criteria such as citizenship, mental competence, lack of a criminal record, and completion of a firearms training course. Thirty-one states have shall-issue laws, and, as exhaustive research by American Enterprise Institute scholar John R. Lott Jr. has shown, they deter crime. Lott found that "the reductions in violent crime are greatest in the most crime prone, most urban areas. Women, the elderly and blacks gained by far the most from this ability to protect themselves."

In contrast, for more than 25 years, D.C. residents have served as guinea pigs in a public-policy experiment in near-total gun prohibition. That experiment has failed catastrophically. Congress can and should end that illegitimate experiment and restore District residents' right to keep and bear arms.

Repeal the Gun Control Act of 1968

The Gun Control Act of 1968, with subsequent amendments, is bad law and bad public policy. It ought to be repealed. Full repeal is not a radical step; Ronald Reagan endorsed it in 1980. But until that can be accomplished, Congress should, at a minimum, repeal the most oppressive sections:

The 1994 Ban on So-Called Assault Weapons

Those guns do *not* fire faster than other guns, nor are they more powerful. Indeed, they fire smaller bullets at lower velocities than do most well-known rifles used for hunting big game. The assault weapons statute is purely cosmetic—banning guns because of politically incorrect features such as bayonet lugs (as if drive-by bayoneting were a problem) or a rifle grip that protrudes ''conspicuously'' from the gun's stock. Police statistics from around the nation show that such guns are rarely used in crime. The federal ban will sunset in 2004, but Congress should repeal it immediately.

The 1994 Ban on Possession of Handguns by Persons under 18

Assuming that such a ban could survive Second Amendment scrutiny, it is a topic that should be addressed by state, not federal, law. The statute does include some exceptions—for example, a parent may take a child target shooting—but, even if the child is under direct and continuous parental supervision, the parent commits a federal crime unless she writes a note giving the child permission to target shoot and the child carries the note at all times. The 1994 prohibition usurps traditional state powers, is overbroad, and encroaches on parental rights, despite a paucity of empirical evidence that the ban will reduce gun accidents or gun-related violence.

The Ban on Gun Possession by Specified Adults

When adult behavior is regulated, the Second Amendment weighs more heavily than when restrictions are imposed on minors. Even if Second Amendment constraints are somehow satisfied, the federal government has no constitutional authority in this area. Particularly unfair, whether imposed by federal or state law, is the ban on gun possession by anyone who is subject to a domestic restraining order, routinely issued by divorce courts without any finding that the subject of the order is a danger to another person. Such provisions ought not to be allowed to stand.

Arm the Pilots

Just as armed citizens can deter aggression on our city streets, they can do so in our nation's skies. On September 11, 2001, a few hijackers armed with box cutters were able to hold scores of airline passengers at bay, secure in the knowledge that American airplanes are gun-free zones. But when we turn planes, airports, schools, and workplaces into gun-free zones, we also turn them into criminal-safe zones. If on the other hand we make it nearly certain that someone will be armed on every commercial flight, the enemies of liberty will have second thoughts about using American aircraft as weapons of mass destruction.

Imagine that you are a terrorist deciding whose plane to use as your next weapon. One airline boasts in its ads, "Our Planes Are Gun-Free Zones." A second, with somewhat less self-righteousness, admonishes that "One or More Employees Will Be Armed on Every Flight." Not much question which one you'd fly. Now picture yourself as a safety-conscious passenger. Still not much question, but the choice won't be the same. That's the case in a nutshell for armed sky marshals and armed pilots.

Let's start with sky marshals. Having an armed federal marshal on every flight would certainly deter terrorists. But the problem is cost. Just one marshal per daily flight would require 35,000 officers—more than twice the number employed by the Federal Bureau of Investigation, the Secret Service, and U.S. Marshals Service combined. Yes, a marshal might be able to average three to four flights each day. Then again, most proposals call for more than one marshal per flight. Put it all together and we're talking about roughly 15 thousand to 20 thousand new employees, salaried at $30,000 and up per year, plus the cost of training.

Transportation Secretary Norman Mineta, hostile to the idea of anyone but federal marshals carrying firearms on U.S. flights, has worked to greatly expand the federal air marshal program. About 6,000 new marshals have been hired since September 11. That rapid expansion has reduced the quality of new hires and left the air marshal program in disarray, according to an August 2002 *USA Today* exposé. According to one disillusioned former marshal, the program has become "like security-guard training at the mall."

Instead of going on a federal hiring binge, why not rely on the talented people the airlines already have? Why not allow pilots to be armed? "These men and women operate $100 million pieces of equipment. They can sure learn to operate a .38 snub-nose if they want to," says aviation consultant Michael Boyd. The Airline Pilots Association, with overwhelming support from its members, wants armed pilots in cockpits. So do the public and Congress. The airlines are opposed only because they fear the trial lawyers.

"Under the old model of hijackings," said a union spokesman, the "strategy was to accommodate, negotiate and do not escalate. But that was before. The cockpit has to be defended at all costs." In a crisis, a pilot's gun would never leave the cockpit because the pilot never would. And if a terrorist were able to penetrate the cockpit, shooting him within the cockpit's door frame would not require a sniper's skill.

An armed pilots program would be strictly voluntary. It would require extensive background screening and psychological testing, as well as classroom and practical training, roughly equivalent to what sky marshals would receive. After all, we now allow weapons on planes if they're carried by sheriffs, FBI and Secret Service agents, postal inspectors, and bodyguards of foreign dignitaries. If those risks are acceptable, then let's arm pilots who can protect *all* passengers' lives. Better yet, leave it up to the individual airlines. They own the property and they can set the rules.

The broader principle is this: On September 11, the United States government failed at its single most important function—protecting American citizens against foreign aggression. Armed civilians can deter aggression. That means safer planes, shopping malls, schools, and other public places. Law enforcement officers can't be everywhere, but an armed, trained citizenry can be.

For too long, elite opinion in America has been implacably opposed to armed self-defense. The underlying philosophy, expressed by Pete Shields, former president of Handgun Control, is that "the best defense is . . . no defense—give them what they want." After September 11, that philosophy is no longer valid, if it ever was. It's time for the 108th Congress to repudiate it.

Suggested Readings

Halbrook, Steven P. "Second Class Citizenship and the Second Amendment in the District of Columbia." *George Mason University Civil Rights Law Journal* 5 (1995).

Kopel, David B. *The Samurai, the Mountie, and the Cowboy: Should America Adopt the Gun Controls of Other Democracies?* Amherst, N.Y.: Prometheus Books, 1992.

Lott, John R. Jr. *More Guns, Less Crime: Understanding Crime and Gun-Control Laws.* 2d ed. Chicago: University of Chicago Press, 2000.

Lund, Nelson. "A Primer on the Constitutional Right to Keep and Bear Arms." Virginia Institute for Public Policy Report no. 7, June 2002.

Snyder, Jeffrey R. "Fighting Back: Crime, Self-Defense, and the Right to Carry a Handgun." Cato Institute Policy Analysis no 284, October 22, 1997.

United States v. Emerson, 270 F.3d. 203 (5th Cir. 2001).

—Prepared by Gene Healy and Robert A. Levy

19. Guns and Federalism

Congress should

- defund Project Safe Neighborhoods and
- reject efforts to bar municipal lawsuits against gun manufacturers.

Members of Congress who support gun rights are currently engaged in a dubious tradeoff: to save the Second Amendment, they've decided to undermine the Tenth. For two years running, Congress has appropriated funds for President Bush's key crime-fighting program, Project Safe Neighborhoods, which is designed to ward off calls for additional gun control by ramping up enforcement of the gun laws already on the books. But the program illegitimately federalizes the prosecution of gun possession crimes ordinarily left to the states. Meanwhile, members of Congress who support gun rights want to use federal power to reform state tort law. They're pushing legislation that would shield firearms manufacturers and sellers from ongoing municipal lawsuits over gun violence. Both of those efforts rely on an expansive interpretation of federal authority that has no constitutional basis; the 108th Congress should abandon both.

Defund Project Safe Neighborhoods

Project Safe Neighborhoods is the public-policy embodiment of the National Rifle Association sound bite "we don't need any new gun control laws; we need to enforce the gun laws on the books." The program funds more than 800 new prosecutors (around 200 federal, 600 state level) who will do nothing but pursue gun-law violations full time.

The federal prosecutors hired under PSN focus on a narrow section of the federal criminal code that duplicates state criminal statutes relating to gun possession. Those provisions prohibit things that are already illegal in all 50 states, such as possession of a handgun by a convicted felon or a drug user or an illegal alien. The problem with federal enforcement of those laws is that most of them ought not to be on the books in the first place. They're based on an overbroad interpretation of Congress's power to regulate commerce among the states. The Commerce Clause was designed to create the original North American free-trade zone by promoting and regularizing commerce among the states. It was never intended to give the federal government general police powers. Indeed, by enumerating only three federal crimes, treason, piracy, and counterfeiting, the Constitution makes it clear that the federal role in criminal law enforcement is narrow. As Alexander Hamilton put it in *Federalist* no. 17, "the ordinary administration of criminal justice" belongs to the states.

PSN takes over the ordinary administration of criminal justice from the states by increasing federalization of crime and dictating state prosecutorial priorities. And if the federal government has the power to prosecute local handgun crimes, it's hard to see why it doesn't also have the power to punish ordinary assault, drunk driving, traffic violations, or anything else we've traditionally left to the states.

More disturbing still is the prospect that PSN will lead to a mindless "zero tolerance" policy for technical infractions of gun laws. Federal prosecutors already operate under an incentive structure that George Washington University Law School professor Jonathan Turley compares with "the body count approach in Vietnam. . . . They feel a need to produce a body count to Congress to justify past appropriations and secure future increases."

This "body count" mentality may help explain the fact that recent federal firearms prosecutions have included Katica Crippen, a Colorado woman who was convicted under the felon-in-possession statutes for posing nude on the Internet with a gun, and Dane Yirkovsky, an Iowa man who was sent to federal prison for 15 years for possession of a single .22-caliber bullet.

We can expect more of the same as PSN ramps up firearms prosecutions because, unlike that of a regular prosecutor, a PSN prosecutor's full-time job is pursuing gun offenders. A PSN prosecutor will not be able to turn to other areas of the criminal code after the worst gun-law violators have been prosecuted. Add to that the fact that a job as a full-time gun prosecutor is likely to appeal disproportionately to attorneys with an ideological hostility toward gun ownership, and PSN begins to sound like something dreamed up by Sarah Brady herself.

Moreover, the program threatens to open a Pandora's box leading to the further politicization of criminal justice. The model set up by PSN practically invites special interest groups to drive prosecutorial priorities via federal funding. What are PSN supporters in Congress going to say when demands are made for federal dollars for local, full-time domestic violence prosecutors or hate crime prosecutors? So long as Congress continues to fund PSN, it will be hard-pressed to say that local crime is not a federal issue.

Leave Tort Reform to the States

Led by the city of Chicago, a number of municipalities have filed suit against gun manufacturers for damages incurred due to the misuse of guns by criminals. Some of the suits allege "negligent marketing"—charging that gun manufacturers flood the suburbs with more guns than legitimate customers will buy, knowing that dealers will sell the excess supply illegally to criminals from the inner city. Others assert that guns are defective and unreasonably dangerous products because manufacturers design their guns without safety features that are purportedly easy and economical to install. At bottom, both legal theories rest on the outlandish proposition that gun makers are responsible for the criminal misconduct of certain of their customers.

A broad coalition of gun-rights supporters in Congress wants to quash those suits with federal tort reform. Two bills moving through the House and Senate provide that gun manufacturers and distributors cannot be sued for damages (or other relief) if someone is injured when a gun is used unlawfully.

It's easy to understand the concerns that spurred those bills. Federal tort reform supporter Rep. Chris John (D-La.) is correct when he calls the gun lawsuits "frivolous" and warns that they "jeopardize a legitimate, legal business that is worth billions of dollars to our national economy." But not every national problem is a federal problem. Advocates of gun rights who back federal tort reform have forgotten the Tenth Amendment's admonition that powers not delegated to the federal government in the Constitution remain with the states or the people. The power to control frivolous lawsuits belongs to the states.

Where in the Constitution could the federal government find authority to ban state and local lawsuits against the gun industry? According to the tort reform bills pending in both the House and the Senate, the answer is the all-purpose Commerce Clause. As the bills' supporters see it, the lawsuits interfere with interstate commerce, and therefore Congress has the authority to stop them.

But the Commerce Clause, properly interpreted, does not give Congress blanket authority to regulate any activity that might affect commerce. Rather, the purpose of the Commerce Clause was functional: to secure the free flow of commerce among the states. That means Congress may act only when actual or imminent state regulations impede free trade among the states, or when it's clear that uniform national regulations are essential for that purpose. Even then, Congress's power ought properly extend no further than to the regulation of (1) channels and vehicles of interstate commerce (such as waterways, airways, and railroads); (2) discrimination by a state against out-of-state interests (for example, restrictions on imported goods); and (3) attempts by a state to exercise sovereignty beyond the state's borders (such as state rules governing national stock exchanges, telecommunications, banking, and broadcast or Internet advertising). Under no credible theory of the commerce power can Congress use that power to regulate noncommercial activities like lawsuits, which are designed to prevent and redress injuries, not to regulate interstate trade.

Yes, lawsuits against gun companies *affect* commerce. But so does just about any state regulation or any court decision. The Commerce Clause could not prevent California, for example, from requiring catalytic converters on cars sold in the state. The Commerce Clause would not permit the federal government to override state minimum wage laws, or state safety regulations on power plants or even on firearms. Yet all of those state rules *affect* interstate commerce.

Companies have a remedy when state courts permit phony lawsuits. They can stop doing business in a state that has an oppressive tort regime. And that remedy honors the federalist idea that the states serve as 50 experimental laboratories. For example, physicians and insurance companies are leaving Mississippi because outrageous damage awards have driven the price of malpractice insurance prohibitively high. Ultimately, the voters in oppressive states will have to choose between access to products and extortionate tort law. As more businesses leave, the choice will become obvious. Yes, there's an effect on commerce when out-of-state companies leave. But the effect is not related to the *interstate* aspect of commerce. There's a similar effect when in-state companies shut down. In Mississippi, in-state and out-of-state insurance companies, or gun companies for that matter, are all exposed to the same tort regime. That's why the Commerce Clause should not apply.

Those supporters of gun rights who would have it otherwise are asking for trouble. Ronald Reagan once noted that a government big enough to give you everything you want is big enough to take it all away. A similar dynamic exists with constitutional interpretation: a Commerce Clause broad enough to solve every national problem is too broad not to be abused. When Congress's authority to regulate commerce is misused to impose federal rules that restrict state gun lawsuits, we should not be surprised that it will also be misused to impose federal rules that restrict gun possession and ownership.

Suggested Readings

Epstein, Richard A. "The Proper Scope of the Commerce Power." *Virginia Law Review* 73 (1987).

Healy, Gene. "There Goes the Neighborhood: The Bush-Ashcroft Plan to 'Help' Localities Fight Gun Crime." Cato Institute Policy Analysis no. 440, May 28, 2002.

Levy, Robert A. "Pistol Whipped: Baseless Lawsuits, Foolish Laws." Cato Institute Policy Analysis no. 400, May 9, 2001.

Reynolds, Glenn Harlan. "Kids, Guns and the Commerce Clause: Is the Court Ready for Constitutional Government?" Cato Institute Policy Analysis no. 216, October 10, 1994.

United States v. Lopez, 514 U.S. 549 (1995).

—Prepared by Gene Healy and Robert A. Levy

MONEY AND BANKING

20. The Limits of Monetary Policy

Congress should

- uphold its constitutional duty to maintain the purchasing power of the dollar by enacting legislation that makes long-run price stability the primary objective of Federal Reserve monetary policy;
- recognize that the Fed cannot fine-tune the real economy but can achieve price stability by limiting the growth of base money to a noninflationary path;
- hold the Fed accountable for achieving expected inflation of 0–2 percent a year;
- abolish the Exchange Stabilization Fund, since the Fed's role is to stabilize the domestic price level, not to stabilize the foreign exchange value of the dollar by intervening in the foreign exchange market; and
- offer no resistance to the emergence of digital currency (money stored in digital form on microchips embedded in computer hard drives or in "smart cards") and other substitutes for Federal Reserve notes, so that free-market forces can help shape the future of monetary institutions.

History has shown that monetary stability—money growth consistent with a stable and predictable value of money—is an important determinant of economic stability. Safeguarding the long-run purchasing power of money is also essential for the future of private property and a free society. In the United States, persistent inflation has eroded the value of money and distorted relative prices, making production and investment decisions more uncertain. In the early 1970s, wage-price controls were imposed that attenuated economic freedom and increased government discretion, thus undermining the rule of law. Although those controls have been removed and inflation appears to be under control, there is no guarantee of future price-level stability.

Current law specifies no single objective for monetary policy and lacks an enforcement mechanism to achieve monetary stability. The multiplicity of goals and the absence of an appropriate penalty-reward structure to maintain stable money are evident from section 2A of the amended Federal Reserve Act:

> The Board of Governors . . . and the Federal Open Market Committee shall maintain long-run growth of the monetary and credit aggregates commensurate with the economy's long-run potential to increase production, so as to promote effectively the goals of maximum employment, stable prices, and moderate long-term interest rates. . . . Nothing in this Act shall be interpreted to require that the objectives and plans with respect to the ranges of growth or diminution of the monetary and credit aggregates disclosed in the reports submitted under this section be achieved.

From 1975 to 1999, the Federal Reserve reported its monetary targets to Congress. *It no longer does.* Alan Greenspan has done a commendable job of keeping inflation relatively low since he took office in 1987, but his performance is no guarantee of future success in achieving money of stable value.

The U.S. monetary system continues to be based on discretionary government fiat money, with no legally enforceable commitment to long-run price stability as the sole objective of monetary policy. Clark Warburton's 1946 characterization of U.S. monetary law as ''ambiguous and chaotic'' still rings true.

The large amount of discretion exercised by the Fed and the uncertainty it entails reflect Congress's failure to provide an adequate legal framework for stable money, as intended in Article I, section 8, of the Constitution. If the Fed were subject to a monetary rule, stop-go monetary policy—an extremely important factor in generating business fluctuations—could be halted. There is a growing consensus among economists and Fed officials that long-run price stability should be the focus of monetary policy, but Congress has yet to enact legislation that would bind the Fed to that objective and hold the chairman accountable for erratic changes in the quantity of money and persistent rises in the price level.

In his July 2000 ''Monetary Report to the Congress,'' Greenspan stated: ''Irrespective of the complexities of economic change, our primary goal is to find those policies that best contribute to a noninflationary environment and hence to growth. The Federal Reserve, I trust, will always remain vigilant in pursuit of that goal.'' But will it? And should the public trust the discretionary power of an ''independent'' central bank not bound by any rule?

William Poole, president of the Federal Reserve Bank of St. Louis and a proponent of zero inflation, has pointed to the market disruption caused by the lack of a clear monetary rule to guide Fed policy:

> The fact that markets so often respond to comments and speeches by Fed officials indicates that the markets today are not evaluating monetary policy in the context of a well-articulated and well-understood monetary rule. The problem is a deep and difficult one.

Congress should face that problem and retain the power to regulate the value of money by mandating that maintaining price stability is the Fed's primary duty.

Mandate Price Stability as the Fed's Primary Duty

The 108th Congress should amend the Federal Reserve Act to make long-run price stability—i.e., expected inflation of 0–2 percent a year— the sole goal of monetary policy. (If price indexes correctly measured inflation, zero expected inflation would be the preferred target. But since price indexes typically understate the extent of quality improvement, zero expected inflation can be in fact deflation.)

The Fed's function is not to set interest rates or to target the rate of unemployment or real growth. The Fed cannot control relative prices, employment, or output; it can directly control only the monetary base (currency held by the public and bank reserves) and thereby affect money growth, nominal income, and the average level of money prices. In the short run, the Fed can affect output and employment, as well as real interest rates, but it cannot do so in the long run.

The tradeoff between unemployment and inflation that is the basis for the Phillips curve is not a viable monetary policy option for the Fed. Market participants learn quickly and will revise their plans to account for the inflationary impact of faster money growth designed to reduce unemployment below its so-called natural rate. The results of those revisions—such as demanding higher money wages to compensate for expected inflation—will frustrate politicians intent on using monetary policy to stimulate the real economy. Cato Institute chairman William Niskanen, in a recent empirical study, made the following points.

- "There is *no* tradeoff of unemployment and inflation except in the same year."
- "In the long term, the unemployment rate is a *positive* function of the inflation rate."
- "The minimum sustainable unemployment rate is about 3.7 percent and can be achieved only by a *zero* steady-state inflation rate."

Evidence also shows that inflation and long-run growth are *inversely* related (Figure 20.1). Inflation introduces distortions in the financial system and impedes the efficient allocation of resources. Those distortions and others have a negative impact on economic growth. Since inflation is primarily a monetary phenomenon (caused by excess growth of the money supply over and above long-run output growth), it cannot increase real growth—but it can *decrease* it. That is why monetary stability and, hence, price-level stability are so important.

The Fed cannot attain more than one policy target with one policy instrument. The only instrument the Fed has direct control over is the

Figure 20.1
Real Growth and Inflation Move in Opposite Directions

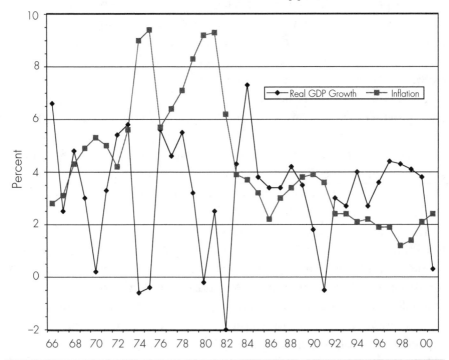

SOURCE: Alan Reynolds, "The Fed's Whimsical Monetary Tinkering," Figure 1, as updated.
NOTE: Inflation is calculated from the GDP chain-type index.

monetary base; the surest target is long-run price stability. The Fed could use either an adaptive feedback rule, such as that proposed by Carnegie Mellon economist Bennett McCallum, or an inflation-targeting rule, such as New Zealand has successfully used. With the feedback rule, the Fed would adjust the growth of the monetary base to keep nominal GDP (or domestic final sales) on a smooth noninflationary growth path. With an inflation target, the Fed would adjust the monetary base so that the growth rate of the price level was approximately zero in the long run. There would be some rises and falls in the price level due to supply-side shocks, either positive or negative, but expected inflation would remain close to zero (in the 0–2 percent range) over time.

Congress need not dictate the exact rule for the Fed to follow in its pursuit of long-run price stability, but Congress should hold the Fed accountable for achieving that goal—and not require the Fed to respond to supply shocks that would lead to one-time increases or decreases in the price level.

The public's trust and confidence in the future purchasing power of the dollar can be permanently increased by a legal mandate directing the Fed to adopt a monetary rule to achieve long-run price stability. According to Poole:

> The logic, and the evidence, both suggest that the appropriate goal for monetary policy should be price stability, that is, a long-run inflation rate of approximately zero. . . . A central bank's single most important job is preserving the value of the nation's money. Monetary policy has succeeded if the public can reasonably trust that a dollar will buy tomorrow what it will buy today. . . . I am confident that our economy's long-run performance would be enhanced by a monetary policy that aims at, achieves, and maintains a zero rate of inflation.

That institutional change—from a fully discretionary monetary authority to one bound by law to a single target—not only would bolster the Fed's reputation but would enhance the efficiency of the price system and allow individuals to better plan for the future. People's property rights would be more secure as a result. Congress should not miss the opportunity to return to its original constitutional duty of maintaining the value of money and safeguarding property rights.

Recognize the Limits of Monetary Policy

The Fed cannot permanently increase the rate of economic growth or permanently lower the rate of unemployment by increasing money growth, nor can it permanently lower real interest rates. But it can throw the economy off track by policy errors—that is, by creating either too much or too little money to maintain stable expectations about the long-run value of the currency. The most grievous error of discretionary monetary policy, as Milton Friedman and Anna Schwartz have shown in *A Monetary History of the United States*, was the Fed's failure to prevent the money supply from shrinking by one-third between 1929 and 1933, which turned a sharp but otherwise ordinary recession into the Great Depression.

Economics, like medicine, is not an exact science. The guiding principle of economic policy should be the great physician Galen's (A.D. 160) admonition to "first do no harm." Instead of pursuing in vain an activist monetary policy designed to fine-tune the economy and achieve all good things—full employment, economic growth, and price stability—Fed policy ought to be aimed at what it can actually achieve.

Three questions Congress must contemplate in its oversight of monetary policy are (1) What can the Fed do? (2) What can't it do? (3) What should it do?

What the Fed Can Do

The Fed can

- control the monetary base through open market operations, reserve requirements, and the discount rate;
- provide liquidity quickly to shore up public confidence in banks during a financial crisis;
- influence the level and growth rate of nominal variables, in particular monetary aggregates, nominal income, and the price level;
- control inflation and prevent monetary instability in the long run; and
- influence expectations about future inflation and nominal interest rates.

What the Fed Cannot Do

The Fed cannot

- target real variables so as to permanently reduce the rate of unemployment or increase economic growth;
- determine real interest rates;
- peg the nominal exchange rate and at the same time pursue an independent monetary policy aimed at stabilizing the price level, without imposing capital controls;

- fine-tune the economy; or
- make accurate macroeconomic forecasts.

What the Fed Should Do

The Fed should

- keep the growth of nominal GDP on a stable, noninflationary path so that expected inflation is close to zero by controlling the monetary base;
- let market forces determine exchange rates so that the dollar and other key currencies are free to find their equilibrium value in the foreign exchange market; and
- avoid predicating monetary policy on stock market performance.

By recognizing the limits of monetary policy, Congress will also recognize the importance of enacting a law that establishes a clear framework for such policy. Mandating long-run price stability as the Fed's sole objective is a goal the public can understand and a target the Fed can achieve and be held accountable for.

Hold the Fed Accountable

If a law making price stability the sole aim of monetary policy is to be effective, the Fed must be held responsible for failure to meet that target. That means the law must clearly state the price-stability target while letting the Fed choose how best to achieve it.

The New Zealand inflation-targeting law is instructive. The Reserve Bank Act of 1989 states that the sole objective of monetary policy is price stability. A target range is set for inflation, as measured by the consumer price index, which the governor of the Reserve Bank must achieve within a specified time horizon, with exceptions made for supply shocks. The governor is required to sign a contract, the Policy Targets Agreement, with the finance minister, in which the governor agrees to a target range for inflation set by the finance minister, the period for achieving it, and the penalty of dismissal for failing to meet the target. That arrangement has served New Zealand well in terms of achieving a low rate of inflation while letting its currency float on the foreign exchange market. Unlike countries with pegged exchange rates and no monetary rule, New Zealand sailed through the Asian financial crisis quite smoothly.

Congress should draw on the experience of New Zealand to create a credible monetary law that holds the chairman of the Fed accountable for achieving long-run price stability.

Abolish the Exchange Stabilization Fund

If the Fed is to focus solely on maintaining the purchasing power of the dollar, then it cannot also use monetary policy to peg the foreign exchange, or external, value of the dollar. The dollar must be free to float without exchange market intervention. Halting such intervention requires that Congress abolish the Exchange Stabilization Fund, which was created in 1934 by the Gold Reserve Act. The ESF has been used by the Treasury to try to ''stabilize'' the external value of the dollar, but without success. It has also been used to make dollar loans to support the currencies of less-developed countries. It is time to get rid of this relic of the New Deal and let markets, not the state, determine the relative price of the dollar.

Welcome the Evolution of Alternatives to Government Fiat Money

While Congress should hold the Fed responsible for maintaining the value of money, in terms of its domestic purchasing power, Congress should also welcome the emergence of alternatives to government fiat money, such as digital cash. New monetary institutions should be allowed to evolve as new technology and information become available.

The growth of electronic commerce will increase the demand for new methods of payment, methods that economize on paper currency. As consumers' trust in electronic cash grows, the demand for the Fed's base money may decrease. That may actually make it easier for a monetary rule to be implemented because the Fed need not worry about complications arising from changes in the ratio of currency to deposits, according to University of Georgia economist George Selgin. Indeed, Milton Friedman's simple rule of zero growth of the monetary base may work quite well in the information age, and it may be a step toward private competing currencies, as advocated by F. A. Hayek. Consumers would have greater monetary freedom and money with the best record of stable purchasing power as a result.

A concrete measure to promote greater monetary choice would be for Congress to repeal the 1 percent tax on bank-issued notes that is still on the books (U.S.C., title 12, section 541), as suggested by Kurt Schuler, an economist with the Joint Economic Committee.

Conclusion

Monetary disturbances have been either a major cause of or a key accentuating factor in business fluctuations. Reducing uncertainty about the future path of nominal GDP and the price level would help remove erratic money as a disrupting influence in economic life. As Friedman has pointed out, one of the most important things monetary policy can do is "prevent money itself from being a major source of economic disturbance."

It is time for Congress to accept its constitutional responsibility by making the Fed more transparent and holding it accountable for long-run price stability. In testimony before the Joint Economic Committee of the U.S. Congress in March 1995, economist David Meiselman summed up the case for limiting Fed discretion and mandating a stable price-level rule:

> It is . . . dangerous folly to expect or depend on the Fed to achieve what is beyond its power to attain. The best possible monetary policy cannot create jobs or production. It can only prevent the instability, the uncertainty, and the loss of employment and income resulting from poor monetary policy. In my judgment, the best possible monetary policy aims to achieve a stable and predictable price level.

Congress should now heed that advice and create an institutional framework that recognizes the limits of monetary policy and sets a firm basis for a credible long-run commitment to stable money in the post-Greenspan era. Monetary policy should not depend on any one individual. It should depend on rules that limit discretion, mandate price stability, and hold the Fed chairman accountable for failing to achieve money of stable value. Financial markets will then show less anxiety upon the departure of the "wise one."

The Greenspan record can be extended by moving from discretion to a clear rule for price stability, thereby converting trust in a particular individual into confidence in a rule that will long outlast any single Fed chairman. Ending stop-go monetary policy will generate social benefits by reducing the uncertainty due to erratic money, making it easier to plan long-term investment projects and increasing the efficiency of resource allocation. Economic growth will be more robust as a result.

The major thrust of this chapter has been to call on Congress to make the Fed accountable for maintaining the long-run value of the currency. But Congress should not limit its vision to a monetary system dominated by a government-run central bank, even if that institution is limited by a monetary rule. Rather, Congress should welcome the vision of a future in which the free market plays an important role in supplying money of stable value, in competition with the Fed. The choice of monetary institutions should ultimately be a free choice, made by the market, not dictated by law.

Suggested Readings

Dorn, James A. "Alternatives to Government Fiat Money." *Cato Journal* 9, no. 2 (Fall 1989): 277–94.

Dorn, James A., ed. *The Future of Money in the Information Age*. Washington: Cato Institute, 1997.

Dorn, James A., and Anna J. Schwartz, eds. *The Search for Stable Money*. Chicago: University of Chicago Press, 1987.

Friedman, Milton. "The Role of Monetary Policy." *American Economic Review* 58 (1968): 1–17.

Gwartney, James, Kurt Schuler, and Robert Stein. "Achieving Monetary Stability at Home and Abroad." *Cato Journal* 21, no. 2 (Fall 2001): 183–203.

Keleher, Robert E. "A Response to Criticisms of Price Stability." Study for the Joint Economic Committee of the U.S. Congress, September 1997, www.house.gov/jec.

McCallum, Bennett T. "Choice of Target for Monetary Policy." *Economic Affairs* (Autumn 1995): 35–41.

Meiselman, David I. "Accountability and Responsibility in the Conduct of Monetary Policy: Mandating a Stable Price Level Rule." Testimony before the Joint Economic Committee of the U.S. Congress on the Humphrey-Hawkins Act. 104th Cong., 1st sess., March 16, 1995.

Niskanen, William A. "On the Death of the Phillips Curve." *Cato Journal* 22, no. 2 (Fall 2002).

––––––. "A Test of the Demand Rule." *Cato Journal* 21, no. 2 (Fall 2001): 205–9.

Poole, William. "Is inflation Too Low?" *Cato Journal* 18, no. 3 (Winter 1999): 453–64.

––––––. "Monetary Policy Rules?" Federal Reserve Bank of St. Louis *Review* 81 (March–April 1999): 3–12.

Reynolds, Alan. "The Fed's Whimsical Monetary Tinkering." *Outlook: Ideas for the Future from Hudson Institute* 1, no. 4 (April 1997): 1–16.

––––––. "The Fiscal Monetary Policy Mix." *Cato Journal* 21, no. 2 (Fall 2001): 263–75.

Schuler, Kurt. "Note Issue by Banks: A Step toward Free Banking in the United States?" *Cato Journal* 20, no. 3 (Winter 2001): 453–65.

Schwartz, Anna J. "Time to Terminate the ESF and the IMF." Cato Institute Foreign Policy Briefing no. 48, August 26, 1998.

Walsh, Carl E. "Accountability in Practice: Recent Monetary Policy in New Zealand." FRBSF Economic Letter no. 96-25, September 9, 1996.

—Prepared by James A. Dorn

21. Financial Deregulation

Congress should

- repeal the Community Reinvestment Act of 1977,
- reject the Federal Deposit Insurance Reform Act of 2002 (H.R. 3717) that calls for increasing the deposit insurance limit to $130,000 and gives the Federal Deposit Insurance Corporation greater discretion in the setting of insurance premiums,
- enact the Bankruptcy Abuse Prevention and Consumer Protection Act of 2002 with stronger provisions, and
- revoke Fannie Mae's and Freddie Mac's federal charters and fully privatize those two government-sponsored enterprises.

With the passage of the Depository Institutions Deregulation and Monetary Control Act of 1980, which removed ceilings on deposit interest rates, Congress began a gradual dismantling of the regulatory barriers that, since the Great Depression, had made the financial services industry among the most regulated sectors of the U.S. economy and the U.S. financial sector among the most regulated in the world. That regulatory burden also made the financial services industry unnecessarily fragile. The deregulatory trend continued with the Federal Deposit Insurance Improvement Act of 1991, which introduced some risk sensitivity to deposit insurance premiums; the Neal-Riegle Interstate Banking Act of 1994, which established nationwide banking networks by removing the geographic restrictions on branching; and the Gramm-Leach-Bliley Act of 1999, which repealed much of the Glass-Steagall Act of 1933 and the Bank Holding Company Act of 1956, created financial holding companies, and ended the artificial separation of insurance companies and commercial and investment banks. Some changes were just the legal recognition of something that was already happening in the marketplace. For instance, the computer and telecommunications revolution made geographic branching restrictions obsolete. Other changes, such as the ones to the FDICIA, were a reaction to crises precipitated by the existence of previous regulations. But while Congress deserves to be congratulated for its past efforts, there is much work left to do to eliminate the inefficiencies and risks created by previous regulations and to allow U.S. financial firms to give consumers the full range of financial services they demand.

The Community Reinvestment Act

One of the major shortcomings of the Gramm-Leach-Bliley Act is that it did not end the Community Reinvestment Act of 1977, a law enacted to encourage banks to help meet the credit needs of their entire communities, including low- and moderate-income neighborhoods, consistent with the safe and sound operation of banks. To the contrary, it gave the CRA more "teeth" by requiring that institutions have a satisfactory CRA rating before a merger involving those institutions can take place or before they engage in any of the new financial activities authorized under that law.

At present, federally insured lending institutions such as banks and thrifts are required to collect data on the loans they make and how those loans are allocated. Federal regulators then evaluate those data in a subjective and arbitrary manner to determine how well the financial institutions are meeting the credit needs of the neighborhoods from which they gather deposits. After all the work is done at considerable expense to the institutions that are rated and taxpayers who fund the agencies that conduct the examinations, about 98 percent of banks receive a satisfactory or better rating. (Banks receive one of four ratings: Outstanding, Satisfactory, Needs Improvement, and Substantial Non-Compliance.)

Some supporters of the CRA maintain that banks are lending in low-income neighborhoods because of the legislation. Others claim that the high percentage of banks that obtains a satisfactory rating or better is an indication that the current legislation is too lax and that it needs to be strengthened. But the fact is that there is no evidence that the CRA has had any discernible effects on lending in low-income or distressed neighborhoods, nor is there evidence that a stronger CRA would benefit low-income neighborhoods. Where profitable investment opportunities exist, banks are already lending. Where they do not, banks are not lending and should not be required to do so.

If the CRA had a real impact, we should expect financial institutions subject to its requirements to lend more aggressively in low-income communities than lending institutions that are not subject to the law. But Jeffery W. Gunther, an economist at the Federal Reserve Bank of Dallas, and others have shown the opposite to be true. Financial institutions subject to the CRA are actually lending less in low-income communities than institutions not subject to the CRA. The elimination of branching restrictions, financial innovations, the new technology that has allowed lenders to screen potential borrowers better (and thus differentiate between good and bad credit risks in the same neighborhoods), and increased competition have increased the availability of financial services to low-income communities. In this new and more competitive environment, banks are unlikely to forgo profitable lending opportunities to otherwise creditworthy borrowers—regardless of race, location, or any other noneconomic characteristic of those borrowers.

There is evidence, however, that the CRA has had at least four negative effects on the communities that it seeks to help. First, outside banks seeking mergers or an expansion of their activities will provide subsidized loans in low-income neighborhoods to avoid CRA-related problems, thus misallocating capital and driving customers away from local institutions that would have otherwise provided credit to local borrowers. Second, the CRA makes it difficult for banks to close branches in distressed areas. The unintended consequence is that other banks that might consider opening new branches in low-income neighborhoods may choose not to do so lest they be unable to close them at a future date. In the end, there is less competition in those areas and consumers suffer. Third, the CRA prevents banks from specializing in servicing specific groups because the banks do not want to be accused of discriminating against other groups. Finally, by increasing the costs to banks of doing business in distressed communities, the CRA makes banks likely to deny credit to marginal borrowers that would qualify for credit if costs were not so high. Chief among those costs is the hundreds of millions of dollars in CRA loans that community activists obtain from banks to give their approval of bank mergers and other bank expansions of activities, in an exercise that can be characterized as legalized extortion.

In the final analysis, the CRA provides few benefits to those it is meant to help, while imposing substantial compliance costs to banks and taxpayers. In addition, there is conclusive evidence that the problem that the CRA was intended to correct—lack of adequate access to credit in low-income neighborhoods—no longer exists. For those reasons, the CRA should not be reformed; it should be repealed.

Deposit Insurance Reform

The House of Representatives passed by a vote of 408 to 18 the Federal Deposit Insurance Reform Act of 2002 (H.R. 3717), a bill introduced by Rep. Spencer Bachus (R-Ala.). Among other things, that legislation would increase the coverage limit for insured deposits from the current $100,000 to $130,000, index the new limit to inflation, and adjust it every five years. It would also give the Federal Deposit Insurance Corporation greater discretion in the way it charges premiums on banks and allow it to charge premiums on banks at all times, regardless of the risk individual banks pose for the FDIC fund or of the size of the fund.

The increase in the coverage limit is the measure that has received the most attention in the press and from policymakers. Higher limits would weaken market discipline by making depositors more indifferent to the risks taken by their banks without improving the welfare of consumers (who already have many opportunities to get FDIC insurance equal to several times $100,000) or the competitive position of small banks (the strongest proponents of the increase) vis-à-vis large banks.

Both the Federal Reserve and the U.S. Treasury are vigorously opposed to the increase. Indeed, in remarks before the Senate Banking Committee in the spring of 2002, Peter Fisher, under secretary of the Treasury for domestic finance, said, "We see no sound public policy purpose that would be served by an increase in current and future coverage limits." Alan Greenspan concurred with that statement, noting that "it is unlikely that increased coverage, even by indexing, would add measurably to the stability of the banking system today."

Sen. Richard Shelby (R-Ala.), the ranking Republican on the Senate Banking Committee, also opposes the increase to $130,000. In an interview with the *American Banker*, Shelby stated his opposition to raising the current limit by saying, "Let's roll [that limit] back to $10,000." Reducing the limit makes sense for at least two reasons. First, depositors would become more vigilant about the risks taken by banks, thus increasing market discipline. That discipline would be even stronger if the limit were to apply to depositors instead of accounts or deposits. Second, depositors can already obtain risk-free U.S. Treasury bills that are equivalent to cash in terms of their liquidity. Thus the coverage limit for insured deposits should be no greater than the minimum denomination for short-term Treasury bills. Today, for instance, the minimum denomination for a four-week Treasury bill is $1,000. Any coverage amount above that represents a potential taxpayer subsidy of the risk-taking activities of banks.

From the point of view of the taxpayer, however, an increase in the coverage limit is not the most dangerous provision of the reform proposals. Giving the FDIC more discretion in the way it charges premiums on banks is the most dangerous provision, because it could very well mean that taxpayers could again be liable for any losses that occurred to the deposit insurance fund, just as they were in the 1980s when the savings-and-loan crisis cost them approximately $150 billion. All four banking regulators are unfortunately in favor of that measure.

Under the current structure, which has been in place since 1991, banks are responsible for any losses to the deposit insurance fund through a system of rapid *required* ex post premiums. If losses to the insurance fund reduce the FDIC's ratio of reserves to insured deposits below 1.25 percent, the FDIC is required to automatically increase premiums to at least 23 basis points if the 1.25 percent ratio is not achieved within one year.

Although many observers consider that system too harsh, because it imposes the highest premiums when banks are the least likely to be able to afford them, it has worked reasonably well in preserving the stability of the banking system—and the pocketbooks of taxpayers. As Loyola University banking and finance professor George Kaufman has written in a recent Cato Institute study, "The threat of a premium increase of 23 basis points serves to encourage banks to pressure the FDIC to resolve insolvencies more quickly and efficiently" and thus avoid regulatory forbearance or negligence.

Giving the FDIC more discretion over premium policy is undesirable because, as Kaufman says, "The longer premiums are not increased . . . the more likely the fund is to go into deficit and the taxpayer to again become liable." Indeed, it is likely that discretion will lead to regulatory forbearance because regulators will be under tremendous pressure from banks and politicians alike to delay the imposition of higher premiums, if and when banks get into trouble.

Furthermore, regulators may view bank failures as a black mark on their records and thus have an incentive to delay the imposition on failed banks of sanctions or even resolution proceedings. In short, regulators have often been poor guardians of the interests of taxpayers.

For that reason, it is important to consider the benefits of private, market-based regulation of banking. Federal deposit insurance is not market priced, despite FDICIA's mandate that the FDIC set premiums according to risk, and so the moral hazard of a government guarantee of deposits remains. To encourage the use of market discipline in the bank supervisory process, Congress should consider establishing a subordinated-debt requirement, so that the holders of that debt provide the main monitoring function in the supervisory process. A subordinated-debt requirement would align the interest of subordinated-debt holders with those of the deposit insurance fund (and hence taxpayers), because they do not profit from a bank's risky investments if those investments turn out to be profitable, but they stand to lose their money if those investments are not profitable. For that reason, holders of subordinated debt would have a very strong incentive to monitor closely the activities of banks. At the same time, yields on subordinated debt provide the market's assessment of the risks taken by banks. Indeed, the interest paid on subordinated debt could serve as a market-determined risk-adjusted insurance premium.

At the very least, the current system of rapid *required* ex post premium increases to fund losses to the FDIC fund should be maintained with a reduction—not an increase—in the coverage limit, lest we compromise the safety and soundness of the U.S. banking system and revert to a system of unlimited taxpayer liability. Beyond that, Congress should consider moving toward a system of voluntary, privately funded and managed deposit insurance.

Real Bankruptcy Reform Needed Now More Than Ever

The 107th Congress passed bankruptcy reform legislation by wide margins in both the House and the Senate, just as the 106th Congress had done. This time, however, the House and Senate bills were reconciled in a conference committee to produce the Bankruptcy Abuse Prevention and Consumer Protection Act of 2002, which had the support of President Bush. Unfortunately, an abortion-related provision in the bankruptcy reform bill once again prevented Congress from enacting a much-needed reform that would curb somewhat the abuses that occur under the existing bankruptcy code, a code that makes filing for bankruptcy very attractive for many debtors, including those who can easily pay their debts.

At present, individual debtors can file for bankruptcy under Chapter 7 or Chapter 13 once every six years. Consumers who file under Chapter 13 agree to a court-approved plan for repaying their debts from future earnings over three to five years. Chapter 13 filers, however, do not have to liquidate their current assets to repay creditors.

Consumers who file under Chapter 7, on the other hand, must use all their present wealth above an exemption to repay their debts, but their postbankruptcy earnings remain untouched. The exemption includes personal items, equity in owner-occupied housing, retirement accounts, and cars. The justification for exempting those items and all future income is that it provides filers with a ''fresh start'' in life after bankruptcy.

But, because the exemption levels are usually very high or filers have few nonexempt assets, in more than 90 percent of Chapter 7 cases, there is no property to be liquidated. The result: creditors get nothing. Consequently, most consumers who file for bankruptcy do so under Chapter 7 rather than Chapter 13.

Under current law, the benefits of filing for bankruptcy greatly outweigh the costs for many households. The costs include the filing fee (usually a few hundred dollars), any attorneys' fees, the amount of debt repaid, and the tarnished reputation that comes from filing. That last item is becoming less significant, however, as the stigma associated with filing for bankruptcy continues to lessen. The benefit is the debt discharged, which, given the leniency of Chapter 7, usually is a large percentage of the total unsecured debt owed. The net financial gain, then, is the difference between the benefits and the costs—a figure that is often substantial. Indeed, Michelle White, an economist at the University of California at San Diego, estimates that about 15 percent of U.S. households could benefit from filing for bankruptcy under the current system.

From a policy perspective, a problem arises because lenders, who have a hard time distinguishing between good and poor credit risks, increase interest rates for *all* consumers to recoup the losses that they incur from unpaid loans. As more and more consumers file for bankruptcy and discharge their debts, interest rates for consumer credit increase to compensate lenders for their losses. White estimates that the average borrower pays $500 a year in extra charges to compensate lenders for those unpaid loans. Thus, to the extent that innocent consumers are paying for the sins of the guilty, the current system works against honest borrowers.

The proposed legislation would reduce the perverse incentives of the current system by introducing a means test for bankruptcy. Consumers who earn more than the median income in their state and have enough disposable income to repay, over a five-year period, at least one-quarter of their debts, or $6,000, whichever is greater, would have to file under Chapter 13. The likely effect is that more people would file under Chapter 13 or refrain altogether from filing after the legislation is implemented.

The legislation, however, would not affect individuals whose incomes are below the regional median. For that reason, the current system, with all its problems, would remain unchanged for a great number of consumers. Indeed, it is estimated that fewer than 15 percent of the people who would otherwise file under Chapter 7 would be forced to file under Chapter 13 under the reform plan. A better reform would require those whose incomes are below the median to pay a (smaller) percentage of their debts based on their ability to pay—but to pay something nonetheless.

The reform legislation also leaves many loopholes, such as the homestead exemption (albeit with tighter limits), contributions of up to 15 percent of gross income to charities, allowances of up to $1,500 per child per year for schooling, contributions to ERISA-approved retirement plans, and an exemption for all tax-free retirement accounts (with a $1 million cap for IRAs), that make it easier for filers not to pay their debts. The legislation does not put in place a minimum level of debt below which debtors should not be able to file for bankruptcy. The establishment of such a threshold would make the system more cost-effective. The 108th Congress has an opportunity to correct those shortcomings.

A bankruptcy system, no matter how stringent, will always allow some debtors to abuse it to the detriment of honest consumers. Those consumers and creditors, however, will likely welcome a reform bill that protects their property rights, enforces contracts more vigorously, and reduces the incentives some people have to cheat. The 108th Congress should put politics aside and get the job done.

Time to Privatize Fannie Mae and Freddie Mac

The Federal National Mortgage Association (Fannie Mae) and the Federal Home Loan Mortgage Corporation (Freddie Mac), the two most important government-sponsored enterprises (GSEs), are an anomaly in today's vibrant and innovative financial markets. GSEs are created by congressional charter and combine characteristics of public and private organizations. Fannie Mae and Freddie Mac are privately owned, publicly traded corporations that have a congressional mandate to provide liquidity in the secondary markets for residential mortgages. They do so mostly by purchasing mortgages from lenders, bundling those mortgages into mortgage-backed securities (MBS), and selling those securities to investors. Since the early 1980s, but especially in the last few years, they have also started to hold directly many of the mortgages they buy and to hold MBS themselves. In the process they have become two of the most profitable and dominant companies in the United States today.

If that success were due to their ability to provide goods and services that consumers want under the same rules as other market participants but at a lower price, then there would be no public policy concerns about Fannie Mae and Freddie Mac. Unfortunately, Fannie Mae and Freddie Mac do not operate under the same rules as other market participants.

They enjoy government-granted benefits and subsidies that give them an unfair advantage over their competitors, create distortions in the allocation of capital, and pose an unnecessary risk to taxpayers.

In exchange for serving a public mission, Fannie Mae and Freddie Mac enjoy an implicit government (taxpayer) subsidy to cover their liabilities. The subsidy results from, among other things, the perception that the government stands behind the obligations of those two companies, which allows Fannie Mae and Freddie Mac to have lower costs of capital than their competitors. The Congressional Budget Office has estimated that in 2000 the implicit subsidy provided by the government amounted to $10.6 billion, of which 37 percent went directly to their shareholders, not to homebuyers. Other government benefits include a $2.25 billion line of credit from the U.S. Department of the Treasury, exemption from Securities and Exchange Commission securities registration requirements, exemption from local and state taxes, and lower capital requirements than are imposed on other financial institutions, which allows them to operate with much greater leverage and earn a higher return on capital than their competitors.

While most public and congressional attention in recent months has concentrated on the fact that the two GSEs are not subject by law to the same disclosure and registration requirements as other publicly traded companies, that criticism should not be the main focus of attention for at least two reasons. First, Fannie Mae and Freddie Mac already disclose voluntarily enough information about their financial activities and condition. Furthermore, they agreed in July 2002 to file quarterly and annual statements and proxies with the SEC (although they did not agree to register their debt and mortgage-backed securities). Second, in this case, what matters is not so much disclosure; after all, Fannie and Fred could disclose that they intend to keep all profits from a very risky investment, if that investment is successful, and to pass most losses on to taxpayers, if it is not, and that disclosure would not make them any less risky. What matters is whether Fannie Mae and Freddie Mac have capital levels that are adequate for the degree of risk they are taking and for the amount of debt they have, because, if they do not, the government will most surely step in and bail them out at a very high cost to taxpayers.

Today that does not seem to be the case, and the two GSEs have no incentive to raise their capital levels or diminish their risk profiles (nor do investors have an incentive to require those actions from them) because of the government guarantee. Fannie Mae and Freddie Mac had a total debt outstanding of $1.3 trillion at the end of 2001 and had guaranteed an additional $1.8 trillion of MBS. Capital levels stood at roughly 3.5 percent of total assets, about a third of the capital levels held by commercial banks in the United States. In addition, they have in recent years begun to hold directly the mortgages they purchase, which exposes them to interest rate risk as well as credit risk, and to enter the subprime mortgage markets, where the credit risk is much higher.

The combination of the high-risk profile of their portfolios, low capital levels, and high levels of debt makes Fannie Mae and Freddie Mac potentially very vulnerable. For that reason, and given that the secondary market for mortgages works very well, Congress should initiate steps— including revoking their federal charters, terminating their Treasury lines of credit, and the presidential appointment of five members to their board of directors—toward the full privatization of Fannie Mae and Freddie Mac.

Conclusion

Technological change and financial innovation have radically transformed the financial services marketplace in the last few years to the benefit of financial services firms and consumers alike. More important, the transformation will likely continue in the coming years and financial regulations are unlikely to be able to keep up with market developments, which could prevent an efficient and sound modernization of the U.S. financial system. Although the process of modernization will not necessarily be smooth, regulators and Congress must resist temptations to go back to the old, rigid structure that came undone with the Gramm-Leach-Bliley Act. Market forces, if allowed to do so, can be very effective in exerting the discipline necessary to minimize conflicts of interest and in correcting any shortcomings that may come along the way. Congress should continue with the elimination of the regulatory burden to which financial services firms are subject and let the shape of the financial marketplace be determined by buyers and sellers of financial services.

Suggested Readings

Benston, George J. "The Community Reinvestment Act: Looking for Discrimination That Isn't There." Cato Institute Policy Analysis no. 354, October 6, 1999, www.cato.org/pubs/pas/pa-354es.html.

Congressional Budget Office. "Federal Subsidies and the Housing GSEs." 2001, ftp://ftp.cbo.gov/28xx/doc2841/GSEs.pdf.

Gunther, Jeffery W. "Should the CRA Stand for 'Community Redundancy Act'?" Regulation 23, no. 3 (2000): 56–60.

Kaufman, George G. "FDIC Reform: Don't Put Taxpayers Back at Risk." Cato Institute Policy Analysis no. 432, April 16, 2002, www.cato.org/pubs/pas/pa-432es.html.

Poole, William. "Financial Stability." Remarks made at the Council of State Governments, Southern Legislative Conference Annual Meeting, New Orleans, August 4, 2002, www.stlouisfed.org/news/speeches/2002/08_04_02.html.

Rodríguez, L. Jacobo. "International Banking Regulation: Where's the Market Discipline in Basel II?" Cato Institute Policy Analysis no. 455, October 15, 2002.

Wallison, Peter J., and Bert Ely. *Nationalizing Mortgage Risk*. Washington: American Enterprise Institute, 2000.

—Prepared by L. Jacobo Rodríguez

22. Enron, WorldCom, and Other Disasters

Congress should

- clarify that the criminal penalties in the Sarbanes-Oxley Act require proof of malign intent and personal responsibility for some illegal act,
- repeal the Williams Act of 1968,
- approve the deduction of *one-half* of dividend payments from the earnings subject to the corporate income tax, and
- eliminate the limit on salaries that may be deducted from the earnings subject to the corporate income tax.

The collapse of the Enron Corporation in late 2001 led to two broad concerns:

- There may be more "Enrons" out there, because many other firms share the characteristics that led to the Enron collapse. This concern was reenforced by the subsequent collapse of Global Crossing, World-Com, and some other large corporations and was reflected by the general weakness of the stock markets and the dollar, even though most of the subsequent economic news was better than expected.
- The revelation of gross accounting violations by these and other firms and the continued weakness of the financial markets have undermined both popular and political support for free-market policies. This effect has already led to the increased regulation of accounting and auditing authorized by the Sarbanes-Oxley Act, proposals for even more regulation, and increased criticism of any proposal for privatization. Any number of critics have been quick to blame many of the problems of the modern world on the corporate culture, with a potential effect similar to that of the muckrakers in shaping and promoting the early progressive legislation.

While these issues deserve further study, some lessons can be drawn now.

Enron Is a Symbol of a Broader Problem

Enron filed for bankruptcy protection on December 2, 2001, a consequence of the combination of too much debt and some unusually risky major investments. Such conditions are characteristic of firms that declare bankruptcy and, by themselves, are not sufficient evidence of a broader problem. The optimal number of bankruptcies is not zero because our broader interests are served by corporations using some amount of debt finance and taking some risks. Moreover, Enron did not collapse because it broke the accounting rules, although it apparently broke some rules to cover up its financial weakness. The collapse of Enron led to huge losses to Enron investors, creditors, and employees but, by itself, had little effect on other parties. The conditions specific to Enron will be adequately sorted out by the market and the courts.

As expressed by one blunt-speaking investment manager, however, "Enron ain't the problem. . . . The unremarked gut issue today is that over the past decade there was a landslide transfer of wealth from public shareholders to corporate managers. Enron was just the tip of the iceberg ready to happen." For the larger community, the important issue is not the specific reasons why Enron collapsed but whether the general rules affecting all corporations lead managers to use too much debt and to incur too many risks. Another important issue raised by the Enron collapse is why these conditions either escaped notice or were not acted upon by any link in the audit chain.

The broader pattern of financial developments since the mid-1990s is clearly more consistent with a description of Enron as "the tip of the iceberg" than with a view that the collapse of Enron was merely a random observation from a stable distribution of potential corporate failures. Something is seriously wrong in corporate America. General shareholders, now a majority of Americans, have a financial interest in correcting the conditions that led to these problems. Those of us who are concerned about maintaining the necessary popular and political support for a market economy have a special political stake in correcting these conditions.

Some Corrective Actions Have Been Taken

The collapse of Enron proved to be a valuable wake-up call to a number of affected groups. The following actions have already been taken by private organizations:

- The Business Roundtable, composed of the chief executives of about 150 large firms, urged corporations to adopt a number of voluntary changes in corporate governance rules, including that a "substantial majority" of corporate boards be independent "both in fact and appearance."
- The New York Stock Exchange and the National Association of Securities Dealers approved major additions and changes in the rules for accounting, auditing, and corporate governance as necessary conditions for listing of a corporation's stock for trade on the exchange. The major continuing uncertainty is how the exchanges will monitor and enforce these rules.
- The International Corporate Governance Network, institutional investors that control about $10 trillion in assets, has approved a set of international standards for corporate governance that its members would use their voting power to promote.
- Merrill Lynch, the nation's largest retail broker, signed an agreement with the New York State attorney general that its stock market analysts "will be compensated for only those activities and services intended to benefit Merrill Lynch investor clients," as determined by their superiors in the research department. This agreement was designed to reduce any conflict of interest between the market analysis and investment banking activities of Merrill Lynch and is expected to be adopted by other major brokerage firms.
- Standard and Poor's, one of the three major credit-rating agencies, has developed a new concept of "core earnings" as a measure of earnings from a company's primary lines of business. Compared with earnings as defined by the generally accepted accounting principles (GAAP), for example, the S&P measure will exclude gains and losses from a variety of financial transactions. S&P plans to report this measure of earnings for all publicly held U.S. companies.

Most important, the long bear market has changed the attitude of many corporate managers and directors. In good times, no one manages the store in firms that make an adequate rate of return, even though other firms may have a significantly higher rate of return. Over the past two years, however, corporate managers have been quicker to reduce employment and close plants in response to weak demand, productivity growth has continued to be high as a consequence, and corporate boards appear to have been more cautious about approving new investments and increased executive compensation. The important test is whether the costly lessons of this period will survive a recovery of demand and another long bull market.

In the meantime, after much sound and fury, Congress approved the Sarbanes-Oxley Act by an overwhelming margin. As is too often the case, Congress responded to a new problem that it does not understand by creating a new bureau, in this case a Public Company Accounting Oversight Board to oversee public accountants. The act also authorized a 64 percent increase in the budget of the Securities and Exchange Commission, a strange reward for the failure of the SEC to uncover any of the major recent accounting violations. The act also makes some minor changes in audit rules and authorizes a substantial increase in criminal penalties for a broader array of white-collar crimes.

The Sarbanes-Oxley Act is a result of a political demand to "do something" about a problem of shared concern. The act was unnecessary, in that the SEC had the authority and had already implemented most of the prescribed actions. The act is expensive, in that the huge increase in the SEC budget is not likely to improve accounting and auditing very much. More disturbing, the major potential problem is an awesome threat that senior corporate managers may be held liable for an illegal action by some subordinate that the senior manager did not direct, condone, or even know about. Congress has wisely refrained from applying this standard to government managers, even though the General Accounting Office reported in 1998 that "significant financial systems weaknesses . . . prevent the government from accurately reporting a large portion of its assets, liabilities, and costs." On first hearing of the Enron breakup, my reaction was that someone ought to go to jail as a consequence; that is an understandable but not very nuanced reaction. Unfortunately, Congress does not seem to have thought much beyond that first reaction. At a minimum, Congress should clarify that the criminal penalties in the Sarbanes-Oxley Act require proof of malign intent and personal responsibility for some illegal act.

Unfinished Business

Most important, the corrective actions taken to date will not be sufficient to reduce the frequency and magnitude of corporate bankruptcies. Enron and other large corporations failed by making unusually bad business decisions, *not* by violating the accounting standards. A blatant violation of accounting rules and auditing procedures clearly offends the general public and the political community, but the losses to a corporation's shareholders, creditors, employees, and local communities are more directly related to the failure of the corporation than to the measures its managers may have taken to delay recognition of its financial weakness. Without changes in the policy-related conditions that contribute to corporate failure, improved accounting and auditing procedures would accelerate bankruptcies with little effect on their frequency or magnitude. Almost all of the public and press attention, however, has focused on reducing the accounting violations, not on those policies that contribute to business failure.

The major lesson from the collapse of Enron and other large corporations is that the rules of corporate governance do not adequately protect the interests of the general shareholders against the increasingly divergent interests of corporate managers. In other words, "the agency problems" that result from the separation of ownership and control posed by Berle and Means in 1932 have not yet been fully solved and may have recently increased. The rules of corporate governance—in effect the "constitution" of a corporation—are a complex combination of federal securities law, the conditions for listing on some stock exchange or for access to credit, the corporate regulations and court decisions of the state in which the firm is incorporated, and company-specific rules.

Over time, moreover, there has been some drift from rules that protect shareholders to rules that protect corporate managers. The first major policy change in this direction was the federal Williams Act of 1968, which substantially increased the cost for outsiders to organize a successful tender offer and entirely removed the potential for surprise. More important were decisions by state legislatures and state courts in the 1980s in response to demands by corporate managers. And the superstar CEOs of the 1990s were able to persuade their passive boards to agree to almost any rule. Over this period, in addition, the major outside shareholder in an increasing number of firms was some pension or mutual fund that had interests so diversified that its management had little interest in the performance of any one stock in the fund's portfolio; these funds very rarely use their voting power to place a representative on a corporate board. Very few corporate boards now include a member with a sufficient portion of the total shares to be a credible threat to incumbent management. As a consequence, according to the leading scholar of the market for corporate control, "it should come as no surprise that, as hostile takeovers declined from 14 percent to 4 percent of all mergers, executive compensation started a steep climb, eventually ending for some companies with bankruptcy and management scandal. . . . Enron is a predictable consequence of rules that inhibit the efficient functioning of the market for corporate control.'' The most important policy lesson from the collapse of Enron is to repeal or reverse those laws, regulations, and court decisions that restrict successful tender offers. The probable results would be a reduction in executive compensation, less pressure to cook the books, an improved allocation of capital, and an increase in the rate of return to general shareholders. Congress should start this process by repealing the Williams Act of 1968.

Another major issue that has been broadly ignored in discussions about the policy lessons from the Enron collapse is that the current U.S. tax code *increases* the conditions that lead to bankruptcy. The corporate earnings subject to tax, for example, exclude interest payments but not dividends; this leads corporations to use more debt finance than would be the case if the tax treatment of interest and dividends were the same. The combined federal and state corporate income tax rate in the United States is now the fourth highest among the industrial nations, so one should expect American corporations to be relatively dependent on debt finance. Second, for most investors, the tax rate on dividend income is much higher than the rate on long-term capital gains; this leads corporations to rely more on retained earnings and capital gains than on dividends as the return to equity. And third, an obscure provision of the 1993 tax law limits to $1 million a year the direct compensation of corporate executives that may be deducted, unless the compensation is ''performance based.'' These biases in the tax code also lead to several other adverse effects— reducing the cash-flow discipline to meet dividend payments, increasing the role of corporate managers relative to investors in the allocation of capital, increasing the use of stock options to compensate corporate executives, and increasing the incentive to inflate the stock price.

Reducing the bias in favor of debt requires reducing the effective tax rate on corporate earnings. Reducing the bias in favor of retained earnings and capital gains requires deducting some amount of dividends from the earnings subject to the corporate income tax *or* reducing the difference between the personal income tax rate on dividends and long-term capital gains. The simplest direct way to reduce both of the first two of these tax-related biases is to allow corporations to deduct *one-half* of their dividend payments from the earnings subject to the corporate income tax. This would make the combined corporate and personal tax rate on capital gains and dividends about the same for most investors without changing any other feature of the corporate or personal income tax code, roughly eliminating those adverse conditions attributable to the current difference in these rates. Over the past several years, in addition, this would have reduced corporate income tax liability by about $60 billion a year, substantially reducing the bias in favor of debt finance. Other tax revenues, of course, would increase due to an improved allocation of capital, increased corporate investment, and higher personal income tax revenues from increased dividend payments. For those who would otherwise be opposed to reducing corporate income tax liability or considering any supply-side benefits of lower tax rates, Cato has long maintained a list of federal corporate welfare spending, the elimination of which would more than offset the reduction of corporate income tax liability. The most important simple change in the federal tax code, thus, would be to authorize corporations to deduct one-half of their dividend payments from the earnings subject to the corporate income tax. The third tax bias in favor of stock-based compensation should be eliminated by the simple repeal of the 1993 limit on the amount of direct compensation that may be deducted. A full elimination of the bias in favor of debt finance would require a more comprehensive tax reform that would either eliminate the corporate income tax *or* any personal taxes on capital gains and dividends.

In summary, Congress should not rest on the faded laurels of the Sarbanes-Oxley Act. More needs to be done to reduce the conditions that lead to corporate failure and to restore American corporations to financial health and integrity. The policy changes recommended in this chapter may be the most important, but other changes are likely to be suggested by completion of Cato's project on the major policy lessons from the collapse of Enron.

Suggested Readings

Gompers, Paul A., Joy Ishii, and Andrew Metrick. "Corporate Governance and Equity Prices." NBER Working Paper no. 8449, August 2001.

Manne, Henry G. "Bring Back the Hostile Takeover." *Wall Street Journal*, June 26, 2002.

Niskanen, William A. "A Preliminary Perspective on the Major Policy Lessons from the Collapse of Enron." Cato Institute white paper, www.cato.org.

Sosnoff, Martin T. "Enron Ain't the Problem." *Directors and Boards*, Spring 2002.

—Prepared by William A. Niskanen

DOMESTIC POLICY

23. The Federal Budget

Congress should

- reduce discretionary spending from 7.1 percent of gross domestic product to 5 percent with program terminations, privatization, management reforms, and transfer of programs to the states (see proposed cuts in the Appendix to this chapter);
- reform Social Security by moving toward a system of individual savings accounts;
- reform Medicare and Medicaid to cut costs and increase efficiency; not add a prescription drug benefit to Medicare unless there is a full one-for-one cost reduction elsewhere in the program;
- establish a "sunset" commission to automatically review all federal programs on a rotating basis and propose major reforms and terminations;
- privatize all government-operated businesses, including Amtrak, the U.S. Postal Service, the Tennessee Valley Authority, and the four power marketing administrations;
- privatize activities in all federal agencies that are commercial in nature, such as air traffic control, marketing support for agriculture, loan and insurance programs for exporters, and research for the energy industry;
- sell excess asset holdings (land, buildings, and inventories) of federal departments such as Interior, Agriculture, and Defense; and
- support aggressive management reforms in the federal bureaucracy, including expanding authority to fire poorly performing workers.

Less Is More

The federal government will spend more than \$2,100,000,000,000 in fiscal year 2003. After taking out the government's core functions of national defense and justice, it will still spend more than $1,700,000,000,000. That amounts to roughly $16,000 for every household in the United States. Clearly, the federal government has taken on a huge range of spending programs beyond its basic responsibilities.

Indeed, the government is so large that the activities of hundreds of federal agencies are beyond the knowledge and understanding of most citizens. The government has become too large even for our representatives in Congress to adequately oversee and control, as scandal after scandal attests. Congress has shown itself to be incapable of running a $2 trillion organization with an adequate degree of competence. For example, the General Accounting Office has not been able to certify as correct the federal government's financial statements five years in a row because of weak accounting controls and widespread mismeasurement of assets, liabilities, and costs.

Modernist architects told us that "less is more" in building design. The same is true in government design. Americans would receive more benefit from the federal government if its size and scope were greatly reduced and they instead received a limited range of much better quality services. The federal government is like a bloated conglomerate corporation that is involved in too many different schemes for the CEO to properly oversee. The government does too much and does few things very well. Reforms must begin to shed all noncore functions of the federal government so that Congress and the administration can focus on delivering high-quality basic services, such as national security.

Short-Term Budget Outlook

The culture of spending in Washington that caused the Democrats to lose control of Congress in 1994 has triumphed again under the Republicans. The spending virus has spread throughout Congress with few members showing immunity. The struggles of fiscal conservatives to bring reforms to federal spending in the mid-1990s have been lost.

In 1994, there was a $203 billion deficit and red ink as far as the eye could see. The president's FY95 and FY96 budgets included no plans to balance federal finances. Ultimately, Congress forced the president's hand, and a plan to end the tide of red ink was passed. Spending constraint, a falling defense budget, and a strong economy produced the first budget surplus in 29 years in FY98.

But fiscal responsibility did not last long, and a gaping deficit appeared just four years later in FY02. Rapid discretionary spending growth averaging more than 7 percent annually between FY98 and FY02 busted the budget (Figure 23.1). The modest fiscal restraint shown in the mid-1990s evaporated, and no lasting lessons on spending discipline were learned by lawmakers.

One way to see how discretionary spending has ballooned is to compare current estimates for FY03 outlays with prior estimates of FY03 outlays. Actual FY03 outlays will be about $788 billion—that is a stunning $193 billion, or 32 percent, more than President Clinton's $595 billion proposal for FY03 in his FY99 budget. There has been a pattern of constant upward revisions in out-year spending in both the defense and nondefense budget categories (Figure 23.2).

Each year, Congress and the administration up the ante on each other's spending plans. Administrations often try to get as much spending as they can for the next budget year but then low-ball the out-years to make the long-term budget plan seem "fiscally responsible." President Bush has presided over huge increases in defense and nondefense discretionary outlays in his first two years (7.4 and 11.7 percent for defense, and 8.9 and 5.3 percent for nondefense, not including the emergency response fund). Yet the administration's July 2002 midsession review would have us believe that discretionary spending will be held to 3.1 percent annual growth from 2003 to 2007. Surely, the only real measure of fiscal responsi-

Figure 23.1
Discretionary Outlays: Defense and Nondefense

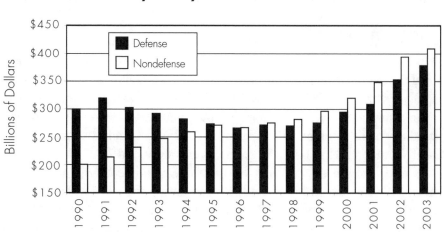

SOURCE: Office of Management and Budget, *Mid-Session Review*, July 2002. Includes emergency response fund.

Figure 23.2
Proposed Discretionary Outlays for FY03

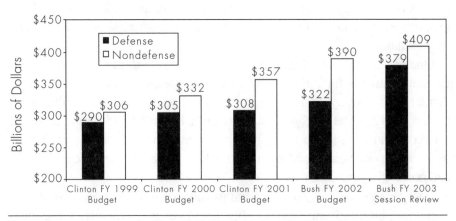

SOURCE: Office of Management and Budget, *Mid-Session Review*, July 2002, and prior budgets of the U.S. government. FY03 midsession review data include emergency response fund.

bility is how much money is being spent right now, not promises of restraint sometime in the future.

It should be obvious to every member of Congress that discretionary spending growth anywhere near recent high rates is not sustainable. The best course would be an immediate hard freeze on discretionary spending followed by large cuts. That is necessary because of the deep fiscal hole that entitlements will dig as health care costs rise and baby boomers begin retiring in a few years. Ultimately, discretionary spending should be reduced from today's 7.1 percent of gross domestic product to no more than 5 percent (see Appendix to this chapter for recommended cuts).

Long-Term Budget Outlook

In the late 1990s, a number of factors lulled Congress into complacency about the need for spending control. First, government revenues expanded rapidly as the economic boom filled federal coffers with income and capital gains tax revenues. Those inflows allowed Congress to increase spending rapidly while still balancing the budget and appearing to be fiscally prudent. That boom in revenues has now ended.

Second, growth of spending on the three major entitlements (Social Security, Medicare, and Medicaid) slowed during the late 1990s. Average annual Social Security growth slowed from 5.4 percent (1991–96) to 4.3 percent (1996–2001); Medicare growth slowed from 10.9 percent to 4.5 percent; and Medicaid growth slowed from 11.9 percent to 7.2 percent.

That slowdown has come to an end. Medicaid is expected to grow at an average annual rate of 8.4 percent during the next decade. For Social Security and Medicare, recent budget growth slowdowns are a brief respite before the spending explosion expected when baby boomers begin retiring in 2008.

All in all, Congressional Budget Office projections show that, under current law, spending on Social Security, Medicare, and Medicaid will increase from 8.3 percent of GDP in 2002 to 15.6 percent by 2040. That 7.3 percentage point increase would be equivalent to about a $750 billion per year tax increase today. By comparison, President Bush's tax rebates saved taxpayers just $40 billion in 2001. Therefore, unless entitlements are reformed, taxpayers will face an added burden rising to almost 20 times the size of the benefit received from the tax rebate in 2001.

Even if one assumed that all other government programs got no larger relative to GDP, the three main entitlements would push federal spending up from 20 percent of GDP today to 27 percent by 2040. State and local governments add about 10 percentage points to that burden, for a total of at least 37 percent of GDP by 2040. Thus without major entitlement reforms, the United States will have a government about as big as many European countries do today. And that outlook will be very optimistic if discretionary spending continues growing at the irresponsible 7 percent rate it has averaged since 1998.

If Americans want to limit the federal government to its current share of GDP, let alone shrink it, then entitlement programs must be thoroughly overhauled and Congress must begin shedding noncore government functions. If reforms are not made, the uniqueness of the United States as a limited-government country will be gone.

At the end of this chapter is a list of $309 billion in proposed spending cuts. These programs should be either terminated immediately, privatized, or transferred to state and local responsibility. It would be a major government reform if the whole list of cuts were made. But even that annual saving of $309 billion represents just 3 percent of GDP. Given that the three main entitlements are projected to impose at least a 7 percentage point cost increase on future taxpayers, these cuts must be paired with major entitlement reforms to solve tomorrow's huge budget problems.

Reform the Entitlements

A special analysis by the CBO in July 2000 found that federal spending on the elderly (through Social Security, Medicare, and other programs)

227

will rise from 35 percent of total federal spending in 2000 to 43 percent by 2010, under baseline assumptions. Spending on the elderly will continue rising rapidly and surpass half the budget by about 2020.

Despite these dramatic cost increases under current law, Congress continues to consider expensive add-ons to programs for the elderly. Most recently, lawmakers have pushed for costly Medicare prescription drug plans. But adding new burdens for taxpayers to pay for programs for the elderly is very unfair. The elderly have had their whole lives to save for their own retirement, yet the massive programs already provided for them create growing tax hurdles for young families trying to make ends meet and save for their own retirement. Victor Fuchs of Stanford University has found that 56 percent of the broadly measured income of the elderly now comes from transfers from the young.

Medicare prescription drug plans will cost hundreds of billions of dollars. In the 107th Congress, the 10-year cost of bills introduced in the Senate ranged from $295 billion for the Hagel-Ensign bill to $594 billion for the Graham-Miller bill. Of course, new programs usually end up costing much more than original estimates. Expanding Medicare when programs for the elderly are already going to blast a huge hole in future budgets is like "putting more people aboard the Titanic," as Sen. Phil Gramm (R-Tex.) observed. A prescription drug plan should be a nonstarter unless the package includes a full one-for-one offset in other Medicare costs.

Unfortunately, it seems difficult to have a sober, nonpartisan debate about entitlement reforms. Even modest reform plans by Democrats, such as Senator Breaux's Medicare plan in the late 1990s, are shot down. Nonetheless, the budgetary and economic necessity of reform is compelling, and ultimately reformers will prevail.

The key piece of the reform solution for Social Security and Medicare is prefunding of future benefits. The only sensible way to do that is through individual savings accounts. Prefunding will allow individuals to begin planning now to help pay for their own retirement, so as to avoid imposing crushing tax hikes on their children and grandchildren. (Medicare reforms are discussed in Chapter 26; Social Security reforms are discussed in Chapter 25.)

Reform Federal Management

A major fiscal theme of the Bush administration is reforming government management. The administration has begun grading federal programs and proposes to move funding away from "ineffective" activities. In addition, each federal agency is being scored with green, yellow, and red grades for performance on various parameters. Of 130 grades given in the baseline scores for 2001, 110 were red for "unsatisfactory." By mid-2002, the administration reported that there were still 109 red grades.

It is to be hoped that these efforts are the start of a major overhaul of the federal bureaucracy. As noted, the federal government has failed five years in a row to produce comprehensive financial statements that could be certified by the General Accounting Office. The sloppiest bookkeeper is probably the $370 billion Defense Department. The GAO has found that the department has "serious financial management problems that are pervasive, complex, longstanding, and deeply rooted in virtually all business operations throughout the department." The Pentagon loses track of assets, mismanages and wastes inventory, deliberately low-balls project costs, and makes billions of dollars of erroneous contractor payments.

New "carrots" should be used to get better performance from federal agencies. For example, pay raises should be contingent on passing grades on the president's new management scorecard. Managers in agencies that receive red grades for "unsatisfactory" should not receive pay raises until they fix problems.

In addition, new "sticks" need to be introduced to the bureaucracy. In the private sector, everyone from CEOs to mailroom clerks faces firing for bad performance. The *Washington Post* reported on August 18, 2002, that 37 percent of departing CEOs of the largest U.S. companies in recent years were fired. By contrast, data from the Office of Personnel Management show that the federal firing rate is stunningly low at just 1 in 4,000 per year. For example, the State Department has fired only 6 employees during the past 18 years. Yet it is hard to believe that there were not more poor performers deserving firing in this 29,000-person agency. Indeed, the State Department has been known for mishandling secret documents, allowing unauthorized people to wander its hallways, and letting Russian spies bug a meeting room down the hall from the former secretary's office.

Americans deserve better performance than that, and Congress is supposed to ensure it through executive branch oversight. But the reality is that the government's size and scope have become so vast that it is probably impossible for Congress to adequately safeguard taxpayer funds. The solution is to greatly cut the size of the government so it can focus on its core mission of national security. Both Ronald Reagan and the Republicans who stormed in to take control of Congress in 1994 sought major program terminations. So far, that understanding of real reform has not sunk into the Bush administration and has been absent from Congress for years. Lawmakers need to regain their commitment to a federal government that works—that means cutting out all the stuff that the government should not be doing and overhauling management of the rest.

Devolve Federal Programs to the States

Congress and the Bush administration seem to have accepted the idea that taxing citizens to send money to Washington and then routing funds back to state officials provides Americans with good government. That is a triumph of hope over experience. Experience shows that when the federal government gains more power over state functions, it results in bureaucratic waste and new layers of regulations for states to deal with.

Greater federal fiscal power also results in unfair redistributions of taxpayer money among the states on the basis of political pull rather than objective need. Some states get swindled by the federal money-go-round year after year in terms of federal taxes paid versus federal spending received. By comparing taxes paid by residents of each state with Census Bureau data on federal spending by state (which include everything from defense to transportation programs), you find that states such as New Jersey, Connecticut, and New Hampshire routinely get less than 75 cents on every dollar sent to Washington.

The federal redistribution of citizens' money gets worse as the federal government amasses more power over state and local functions, such as transportation and education. Aside from the unfairness and inefficiency involved in channeling money through Washington, it is clear that, if the government is spending its time worrying about potholes in Pittsburgh and SAT scores in St. Louis, then it is not devoting full attention to national security and other crucial concerns.

We have seen the most aggressive recent federal expansion of spending on education, which was traditionally a local function. In 1995, the House Republicans had slated the Department of Education for closing. Under President Clinton, education outlays rose fairly modestly from $30 billion in FY93 to $36 billion in FY01. But under President Bush, the department's outlays skyrocketed to $56 billion in FY03.

Much of the Department of Transportation's activities are properly state and private-sector responsibilities. It makes no sense to collect gasoline taxes from citizens, send them to Washington, then dole the money back to the states—minus the costs of the 100,000-plus-person DOT bureaucracy and its meddlesome rules. For example, federal funds come with

Davis-Bacon strings attached requiring union-level wages on highway projects. Moreover, Congress uses the DOT budget to deliver pork-barrel projects of dubious value. The federal government should end the federal gasoline tax and cease its highway, road, and mass transit spending functions.

In FY03, the federal government will pay out about $376 billion in grants in aid to state and local governments for health care, transportation, housing, education, and other programs. Congress should begin transferring these programs back to the states and reduce federal taxes by an equal amount. State and local governments are in a much better position to determine whether citizens are receiving value for their tax money on roads, schools, and other items. By federalizing such spending we are asking the U.S. Congress to do the impossible—to accurately balance in a neutral and selfless way the competing needs of a massive and diverse country of 280 million individuals.

Privatize Federal Assets

The federal government owns about one-third of the land in the United States and continues to accumulate more holdings. Yet only a fraction of federal land is of environmental significance, and the government has proven itself to be a poor land custodian. The process of federalizing the nation's land should be reversed by identifying low-priority holdings to sell back to citizens.

In addition to excess land, the federal government owns billions of dollars worth of other excess assets, including mineral stockpiles and buildings. For example, the Department of Defense operates large numbers of excess supply and maintenance depots, training facilities, medical facilities, research labs, and other installations that should be closed. In a positive move, DoD has begun to dispose of 80 million square feet of excess buildings it owns.

The federal government should also sell the operating businesses that it owns, including the U.S. Postal Service, Amtrak, electric utilities, and other agencies. Privatization has swept the world as governments abroad have recognized the superiority of private competitive markets. If a private postal system works in Germany and private air traffic control works in Canada, those industries ought to be private here, too (for further information, see Chapter 32).

Establish a Federal Sunset Commission

To structure the process of terminating federal agencies, Congress should establish a federal ''sunset'' commission. Sunsetting is a process of automatically terminating government agencies and programs after a period of time unless they are specifically reauthorized. Sunset legislation was introduced in the 107th Congress by Rep. Kevin Brady (R-Tex.). A sunset commission would review federal programs on a rotating basis and recommend major overhauls, privatization, or elimination.

Since the 1970s, numerous state governments have adopted the sunset process, and it is currently used in about 16 states. In the late 1970s, there was strong bipartisan support to pass a federal sunset law introduced by Sen. Edmund Muskie (D-Maine) that would have sunset most federal programs every 10 years. Supporters at the time ranged from Jesse Helms (R-N.C.) to Edward Kennedy (D-Mass.). Although it gained strong support in the Senate, the legislative effort failed in the House.

Today, sunsetting is needed more than ever. There is no structured method for reforming or terminating agencies when they no longer serve a public need or when better private alternatives become available. As a result, government agencies rarely disappear. For example, the Rural Utilities Service (formerly the Rural Electrification Administration) was created in the 1930s to bring electricity to rural homes. Virtually all American homes have had electricity for 20 years or more, yet the agency still survives.

A sunsetting process could help eliminate such agencies and add teeth to the Bush administration's efforts to move funds away from poorly performing programs. Programs that the administration grades as ''ineffective'' five years in a row could be automatically reviewed by the sunset commission and subject to termination. An alternative would be a new congressional procedure requiring a stand-alone vote on terminating an agency or program if the administration grades it as ineffective for five years.

Recent corporate scandals have illustrated that poor management and financial malfeasance can occur in any organization in society. But the scandals also show that private markets have mechanisms to correct excesses and rule breaking. In the private sector, poor performers are weeded out, executives and managers are sacked, and resources are shifted to better-run competitors. By contrast, the executive branch of government has no mechanism for creating the renewal that all organizations need in our fast-changing modern society. A federal sunset law would help to create renewal and reform in government.

Other Budget Process Reforms

Congress has done little to reform the budget rules that skew political decisionmaking in favor of ever-larger outlays. Now that the federal budget again has huge deficits, it is even more clear that lasting budget process reforms are needed. There has been much debate about which particular reforms would best restrain spending. But there is little to lose by experimenting with different budget control mechanisms, and any or all of the following reforms should be pursued.

Discretionary Spending Caps with a Freeze or Cut on Outlays

Caps on discretionary spending enacted in 1990, as extended, expired at the end of FY02. The caps, while far from perfect, did play a role in bringing discipline to spending in the 1990s. The caps should be extended and frozen at today's nominal total for discretionary outlays, or, even better, outlays should be put on a downward glide path. At the same time, rules on such items as emergency spending and advance appropriations need to be tightened to prevent Congress from bypassing the caps.

Tax and Expenditure Limitation

The federal government should implement a cap on overall annual budget growth, in the manner of the 26 states that have either statutory or constitutional limits on tax revenue or spending growth. Colorado's Taxpayer Bill of Rights is probably the most successful budget cap. It provides an automatic tax refund to citizens when tax revenues grow faster than the sum of inflation plus population growth. Such limits prevent governments from overexpanding during boom years, thus making it easier to balance the budget during recessions.

Balanced-Budget Amendment

Fiscal conservatives have long sought a balanced-budget amendment (BBA) to the U.S. Constitution. The return to large deficits shows that, once again, Congress cannot control its spending appetite and that further constraints are needed. However, there is a concern that a BBA could cause politicians to raise taxes during economic slowdowns to balance the budget. For that reason, a BBA should be paired with a supermajority tax limitation amendment that makes it more difficult for Congress to raise taxes.

Supermajority Tax Limitation Amendment

With or without a BBA in place, a supermajority requirement for tax increases makes sense. Under a supermajority tax limitation, any tax increase would require a two-thirds vote in the House and Senate for passage. When the economy grows, federal tax revenues tend to grow faster than incomes—even without legislated increases. Given this automatic upward tax bias, taxpayers should be provided with the extra protection of such a limitation against any legislated tax increases. (Note that a supermajority tax limitation amendment or the BBA would need a two-thirds vote in Congress and ratification by three-quarters of the states to become law.)

Reject Spending Programs as Unconstitutional

The U.S. Constitution confines federal spending authority to a few limited areas. Article I, section 8, allows for spending mainly on basic functions, such as establishing courts, punishing crime, and maintaining an army and navy. The General Welfare Clause in section 8 is said to provide a justification for much of today's $2.1 trillion in federal spending. But much of federal spending is not for "general welfare" at all. Rather, it is for the benefit of particular groups and individuals. For example, federal export loans of more than $1 billion to Enron, and other corporate welfare spending, are aimed at narrow interests, not the general interest. Members of Congress take an oath to uphold the Constitution. They should start taking that oath seriously. When a dubious program comes before them, they should ask whether there is proper constitutional authority for it given the limited role that is reserved for federal spending power.

Conclusion: Time for Bold Reforms

Bold fiscal reforms need to be pursued at both ends of Pennsylvania Avenue. The administration is under the shortsighted illusion that it can have bigger government in the selected areas it wants, such as defense, agriculture, education, and Medicare prescription drugs, but have tight limits on spending elsewhere. But that strategy leads to larger government everywhere because Congress is spurred to demand higher spending for all its favorite programs. Both Congress and the administration must end their shortsighted jostling for more taxpayer cash. Not only is the government running huge deficits again, but the looming explosion in entitlement costs demands that all aspects of the federal spending empire be overhauled.

Appendix: Proposed Program Terminations, Privatizations, and Transfers to the States (FY02 outlays in $ millions)

Department of Agriculture

Economic Research Service	$70
National Agricultural Statistics Service	$118
Agricultural Research Service	$1,104
Cooperative State Research, Educ., and Extension Serv.	$1,069
Agricultural Marketing Service	$770
Risk Management Agency	$2,978
Farm Services Agency (subsidies, loans, insurance)	$23,732
Rural Development	$946
Rural Housing Service	$287
Rural Business Cooperative Service	$76
Rural Utilities Service	$106
Foreign Agricultural Service	$1,167
Food and Nutrition Services	$38,003
Land Acquisition Programs	$101
Forest Service, State and Private Forestry	$441
Total Department of Agriculture	$70,968

Department of Commerce

Economic Development Administration	$493
International Trade Administration	$342
Export Administration	$80
Minority Business Development Agency	$25
National Ocean Service	$435
National Marine Fisheries Service	$675
National Environmental Satellite, Data, & Info. Serv.	$147
Advanced Technology Program	$187
Manufacturing Extension Program	$111
Other Nat. Inst. of Standards & Tech. Programs	$361
National Telecommunications & Info. Admin.	$112
Total Department of Commerce	$2,968

Department of Defense (see Chapter 48)

Department of Education
Total—terminate, privatize, or transfer to states all programs $47,587

Department of Energy
General Science, Research, and Development	$3,240
Energy Supply	$695
Fossil Energy, Research and Development	$544
Energy Conservation	$831
Strategic Petroleum Reserve	$166
Energy Information Administration	$80
Clean Coal Technology	$75
Power Marketing Administration subsidies	$145
FreedomCAR	$150
Total Department of Energy	$5,926

Department of Health and Human Services
Indian Health Service	$2,874
Substance Abuse and Mental Health Serv. Admin.	$2,918
Agency for Health Care Research and Quality	$91
Temporary Assistance for Needy Families	$18,334
Payments to States for Family Support Programs	$3,558
Low-Income Home Energy Assistance	$1,831
Promoting Safe and Stable Families	$300
Child Care Entitlements to States	$2,536
Block Grants to States for Child Care and Dev.	$1,917
Social Services Block Grant	$1,803
Payments to States for Foster Care and Adoption	$6,098
Violent Crime Reduction Programs	$25
Administration on Aging	$1,137
Total Department of Health and Human Services	$43,422

Department of Housing and Urban Development
Total—terminate, privatize, or transfer to states all programs $30,948

Department of the Interior
Bureau of Indian Affairs	$2,217
Bureau of Reclamation	$999
U.S. Geological Survey	$923
Sport Fish Restoration Fund	$312
Land Acquisition Programs	$271
Total Department of the Interior	$4,722

Department of Justice
    Juvenile Justice Programs $208
    Community Oriented Policing Services $1,057
    State and Local Law Enforcement Assistance $1,722
    Weed and Seed Program $41
    Drug Enforcement Administration $1,537
    Interagency Crime and Drug Enforcement $335
Total Department of Justice $4,900

Department of Labor
    Training & Employment Services $5,860
    Welfare to Work $491
    Community Service Employ. for Older Americans $469
    Trade Adjustment Assistance $415
Total Department of Labor $7,235

Department of State/International Assistance Programs
    United Nations Organizations $595
    United Nations Peacekeeping Activities $1,565
    United Nations Arrearage Payments $826
    Inter-American Organizations $126
    North Atlantic Treaty Organization $42
    Org. for Economic Cooperation & Dev. $49
    Migration and Refugee Assistance $762
    Int. Narcotics Control & Law Enforcement $350
    Andean Counterdrug Initiative $409
    Economic Support Fund $2,955
    Foreign Military Financing Program $4,237
Total Department of State/International Assistance Programs $11,916

Department of Transportation
    Federal Railroad Administration $1,089
    Federal Transit Administration $6,112
    Grants-in-Aid for Airports $2,801
    Essential Air Service program $53
    Air Traffic Control operations $5,792
    Maritime Administration $651
    Federal Highway Administration $28,729
Total Department of Transportation $45,227

Department of the Treasury
    Customs Service, Air and Marine Interdiction $198
    Community Development Financial Institutions $115
    Interagency Crime and Drug Enforce. Task Force $92
Total Department of the Treasury $405

Department of Veterans Affairs
    V.A. Health Care Facilities Construction $398
Total Department of Veterans Affairs $398

Other Agencies and Activities
    Agency for International Development $3,390
    Assistance for Eastern Europe $402
    Assistance for Former Soviet Union $484
    African Development Fund $57
    Appalachian Regional Commission $109
    Commission on Civil Rights $9
    Corporation for National and Community Service $433
    Corporation for Public Broadcasting $375
    Corps of Engineers $4,975
    Equal Employment Opportunity Commission $331
    Cargo Preference Program $673
    Export-Import Bank $1,044
    Federal Drug Control Program $457
    Federal Labor Relations Board $29
    International Assistance Programs (multilateral) $2,089
    Legal Services Corporation $329
    NASA $14,484
    National Endowment for the Arts $113
    National Endowment for the Humanities $125
    National Labor Relations Board $238
    Neighborhood Reinvestment Corp. $105
    Overseas Private Investment Corporation $207
    Peace Corps $284
    Selective Service System $25
    Small Business Administration $1,439
    Trade and Development Agency $55
Total Other Agencies and Activities $32,261

Total Proposed Budget Savings $308,883

Suggested Readings

Congressional Budget Office. "Federal Spending on the Elderly and Children." July 28, 2000, www.cbo.gov.

_____. "A 125-Year Picture of the Federal Government's Share of the Economy, 1950 to 2075." July 3, 2002, www.cbo.gov.

Edwards, Chris. "Controlling Defense Costs." Cato Institute Tax & Budget Bulletin no. 8, May 2002.

_____. "Sunsetting to Reform and Abolish Federal Agencies." Cato Institute Tax & Budget Bulletin no. 6, May 2002.

Moore, Stephen, and Stephen Slivinski. "The Return of the Living Dead: Federal Programs That Survived the Republican Revolution." Cato Institute Policy Analysis no. 375, July 24, 2000.

New, J. Michael. "Limiting Government through Direct Democracy: The Case of State Tax and Expenditure Limitations." Cato Institute Policy Analysis no. 420, December 13, 2001.

Penny, Tim, and Major Garrett. *The Fifteen Biggest Lies in American Politics*. New York: St. Martins, 1998.

—Prepared by Chris Edwards

24. Tax Reform

Congress should

- make permanent and accelerate the phase-in of tax cuts enacted in 2001, including rate reductions, estate tax repeal, and pension liberalization;
- repeal the individual and corporate alternative minimum taxes;
- reduce the taxation of capital by lowering personal taxes on capital gains and dividends, which are currently taxed at both the corporate and individual levels;
- expand Roth individual retirement accounts by greatly increasing contribution and income limits and repealing withdrawal restrictions to create a large all-purpose savings account available to every American;
- index individual income tax brackets to nominal income growth rather than inflation to prevent hidden tax increases caused by "real bracket creep";
- make permanent the 30 percent expensing provision for capital investment enacted in 2002, and expand it to ultimately allow 100 percent expensing;
- ensure that all tax cuts are consistent with replacing the income tax with a low-rate consumption-based tax, such as a Hall-Rabushka flat tax, a savings-exempt income tax, or a national retail sales tax; and generally
- make all federal taxes lower, flatter, and simpler.

Introduction

At the beginning of the 20th century, federal taxes accounted for just 3 percent of the nation's gross domestic product, and the tax code and related regulations filled just a few hundred pages. Today, federal taxes account for more than 18 percent of GDP (after peaking at about 21 percent in 2000), and federal tax rules span 45,662 pages.

The annual extraction of $2 trillion in federal taxes from families and businesses comes at an enormous cost. The most obvious cost is that Americans are left with less money to meet their needs for food, clothing, housing, and other items, and businesses are left with fewer funds to reinvest to build the economy. Today's huge tax burden exacerbates every problem of the federal tax code, including the bias against saving and investment, complexity, unequal treatment, and wasteful tax avoidance and evasion.

Reducing the overall tax burden should be the top priority for Congress (Chapter 23 provides federal budget reduction ideas). The tax system can be redesigned to greatly reduce its high costs. That is particularly true of the income tax on individuals and corporations. The current high-rate income tax is excessively complex, discourages saving and investment, and creates large inefficiency costs that stunt economic growth. Any of those problems alone should give Congress a strong motive for major reforms. Taken together, they make major tax reform a necessity.

This chapter looks first at problems inherent in the current income tax that would be greatly reduced by a low-rate consumption-based tax. Short-term reform options are then proposed to make the tax code simpler and less burdensome. Finally, long-term consumption-based tax reforms are discussed.

Excessive Complexity

In 1976, president-to-be Jimmy Carter called for "a complete overhaul of our income tax system. I feel it's a disgrace to the human race." Since Carter's attack, the number of pages of federal tax rules has more than doubled. And now, Treasury Secretary Paul O'Neill calls the tax system an "abomination." Clearly, reform is long overdue.

The income tax's complexity creates a huge compliance burden, requires high enforcement costs, causes high error rates, impedes economic decisionmaking, leads to inequitable treatment of citizens, and promotes tax avoidance and evasion.

Compliance Burden

Estimates reported by the Office of Management and Budget show that Americans spend more than 6 billion hours each year filling out tax forms, keeping records, and learning tax rules. The complexity of the tax system has spawned a huge public and private "tax industry" to perform administrative, planning, and enforcement activities. Those activities represent a pure loss to the economy since they consume resources and human effort that could otherwise be used to create useful goods and services. The costs of complying with federal income taxes are estimated to be roughly $200 billion per year. That huge burden falls on individuals both directly and indirectly through the burdens imposed on businesses. For example, a large corporate tax filing with related paperwork can run more than 10,000 pages. All Americans would gain if businesses spent less time on such paperwork and tax avoidance strategies and more time creating better products.

Enforcement Costs

In addition to the basic compliance costs of filing returns and tax planning, taxpayers incur large costs responding to IRS audits, notices, liens, levies, and seizures. The IRS assesses about 30 million penalties each year, thus imposing more costs on taxpayers. Because of the complexity of the tax system, many penalties are erroneous and thus a waste of effort all around.

Errors

Tax complexity causes taxpayers, the IRS, and tax experts to make frequent and costly errors. The IRS routinely gets up to half the answers to taxpayer phone inquiries wrong. *Money* magazine's annual test of tax experts, who are asked to compute taxes for a hypothetical family, consistently shows wide variations in experts' answers as a result of tax law complexity.

Economic Decisionmaking

Tax complexity impedes efficient decisionmaking by families and businesses. For example, the growing number of saving vehicles under the income tax, including 401(k)s and individual retirement accounts (IRAs), greatly confuses family financial planning. The wrong saving choice could result in lower returns, less liquidity, and payment of withdrawal penalties. Today's complex savings choices would be vastly simplified under a low-rate consumption-based tax.

The continual change in tax rules injects great uncertainty into long-term economic decisions, such as planning for business investment or retirement. The 2001 tax cut law alone had 85 major provisions and created 441 separate changes to the tax code. Each change in the law sets off changes in tax regulations, requests for IRS guidance, changes to tax forms, and higher error rates. Income tax complexity also creates taxpayer confusion about the effects of current laws, let alone future changes. With regard to disagreements on business tax items, audits, appeals, and litigation with the IRS can drag on for years with no clear answer as to the correct tax payment amount.

Inequity and Unfairness

The many complex features of the income tax create unfairness because similar families end up paying different tax amounts. As Congress has larded up the income tax code with special preferences, inequities have increased. Tax incentives for education, home ownership, and savings plans reward some families but not others. Polls have found that most Americans believe that the income tax is "unfair." No doubt such feelings have been fueled by the many special preferences carved into the tax code. A consumption-based tax would be simpler and fairer.

Avoidance and Evasion

Tax complexity leads to noncompliance with the tax system caused by both confusion and a desire to evade taxes. Complexity fosters multiple interpretations of the law and aggressive tax planning. Taxpayers take risks on their tax returns in the hope that complexity will hide their strategies from the IRS. The economy would be better off if tax rules were simple and transparent so that businesses could spend their energies on their operations, not playing cat-and-mouse games with the IRS.

Bias against Saving

The income tax system distorts the crucial economic tradeoff between consumption and saving. Saving is a primary source of economic growth because it provides businesses with the investment funds they need to expand and modernize the nation's capital stock. It is widely recognized that the income tax system is biased against saving because the returns to saving can face high tax rates, whereas current consumption does not.

That income tax bias has contributed to much of the interest in fundamental tax reform in recent years. Nearly all recent tax reform proposals would adopt a consumption base in order to eliminate saving and investment disincentives and to boost capital formation and growth. Also, a consumption tax base would increase economic efficiency by equalizing the treatment of all types of capital income. By contrast, the current tax system distorts corporate financing. For example, interest payments are deductible at the corporate level, but dividend payments are not. Many experts believe that this disparate treatment has led American companies to take on too much debt relative to equity. That causes greater numbers of bankruptcies and exacerbates economic instability.

At the individual level, removing tax barriers to all types of saving would allow families to gain greater financial security. With larger pools of savings, families could better plan for their future and guard against unforeseen financial problems. Consumption-based tax plans would treat personal saving under rules similar to those that govern either regular IRAs or Roth IRAs. In the first case, saving is initially deducted but withdrawals are later taxed. In the second case, no deduction is given for saving initially but qualified withdrawals are not taxed. The Hall-Rabushka flat tax adopts savings treatment similar to that of the Roth IRA by taxing initial wage earnings but exempting dividends, interest, and capital gains from taxation at the individual level. If made universal for all types of savings and for all families, that treatment would greatly increase saving incentives and remove large paperwork headaches that taxpayers face under the current plethora of different savings vehicles, each with unique rules and limitations.

Economic Inefficiency

A $1 million government spending program does not cost taxpayers just $1 million. It costs them much more. That is because taxes cause large distortions in the efficient functioning of the market economy by changing prices and altering behavior. Those distortions are called ''deadweight losses.'' For example, consider a woman with a wage job who is considering launching a small business on the side to earn more income. If the government hikes marginal tax rates and dissuades her from those entrepreneurial plans, the nation loses the additional production and the innovative ideas that she could have added to the economy.

High marginal tax rates greatly increase the economic damage or deadweight losses of income taxes. That is because deadweight losses increase more than proportionally to increases in tax rates. In particular, deadweight losses rise by the square of the increased tax wedge between pre- and posttax income for income taxes. For example, a doubling of the tax wedge causes deadweight losses to quadruple. As a consequence, a flatter

tax rate structure would be much more efficient than today's highly graduated tax rate structure.

Economic research indicates that deadweight losses represent at least
25 percent of each additional dollar of federal income tax revenue. Indeed,
the Office of Management and Budget incorporates a 25 percent deadweight loss measure into federal cost/benefit analyses. That means that
for new government spending projects to even begin making economic
sense, they must generate benefits at least 25 percent greater than their
explicit tax costs because of the extra 25 cents on the dollar damage
created by raising taxes.

Conversely, tax rate reductions benefit taxpayers by substantially more
than the amount by which taxpayers' explicit liabilities are reduced. For
example, an estimate of President Bush's original tax cut plan by Harvard
professors Martin Feldstein and Daniel Feenberg in 2001 found that it
would reduce deadweight losses by 38 percent of the value of the $1.6
trillion tax reduction, or about $600 billion over 10 years.

Tax rate cuts reduce deadweight losses by increasing rewards for work,
savings, entrepreneurial activity, and business investment and by shifting
economic activity into more productive areas. For example, a series of
statistical studies by tax economists Robert Carroll, Douglas Holtz-Eakin,
Mark Rider, and Harvey Rosen has found that personal income tax rate
cuts, such as occurred in 1986, have a substantial positive effect on small
business hiring, investment, and growth.

Short-Term Reforms

In 2001, Congress enacted the Economic Growth and Tax Relief Reconciliation Act based on the outline of President Bush's tax reduction plan.
The 2001 tax law took a number of very positive steps, including reducing
individual statutory tax rates, liberalizing the tax rules on retirement savings, and repealing the estate tax. However, all those provisions are set
to expire on December 31, 2010, which would impose a massive tax hike
on Americans at that time. The tax law also included absurdly extended
phase-in periods for tax reductions such that taxpayers will experience
the benefits of some tax cuts for just a year or two before having them
snatched away at the end of 2010. The first priority of the 108th Congress
should be to fix the severe shortcomings of the 2001 tax law.

Make 2001 Tax Cuts Permanent and Effective Immediately

Under the 2001 tax law, individual tax rate cuts are not fully phased
in until 2006, the estate tax is fully repealed for only one year in 2010, and

IRA liberalization is not fully phased in until 2008. Most other provisions in the law also have delayed effective dates. Congress should make all provisions in the 2001 tax law effective immediately. After all, the law's provisions help to solve long-standing problems with the tax code and help to spur economic growth. It makes sense to provide taxpayers with those promised future benefits today.

Expand and Make Permanent New Capital Expensing Rules

In 2002, Congress enacted a tax cut designed to stimulate the economy by allowing companies a 30 percent first-year tax write-off ("expensing") for investment in qualified business equipment. That provision is effective for only three years. Yet expensing has long been proposed as a permanent tax code fix to spur investment and long-term economic growth. The expensing provision should be made permanent and ultimately expanded to allow 100 percent expensing. Full expensing would be the treatment received by capital investment under most major tax reform plans, such as the Hall-Rabushka (or Dick Armey) flat tax and the USA tax plan of Rep. Phil English (R-Pa.). Such treatment would not only boost economic growth; it would also greatly simplify the tax code by ridding it of all the complex depreciation rules.

Greatly Liberalize the Roth IRA

Individual-level taxes on capital income need to be reduced all around. One promising approach to that end would be to liberalize the Roth IRA. The Roth IRA, created in 1997, has become a popular way to save; 12 million U.S. households now hold accounts, according to the Investment Company Institute. Contributions to Roth IRAs are from after-tax earnings, but investment returns and qualified withdrawals are tax-free. But Roth IRAs have strict limitations that should be greatly liberalized so that families can build up larger pools of savings to achieve more financial security.

Roth IRAs have income limits, low caps on annual contributions, and restrictions on withdrawals before retirement age. Under the 2001 Bush tax cut, the annual contribution limit for Roth IRAs rises from $3,000 in 2002 to $5,000 by 2008. That limit should be raised to at least $20,000 immediately. Another key problem is that because a 10 percent penalty is placed on most withdrawals prior to retirement, the liquidity of these savings vehicles is greatly reduced. The result is that individuals save much less because they fear that they may need their money before the government permits them penalty-free access. Thus, Roth IRAs should be liberalized and turned into universal-purpose savings accounts allowing withdrawals for any reason, not just for purposes specified by the government.

As currently designed, Roth IRAs are aimed at encouraging retirement savings. But tax code barriers to all types of savings, not just retirement savings, should be removed. Not only would that stimulate economic growth, it would encourage individuals to build up larger financial pools that could be used for any family contingency, such as medical expenses, home buying, unemployment, college, or unexpected crises. All individual savings are beneficial to long-term economic growth, and all savings contribute to individual financial stability.

Congress should create a universal savings account by removing income limits, contribution limits, and withdrawal restrictions on Roth IRAs. There would be no tax on dividends, interest, and capital gains earned within these new accounts because initial contributions would come from after-tax earnings. The revenue loss to the government in the short term would be small. Such a plan would greatly simplify the individual tax code by steering much of future individual savings into these simple accounts, and away from all the current complex and special-purpose savings plans.

Fix Real Bracket Creep

During economic expansions, individual taxes are steadily and stealthily increased by the phenomenon of "real bracket creep." Much of the individual income tax code is indexed for inflation but not for real economic growth. As a consequence, increasing shares of Americans' incomes are moved into higher tax brackets each year as the economy expands. That occurs because of the steeply graduated rate structure of the income tax and provisions such as the standard deduction that are also not indexed for real economic growth.

A substantial share of the benefits from the 2001 tax cut may be eaten away by real bracket creep. Congress should index individual income tax brackets and other tax code provisions to nominal income growth, rather than inflation, to prevent real bracket creep. Implementing a low flat-rate tax would also eliminate the problem.

Reduce Taxation of Dividends and Capital Gains

Congress should follow a general policy of steadily reducing the excessive taxation of capital income. Top tax cut priorities include reducing the corporate income tax rate and reducing individual taxes on dividends and capital gains. The United States is out of step with many of its major trading partners who have reduced capital income taxation in recent years. In fact, the United States has the fourth highest corporate income tax rate among the 30 major nations of the Organization for Economic Cooperation and Development. The average rate across the 30 OECD countries fell from 37.6 percent in 1996 to 31.4 percent in 2002 (including national and subnational taxes).

Regarding dividends, the United States has the fourth highest corporate plus individual tax burden on earnings distributed as dividends among OECD countries. About two-thirds of OECD countries—but not the United States—partially or fully relieve the double taxation of dividends, typically by providing shareholders with a tax reduction on dividends received.

The United States also lags behind on capital gains taxation. For example, Austria, Belgium, the Czech Republic, Germany, Greece, Hong Kong, Mexico, the Netherlands, New Zealand, Poland, and Switzerland all have a tax rate of zero on individual capital gains (holding periods or other conditions apply in some cases).

Enact Simplification Measures

Congress has taken a few very small steps to deal with the tax complexity problem. In April 2001, the Joint Committee on Taxation released a 1,300-page report on the topic. The study cataloged the excessive complexity of federal taxes and proposed more than 100 specific reforms. There is no reason why Congress should not move forward with these reforms, most of which are not controversial.

Congress should also move forward on tax reforms for international businesses. Many good reforms were proposed by House Ways and Means Committee chairman Bill Thomas (R-Calif.) in the 107th Congress. The U.S. tax rules on multinational corporations are perhaps the most complex in the world. The complexity of the rules causes U.S. companies to spend far too much time and energy on tax planning activities rather than more productive pursuits. Glenn Hubbard, chairman of the Council of Economic Advisers, and James Hines have in the past concluded that "the present U.S. system of taxing multinationals' income may be raising little U.S. tax revenue, while stimulating a host of tax-motivated financial transactions." It is time to move ahead on both business and individual tax simplification reforms.

Reform U.S. International Business Taxation

Not only are U.S. tax rules on international businesses complex, many experts agree that they put U.S.-based companies at a competitive disadvantage in world markets. Consumption-based taxes, including the flat tax, would eliminate most international tax rules because they are "territorial" taxes, which do not tax the foreign operations of U.S. businesses. About half of OECD countries have territorial business tax systems. Moving to a territorial system would allow U.S. companies to compete on a level playing field in foreign markets with corporations headquartered in other countries.

Repeal the Alternative Minimum Tax

The corporate and individual alternative minimum taxes (AMTs) are complex income tax systems that operate parallel to the ordinary income tax systems. There is broad agreement that the ill-conceived AMTs should be repealed. For example, AMT repeal has been recommended by the Joint Committee on Taxation and the American Bar Association. Former IRS national taxpayer advocate Val Oveson called the AMT "absolutely, asininely stupid" in a speech in 2000. Under JCT projections, 36 million taxpayers will be subject to the "asinine" individual AMT by 2010 unless Congress acts to repeal it.

Reform the Tax Policy Process

When Congress is considering raising or cutting taxes, expected changes in revenues are officially estimated by the JCT. The Treasury's Office of Tax Analysis performs a similar function for the administration. Those estimates are very important in policy debates about the desirability of tax changes, yet they are often erroneous and incomplete. Unfortunately, tax reforms that are desirable because they would raise Americans' incomes are often held up because of faulty estimates of the federal budgetary impact and because broad economic benefits are not taken into account. The current tax policy process in Washington stacks the deck against pro-growth tax reforms.

Revenue estimates by the JCT and OTA generally assume that tax changes will not affect the overall economy; thus they are termed "static" estimates. Yet major reductions in marginal tax rates, for example, would substantially boost economic activity and individual incomes, thus generating an offsetting increase in federal revenues. Revenue estimates that include such economic feedbacks are called "dynamic" estimates. Congress should introduce procedures to present dynamic revenue estimates alongside current static estimates for major tax bills.

Other aspects of the tax policy process also need reform. The current process is closed to public scrutiny and is resistant to change. Information provided to policymakers is based on particular economic and tax theories that should be more open to peer review. In addition, the presentation of tax information to policymakers and the general public needs to be overhauled. For example, politically important presentations on the "distributional" effects of proposed tax changes (effects presented by income groups) can be very misleading. Congress should reexamine the way such information on tax changes is presented to ensure fairness and accuracy.

Long-Term Reforms

Raising the bulk of federal revenue from broad-based individual and corporate income taxes was a historic mistake. It has led to excessive complexity, a powerful bias against saving and investment, economic inefficiency, and a reduction in U.S. economic growth. To correct those problems, nearly all major tax reform proposals of recent years would replace the individual and corporate income taxes with a low-rate consumption-based tax.

Current System Has Complex and Damaging Tax Base

The key economic differences between income and consumption-based taxes regard the treatment of saving and investment. The federal income tax is loosely based on a very broad measure of income called Haig-Simons income. That basis results in heavy taxation of saving and investment. For example, a full Haig-Simons-based tax would tax all capital gains accrued on paper every year, whether or not those gains were actually received. It would also tax items that individuals would not normally think of as income, such as the implicit rent received from owning one's home and the buildup of wealth in life insurance policies.

Many tax policy experts traditionally supported taxing an expansive Haig-Simons income base. Yet there is no good economic argument for such a tax base. For example, the accrual taxation of capital gains would result in double taxation of investment. (A rise in an asset's projected future return would lead to an immediate taxable capital gain. Then, the return would be taxed again as the asset generated revenues in future years.) The attraction of a Haig-Simons income tax base seems to stem mainly from the egalitarian impulse to impose a heavy load of taxation on those with high incomes.

Taxing a broad income base is very impractical and complex. As a result, the current income tax has fallen back on an array of ad hoc and inconsistent rules for defining individual and business income. Some income is exempt from tax, some income is taxed once, and other income is taxed multiple times. There is no consistent standard under present tax policy for what constitutes income or when it should be taxed.

In addition, inflation wreaks havoc with broad-based income taxes, making items such as capital gains and depreciation very difficult to measure properly. The many jury-rigged fixes under the income tax create decisionmaking difficulties and paperwork burdens for individuals and businesses. For example, the current income tax treats capital gains on a realization basis, which adds a great deal of planning difficulties for investors who must try to optimally time asset sales and offset gains with losses.

There is a growing realization among economists, tax experts, and taxpayers that the current income-based system cannot be made simple. What is needed is a fundamental overhaul that would create a simple and transparent consumption-based tax, in place of the complex and uncompetitive federal income tax.

Reforming Taxation with a Low-Rate Consumption-Based Tax

Congress should begin replacing the individual and corporate income taxes with a low-rate consumption-based tax. That goal can be reached gradually by following the short-term reforms listed above, or it can be implemented by an immediate replacement combined with various transition rules. Leading consumption-based tax proposals have included the Hall-Rabushka flat tax, a national retail sales tax, and variants of a consumed-income tax. The flat tax was originally proposed by Robert Hall and Alvin Rabushka of the Hoover Institution and was most recently championed by former house majority leader Dick Armey. Leading retail sales tax proposals have included a plan by Rep. Billy Tauzin (R-La.) to replace income taxes and the estate tax with a 15 percent retail sales tax; Rep. John Linder's (R-Ga.) plan would replace those taxes plus federal payroll taxes with a 23 percent sales tax called the "FairTax." Rep. Phil English (R-Pa.) has introduced a plan based on the consumed-income tax approach.

Those plans are similar in economic thrust as they all would reduce the taxation of saving and investment. They would, however, differ in

Table 24.1
Advantages of a Low-Rate Consumption-Based Tax
Economic and simplification advantages
of a Hall-Rabushka-style tax compared with the current income tax

---

Advantages for Individuals

Low tax rate: Increased incentives for working, saving, and entrepreneurial activities. With lower rates, more than 20 million small businesses and the self-employed who file under the personal tax system would have added incentives to hire and invest.

Personal savings: No taxation of interest, dividends, and capital gains. That would greatly enhance financial privacy and increase the ability and incentive for families to save for their own retirement and other future expenses. No need for half a billion 1099s and other IRS forms.

Capital gains: Eliminating capital gains taxation would get rid of multiple tax rates and holding periods and complexities such as the timing of realizations, matching gains with losses, and calculating basis. Great boon for entrepreneurial growth companies, which rely on investors who earn returns through capital gains.

Interest: Interest income and interest expense complications and distortions eliminated, such as the municipal bond preference.

Savings vehicles: Current plethora of savings vehicles, including 401(k)s and IRAs, would be phased out as tax hurdles were removed for all types of savings. Families would save for reasons of their own choosing, would withdraw funds without penalties, and would not have to sort through pages of rules to make savings decisions. Saving would become individually based instead of being tied to the risks of company pension plans.

Social engineering: Fairness would be increased as items that specially favor some taxpayers were eliminated, such as the five different current education tax preferences related to savings and interest.

Advantages for Businesses

Low tax rate: Increased incentives for all businesses to hire and invest. Greater attraction of foreign investment would help build the U.S. economy. Reduced efforts put into wasteful tax avoidance, evasion, compliance, and enforcement activities.

Capital income: All types of capital income would receive the same neutral treatment and be taxed only once. Distortions that change business and financial structure, such as the current corporate bias in favor of debt financing, would be eliminated.

(continued)

Table 24.1
(continued)

Depreciation: Complex and distortionary tax rules for capital purchases eliminated. Business investment would receive a huge boost, which would spur long-term economic growth.

Capitalization issues: Aside from depreciation, other tax rules that relate to the timing of income and deductions would be eliminated, such as the complex rules for business inventory.

Capital gains: Elimination of corporate capital gains would reduce complexities of business reorganizations and investment activities.

Inflation: Distortions caused by inflation under the income tax for such items as for depreciation, inventory, and capital gains would be eliminated under a consumption-based tax.

International tax rules: Businesses would be taxed on a territorial basis under a consumption-based tax, thus eliminating many complex tax provisions, such as the foreign tax credit.

Business structure: Uniform business taxation would replace C and S corporations, LLCs, sole proprietorships, and partnerships. Business and financial planning would be greatly simplified, as would be the tax treatment of mergers and acquisitions.

---

their mechanics and pose trade-offs with regard to administration, simplicity, and civil liberties. Nonetheless, they would all represent major improvements on the current federal income tax mess.

Table 24.1 summarizes the dramatic economic and simplification gains that could be achieved under a structure like the Hall-Rabushka flat tax, which would incorporate simple and low-rate business and individual-level taxes. Similar gains may be achieved under other low-rate consumption-based tax plans.

Conclusion

Consumption-based tax proposals have gained widespread support because they would reduce the tax burden on saving and investment and spur greater economic growth. In addition, replacing the current income tax with a consumption-based tax promises vast simplification of the complicated federal tax code.

Given the nine-decade reign of the income tax, it is surprising what a weak case there is for it compared with a consumption-based tax. In congressional testimony a few years ago, the current chairman of the Council of Economic Advisers, Glenn Hubbard, called the income tax "fundamentally flawed" because of its inefficiency, complexity, and unfairness. It is time to replace the flawed income tax with a lower, flatter, simpler alternative.

As discussed, there are many good short-term reforms that Congress should pursue, such as reducing overall marginal tax rates, eliminating the AMT, and cutting taxes on dividends and capital gains. All changes should aim for the ultimate goal of enacting a low-rate consumption-based system in place of the fundamentally flawed income tax.

Suggested Readings

Adams, Charles. *Those Dirty Rotten Taxes: The Tax Revolts That Built America*. New York: Free Press, 1998.

Burton, David. "Reforming the Federal Tax Policy Process." Cato Institute Policy Analysis no. 463, December 17, 2002.

Burton, David, and Dan R. Mastromarco. "Emancipating America from the Income Tax: How a National Sales Tax Would Work." Cato Institute Policy Analysis no. 272, April 15, 1997.

Edwards, Chris. "Economic Benefits of Personal Income Tax Rate Reductions." U.S. Congress, Joint Economic Committee, April 2001.

———. "New Data Show U.S. Has Fourth Highest Corporate Tax Rate." Cato Institute Tax & Budget Bulletin no. 3, April 2002.

———. "Simplifying Federal Taxes: The Advantages of Consumption-Based Taxation." Cato Institute Policy Analysis no. 416, October 17, 2001.

———. "Top Ten Civil Liberties Abuses of the Income Tax." Cato Institute Tax & Budget Bulletin no. 4, April 2002.

Hall, Robert, and Alvin Rabushka. *The Flat Tax*. 2d ed. Stanford: Hoover Institution Press, 1995.

McCaffery, Edward. "Grave Robbers: The Case against the Death Tax." Cato Institute Policy Analysis no. 353, October 4, 1999.

Metcalf, Gilbert. "The National Sales Tax: Who Bears the Burden?" Cato Institute Policy Analysis no. 289, December 8, 1997.

Moore, Stephen, and John Silvia. "The ABCs of the Capital Gains Tax." Cato Institute Policy Analysis no. 242, October 4, 1995.

—Prepared by Chris Edwards

25. Social Security

Congress should allow young workers to redirect their payroll taxes to individually owned, privately invested retirement accounts.

The debate over Social Security reform was poorly served by the 2002 congressional elections. With a declining stock market as a backdrop for dueling attack ads, too many candidates became embroiled in a pointless debate over the meaning of the word ''privatization.'' The public was left without a clear presentation of the problems facing Social Security or of the pros and cons of various solutions. But as campaigning gives way to governing, Congress must recognize that Social Security is facing serious problems and must be reformed.

Why Reform Social Security?

There are five main reasons to reform Social Security.

Keeping Social Security Solvent

Social Security is going bankrupt. The federal government's largest spending program, accounting for nearly 22 percent of all federal spending, faces irresistible demographic and fiscal pressures that threaten the future retirement security of today's young workers. According to the 2001 report of the Social Security system's Board of Trustees, in 2017, just 14 years from now, the Social Security system will begin to run a deficit (Figure 25.1) That is, it will begin to spend more on benefits than it brings in through taxes. Anyone who has ever run a business—or balanced a checkbook—understands that when you are spending more than you are bringing in, something has to give: you need to start either earning more money or spending less to keep things balanced. For Social Security, that means either higher taxes or lower benefits.

Figure 25.1
Social Security Cost and Income

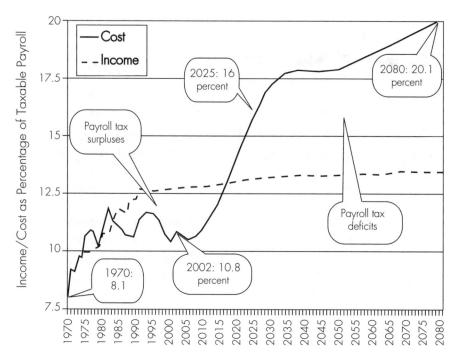

In theory, Social Security is supposed to continue paying benefits after 2017 by drawing on the Social Security Trust Fund. The trust fund is supposed to provide enough money to guarantee benefits until 2041, when it will be exhausted. But one of Washington's dirty little secrets is that there really is no trust fund. The government spent that money long ago to finance general government spending and hide the true size of the federal budget deficit. The trust fund now consists only of IOUs—promises that at some time in the future the government will replace that money, which can only be done by collecting more taxes or issuing even more debt.

Even if Congress can find a way to redeem the bonds, the trust fund surplus will be completely exhausted by 2041. At that point, Social Security will have to rely solely on revenue from the payroll tax. But that revenue will not be sufficient to pay all promised benefits.

There are limited options available. Former president Bill Clinton pointed out the choices: (a) raise taxes, (b) cut benefits, or (c) get a higher rate of return through investment in real capital assets. Henry Aaron of the Brookings Institution, a noted opponent of privatization, agrees. "Increased funding to raise pension reserves is possible only with some combination of additional tax revenues, reduced benefits, or increased investment returns from investing in higher yielding assets," he told Congress in 1999.

The tax increases and benefit cuts would have to be large. To maintain benefits after the system starts running a deficit in 2017, the government must acquire new funds equivalent to $103 per worker. By 2030, the additional tax burden increases to $1,543 per worker, and it continues to rise thereafter. Functionally, that would mean an increase in payroll taxes of roughly 50 percent, or an equivalent increase in income or other taxes.

If both individual accounts and tax increases are off the table, then, *by law*, benefits will have to be cut. Current estimates suggest that benefits may have to be reduced by as much as a third. That would have a devastating effect on those Americans most dependent on Social Security for retirement income. Studies indicate that as many as 20 percent of American seniors receive nearly all their retirement income from Social Security.

It is important to realize that doing nothing is the same as endorsing benefit cuts. Since, by law, once Social Security no longer has enough revenue to pay benefits, without reform, benefit cuts are inevitable. In this case, not to act is to act.

A Better Deal for Young Workers

Even if Social Security did somehow manage to pay all its promised benefits, the taxes paid by today's young workers are already so high that promised benefits would be a bad deal in return for those taxes. Those benefits represent a low, below-market rate of return, or effective interest rate, on the taxes workers and their employers have to pay into the system throughout their careers (Table 25.1). Studies show that investing those tax funds instead in private savings and insurance would likely yield three or more times the benefits Social Security promises to today's young workers. In fact, retiring workers will receive returns from Social Security that are below those of risk-free government bonds.

Look at it another way: A single worker born in 1965, paying the maximum in Social Security taxes, and retiring in 2030 would have to live to over age 90 just to get back what he or she had paid into the system (Table 25.2). This means that entire generations will lose money under the current Social Security system.

Table 25.1
Real Rates of Return Falling for All Retirees
(assumes no change in law, retirement at age 65)

Birth Year	Single Male (medium wages)	Single Female (medium wages)	Single-Earner Couple (medium wages)	Two-Earner Couple (medium/low wages)
1970	1.13	1.59	3.42	2.24
1980	0.91	1.36	3.31	2.08
1990	0.88	1.29	3.14	1.97
2000	0.86	1.25	3.02	1.88

SOURCE: Social Security Office of the Actuary calculations, May 27, 2001.

Table 25.2
What Age Must You Reach to Get Back What You've Paid In?

Year of Birth	Age an Average Earner Gets Back Taxes Paid into the Retirement Portion of Social Security	Total Life Expectancy for Individual Reaching Age 65	
		Male	Female
1875	65.2	77.7	79.7
1895	66.1	78.2	82.4
1915	67.8	79.7	83.9
1936	81.8	81.3	84.6
1945	85.2	81.9	85
1955	89.7	82.5	85.6
1965	91.9	83	86.1

SOURCE: Congressional Research Service, "Social Security: The Relationship of Taxes and Benefits for Past, Present, and Future Retirees," June 22, 2001; updated via telephone conversation with author. Under the intermediate assumptions of the 2001 Trustees Report and taking into account benefit increases and continued accrual of interest after retirement but not the taxation of benefits. The retirees are assumed to begin work at age 22 and retire in January of the year in which they turn 65. Assumes contributions earn interest equal to the long-term government bond rate.

Moreover, this may understate the problem since it assumes that Social Security will continue to pay promised benefits without increased taxes. But, as we have seen above, that is impossible.

Savings and Economic Growth

Social Security operates on a pay-as-you-go basis; almost all of the funds coming in are immediately paid out to current beneficiaries. This system displaces private, fully funded alternatives under which the funds coming in would be saved and invested for the future benefits of today's workers. The result is a large net loss of national savings, which reduces capital investment, wages, national income, and economic growth. Moreover, by increasing the cost of hiring workers, the payroll tax substantially reduces wages, employment, and economic growth as well.

Shifting to a system of individual accounts, with hundreds of billions of dollars invested in private capital markets, could produce a large net increase in national savings, depending on how the government financed the transition. This would increase investment, productivity, wages, and jobs. Replacing the payroll tax with private retirement contributions would also improve economic growth, because the required contributions would be lower and those contributions would be seen as part of a worker's direct compensation, stimulating more employment and output.

Helping the Poor

Low-income workers would be among the biggest winners under a private system. The higher returns and benefits of a system that relies on private investment would be most important to low-income families, as they most need the extra funds. The funds saved in the individual retirement accounts, which could be left to the children of the poor, would also greatly help families break out of the cycle of poverty. Similarly, the improved economic growth, higher wages, and increased jobs that would result from reforming Social Security would be most important to the poor. Moreover, if we continue on our current course, low-income workers will be hurt the most by the higher taxes or reduced benefits that will be necessary. Averting a financial crisis and its inevitable results would consequently be most important to low-income workers.

In addition, with average- and low-wage workers accumulating large sums in their own investment accounts, the distribution of wealth throughout society would become far broader than it is today. That would occur, not through the redistribution of existing wealth, but through the creation of new wealth, far more equally held. Because Social Security investment accounts would make every worker a stockowner, the old, senseless division between labor and capital would be eroded. Every laborer would become a capitalist. The socialist dream of the nation's workers owning its businesses and industries would be effectively achieved. At the same time, as the nation's workers became capitalists, support for free-market, pro-growth economic policies would increase in all sectors of society.

That social effect is one of the least cited but most important reasons for giving workers more control over their retirement savings.

Ownership and Control

After all the economic analysis, however, perhaps the single most important reason for privatizing Social Security is that it would give American workers true ownership of and control over their retirement benefits.

Many Americans believe that Social Security is an earned right. That is, because they have paid Social Security taxes they are entitled to receive Social Security benefits. The government encourages this belief by referring to Social Security taxes as "contributions," as in the Federal Insurance Contributions Act. However, the U.S. Supreme Court has ruled, in *Flemming v. Nestor,* that workers have no legally binding contractual or property right to their Social Security benefits, and those benefits can be changed, cut, or even taken away at any time.

As the Court stated, "To engraft upon Social Security a concept of 'accrued property rights' would deprive it of the flexibility and boldness in adjustment to ever changing conditions which it demands." That decision built on a previous case, *Helvering v. Davis,* in which the Court had ruled that Social Security is not a contributory insurance program, stating that "the proceeds of both the employer and employee taxes are to be paid into the Treasury like any other internal revenue generally, and are not earmarked in any way."

In effect, Social Security turns older Americans into supplicants, dependent on the political process for their retirement benefits. If they work hard, play by the rules, and pay Social Security taxes their entire lives, they earn the privilege of going hat in hand to the government and hoping that politicians decide to give them some money for retirement.

In contrast, under a system of individual accounts, workers would have full property rights in their private accounts. They would own their accounts and the money in them the same way they own their individual retirement accounts (IRAs) or 401(k) plans. Their retirement benefits would not depend on the whims of politicians.

The President's Commission

In May 2001, President Bush appointed former senator Daniel Patrick Moynihan and AOL/Time Warner executive Richard Parsons to co-chair the President's Commission to Strengthen Social Security. The 16-member bipartisan commission was charged with devising Social Security reform proposals according to the following principles: modernization must not change Social Security benefits for retirees or near retirees; the entire Social Security surplus must be dedicated to Social Security only; Social Security payroll taxes must not be increased; the government must not invest Social Security funds in the stock market; modernization must preserve Social Security's disability and survivors' components; and modernization must include individually controlled, voluntary personal retirement accounts, which will augment the Social Security safety net.

Three members of the commission, Lea Abdnor, Sam Beard, and former representative Tim Penny (D-Minn.), have worked with Cato's Project on Social Security Choice. Cato Social Security analyst Andrew Biggs served as a staff member to the commission.

In August 2001 the commission released its interim report, which outlined the demographic pressures on the current pay-as-you-go program and argued that the current trust fund financing mechanism did not effectively save today's payroll tax surpluses to fund future benefit obligations. Over the remainder of the year, the commission held a number of public hearings and meetings, which often became the target of protests from opponents of personal retirement accounts.

Nevertheless, in December the commission delivered its recommendations to the president. Those included three proposals illustrating how personal retirement accounts could be integrated into the current Social Security program, strengthening the system for the future while giving workers ownership of and control over at least a part of their payroll taxes.

The commission's Plan 1 did nothing other than add voluntary personal accounts to Social Security. Workers could choose to invest 2 percent of their wages in a personal account. In return, workers with accounts would give up a portion of their traditional retirement benefits. While Plan 1 did not bring the system back to solvency, it illustrated that individual accounts could increase benefits for all retirees while improving the financing health of the program.

The commission's Plan 2 allowed workers to divert 4 percentage points of their payroll taxes to a personal account, up to an annual maximum of $1,000 (which would be indexed annually to the growth of wages). To bring the traditional program back to financial balance, Plan 2 would increase the initial benefits each cohort of new retirees receives by the rate of price growth, rather than wage growth as under current law. This "price indexing" of initial benefits would bring the program back to solvency and eventually deliver substantial payroll tax surpluses. In addition, Plan 2 contained new protections for low-wage workers and lower-income widows. Plan 2 would be substantially cheaper than the current system, requiring general revenue transfers 68 percent smaller (measured in today's dollars).

The commission's Plan 3 would allow workers to divert 2.5 percentage points of their payroll taxes to a personal account (up to an annual maximum of $1,000), provided they voluntarily deposited an additional 1 percent of their wages in the account. Plan 3 would pay all retirees a larger benefit than that promised by the current program—and at a substantially lower cost over the long term. Measured in today's dollars, the general revenue cost of Plan 3 was less than half that of maintaining the current program. Like Plan 2, Plan 3 contained new protections for low-wage retirees and lower-income widows.

Together, the three commission plans show that personal accounts enable a reformed Social Security program to pay higher benefits at lower cost than the current pay-as-you-go method of financing.

Principles for Reform

As it approaches the historic debate over Social Security reform, Congress should keep in mind five basic principles.

Solvency Is Not Enough

Workers deserve the best possible deal for their dollar. With Social Security facing a financial crisis—it will begin running a deficit in just 14 years—much attention has been focused on ways to keep the program solvent. Theoretically, that could be accomplished by raising taxes or cutting benefits. But Social Security faces a second crisis as well: Young workers will receive a negative rate of return from the program. They will get less back in benefits than they pay in taxes. That low return, and other inequities, particularly disadvantages women, the poor, and minorities. Any Social Security reform must reverse this trend, raising the rate of return and providing higher retirement benefits.

Individuals, Not Government, Should Invest

The only way to increase Social Security's rate of return is to invest Social Security taxes in real capital assets. This should be done through the creation of individually owned accounts, not by allowing the government to directly invest payroll taxes. Individual accounts would give workers ownership of and control over their retirement funds, allowing them to accumulate wealth and pass that wealth on to their heirs; it would also give them a greater stake in the American economic system. Government investment would allow the federal government to become the largest shareholder in every American company, posing a potential threat to corporate governance and the specter of social investing.

Maximize Consumer Choice

Workers should be given as wide a range of investment opportunities as possible, consistent with regulatory safeguards against fraud or speculation. While investing in "Singapore derivatives" is clearly not envisioned, there is no reason to limit workers to only two or three index funds. As much as possible, the existing retirement savings infrastructure should be used, meaning workers would have a large number of safe and secure options. Moreover, a safety net would guarantee that no senior would end up in poverty as a result of bad investments.

Don't Touch Grandma's Check

Benefits to the currently retired and nearly retired should not be reduced. Indeed, by explicitly recognizing benefits owed to current retirees, Social Security reform would guarantee those benefits in a way that the current political system does not. Making the transition to a new system while guaranteeing current benefits means that the government will have to issue debt, cut current spending, or sell assets, but those "transition costs" will be substantially less than the costs of maintaining the current system.

More Investment Is Better Than Less

You don't cut out half a cancer. Given the advantages of individual accounts, there is no excuse for stopping at only 2–3 percent of payroll taxes. Once Congress has conceded that private capital investment can provide better and more secure retirement benefits, it should press on and allow workers to control the maximum feasible amount of their retirement income.

Answering the Objections

The Transition

The most difficult issue associated with any proposed reform of Social Security is the transition. Put quite simply, regardless of what system we choose for the future, we have a moral obligation to continue benefits to today's recipients. But if current workers divert their payroll taxes to individual accounts, those taxes will no longer be available to pay benefits. The government will have to find a new source of funds.

However, it should be understood that this is not a new cost. It is really just making explicit an already existing unfunded obligation. The federal government already cannot fund as much as $25 trillion of Social Security's promised benefits. Reforming Social Security, therefore, will actually reduce the amount of debt we owe.

The tradeoffs in refinancing a home mortgage provide a useful analogy. There are costs associated with achieving a lower interest rate, such as points, title insurance, a title search, attorneys' fees, a credit report, and the like. The decision to refinance is based not only on the lower interest rate but on those costs as well. If the present value of the costs and the lower interest expense is less than the present value of the existing mortgage interest expense, then there is a net benefit from refinancing even though costs are incurred to achieve it. With Social Security, the cost of paying for the transition to a system of individual accounts will be less than the cost of preserving the current system.

Of course there will be a temporary cash flow problem while we make the transition. We will have to find the revenues to pay benefits to current retirees. Any financing mechanism will be political, involving some combination of debt, transfers from general revenues, asset sales, and the like. If both parties are willing to forgo new spending programs and junk tax cuts, we can begin the transition to a new, improved Social Security system.

There are several methods of financing the transition. For example, a small portion of the payroll tax could be continued temporarily. Workers could be allowed to invest their half of the payroll tax (6.2 percentage points of 12.4 percent) with the remainder temporarily being used to fund a portion of continued benefits. Congress could also identify additional spending cuts and use the funds saved to finance the transition. Because much federal government spending is wasteful or counterproductive, such cuts would not be any sacrifice for society—indeed, the cuts themselves might provide many benefits. A list of potential cuts can be found in Chapter 23. The government could also sell many assets that it currently owns. Finally, the government could issue bonds to spread the cost of transition over several generations. It is important to understand that this is not new debt; it is simply the explicit recognition of an existing implicit debt under the current system.

Risk

Last year's turmoil in the stock market provided ample evidence that in any given year stocks can go down as well as up. But, in truth, the year-to-year fluctuations of the stock market are irrelevant. What really counts is the long-term trend of the market over a person's entire working lifetime, in most cases 40 or 45 years. Given that long-term perspective, there is no period during which the average investor would have lost money by investing in the U.S. stock market. In fact, during the worst 20-year period in U.S. history, which included the Great Depression, the stock market produced a positive real return of more than 3 percent.

As Figure 25.2 shows, even with the recent stock market decline, a worker investing only in stocks would receive benefits 2.8 times higher than he would had he "invested" the same amount of money in the current program.

Put another way, the recent decline in stock prices means the worker's personal account would be worth the same today as it was worth in 1997. But that worker's Social Security "savings" would be worth today only what the personal account was worth in the late *1980s*. It would take a

Figure 25.2
Value of Personal Accounts and Social Security Benefits

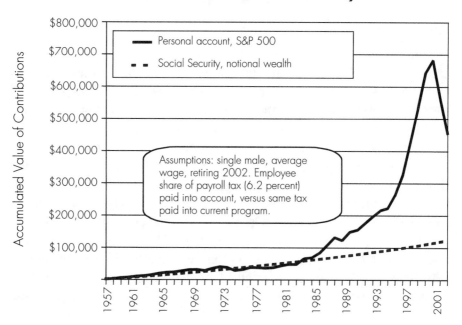

Figure 25.3
Total Benefits

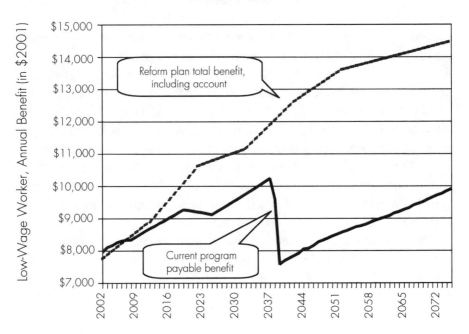

much larger decline than the one we have seen for a personal account to be a worse deal than the current program.

Benefit Cuts

Many opponents of individual accounts charge that creating such accounts would lead to benefit cuts. However, that claim is based on two faulty premises. First, opponents compare privatization proposals with current law and suggest that those proposals will provide lower benefits, or at least lower government-provided benefits. Second, they suggest that transition costs to a privatized system will require tax increases.

But as Charles Blahous, executive director of the President's Commission to Strengthen Social Security, has pointed out, "The essential problem with comparing reform plans with 'current law' is that 'current law' allows the system to go bankrupt." Or, as David Walker, comptroller of the United States, warned: "There's a lot of people that want to compare Social Security reform proposals to promised benefits. That is fundamentally flawed and unfair because all of funded benefits are not funded." A fair test of Social Security reform proposals, including those that include

Experts Speak Out on the Trust Fund

Congressional Budget Office: "The size of the balance in the Social Security Trust Funds—be it $2 trillion, $10 trillion, or zero—does not affect the obligations that the federal government has to the program's beneficiaries. Nor does it affect the government's ability to pay those benefits."

General Accounting Office: Social Security's "Trust Funds are not like private Trust Funds. They are simply budget accounts used to record receipts and expenditures earmarked for specific purposes. A private Trust Fund can set aside money for the future by increasing its assets. However, under current law, when the Trust Funds' receipts exceed costs, they are invested in Treasury securities and used to meet current cash needs of the government. These securities are an asset to the Trust Fund, but they are a claim on the Treasury. Any increase in assets to the Trust Funds is an equal increase in claims on the Treasury."

Congressional Research Service: "What often confuses people [about the Trust Funds] is that they see these securities as assets for the government. When an individual buys a government bond, he or she has established a financial claim against the government. When the government issues a security to one of its own accounts, it hasn't purchased anything or established a claim against some other person or entity. It is simply creating an IOU from one of its accounts to another."

Clinton Administration 2000 Budget: "[Trust Fund] balances are available to finance future benefit payments and other Trust Fund expenditures—but only in a bookkeeping sense. . . . They do not consist of real economic assets that can be drawn down in the future to fund benefits. Instead, they are claims on the Treasury that, when redeemed, will have to be financed by raising taxes, borrowing from the public, or reducing benefits or other expenditures. The existence of large Trust Fund balances, therefore, does not, by itself, have any impact on the government's ability to pay benefits."

individual accounts, is to compare them, not to promised benefits, but to benefits that can actually be paid. By that standard, proposals to create individual accounts come out far ahead.

Moreover, opponents of individual accounts frequently omit the funds accumulating in those accounts when making comparisons. They compare only government-provided benefits with government-provided benefits. But that omits half the story. When *total* benefits under individual account plans, that is benefits from the accounts plus government-provided benefits, are considered, these plans provide benefits in excess of what Social Security has promised, let alone what it can pay (Figure 25.3).

Conclusion

The American people have shown themselves ready for fundamental Social Security reform. Now is the time for Congress to act. There is little that the 108th Congress could do that would have a more profound impact on the lives of the American people.

Suggested Readings

Biggs, Andrew. "Personal Accounts in a Down Market: How Recent Stock Market Declines Affect the Social Security Reform Debate." Cato Institute Briefing Paper no. 74, September 10, 2002.

————. Perspectives on the President's Commission to Strengthen Social Security." Cato Institute Social Security Paper no. 27, August 22, 2002.

Ferrara, Peter, and Michael Tanner. *A New Deal for Social Security*. Washington: Cato Institute, 1998.

————. *Common Cents, Common Dreams: A Layman's Guide to Social Security Privatization*. Washington: Cato Institute, 1998.

O'Neill, June. "The Trust Fund, the Surplus, and the Real Social Security Problem." Cato Institute Social Security Paper no. 26, April 9, 2002.

Piñera, José. "Empowering Workers: The Privatization of Social Security in Chile." *Cato's Letters* no. 10, May 1996.

Rounds, Charles. "Property Rights: The Hidden Issue of Social Security Reform." Cato Institute Social Security Paper no. 19, April 19, 2000.

Tanner, Michael. "No Second Best: The Unappetizing Alternatives to Individual Accounts." Cato Institute Social Security Paper no. 24, January 29, 2002.

—Prepared by Michael Tanner

26. Public Health Care

Congress should

- fundamentally restructure Medicare to expand competitive private health plan choices;
- not add comprehensive prescription drug benefits to Medicare unless and until it enacts structural reform of the entire program;
- encourage states to adjust Medicaid eligibility criteria and covered benefits to serve fewer nondisabled, lower-income individuals—but then provide remaining beneficiaries with higher-quality core health services and make greater use of cost-sharing incentives; and
- facilitate state efforts to adapt defined-contribution-style financing as an option for Medicaid beneficiaries.

Over the past two years, Congress has again backed away from taking on necessary restructuring of Medicare while private health options under the Medicare + Choice program have continued to shrink rather than expand. Meanwhile, efforts to add a new runaway entitlement program for prescription drug benefits came up short in the Senate after the House narrowly approved its own flawed measure that strained to preserve the appearance, but not the reality, of competitive and privately managed Medicare drug insurance.

Congress also entertained proposals to expand eligibility for Medicaid coverage to uninsured lower-income workers, to increase the federal matching payments to state Medicaid programs, and to begin a federal takeover of certain subsidy payments to "dual eligible" Medicare/Medicaid beneficiaries; none of those measures became law.

In short, the status quo prevailed. Congress refrained from doing more harm in both programs, but it also failed to make any progress toward moving current and future beneficiaries away from unsustainable dependence on two aging Great Society entitlement programs born in 1965 that suffer from their own sets of worsening chronic conditions and disabilities.

Medicare's Midlife Crisis

Despite a few recent years of improved financial performance, Medicare remains fundamentally flawed after 37 years in operation, and it is unsustainable on a long-term basis. The Balanced Budget Act of 1997 launched a new round of arbitrary price controls, regulatory complexity, and overzealous "fraud and abuse" enforcement that temporarily slowed the rate of growth of Medicare spending. But Medicare's Hospital Insurance (Part A) trust fund will resume spending more than it collects in taxes in 2016, and it faces a long-term actuarial deficit of 2 percent of taxable payroll. The Supplementary Medical Insurance (Part B) side of Medicare will continue to grow faster than both Part A and the overall economy. It will double its share of gross domestic product within 30 years.

The *2001 Financial Report of the United States Government,* prepared by the Financial Management Service of the Department of the Treasury, provides a more comprehensive view of the mounting burden that Medicare will impose on current and future taxpayers. Medicare spending exceeded the program's tax receipts and premiums by $59 billion in fiscal 2000, and the annual gap will grow to an estimated $216 billion (using constant dollars) in 2020. In 2002, Medicare program actuaries at the Centers for Medicare and Medicaid Services conservatively projected that the discounted net excess of cash spending over cash income during the next 75-year period would be $5.1 trillion (even after including Medicare trust funds' balances and future interest income, as well as general revenue transfers to Part B). However, the *Financial Report* calculations from one year earlier, using accrual accounting under generally accepted accounting principles and therefore excluding interest payments and other intragovernmental transfers, estimated that the net present value of negative cash flow (funds needed to cover projected shortfalls) was $4.7 trillion for Part A and an additional $8.1 trillion for Part B (Table 26.1).

Working Americans remain on the hook for a rising share of the imminent cost explosion. Federal general revenues already finance 25 percent of Medicare spending; that share will rise to more than half within 30 years. More than 37 years after it began in 1965, Medicare remains one of the most volatile and uncontrollable programs in the federal budget. Its unrestrained appetite will squeeze out other national priorities and jeopardize opportunities for future generations.

Table 26.1
U.S. Government Statement of Social Insurance
Present Value of Long-Range Actuarial Projections[1]

	Contributions and Earmarked Taxes[2]		Benefit Payments[3]		Benefit Payments in Excess of Contributions and Earmarked Taxes	
	2001	2000	2001	2000	2001	2000
Participants Who Are Currently Receiving Benefits:						
Federal Hospital Insurance (Medicare Part A)	113	97	1,693	1,681	1,580	1,584
Federal Supplementary Medical Insurance (Medicare Part B)	258	234	1,159	1,051	901	817
Participants Who Are Not Currently Receiving Benefits:						
Federal Hospital Insurance (Medicare Part A)	4,136	3,757	8,568	6,702	4,432	2,945
Federal Supplementary Medical Insurance (Medicare Part B)	1,845	1,527	7,415	6,094	5,570	4,567
Future Participants:[4]						
Federal Hospital Insurance (Medicare Part A)	3,507	3,179	2,225	1,349	(1,282)	(1,830)
Federal Supplementary Medical Insurance (Medicare Part B)	593	404	2,206	1,514	1,613	1,110

(continued)

273

Table 26.1
(continued)

	Valuation Period	Valuation Date	Net Present Value of Negative Cash Flow[5]
Federal Hospital Insurance (Medicare Part A) 2000	1/1/2000–12/31/2074	1/1/2000	2,699
Federal Hospital Insurance (Medicare Part A) 2001	1/1/2001–12/31/2075	1/1/2001	4,730
Federal Supplementary Medical Insurance (Medicare Part B) 2000	1/1/2000–12/31/2074	1/1/2000	6,494
Federal Supplementary Medical Insurance (Medicare Part B) 2001	1/1/2001–12/31/2075	1/1/2001	8,084

SOURCE: *Financial Report*, United States Government Stewardship Information for the Years Ended September 30, 2001, and September 30, 2000 (unaudited).

Note: figures are billions of dollars.

[1] Present values are computed based on the economic and demographic assumptions believed most likely to occur (the intermediate assumptions) as set forth in the related Trustees' reports.

[2] Contributions and earmarked taxes consist of payroll taxes from employers, employees, and self-employed persons; revenue from Federal income taxation of OASDI; and monthly Medicare Part B premiums paid by, or on behalf of, beneficiaries. Contributions and earmarked taxes for the Medicare Part B program presented in this report are presented on a consolidated perspective. Interest payments and other intergovernmental transfers have been eliminated. The Centers for Medicare & Medicaid Services' (CMS), formerly known as the Health Care Financing Administration (HCFA), 2001 Annual Report presents income from the trust fund's perspective, not a Government-wide perspective. Therefore, CMS's Annual Report includes $8,084 billion for the present value of transfers from the general fund of the Treasury to the Medicare Part B Trust Fund that have been eliminated in this *Financial Report*.

[3] Benefit payments include administrative expenses.

[4] Includes births during the period and individuals below age 15 as of January 1 of the valuation year.

[5] The net present value of negative cash flow is the current amount of funds needed to cover projected shortfalls, excluding trust fund balances, over the 75-year period. The trust fund balances at the beginning of the valuation period that were eliminated for this consolidation were: $177 billion—Medicare Part A and $44 billion—Medicare Part B. The projection period for new entrants covers the next 75 years for the Medicare program. The projection period for current participants (or "closed group") would theoretically cover all of their working and retirement years, but as a practical matter, the present values of future payments and contributions for/from current participants beyond 75 years are not material. The actuarial present value of the excess of future benefit payments to current participants (that is, to the closed group of participants) over future contributions and tax income from them or paid on their behalf is calculated by subtracting the actuarial present value of future contributions and tax income by and on behalf of current participants from the actuarial present value of the future benefit payments to them or on their behalf.

Moreover, simply struggling to preserve the current Medicare program, without substantial improvements and structural change, would ignore the needs of current and future beneficiaries. Medicare's basic benefit package has become increasingly outdated and inflexible. Traditional coverage fails to protect seniors against catastrophic medical bills or against almost any outpatient prescription drug expenses at all. Resolution of many coverage and reimbursement issues is hampered by inefficient, interminable, and inconsistent administrative determinations. For example, Medicare administrators took an average of 383 days to make and implement a national coverage decision in FY01. But, according to the Advanced Medical Technology Association, it then may take the Centers for Medicare and Medicaid Services an additional two years or more to assign codes and set payment rates for a new technology or service.

Physicians face mounting burdens of Medicare paperwork and incomprehensible regulatory edicts that reduce the time they can spend with their patients. Doctors also fear unwarranted accusations of fraud and harsh sanctions by Medicare enforcement officials, according to the Medicare Payment Advisory Commission. On top of that, Medicare reimbursement formulas cut payments to doctors by more than 5 percent in 2002. Current law requires overall reductions of 17 percent in Medicare fees paid for each medical service from 2002 to 2005. Not surprisingly, growing numbers of physicians are refusing to take new Medicare patients.

Although the 1999 bipartisan commission on Medicare sketched out some promising structural reforms, further actions to follow up on them and overhaul Medicare have languished, at best, in Congress. Instead, Congress has preferred to debate to a standstill an expanded Medicare entitlement to prescription drug coverage.

The next round of Medicare reform should emphasize structural change over short-term budget savings targets. The bungled experiment in Medicare + Choice must be repaired. Although the M + C program aimed at offering consumers more choice, a smaller percentage (14 percent) of Medicare beneficiaries was enrolled in private plans during 2001 than before the program was launched in 1997. The program has been plagued by withdrawals of and service reductions by private health plans. Very few insurers offered non-health-maintenance-organization (HMO) options, such as preferred provider organizations (PPOs) or private fee-for-service plans, and no carrier has ever offered a medical savings account (MSA) plan.

New payment methods established by the Balanced Budget Act largely failed to achieve their goal of limiting geographic variation in M + C payment rates, but they had the unintended consequence of paying too little in the most promising markets for expansion of private plan options. Early bureaucratic efforts at full risk adjustment in payments to plans were ineffective and suspended.

Congress needs to begin again with a blank sheet of paper and proceed to eliminate the uncertainties and excesses of its complex regulatory requirements, time limits, and payment methodologies for the faltering M + C program. Creation of a sustainable framework for Medicare modernization requires moving from an antiquated defined-benefit structure (which covers a specific set of health services) to a defined-contribution model, under which seniors could choose among competing packages of health benefits with taxpayers' costs capped at preset levels.

It is crucial that the traditional Medicare fee-for-service coverage program be required to improve by competing for market share on a level playing field. Many Medicare reformers emphasize the enhanced benefits and higher-quality care that new private plan options might make available to beneficiaries, but they tend to underplay, if not neglect, the key ingredients needed to make those improvements affordable. One necessary element includes a payment system under which private plans bid to provide required benefits, beneficiaries capture the savings from choosing less-costly options, and the government's share of Medicare funding reflects the enrollment-weighted average costs of the mandatory benefits provided in all plans (including traditional Medicare).

Seniors seeking additional supplemental benefits would pay higher premiums for them that would reflect their marginal costs. Because the same insurer would provide both the required benefits and the supplemental benefits, separate Medigap insurers that currently remove cost-sharing incentives within basic coverage would no longer be able to pass on to taxpayers the higher costs of additional spending. Medicare beneficiaries who accepted greater individual responsibility would be rewarded with broader health coverage choices and possible cash rebates.

Defined-contribution payments must be determined by competitive market prices, instead of remaining linked to the politically driven and bureaucratically administered price controls of the traditional Medicare program. Competitive bidding mechanisms and reasonable ground rules for periodic open enrollment choices offer great promise for ending distorted prices and poor information.

Other fundamental Medicare reforms include scrapping the mirage of trust fund financing, particularly the arbitrary shell game distinctions between the Part A trust fund (financed by payroll taxes) and the Part B trust fund (financed approximately three-quarters by general revenues and one-quarter by beneficiary premium payments).

Adding prescription drug benefits to Medicare should accompany, not precede, such structural reform. An updated M + C program and a restructured version of traditional Medicare could offer a range of enhanced drug options to beneficiaries willing to pay for them, perhaps through greater cost sharing for other covered benefits. Encouraging insurers to assemble packages of linked benefits would provide the greatest value by coordinating tradeoffs between drugs, surgery, hospitalization, and outpatient care as treatment options.

Congress must continue to resist the impulse to spread a wide and thin layer of visible, first-dollar drug subsidies to all Medicare beneficiaries, regardless of need, rather than target them more narrowly to support more generously those seniors most in need of assistance. Simply adding a new round of underfunded, irresponsible promises to Medicare will stimulate beneficiary demand for ''cheap'' drugs and overuse of those benefits. It is sure to be followed by exploding budgetary costs and increases in the ''unsubsidized'' price of Medicare's prescription drugs. Next will come waves of drug coverage rollbacks, regulatory restrictions, tighter drug formularies, and price controls that chill future innovative research and snuff out the next round of life-saving drugs.

It's the same old dead-end path to the Medicare Money Pit that we've already traveled down for hospital and physician services. The full costs of government-mandated ''price discounts'' eventually include reduced access to quality care and destabilized health care markets.

If Congress cannot resist the urge to add drug benefits without tackling fundamental Medicare reform, it should at least do less harm by emphasizing higher deductibles and catastrophic loss protection for prescription drug coverage, targeted assistance to lower-income seniors, and reformed coverage for individual Medigap purchasers. Under no circumstances should the door be opened to universal subsidies to seniors for routine, manageable drug expenses.

The average out-of-pocket drug expenditure for all Medicare enrollees in 2001 was about $650. Let's place the prescription drug issue in perspective by first dealing effectively with the small slice of Medicare beneficiaries (fewer than 10 percent) that faces more than $2,000 a year in out-of-pocket drug expenses, as well as with lower-income beneficiaries just beyond the eligibility limits for Medicaid drug assistance.

An initial round of the intermediate reform measures suggested above would help realign the current Medicare structure to allow its later transformation into a fully privatized system of health care choices for seniors. Congress should give careful consideration to eventually making it possible for younger workers to divert some or all of their Medicare payroll taxes into savings vehicles that would prefund their purchase of private health insurance when they reach retirement age. Transitional finance issues may slow the evolution toward this ultimate objective, but a full return to individual responsibility and private-sector health care offers the only long-term hope for surmounting the chronic financial crises and bureaucratic morasses of Medicare as we know it.

Up and Away from Medicaid Dependence

Over the past 15 years, Medicaid program outlays grew more than any other area of federal entitlement spending. Medicaid trails Social Security and Medicare as the third largest entitlement program. When Medicaid spending grew by 11 percent in FY01, it marked the fifth consecutive year that the program's spending growth accelerated. The Congressional Budget Office estimates that the federal share of Medicaid spending will grow at an average rate of 8.5 percent over the next 10 years.

Medicaid is a complex, patched-together assortment of four different types of public insurance programs for various categories of low-income Americans. It provides medical insurance for low-income women and their children. It pays medical bills for the low-income disabled. It finances a large portion of nursing home expenses for the elderly. It also picks up some of the other health costs of the "dual eligible" elderly that are not covered by Medicare (such as deductibles, coinsurance, Part B premiums, and outpatient prescription drugs).

The program is not just terribly costly, it is prone to mismanagement as an unwieldy mix of shared federal and state administrative responsibilities. More fundamentally, Medicaid is handicapped by its flawed welfare entitlement structure that still largely remains linked to one-size-fits-none sets of defined benefits. Medicaid continues to be plagued by poor quality health care and inadequate reimbursement levels. It keeps trying to promise more yet delivers less and less.

Federal policy encouraged states to expand eligibility for and services covered by their Medicaid plans over the last decade. State governments were eager to do so, because federal taxpayers picked up roughly 50 percent to 83 percent of Medicaid costs under matching formulas, depending on the particular state involved. States even exploited program funding loopholes to funnel more federal dollars into their coffers through such devices as phony "tax payments and donations" from providers and artificially higher state payments to public medical facilities that qualified for disproportionate share assistance.

The states belatedly discovered that they had indulged in too much of a good thing in leveraging their share of Medicaid financing. Over the last two years in particular, state Medicaid spending exploded at the same time that state revenue growth first slowed and then declined. Although state Medicaid program directors are beginning to learn that they cannot make up their losses on more volume, they have remained reluctant to cut back on their irrationally exuberant eligibility expansions of the 1990s. Instead, they generally have preferred to keep provider reimbursement rates well below market levels, blame pharmaceutical manufacturers for rising drug costs, and beg for larger federal matching payments.

Congress should resist pressure to expand the Medicaid program to new classes of beneficiaries, and it should encourage the states to put their own fiscal houses in order. The Bush administration's aggressive use of Medicaid waivers has provided more flexibility for state Medicaid programs. Its Health Insurance Flexibility and Accountability initiative allows states to reduce benefits and increase cost sharing, but with an unfortunately one-sided bias toward expanding the number of beneficiaries covered. The political danger of buying greater "market share" for Medicaid at loss-leader prices is that initial limits on benefits and coverage levels might not be politically sustainable.

State Medicaid programs need to rethink their policy priorities in balancing Medicaid spending with other claims on overstretched budget dollars. They should adjust eligibility criteria and covered benefits to serve fewer nondisabled and (relatively) higher-income individuals—but then provide those beneficiaries with higher quality health services. Instead of finding new ways to pay medical providers even less money per billable charge, they should focus on paying primary care doctors more adequately, making greater use of copayments and cost-sharing incentives, and reducing other optional Medicaid services. It's also more important to maximize coverage of the lowest-income individuals and families that are eligible for Medicaid but have few other insurance alternatives than to expand coverage to relatively higher-income groups.

Benefit payments for low-income adults and children are not major cost drivers. Those people represent about three-fourths of eligible beneficiaries, but they account for only about one-fourth of total program costs. Disabled individuals below age 65 constitute the fastest growing group eligible for Medicaid and account for the fastest growing slice of Medicaid spending. Medicaid spending per capita is highest for the low-income elderly, primarily in the form of payments for long-term care in nursing homes.

Although the cost of Medicaid drug benefits has been growing at eye-popping rates in recent years, it totaled just 11 percent of Medicaid spending in 2000. Medicaid beneficiaries who are either elderly or disabled accounted for almost 80 percent of those drug expenditures. Yet the health of the elderly has been improving since the early 1980s, particularly in terms of reduced rates of disability, because of improvements in medical technology and health knowledge. Given that development of innovative drug treatments has played a large role in this progress, recent state efforts to leverage further price rebates out of drug makers through tighter formularies and ''reference price'' ceilings may end up being penny-wise and pound-foolish in terms of overall Medicaid costs if they cut off access to new breakthrough drugs. Greater use of multitiered cost sharing provides a more flexible mechanism for slowing skyrocketing rates of prescription drug cost growth without arbitrarily restricting access to therapeutically necessary medicines.

Ironically, disability rates among younger Americans (and eligibility for Medicaid benefits) have been growing. This problem is best addressed by reexamining loosened requirements for disability eligibility; improving incentives for many disabled beneficiaries to build capital, reenter the workforce, and regain self-sufficiency; and expanding promising ''Cash and Counseling'' demonstration projects already under way in several states.

The benefits of more generous state Medicaid policies for nursing home reimbursement have largely accrued to children who would otherwise have to support and live with their elderly parents. Eligibility for Medicaid assistance in paying nursing home costs should be targeted more narrowly to the genuinely needy in order to provide stronger financial incentives for aging baby boomers and future generations to purchase private long-term care insurance.

Despite early enthusiasm on the part of many state governments for contracting with private HMOs to coordinate medical care for Medicaid recipients, a recent empirical review by Mark Duggan of the University of Chicago demonstrated that switching from fee-for-service to Medicaid managed care was associated with a substantial increase in government spending but no observable improvement in health outcomes.

A more ambitious intermediate-range Medicaid reform agenda should include more efforts to adapt defined-contribution-style financing as an option for beneficiaries so that they could control more of the content of their benefits packages and capture the gains from spending less on covered health services. Health care value is maximized better by "fixing" the total cost of benefits under an insurance model that then allows eligibility, the scope of benefits, and service quality to vary. Traditional Medicaid program rules instead concentrate on fixing the scope of benefits and eligibility criteria under an entitlement model that then focuses on budget costs as the key variable (and treats quality and access as less important considerations). Federal waiver authority should allow individual Medicaid beneficiaries to claim their "share" of annualized capitated payments within state managed care programs as a private health insurance voucher. Those beneficiaries who chose to opt out of such programs could then purchase other forms of private insurance coverage, as defined in the Health Insurance Portability and Accountability Act. States would be allowed to waive certain mandatory Medicaid benefits requirements to allow greater cost-sharing and economizing incentives.

Long-term reform will require that states be weaned from the federal matching rate formula that encourages them to chase their fiscal tails in search of federal dollars even as their state budgets plummet deeper into fiscal holes.

Suggested Readings

Blevins, Sue A. *Medicare's Midlife Crisis*. Washington: Cato Institute, 2001.

Ferrara, Peter. "The Next Steps for Medicare Reform." Cato Institute Policy Analysis no. 305, April 29, 1998.

Hyman, David A. "HIPAA and Health Care Fraud: An Empirical Perspective." *Cato Journal* 22, no. 1 (Spring–Summer 2002).

Miller, Tom. "Competitive Alternatives to Medicare." In *Privatization 2002: 16th Annual Report on Privatization*. Reason Public Policy Institute, 2002.

———. "Improving Access to Care without Comprehensive Health Insurance." In *Covering America: Real Remedies for the Uninsured,* Edited by Elliot K. Wickes and Jack A. Meyer. Washington: Economic and Social Research Institute, 2002.

———. "The Medicare Drug War Escalates: Bush Opens Up a New Front—Comprehensive Reform." Cato Institute White Paper, September 8, 2000.

Moses, Stephen. "LTC Choice: A Simple, Cost-Free Solution to the Long-Term Care Financing Puzzle." Center for Long-Term Care Financing, September 1, 1998.

Teske, Richard. "Abolishing the Medicaid Ghetto: Putting 'Patients First.'" In *The State Factor*. American Legislative Exchange Council, April 2002.

U.S. Department of the Treasury, Financial Management Service. *2001 Financial Report of the United States Government*. Washington: Government Printing Office, 2001, www.fms.treas.gov/fr/index.html.

—Prepared by Tom Miller

27. Private Health Care

Congress should

- offer a simplified set of flexible medical savings account options to all Americans;
- provide a tax credit option for taxpayers who choose to purchase health insurance that is not sponsored by their employers;
- expand consumer choices that increase market-based accountability of health plans; and
- improve access to health care through incentives to purchase less-comprehensive insurance, expand high-risk pool coverage, finance charitable safety net care, and deregulate state insurance regulation.

In the past two years, Congress finally may have exhausted its exploration of incremental health care proposals that lacked any consistent and coherent vision of free-market health care reform. The 107th Congress ultimately backed away from reconciling yet another set of different House and Senate versions of so-called patient's bill of rights legislation. Congress could not decide whether to herd more low-income uninsured Americans into Medicaid coverage or to accomplish income redistribution objectives through refundable tax credits for health insurance. The saving grace for a "do-nothing" Congress was that it did nothing to substantially expand federal control over the U.S. health care system. However, it also failed to begin to restore fundamental control of health care decisionmaking to individual consumers within a competitive free market.

Freeing Medical Savings Accounts from a Regulatory Lockbox

One of the primary factors driving health care costs higher has been the increased share of medical bills paid by third-party payers such as private health insurers, employers, and government health program administrators. On average, more than three out of every four dollars used to purchase health care are actually paid by someone other than the consumer who incurs the bill.

The centerpiece of market-oriented health care that can reverse this trend remains medical savings accounts (MSAs). MSAs combine two elements—a savings account controlled by the insured individual to be used to pay for routine health care expenses and a high-deductible (catastrophic) insurance policy to cover more substantial health care needs. With MSAs, a much smaller share of health care spending is funneled through third-party insurance. MSAs provide workers strong market incentives to control the costs of their health care, because account holders are effectively spending their own money for routine health items. That, in turn, stimulates real cost competition among and price disclosure by doctors and hospitals.

The 1996 Health Insurance Affordability and Accountability Act authorized up to 750,000 "tax-qualified" MSAs over a four-year period (later extended to December 31, 2003). Unlike previous MSAs, those so-called Archer MSAs featured tax-deductible treatment of MSA deposits and tax-exempt treatment of investment earnings accumulated with the MSAs. However, the potential of Archer MSAs has been hampered by eligibility limits and other design flaws mandated by HIPAA.

The next Congress should authorize MSAs permanently and open MSA eligibility to anyone covered by qualified high-deductible insurance. Market-oriented MSA rules also should provide more flexibility in deductible levels, contribution amounts, and fund withdrawal options. The best way to bring down health costs and improve health care quality remains a simple one—let workers and patients control more of their own health care dollars.

Facilitating Defined-Contribution Employer Health Benefits

A growing number of employers are beginning to offer defined-contribution-style (DC) health benefits plans, in which the employer purchases less-comprehensive, high-deductible group insurance coverage for workers covered by the plan and then makes cash contributions to those workers' individual health accounts. DC plans help employers cope with rising health insurance costs by capping their total health benefits contributions, increasing employee cost sharing, and empowering workers to handle more routine health care decisions.

Fewer than half (43 percent) of workers covered by employer-sponsored insurance (ESI) are satisfied with the overall performance of their current health plan, according to a Watson Wyatt Worldwide survey in 2001 (Figure 27.1). Fewer than half (48 percent) trust their employer to design a health plan that will provide the coverage they need, and approximately the same number of employees think better health plans are available for the same cost (Figure 27.2). Almost 4 of 10 employees want their employer to contribute a fixed-dollar amount toward the premium for any health plan—even if it means the employees have to find their own health plans.

A "purer" form of DC plan would allow employees to select their own individual insurance coverage, with the assistance of their employer's original contribution. Whether individual employees pay just the extra cost of additional out-of-pocket health spending or the extra cost of more generous insurance coverage as well, DC plans provide incentives for

Figure 27.1
Most Employees Are Less Than Satisfied with Health Plan Performance

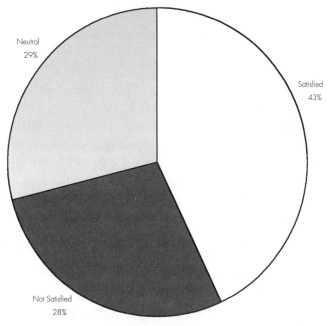

Neutral
29%

Satisfied
43%

Not Satisfied
28%

SOURCE: Based on Watson Wyatt, "Maximizing the Return on Health Benefits: 2001 Report on Best Practices in Health Care Vendor Management," www.watsonwyatt.com/research/resrender.asp?id + W-446&page3.

Figure 27.2
Employees Want More Options and Greater Involvement in Selecting a Health Plan

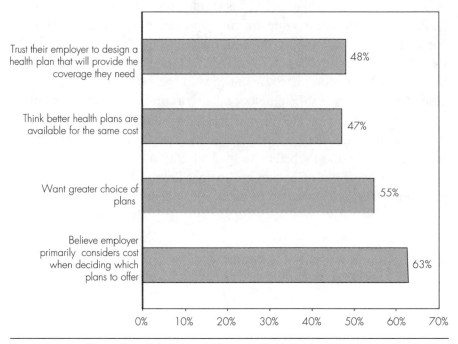

SOURCE: Based on Watson Wyatt, "Maximizing the Return on Health Benefits: 2001 Report on Best Practices in Health Care Vendor Management," www.watsonwyatt.com/research/resrender.asp?id+W-446&page3.

people to compare the value of the health care they receive with that of other goods and services they might want.

DC plans might provide a halfway house in the transition from comprehensive ESI to high-deductible MSA plans. Value-conscious employers and employees could insist that insurers ''spin off'' (not insure) items about which little uncertainty exists or for which the typical treatment cost is relatively low compared with the paperwork required to process the claim. Whereas MSA plans rely on much higher deductible levels for accompanying catastrophic insurance policies and treat all insured services equally, two-tiered DC plans could provide certain ''preventive care'' health services with first-dollar coverage, while others might not be covered at all.

Despite the potential benefits of two-tiered DC plans, as well as recent tax guidance issued by the Internal Revenue Service clarifying how accumulated balances in an individual employee's health reimbursement account may be treated when rolled over at the end of a year, several regulatory barriers to the future growth of DC plans still need to be removed.

First, "pure" DC plans for fully insured employer groups, in which an employer distributes defined health benefits contributions to each eligible employee and allows employees to purchase their own individual or non-employer-group insurance coverage, run the risk of being regulated inconsistently. They might be treated both as employee welfare benefit "group" plans and as "individual" health plans under state law.

Congress should clarify the regulatory treatment of this kind of DC plan so that it is not considered an "employee welfare benefit plan" for regulatory purposes under the Employee Retirement Income Security Act. However, such plans or funds should retain their "group" tax exclusion benefits under the Internal Revenue Code. One possible version of such hybrid treatment (group for tax purposes, individual for regulatory purposes) was proposed in the Health Care Act of 2001 (H.R. 2658).

Second, the defined contributions that employers make to individual employees in pure DC plans, to be used to purchase individual health insurance coverage, should be allowed to vary on the basis of health status in the event the employer uses an approved risk-adjustment mechanism. Congress should amend HIPAA rules to allow employers to make larger contributions to workers with poorer health status to offset the higher premiums they face when they seek to purchase individual coverage.

Third, recent IRS guidance regarding the tax-free rollover status of employer contributions to health reimbursement accounts still does not allow accumulated funds to become vested for other non-health-spending purposes. Nor does it allow employees to contribute their own money to such tax-advantaged accounts. To a large extent, allowing annual rollovers of flexible spending account (FSA) fund balances, or expanding the availability of MSAs, would bypass most of this problem if Congress does not address it more directly.

Tax Equity and Efficiency

MSAs and DC health plans provide a foundation for free-market health reform, but Congress also needs to enact more fundamental changes in the tax treatment of health care benefits. The tax system should promote economic efficiency and be perceived as fair. Its compliance and administrative costs should be kept to a minimum. Tax policy proposals that try to target more narrow objectives must be structured to reinforce, not undercut, those fundamental principles.

Federal tax law excludes the cost of employer-sponsored health insurance benefits from the taxable income of individual workers. Many employers also offer their employees tax-exempt FSAs for health care reimbursements. However, those job-based tax benefits for health care spending put employers, instead of employees, in charge of selecting health care benefits. Special tax treatment of ESI via the so-called tax exclusion forces many working Americans to accept the only health plan offered by their employer or pay higher taxes.

The tax exclusion also raises the comparative after-tax price of other non-employer-based insurance alternatives. Although similar tax subsidies are available to the self-employed, the tax exclusion provides no assistance at all to other individuals (such as Americans working in firms that do not provide health insurance) who might wish to purchase health insurance on their own.

The tax exclusion distorts health care purchasing choices by favoring the financing of medical services through insurance and providing the greatest tax benefits for the most costly versions of employer-sponsored coverage. It encourages workers to think that someone else (their employer) pays for their health care, and it reduces their sensitivity to the cost of health insurance choices. The tax exclusion disconnects the consumption decisions of insured workers and their families from the payment decisions of employers and their insurers. Tax subsidies for health insurance over-stimulate the demand for health care and, perversely, increase its total cost, creating net welfare losses estimated at 20 percent to 30 percent of total insurance spending.

The current tax subsidy for health insurance is inefficient and unfair. It should be reformed to place individuals, not employers or government, in charge of choosing something as personal as health care.

The best way to remove tax policy distortions from the health insurance market would be to eliminate tax subsidies for employment-based health insurance altogether. Implementing a flat income tax or a national sales tax would provide the best comprehensive solution. Fundamental tax reform would render neutral the federal government's tax treatment of all goods and services, including health care. Employer-paid health benefits either would be treated as taxable income earned by employees (flat tax) or would be subject to a sales tax like other goods and services (national sales tax).

However, repeal of the tax exclusion would need to be phased in gradually and be accompanied by offsetting reductions in marginal income tax rates and increases in income tax bracket thresholds, in order to minimize economic distortions and return the money to the American workers who earn it.

Absent a broad restructuring of the tax code, the next-best policy would be to offer a new federal tax credit option, most likely amounting to 30 percent of the cost of qualified insurance coverage. The tax credit option would not eliminate the current tax exclusion; it would provide a competitive alternative for workers to choose in place of the tax exclusion. It would encourage a more gradual transition to other forms of private insurance coverage. The tax credit option also would be made available to other individuals and families that currently do not qualify for the tax exclusion because they lack access to ESI coverage.

Employers that continue to offer ESI should be required to report the value of the employer-financed share of that coverage to individual employees on their regular periodic pay statements and annual W-2 forms. The default setting for such disclosure would assume that workers in employer-group plans are community rated within the firm and the employer contributions for coverage are identical for each worker (such as the periodic equivalent of the firm's per employee COBRA premium). In the event that employers were allowed to adjust health plan contributions to reflect factors specific to individual workers, they could report those different amounts instead.

The new tax credits would be assignable to insurers and advanceable, but not refundable. The maximum tax credit available to any eligible individual would be no greater than that individual's total federal income tax and FICA payroll tax liability (including both the employee and employer shares) for the previous calendar year. Only taxpayers would receive tax credit "relief" for health insurance costs.

The net effect of the above tax reform would be to encourage workers and their families either to move from ESI coverage to individually purchased insurance or to ensure that the ESI plan they select represents the best competitive value they can find.

Congress should consider using the new tax credit option to leverage other market-opening reforms. In that case, consumers wishing to use the tax credit would have to purchase an insurance package that covered a minimum set of health services and included a minimum, but significant, front-end deductible (along with maximum out-of-pocket "stop-loss" limits). Qualified insurance policies might provide separately priced guaranteed renewal options in return for exemption from HIPAA's guaranteed renewal requirements. Those policies also should be exempt from individual state benefit mandates. New voluntary purchasing pools could be authorized to accept tax credit funds to pay for such qualified insurance in return for federal preemption of state benefit mandates, fictitious group laws, or rating laws that would otherwise interfere with their operations.

Providing a new tax credit option could jump-start the evolution toward an employee benefits environment in which workers more directly control their health care benefits and insurance choices. It would ensure sufficient consumer demand for individually selected insurance arrangements and provide a competitive alternative to ESI coverage.

Improving Access to Health Care for the Low-Income Uninsured

Any new tax credits for health care should not try to finance comprehensive insurance for all uninsured, low-income Americans. Most refundable tax credit proposals are designed to award tax "cuts" to individuals who pay little, or no, federal taxes. But endorsing a new round of income redistribution and federal spending via the tax code (in the name of health care) is contradictory and counterproductive. Refundable health tax credits blur necessary policy distinctions between how to set the appropriate level of income-based welfare assistance and how to neutralize the many distortions caused by our complex tax system. The politics of refundable tax credit proposals also has unfortunately steered recent health care debates away from broad, individual empowerment tax reforms and toward a narrow, cramped version of targeted handouts to smaller slices of the low-income uninsured population. The alternative budgetary end game of traveling down the road to a universal fixed-dollar tax credit is likely to involve financing new subsidies for nontaxpayers by reducing the current health insurance tax benefits available to higher-income Americans (in other words, the old politics of trying to soak the rich to subsidize the poor).

Refundable tax credits combine bad tax policy, bad welfare policy, and bad health policy. They reinforce the mistaken stance of those who argue that cuts in marginal tax rates are somehow "unfair" when they provide most of their benefits to those who pay the largest share of federal income taxes. Refundable credits also are prone to carrying the lumpy baggage of complex income-based, phase-out levels; tight restrictions on the contents of eligible health benefits packages; and narrow rules for eligible insurers.

Making health tax credits refundable would endorse expansion of current taxpayer-financed "entitlements" to health insurance coverage. It would adopt the view that health insurance is a "merit good" for everyone and that necessary access to health care cannot be adequately financed without even greater subsidies from taxpayers for insurance coverage. Many lawmakers who salute the remarkable benefits gained from limiting the magnitude and duration of cash assistance to low-income beneficiaries on the welfare rolls nevertheless appear poised to dole out a new round of permanent "welfare" checks to the working poor, hidden beneath a refundable health tax-credit label.

For low-income individuals lacking access to health insurance, the better policy solutions include safety net reforms that strengthen state high-risk pools and encourage charitable contributions to provide health services through nonprofit intermediaries. Dollar for dollar, investing in safety net assistance that directly delivers care to the uninsured is more effective and productive than trying to coax them to purchase health insurance with modest tax subsidies. In the long run, improving the quality of education that lower-income individuals receive, expanding their personal control of health care decisions, and reversing regulatory policies that increase the cost of their health care will yield even greater returns in improved health outcomes.

Managed Care and Consumer Empowerment

Although the growth of managed care insurance coverage during the 1990s helped to restrain the rate of growth of health care costs, consumers increasingly became dissatisfied with managed care's limits on covered treatments and restrictions on their choice of physicians. Various "patient's bill of rights" (PBOR) measures have been proposed in Congress to respond to (or at least exploit) those cost and quality conflicts.

In the 107th Congress, both House and Senate bills advanced that would have extended the tentacles of federal regulation more tightly over health insurance arrangements and health care delivery. A multitude of new federal commands was buttressed by the usual vague, undefined terms and weasel words, sure to expand bureaucratic discretion and control in future rounds of reinterpretation and elaboration. Even without more explicit rights to sue health plans over coverage denials, approval of PBOR mandates would have opened the door to federal micromanagement of complex health care decisions and provided the foundation for lawsuits based on alleged violations of mandatory standards.

Ironically, while Capitol Hill politicians again reached a dead end in negotiations over a final PBOR bill, they were essentially still fighting the last war. The marketplace had moved on. The pure vision of HMO-style health care failed several years ago. HMOs reduced costs primarily by gaining bargaining leverage and squeezing the wallets of providers on fees, but their claims of evidence-based health care management and cost-saving preventive care often were more illusion than reality. Other forms of managed care became more widespread and more attractive to employers. Employers shifted their health plans to preferred provider organizations with broad networks and fewer limits on access to care. When workers insisted on more choices and fewer hassles, their employers generally responded. However, part of the price of loosened management of health care services may have been the recent return of annual double-digit percentage increases in health insurance premiums.

The most immediate victims of PBOR-style regulation would be the consumers who don't want, or cannot afford to pay for, the type of minimum contract terms that the legislation would mandate. Raising the cost of health insurance and regulating away low-cost HMO options will hurt low-income workers the most. They will either have to pay the higher price of upper-middle-class medical care expectations or have to go without any insurance at all. Price-sensitive small employers who could no longer find low-cost HMO options also would be squeezed out of the insurance market.

Instead of offering consumers another set of unreliable third-party guardians (regulators, independent medical reviewers, and courts), Congress should emphasize greater tax equity for all health care purchasers and expanded pooling options outside the workplace so that disgruntled consumers could choose and control the types of health plan and benefits packages for which they are willing to pay.

A policy environment friendlier to value-driven consumer choice would hold managed care insurers and self-insured employers more accountable to their true customers. Consumers would rely on voluntary contracts and competitive markets, instead of random lawsuits, to stimulate better service, relevant disclosure, benefits flexibility, and health care innovation. Or they would switch insurers.

Legitimacy and acceptance of after-the-fact results in health care require before-the-fact opportunities to choose. Many consumers may not want to manage personally most details of their health care decisions, but they should get to decide who will decide for them.

Insurers or employers that still choose to more actively manage health care decisions or supervise in-network providers should be exposed to vicarious liability for medical malpractice and other negligent treatment decisions. Liability rules should clarify the differences between contractual obligations (delivering what it promised by the written terms of a health insurance policy) and tort liability (providing compensation for personal injuries and other losses arising from care rendered by health care providers under the contract between a health plan and a purchaser of its coverage). Augmenting ERISA contract remedies for wrongful denial of coverage could be handled through early offer settlement incentives and a worker's compensation–like schedule of recoveries tied to the cost of denied benefits.

For the last six years, Congress has remained both fixated on and stalemated over how to hold managed care plans more accountable for adverse medical treatment outcomes but avoid crushing them under an avalanche of personal injury lawsuits. If the next Congress cannot remain away from the PBOR bargaining table, it should at least reconsider the applicable standard that it sets for external review of coverage decisions. Review should focus on interpreting and enforcing the actual contractual terms of a particular health plan—rather than on making de novo "expert" judgments about what constitutes "medically necessary" treatment according to a uniform standard of care.

Restoring the role of consensual contracts, instead of expanding the role of adversarial tort lawsuits and political micromanagement, would improve the range of competitive health care choices for consumers and encourage better monitoring of health care quality.

Conclusion

We cannot afford to allow the market vision of health care reform to be dimmed and obscured by cut-rate compromises that lead to a slow, steady drift toward centralized, politicized control of health spending decisions. Every calculated attack on private health insurance markets should be resisted before a series of "small" proposals steadily accumulates to make private coverage ever more expensive and difficult to obtain.

Health care costs will remain too high, the value of health insurance too inadequate, and the quality of health care too low until we restore a genuine free market in health care, from cradle to grave.

Suggested Reading

Bunce, Victoria C. "Medical Savings Accounts: Progress and Problems under HIPAA." Cato Institute Policy Analysis no. 411, August 8, 2001.

Miller, Tom. "Improving Access to Health Care without Comprehensive Health Insurance Coverage." In *Covering America: Real Remedies for the Uninsured.* Edited by Elliot K. Wicks and Jack A. Meyer. Washington: Economic and Social Research Institute, 2002.

————. "Nickles-Stearns Is Not the Market Choice for Health Care Reform." Cato Institute Policy Analysis no. 210, June 13, 1994.

————. "A Regulatory Bypass Operation," *Cato Journal* 22, no 1 (Spring–Summer 2002).

Miller, Tom, and Gregory Conko. "Getting beyond the Managed Care Backlash." *Regulation* 21, no. 4 (Fall 1998).

Miller, Tom, and Scott E. Harrington. "Competitive Markets for Individual Health Insurance." *Health Affairs*, October 23, 2002.

Morreim, E. Haavi. "Defined Contribution: From Managed Care to Patient-Managed Care." *Cato Journal* 22, no. 1 (Spring–Summer 2002).

————. "The Futility of Medical Necessity." *Regulation* 24, no. 2 (Summer 2001).

Scandlen, Greg. "Legislative Malpractice: Misdiagnosing Patients' Rights." Cato Institute Briefing Paper no. 57, April 7, 2000.

Tanner, Michael. "Medical Savings Accounts: Answering the Critics." Cato Institute Policy Analysis no. 228, May 25, 1998.

—Prepared by Tom Miller

28. Department of Education

Congress should

- abolish the Department of Education and
- return education to the state, local, or family level, as provided by the Constitution.

The powers not delegated to the United States by the Constitution, nor prohibited by it to the States, are reserved to the States respectively, or to the people.

—Tenth Amendment to the U.S. Constitution

The U.S. Department of Education, formed in 1979 during the Carter administration, represents an intrusion by the federal government into an aspect of American society for which there is no constitutional authority. The U.S. Constitution gives Congress no authority whatsoever to collect taxes for, fund, or operate schools. Therefore, under the Tenth Amendment, education should be entirely a state and local matter.

For more than 200 years, the federal government had left education to those who were in the best position to oversee it—state and local governments and families. Richard L. Lyman, president of Stanford University, who testified at the congressional hearings on forming the new department, pointed out that "the two-hundred-year-old absence of a Department of Education is not the result of simple failure during all that time. On the contrary, it derives from the conviction that we do not want the kind of educational system that such arrangements produce."

Without question, the Framers intended that most aspects of American life would be outside the purview of the federal government. They never envisioned that Congress or the president would become involved in funding schools or mandating policy for classrooms. As constitutional scholar Roger Pilon has said: "From beginning to end the [Constitution] never mentioned the word 'education.' The people, in 1787 or since, have never given the federal government any power over the subject—despite a concern for education that surely predates the Constitution.''

Why then was the Department of Education created? President Jimmy Carter, during whose watch the new department came into being, had promised the department to the National Education Association. Contemporary editorials in both the *New York Times* and the *Washington Post* acknowledged that the creation of the department was mainly in response to pressure from the NEA. According to Rep. Benjamin Rosenthal (D-N.Y.), Congress went along with the plan out of ''not wanting to embarrass the president.'' Also, many members of Congress had made promises to educators in their home districts to support the new department. The *Wall Street Journal* reported the admission of one House Democrat: ''The idea of an Education Department is really a bad one. But it's NEA's top priority. There are school teachers in every congressional district and most of us simply don't need the aggravation of taking them on.'' Former house minority leader Bob Michel termed the Department of Education the ''Special Interest Memorial Prize'' of the year.

The new department started with a $14 billion budget and more than 4,000 employees, all transferred from other departments. Proponents claimed that cost savings would be realized, but opponents pointed out that a new department would require not only a new secretary but also the corresponding assistant secretaries, under secretaries, support staff, office space, regional offices, cars, and other amenities. All of those would be necessary for the new department to look and act like a bona fide cabinet department. Critics of the department also pointed to the Department of Energy, formed two years earlier, which had been the subject of a tangle of regulations and confusing policies. Rep. John Rousselot (R-Calif.) said: ''If you like the Department of Energy, you'll love the Department of Education. You'll have every bureaucrat in Washington looking at your school district.''

Has the Department of Education produced budget savings or a streamlining of federal education programs? No. The department's budget has continually increased, from $14.5 billion in 1979 to $47.6 billion in 2002. According to analyses of federal education spending before and after the creation of the Department of Education, after its creation, federal spending on education increased at twice the rate it had before.

Chester Finn, who served as assistant secretary of education from 1985 until 1988, made the following observation about why education spending increased faster once we had a Department of Education:

When budget time rolls around, a department is able to exert more clout in pressing for larger funding from Congress than can smaller agencies. It carries a bureaucratic momentum and muscle all its own. Since it no longer has to compete with health and welfare, as it did under HEW, the new department will be able to exert the full brunt of the education lobby in its behalf upon the Congress. Make no mistake about it, the principal reason the NEA and the administration wanted to elevate the Office of Education to a full-fledged department was to give it the political power and prestige to seek bigger budget increases for federal education programs.

Along with the budget, the maze of federal education programs continues to expand under the Department of Education. Wayne Riddle, representing the Congressional Research Service, testified before a 1995 congressional hearing that the potential overlap of Department of Education programs with those of other federal agencies has probably increased since 1979 in such areas as vocational education and job training, science education, and early childhood education. Last year, the House Education and Workforce Committee reported that there were more than 760 education-related programs spread across 39 federal agencies costing taxpayers $120 billion per year. President Bush's 2003 budget calls for federal spending on myriad education programs that are clearly local in nature—from special reading and after-school programs to tutoring preschoolers to job training for their parents.

Also, the Department of Education and its nearly 5,000 employees have had virtually no positive effect on the performance of schools or the academic gains of school children. The department's own national history report card issued in May 2002 found that only 43 percent of the nation's 12th graders had at least a basic understanding of U.S. history, unchanged from 1994, the last time the test was given. On one question, the majority of high school seniors chose Germany, Japan, or Italy as a U.S. ally in World War II. Diane Ravitch, education adviser to the Bush administration and professor of education at New York University, called the results "truly abysmal." "Since the seniors are very close to voting age or have already reached it," she observed, "one can only feel alarm that they know so little about their nation's history and express so little capacity to reflect on its meaning." Comparisons of U.S. students with students in other countries show that U.S. students still lag behind students in countries such as Finland, Australia, and New Zealand.

It's fair to say that the Department of Education has had no apparent positive effect on the academic performance of U.S. school children.

Instead, its major effect has been to move the focus on improving education from parents and local districts to Washington, D.C. Federal guidelines now cover topics such as how schools discipline students, the content of sex education courses, and the gender of textbook authors. Former secretaries of education Lamar Alexander and William Bennett have stated that the department has "an irresistible and uncontrollable impulse to stick its nose into areas where it has no proper business. Most of what it does today is no legitimate affair of the federal government. The Education Department operates from the deeply erroneous belief that American parents, teachers, communities and states are too stupid to raise their own children, run their own schools and make their own decisions."

American taxpayers have spent virtually billions of dollars on the Department of Education since its founding in 1979, yet test scores and other measures indicate no improvement in American education (Figure 28.1). The benefits promised by the proponents of the department plainly have not materialized. There is simply no legitimate reason to continue this failed experiment.

Figure 28.1
Average Student Performance and Cost

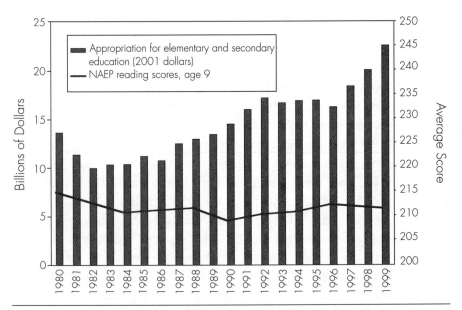

SOURCE: U.S. Department of Education, National Center for Education Statistics, National Assessment of Educational Progress, 1999 Long Term Trend Assessment, www.nces.ed.gov/nationsreportcard/reading/trends-national.asp; and U.S. Department of Education, Budget Office, Education Department Budget by Major Program, www.ed.gov/offices/OUS/Budget02/History.pdf.

No Child Left Behind Act

The foremost policy initiative of the Bush administration to date has been the No Child Left Behind Act, a comprehensive plan to encourage states to improve the performance of American public schools through mandatory testing and an accountability plan that requires states to determine which schools are failing. The supporters of the NCLBA assure us that these actions will improve schools. But the response of public school districts to the federal mandate thus far shows how resistant the education establishment is to change. Most districts have designated only a few schools as alternatives to those schools in their districts categorized as failing, leaving students with little choice of an alternative. And in many cases, the designated alternative schools are not much better than the school the child would be leaving. Some districts, like Washington, D.C., have nowhere to send children who wish to leave poorly performing schools. D.C. School Board president Peggy Cooper Cafritz noted that all D.C. high schools, except four, "are generally lousy, so where do we send the children?" Few school districts have published user-friendly information about available schools, and some districts do not even allow parents to designate on the transfer application where they want their child to go.

Although the bill requires that schools show "adequate yearly progress," there is no consensus about what amount of progress is adequate, so states can formulate a definition that shows most schools as successful, even if the parents are dissatisfied with the results. In July 2002 Arkansas, for example, reported zero failing schools, while Michigan reported 1,513 failing schools. This is a highly dubious situation since Arkansas ranked 42nd in the nation and Michigan ranked 26th on the American Legislative Exchange Council's recent "Report Card on American Education," which ranks states on the basis of K–12 academic achievement.

The NCLBA is also a funding initiative that gives billions of additional federal dollars to failing schools. The Washington, D.C., school district, a school system with a long string of documented inefficiencies and a history of waste and corruption, already spends the second largest amount per student in the nation. Under the new federal program, the D.C. public schools will receive $149.8 million in additional funding. No reasonable person who is familiar with the D.C. system would expect to see any benefit result from placing those funds in the hands of the people who are in charge of running the failing D.C. schools.

The NCLBA provides the Department of Education with $26.5 billion for spending on the program and perpetuates most of the old federal education programs, most of which are ineffective and wasteful. The total could climb to $37 billion a year by the end of the six-year authorization period. If past experience is any guide, those dollars will go primarily to feeding the hungry bureaucracy and will have little positive impact on public school students.

Instead of decreasing the role of the federal government in education, the NCLBA allows the federal government to intervene more than ever in what should be strictly a local and state matter. While the act provides school districts with increased flexibility in spending some of their federal subsidies, mandated testing and staff restructuring represent an unprecedented usurpation of the authority of local communities to run their own schools.

During his presidential campaign, Bush emphasized that he did not want to become the "federal superintendent of schools." But the NCLBA gives the president and the federal government far too much power over local schools and classrooms. Instead of proposing more top-down fixes for education, the president should use his position to push for the return of control of education to states and localities and urge state-level reforms that return the control of education to parents.

New Directions

There is a growing awareness that parents, not distant government bureaucrats, should have more power over their children's education. After years of legal battles over school choice in places like Cleveland, Ohio, and Milwaukee, Wisconsin, the U.S. Supreme Court ruled in June 2002 that school vouchers were constitutional and that parents could use them at either secular or religious private schools. School choice programs now exist in Ohio, Wisconsin, Florida, Pennsylvania, Arizona, Maine, Vermont, and Illinois. Many more states will consider school choice legislation during the coming two years.

The way for Congress to improve American education is to step aside and let the states experiment with choice in a variety of ways. Some will expand charter schools or experiment with private management. Others will institute scholarship tax credits, parental tax credits, or vouchers either on a limited basis or open to all students. The most successful policies and programs will be emulated by other states.

Nine Reasons to Abolish the Department of Education

1. The Constitution provides no authority whatsoever for the federal government to be involved in education. Eliminating the department on those grounds would help to reestablish the original understanding of the enumerated powers of the federal government.

2. No matter how brilliantly designed a federal government program may be, it creates a uniformity among states that is harmful to creativity and improvement. Getting the federal government out of the picture would allow states and local governments to create better ways of addressing education issues and problems.

3. If education were left at the local level, parents would become more involved in reform efforts. Differences in school effectiveness among states and communities would be noted, and other regions would copy the more effective programs and policies.

4. The contest between Congress and state legislatures to demonstrate who cares more about education would be over, allowing members of Congress to focus on areas and problems for which they have legitimate responsibility.

5. Since most information about the problems and challenges of education is present at the local level, Congress simply does not have the ability to improve learning in school classrooms thousands of miles away. These problems are best understood and addressed by local authorities and parents.

6. The inevitable pattern of bureaucracy is to grow bigger and bigger. The Department of Education should be eliminated now, before it evolves into an even larger entity consuming more and more resources that could be better spent by parents themselves.

7. The $47.6 billion spent each year by the Department of Education could be much better spent if it were simply returned to the American people in the form of a tax cut. Parents themselves could then decide how best to spend that money.

8. The Department of Education has a record of waste and abuse. For example, the department reported losing track of $450 million during three consecutive General Accounting Office audits.

9. The Department of Education is an expensive failure that has added paperwork and bureaucracy but little value to the nation's classrooms.

Since Congress has no authority under the Constitution to collect taxes for, fund, or regulate schools, it should not tax Americans to fund a huge federal education bureaucracy that exercises dictatorial control over curriculum, standards, and policy. The only actions that should be taken at the federal level are those that deregulate education. For example, Congress should repeal the many regulations and mandates governing special education and allow states to set up their own programs for educating special needs children. Instead of mandating tests or other accountability measures and subsidizing the public school monopoly, it should free states from their addiction to federal funds, eliminate the myriad unnecessary and unconstitutional federal programs, and allow the states to take the lead in reforming education.

Except in Washington, D.C., where Congress has constitutional authority over legislative matters, it should not set up demonstration projects or fund voucher programs. Federal tax credits for parents who use private schools may seem attractive, but, since Congress has no constitutional authority to collect taxes for education, it would be better to simply institute a tax cut for all Americans, eliminate the wasteful and meddlesome Department of Education, and allow individual Americans to decide how best to spend that money. We must remember that parents, not politicians, are in the best position to make decisions about the education of their children.

James Madison, who proclaimed that the powers of the federal government should be few and enumerated, would be shocked at what the president and Congress are doing today in relation to an aspect of family life that was never intended to come under the control of Congress, the White House, or any federal agency. Congress should take the enlightened view, consistent with that of the nation's Founders, and draw a line in the sand that won't be crossed. Education is a matter reserved to the states, period.

Suggested Readings

Boaz, David, ed. *Liberating Schools: Education in the Inner City.* Washington: Cato Institute, 1991.

Finn, Chester E. Jr., and Michael J. Petrilli. ''Washington versus School Reform.'' *Public Interest* 133 (Fall 1998).

Coulson, Andrew. *Market Education: The Unknown History.* New Brunswick, N.J.: Transaction, 1999.

Harmer, David. *School Choice: Why You Need It, How You Get It.* Washington: Cato Institute, 1994.

Lieberman, Myron. *Public Education: An Autopsy.* Cambridge, Mass.: Harvard University Press, 1993.

Richman, Sheldon. "Parent Power: Why National Standards Won't Improve Education." Cato Institute Policy Analysis no. 396. April 26, 2001.

Subcommittee on Oversight and Investigations of the House Committee on Education and the Workforce. "Education at the Crossroads: What Works and What's Wasted in Education Today." 105th Cong., 2d sess., July 17, 1998.

—Prepared by David Salisbury

29. Special Education

Congress should

- devolve responsibility for special education to the states,
- eliminate federal regulations that waste resources and pit parents against teachers, and
- refuse to turn the Individuals with Disabilities in Education Act into an entitlement for state governments.

Since 1975, the law now known as the Individuals with Disabilities in Education Act has promised a "free appropriate public education" to all children with disabilities. Local public schools have been required to accept all disabled students and provide them with an educational plan in compliance with various federal procedural requirements. In return, the act provides for some discretionary federal funding to assist school districts in establishing programs and procedures to meet the special needs of students with disabilities. Students with disabilities must be educated in the "least restrictive environment," meaning that they should be accommodated in regular classrooms where possible.

IDEA was part of an important effort in the 1970s to end discrimination against disabled children by states and local school districts. Disabled students' civil rights are protected by the Equal Protection Clause and Due Process Clause of the Constitution and by an anti-discrimination law commonly known as Section 504. When it became clear that disabled children were not being treated fairly under the law by public school systems, Congress passed IDEA in an effort to provide a regulatory framework, or process, as well as some funding to help states ensure that disabled children would not suffer from further discrimination.

IDEA is often conflated with the constitutional rights of disabled children by defenders of the status quo. They wrongly argue that changes to IDEA would amount to a denial of equal protection to students with special needs. In fact, IDEA is a regulatory process—a mechanism—for helping to achieve the goal of equity for disabled students. Although IDEA has been successful in providing disabled children with greater access to public schools, it has largely failed to ensure an appropriate education for children with disabilities.

IDEA's Failed Dispute Resolution Model

IDEA's central failure is the complex and adversarial process required to determine the size and nature of each disabled child's entitlement to special services. Recognizing that the educational needs of disabled children differ widely, the act mandates that each child's "individual education plan," or IEP, be created out of whole cloth by his or her local school district in a series of meetings and due process procedures.

The process mandated by the statute has not only failed to achieve its purpose of ensuring an appropriate education for each disabled child. It also has marginalized the parents it was intended to empower and has created a barrage of compliance-driven paperwork so overwhelming that special educators are driven to quit the profession. Federal survey results show that special education teachers spend between a quarter and a third of each week on IDEA-mandated bureaucratic chores.

Worse, IDEA's adversarial nature has undermined relationships between parents and educators, pitting parent against school in a bitter struggle over limited resources. Because the act's procedures require savvy, aggressive navigation, its benefits flow disproportionately to wealthy families, often leaving lower-income children poorly served.

IDEA has also encouraged incorrect labeling of many students as learning disabled. The growth of special education can be attributed largely to a sharp rise in the number of children categorized as learning disabled. The number of children identified in this category grew by an extraordinary 242 percent between 1979 and 1997 (Figure 29.1). The number of children served in all the other disability categories combined increased by only 13 percent during the same period. Today, children diagnosed as learning disabled account for nearly 50 percent of children in special education.

Although the 1997 amendments to IDEA sought to alleviate this problem by changing federal fiscal policy, schools will continue to overidentify children as learning disabled as long as funds that follow a disabled child into a school are controlled by the school rather than by the child's parents. Under IDEA's current dispute resolution model for determining benefits, funds received from state and federal sources for each identified child

Figure 29.1
Number of Children in Federally Supported Programs for the Disabled, by Category (thousands)

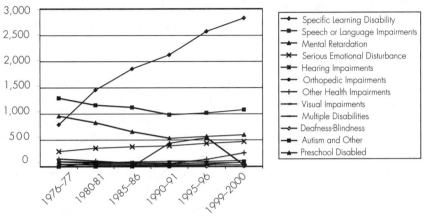

SOURCE: National Center for Education Statistics, *Digest of Education Statistics, 2001* (Washington: U.S. Department of Education, 2002), Table 52.

need not actually be spent on that child. If the school can identify a child in need of few special services, that child's special education funds can be shifted to other children with more expensive needs, or to cover the bureaucratic costs of administering the program. Because learning disabilities have no known organic basis and require fewer services than most other types of disabilities, the label is especially ripe for abuse.

Unsurprisingly, IDEA has precipitated a financial crisis in schools. In 1977 services for disabled students accounted for 16.6 percent of total education spending. Today the $78.3 billion spent on special education students at the local, state, and federal levels accounts for 21.4 percent of the $360.2 billion spent on elementary and secondary public education in the United States. The number of school-age children receiving special education services also increased during this period, from about 8.5 percent in 1977–78 to nearly 13 percent in 1999–2000.

Regulatory compliance and litigation costs related to IDEA's failed dispute resolution framework are soaking up precious resources needed for education. For the year 1999–2000, the American Institutes for Research estimates that $6.7 billion was spent at the state and local levels for "assessment, evaluation and IEP related activities." Moreover, the $6.7 billion estimate does not appear to include many due process and litigation expenses, nor does it include fee awards to successful plaintiffs' attorneys.

307

Choice-Based Reform

The battle between parents and schools over each child's educational plan must end with a decisive victory for parents in the form of portable benefits. Special education should be reformed to allow parents to control how their child's educational dollars are spent in the public or private school of their choice.

Choice-based reform would improve educational outcomes by allowing parents to choose their child's very best option, and successful schools would be those that served parents and children well. Accompanied by massive deregulation, thoughtful choice-based reform will free teachers to teach and allow funds currently wasted on administration to be returned to the classroom.

Devolution of all responsibility for special education to the states would be optimal. If complete devolution is not immediately possible, Congress should amend IDEA to allow states to opt into a reformed special education system, which would eliminate the failed dispute resolution model entirely in favor of a state-administered, largely state-funded system based on parental choice.

A state would opt into the program by creating a matrix of disability categories and monetary contributions designed to represent the total average cost of both general and special services required to educate a child in each category of disability. The state would then create a menu of special education services no less comprehensive than those currently available in each school district and their estimated cost per child per hour or per semester, as appropriate.

Parents in a reformed special education system would find themselves transformed from combatants into customers. Instead of fighting each year over educational programming, parents would be invited to their local school to select from the menu of available special services with the advice of special educators or anyone else the parent felt was appropriate, up to the amount of the child's defined monetary contribution under the matrix. Or the parent could take his or her child's total educational allowance to a private school of choice.

Because parental choice would replace negotiation as the method of determining a child's educational plan, Congress should exempt states opting into a reformed system from all of the IEP and due process requirements of IDEA, and they should no longer be subject to civil suit under the act. The sole remaining potential dispute in a reforming state would be the accuracy of a child's diagnosis and, accordingly, the size of his or her monetary contribution. Congress should ask those states to create rules for genuinely independent binding arbitration of disputes related to the diagnosis of a child covered by IDEA.

The end result for a state opting for reform would be a state-administered, largely state-funded portable benefits plan that would avoid IDEA's worst problems.

Choice-Based IDEA Reform Will Reduce Waste, Empower Parents

States opting for choice-based reform would each save tens of millions of dollars, now devoted to procedural compliance, legal posturing, and litigation. If even half of the annual $6.7 billion devoted to "assessment, evaluation and IEP related expenditures" were eliminated, $3.35 billion could be saved nationally on those items alone. States and parents would also save millions more on IDEA attorneys' fees and other legal expenses.

Choice-based reform will also alleviate the problem of overidentification of children as having disabilities, a phenomenon that has contributed to IDEA's increasing costs. By tying an agreed level of funding directly to each disabled child, and giving each family control over how those funds are spent, reform states will reduce any remaining tendencies of school districts to compete for extra funds through overdiagnosis.

Choice-based reform should also be effective in increasing the quality of education available to most disabled children. Choices are particularly beneficial to special education students because of the variety of disability types and because significant advances are being made in special education. Public institutions by their nature change too slowly to keep pace with rapidly evolving techniques and technologies in special education.

Parents have better information and better incentives than do school districts to make optimal decisions for their children. Although parents often lack the professional expertise of special educators, they have an incentive to seek out the very best sources of information and advice. A public school district will never be similarly motivated to spend weeks and months researching educational alternatives for a single child. Accordingly, choice-based reform should result in better educational outcomes for disabled children.

Choice-based reform will also relieve parents of their current Hobson's choice—accept an objectionable plan created by the school district or face the financial and personal costs of a potentially years-long hearing and appeals process. Similarly, the elimination of the IEP and due process regimens will free special educators from the meetings and paperwork that have come to dominate their days, allowing them to focus once again on teaching children.

Perhaps most critically, replacement of the dispute resolution model of IDEA with parental choice will restore trust between parents and educators, whose interests will no longer be misaligned. With the size of a child's benefit no longer in question, teachers can collaborate with parents to determine how the child's allotment might best be spent. If the two cannot agree, the parent is welcome to find another teacher or school with which to work. As are other consensual fiduciary relationships—doctor and patient, attorney and client—the new teacher-parent relationship will be built on trust, honesty, and results. Successful special educators and schools will be those that serve parents and children well.

Congress Must Not Create an Entitlement for State Governments

State agencies are pressuring Congress to make an open-ended commitment to cover 40 percent of all costs labeled "special education" by states. Congress must decline to create a new federal entitlement program for state governments.

In addition to further expanding federal influence in what should be a state and local matter, education, an entitlement for state governments in the form of an open-ended funding commitment would provide states with huge incentives to expand the portion of the state educational system designated as "special education." That in turn would mean more overidentification of students as disabled, one of the problems lawmakers should be trying to solve, not worsen.

Moreover, large funding increases would be counterproductive to state-level reform efforts, because they would discourage states from turning down federal funds in order to escape IDEA's suffocating regulatory compliance requirements. Congress would essentially be bribing states to stick with IDEA's failed dispute resolution model. By contrast, keeping the federal contribution small (recently around 15 percent of special education costs) would encourage states to reform their special education programs individually, discarding the federal money as not worth the compliance and litigation costs associated with IDEA.

Suggested Readings

American Institutes of Research. *What Are We Spending on Special Education Services in the United States, 1999–2000?* Advance Report no. 1, Special Education Expenditure Project. Washington: American Institutes of Research, March 2002.

Bolick, Clint. "A Bad IDEA Is Disabling Public Schools." *Education Week*, September 5, 2001.

Finn, Chester E., et al., eds. *Rethinking Special Education for a New Century*. Washington: Thomas B. Fordham Foundation and Progressive Policy Institute, 2001.

Gryphon, Marie, and David Salisbury. "Escaping IDEA: Freeing Parents, Teachers, and Students through Deregulation and Choice." Cato Institute Policy Analysis no. 444, July 10, 2002.

Hettleman, Kalman R. "Still Getting It Wrong: The Continuing Failure of Special Education in the Baltimore City Public Schools." Baltimore: Abell Foundation, 2002.

Kolter, Martin A. "The Individuals with Disabilities in Education Act: A Parent's Perspective and Proposal for Change." *University of Michigan Journal of Law Reform* 27 (1994).

Worth, Robert. "The Scandal of Special Ed." *Washington Monthly*, June 1999.

—Prepared by Marie E. Gryphon

30. Agricultural Policy

Congress should

- reduce greatly the per farm subsidy cap as a first step to control the excesses of federal agriculture subsidies;
- repeal the new crop price supports included in the 2002 farm law, which are unnecessary add-ons to existing subsidy mechanisms;
- phase out other crop subsidies, a process that began under the 1996 Freedom to Farm Act;
- move toward a system of private insurance and use of other financial instruments to protect farmers against market and weather fluctuations; and
- eliminate federal controls that perpetuate producer cartels in markets such as those for milk and sugar.

Reversal of the 1996 Reforms

With strong support from the Bush administration, Congress passed a huge farm bill in 2002 that moved away from the "Freedom to Farm" reforms of 1996. Farm subsidies are now projected to cost taxpayers more than $180 billion over the next decade. The costs may end up being much higher; subsidies under the 1996 farm law were expected to cost $47 billion over seven years but ended up costing about $123 billion.

The landmark 1996 farm law aimed to move agriculture away from the command-and-control regime in place since the 1930s. The law increased farmers' flexibility to plant and eliminated some crop price supports. The law was supposed to phase down subsidy levels between 1996 and 2002. But after enactment, Congress ignored agreed-upon subsidy limits and passed huge supplemental subsidy bills every year beginning in 1998. As a result, direct farm subsidies have soared to more than $20 billion per year from an average of $9 billion per year in the early 1990s (see Figure 30.1). Since the passage of the 2002 bill, some lawmakers have already clamored for further supplemental spending because of drought conditions in some regions.

Politically Favored Crops

Not all farmers receive direct subsidies from the federal government. Indeed, commodities that get federal payments account for just 36 percent of U.S. farm production. Commodities, such as fruits and vegetables, that are not on the federal dole account for 64 percent of U.S. farm production. More than 90 percent of direct federal subsidies go to farmers of just five crops—wheat, corn, soybeans, rice, and cotton.

In addition to those direct subsidies, the U.S. Department of Agriculture runs a massive array of marketing, loan, statistical, research, and other support programs. Also, legal restrictions and tariffs manipulate markets for products such as sugar and dairy foods. All in all, about 70,000 employees of the USDA work on farm-related programs. No other industry in America is so coddled.

Figure 30.1
Direct Federal Farm Subsidies, 1990–2001

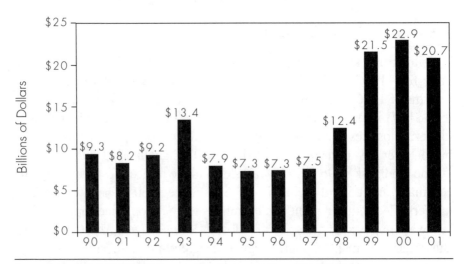

SOURCE: Calendar year USDA farm income data at www.ers.usda.gov/data/farmincome.

The Structure of Crop Subsidies

Large-scale federal manipulations of agriculture began as "temporary" measures in the 1930s under the New Deal. Farm programs have flourished ever since, despite a dramatic drop in the importance of agriculture to the U.S. economy. Crop subsidies have usually been delivered in the form of price supports, which create chronic problems of crop overproduction, which necessitate other programs to control output.

Prior to 1996, the main farm subsidy program paid "deficiency" payments based on legislated price levels called target prices. Eligible commodities included major field crops, such as wheat, corn, and rice. Farmers were paid for their base acreage in each particular crop and were stuck producing certain crops if they wanted to get the full subsidy. To stem overproduction, the government paid farmers not to farm on set-aside land.

The resulting absence of planting flexibility and land idling created large "deadweight" economic losses or inefficiency costs. The most efficient selection of crops was not being planted, and farmland was going unused. Those inefficiencies provided an important justification for the 1996 reforms. At that time, a combination of high commodity prices and the Republican takeover of Congress created support for reducing government intervention in the farm sector under the 1996 farm law.

1996 Reforms

The centerpiece of the 1996 farm law was the replacement of price support payments with production flexibility contracts (PFCs) that were fixed payments decoupled from market prices. The government set total PFC subsidy payments on a declining scale from $6 billion in 1996 to $4 billion in 2002.

The reforms affected farmers of corn, wheat, grain sorghum, barley, oats, cotton, and rice. Farmers of those crops were now allowed to plant any crop they chose and their subsidy payment would be at a fixed level decoupled from planting decisions. The new rules under the 1996 law led to significant reductions in deadweight economic losses and allowed farmers to better respond to changing market conditions.

Nonetheless, the new PFC subsidies still promote oversupply since they increase farmer wealth and income, thus encouraging farm expansion. Also, oversupply incentives continue under programs not reformed in 1996, such as the marketing loan program. That program was designed to provide short-term financing to farmers before crops were sold, but it has morphed into another multi-billion-dollar subsidy program. Eligible crops include corn, wheat, cotton, rice, sorghum, oats, barley, and soybeans. The program's cost has exploded to more than $5 billion per year in recent years.

Yet another major direct subsidy program for farmers is the conservation reserve program (CRP), which was created to idle millions of acres of farmland by paying farmers not to farm. The taxpayer cost of the CRP has averaged about $1.5 billion per year. Almost one-third of land idled under the CRP is owned by retired farmers, so many recipients do not even have to work to get subsidies. A simpler way to reduce overproduction and help the environment would be to eliminate all government farm subsidies.

Welfare for the Well-to-Do

Politicians love to discuss the plight of the small farmer. Yet the bulk of direct farm subsidies goes to the largest farms. For example, the largest 7 percent of farms received 45 percent of all farm subsidy payments in 1999. Much of the farm subsidy payout goes to individuals and companies that clearly do not need taxpayer help. A Washington, D.C., think tank has posted individual farm subsidy recipients on its Web page at www.ewg.org to illustrate the unfairness of farm welfare for the well-to-do. Farm subsidy recipients include Fortune 500 companies, members of Congress, and millionaires such as Ted Turner.

USDA figures show that, compared with other Americans, farmers are quite well off. The average farm household income was $61,947 in 2000, which is 8.6 percent higher than the average U.S. household income of $57,045. Commercial farms, as defined by the USDA, get about half of all farm subsidies, had average household incomes of $118,450 in 2000, and received an average subsidy of $43,379. So even if one accepts the notion that the government should redistribute wealth from rich to poor, farm subsidies do the reverse by giving taxpayer money to those with above-average incomes.

2002 Farm Bill—Taxpayers Take Bipartisan Beating

The 2002 farm bill is expected to cost taxpayers more than $180 billion in subsidy costs over the next 10 years. The ultimate taxpayer cost will be higher if Congress doles out further supplemental spending.

Aside from the taxpayer costs, the 2002 farm bill reverses progress made in 1996 toward reducing agriculture market distortions by introducing new price supports. Experts widely agree that price supports are counterproductive. Indeed, the USDA noted in a major report in September 2001 that "government attempts to hold prices above those determined by commercial markets have simply made matters worse time after time" by encouraging unneeded output and inflating land prices. Nonetheless, the president signed into law the 2002 farm bill, which added a new price support, or "countercyclical," program to provide big subsidies when prices are low. In addition, the marketing loan program, which also acts as a price support, was expanded in the 2002 bill to cover chickpeas, lentils, dry peas, honey, wool, and mohair.

The 2002 bill also retains the multi-billion-dollar PFC subsidy program. The intent of the PFC program introduced in 1996 was to gradually wean farmers from subsidies. Instead, the 2002 farm bill simply turns the program into yet another long-term handout.

Many other agricultural products received continued support under the new farm bill. Protectionist sugar measures that cost consumers billions of dollars are kept in place. Complex milk supports and regulations are retained, and an additional National Dairy Program is created that will cost taxpayers millions more dollars. The quota system for peanuts is being bought out at great taxpayer expense, and peanut farmers are now eligible for direct subsidies under other farm programs.

A final taxpayer insult of the 2002 bill was the audacious defense of the law after enactment in a glossy full-color booklet titled "The Facts on U.S. Farm Policy," published by the House Agriculture Committee. The propaganda piece attacks the "myths" of people who dared question the bill. Throughout the booklet are pictures of famous Americans from Thomas Jefferson to Ronald Reagan with assorted quotes meant to imply that these great men would have supported the profligate farm bill.

Repealing Farm Subsidies Is Economically and Politically Feasible

Despite the reversal in 2002, farm reform efforts will return because economic reality always intrudes on the best-laid plans of the central planners. During the debate over the 2002 farm bill, Sen. Richard Lugar (R-Ind.) offered an interesting alternative to the current system. His plan would have phased out current subsidies and replaced them with a voucher system promoting reliance on insurance and other financial instruments.

While Lugar's reforms would not go far enough, they indicate that with some innovative thinking and political courage Congress may eventually come around to real reforms.

The experience of New Zealand in the 1980s shows that complete subsidy removal makes sense economically and politically. In 1984 New Zealand's Labour government took the dramatic step of ending all farm subsidies. That was a remarkably bold policy action since New Zealand's economy is roughly five times more dependent on farming than is the U.S. economy.

Subsidy elimination in New Zealand was swift and sure. There was no extended phaseout of farm payments, as was promised under U.S. reforms in 1996. Although the plan was initially met with massive protests, the subsidies were ended and New Zealand farming has never been healthier. The value of farm output in New Zealand has soared since subsidies were repealed, and farm productivity has grown strongly.

Forced to adjust to new economic realities, New Zealand farmers cut costs, diversified their land use, sought nonfarm income, and altered production as market signals advised. As a report by the Federated Farmers of New Zealand noted, the country's experience "thoroughly debunked the myth that the farming sector cannot prosper without government subsidies." Reformers in Congress should continue working to eventually debunk that myth in this country.

Suggested Readings

Edwards, Chris, and Tad DeHaven. "Farm Reform Reversal." Cato Institute Tax & Budget Bulletin no. 2, March 2002.

_____. "Farm Subsidies at Record Levels As Congress Considers New Farm Bill." Cato Institute Briefing Paper no. 70, October 18, 2001.

Federated Farmers of New Zealand. "Life after Subsidies." www.fedfarm.org.nz/homepage.html.

McNew, Kevin. "Milking the Sacred Cow: A Case for Eliminating the Federal Dairy Program." Cato Institute Policy Analysis no. 362, December 1, 1999.

Orden, David. "Reform's Stunted Crop." *Regulation* 25, no. 1 (Spring 2002).

Orden, David, Robert Paarlberg, and Terry Roe. *Policy Reform in American Agriculture: Analysis and Prognosis.* Chicago: University of Chicago Press, 1999.

—Prepared by Chris Edwards and Tad DeHaven

31. Cultural Agencies

Congress should

- eliminate the National Endowment for the Arts,
- eliminate the National Endowment for the Humanities, and
- defund the Corporation for Public Broadcasting.

In a society that constitutionally limits the powers of government and maximizes individual liberty, there is no justification for the forcible transfer of money from taxpayers to artists, scholars, and broadcasters. If the proper role of government is to safeguard the security of the nation's residents, by what rationale are they made to support exhibits of paintings, symphony orchestras, documentaries, scholarly research, and radio and television programs they might never freely choose to support? The kinds of things financed by federal cultural agencies were produced long before those agencies were created, and they will continue to be produced long after those agencies are privatized or defunded. Moreover, the power to subsidize art, scholarship, and broadcasting cannot be found within the powers enumerated and delegated to the federal government under the Constitution.

The National Endowment for the Arts, an "independent" agency established in 1965, makes grants to museums, symphony orchestras, and individual artists "of exceptional talent" and organizations (including state arts agencies) to "encourage individual and institutional development of the arts, preservation of the American artistic heritage, wider availability of the arts, leadership in the arts, and the stimulation of non-Federal sources of support for the Nation's artistic activities." Among its more famous and controversial grant recipients were artist Andres Serrano, whose exhibit featured a photograph of a plastic crucifix in a jar of his own urine, and the Institute of Contemporary Art in Philadelphia, which sponsored a traveling exhibition of the late Robert Mapplethorpe's homoerotic photographs. (Thanks to an NEA grantee, the American taxpayers once paid $1,500 for a poem, "lighght." That wasn't the title or a typo. That was the entire poem.) The NEA's fiscal 2002 budget was $115 million, back up after modest cuts by the 104th and 105th Congresses.

The National Endowment for the Humanities, with a fiscal year 2002 budget of $124.5 million, "funds activities that are intended to improve the quality of education and teaching in the humanities, to strengthen the scholarly foundation for humanities study and research, and to advance understanding of the humanities among general audiences." Among the things it has funded are controversial national standards for the teaching of history in schools, the traveling King Tut exhibit, and the documentary film *Rosie the Riveter*.

The 35-year-old Corporation for Public Broadcasting—FY02 budget, $350 million—provides money to "qualified public television and radio stations to be used at their discretion for purposes related primarily to program production and acquisition." It also supports the production and acquisition of radio and television programs for national distribution and assists in "the financing of several system-wide activities, including national satellite interconnection services and the payment of music royalty fees, and provides limited technical assistance, research, and planning services to improve system-wide capacity and performance." Some of the money provided local public radio and television stations is used to help support National Public Radio and the Public Broadcasting Service.

Note that the amount of arts funding in the federal budget is quite small. That might be taken as a defense of the funding, were it not for the important reasons to avoid *any* government funding of something as intimate yet powerful as artistic expression. But it should also be noted how small federal funding is as a percentage of the total arts budget in this country. The NEA's budget is about 1 percent of the $11.5 billion contributed to the arts by private corporations, foundations, and individuals in 1996. According to the American Arts Alliance, the nonprofit arts are a $53 billion industry. Surely they will survive without whatever portion of the NEA's budget gets out of the Washington bureaucracy and into the hands of actual artists or arts institutions. Indeed, when the NEA budget was cut in 1995, private giving to the arts rose dramatically.

The 104th Congress voted to phase out the NEA over three years. The 108th Congress should revive that commitment and also end federal involvement with the National Endowment for the Humanities and the Corporation for Public Broadcasting.

Poor Subsidize Rich

Since art museums, symphony orchestras, humanities scholarship, and public television and radio are enjoyed predominantly by people of greater-than-average income and education, the federal cultural agencies oversee a fundamentally unfair transfer of wealth from the lower classes up. It's no accident that you hear ads for Remy Martin and "private banking services" on NPR, not for Budweiser and free checking accounts. *Newsweek* columnist Robert J. Samuelson is correct when he calls federal cultural agencies "highbrow pork barrel." As Edward C. Banfield has written, "The art public is now, as it has always been, overwhelmingly middle and upper-middle class and above average in income—relatively prosperous people who would probably enjoy art about as much in the absence of subsidies." Supporters of the NEA often say that their purpose is to bring the finer arts to those who don't already patronize them. But Dick Netzer, an economist who favors arts subsidies, conceded that they have "failed to increase the representation of low-income people in audiences." In other words, lower-income people are not interested in the kind of entertainment they're forced to support; they prefer to put their money into forms of art often sneered at by the cultural elite. Why must they continue to finance the pleasures of the affluent?

Corruption of Artists and Scholars

Government subsidies to the arts and humanities have an insidious, corrupting effect on artists and scholars. It is assumed, for example, that the arts need government encouragement. But if an artist needs such encouragement, what kind of artist is he? Novelist E. L. Doctorow once told the House Appropriations Committee, "An enlightened endowment puts its money on largely unknown obsessive individuals who have sacrificed all the ordinary comforts and consolations of life in order to do their work." Few have noticed the contradiction in that statement. As author Bill Kauffman has commented, Doctorow "wants to abolish the risk and privation that dog almost all artists, particularly during their apprenticeships. 'Starving artists' are to be plumped up by taxpayers. . . . The likelihood that pampered artists will turn complacent, listless, and lazy seems not to bother Doctorow." Moreover, as Jonathan Yardley, the *Washington Post*'s book critic, asked, "Why should the struggling young artist be entitled to government subsidy when the struggling young mechanic or accountant is not?"

321

Politicizing Culture

James D. Wolfensohn, former chairman of the Kennedy Center for the Performing Arts, decried talk about abolishing the NEA. "We should not allow [the arts] to become political," he said. But it is the subsidies that have politicized the arts and scholarship, not the talk about ending them. Some artists and scholars are to be awarded taxpayers' money. Which artists and scholars? They can't all be subsidized. The decisions are ultimately made by bureaucrats (even if they are advised by artists and scholars). Whatever criteria the bureaucrats use, they politicize art and scholarship. As novelist George Garrett has said: "Once (and whenever) the government is involved in the arts, then it is bound to be a political and social business, a battle between competing factions. The NEA, by definition, supports the arts establishment." Adds painter Laura Main, "Relying on the government to sponsor art work . . . is to me no more than subjecting yourself to the fate of a bureaucratic lackey."

Mary Beth Norton, a writer of women's history and a former member of the National Council on the Humanities, argues that "one of the great traditions of the Endowment [for the Humanities] is that this is where people doing research in new and exciting areas—oral history, black history, women's history to name areas I am familiar with—can turn to for funding." When the NEH spent less money in the mid-1980s than previously, Norton complained, "Now, people on the cutting edge are not being funded anymore." But if bureaucrats are ultimately selecting the research to be funded, how cutting-edge can it really be? How can they be trusted to distinguish innovation from fad? And who wants scholars choosing the objects of their research on the basis of what will win favor with government grant referees?

Similar criticism can be leveled against the radio and television programs financed by the CPB. They tend (with a few exceptions) to be aimed at the wealthier and better educated, and the selection process is inherently political. Moreover, some of the money granted to local stations is passed on to National Public Radio and the Public Broadcasting Service for the production of news programs, including *All Things Considered* and the *Newshour with Jim Lehrer.* Why are the taxpayers in a free society compelled to support news coverage, particularly when it is inclined in a statist direction? Robert Coonrod, president of CPB, defends his organization, saying that "about 90 percent of the federal appropriation goes back to the communities, to public radio and TV stations, which are essentially community institutions." Only 90 percent? Why not leave 100 percent in the communities and let the residents decide how to spend it? Since only 13 percent of public broadcasting revenues now come from the federal government, other sources presumably could take up the slack if the federal government ended the appropriation.

It must be pointed out that the fundamental objection to the federal cultural agencies is not that their products have been intellectually, morally, politically, or sexually offensive to conservatives or even most Americans. That has sometimes, but not always, been the case. Occasionally, such as during the bicentennial of the U.S. Constitution, the agencies have been used to subsidize projects favored by conservatives. The brief against those agencies would be the same had the money been used exclusively to subsidize works inoffensive or even inspiring to the majority of the American people.

The case also cannot be based on how much the agencies spend. In FY02 the two endowments and the CPB were appropriated about $590 million total, a mere morsel in a $2 trillion federal budget. (Total federal support for the arts—ranging from military bands to Education Department programs to the Kennedy Center for the Performing Arts—amounts to $2 billion, not a minuscule amount. Congress should critically review all of those expenditures in light of the lack of constitutional authority for such programs, the burden they place on taxpayers, and the principle of subsidiarity or federalism.) The NEA's budget is about 0.2 percent of the total amount spent on the nonprofit arts in the United States.

No, the issue is neither the content of the work subsidized nor the expense. Taxpayer subsidy of the arts, scholarship, and broadcasting is inappropriate because it is outside the range of the proper functions of government, and as such it needlessly politicizes, and therefore corrupts, an area of life that should be left untainted by politics.

Government funding of anything involves government control. That insight, of course, is part of our folk wisdom: "He who pays the piper calls the tune." "Who takes the king's shilling sings the king's song."

Defenders of arts funding seem blithely unaware of this danger when they praise the role of the national endowments as an imprimatur or seal of approval on artists and arts groups. Former NEA chair Jane Alexander said: "The Federal role is small but very vital. We are a stimulus for leveraging state, local and private money. We are a linchpin for the puzzle of arts funding, a remarkably efficient way of stimulating private money." Drama critic Robert Brustein asks, "How could the NEA be 'privatized' and still retain its purpose as a funding agency functioning as a stamp of approval for deserving art?"

The politicization of whatever the federal cultural agencies touch was driven home by Richard Goldstein, a supporter of the NEH. Goldstein pointed out:

> The NEH has a ripple effect on university hiring and tenure, and on the kinds of research undertaken by scholars seeking support. Its chairman shapes the bounds of that support. In a broad sense, he sets standards that affect the tenor of textbooks and the content of curricula. . . . Though no chairman of the NEH can single-handedly direct the course of American education, he can nurture the nascent trends and take advantage of informal opportunities to signal department heads and deans. He can "persuade" with the cudgel of federal funding out of sight but hardly out of mind.

The cudgel (an apt metaphor) of federal funding has the potential to be wielded to influence those who run the universities with regard to hiring, tenure, research programs, textbooks, curricula. That is an enormous amount of power to have vested in a government official. Surely, it is the kind of concentration of power that the Founding Fathers intended to thwart.

Separation of Conscience and State

We might reflect on why the separation of church and state seems such a wise idea to Americans. First, it is wrong for the coercive authority of the state to interfere in matters of individual conscience. If we have rights, if we are individual moral agents, we must be free to exercise our judgment and define our own relationship with God. That doesn't mean that a free, pluralistic society won't have lots of persuasion and proselytizing—no doubt it will—but it does mean that such proselytizing must remain entirely persuasive, entirely voluntary.

Second, social harmony is enhanced by removing religion from the sphere of politics. Europe suffered through the Wars of Religion, as churches made alliances with rulers and sought to impose their theology on everyone in a region. Religious inquisitions, Roger Williams said, put towns "in an uproar." If people take their faith seriously, and if government is going to make one faith universal and compulsory, then people must contend bitterly—even to the death—to make sure that the *true* faith is established. Enshrine religion in the realm of persuasion, and there may be vigorous debate in society, but there won't be political conflict—and people can deal with one another in secular life without endorsing the private opinions of their colleagues.

Third, competition produces better results than subsidy, protection, and conformity. "Free trade in religion" is the best tool humans have to find the nearest approximation to the truth. Businesses coddled behind subsidies and tariffs will be weak and uncompetitive, and so will churches, synagogues, mosques, and temples. Religions that are protected from political interference but are otherwise on their own are likely to be stronger and more vigorous than a church that draws its support from government.

If those statements are true, they have implications beyond religion. Religion is not the only thing that affects us personally and spiritually, and it is not the only thing that leads to cultural wars. Art also expresses, transmits, and challenges our deepest values. As the managing director of Baltimore's Center Stage put it: "Art has power. It has the power to sustain, to heal, to humanize ... to change something in you. It's a frightening power, and also a beautiful power. ... And it's essential to a civilized society." Because art is so powerful, because it deals with such basic human truths, we dare not entangle it with coercive government power. That means no censorship or regulation of art. It also means no tax-funded subsidies for arts and artists, for when government gets into the arts funding business, we get political conflicts. Conservatives denounce the National Endowment for the Arts for funding erotic photography and the Public Broadcasting System for broadcasting *Tales of the City,* which has gay characters. (*More Tales of the City,* which appeared on Showtime after PBS ducked the political pressure, generated little political controversy.) Civil rights activists make the Library of Congress take down an exhibit on antebellum slave life, and veterans' groups pressure the Smithsonian to remove a display on the bombing of Hiroshima. To avoid political battles over how to spend the taxpayers' money, to keep art and its power in the realm of persuasion, we would be well advised to establish the separation of art and state.

Suggested Readings

Banfield, Edward C. *The Democratic Muse.* New York: Basic Books, 1984.

Boaz, David. "The Separation of Art and the State." *Vital Speeches,* June 15, 1995. www.cato.org/speeches/sp-as53.html.

Cowen, Tyler. *In Praise of Commercial Culture.* Cambridge, Mass.: Harvard University Press, 1998.

Gillespie, Nick. "All Culture, All the Time." *Reason,* April 1999.

Grampp, William. *Pricing the Priceless.* New York: Basic Books, 1984.

Kauffman, Bill. "Subsidies to the Arts: Cultivating Mediocrity." Cato Institute Policy Analysis no. 137, August 8, 1990.

Kostelanetz, Richard. "The New Benefactors." *Liberty,* January 1990.

Lynes, Russell. "The Case against Government Aid to the Arts." *New York Times Magazine,* March 25, 1962.

Samuelson, Robert J. "Highbrow Pork Barrel." *Newsweek,* August 21, 1989.

Subcommittee on Oversight and Investigations of the House Committee on Education and the Workforce. *The Healthy State of the Arts in America and the Continuing Failure of the National Endowment for the Arts.* 105th Cong., 1st sess., September 23, 1997. Serial no. 105-A.

—Prepared by Sheldon Richman and David Boaz

32. Privatization

Amtrak

For 30 years, Amtrak has provided second-rate passenger rail service to Americans at higher-than-competitive costs while consuming more than $25 billion in federal subsidies. Today, Amtrak passengers pay a higher fare per mile than the average airline or bus passenger—and that is on top of all the taxpayer costs.

Against the backdrop of rail privatization in numerous foreign countries, Congress created the Amtrak Reform Council in 1997 to study major rail reforms. One ARC goal was to assess whether Amtrak could break even by the end of 2002 with fares covering operating costs. In December 2001, ARC issued a finding that Amtrak could not meet that target. ARC then developed reform plans that would end Amtrak's monopoly on passenger service, spin off its Northeast Corridor infrastructure, and permit states and private entities to bid for Amtrak routes.

Around the world, momentum for rail privatization is strong, although there have been a few setbacks. For example, Railtrack, the private owner of British Rail's infrastructure (track and stations), went bankrupt. But big mistakes were made in the structure of British reforms. British Rail privatization involved the separation of infrastructure from newly created private train operating companies. As it turned out, the operating companies were so successful at increasing passenger and freight volume (up 26 percent and 34 percent, respectively, in four years) that traffic overwhelmed Railtrack's infrastructure. The infrastructure had suffered decades of low investment under government ownership. Because 90 percent of Railtrack's revenue came from fixed charges, it had little incentive to expand capacity to meet the new demands.

The fatal flaw in Railtrack's privatization was the separation of track from operations. Most countries that have privatized their rail systems, including Argentina, Australia, Japan, and New Zealand, have maintained vertical integration in the rail system (sometimes with separate regional companies). Australia recently sold two more such regional vertically integrated rail units. The Japanese government plans to sell its remaining stakes in three privatized railroad firms: JR East (of which it still owns 13 percent), JR West (32 percent), and JR Tokai (40 percent). The German government is dropping plans to separate track from train operations as it prepares to privatize Deutsche Bahn by 2005.

The United States should not fall behind the worldwide trend of rail privatization. Amtrak should be sold as a single unit including operations, maintenance, stations, rails, and trains. Americans deserve better rail service than the government has provided, and taxpayers deserve an end to federal subsidies.

Air Traffic Control

President Bush was right in saying that air traffic control (ATC) is not "an inherently governmental function" when he signed Executive Order

13180. That order is a first step toward ATC privatization in that it sets up a performance-based federal ATC agency.

During the past 15 years, nearly two dozen countries have partly or fully privatized ATC services. Some, such as Germany, have created self-supporting government corporations for ATC. Others, such as Canada, have created fully private nonprofit corporations. Canada's reforms provide an excellent model for future U.S. reforms. Nav Canada was set up in 1996 to take over all Canadian ATC responsibilities. As a nonprofit company, it has a board of directors made up of various aviation stakeholders. It is fully self-supporting from fees and charges paid by aviation users. The new Canadian system has received rave reviews for investing in the newest technology and substantially reducing air congestion.

In Britain, ATC has been moved to the National Air Traffic Services company. NATS has a public-private corporate structure with 46 percent of shares owned by the Airline Group (a consortium of the U.K.'s main airlines), 49 percent of shares owned by the government, and 5 percent of shares owned by employees. Like Canada's system, NATS is self-supporting from fees and charges.

The cutbacks in air travel following the terrorist attacks in 2001 have created challenges for the privatized ATC corporations. But Nav Canada and NATS have responded nimbly by reducing costs and postponing new expansion projects. Meanwhile, the U.S. government's ATC in the Federal Aviation Administration has done just the opposite. In response to falling traffic, it has requested more money from Congress.

The United States should be a leader rather than a follower in air traffic control, especially given this country's remarkable legacy of aviation innovation during the past century. Privatized ATC can help reduce transportation congestion, increase cost efficiencies, and provide Americans with greater safety by speeding the adoption of new technologies.

Opt-Out Program for Federal Airport Security

The federal takeover of airport passenger screening was a big mistake and has run into serious troubles. After the terrorist attacks in 2001, legislation was passed allowing the new Transportation Security Administration to take over screening of passengers and baggage at all 429 U.S. commercial airports. The TSA needs to hire and train 33,000 passenger screeners and 21,600 baggage screeners. The huge hiring demands have created large problems.

To ease the problems, a modest pilot program that allows some airports to opt out of the new government-run passenger screening system should be expanded. In enacting the new airport security legislation, Congress compromised between the Senate's bill, which called for 100 percent federal screening, and the House bill, which would have left to each airport director the decision of whether to use federal workers or outside security firms. The compromise permitted five airports to opt out of federal security as of November 2002 and allowed other airports to opt out as of November 2004.

A significant expansion of the initial pilot program is needed for a number of reasons. First, five airports with private screening are a sample far too small to provide good comparisons between private and government screening. Allowing at least 40 airports to opt out would provide far better comparative information. Second, the more airports that opt to use private contractors, the smaller the workforce that TSA needs to recruit and train. Judging by the high demand of airports to get one of the five initial opt-out chances, a large share of all U.S. airports would choose to opt out if allowed to.

Airports have important reasons for wanting to opt out of government-run screening. One is the possibility of obtaining a higher-quality workforce. For example, New York's JFK International Airport applied for the opt-out program with a proposal calling for screening by a security firm staffed by retired law enforcement officers—people with experience in explosives, weapons, interrogation, and crowd control. Unfortunately, JFK's proposal was turned down.

Another reason cited by airport directors for favoring private contractors is greater staffing flexibility. For example, flight activity levels at airports often change rapidly. Unless the passenger screening system can quickly staff up and down in response, there are unacceptable delays in screening passengers.

The United States has nationalized its airport screening, but European airports have successfully used private contractors for years. Nearly all large airports in Europe and Israel (32 of 34) have shifted from civil service workers for passenger and baggage screening to private security firms in the past decade. In those countries, the government sets training and performance standards and provides strong oversight of private contractors. By contrast, prior to September 11, 2001, U.S. airports generally used low-bid contractors for passenger screening instead of focusing on quality service.

Congress should also think further about the government's longer-term role once all airports are allowed to opt out in November 2004. Europe's experience suggests that airport security works best under a unified approach controlled by the airport director. That differs from the new U.S. approach, which has some parts of security under TSA and other parts under airport responsibility. Note also that a clear conflict of interest exists in having the TSA be both a provider of airport security and the airport security regulator.

After 2004, TSA should focus only on standard setting and regulatory oversight, and airports should adopt privatized security. The TSA has ample time before 2004 to fine-tune standards and procedures and to train a high-quality airport screening workforce. That workforce would eventually go to work for airports, either directly as employees or indirectly as employees of qualified screening contractors hired by airports.

Federal Electric Utilities

The federal government is the nation's largest electric power organization, as owner and manager of the Tennessee Valley Authority and four power marketing administrations (PMAs), which have operations that span much of the country outside the Northeast. These electricity businesses, along with federally subsidized cooperative and municipal utilities, are poorly managed and out of step with the new environment of electricity competition.

Government-owned electric power generation originally had two justifications. First, it was thought that private electricity companies would not find enough profit in electrifying rural America, thus requiring that government step in and serve those areas. Second, it was thought that government could provide power to consumers at lower prices than could private companies because it could set prices "at cost" without worrying about profit margins.

The first justification is now irrelevant because rural America has been thoroughly electrified. Moreover, 60 percent of rural America is served by investor-owned utilities. The second justification—that government power would be cheap—was socialist pie-in-the-sky thinking. Government electricity generation has proven to be more costly than private generation.

The United States lags behind other countries in freeing itself from government-owned power generation. Indeed, between 1990 and 1999 the value of worldwide electric utility privatization was $65 billion, according to Reason Foundation figures. Major countries, such as Australia, Britain,

Canada, and Germany, have launched electricity privatization programs in recent years.

Other countries have privatized electricity for numerous reasons. One reason has been to improve the efficiency and performance of backward electric power systems. Another reason is that countries have sought to raise funds to reduce government budget deficits. Both objectives are applicable to the United States. In 1996, the Clinton administration did propose privatizing the PMAs, but Congress and various anti-reform groups shot down the proposal.

The sale of all the federal power enterprises could raise between $20 billion and $35 billion to help reduce the federal deficit. The Clinton plan was estimated to bring in between about $3 billion and $9 billion. The Congressional Budget Office has estimated that sale of the three smallest PMAs and related hydropower assets would bring in from $8 billion to $11 billion. Sale of the Bonneville Power Administration would bring in about $9 billion. The former head of the TVA estimates that that utility could sell for as much as $10.5 billion.

Government-owned power generation is a throwback to early 20th-century thinking that governments could operate business enterprises in a cost-effective and high-quality manner. Few economists believe that today, and it is time for the U.S. government to catch up to electricity reforms made in other countries to establish private competitive electricity systems for the 21st century.

Federal Competitive Outsourcing

A major fiscal theme of the Bush administration is reform of the federal bureaucracy to make it work more efficiently. As part of that agenda, the administration is promoting the contracting out of many federal functions to private companies. Indeed, surveys of private companies have found that firms are seeing substantial increases in revenue from federal contracting in recent years. In addition to the Bush initiatives, earlier legislation, including the 1994 Federal Acquisition Streamlining Act and the 1998 Federal Activities Inventory Reform Act, helped increase the level of outsourcing.

As legislation has removed barriers to outsourcing, agency demand for outsourcing has grown as staffing challenges have increased. For example, federal spending on information technology is expected to continue climbing. Yet many federal technology workers are expected to retire in coming years, thus creating difficulty in continuing to provide technology services in-house. As a result, outsourcing will likely grow in importance.

The Bush administration is promoting ambitious goals for federal outsourcing. The administration plans to have agencies competing 15 percent of all positions by 2004 and 20 percent per year after that. Under the FAIR act, agencies in 2001 identified about 850,000 positions as commercial in nature and possibly subject to outsourcing. President Bush's ultimate goal is to have agencies put half of those jobs to competition with private providers.

Both the FAIR act and the government's process for outsourcing (under Office of Management and Budget Circular A-76) have been controversial. The General Accounting Office has convened a panel to examine outsourcing in general and Circular A-76 and FAIR in particular. The Commercial Activities Panel held a series of hearings in 2001 and provided recommendations to Congress in May 2002. The recommendations strongly supported continued emphasis on contracting out.

The president's outsourcing goals do face numerous hurdles. Many agencies have been slow to embrace the challenge. For example, in January 2002 the Department of Defense announced that it would halt all competitions of its workforce. But soon after, the DoD said that it was back on board with a plan to outsource roughly 70,000 jobs over the next two years. Congress should strongly support the administration's goal of reforming the federal workforce.

Privatization of Military Support Services

Military Housing

Recent efforts have sought to make military service more attractive. At the top of the list of needed reforms is improved housing. In 1996, the Department of Defense identified about 177,000 of its 290,000 family housing units as inadequate. Initial estimates suggested that it would take 30 years to fix the housing problem using traditional military construction. In a reform spirit, Congress passed new laws to enable DoD to use private-sector financing and expertise for housing. As a result, DoD believes that it will have all military families adequately housed by 2008—more than a decade and a half sooner and more inexpensively than would have been possible using standard methods.

The fiscal year 1996 defense authorization act granted DoD broad flexibility to work with the private sector to build and renovate military housing. The DoD could obtain private capital to leverage government dollars and to enter into limited partnerships with private developers to construct, renovate, and maintain housing. Among other benefits, the new flexibility allows DoD to deal with variations in local real estate markets.

Fort Carson in Colorado is DoD's largest privatization effort so far, and it is the first installation to fully privatize all its on-post housing. In 1999, Fort Carson Family Housing, LLC, assumed the operation and maintenance of 1,823 family housing units. The company agreed to renovate those units by 2005 and to build 840 new units by 2004. The company will own, operate, and maintain all housing on Fort Carson for at least the next 50 years. Fort Carson is being heralded as a big success, and privatization is being seen as a good way to quickly and permanently fix military housing problems.

Other military housing upgrades being performed by the private sector include those at the naval station in Everett, Washington, Camp Pendleton in California, and Elmenorf Air Force Base in Arkansas. Estimates show that all those projects will cut construction costs substantially and save federal taxpayers millions of dollars.

Military Utilities

As part of the FY98 defense authorization act, Congress passed a military utilities privatization initiative. The law allowed military services to enter into agreements with private utilities for service provision and to retain any cost savings realized. Those reforms were prompted after reviews found that DoD was wasting millions of dollars on utilities that were obsolete and unreliable.

The U.S. military currently has about 2,700 electric, gas, water, and wastewater systems on bases. About 1,000 of those are leased from contractors, owned by utility companies, or must be operated by the military for security reasons. As of 2002, only 29 of the other 1,700 systems had been privatized. The effort has been delayed by the complexity of privatization, the deregulation of the electric industry, and the California energy crisis. Also, the military has been releasing too many requests for proposals simultaneously, thus overwhelming contractors who can bid on only so many projects at a time. The original plan was to have privatized about 1,600 utilities by September 2003, but that goal has proved to be too optimistic.

More flexibility needs to be added to the process. Some observers argue that the slow pace of contracting has resulted from unattractive bids. But DoD should be able to look beyond initial bid costs and evaluate long-term benefits from enhanced operational qualities of private utility systems.

Also, new guidelines should allow the different military services to take different approaches to privatization. Privatization of functions that have always been performed by the government can be a learning experience, but the large potential benefits are well worth the hard efforts.

Suggested Readings

Bacon, R. W., and J. Besant-Jones. "Global Electric Power Reform: Privatization and Liberalization of the Electric Power Industry in Developing Countries." *Annual Review of Energy and Environment* (2001): 331–59, http://energy.annualreviews.org.

Butler, Viggo, and Robert W. Poole Jr. "Rethinking Checked-Baggage Screening." Reason Public Policy Institute Policy Study no. 297, July 2002.

Poole, Robert W. Jr. "Replacing Amtrak: A Blueprint for Sustainable Passenger Rail Service." Reason Public Policy Institute Policy Study no. 235, October 1997.

————. "Revisiting Federalized Passenger Screening." Reason Public Policy Institute Policy Study no. 298, August 2002.

Poole, Robert W. Jr., and Viggo Butler. "How to Commercialize Air Traffic Control." Reason Public Policy Institute Policy Study no. 278, February 2001.

U.S. Department of Defense, Office of the Deputy Undersecretary for Installations and Environment. Utilities privatization website, www.acq.osd.mil/ie/utilities/privatization.htm.

U.S. Department of Defense, Office of the Undersecretary for Acquisition, Technology, and Logistics. Military housing privatization website, www.defenselink.mil/acq/installation/hrso.

U.S. General Accounting Office. "Federal Power: The Role of the Power Marketing Administrations in a Restructured Electricity Industry." GAO report AIMD-99-229, June 24, 1999.

Vranich, Joseph, and Edward L. Hudgins. "Help Passenger Rail by Privatizing Amtrak." Cato Institute Policy Analysis no. 419, November 1, 2001.

—Prepared by Geoffrey F. Segal

33. Corporate Welfare

Congress should

- end programs that provide direct grants to businesses,
- end programs that provide marketing and other commercial services to businesses,
- end programs that provide subsidized loans and insurance to businesses,
- eliminate foreign trade barriers that try to protect U.S. industries from foreign competition at the expense of U.S. consumers,
- eliminate domestic regulatory barriers that favor particular companies with monopoly power against competitors, and
- create financial transparency with a detailed listing in the federal budget of companies that received direct business subsidies and the amounts received.

In fiscal year 2002, the federal government spent about $93 billion on programs that subsidize businesses. There have been numerous efforts to cut these wasteful and unfair uses of taxpayer money, but total corporate welfare spending keeps rising. A serious attempt was made after the Republicans took control of both houses of Congress in the 1990s to eliminate corporate welfare, but those efforts met with few successes.

The Bush administration has promised a renewed attack on corporate welfare. Indeed, Budget Director Mitch Daniels stated that it was "not the federal government's role to subsidize, sometimes deeply subsidize, private interests." While taxpayers wait for reforms, the government continues to subsidize private interests *directly* through such programs as aid to farmers and subsidized loans for exporters. And private interests continue to receive billions of dollars of *indirect* subsidies through programs such as those for federal energy research. With the federal budget again in deficit by more than $100 billion, corporate welfare is the perfect place to start cutting excess spending.

What Is Corporate Welfare?

Corporate welfare consists of government programs that provide unique benefits or advantages to specific companies or industries. Corporate welfare includes programs that provide direct grants to businesses, programs that provide indirect commercial support to businesses, and programs that provide subsidized loans and insurance.

Many corporate welfare programs provide useful services to private industry, such as insurance, statistics, research, loans, and marketing support. Those are all functions that many industries in the private sector do for themselves. If the commercial activities of government are useful and efficient, then private markets should be able to support them without subsidies.

In addition to spending programs, corporate welfare includes barriers to trade that attempt to protect U.S. industries from foreign competition at the expense of U.S. consumers and U.S. companies that use foreign products. Corporate welfare also includes domestic legal barriers that favor particular companies with monopoly power over free-market competitors.

Corporate welfare sometimes supports companies that are already highly profitable. Such companies clearly do not need any extra help from taxpayers. In other situations, corporate welfare programs prop up businesses that are failing in the marketplace. Such companies should be allowed to fail because they weigh down the economy and reduce overall U.S. income levels.

Which Agencies Dish It Out and Who Receives It?

The federal budget supports a broad array of corporate welfare programs. The leading corporate welfare providers are the Departments of Agriculture, Health and Human Services, Transportation, and Energy (Table 33.1). Many smaller independent federal agencies, such as the Export-Import Bank, also dole out corporate welfare.

Corporate welfare is a multiagency problem, so any one congressional committee cannot reduce the corporate welfare budget across the board. Indeed, congressional committees try to maximize corporate welfare handouts within their jurisdictions. For example, the agriculture committees appeal to farm voters with farm pork. Leadership to cut corporate welfare in the broader public interest must come from the budget committees, the senior congressional leadership, and the president.

Table 33.1
Corporate Welfare Spending by Department
(budget authority, $ millions)

Department	FY02	Share (%)
Agriculture	$35,049	38
Health & Human Services	$9,156	10
Transportation	$10,702	12
Energy	$5,873	6
Housing & Urban Dev.	$7,802	8
Defense	$4,003	4
Interior	$1,967	2
Commerce	$1,967	2
All other agencies	$16,144	17
Total	$92,663	100

SOURCE: Cato estimates based on the *Budget of the U.S. Government, FY 2003*.

Many corporate welfare recipients are among the biggest companies in America, including the Big 3 automakers, Boeing, Archer Daniels Midland, and now-bankrupt Enron. Most of the massive handouts to agricultural producers go to large farming businesses. Once companies are successful in securing a stream of taxpayer goodies, they defend their stake year after year with the help of their state's congressional delegation. But with corporate governance reform currently in vogue, it would seem to be a good time for Congress to cut off this unjustified source of corporate profit.

A Sampler of Corporate Welfare Programs to Cut

The following are some corporate welfare programs that are long over-due for cutting. Spending totals given are budget authority for FY02.

Direct Subsidies

- Agriculture Department—Market Access Program ($90 million). This program gives taxpayer dollars to exporters of agricultural products to pay for their overseas advertising campaigns.
- Commerce Department—Advanced Technology Program ($187 million). This program gives research grants to high-tech companies. Handouts to successful firms make no sense because they could have relied on private venture capital instead. Handouts to unsuccessful firms with poor ideas also make no sense because taxpayers end up paying for economic waste.

339

- Foreign Military Financing ($3.7 billion). U.S. taxpayers fund weapons purchases by foreign governments through this program. That seems contrary to weapons nonproliferation policy, and the program runs the risk that weapons recipients may not be U.S. allies in the future.
- Amtrak ($621 million). The federal passenger rail company should be fully privatized to allow it to compete fairly with other modes of transportation.

Subsidized Loans and Insurance

- Export-Import Bank ($1.2 billion). This program uses taxpayer dollars to subsidize the financing of foreign purchases of U.S. goods. It makes loans to foreigners at below-market interest rates, guarantees the loans of private institutions, and provides export credit insurance.
- Overseas Private Investment Corporation ($188 million). OPIC provides direct loans, guaranteed loans, and risk insurance to U.S. firms that invest in developing countries. Enron, a top beneficiary of both OPIC and Ex-Im programs in the late 1990s, provides a glaring example of corporate welfare waste.
- Maritime Administration—guaranteed loan program ($250 million). Provides loan guarantees for purchases of ships from U.S. shipyards. The United States has vast and liquid financial markets making credit available to all businesses that have reasonable risks. It makes no sense to use taxpayer funds to duplicate functions of private financial markets.

Indirect Subsidies to Businesses

- Agriculture Department—research and marketing services ($2 billion). Agricultural research and marketing programs aim to improve product quality, find new uses for products, generate market data, and support promotions for a variety of agriculture products. In most industries, such commercial activities are carried out by private businesses.
- Energy Department—energy supply research ($670 million). This program aims to develop new energy technologies and improve existing ones. The energy industry itself and private research institutes should fund such work.
- The Small Business Administration ($1.6 billion). The SBA provides subsidized loans and loan guarantees to small businesses and has a poor record of selecting businesses to support since its loans have a very high delinquency rate.

What Is Wrong with Corporate Welfare?

As some of the above examples illustrate, there are many problems with corporate welfare programs. Here are seven:

1. Corporate welfare is a big drain on the taxpayer. In FY02, $93 billion of taxpayer money was spent on programs that subsidize businesses. By eliminating these programs, Congress could provide every household in the country with an $860 per year tax cut.

2. Corporate welfare creates an uneven playing field. By giving selected businesses and industries special advantages, corporate subsidies put businesses that are less politically connected at an unfair disadvantage.

3. Corporate welfare programs are anti-consumer. By helping particular businesses, the government often damages consumers. For example, the protectionist federal sugar program costs consumers several billion dollars per year in higher product prices.

4. The government does a poor job of picking winners. Federal loan programs, such as those operated by the SBA, have high delinquency rates, indicating that the difficult job of analyzing business risks should be left to the private sector. With regard to technology subsidies, the federal government has a long history of wasting money on failed ideas. It is the role of private entrepreneurs and investors to take technology risks through institutions such as "angel" financing, venture capital, and stock markets. Government should not use taxpayer money on risky schemes.

5. Corporate welfare fosters corruption. Corporate welfare generates an unhealthy—sometimes corrupt—relationship between business and the government. For example, a Maritime Administration program aided shipbuilders by guaranteeing a $1.1 billion loan to build cruise ships in Sen. Trent Lott's hometown. Before the ships were completed, the company went bankrupt and left taxpayers with a $200 million tab. Steering taxpayer funds into risky private schemes in important politicians' districts should be stopped.

6. Corporate welfare depletes private-sector strength. While "market entrepreneurs" work hard to create new businesses, corporate welfare helps create "political entrepreneurs" who spend their energies seeking government handouts. Corporate welfare draws talented people and firms into wasteful subsidy-seeking activities and away from more productive pursuits. Besides, companies receiving subsidies usually become weaker and less efficient, not stronger.

7. Corporate welfare is unconstitutional. Corporate subsidy programs lie outside Congress's limited spending authority under the U.S. Constitution. Nowhere in the Constitution is the government granted the authority to spend taxpayer dollars on boondoggles such as subsidizing Enron to build power plants in India.

Congress Needs to Work with the Administration to Achieve Cuts

The Bush administration has launched an effort to grade the effectiveness of federal activities and move funds away from poorly performing programs. As part of that effort, the FY03 budget proposed some modest corporate welfare cuts. Overall, it proposed reducing corporate welfare from $93 billion in FY02, to $86 billion in FY03, according to Cato estimates.

The administration has proposed reductions in the Manufacturing Extension Partnership and the Advanced Technology Program. The Corps of Engineers has also been slated for budget reductions. Unfortunately, Congress usually ignores such cut proposals unless the administration presses hard and starts to veto spending bills to gain leverage.

The administration did zero out the failed Partnership for a New Generation of Vehicles subsidy program for U.S. automakers in its FY03 budget. Despite $1.5 billion in subsidies over eight years, U.S. carmakers did not deliver a promised hybrid car to consumers. Meanwhile, unsubsidized Honda and Toyota did introduce successful models. Unfortunately, the administration replaced PNGV with a new carmaker subsidy called FreedomCar at $150 million per year.

There are many good corporate welfare targets for Congress to cut. In the wake of the Enron scandal, reformers should push for elimination of the Ex-Im Bank and OPIC. These federal entities loaned Enron more than $1 billion for far-flung schemes around the world from which taxpayers did not get their money back. Also, reformers should get on board with the administration and cut the Community Development Block Grant program, which was criticized in the FY03 budget for doling out pork projects to high-income communities.

Eliminating Corporate Welfare

A two-pronged attack should be made to overcome the political difficulty of ending corporate welfare. Because corporate welfare is doled out by dozens of federal agencies, it is difficult for taxpayers to find out which firms are receiving what amounts of money. A first reform step should be financial transparency. The administration should begin providing a detailed cross-agency listing of companies that received direct business subsidies and the amounts received in its annual budget documents.

In addition to full disclosure, a corporate welfare termination commission should be established, akin to the successful military base closing commissions of the 1990s. The commission would present a list of cuts to Congress, which would be required to vote on all the cuts together with no amendments allowed. As an added way for members to gain support for the measure, the full value of savings could go to immediate tax rebates for all taxpayers.

Suggested Readings

Congressional Budget Office. "Federal Financial Support of Business." July 1995.

Edwards, Chris, and Tad DeHaven. "Corporate Welfare Update." Cato Institute Tax & Budget Bulletin, no. 7, May 2002.

Hartung, William. "Corporate Welfare for Weapons Makers: The Hidden Costs of Spending on Defense and Foreign Aid." Cato Institute Policy Analysis no. 350, August 12, 1999.

Lukas, Aaron, and Ian Vásquez. "Rethinking the Export-Import Bank." Cato Institute Trade Briefing no. 15, March 12, 2002.

Moore, Stephen, and Dean Stansel. "Ending Corporate Welfare As We Know It." Cato Institute Policy Analysis no. 225, May 12, 1995.

Rodgers, T. J. "Silicon Valley versus Corporate Welfare." Cato Institute Briefing Paper no. 37, April 27, 1998.

_____. "Why Silicon Valley Should Not Normalize Relations with Washington, D.C." Cato Institute monograph, February 9, 2000.

Slivinski, Stephen. "The Corporate Welfare Budget: Bigger Than Ever." Cato Institute Policy Analysis no. 415, October 10, 2001.

—Prepared by Chris Edwards and Tad DeHaven

REGULATION

34. Labor Relations Law

Congress should

- eliminate exclusive representation, or at least pass a national right-to-work law, or codify the U.S. Supreme Court's decisions in *NLRB v. General Motors* (1963) and *Communications Workers of America v. Beck* (1988);
- repeal section 8(a)2 of the National Labor Relations Act, or at least permit labor-management cooperation that is not union-management cooperation only;
- codify the Supreme Court's ruling in *NLRB v. Mackay Radio & Telegraph* (1938) that employers have an undisputed right to hire permanent replacement workers for striking workers in economic strikes;
- overturn the Supreme Court's ruling in *U.S. v. Enmons* (1973) that prohibits federal prosecution of unionists for acts of extortion and violence when those acts are undertaken in pursuit of "legitimate union objectives";
- overturn the Supreme Court's ruling in *NLRB v. Town & Country Electric* (1995) that forces employers to hire paid union organizers as ordinary employees;
- protect the associational rights of state employees by overriding state and local laws that impose NLRA-style unionism on state and local government employment;
- proscribe the use of project labor agreements on all federal and federally funded construction projects; and
- repeal the 1931 Davis Bacon Act and the 1965 Service Contract Act.

In a market economy it makes little sense to distinguish between producers and consumers because most people are both. It also makes no sense, outside discredited Marxist theory, to distinguish between management and labor because both are employed by consumers to produce goods and services. Management and labor are complementary, not rivalrous, inputs to the production process. Unfortunately, U.S. labor relations law is based on the mistaken ideas that management and labor are natural enemies; that labor is at an inherent bargaining power disadvantage relative to management; and that only unions backed by government power, which eliminate competition among sellers of labor services, can redress that situation. The National Labor Relations Act, as amended, is based on ideas that might have seemed sensible in the 1930s but do not make any sense in today's information age. That act is an impediment to labor market innovations that are necessary if the United States is to continue to be the world's premier economy. The NLRA ought to be scrapped, or at least substantially amended so it reflects modern labor market realities.

The Labor Front Today

Unions represent a small and declining share of the American labor market. In 2001 only 9.0 percent of the private-sector workforce was unionized. That figure has been declining since 1953 when it was 36 percent, and soon it will be no higher than 7 percent—exactly where it was in 1900. Unions, at least in the private sector, are going the way of the dinosaur. They are institutions that cannot succeed in the competitive global economy of the future. Firms and workers must be more innovative and have the freedom to adjust to changing market conditions if they are to reap the rich rewards of a more prosperous world economy.

Further, nearly half of union members now work for federal, state, and local governments. In 2001, 37.4 percent of the government-sector workforce was unionized. Even that number has declined from its 1995 peak of 38.8 percent. Yet, despite the decline of unions, the old regime that supports them is still in place.

Exclusive Representation and Union Security

The principle of exclusive representation, as provided for in sec. 9(a) of the NLRA, mandates that if a majority of employees of a particular firm vote to be represented by a particular union, that union is the sole representative of all workers whether an individual worker voted for or against it or did not vote at all. Individual workers are not free to designate representatives of their own choosing. While workers should be free, on an individual basis, to hire a union to represent them, they should not be forced to do so by majority vote. Unions are not governments; they are private associations. For government to tell individual workers that they must allow a union that has majority support among their coworkers to represent them is for government to violate those workers' individual freedom of association. Freedom of religion is not subject to a majority vote; neither should freedom of association be.

Union security is the principle under which workers who are represented by exclusive bargaining agents are forced to join, or at least pay dues to, the union with monopoly bargaining privileges. In the 22 right-to-work states such coercive arrangements are forbidden by state law. (Sec. 14[b] of the NLRA gives states the right to pass such laws.) The union justification for union security is that some workers whom unions represent would otherwise get union-generated benefits for free. But if exclusive representation were repealed, only a union's voluntary members could get benefits from the union because the union would represent only its voluntary members. The right-to-work issue would be moot. Forced unionism would, at long last, be replaced by voluntary unionism.

The NLRA serves the particular interests of unionized labor rather than the general interests of all labor, and it abrogates one of the most important privileges and immunities of U.S. citizens—the right of each individual worker to enter into hiring contracts with willing employers on terms that are mutually acceptable. Unfortunately, no court has had the courage to take up the issue since the 1930s. It is time for Congress to do so.

Congress has three options for remedying the current situation:

- Eliminate exclusive representation. Ideally, the current restrictions on the freedom of workers to choose who if anyone represents them should be eliminated. The 1991 New Zealand Employment Contracts Act would be an excellent model to follow. Although 85 percent of that country's population opposed that approach in 1991, in 1999, 73 percent of employees reported that they were ''very satisfied'' or ''satisfied'' with their working conditions and terms of employment. Still, initially it might be politically difficult to pass a similar act in the United States. Thus, several short-term options are available.
- Adopt a national right-to-work law. Under this option workers would still be forced to let certified unions represent them, but no worker would be forced to join, or pay dues to, a labor union. This is a poor second best to members-only bargaining.

- Codify the U.S. Supreme Court's decisions in *NLRB v. General Motors* (1963) and *Communications Workers of America v. Beck* (1988) by passing a federal "payroll protection" statute that guarantees that union members as well as nonmember agency-fee payers can opt out of union political activities. This is a third-best alternative to members-only bargaining.

In *General Motors* the Court declared that the only permissible form of compulsory union membership under the NLRA is the payment of union dues. Neither unions nor employers are allowed to compel "full membership in good standing." Notwithstanding this decision, the NLRB and the Court still allow unions and employers in non-right-to-work states to include union security clauses in collective bargaining contracts that assert that workers must become and remain members of unions in good standing as a condition of continued employment.

On November 3, 1998, a unanimous Supreme Court, in *Marquez v. Screen Actors Guild*, decided that union security clauses may continue to state that "membership in good standing" is required as a condition of employment. It remains true that, in this context, "membership in good standing" does not mean what almost everyone thinks it means. It means only that "members" must pay some money to the union that represents them in order to keep their jobs. But unions and employers are now free to continue to deceive workers into thinking that ordinary union membership is required as a condition of employment. Only Congress can put this travesty right.

In *Beck* the Court declared that the compulsory dues and fees collected by unions from workers they represent could not be used for purposes not directly related to collective bargaining, principally for political contributions. Many unions have effectively nullified *Beck* by creative bookkeeping. In 1996 the NLRB turned a blind eye to such deceit in its *California Saw and Knife Works* decision. In that case the board accepted the union's own staff accountants' categorization of expenditures on activities related to and not related to collective bargaining. It stated that, under *Beck,* dissenting workers had no right to an independent audit of the union's books. In this regard, Congress should incorporate, for private-sector workers, the procedural and substantive protections that were granted to government workers who are forced dues payers in *Chicago Teachers Union v. Hudson* (1986). Among them is an indisputable right of dissenting government workers to independent audits in all cases involving disputes over union uses of forced dues and fees. The Supreme Court is eventually likely to take up the issue of the applicability of *Hudson* to the private sector because of a conflict between two circuit courts of appeal. The D.C. Circuit, in *Ferriso v. NLRB* (1997), ruled that *Hudson* does apply, and the Seventh Circuit, in *Machinists v. NLRB* (1998), ruled that it does not.

A related problem concerns whether union expenditures for organizing union-free workers are chargeable to private-sector agency-fee payers. In *Ellis v. Railway Clerks* (1984), the Supreme Court explicitly said that organizing expenses are not chargeable to agency-fee payers under the Railway Labor Act, which sets the rules of unionism for workers in the railroad and airline industries. Until October 7,1999, most experts assumed that the *Ellis* rule would also apply to workers under the NLRA. However, on that date the NLRB ruled in two cases (*United Food and Commercial Workers*, and *Meijer, Inc.*) that the *Ellis* rule does not apply. In June 2001 a three-judge panel of the Ninth Circuit Court of Appeals overruled the NLRB in *Meijer*, but in April 2002 that same court, sitting en banc, reversed the panel and sided with the NLRB.

The issue of which procedural rules apply and which union expenses are and are not chargeable to nonmember agency-fee payers is a morass. It keeps a lot of judges, lawyers, arbitrators, and accountants busy, but not in the public interest. Congress must act to establish fair labor laws.

A "paycheck protection" statute that codifies *Beck, Ellis,* and *Hudson* protections for nonmember agency-fee payers does not go far enough. Because of exclusive representation, individual union members should also be protected by requiring unions annually to get written permission from a dues payer before spending any of his or her dues on politics. Under exclusive representation many workers may choose to be union members to get to vote on the collective bargaining agreements that affect them. Those workers also deserve to be able to opt out of union political activities. Not even a national right-to-work act would protect those workers against misuse of their dues for politics. Without exclusive representation no worker would be subject to the terms of a collective bargaining agreement unless he or she chose to be a union member. Union membership would be genuinely voluntary. If Congress abolished exclusive representation, and protected individual workers from union violence, there would be no need for payroll protection.

The history of attempts to enforce *Beck* and related cases demonstrates how complicated the issues are and how expensive it is to litigate them. Congress created these problems, and only Congress can eliminate them.

Repeal Section 8(a)2 of the NLRA

This is the section that outlaws so-called company unions. More important, it is the section that unions have discovered they can use to block any labor-management cooperation that is not union-management cooperation. Labor-management cooperation is crucial to America's ability to compete in the global market. The Employment Policy Foundation in Washington, D.C., has found that employee involvement plans increase productivity by from 30 percent to more than 100 percent. Under existing law union-free firms in America are not allowed to implement such plans unless they agree to take on the yoke of NLRA-style unions, and doing so usually reduces productivity in other ways.

Workers who want to have a voice in company decisionmaking without going through a union should be free to do so. A 1994 national poll of employees in private businesses with 25 or more workers, conducted by Princeton Survey Research Associates, revealed that 63 percent preferred cooperation committees to unions as a way of having a voice in decision-making. Only 20 percent preferred unions.

In the 1992 *Electromation* case, the NLRB declared that several voluntary labor-management cooperation committees, set up by management and workers in a union-free firm to give employees a significant voice in company decisionmaking, were illegal company unions. The Teamsters, who earlier had lost a certification election at the firm, then argued that the only form of labor-management cooperation the government would allow was union-management cooperation. On the basis of that argument, the Teamsters won a slim majority in a second certification election. As a result of the *Electromation* decision, Polaroid Corp. was forced to disband voluntary labor-management cooperation committees that had been in existence for 40 years.

In the 1993 *DuPont* case, the NLRB ruled that labor-management cooperation committees in a unionized setting were illegal company unions because they were separate from the union. The voluntary committees were set up to deal with problems with which the union either could not or would not deal. Under exclusive representation, management must deal only with a certified bargaining agent in a unionized firm. The solution is simply to abolish exclusive representation.

The report that was issued by the Dunlop commission on January 9, 1995, recommends "clarifying" rather than doing away with sec. 8(a)2. It says that voluntary worker-management cooperation programs "should not be unlawful simply because they involve discussion of terms and conditions of worker compensation where such discussions are incidental to the broad purposes of these programs.'' That will do little to solve the problem. What is ''incidental"? Who will decide? Answer: the NLRB that has already given us the *Electromation* decision.

It is time for Congress to state unequivocally that employers and workers may formulate and participate in any voluntary cooperation schemes they like so long as any individual worker may join and participate in any union he or she chooses without penalty.

Short of repealing sec. 8(a)2 outright, Congress should amend it to permit labor-management cooperation that is not union-management cooperation.

The Teamwork for Employees and Managers Act (H.R. 473 and S. 295), passed by Congress but vetoed by President Clinton in 1996, is an excellent second-best model. Unions supported Clinton's veto because they do not wish to compete on a level playing field with alternative types of labor-management cooperation.

Codify the Supreme Court's Ruling in NLRB v. Mackay Radio & Telegraph (1938)

Once and for all, it should be made clear that, although strikers have a right to withhold their own labor services from employers who offer unsatisfactory terms and conditions of employment, strikers have no right to withhold the labor services of workers who find those terms and conditions of employment acceptable. Strikers and replacement workers should have their constitutional right to *equal* protection of the laws acknowledged in the NLRA.

Overturn the Supreme Court's Ruling in U.S. v. Enmons (1973)

The federal Anti-Racketeering Act of 1934 was enacted to cope with the violence, intimidation, and injury to persons and property associated with organized crime. For example, it prohibits the use of violence, intimidation, and injury to extort money or other things of value from people or to force individuals to join or make payments to organizations they don't like. While this legislation was wending its way through Congress, the American Federation of Labor noticed that its provisions could apply just as well to many union activities as to the activities of the mob. To forestall that use of the law, the AFL lobbied to exempt union activities from the provisions of the statute. Congress obliged by adding a clause that says, ''No court of the United States shall construe or apply any of the provisions of this act in such a manner as to impair, diminish or in any manner affect the rights of bona-fide labor organizations in *lawfully* carrying out the legitimate objects thereof, as such rights are expressed in existing statutes of the United States'' (emphasis added). Notwithstanding that the clear language of the statute protected only *lawful* actions of the unions, courts soon interpreted the act to protect violence and intimidation by unions during strikes on the preposterous grounds that strikes are legal and they are undertaken to achieve legal ends such as improvements in the terms and conditions of employment for strikers. The Supreme Court made this interpretation of the law official in *United States v. Local 807, International Brotherhood of Teamsters* (1942).

Congress reacted swiftly to the *Local 807* decision by enacting the Hobbs Act amendments to the Anti-Racketeering Act over President Truman's veto in 1946. The clear intent of Congress was to proscribe acts of violence and intimidation by unions as well as organized crime. However, the federal judiciary refused to go along. They continued to apply the *Local 807* decision in most cases of union violence and intimidation during strikes. Unions continued to get away with egregious attacks against persons and property, including robbery and arson, whenever any case could be made that such aggression was in pursuit of "legitimate union objectives." The Supreme Court removed all doubt concerning union immunity to federal anti-racketeering laws in 1973 with its ruling in *U.S. v. Enmons.* By a 5–4 decision the Court upheld the right of strikers under federal law to fire high-powered rifles at three utility company transformers, to drain oil from and thus ruin a transformer, and to blow up a transformer substation. The Court said it was up to state and local officials to prosecute such behavior. The federal government had to stay out of it because it involved a legal strike under the NLRA.

Congress must try again to make it clear that violence and intimidation are not acceptable no matter who initiates them and no matter for what purpose they are initiated. Equal protection of the laws is an important constitutional principle. Victims of union thuggery deserve as much protection as victims of mob thuggery. The Freedom from Union Violence Act (S. 764) proposed in the 106th Congress is a good model for the 108th Congress to adopt.

Overturn the Supreme Court's Ruling in NLRB v. Town & Country Electric (1995)

Sec. 8(a)3 of the NLRA makes it an unfair labor practice for an employer to discriminate against a worker on the basis of union membership. According to the Supreme Court, that means that an employer cannot refuse to hire or cannot fire any employee who is a paid union organizer. Unions send paid organizers (salts) to apply for jobs at union-free firms and, if employed, to foment discontent and promote pro-union sympathies. In the *Town & Country Electric* decision the Court said that employers could not resist that practice by firing or refusing to hire salts. In other words, employers must hire people whose main intent is to subvert their business activities. That is like telling a homeowner that it is illegal to exclude visitors whose principal intent is to burglarize his home. Congress should allow employers to resist this practice. The Truth in Employment Act (H.R. 758), which was quashed by the threat of a filibuster in the 105th Congress, is a good model for the 108th Congress to adopt.

Protect the Associational Rights of State Employees with a Federal Statute

Congress has constitutional authority under the Fourteenth Amendment to protect the privileges and immunities of citizens of the United States. Thus it is not necessary to undo the harm of government employee unionism state by state.

The principles of exclusive representation and union security abrogate the First Amendment rights of government employees who wish to remain union free. Government is the employer; hence there is sufficient government action to give rise to Bill of Rights concerns.

Under the Bill of Rights, government is not supposed to intrude on an individual citizen's right to associate or not associate with any legal private organization. A voluntary union of government employees is a legal private organization. But forcing dissenting workers to be represented by, join, or pay dues to such an organization is an abridgment of those workers' freedom of association.

Moreover, in government employment, mandatory bargaining in good faith (a feature of the NLRA incorporated into 31 state collective bargaining statutes) forces governments to share the making of public policy with privileged, unelected private organizations. Ordinary private organizations can lobby government, but only government employee unions have the privilege of laws that force government agencies to bargain in good faith with them. Good-faith bargaining is conducted behind closed doors. It requires government agencies to compromise with government employee unions. Government agencies are forbidden to set unilaterally terms and conditions of government employment (questions of public policy) without the concurrence of government employee unions. Not even the Sierra Club has that special access to government decisionmakers or that kind of influence over decisionmaking. In short, government employee unionism, modeled on the NLRA, violates all basic democratic values. It should be forbidden. That is why Title VII of the 1978 Civil Service Reform Act greatly restricts the scope of bargaining with federal employee unions and forbids union security in federal employment. It ought also to forbid exclusive representation and mandatory good-faith bargaining in federal employment.

Incredibly, in the 106th Congress there was bipartisan support for a statute (S. 1016 and H.R. 1093) that would force all states to give exclusive representation, mandatory bargaining, and union security privileges to unions representing police and firefighters. That same measure was promoted by many members of the 107th Congress under cover of the September 11, 2001, terrorist attacks. It is a measure to benefit union leaders, not firefighters and police on the front lines. The record of disaster in the states that already give public safety unions such privileges is clear. Firefighters who are prohibited by union leaders from fighting fires and police who are prohibited by union leaders from maintaining order and preventing crimes during strikes undermine civil society. The public safety strikes in San Francisco during the 1970s prove the point. The proposed legislation would expose the 20 states that now deny NLRA-style privileges to public safety unions to the same predation. It proscribes strikes by public safety personnel, but the record is clear. Public-sector unions with NLRA-style privileges are almost never deterred by laws that make strikes illegal. Moreover, once states are forced to give public safety unions such privileges, the teachers' unions and other public-sector unions will demand equal treatment. The 108th Congress should drive a stake through the heart of this idea as soon as possible.

Proscribe the Use of Project Labor Agreements on All Federal and Federally Funded Construction Projects

A project labor agreement (PLA) is a device used by unions in the construction industry to make it extremely difficult for union-free contractors to bid successfully for construction projects funded by taxpayer money. In 1947 construction unions had an 87 percent market share nationwide. In 2001 that figure was only 18.4 percent. Failing the market test, construction unions have turned to politics at all levels. Construction unions lobby politicians to require that open-shop (union-free) contractors sign agreements to operate according to union rules before they are permitted to bid on any project funded, in whole or in part, with taxpayer money.

An open-shop contractor that signs a PLA in order to be able to bid agrees to (1) force all its employees to either join, or pay dues to, the unions specified in the PLA; (2) do all new hiring associated with the PLA through designated union hiring halls; (3) operate according to union work rules and craft jurisdiction definitions; and (4) force its employees to pay (or agree to pay on their behalf) into union welfare, benefits, and pension funds. Since it usually takes at least five years for workers to become vested in such funds, and most projects last less than five years, the money is forfeited to the unions when the projects are completed. Moreover, unless employees are to lose their regular benefits and pension plans, payments to them must be maintained during the life of the PLA project.

PLAs should not be confused with "prevailing wage" regulations in taxpayer-funded construction. The federal Davis-Bacon Act (see below) forces successful union-free bidders to pay their employees union wages on taxpayer-funded projects. But even when forced to pay union-scale wages, union-free contractors have cost advantages over union-impaired contractors that enable them to bid lower to get contracts. The unions' restrictive work rules and job classifications drive up costs substantially. The obvious solution from the unions' point of view is, through PLAs, to remove all union-free cost advantages.

Unions claim that PLAs are a way of ensuring safe, on-budget quality work without labor disputes and project delays. Facts belie those claims.

A nationwide study in 1995 by Charles Culver, a former Occupational Safety and Health Administration official, revealed that on-the-job fatalities were significantly lower in union-free construction than in comparable unionized construction in every year from 1985 through 1993. Moreover, the quality of union-free work is usually just as good as unionized work, and it is often better. It is revealing to note that union-free contractors deemed unqualified to do a job all of a sudden are deemed well qualified when they sign a PLA.

PLAs are not even effective guarantees against strikes by the unions on the jobs they win. For example, the San Francisco Airport PLA includes a no-strike pledge that has been violated at least three times. And PLAs are not effective guarantees against project completion delays. The Boston "Big Dig" PLA has resulted in substantial delays. The project was supposed to be completed in 1998; now the earliest possible completion date is 2004. As for on-budget performance, the original budget for the Big Dig was $2.5 billion. Best estimates now put the cost at $15 billion.

On February 17, 2001, President Bush signed Executive Order 13202, which prevents federal government agencies from including PLAs as bid specifications on federal construction projects. Under the executive order, union-free firms can use their cost advantages to try to win the bid, but if a contractor submits a winning bid for a federal construction project he is thereafter free to agree with construction unions that he and his subcontractors will work on a union-only basis. The reason the executive order permits union-only agreements *after* bids are won is that after a contract is awarded all subsequent labor relations questions are controlled by the NLRA, which clearly permits union-only agreements among private parties. All the president can do is prohibit federal agencies from requiring PLAs as a condition for bidding.

The legality of PLAs at the state level was affirmed in 1993 by the U.S. Supreme Court in the *Boston Harbor* case. This involved a massive cleanup of Boston Harbor. The Massachusetts Water Resources Authority said that no union-free contractors could bid on the project unless they first agreed to the terms of a PLA. Opponents of the PLA argued that the NLRA preempted state authority to impose a PLA. The Court upheld the PLA on the grounds that MWRA was acting as an owner-developer of the project, not the employer of the employees who actually worked the project. The NLRA controls relations among employers, employees, and unions, not relations between owner-developers and the employers with whom they contract. So, under *Boston Harbor,* a state agency is free to choose whether or not to impose a PLA as a bid qualification.

Labor unions and their logrolling partner, the Sierra Club, immediately challenged the legality of Bush's executive order in federal district court, and on November 7, 2001, Judge Emmet Sullivan declared, on the basis of the *Boston Harbor* case, that the executive order was preempted by the NLRA. This was a manifestly silly ruling because in *Boston Harbor* the Supreme Court ruled that the NLRA does *not* preempt *state* PLAs if the state agency involved is an owner-developer rather than an employer. If *Boston Harbor* says anything about federal PLAs, it says that the president, as owner-developer of federal projects, is free to permit or forbid PLAs. Judge Sullivan's decision was overturned by the D.C. Circuit Court of Appeals on July 15, 2002.

Congress should settle this issue by enacting legislation that goes beyond Bush's executive order to preserve open competition at all stages of federal construction projects including subcontracting. Primary contractors should not be permitted to discriminate against subcontractors on the grounds of whether they are unionized or not. The rule in federal contracting should be that the lowest bidder who is capable of doing the specified job always wins. That would save taxpayers millions of dollars each year, and it would set a good model for states to follow.

Union-only agreements between private parties would be unobjectionable if labor union participation were a matter of free choice for all individual workers. However, as long as we have compulsory unionism (exclusive representation, union security, and mandatory good-faith bargaining), taxpayers need protection against the inflated costs that inevitably follow.

Repeal the 1931 Davis-Bacon Act and the 1965 Service Contract Act

The Davis-Bacon Act, passed at the beginning of the Great Depression, had two purposes: to stop prices and wages from falling and to keep blacks from competing for jobs that had previously been done by white unionized labor. Both of its purposes were wrong. Falling wages and prices were precisely what were needed to reverse the collapse of real income and employment in the early 1930s. (Both fell from 1929 to 1933, but prices fell by more than wages. Thus the real cost of hiring workers increased during that time period.) The purchasing power fallacy that misled first Herbert Hoover and later Franklin Roosevelt (e.g., the National Industrial Recovery Act) did as much to deepen and prolong the Great Depression as did the Smoot-Hawley tariff.

The racist motivation behind the legislation is plain for anyone who reads the *Congressional Record* of 1931 to see. For example, Rep. Clayton Allgood, in support of the bill, complained of "cheap colored labor" that "is in competition with white labor throughout the country."

While most current supporters of Davis-Bacon are not racists, the law still has racist effects. There are very few minority-owned firms that can afford to pay union wages. As a result, they rarely are awarded Davis-Bacon contracts, and many of them stop even trying for those contracts.

Moreover, Davis-Bacon adds over a billion dollars each year directly to federal government expenditures, and billions more to private expenditures on projects that are partially funded with federal funds, by making it impossible for union-free, efficient firms to bid on construction contracts financed in whole or in part with federal funds. Today Davis-Bacon serves no interest whatsoever other than protecting the turf of undeserving, white-dominated construction trade unions.

The claim, on January 6, 1995, by Robert A. Georgine, president of the AFL-CIO Building and Construction Trades Department, that Davis-Bacon has long been supported by the GOP because it adheres to "free market principles by recognizing existing wages within each community set by the private marketplace, not by imposing an artificial standard or deleterious government interference," is self-serving nonsense. Prices set by the free market do not need any government enforcement at all. They are the prices at which the production and exchange plans of buyers and sellers of inputs and outputs are coordinated with each other. They are the prices that would exist in the *absence* of any government involvement. The AFL-CIO and its constituent unions want government to impose prices that are more favorable to their members and officers than the marketplace would produce. The "prevailing wage" or "community wage" set by the Department of Labor under the Davis-Bacon Act is almost always the union wage—not the free-market wage. After all, unions insist that they make wages higher than market-determined wages. Only members of the GOP in thrall to unions' in-kind and financial bribes would support Davis-Bacon. No member of Congress, of either party, who supports the free market can be against repealing Davis-Bacon.

Several states have their own "little Davis Bacon Acts." In 1994 a federal district court in Michigan found that state's prevailing wage law violated federal Employee Retirement Income Security Act regulations. As a result the Michigan law was suspended between 1994 and 1997 when an appellate court reinstated it. According to a study done for the Mackinac Center for Public Policy, as a direct result of the suspension more than 11,000 new jobs were created. Comparing the costs of state government construction projects during the suspension with their costs under the prevailing-wage rules suggests that those regulations add at least $275 million per year.

The Service Contract Act does for federal purchases of services what the Davis-Bacon Act does for federally funded construction. It wastes billions of taxpayer dollars for the sole purpose of attempting to price union-free service providers out of the market. Both acts should be placed in the dustbin of history along with the syndicalist sympathies that inspired them.

Conclusion

The more integrated global economy of the new millennium offers greater opportunities for American enterprises and workers to prosper. Greater productivity worldwide means more wealth for those who can exchange their services with willing customers. But to do so, American workers and the enterprises that employ them must be empowered to act quickly to meet market demands. That means eliminating the laws and regulations that destroy jobs and make workers a burden rather than an asset to employers. The outmoded perceptions of the 1930s should not be allowed to shackle the American economy of the 21st century.

Suggested Readings

Baird, Charles W. "Are Quality Circles Illegal? Global Competition Meets the New Deal." Cato Institute Briefing Paper no. 18, February 10, 1993.

———. "Outlawing Cooperation: Chapter Two." *Regulation*, no. 3 (1993).

———. "The Permissible Uses of Forced Union Dues: From *Hanson* to *Beck*," Cato Institute Policy Analysis no. 174, June 30, 1992.

———. "The PLA Hustle." *Ideas on Liberty*, August 2002.

———. "Right to Work before and after 14(b)." *Journal of Labor Research* 19, no. 3 (Summer 1998).

———. "Salt without Savor." *Freeman*, May 1998.

———. "Toward Voluntary Unionism." *Journal of Private Enterprise* 17, no. 1 (Fall 2001).

———. "Unchaining the Workers." *Regulation* 24, no. 3 (Fall 2001).

Bernstein, David. "The Davis-Bacon Act: Let's Bring Jim Crow to an End." Cato Institute Briefing Paper no. 17, January 18, 1993.

Culver, Charles A. *Comparison of Nonunion and Union Contractors Construction Fatalities*. Gainesville, Fla.: National Center for Construction Education and Research, 1995.

Deavers, Ken, Anita Hattiangadi, and Max Lyons. *The American Workplace 1998*. Washington: Employment Policy Foundation, 1998.

Moore, Cassandra Chrones. "Blocking Beck." *Regulation*, Spring 1998.

Nelson, Daniel. "The Company Union Movement, 1900–1937: A Reexamination." *Business History Review* 56 (Autumn 1982).

Reynolds, Morgan O. *Making America Poorer: The Cost of Labor Law*. Washington: Cato Institute, 1987.

Summers, Robert S. *Collective Bargaining and Public Benefit Conferral: A Jurisprudential Critique*. Ithaca, N.Y.: Cornell University, Institute of Public Employment, 1976.

Theiblot, Armand J., Thomas R. Haggard, and Herbert R. Northrup. *Union Violence: The Record and the Response by Courts, Legislatures, and the NLRB*. Fairfax, Va.: George Mason University Press, 1999.

Vedder, Richard. *Michigan's Prevailing Wage Law and Its Effects on Government Spending and Construction Employment*. Midland, Mich.: Mackinac Center for Public Policy, 1999.

—Prepared by Charles W. Baird

35. Health and Safety Policy

> **Congress should**
> - eliminate goals of zero risk in statutes governing occupational and environmental health and
> - establish the purpose of safety and health agencies as the identification of opportunities to improve safety and health at costs that are much less than the market value of the benefits.

Before the 1970s, the health and safety regulations that we now take for granted were completely absent from the American economy, with the exception of selected regulations for food safety and prescription drugs. The rise of the consumer movement and environmental concerns led to the establishment of the National Highway Traffic Safety Administration in 1966, the Occupational Safety and Health Administration in 1970, the Environmental Protection Agency in 1970, the Consumer Product Safety Commission in 1972, and the Nuclear Regulatory Commission in 1974.

Scholarly assessment of the more than three decades of experience with regulation and government oversight concludes that health and safety regulations have largely failed to fulfill their initial promise, but many of the initial promises were infeasible goals. There continue to be major opportunities to improve regulatory performance by targeting existing inefficiencies and using market mechanisms (rather than strict command-and-control mechanisms) to achieve regulatory goals.

Why Should the Government Regulate Risk?

Government action in the health and safety arena can be justified when there are shortcomings in risk information. The goal of regulatory agencies that address health and safety risks should be to isolate instances in which misinformation about health risks prevents people from making optimal tradeoffs and to isolate instances in which health risks are not internalized in market decisions.

The existence of a health risk does not necessarily imply the need for regulatory action. For example, as long as workers understand the risks they face in various occupations, they will receive wage compensation through normal market forces sufficient to make them willing to bear the risk; the health risk is internalized into the market decision.

In situations in which the risks are not known to workers, as in the case of dimly understood health hazards or situations in which the labor market is not competitive, market forces might not operative effectively to internalize the risk. Those cases provide an opportunity for constructive, cost-effective government intervention.

Zero vs. Optimal Risk

Unfortunately, the rationale of correcting market failures has never been a major motivation of regulatory intervention. The simple fact that risks exist has provided the impetus for the legislative mandates of the health and safety regulatory agencies. To this day, very few regulatory impact analyses explore in any meaningful way the role of potential market failure in the particular context and the constructive role that market forces may already play in that context.

The conventional regulatory approach to health and safety risks is to seek a technological solution either through capital investments in the workplace, changes in the safety devices in products, or similar kinds of requirements that do not entail any additional care on the part of the individual. Stated simply, the conventional view is that the existence of risks is undesirable and, with appropriate technological interventions, we can eliminate those risks. That perspective does not recognize the cost tradeoffs involved; the fact that a no-risk society would be so costly as to make it infeasible does not arise as a policy concern of consequence.

The economic approach to regulating risk is quite different. The potential role of the government is not to eliminate the risk but rather to address market failures that lead to an inefficient balance between risk reduction and cost. The task of government regulatory agencies is to identify cases in which regulation can generate benefits to society that are worth more than the costs that are incurred and to address market failures using a cost-effective approach. To achieve those goals, the focus should not simply be on rigid technological standards but on flexible regulatory mechanisms that meet the performance goals.

How Should Risks Be Evaluated?

Because government policies reduce risks of death rather than eliminate certain death for identified individuals, the correct benefit value is society's willingness to pay for the reduction in risk. For example, if a regulation would reduce risk by 1 in 1 million to everyone in a population of 1 million, then the regulation would save 1 statistical life. If the average willingness to pay for that risk reduction is $6 per person, then the value of a statistical life is $6 million.

Using detailed data on wages and prices, economists have estimated people's tradeoffs between money and fatality risk, thus establishing a value of statistical lives based on market decisions. For workers in jobs of average risk, the estimates imply that, in current dollars, workers receive premiums in the range of $600 to face an additional annual work-related fatality risk of 1 chance in 10,000. Put somewhat differently, if there were 10,000 such workers facing an annual fatality chance of 1 in 10,000, there would be 1 statistical death. In return for that risk, workers would receive total additional wage compensation of $6 million. The compensation establishes the value of a statistical life, based on workers' own attitude toward risks.

The estimates suggest that in situations in which there is an awareness of the risk, market forces are enormously powerful and create tremendous safety incentives. Thus, we are not operating in a world in which there are no constraints other than regulatory intervention to promote our safety. Powerful market forces already create incentives for safety that should not be overridden by intrusive regulations. We should define the overall economic framework in which regulatory interventions can potentially complement the already significant market forces at work.

Assessing Regulatory Performance

Although many agencies use reasonable measures of the value of a statistical life for the purpose of assessing benefits, the cost per life saved by the regulations actually promulgated often far exceeds the estimated benefits. The restrictive nature of agencies' legislative mandates often precludes consideration of costs in the regulatory decision.

Table 35.1 lists various health and safety regulations and their estimated cost per life saved. The table also lists the cost per normalized life saved (in 1995 dollars), which accounts for the duration of life lost and the existence of discounting of future lives. Because the legislative mandate

363

Table 35.1
A Sample of U.S. Health and Safety Regulations and Their Cost per Life Saved

Regulation	Year	Agency	Cost per Life Saved (millions of 1990 $)	Cost per Normalized Life Saved (millions of 1995 $)
Unvented space heater ban	1980	CPSC	0.1	0.1
Aircraft cabin fire protection standard	1985	FAA	0.1	0.1
Seatbelt/air bag	1984	NHTSA	0.1	0.1
Steering column protection standard	1967	NHTSA	0.1	0.1
Underground construction standards	1989	OSHA	0.1	0.1
Trihalomethane in drinking water	1979	EPA	0.2	0.6
Aircraft seat cushion flammability	1984	FAA	0.5	0.6
Alcohol and drug controls	1985	FRA	0.5	0.6
Auto fuel system integrity	1975	NHTSA	0.5	0.5
Auto wheel rim servicing	1984	OSHA	0.5	0.6
Aircraft floor emergency lighting	1984	FAA	0.7	0.9
Concrete and masonry construction	1988	OSHA	0.7	0.9
Crane-suspended personnel platform	1988	OSHA	0.8	1.0
Passive restraints for trucks and busses	1989	NHTSA	0.8	0.8
Auto side-impact standards	1990	1990	1.0	1.0
Children's sleepwear flammability ban	1973	1973	1.0	1.2
Auto side-door supports	1970	NHTSA	1.0	1.0
Low-altitude windshear equipment	1988	FAA	1.6	1.9
Metal mine electrical equipment standards	1970	MSHA	1.7	2.0
Trenching and excavation standards	1989	OSHA	1.8	2.2
Traffic alert/collision avoidance systems	1988	FAA	1.8	2.2

Regulation	Year	Agency	Cost per Life Saved (millions of 1990 $)	Cost per Normalized Life Saved (millions of 1995 $)
Hazard communication standard	1983	OSHA	1.9	4.8
Truck, bus, and MPV side-impact standard	1989	NHTSA	2.6	2.6
Grain dust explosion prevention standards	1987	OSHA	3.3	4.0
Rear lap/shoulder belts for cars	1989	NHTSA	3.8	3.8
Stds for radionuclides in uranium mines	1984	EPA	4.1	10.1
Benzene NESHAP (original)	1984	EPA	4.1	10.1
Ethylene dibromide in drinking water	1991	EPA	6.8	17.0
Benzene NESHAP (revised)	1988	EPA	7.3	18.1
Asbestos occupational exposure limit	1972	OSHA	9.9	24.7
Benzene occupational exposure limit	1987	OSHA	10.6	26.5
Electrical equipment in coal mines	1970	OSHA	11.0	13.3
Arsenic emissions from glass plants	1986	MSHA	16.1	40.2
Ethylene oxide occupational exposure limit	1984	EPA	24.4	61.0
Arsenic/copper NESHAP	1986	EPA	27.4	68.4
Petroleum sludge hazardous waste listing	1990	EPA	32.9	82.1
Cover/move uranium mill tailings (inactive)	1983	EPA	37.7	94.3
Benzene NESHAP (revised)	1990	EPA	39.2	97.9
Cover/move uranium mill tailings (active)	1983	EPA	53.6	133.8
Acrylonitrile occupational exposure limit	1978	OSHA	61.3	153.2
Coke ovens occupational exposure limit	1976	OSHA	75.6	188.9

(continued)

Table 35.1
(continued)

Regulation	Year	Agency	Cost per Life Saved (millions of 1990 $)	Cost per Normalized Life Saved (millions of 1995 $)
Lockout/tagout	1989	OSHA	84.4	102.4
Arsenic occupational exposure limit	1978	OSHA	127.3	317.9
Asbestos ban	1989	EPA	131.8	329.2
Diethylstilbestrol cattle feed ban	1979	FDA	148.6	371.2
Benzene NESHAP (revised)	1990	EPA	200.2	500.2
1,2-Dichloropropane in drinking water	1991	EPA	777.4	1,942.1
Hazardous waste land disposal ban	1988	EPA	4,988.7	12,462.7
Municipal solid waste landfills	1988	EPA	22,746.8	56,826.1
Formaldehyde occupational exposure limit	1987	OSHA	102,608.5	256,372.7
Atrazine/alachlor in drinking water	1991	EPA	109,608.5	273,824.4
Wood preservatives hazardous waste listing	1990	EPA	6,785,822.0	16,952,364.9

SOURCE: W. Kip Viscusi, Jahn K. Hakes, and Alan Carlin, ''Measures of Mortality Risks,'' *Journal of Risk and Uncertainty* 14 (1997): 213–33.

varies across regulations, one sees great variance in the cost per life saved. Indeed, the cost varies even within certain regulatory agencies. For example, EPA's regulation of trihalomethane in drinking water has an estimated cost per normalized life saved of $600,000, whereas the regulation of atrazine/alachlor in drinking water has an estimated cost per normalized life saved of $274 billion. A regulatory system based on sound economic principles would reallocate resources from the high- to the low-cost regulations. That would result in more lives saved at the same cost to society (or, equivalently, shifting resources could result in the same number of lives saved at lower cost to society).

The focus of policy debates should not be on whether regulations that cost $7 million per life saved or $12 million per life saved are desirable. Rather, policy debates should emphasize the enormous opportunity costs associated with regulations that cost hundreds of millions of dollars or even billions of dollars per statistical life saved.

Effect of Regulation on Accident Rates

What has been the overall effect of health and safety regulations since the early 1970s? One yardstick of performance is to see whether accident rates have declined. Figure 35.1 summarizes fatality rates of various kinds, including motor vehicle accidents, work accidents, home accidents, public no-motor-vehicle accidents, and an aggregative category of all accidents.

Since the 1970s, accidents of all kinds have declined. Improvements in safety over time typically lead to annual press releases on the part of the regulatory agencies in which they take credit for the improvements and attribute the gains to their regulatory efforts. There are exceptions, as

Figure 35.1
Accidental Death Rates

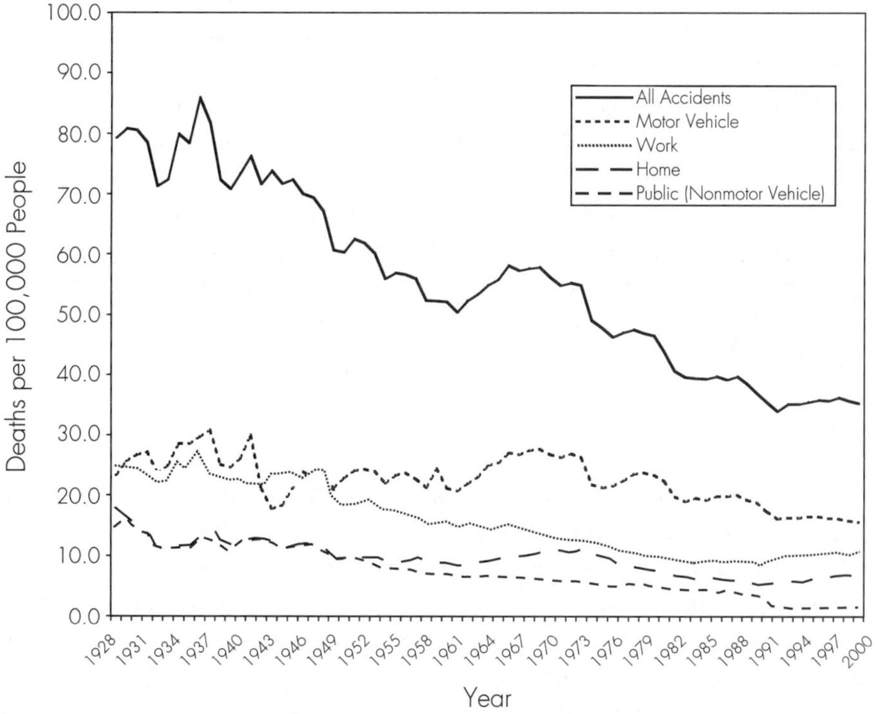

SOURCE: National Safety Council, *Accident Facts* (Itasca, Ill.: NSC, 2001), pp. 34–35.

there are some years in which accident rates increase—and regulatory officials typically blame cyclical factors for such trends.

The basic message of Figure 35.1 is that accident rates have been declining throughout the past 100 years. The improvement in our safety is not a new phenomenon that began with the advent of regulatory agencies commissioned to protect the citizenry. There is, for example, no significant downward shift in Figure 35.1's trend for job fatality risk after the establishment of OSHA.

Perhaps the main exception has been motor vehicle accidents, but assessments of annual death rates associated with motor vehicles are complicated by the fact that many more people drive than did in previous years, and there have been considerable changes in the amount of driving, traffic congestion, and highway design.

Figure 35.2 provides an explanation of motor vehicle accident rates that attempts to adjust to some of the aspects of driving intensity rather than simply tallying the motor vehicle fatality rate per person. As can be seen from the figure, deaths per 10,000 motor vehicles as well as deaths per 100 million vehicle miles have declined steadily throughout the last 100 years. As in the case of the other accident statistics, there is no evidence of a sharp, discontinuous break in the downward trend occurring with the advent of regulatory policies.

Although regulation may play a beneficial safety-enhancing role, the steady decrease in risk throughout the century supports the hypothesis that improvements in societal wealth have greatly increased our demand for safety over time. Coupling that wealth with technological improvements— many of which have been stimulated by the greater demand for safety— has led to dramatic improvements in our individual well-being. Market forces rather than regulatory policy have likely been the most important contributor to safety improvements since early last century.

Reform Agenda

Almost from its inception, health and safety regulation has been the target of proposed reform. Some policy improvements have occurred, such as elimination of some of the nitpicking of safety standards, the increased use of informational approaches to regulation, and enhanced enforcement efforts. However, health and safety regulations have fallen short of any reasonable standard of performance.

The underlying difficulty can be traced to the legislative mandates of the regulatory agencies. Instead of focusing regulations on instances of

Figure 35.2
Motor Vehicle Death Rates

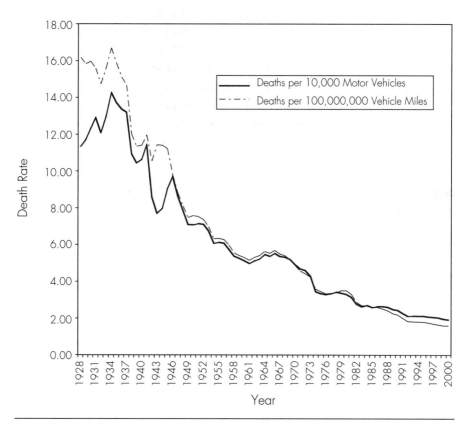

SOURCE: National Safety Council, *Accident Facts* (Itasca, Ill.: NSC, 2001), pp. 108–9.

market failure, the emphasis is on reductions of risk irrespective of cost. The regulatory approach has also been characterized by an overly narrow conceptualization of the potential modes of intervention. The emphasis has been on command-and-control regulations rather than performance-oriented standards. More generally, various forms of injury taxes that would parallel the financial incentives created by workers' compensation or various environmental tradable permits programs could establish incentives for safety while at the same time offering firms leeway to select the most cost-effective means of risk reduction. A glaring omission from the regulatory strategy has been adequate attention devoted to the role of consumer and worker behavior and the potential for exploiting the benefits that can derive from promoting safety-enhancing actions by individuals rather than relying simply on technological controls.

369

Defenders of the current regulatory approach have long seized the moral high ground by claiming that their uncompromising efforts protect individual health; less consequential concerns such as cost should not interfere with that higher enterprise. The fallacy of such thinking is that high-cost, low-benefit safety regulations divert society's resources from a mix of expenditures that would be more health enhancing than the allocations dictated by the health and safety regulations. Agencies that make an unbounded financial commitment to safety frequently are sacrificing individual lives in their symbolic quest for a zero-risk society. It is unlikely that this situation will be remedied in the absence of fundamental legislative reform.

Suggested Readings

Adams, John. "Cars, Cholera, and Cows: The Management of Risk and Uncertainty." Cato Institute Policy Analysis no. 335, March 4, 1999.

Hahn, Robert W., and Jason K. Burnett. "A Costly Benefit." *Regulation* 24, no. 3 (2001).

Kniesner, Thomas J., and John D. Leeth. "Abolishing OSHA." *Regulation* 18, no. 4 (1995).

Miller, Henry I., and Peter VanDoren. "Food Risks and Labeling Controversies." *Regulation* 23, no. 1 (2000).

Niskanen, William A. "Arsenic and Old Facts." *Regulation* 24, no. 3 (2001).

Scalia, Eugene. "OSHA's Ergonomics Litigation Record: Three Strikes and It's Out." Cato Institute Policy Analysis no. 370, May 15, 2000.

Viscusi, W. Kip, and Ted Gayer. "Safety at Any Price?" *Regulation* 25, no. 3 (2002).

Wilson, Richard. "Regulating Environmental Hazards." *Regulation* 23, no. 1 (2000).

———. "Underestimating Arsenic's Risk." *Regulation* 24, no. 3 (2001).

—Prepared by Peter VanDoren

36. Transportation Policy

Congress should

- close the U.S. Department of Transportation;
- eliminate the federal gasoline tax;
- end all federal transportation subsidies;
- entrust states and municipalities with maintaining infrastructure such as highways, roads, bridges, and subways;
- repeal the Urban Mass Transit Act of 1964;
- repeal the Railway Labor Act of 1926 and the Railroad Retirement Act of 1934;
- privatize Amtrak;
- privatize the air traffic control system;
- eliminate all federal regulations that prevent airports from being privately owned or operated;
- repeal laws that prevent foreign airlines from flying domestic routes in the United States; and
- repeal the Jones Act.

Historically, the federal government regulated the U.S. transportation system with a heavy hand. Beginning in the 1950s, a series of academic studies showed that regulation protected incumbent firms rather than the public. The result was higher prices and poorer service.

Deregulation of the Airlines

Congress passed the Airline Deregulation Act in October 1978. This legislation eliminated federal control over routes by December 1981 and over fares by January 1983. The Civil Aeronautics Board, which directed much of federal regulation of air transportation, was abolished at the end of 1984. The new law authorized airlines to abandon routes but established an Essential Service Air Program to provide subsidies for service to small communities.

The effect of this legislation on the market value of the various airlines has been remarkable. Southwest has gone from virtually "zero" to a market capitalization of more than $14 billion. On the other hand, United's market value declined in real terms from $2 billion to less than three-quarters of a billion dollars at the end of 2001. However, the total valuation of the major airlines today is more than double that of all the trunk and regional carriers together in 1976, before any deregulation. It is even 45 percent more than in 1983. Although some of the carriers, such as United, Northwest, TWA, and Pam Am, have suffered or even gone out of business, the industry has done well.

The percentage of passengers traveling on discount fares has increased dramatically. In 1976, on long flights, only 27 percent of those flying in coach between major metropolitan areas managed to get discount tickets; by 1983, 73 percent were getting special fares. Virtually all passengers today, except for a handful of business travelers, are paying less than the full coach fare. From 1977 to 1996, after adjusting for inflation, airfares fell some 40 percent. Figure 36.1 shows how the average fare has declined

Figure 36.1
Average Fare per Mile Adjusted for Inflation
(systemwide operations, 1996 dollars)

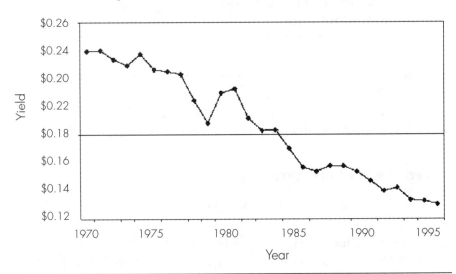

SOURCE: Steven A. Morrison, Statement before House Committee on the Judiciary, November 5, 1997.

since the early 1970s. The Federal Trade Commission estimated in 1988 that, after adjusting for fuel costs, the flying public was paying 25 percent less because of deregulation. Stephen Morrison, professor of economics at Northeastern University, calculated that deregulation produced a net benefit, in 2001 dollars, of about $15 billion, most of which was in the form of lower prices for consumers.

Lower fares have boosted load factors—from 49 percent in 1976 to 58 percent in 2000—which means that travelers are finding planes and airports far more crowded. Higher load factors, however, make it possible for the airlines to make money at lower prices. Over the quarter of a century since deregulation, the number of passengers flying has roughly doubled while passenger-miles have nearly tripled, proving the success of deregulation.

Deregulation of Air Freight

While passenger airlines were receiving greater authority to compete, Federal Express was lobbying to open up freight air traffic. The Civil Aeronautics Board had granted it only a commuter license that limited FedEx to small aircraft, restricting its ability to compete. It wanted authorization to fly large aircraft to and from any state or city in the country. In 1976 the CAB recommended that air freight transportation be largely deregulated. With support for less federal control from other freight carriers and no visible opposition, President Jimmy Carter, in November 1977, signed H.R. 6010, which deregulated air freight transportation.

Although little attention has been paid to the abolition of air freight regulation, it has been hugely successful. Prior to deregulation, air freight had been growing around 11 percent per year. In the first year of decontrol, 1978, revenue ton-miles jumped by 26 percent. That early success helped build support for exempting passenger transportation from control.

Deregulation of Rail Freight

In the fall of 1980 Congress passed the Staggers Act to provide additional pricing and route abandonment freedoms to the railroad industry. The Staggers Act gave railroads the ability to set prices within wide limits. Rail lines could enter into contracts with shippers to carry goods at agreed-upon rates. Tariffs could not be considered unreasonable, even for "captive" shippers, unless they exceeded 180 percent of variable costs. To qualify as "captive," shippers also had to prove that there was no effective competition, a provision designed to protect coal, chemical, and other bulk commodity shippers. Railroads were also given new authority to abandon routes.

The Interstate Commerce Commission was abolished and the Surface Transportation Board established on January 1, 1996, as an independent body housed within the U.S. Department of Transportation, with jurisdiction over certain surface transportation economic regulatory matters. Its authority is largely confined to railroad pricing and merger issues. This act also effectively deregulated intrastate controls on motor carriers, which had been blocking a fully competitive trucking industry.

The Staggers Act was highly beneficial for carriers as well as for shippers. The rail industry withstood well the sharp recession of 1981–82 and enjoyed record profit levels in 1983, notwithstanding a sharp drop in revenue per ton-mile. By 1988 railroad rates had fallen from 4.2 cents per ton-mile in the 1970s to 2.6 cents. After 1984 rail rates continued to fall, declining over the following 15 years by 45 percent. Competition and the Staggers Act have been a great success.

Deregulation of Trucking

Deregulation of the trucking industry, completed only in the 1990s, resulted in lower rates and better service to shippers. It also resulted in lower wages for truck drivers as the Teamsters Union lost power. The price of trucking licenses, which had been as much as millions of dollars, declined significantly to a few thousand dollars as the ICC made new licensing relatively simple and easy. Even though bankruptcies increased, the number of licensed trucking firms increased sharply in the first few years of deregulation.

Standard & Poor's found that the cost of shipping by truck had fallen by $40 billion from the era of regulation to 1988. Improved flexibility enabled business to operate on the basis of ''just-in-time delivery,'' thus reducing inventory costs. The Department of Transportation calculated that the outlays necessary to maintain inventories had plummeted in today's dollars by more than $100 billion.

Further Reform

Although great progress has been made in reducing regulation of transportation, further steps would improve the U.S. system. Currently, the motor carrier industry is subject to no economic controls; consequently there need be no change in policy. The restrictions on Mexican truckers should be lifted, but that is mainly a trade and protectionism issue.

Railroads are still subject to some price controls, limits on abandonment, and control over mergers. Rail passenger service, particularly Amtrak, has been a problem ever since it was established in the 1970s.

Government limits on air passenger transportation continue through cabotage restrictions, federal administration of air traffic controllers, and government ownership of airports. Finally, as a result of the September 11, 2001, attacks, security considerations have burgeoned, making air travel more expensive, more time-consuming, and perhaps safer.

Water transportation regulation and subsidies have not been a part of the regulatory reforms of the last 25 years and remain stubbornly resistant to change.

Rail Freight

Today, the rail industry remains the most closely supervised mode of transport with limits on abandonment; mergers; labor usage; ownership of other modes; and even, in certain situations, pricing. The Surface Transportation Board oversees the rail industry and administers the Staggers Act, under which the board must ensure that rates charged to ''captive shippers'' are fair.

Under federal law, the STB can exempt railroad traffic from rate regulation whenever it finds such control unnecessary to protect shippers from monopoly power or wherever the service is limited. Congress has legalized individual contracts between shippers and rail carriers, allowing competitive pricing. The Staggers Act authorizes railroads to price their services freely, unless a railroad possesses ''market dominance.'' Congress continues a prohibition on intermodal ownership and requires the maintenance of labor protection.

All rail mergers, for example, require STB approval; once given the green light, however, those mergers are relieved from challenge under the antitrust laws or under state and local legal barriers. Railroads face a stringent review by the STB that, in addition to general antitrust considerations, includes the effect on other carriers, the fixed charges that would arise, and the effect on employees. In particular, the board must provide protection in any consolidation for employees who might be adversely affected. That provision is very popular with rail labor unions; the industry views it as employment protection, which makes achieving significant savings from mergers difficult.

Under current law, railroads must seek STB permission to abandon lines, build new track, or sell any service. Because users and other interested parties employ the law to slow or even block change, which adds to costs, those rules should be repealed.

Federal law also enjoins the STB to regulate rates charged ''captive shippers''—those that can ship by only one line and enjoy no satisfactory alternative. Coal and grain companies have exploited this provision to gain lower rates. The markets for coal and grain are highly competitive, so the producers cannot sell their output at more than the market price. Consequently, a railroad that drives shipping costs up to the point where the cost of producing the coal or grain and then moving it exceeds the competitive price will find that it has no traffic. In other words, although the railroad has no direct competition, it, too, is constrained by the market.

If a coal company enjoys significantly lower costs because of a favorable location or a rich and easily exploited mine, it could reap higher profits than less favorably sited enterprises. However, if the mine has only one option for shipping its product, that is, a single railroad, the rail carrier will be able to secure much of that above-normal profit. In that case, the stockholders of the railroad will gain at the expense of the stockholders of the mining corporation. There exists no rationale for the government to intervene by favoring one company over another. The captive shipper clause must go.

Congress should also repeal the ban on railroads' owning trucking companies or certain water carriers. Federal regulations proscribe railroad ownership of trucking firms, although the STB and the ICC, in earlier decades, have granted many exceptions. From the time of the building of the Panama Canal, the Interstate Commerce Act has prohibited railroad possession of water carriers that ply that waterway. Early in the 20th century, the public believed that those huge companies needed the competition of water carriers to keep down transcontinental rates. Like the prohibition on ownership of water carriers, the ban on owning trucking firms stems from the unwarranted fear of railroad power. With the plethora of options available to shippers today, such rules are totally unnecessary. The restrictions simply limit the ability of railroads, trucking firms, and water carriers to offer the most efficient multimodal services.

The Staggers Act authorized railroads to negotiate contracts with shippers but only with government approval. In addition, all rates must be filed with the STB, and tariffs that are either ''too high'' or ''too low'' can be disallowed. Congress should repeal these vestigial regulatory powers. At best, they add to paperwork and to the cost of operation; at worst, they slow innovation and reduce competition.

Amtrak

The STB retains jurisdiction over passenger transportation by rail. In particular, it arbitrates between Amtrak and freight railroads, which own most of the track used by the government-owned passenger railroad. Ideally, Congress should privatize Amtrak and let it negotiate with freight railroads over its use of trackage. Assuming that a mutually profitable arrangement exists, private arrangements will develop.

In 1997, given the dismal financial performance of Amtrak, Congress gave it $2.2 billion to modernize its system, with the stipulation that it would be operating without federal aid in five years. Congress established the Amtrak Reform Council to draw up a plan to reconstitute rail passenger transportation if the government railroad was unable to eliminate its constant deficits. In November 2001, the ARC determined unanimously that, in the words of Chairman Carmichael Friday, the passenger train company had "failed terribly. It hasn't produced a modern system, it's done a lousy job of raising money and the Northeast Corridor, the one corridor it controls, is far behind on maintenance and improvements."

The council has recommended to Congress that Amtrak be broken up and competition be introduced. A new company would own the Northeast Corridor infrastructure and other Amtrak properties, and a second company would operate the trains. Amtrak itself would manage rail passenger franchise rights, secure funding from Congress, and oversee performance. Eventually, certain corridors would be franchised to private companies or to the states. There would be no expectation that passenger transportation could be made profitable. In fact, the ARC's plan would simply waste more of the taxpayers' money.

Over 30 years, Amtrak has already spent some $25 billion in an effort to turn itself into a self-sustaining enterprise. In 2001 Amtrak asked for $3.2 billion to cope with *new* business. Even this money, the ARC believes, will not result in a company that can pay its bills without subsidy. The report of the council to Congress finds that instead of moving toward self-sufficiency, Amtrak is weaker financially today than it was in 1997. It singles out long-haul passenger trains as inherent money losers that under any circumstances will have to be subsidized or abandoned.

Congress should face the facts: passenger rail transportation cannot be made profitable, except in a few corridors, such as between Washington and New York and perhaps Boston. That portion of the system can probably cover its operating costs but most likely will be unable to cover its capital costs. With a few minor exceptions, passenger rail is not profitable anywhere in the world; there is no reason to believe it can be made profitable here. The appropriate policy would be to auction off the assets of the current system, favoring investors who would attempt to continue some passenger service. It seems likely that the East Coast corridor between Washington and points north would survive, albeit with a lower paid workforce. If all union contracts and employees are kept, as the ARC recommends, the system can survive only with taxpayers' funds.

Air Travel

Although airline deregulation has been a great success, the industry has been plagued with crowding; delays; and, on some routes, dominance of a single carrier. The causes lie in the failure to deregulate other essential features of the industry. The air traffic control system, in particular, remains a ward of the FAA. Government entities own virtually all airports. The recent move to federalize airport security will add more government bureaucracy without adding more security.

Air Traffic Control. The FAA runs the current air traffic control (ATC) system. Because the FAA is a government agency, annual congressional appropriations control its finances. Its rules follow normal bureaucratic practices with congressional committees looking over its actions. Moreover, the FAA must regulate itself—a major conflict of interest.

As a government agency, the FAA has been unable to bring on line quickly new technologies that would improve safety and reduce delays. While computer technology changes every year or two, the FAA's procurement processes require five to seven years to complete. It still has 1960-era mainframe computers, equipment that depends on vacuum tubes, and obsolete radars. As a consequence, equipment breaks down frequently and planes must be spaced farther apart than would be necessary with state-of-the-art computers and radars.

Congress has held numerous hearings and put great pressure on the FAA to modernize, but it has been unable to improve matters significantly. To create and maintain a modern system, air traffic controls must be separated from the FAA. The Clinton administration recommended a government corporation to run the ATC system; but another government corporation, such as the post office or Amtrak, although it would probably be an improvement over the current arrangement, is not the solution.

A number of other countries—Canada, the Czech Republic, Germany, Latvia, New Zealand, South Africa, Switzerland, Thailand, and the United Kingdom—have wrestled with this problem and have found that separating the ATC system from government oversight while maintaining government safety regulations works well.

Although no country has fully privatized its ATC system, Canada has created a private nonprofit corporation owned by the users. Its system has successfully reduced delays. The other freestanding ATC systems are at least partially government owned. Given the restrictions that the federal government puts on its government-owned corporations, such as Amtrak and the post office, it would be preferable to follow Canada's example by establishing a nonprofit corporation owned and controlled by airlines and other users of the ATC system.

Most ATC systems are funded through user fees. The problem that arises is what to charge general aviation. Because the FAA currently subsidizes general aviation, owners and pilots oppose any notion of a freestanding corporation dependent on user fees. Nevertheless, client pay is a good rule. Noncommercial general aviation pilots, who typically fly single-engine planes, should be charged only when they file a flight plan or land at an airport with a control tower. Commercial general aviation planes, such as corporate jets, should pay their share of the costs of the system.

Airline Cabotage. It is time for the United States to drop its restrictions on foreign ownership and operation of air carriers. Under current law, non-Americans can own no more than 25 percent of the voting stock of U.S. airlines. America has no similar restrictions on investment in steel, autos, or most other industries. There is no reason to make an exception for the airlines. Other private carriers should be free to invest in the United States. At the moment, several U.S. carriers are in financial difficulties. Purchase by a healthy foreign airline would make great sense, bringing new capital and new competition to the American market. Virgin Atlantic Airways, for example, is interested in building a low-cost U.S. carrier to feed its international service.

At the same time, the longstanding policy of negotiating "open skies" agreements with other governments should be based not on what U.S. carriers get out of the agreement but on the benefits to American travelers. Cathay Pacific, based in Hong Kong, could offer improved service and competition both in the domestic market and internationally. British Air might invest in US Air to provide nationwide connections to Europe. The introduction of such foreign carriers would strengthen competition in the American market, bringing additional benefits to travelers.

Airport Privatization. Because the Airport and Airways Trust Fund moneys have been available only to government-owned airports, private airports are ineligible for any of the funds that are raised from taxes on fuel and passengers. Because those airports eligible for grants are subject to federal appropriations, even state- and local government–owned airports cannot plan and count on money from the trust fund. Repealing the federal taxes on aviation and allowing airports to impose their own fees, which could vary by time of day to reflect peak use, would give airports incentives to expand their capacity and introduce technologies that would reduce delays.

Airport Security. September 11, 2001, sharply increased the public's demand for greater security at airports. The federal government responded, after considerable wrangling in Congress, by federalizing the security personnel at all major airports. The bill passed requires all airports, except for five participating in a pilot program, to use federal employees, who must be American citizens, to screen passengers and luggage. Those security personnel would be employed by the Department of Transportation but presumably would not enjoy the security of civil service workers. One airport from each of five size categories, from biggest to smallest, will experiment with private screeners supervised by federal employees. After three years, all airports could opt out of the government employee system and use private screeners overseen by federal agents.

Federalizing the screeners may produce less security than we enjoyed before September 11. Although the legislation specified that the new federal employees would not have the same civil service protections as other Department of Transportation employees, there will be a tendency over time to give them more employment security. Already, there are efforts to allow aliens to remain as security guards. Firing incompetent workers will be much more difficult under this legislation than it was when private companies managed security. What is changing is not the nature of the security personnel but their employer.

Maritime Policy

Unlike the regulations affecting other transportation sectors, maritime regulations and subsidies have been strikingly resistant to reform. A hodgepodge of conflicting and costly policies—subsidization, protectionism, regulation, and taxation—unnecessarily burdens the U.S.-flag fleet, forces U.S. customers to pay inflated prices, and curbs domestic and international trade. The list of rules and regulations governing shipping is too exhaustive to catalog here, but one thing is clear: shipping policies must be thoroughly reviewed and revamped. Congress should pay special attention to deregulation of ocean shipping and other trade- and consumer-oriented reforms.

In particular, Congress should repeal the Jones Act (sec. 27 of the Merchant Marine Act of 1920). The Jones Act prohibits shipping merchandise between U.S. ports "in any other vessel than a vessel built in and documented under the laws of the United States and owned by persons who are citizens of the United States." The act essentially bars foreign shipping companies from competing with American companies. A 1993 International Trade Commission study showed that the loss of economic welfare attributable to America's cabotage restriction was some $3.1 billion per year. Because the Jones Act inflates prices, many businesses are encouraged to import goods rather than buy domestic products.

The primary argument made in support of the Jones Act is that we need an all-American fleet on which to call in time of war. But during the Persian Gulf War, only 6 vessels of the 460 that shipped military supplies came from America's subsidized merchant fleet. Repealing the Jones Act would allow the domestic maritime industry to be more competitive and would enable American producers to take advantage of lower prices resulting from competition among domestic and foreign suppliers. Ships used in domestic commerce could be built in one country, manned by citizens of another, and flagged by still another. That would result in decreased shipping costs, with savings passed on to American consumers and the U.S. shipping industry. The price of shipping services, now restricted by the act, would decline by an estimated 25 percent.

Highway Infrastructure, Mass Transit, and Gasoline Taxes

This final section analyzes highway and transit infrastructure, which is owned and operated by government. The U.S. Department of Transportation should be abolished and public roads, national highways, and urban mass transit systems returned to the states and municipalities and the private sector. Whatever justification there may once have been for a national transportation department has disappeared; the goal of creating a national road network was achieved long ago.

If states were allowed to assess and fund their own infrastructure needs, they would be able to select the transportation systems that best suited local conditions. If necessary, they could reintroduce gasoline taxes at the current level, or at higher or lower levels, to pay for their systems. But that is unlikely to be necessary. Ken Small and his colleagues demonstrated more than a decade ago that efficient congestion and axle-weight-related fees on trucks could finance an interstate highway system without the use of a gasoline tax. And the Chilean experience described by Eduardo Engel and his coauthors provides a blueprint for private road franchise contracts that could be used in the United States.

The Urban Mass Transit Act of 1964 should be repealed. Transit accounted for fewer than 2.0 percent of total daily trips in 1995 and 3.2 percent of work trips. Average transit load (passenger-miles divided by available seat-miles) is only 16 percent. Only New York City rail transit has more passenger-miles per route-mile (approximately 40,000) than average urban freeway passenger-miles per lane-mile (approximately 25,000). And light rail transit is only 18 percent as productive (4,523/25,385) as urban freeways. Most of the time, buses and subways are running empty.

The net result is that even though government spent $70 billion on new mass transit projects in the 1990s, the number of people using transit to go to work actually decreased slightly from 1990 to 2000 according to the 2000 census. Yet the outdated transit act provides incentives to local governments to build urban rail and subway systems by providing up to 75 percent of construction funds.

Conclusion

Transportation is inherently competitive. Since elimination of most of the economic controls on trucking, railroads, and airlines, those industries have flourished. Although the performance of those sectors has improved greatly since the 1970s when the federal government controlled entry, rates, and routes, problems remain. The difficulties stem in part from the success of deregulation, which, for example, has democratized air travel while the infrastructure has remained in government hands. Decontrol has demonstrated that the market works much better free from government controls than with government oversight. We need to apply that lesson to the remaining problems and remove federal ownership and control from administration of air traffic control, the airports, and the security system.

The government should free the freight railroads from the remaining constraints on that industry. The government should recognize that passenger rail transport is never going to be profitable, especially when run by the government. Only the private sector can possibly run a profitable passenger train system and then only if free from government controls on labor and pricing.

Unlike other transportation policies, maritime, highway, and mass transit policies have been resistant to reform and thus should receive the immediate attention of reform-minded members of Congress.

Suggested Readings

Button, Kenneth. "Toward Truly Open Skies." *Regulation* 25, no. 3 (2002).

Engel, Eduardo, Ronald Fischer, and Alexander Galetovic. "A New Approach to Private Roads." *Regulation* 25, no. 3 (2002).

Moore, Thomas Gale. "Moving Ahead." *Regulation* 25, no. 2 (2002).

Poole, Robert W. Jr., and Viggo Butler. "Airline Deregulation: The Unfinished Revolution." *Regulation* 22, no. 1 (1999).

Small, Kenneth A., Clifford Winston, and Carol Evans. *Road Work.* Washington: Brookings Institution, 1989.

Vranich, Joseph, Cornelius Chapman, and Edward L. Hudgins. "A Plan to Liquidate Amtrak." Cato Institute Policy Analysis no. 425, February 8, 2002.

Winston, Clifford. *Alternate Route.* Washington: Brookings Institution, 1998.

—Prepared by Peter VanDoren

37. Insurance Regulation and Government Insurance

Congress should

- keep the federal government out of the business of regulating insurance companies;
- authorize tax-deferred treatment of private insurers' catastrophe reserves; and
- reduce the scope of current government insurance programs, terminate the new terrorism reinsurance program within three years (if not sooner), and not launch any other new federal reinsurance schemes.

In recent years, most congressional efforts to expand the federal role in insurance regulation and insurance assistance have focused on the mounting cost of federal outlays for disaster assistance involving earthquakes, floods, hurricanes, droughts, and other weather-related events. When devastating losses from the terrorist attack on the World Trade Center rocked private insurance markets in the fall of 2001, they also revived political momentum for even broader federal reinsurance guarantees to cover the depleted reserves of insurers and fill growing gaps in private reinsurance coverage.

The 107th Congress approved creation of a federal backstop for private-sector terrorism insurance coverage in response to the events of September 11, 2001. Like other federal insurance programs, that approach to shielding the private sector from loss runs the risk of creating sizable taxpayer-financed subsidies that would undermine private-sector incentives for risk management. The broader, long-run issue is the extent to which the federal government should provide reinsurance protection for large losses from disasters, whether natural or man-made, as opposed to taking actions that would expand private-sector capacity for insuring such losses. The preferred alternative is to reduce the scope of current federal insurance programs with their inherent subsidies and disincentives for risk management, avoid creating new federal insurance and reinsurance programs, and modify the tax code to reduce double taxation of the income from the large reserves that insurers must hold to credibly insure large losses from catastrophic events.

Government-provided programs for crop insurance and flood insurance, as well as other interventions in private disaster insurance markets, often are justified as necessary to overcome the failure of private markets to offer adequate and affordable disaster insurance. Defenders of government insurance programs claim that they reduce dependence on "free" disaster assistance and promote efficient risk management by property owners and farmers.

But government policies are the cause of, not the cure for, the limited supply and narrow scope of private-sector disaster insurance. Demand for private coverage is low in part because of the availability of disaster assistance, which substitutes for both public and private insurance. Moreover, a government that cannot say no to generous disaster assistance is unlikely to implement an insurance program with strong incentives for risk management. The subsidized rates and limited underwriting and risk classification within current federal government insurance programs aggravate adverse selection, discourage efficient risk management, and crowd out market-based alternatives.

Federal tax policy reduces supply by substantially increasing insurers' costs of holding capital to cover very large but infrequent losses. State governments also intrude on insurance markets by capping rates, mandating supply of particular types of insurance, and creating state pools to provide catastrophe insurance or reinsurance coverage at subsidized rates.

By reducing both the supply and demand sides of private insurance protection, government intervention leads to greater reliance on politically controlled disaster assistance and higher costs for taxpayers. A clear outcome is larger government.

Disaster Assistance vs. Government Insurance

The federal government seems unable to withhold disaster assistance from persons who fail to buy private or government insurance. Government insurance might be seductive to some efficiency-minded economists because, unlike free disaster assistance, it should encourage property owners and farmers to reduce risky activities and take loss-limiting measures. In practice, however, the same political pressures that make disaster assistance inevitable prevent the government from offering insurance at prices that reflect the full costs of coverage. Given low demand, government disaster insurance must be subsidized heavily or coverage must be compelled. By subsidizing high-risk properties, adopting loose underwriting and risk classification rules, and continuing to make disaster assistance widely available, the federal government discourages efficient risk management.

If the scope of insurance coverage were relatively narrow and the total cost of subsidies were small, government insurance would reduce costs. But as coverage and subsidies increase, there is a point at which the total cost of a subsidy-and-assistance program exceeds that of an assistance-only program. It is not obvious that a disaster-assistance-only program would cost more.

Private-Sector Risk Bearing vs. Inefficient Government Insurance

The terrorist attack on the World Trade Center depleted capital reserves of insurers and reinsurers and contributed to significant short-run turmoil in property insurance markets. The losses aggravated ongoing price increases that began in late 1999 following a decade-long "soft" insurance market (marked by low prices and expanded coverage). Insurers subsequently filed for and most states approved exclusions of most terror losses in standard form property-casualty insurance policies, except workers' compensation insurance. As the events of September 11 were digested and no new attacks occurred, a substantial amount of new capital flowed into the sector. A number of new entities were formed to sell property insurance and reinsurance. Coverage for losses from terror generally is available, albeit at a steep price in many instances, particularly for large buildings in major cities. In response to those price increases, many properties are being insured for lower limits of coverage and in some cases are going "bare" (without any insurance).

After the insurance, banking, construction, and real estate industries vigorously pressed for federal intervention to create a "backstop" for private-sector coverage for losses from terrorist attacks, the Bush administration proposed direct federal reimbursement of a large proportion of terrorist claims for three years. In November 2001 the House passed a complicated bill that would advance federal funds to pay a large proportion of losses above individual insurer and industrywide retentions but would require insurers to pay back any federal funds with premium-based assessments and possible direct surcharges on policyholders. The House bill included stiff tort limitations to prevent profiteering by the plaintiffs' bar. Last June the Senate passed its own bill, which authorized the federal government to pay a large proportion of losses above specified individual insurer and industrywide loss thresholds, without any payback provision or tort limitations. In November, Congress finally approved final legislation that reflected most of the Senate bill's approach, with low loss thresholds, very limited payback provisions, and no significant restrictions on tort lawsuits.

The World Trade Center's destruction and the subsequent debate over federal intervention in terrorism insurance highlight fundamental issues associated with government insurance or reinsurance. Insurance involves a basic tension between risk-sharing protections and risk-reducing incentives. The public and policymakers appreciate the benefits of risk sharing; the dulling of incentives to reduce risky activity and take precautions to control loss that often accompanies insurance is less visible. Private insurance markets limit that moral hazard by charging premiums that are closely aligned with a policyholder's risk of loss, thus providing appropriate incentives to reduce loss. Insurers that fail to price policies accurately suffer adverse selection and lose money. Insurers also have strong incentives to settle claims efficiently.

Government insurance operates differently. It invariably results in subsidized rates that are crudely related to the risk of loss, thus aggravating moral hazard and adverse selection. Incentives for economy in claim settlement are relatively weak. In the two main federal insurance programs, crop and flood insurance, the government insures a disproportionate number of high-risk entities at inadequate rates, thus requiring large taxpayer subsidies. Rather than lose money and disappear, federal insurance programs tend to lose money and expand, crowding out viable private-sector coverage. Risky activity and the amount of losses increase as parties adapt risk management to the terms of subsidized coverage. Subsidized federal insurance or reinsurance of large losses that result from disasters—whether natural or man-made—can make citizens more vulnerable to harm by discouraging rational responses to those losses and the risk of future loss.

In the wake of the new federal terrorism insurance program, pressure for Congress to enact federal reinsurance for natural disasters will likely resurface, such as the Homeowners' Insurance Availability Act, which would authorize the secretary of the treasury to sell "excess-of-loss" reinsurance contracts for insured natural catastrophe losses on residential properties. That pressure should be resisted. There is no need for such a federal reinsurance program. Although temporary pressure has been exerted since the events of September 11, private reinsurance capacity has expanded substantially since the early 1990s, and the development of new financial instruments to fund catastrophe coverage has further expanded the supply of private catastrophe insurance and reinsurance. The proposed reinsurance program would crowd out much private-sector coverage and would encourage creation of state insurance programs. As with federal flood and crop insurance, pressure would likely build for artificially low prices and program expansion—with similar results: less private coverage, higher costs for taxpayers, and poorer risk management by property owners.

Worst-case scenarios can always be imagined that overwhelm the current capacity of private insurers and capital markets. However, we should not pretend that levels of catastrophic risks that truly are "uninsurable" could be managed efficiently with hastily constructed public-private "partnerships" that masquerade as insurance and corrupt private markets. To handle those most unlikely events, it would be better if private insurers encouraged the federal government to set clearer *ex ante* guidelines for the *ex post*, compassionate relief needed for eligible injured parties and pressed for removal of tax and regulatory disincentives that impede the growth of private-sector risk-bearing capacity.

Expanding the Supply of Private Disaster Insurance

Given the past failures of Congress to exercise self-restraint and resist political demands for more subsidized government insurance, a more fruitful reform strategy should focus on expanding the supply of prefunded capital reserves that stand behind private insurance—both to strengthen the role of insurers as efficient risk managers and to serve as a necessary "buffer" against the risk of insurer insolvencies. Congress should reexamine in particular the counterproductive impact of federal tax policy on the availability of private insurance coverage for low-probability, high-cost events.

Federal corporate income taxes increase insurers' costs of holding capital and, in turn, the premiums they must charge for a given level of disaster coverage. Because private insurers cannot set up tax-deferred reserves, they must increase premiums by enough to cover the taxes on investment income in order to generate returns equivalent to those that investors could earn elsewhere. This tax disadvantage is especially pronounced for disaster insurance because insurers must hold huge amounts of capital to pay claims that have a low probability of occurrence. Moreover, premium increases to cover taxes on investment income result in higher expected before-tax income, thus further increasing expected taxes and premiums. Loss carry-back and carry-forward provisions in the tax code result in high taxes in years when disaster claims are low but yield limited deductions in years with high claims.

The tax loading on premiums is inversely related to the probability of loss and significantly increases the premium rates needed to cover large disaster losses that have a low probability of occurrence. Insurers and reinsurers can reduce the tax loading in disaster insurance premiums by, for example, substituting debt for equity financing; purchasing reinsurance from non-U.S. insurers; or, at least for the time being, moving operations offshore. The tax code nonetheless discourages the private supply of coverage for relatively rare but potentially large catastrophe losses. It contributes to possibly severe short-run consequences in the event of a large disaster, namely, increased insurer insolvency, higher rate increases, more cancellations and nonrenewals, and pressure for more government intervention.

A federal reinsurance program would threaten to crowd out much private-sector coverage, because its coverage thresholds to trigger payments would be far too low compared to current private-sector capacity. The federal government also inevitably would extend its reach to the pricing and underwriting of individual policies backed by federal reinsurance.

Preserve State Regulation of Competitive Insurance Markets

Concern over state regulation of property-casualty insurance rates and policy forms (contract language) for all types of insurance already has generated pressure for Congress to enact legislation that would allow insurers to obtain an optional federal charter and be regulated primarily by federal regulators. Despite the obvious sins of state regulation as practiced in some states, the potential efficiencies from optional federal chartering are speculative and small. The risks, however, are large, including the possibility of inefficient regulation of rates and underwriting at the federal level, which would undermine incentives for private risk management, and creation of a broad federal guaranty of insurers' obligations patterned after federal deposit insurance, which would aggravate moral hazard and undermine incentives for safety and soundness in private insurance markets. The preferred alternative to federal chartering and regulation of insurance is additional reforms at the state level.

The McCarran-Ferguson Act was enacted in 1945 in response to the Supreme Court's decision that insurance transacted across state lines was interstate commerce and subject to federal antitrust law. The ruling challenged the legitimacy of state regulation and insurers' cooperative arrangements to fix prices through rating bureaus. The act stipulates that state regulation is in the public interest, that federal law does not apply to insurance unless specifically indicated, and that federal antitrust law does not apply to insurance for activities that are regulated by the states and that do not involve boycott, coercion, or intimidation.

Although the long-term trend in property-casualty insurance regulation has been toward greater reliance on market competition and less reliance on rate regulation, progress has been slow. The last decade has seen significant, albeit uneven, progress toward greater reliance on competitive pricing. The sporadic movement toward less rate regulation reflects (1) expanded recognition of rate regulation's inability to make insurance more affordable and the adverse effects of attempting to do so; (2) increased concern with the direct and indirect costs of state regulation of prices, policy forms, and producer licensing; (3) accumulating evidence that competitive rating works; (4) broader support for competitive rating by insurance companies that have tasted regulatory rate suppression; and (5) favorable trends in claim costs for auto and workers' compensation insurance in the 1990s, which allowed deregulation to be accompanied by rate reductions or slower rate increases.

Prior approval regulation in some states is relatively benign. The main problem lies in states where regulation materially delays rate and form changes, chills competition and innovation, produces chronic cross-subsidies, or has more than one of those effects. When it comes to insurance, some voters are inclined to support command-and-control policies, even if they reject such policies generally. Sizable rate increases and "unaffordable" rates create large constituencies that favor rate suppression, especially when its adverse consequences may be opaque in the short run. Regulatory bureaucracies resist reform. Interest groups that benefit from high claim costs may oppose regulatory reform in some states out of fear that it might increase pressure for public policies to control costs (such as tort reform).

Problems with Optional Federal Chartering

The enactment of the Graham-Leach-Bliley Act (GLB) in 1999 increased debate over the residual sins of state regulation, in particular the direct and indirect costs of state regulation of rates, forms, and producer licensing in an environment of financial modernization and global competition. Representatives of many large property-casualty insurers specializing in business insurance and their main trade association (the American Insurance Association) advocate optional federal chartering and regulation as a means of regulatory modernization (that is, of escaping inefficient state regulation of rates and certain forms). Representatives of many life insurance and annuity companies and the American Council of Life Insurers favor optional federal regulation as a way to escape inefficient form regulation and compete more effectively with banks that offer similar products.

The American Bankers Insurance Association has proposed an optional federal chartering bill patterned largely after bank regulation. Rep. John LaFalce (D-N.Y.) and Sen. Charles Schumer (D-N.Y.) also proposed optional federal chartering bills with a number of similar features. The American Insurance Association has advanced optional federal chartering for property-casualty insurers, and the American Council of Life Insurers has urged chartering legislation for life and annuity insurers.

State responses to increased concern about antiquated regulatory practices and to the threat of federal chartering include the elimination of prior approval regulation of rates and policy forms for "large" commercial buyers in many states. Many states also approved laws to meet GLB provisions dealing with reciprocity for nonresident producer licensing and to prevent federal licensing of producers. The National Association of Insurance Commissioners is pressing for an interstate compact for one-stop approval of policy forms for life, annuity, disability, and long-term-care insurance and for modernization of rate filing and review processes for property-casualty insurance.

In theory, optional federal chartering of insurers might enhance competition by streamlining, centralizing, or eliminating antiquated regulations of multistate insurers and producers. It might provide federally chartered insurers with a broad exemption from state rate and form regulation. It might promote beneficial regulatory competition between federal and state regulators. It might avoid excessively burdensome consumer protections and eschew mandates that would force policyholders to subsidize particular sectors or groups. The problem is that optional federal chartering might achieve few or none of those results and might instead harm competition, safety, and soundness.

Because the need for and terms of insurance coverage are closely linked to substantive state law (for example, workers' compensation and motor vehicle accident reparations law), property-casualty insurance markets have an inherently local dimension. The scope of possible gains from centralization is correspondingly limited. Federal chartering would be unlikely to exempt federally chartered insurers from participation in state residual markets, given legitimate state interests in ensuring the availability of mandatory coverage. State regulation of residual market rates might therefore still be used to cap rates for high-risk buyers and produce chronic cross-subsidies. More broadly, the temptation to use insurance regulation to redistribute wealth need not be lower at the federal level.

Misguided state regulation is largely unable to achieve subsidies across lines of insurance within a state or across states. Federal regulation might be able to achieve both, especially if redistributive policies were mandated for state and federal insurers. For politically sensitive insurance coverage, federal regulation could ultimately lead to restrictions on rates with harmful effects on private-sector risk management and resource allocation. Past examples such as the Home Mortgage Disclosure Act, the Community Reinvestment Act, various consumer group proposals, and recent congressional hearings on sub-prime lending and credit life insurance suggest that federal insurance regulation would be subject to many of the same pressures that produce controls on rates and underwriting in some states.

If most insurers could switch charters at relatively low cost, dual chartering could promote regulatory competition, help discipline regulatory excesses, and provide strong motivation for further state reforms. But, as long as the threat of tighter federal regulation is credible, additional gains from actual competition between state and federal regulators may be modest. Moreover, the largely fixed costs of adopting a federal charter might discourage many smaller insurers from seeking a federal charter, and the cost for multistate, federally chartered insurers to return to state regulation could be large, thereby undermining regulatory competition for charters.

Federal deposit insurance protects depositors of both federal and state banks. A federal guaranty covering the obligations of *all* insurers is likely to be a precondition for effective regulatory competition on other dimensions. The potential benefits from increased regulatory competition should be assessed in relation to the disadvantages of an inclusive federal guaranty program. It is highly probable that federal guarantees of both federally chartered and state-chartered insurers would be inevitable with dual chartering. Even if initial dual chartering legislation eschewed federal guarantees and required federally chartered insurers to participate in state guaranty funds (as in the insurance trade group proposals) or established a federal guaranty system for federal insurers (as in the banking group, LaFalce, and Schumer proposals), predictable political incentives are likely to result in federal guarantees for all insurers.

An optional chartering system that required federally chartered insurers to participate in the state guaranty system without a federal guaranty would be unstable. Insolvency of a federally chartered insurer or a number of state-chartered insurers would create strong pressure for a federal guaranty patterned after deposit insurance. In any event, the state guaranty system would likely be seriously weakened without participation of federally chartered insurers.

The danger is that federal guarantees would repeat some of the mistakes of federal deposit insurance. The scope of protection of insurance buyers against loss from insurer insolvency might be expanded materially (for example, by reflecting a policy, de facto or de jure, of "too big to fail"). Such expansion would materially undermine incentives for safety and soundness. More regulatory constraints on insurer operations would eventually ensue. The ultimate result of optional federal chartering would therefore be less reliance on market discipline and more reliance on regulation.

Current proposals for optional federal chartering would eliminate the antitrust exemption for federally chartered insurers, which could undermine the integrity and value of current systems of information sharing and thus reduce competition, increase costs of ratemaking, and reduce safety and soundness, with disproportionate effects on small insurers. Optional federal chartering also would involve protracted litigation over the scope of federal preemption of state insurance law and permissible cooperative practices for federally chartered insurers.

Regulatory policies in some states that interfere with competitive insurance pricing are clearly inefficient; they reduce gross domestic product and consumer welfare. Although optional federal chartering might hasten the demise of such policies, that result is hardly ensured. The unsatisfactory pace of state reforms does not imply that optional federal chartering is desirable.

Conclusion

Despite the obvious shortcomings of regulation of insurance rates and policy forms in some states, optional federal chartering of property-casualty insurers is not in the best interests of policyholders and taxpayers. The possible benefits from optional federal chartering—a reduction in ineffi-cient state rate and form regulation, achievement of regulatory scale econo-mies, and promotion of regulatory competition—are speculative, subject to real uncertainties, and probably modest at best. The potential risks and costs are comparatively large, including modifications in insurance guaranty funds and data-sharing arrangements that would undermine safety, soundness, and healthy competition. Optional federal chartering also could ultimately produce broader restrictions on insurance pricing and underwriting, which would increase cross-subsidies among policyholders, place taxpayers at risk, and inefficiently distort policyholders' incentives to reduce the risk of loss. The better and more prudent policy is to reject federal chartering and encourage and support further modernization of state regulation.

The recent enactment of terrorism insurance legislation notwithstanding, Congress should avoid creating new federal insurance and reinsurance schemes and strive to make existing government programs more efficient. Although politically difficult, it should encourage better risk management by requiring current federal government insurance programs to apply private-sector underwriting and risk classification techniques; increase private-sector risk bearing; and, if necessary, target any remaining premium subsidies more narrowly. Congress should also promote the accumulation of additional private-sector capacity for bearing catastrophic risk. The most direct approach—apart from fundamental tax reform—is to allow private insurers to offer more affordable coverage by allowing them to establish tax-deferred reserves for catastrophic risks.

Suggested Readings

Harrington, Scott E. *Optional Federal Chartering of Property/Casualty Insurance Com-panies.* Downers Grove, Ill.: Alliance of American Insurers, 2002.

———. "Repairing Insurance Markets." *Regulation* 25, no. 2 (Summer 2002).

———. "Rethinking Disaster Policy." *Regulation* 23, no. 1 (2000).

———. "Taxes and the High Cost of Catastrophe Insurance: The Case for Tax-Deferred Reserves." Competitive Enterprise Institute Insurance Reform Project, October 1999.

Harrington, Scott E., and Tom Miller. "Insuring against Terror." *National Review Online Financial*, November 5, 2001.

Harrington, Scott E., and Greg Niehaus. "Government Insurance, Tax Policy, and the Availability and Affordability of Catastrophe Insurance." *Journal of Insurance Regu-lation* 19 (Summer 2001).

Skees, Jerry R. "Agricultural Risk Management or Income Enhancement." *Regulation* 22, no. 1 (1999).

VanDoren, Peter, Tom Miller, and John Samples. "A Risky Business: Government Is Not the Cure for Insurance Markets." *National Review Online Financial*, January 25, 2002.

—Prepared by Scott E. Harrington and Tom Miller

38. Antitrust

Congress should

- repeal the Sherman Act of 1890;
- repeal the Clayton Act of 1914;
- repeal the Federal Trade Commission Act of 1914;
- repeal the Robinson-Patman Act of 1936;
- repeal the Celler-Kefauver Act of 1950;
- repeal the Antitrust Procedures and Penalties Act of 1975;
- repeal the Hart-Scott-Rodino Act of 1976; and
- pending repeal, strip the states' authority to enforce federal antitrust laws.

Introduction

Antitrust is thought by some to be the bulwark of free enterprise. Without the continued vigilance of the Justice Department and the Federal Trade Commission, so the argument goes, large corporations would ruthlessly destroy their smaller rivals and soon raise prices and profits at consumers' expense. When megamergers grab headlines and a federal judge decides that the nation's leading software company should be dismembered, the importance of vigorous antitrust law enforcement seems to be obvious.

But antitrust has a dark side. The time for modest reform of antitrust policy has passed. Root-and-branch overhaul of what Federal Reserve chairman Alan Greenspan a generation ago referred to as a "jumble of economic irrationality and ignorance"—and what modern scholarship has shown over and over again to be a playground of special pleaders—is called for.

Here are seven reasons why the federal antitrust laws should be repealed.

No. 1: Antitrust Debases the Idea of Private Property

Frequently when government invokes the antitrust laws, it transforms a company's private property into something that effectively belongs to the public, to be designed by government officials and sold on terms congenial to rivals who are bent on the market leader's demise. Some advocates of the free market endorse that process, despite the destructive implications of stripping private property of its protection against confiscation. If new technology is to be declared public property, future technology will not materialize. If technology is to be proprietary, then it must not be expropriated. Once expropriation becomes the remedy of choice, the goose is unlikely to continue laying golden eggs.

The principles are these: No one other than the owner has a right to the technology he created. Consumers can't demand that a product be provided at a specified price or with specified features. Competitors aren't entitled to share in the product's advantages. By demanding that one company's creation be exploited for the benefit of competitors, or even consumers, government is flouting core principles of free markets and individual liberty.

No. 2: Antitrust Laws Are Fluid, Nonobjective, and Often Retroactive

Because of murky statutes and conflicting case law, companies never can be quite sure what constitutes permissible behavior. If a company cannot demonstrate that its actions were motivated by efficiency, conduct that is otherwise legal somehow morphs into an antitrust violation. Normal business practices—price discounts, product improvements, exclusive contracting—become violations of law. When they're not accused of monopoly price gouging for charging too much, companies are accused of predatory pricing for charging too little or collusion for charging the same!

No. 3: Antitrust Is Based on a Static View of the Market

In real markets, sellers seek to carve out minimonopolies. Profits from market power are the engine that drives the economy. So what might happen in a utopian, perfectly competitive environment is irrelevant to the question of whether government intervention is necessary or appropriate. The proper comparison is with the marketplace that will evolve if the antitrust laws, by punishing success, eliminate incentives for new and improved products. Markets move faster than antitrust laws could ever move. Consumers rule, not producers. And consumers can unseat any product and any company no matter how powerful and entrenched. Just ask WordPerfect or Lotus or IBM.

No. 4: Antitrust Remedies Are Designed by Bureaucrats Who Don't Understand How Markets Work

Economic losses from excessive regulation can do great damage to producers and consumers. But government moves forward in the name of correcting market failure, apparently without considering at all the possibility of government failure. Proponents of antitrust tell us that government planners know which products should be withdrawn from the market, no matter what consumers actually prefer. The problem with that argument is that it leads directly to paternalism, to the idea that an elite corps of experts knows our interests better than we do—and can regulate our affairs to satisfy those interests better than the market does.

The real issue is not whether one product is better than another but who gets to decide—consumers, declaring their preferences by purchases in the market, or specialists at the Justice Department or the Federal Trade Commission rating the merits of various goods and services. When we permit government to make such decisions for us and allow those decisions to trump the subjective choices of consumers, we abandon any pretense of a free market. In the process, we reduce consumer choice to a formalistic appraisal centering on technical features alone, notwithstanding that products are also desired for quality, price, service, convenience, and a host of other variables.

No. 5: Antitrust Law Is Wielded by Business Rivals and Their Allies in the Political Arena

Instead of focusing on new and better products, disgruntled rivals try to exploit the law—consorting with members of Congress, their staffers, antitrust officials, and the best lobbying and public relations firms that money can buy. Soon enough, the targeted company responds in kind. Microsoft, for example, once conspicuously avoided Washington, D.C., politicking—but no longer. And America's entrepreneurial enclave, Silicon Valley, has become the home of billionaire businesspeople who use political influence to bring down their competitors. That agenda will destroy what it sets out to protect. Politicians are mostly order takers. So we'll get the kind of government we ask for—including oppressive regulation. Citizens who are troubled by huge corporations dominating private markets should be even more concerned if those same corporations decide that political clout better serves their interest—politicizing competition to advance the private interests of favored competitors.

No. 6: Barriers to Entry Are Created by Government, Not Private Businesses

Under antitrust law, the proper test for government intervention is whether barriers to entry foreclose meaningful competition. But what is a "barrier"? When a company advertises, lowers prices, improves quality, adds features, or offers better service, it discourages rivals. But it cannot bar them. True barriers arise from government misbehavior, not private power—from special-interest legislation or a misconceived regulatory regime that protects existing producers from competition. When government grants exclusive licenses to cable, electric, and telephone companies, monopolies are born and nurtured at public expense. When Congress decrees targeted tax benefits, subsidies, insurance guarantees, and loans or enacts tariffs and quotas to protect domestic companies from foreign rivals, that creates the same anti-competitive environment that the antitrust laws were meant to foreclose. The obvious answer, which has little to do with antitrust, is for government to stop creating those barriers to begin with.

No. 7: Antitrust Will Inevitably Be Used by Unprincipled Politicians as a Political Bludgeon

Too often, the executive branch has exploited the antitrust laws to force conformity by "uncooperative" companies. Remember that when President Nixon wanted to browbeat the three major TV networks, he used the threat of an antitrust suit to extort more favorable media coverage. On a widely publicized tape, Nixon told his aide, Chuck Colson: "Our gain is more important than the economic gain. We don't give a goddamn about the economic gain. Our game here is solely political. . . . As far as screwing the networks, I'm very glad to do it." If Nixon were the only culprit, that would be bad enough. But former *New York Times* reporter David Burnham, in his 1996 book, *Abuse of Power*, shows that presidents from Kennedy through Clinton routinely demanded that the Justice Department bend the rules in pursuit of political ends.

The lesson is clear. The threat of abusive public power is far larger than the threat of private monopoly. It's time for Congress to get rid of the federal antitrust laws. Meanwhile, pending repeal of those laws, Congress must ensure that enforcement by state authorities does not duplicate federal enforcement. Government must not be given two bites at the antitrust apple, nor should defendants be exposed to double jeopardy.

Strip the States' Authority to Enforce Federal Antitrust Laws

It's time to rein in the power of state attorneys general. For most of American history they did vital, but routine and distinctly unglamorous, legal work for their states. But beginning in the 1980s, some attorneys general challenged the Reagan administration's policies in antitrust and environmental law, pursuing their own agendas through litigation. In the antitrust context, activist attorneys general have relied on their so-called *parens patriae* power to sue on behalf of state residents under federal statutes.

The Microsoft case is perhaps the most egregious example of duplicative federal and state antitrust enforcement. Nine states—relying on the same trial, the same facts, the same conclusions of law, and the same injuries to the same people—want to override a settlement between Microsoft and the federal government, supported by 41 of the 50 states. In a legal brief to a federal judge, the Justice Department offered persuasive reasons why the states should not be allowed an end run around the federal settlement.

First, "The United States is the sole enforcer of the federal antitrust laws on behalf of the American public." Second, the states' remedies would affect competition and consumers outside their borders—raising "for the very first time the prospect that a small group of states, with no particularized interests to vindicate, might somehow obtain divergent relief with wide-ranging, national economic implications." Third, "The public interest is best served when federal and state antitrust activity is complementary, not duplicative or conflicting." Fourth, the nine holdout states had "neither the authority nor the responsibility to act in the broader national interest, and the plaintiff with that authority and responsibility [that is, the United States] has taken a different course."

Still worse, continued the Justice Department, the relief sought by the nonsettling states "may harm consumers, retard competition, chill innovation, or confound compliance" with the federal settlement. Echoing the Supreme Court, the Justice Department warned that antitrust redress requires a showing of "harm to competition not competitors." Remedies must be crafted for the benefit of the public, not for the private gain of politically favored rivals.

Consider the remarks of respected Judge Richard Posner of the Seventh Circuit Court of Appeals, who mediated an abortive Microsoft settlement two years ago. Posner offered these recommendations in a recent issue of the *Antitrust Law Journal:* "I would like to see, first, the states stripped of their authority to bring antitrust suits, federal or state, except . . . where the state is suing firms that are fixing the prices of goods or services that they sell to the state. . . . [States] are too subject to influence by . . . competitors. This is a particular concern when the [competitor] is a major political force in that state. A situation in which the benefits of government action are concentrated in one state and the costs in other states is a recipe for irresponsible state action."

Congress is constitutionally authorized to intervene whenever actual or imminent state practices threaten the free flow of commerce. Congress should use that power and revoke the *parens patriae* authority of the states to enforce federal antitrust laws. Otherwise, some states will continue to abuse their existing authority—exercising it to impose sovereignty beyond their borders and catering to the parochial interests of influential constituents.

Would constraints on state antitrust enforcement powers violate time-honored principles of federalism? Not at all. Federalism isn't simply a matter of states' rights. Nor is it exclusively about devolution of power or promoting efficient government. First and foremost, federalism is about checks and balances based on dual sovereignty. Most often, the states are a counterweight to excessive power in the hands of the federal government. Yet antitrust is an obvious case in which the federal government must curb excessive power in the hands of the states.

Conclusion

More than two centuries ago, in the *Wealth of Nations*, Adam Smith observed that "people of the same trade seldom meet together . . . but the conversation ends in a conspiracy against the public or in some contrivance to raise prices." Coming from the father of laissez faire, that warning has been cited ad nauseam by antitrust proponents to justify all manner of interventionist mischief. Those same proponents, whether carelessly or deviously, rarely mention Smith's next sentence: "It is impossible indeed to prevent such meetings, by any law which either could be executed, or would be consistent with liberty and justice.''

Antitrust is bad law, bad economics, and bad public policy. It deserves an ignominious burial—sooner rather than later.

Suggested Readings

Armentano, Dominick T. *Antitrust and Monopoly: Anatomy of a Policy Failure.* New York: Wiley, 1982.

DeBow, Michael. ''Restraining State Attorneys General, Curbing Government Lawsuit Abuse.'' Cato Institute Policy Analysis no. 437, May 10, 2002.

Greenspan, Alan. ''Antitrust.'' In *Capitalism: The Unknown Ideal.* Edited by Ayn Rand. New York: Signet, 1966.

Levy, Robert A. ''Microsoft Redux: Anatomy of a Baseless Lawsuit.'' Cato Institute Policy Analysis no. 352, September 30, 1999.

Shughart, William F. II. ''The Government's War on Mergers: The Fatal Conceit of Antitrust Policy.'' Cato Institute Policy Analysis no. 323, October 22, 1998.

—Prepared by Robert A. Levy

39. The Food and Drug Administration

> **Congress should**
>
> - modify the Food, Drug and Cosmetics Act of 1938 to allow pharmaceutical companies to opt out of Food and Drug Administration testing requirements and to use alternative organizations to certify product safety and efficacy and
> - allow individuals the freedom to use any non-FDA-approved product.

Under current law, the Food and Drug Administration must approve all pharmaceuticals and medical devices before they can be marketed. Although the process is often termed an FDA testing program, that agency does little if any actual testing. For example, the developer of a new drug uses its own labs or hires another private company to conduct animal tests on the drug for safety before proceeding to clinical trials for safety and efficacy in people. These tests often are conducted by a medical school department or a consulting firm. When each phase of the testing is completed, the pharmaceutical company submits the details of the testing process, evidence of adherence to FDA protocols, and the test results to the FDA.

FDA officials review the test results at each step, and if they are satisfied, they give the pharmaceutical company permission to proceed to the next step in the testing process. When all the tests and trials are complete, FDA officials review all the information—often measured in hundreds of pounds or linear feet of reports rather than number of pages—and decide whether the company can market the drug and advertise it to physicians for the treatment of specific diseases and conditions. The FDA exercises very strict authority over what manufacturers can say about their products. Interestingly, over half of product uses are so-called off-label uses as physicians discover that products approved to counter one ailment can be helpful in preventing or treating other problems. For example, aspirin designed for pain relief turns out to be effective in preventing heart attacks.

Up to 10 years may be necessary to complete the development, testing, and approval process. Some estimates suggest that the cost of bringing a new product from conception to market is on average $400 million. According to the Office of Technology Assessment, the cost of bringing a new pharmaceutical to market is so great that most companies will begin the process only if the market for the drug is expected to be greater than $100 million a year. As a result, companies focus on drugs expected to be "blockbusters," which can be used by essentially everyone with a disease in the expectation that the drug will ameliorate or cure the disease with a marginal risk of causing adverse side effects.

In response to complaints about constantly increasing delays in the drug approval process, the federal government devised a method by which pharmaceutical manufacturers pay FDA to hire and retain additional drug application reviewers. The user charge system has reduced the time needed for some phases of the approval process.

The Human Costs of FDA Delays

As an agency, the FDA has a strong incentive to delay allowing products to reach the market. After all, if a product that helps millions of individuals causes adverse reactions or even death for a few, the FDA will be subject to adverse publicity with critics asking why more tests were not conducted. Certainly, it is desirable to make all pharmaceutical products as safe as possible. But every day that the FDA delays approving a product for market, many patients who might be helped suffer or die needlessly.

For example, Dr. Louis Lasagna, director of Tufts University's Center for the Study of Drug Development, estimates that the seven-year delay in the approval of beta-blockers as heart medication cost the lives of as many as 119,000 Americans. During the three and half years it took the FDA to approve the drug Interleukin-2, 25,000 Americans died of kidney cancer even though the drug had already been approved for use in nine other countries. Eugene Schoenfeld, a cancer survivor and president of the National Kidney Cancer Association, maintains that "IL-2 is one of the worst examples of FDA regulation known to man."

In the past two decades patients' groups have become more vocal in demanding timely access to new medication. AIDS sufferers led the way. After all, if an individual is expected to live for only two more years, three more years spent testing the efficacy of a prospective treatment does that person no good. The advent of the Internet has allowed individuals suffering from specific ailments and patient groups to use websites and chat rooms to exchange information and to give them an opportunity to take more control of their own treatment. They now can track the progress of possible treatments as they are tested for safety and efficacy and are quite conscious of how FDA-imposed delays can stand in the way of their good health and even their lives.

Reforming Access to Drugs

So long as the FDA maintains a monopoly on drug approval, however, the agency will remain a bottleneck, slowing the advent of new drugs and the use of "old" drugs in new circumstances.

It is time for Congress to break the FDA's monopoly on drug and medical device approval, and on information dissemination about drugs and devices, and to allow individuals to take better control of their own health care.

First, the Food, Drug and Cosmetics Act of 1938 should be changed to allow drug companies to seek certification of their products from nongovernmental organizations. Those organizations would have an incentive to move quickly to design and execute the laboratory tests and human studies that are appropriate for evaluating the safety and efficacy of personalized drugs. Instead of the FDA's approval being required before drugs are marketed, the nongovernmental organizations would be allowed to certify new drugs for particular uses and new uses of old drugs. Those certification organizations would have incentives to allow products on the market as quickly as possible but also incentives to be as honest as possible in evaluating the safety and efficacy of products. After all, like Underwriters Laboratory, those organizations are selling their reputations, which, if damaged, would cause them to lose their customers.

Different kinds and levels of certification should be allowed, with full disclosure of information on safety and efficacy. For example, a testing organization might classify a certain drug as "risky," with the recommendation that it be used only in life-threatening situations when no other therapy is available. Pharmaceutical manufacturers would be permitted to certify their own products if they chose to forgo the use of an independent certification organization. As a compromise with a fully free system of certification, manufacturers as well as private testing organizations might be required to label their products "Not FDA Approved."

Some pharmaceutical manufacturers might oppose breaking the FDA's monopoly. Larger companies especially are used to doing business with the agency; they are comfortable with the confidence the public has in FDA-approved drugs; and they could see continuing FDA regulations imposing costs that they could absorb but that their smaller competitors could not. Those attitudes are even more reason to allow private certification.

More fundamentally, in a free society individuals should be free to take care of their physical well-being as they see fit. The advent of the Internet gives individuals even more access to information about medical products and treatments. Individuals should be allowed to choose the treatments they think best. Such liberty does not open the door for fraud or abuse any more than does a free market in other products. In fact, informed consent by patients probably will become more sophisticated as the market for information about medical treatments becomes more free and open.

Suggested Readings

Campbell, Noel D. ''Replace FDA Regulation of Medical Devices with Third-Party Certification.'' Cato Institute Policy Analysis no. 288, November 12, 1997.

Goldberg, Robert M. ''Breaking Up the FDA's Medical Information Monopoly.'' *Regulation* 18, no. 2 (1995).

Higgs, Robert. ''Wrecking Ball: FDA Regulation of Medical Devices.'' Cato Institute Policy Analysis no. 235, August 7, 1995.

Hollis, Aidan. ''Closing the FDA's Orange Book.'' *Regulation* 24, no 4 (2001).

Miller, Henry I. *To America's Health: A Proposal to Reform the Food and Drug Administration.* Stanford, Calif.: Hoover Institution Press, 2000.

Olson, Mary K. ''How Have User Fees Affected the FDA?'' *Regulation* 25, no. 1 (2002).

Tabarrok, Alexander. ''The Blessed Monopolies.'' *Regulation* 24, no. 4 (2001).

—Prepared by Peter VanDoren

40. Intellectual Property

> **Congress should**
>
> - reject proposals to *ban* new technologies or business models to solve copyright problems (examples include file sharing, copy protection, and "collusion" among creators);
> - reject proposals to *impose* new technologies or business models to solve copyright problems (examples include federally certified copy protection standards and compulsory licensing);
> - Phase out compulsory licensing for all communications content industries and avoid extending it to future services such as online downloading and streaming; and
> - take the constitutional principle of "promot[ing] the progress of science and useful arts" seriously, but don't extend copyright protections far beyond reasonable terms.

The "Napsterization" of just about everything digitizable—books, music, movies, and, of course, software itself—has brought copyright issues to the forefront as never before, reenergizing the debate over questions such as the following:

- Why do we protect intellectual property at all?
- Do we really have "property rights" to our intangible creations the same way we do to our homes or the land on which they rest?
- Are there more effective market-oriented ways of encouraging artistic creation and scientific discovery than through the use of copyright and patent laws that protect a limited monopoly?

Those questions are hardly new, of course. Indeed, the debate over the nature and scope of intellectual property law is centuries old. More than 200 years ago, these questions concerned our Founding Fathers, who included a utilitarian compromise within the Constitution to ensure that science and the useful arts would be promoted by offering limited protection. They arrived at the balancing act contained in Article 1, section 8, clause 8, which gave Congress the power to "promote the progress of science and useful arts, by securing for limited times to authors and inventors the exclusive right to their respective writings and discoveries."

But the inclusion of this clause in the Constitution did not answer specific questions regarding such matters as the lengths of copyright or patent protections for various artistic or scientific creations, or what "fair use" or "prior art" were to mean. These highly subjective legal concepts didn't yet exist; the question of their meaning was left open to future generations of jurists, legal theorists, economists, and politicians.

And so today, in the midst of an explosion of digital and online creativity, the concept of intellectual property (IP) is being challenged as it has never been before. The current debate pits those who fear file-sharing technologies such as Napster and Kazaa, against those who are afraid that IP rights holders will lock up content with new copy protection scheme such as digital rights management (DRM), which includes a variety of tools and methods the creative community hopes to use to control access to, and reproduction of, various forms of entertainment and information content.

In the United States, the extremes manifest themselves in legislative proposals by file-sharing companies for compulsory licensing, on the one hand, and government-mandated DRM schemes to *prevent* file sharing on the other. But to the extent the market can be capable of self-protection, it can reduce the sphere of disagreement by minimizing the amount of legal protection required. For example, the market alternative to shutdown of file sharing, or targeting individual file swappers, may well be the improvement of digital rights management technologies to protect intellectual property. Perhaps such private, "barbed-wire" solutions can be superior. Indeed, some people must think so, because they argue that DRM technologies will be able to lock up content and violate fair use. But not yet: new copy-protected CDs have already been cracked by users who found they could use a 99-cent felt-tip pen to mark around the edges of the disc and defeat the DRM system. So even low-tech hacking techniques can sometimes cause headaches for industry.

It seems that even with legal protections of IP in the digital age, the reality of copying has confronted us with a need to find incentives to encourage artistic creation and scientific innovation if legal protections no longer work. If the market can do some of its own self-protecting and provide some incentives, is that enough? Or, paradoxically, is it too much?

410

There are certain things Congress should *not* do as we search for the answers.

IP and First Principles

Governments exist to protect property rights among other natural rights. But the property status of intangibles has always been unclear from a natural law perspective. Novelist-philosopher Ayn Rand wrote, "Patents and copyrights are the legal implementation of the base of all property rights: a man's right to the product of his mind." Other theoreticians claim that there is no right to own intangible ideas, which are not scarce in the sense that physical property is. To this group, the cost of protecting IP is just another cost of doing business, so why socialize it?

A good argument can be made, however, that, in a world without any IP protection, some individuals would be discouraged from producing important goods or ideas (consider pharmaceuticals or genetically altered foods to feed hungry populations). Indeed, those who advocate the abolition of copyright or patent law might ask themselves why the same arguments and reasoning should not be applied to tangible property.

Nonetheless, it is clear that some creators seek and receive excessive terms of protection—which, by extending far beyond the life of the author, seemingly go beyond any reasonable possibility of motivating creators, who often are deceased. Other people seek to expand what is covered by copyright and patent law in the first place, such as "One-Click" Internet shopping (which Amazon.com patented) or even hyperlinking itself (which British Telecommunications claims it patented and on which it therefore deserves to collect fees).

So, succinctly stated, Congress's problem is balancing artistic and entrepreneurial incentives to create with the interests of the larger community of users in an unhindered exchange of ideas and products.

The Internet Changes Things

Previous technological innovations such as photocopiers and VCRs forced society to reconsider the proper balance of IP protections. Nonetheless, the shifts brought about by the modern communications and computing revolution are more profound because today's copies are perfect reproductions. Thus record companies and Hollywood claim that their intellectual property rights are under attack as never before, threatening their economic livelihood and making it less likely they will want to put anything at all in the public realm.

In response, critics claim that copyright and patent law has been corrupted, that the balance has tilted too far in favor of copyright holders, and that digital technologies and other market developments have so fundamentally altered the nature of intellectual property that we need to radically shorten established terms of protection or eliminate them altogether. Those thinkers hold that information transmitted in electronic or digital formats should not be ''bottled up'' and controlled by its creators. They fear that copy protection technologies can go too far—even further than existing legal protections—and erode fair use rights that individuals have come to expect, as well as pose a technological threat to free speech. Thus they want assurances that noninfringing uses of materials and rights of fair use are preserved in the law.

Under the Digital Millennium Copyright Act of 1998, for example, one's intent to infringe is not relevant; rather, a person engaged in the development or distribution of circumvention technology, even for a benign purpose such as research or archiving, is at risk of being held criminally or civilly liable. There is no defense under the act even if there is no underlying copyright infringement. That's too extreme.

Potential Common Ground Solutions

Is there any common ground in this debate? Perhaps. The justification for copyright law is to create incentives. But if markets can create them, law may not need to play as great a role. Sometimes a private security guard and barbed wire may be superior to the policeman and the court. Then again, when someone breaks into your house and steals your property, you call the cops.

The first step toward common ground is to take the principle ''To Promote the Progress of Science and Useful Arts'' more seriously. Many agree on the concept of the protection of property; the disputes often arise over such matters as how long property should be protected. Any term set by law will be unavoidably arbitrary.

But copyright protection that extends far beyond the life of the originator provides diminishing incentives for that person to innovate (even if one assumes he is innovating on behalf of yet-unborn descendants). Thus terms of protection may need to be rethought; indeed a new Supreme Court case is challenging the 1998 ''Sonny Bono Copyright Term Extension Act,'' which extended copyright protection terms to life of the author plus

70 years (up from 50 years) (Table 40.1). Some jokingly call it the "Mickey Mouse Protection Act."

Rights owners certainly expend great energy on extending the legal monopoly granted by copyright. This is the widespread criticism of the Copyright Term Extension Act, in that new protections were given *retroactively*. The middlemen—and heirs—continue to want to be paid, an impulse having little to do with Walt Disney's initial inspiration to invent Mickey Mouse. Similarly, the heirs of Margaret Mitchell, author of *Gone with the Wind*, protested the derivative work *The Wind Done Gone* by Alice Randall. Although decisions about copyright terms inevitably will be arbitrary, there seems little reason to provide retroactive legal protection decades after a creator is dead.

Anger at the middleman (or heirs) is understandable: one exploring and sampling, say, roots-country music, would not be thrilled about paying BMG/RCA for the privilege when artists have been dead for more than 60 years. More consciously adhering to the Constitution's goal of promoting the progress of science and the useful arts—rather than promoting unnecessary government monopoly—seems a sensible course. Copyright laws that instead extend terms of protection to benefit a middleman do little to "incentivize" true creative activity.

One possible solution to the perceived problem of duplicating digital content that is still protected has been suggested by Wayne State University law professor Jessica Litman, who calls for revisions to "recast . . . copyright as an exclusive right of commercial exploitation." She would focus less on whether copies were made of a work and instead focus more narrowly on ensuring that copyright holders retain the sole opportunities for commercial exploitation of their work. Under this model, she points out, individual trading of song files wouldn't be actionable, but perhaps Napster's facilitation of large-scale sharing would be because of its signifi-

Table 40.1
Ever-Increasing Copyright Terms of Protection

Year	Term of Copyright Protection
1790	28 years (14 years of protection + possible 14-year renewal)
1831	42 years (28 years of protection + possible 14-year renewal)
1909	56 years (28 years of protection + possible 28-year renewal)
1976	Life of the author + 50 years
1998	Life of the author + 70 years

cant interference with rights holders' commercial opportunities. Such an approach would put the law back in line with the public's typical understanding of the copyright bargain and fair use.

The second step toward establishing common ground is for Congress to reject the impulse to either *ban* or *impose* new technologies or business models to solve copyright problems. Examples of bans include bans on file-sharing programs, restrictions on copy protection, and prohibitions on "collusion" among creators seeking to shelter their content. Examples of technology impositions would include federally certified copy protection standards and compulsory licensing.

Calls to ban file sharing came early. The response to Napster was a perfect example of creators wanting the government to ban or restrict file-sharing technologies that reduce copyright control. Today—now that peer-to-peer file sharing has become even more widespread despite Napster's demise—some people go so far as to endorse measures such as Sen. Ernest Hollings' (D-S.C.) Consumer Broadband and Digital Television Promotion Act. This bill would require federally certified DRM controls on any devices capable of manipulating and copying digital content, such as computers and personal digital assistants ("palm pilots"). The idea would be to ensure that those who copy files do so only with permission, on approved equipment. Manufacturers would be forbidden to make devices that didn't include the copy protection technology.

While some people inappropriately want to ban file-sharing capabilities, others—equally inappropriately—want to ban copy protection technologies designed to halt file sharing. Those who eagerly share copyrighted files often condemn experimental DRM technologies by which copyright holders hope to shield works from reproduction, such as digital watermarking and enhanced encryption. As noted, some regard such efforts as threats to free expression (which is ironic, given that many in the next breath will assert that encryption or watermarking can always be cracked—and so far, that's been true).

Many opponents of copy protection also want government to impose a different type of technology mandate—a compulsory license—that would require content providers to license their products to others at a government-regulated rate. So while opposing mandatory DRM schemes, this crowd simultaneously endorses forced "contracts" and their accompanying government-set royalty fees, which are little more than price controls. Reps. Rick Boucher (D-Va.) and Chris Cannon (R-Utah) have pushed for a "Music Online Competition Act," which would implement a version of this plan.

The legislative extremes of either banning or imposing particular technologies or business models should be avoided.

A New Model for the Future

Finally, when thinking about the future, it helps conceptually if we break up intellectual property into "A, B, and C" components. A is what's in the public domain. B is the stuff protected now, which we're fighting over. C is what hasn't been created yet. If Congress allows market mechanisms to take over C, then, over time, C and A will dwarf B.

In other words, we need to think of ways of making the role of government smaller. Avoiding interference with technological experimentation can do that. For example, digital rights management—although it will never fully prevent copying—can make it inconvenient enough so that cracking encrypted songs may not be worth the trouble. Perhaps a 19-cent music download, certified virus free, that also includes liner notes, lyrics, photos, and discount coupons on merchandise and concerts is a better deal than a free song.

And the fair use issue may not be as thorny as some people expect. First, it is not in the interest of profit-maximizing companies to restrict intellectual output and software research. In striking the balance, companies face market-induced incentives to avoid devising copy protection schemes so inconvenient or cumbersome that they go beyond the goal of deflecting piracy. For example, although one isn't necessarily entitled to a perfect digital copy as a matter of fair use, record companies are nonetheless experimenting with putting multiple versions of songs on CD as a way to alleviate fair use concerns and give people the portability they want.

Moreover, as University of Texas economics professor Stan Liebowitz notes, while digital rights management technologies won't prevent all copying, the imperative is to prevent massive unauthorized duplication. With respect to fair use, Liebowitz argues that, given technologies such as micropayments, voluntary DRM schemes will not restrict the output of intellectual property at all as IP pricing techniques are improved.

Technological experimentation may offer artists and inventors the option of "opting out" of the IP legal regime entirely and instead relying on new technologies and unique business models to protect their property and receive compensation for it. Digital distribution even gives producers and artists the option of avoiding the existing music companies and movie studios. Artists often claim to be ripped off, which is another fight within the wide-ranging copyright debate of today. (MP3.com was one of those

415

options—artists-direct-to-the-customer model.) Of course, if artists rather than middlemen control their copyrights, it won't end disputes over length of protection, but it could remove one layer of the dispute.

The bottom line is that Congress should not imagine that it has all the answers to practical problems of digital copy protection as ''Napsterization'' continues to unfold. Perhaps technology can be a better means of controlling use of one's creations, in some applications, than can law— even if law is in place as a backup.

Also, to lessen the reliance on traditional copyright protections, policymakers should ensure that unintentional government barriers don't stand in the way of private efforts by individuals to protect their intangible creations. For example, overzealous antitrust enforcement might hamper collective private efforts to license songs, such as the MusicNet and Pressplay services. Restrictive contracts that antitrust law might eye suspiciously could in fact benefit consumers by ensuring returns for producers, preserving their incentives to create. Indeed, some academics have suggested that regulation such as antitrust law may force the ''need'' for more intellectual property law and enforcement than would otherwise be warranted.

Suggested Readings

Crews, Clyde Wayne Jr. ''Musical Mandates: Must the Pop Music Industry Submit to Compulsory Licensing?'' Cato Institute TechKnowledge no. 16, August 15, 2001, www.cato.org/tech/tk/010815-tk.html.

Crews, Clyde Wayne Jr., and Adam Thierer. ''When Rights Collide: Principles to Guide the Intellectual Property Debate.'' Cato Institute TechKnowledge no. 10, June 4, 2001, www.cato.org/tech/tk/010604-tk.html.

Liebowitz, Stan. ''Policing Pirates in the Networked Age.'' Cato Institute Policy Analysis no. 438, May 15, 2002, www.cato.org/pubs/pas/pa-438es.html.

Litman, Jessica. *Digital Copyright.* Amherst, N.Y.: Prometheus Books, 2001.

Thierer, Adam, and Clyde Wayne Crews Jr., eds. *Copy Fights: The Future of Intellectual Property in the Information Age.* Washington: Cato Institute, 2002.

—Prepared by Clyde Wayne Crews Jr. and Adam Thierer

41. Telecommunications and Broadband Policy

Congress should

- end regulatory asymmetry by placing all carriers on an equal legal footing and comprehensively deregulate all carriers to accomplish this goal,
- end the open-access crusade at the FCC,
- reform and devolve universal service subsidies and the "E-Rate" program,
- enact comprehensive spectrum reform and privatization,
- end the failed HDTV transition and reallocate that spectrum for other uses,
- end arbitrary regulatory "public interest standard" decision-making, and
- clean up the telecom industry tax mess.

The American telecommunications sector went into freefall in 2002. Telecom stocks tanked as once-proud industry giants and smaller carriers alike were financially decimated. Numerous providers were forced to declare bankruptcy. And the reverberations were felt well beyond the boundaries of the telecom sector as upstream and downstream industries took a hit as well.

There are many obvious business reasons for this market meltdown. Excessive debt loads, overcapacity, lack of consumer demand, and even accounting scandals have all contributed to the current downturn. But public policy has had an equally important impact on this sector. While markets and technologies have evolved rapidly, the communications policy landscape remains encumbered with outdated rules and regulations.

This is largely due to the fact that when Congress last attempted to address these matters seven years ago by implementing the Telecommunications Act of 1996, legislators intentionally avoided providing clear deregulatory objectives to the Federal Communications Commission and instead delegated broad and remarkably ambiguous authority to the agency. That left the most important deregulatory decisions to the FCC and, not surprisingly, the agency did a very poor job of following through with a serious liberalization agenda.

The Failed Promise and Premise of the Telecom Act

The Telecom Act's most serious flaw was its backward-looking focus on correcting the market problems of a bygone era. Instead of thoroughly cleaning out the regulatory deadwood of the past, legislators and regulators decided to instead rework archaic legal paradigms and policies that were outmoded decades ago. It kept in place increasingly unnatural legal distinctions, such as the artificial separation of local and long-distance wireline telephone services even though these two services can be bundled and sold as one service as they are by wireless cellular providers.

The Telecom Act did not address the underlying regulatory asymmetry that governs formerly distinct industry sectors. That is, regulators have traditionally grouped providers into categories such as common carriers, cable services, wireless, and mass media and broadcasting. But the increasing reality of technological convergence means these formerly distinct industry sectors and companies are now integrating and searching for ways to offer consumers a bundled set of communications services under a single brand name. Increasingly, providers are referring to themselves as information services providers, broadband providers, or network services providers. Yet the Telecom Act endorsed the paradigms of the past and allowed increasingly interchangeable services to be regulated under different legal standards.

The first step Congress must take to begin seriously reforming communications policy is to end this asymmetry, not by "regulating up" to put everyone on an equal footing, but rather by "deregulating down." Placing everyone on the same *deregulated* level playing field should be at the heart of telecommunications policy to ensure nondiscriminatory regulatory treatment of competing providers and technologies by all levels of government.

Two controversial bills were proposed in the 107th Congress to clarify the law in this regard. One bill, the Internet Freedom and Broadband Deployment Act of 2001 (H.R. 1542), was sponsored by House Committee on Energy and Commerce chairman Billy Tauzin (R-La.) and ranking member John Dingell, (D-Mich.). The hotly debated Tauzin-Dingell bill would allow incumbent local telephone exchange carriers, or "Baby Bells," to provide customers with broadband services the same way cable and satellite companies are currently allowed to, largely free of the infrastructure-sharing mandates. On February 27, 2002, after months of acrimonious debate, the House of Representatives finally passed a watered-down version of the bill and passed it along to the mostly unsympathetic Senate Commerce Committee, chaired by longtime Baby Bell critic Ernest Hollings (D-S.C.). Hollings and a number of his colleagues denounced the Tauzin-Dingell bill and vowed to kill the measure or to go further and introduce legislation to actually impose new regulations on telecom and broadband markets.

Despite the generally hostile reception that the Tauzin-Dingell measure received in the Senate, a second measure, S. 2430, the Broadband Regulatory Parity Act of 2002, was introduced by Sens. John Breaux (D-La.) and Don Nickles (R-Okla.); that measure would require the FCC to ensure regulatory parity among the various providers of broadband services. The Breaux-Nickles bill would achieve this parity not by "regulating up" but by "deregulating down." The bill states that "all providers of broadband service, and all providers of broadband access services, are subject to the same regulatory requirements, or no regulatory requirements" and requires that those provisions be "implemented without increasing the regulatory requirements applicable to any provider of broadband services." Through those provisions, the bill establishes a simple legal standard to help level the playing field in the broadband marketplace. Both of these bills provide a refreshing break from the past and represent the simplest path to communications policy symmetry.

The Open-Access Crisis

The second serious problem with the Telecom Act was its fundamentally flawed premise that competition could be micromanaged into existence through "open-access" mandates. The act included provisions that required incumbent local telephone companies to share elements of their networks with rivals at a regulated rate. The theory behind these interconnection and unbundling rules was that smaller carriers needed a chance to get their feet wet in this market before they could invest in facilities of their own to serve consumers. To encourage entry by smaller carriers, Congress delegated broad and undefined authority to the FCC to create rules that would allow independent carriers to lease capacity from incumbent network owners at a regulated (and very low) price so that the new rivals could resell that capacity to customers and still earn a profit.

The danger inherent in this scheme should have been apparent from the start: If regulators went to the extreme and set the regulated rate for leased capacity too low, then new rivals would come to rely on infrastructure sharing as their core business model and avoid making the facilities-based investments necessary for true competition to develop. That is essentially what happened in the wake of the Telecom Act's passage as the FCC overzealously implemented the act's network-sharing provisions. This encouraged new entrants to engage in a crude form of regulatory arbitrage as they pushed for regulators to constantly suppress the regulated price of access to existing telephone networks. Meanwhile, they largely ignored investment in new networks of their own through which legitimate competition could have developed.

Despite the consistent and tireless efforts of federal and state regulators to prop up this regulatory house of cards, this system essentially collapsed under its own weight in 2001. Regulators pushed the rules as far as they possibly could until it became painfully obvious that industry investment was being seriously discouraged. Moreover, litigation by incumbents tied the hands of regulators somewhat. More important, markets and investors came to realize that business models that are heavily dependent on a forced-access regulatory regime are not sustainable in the long run. Consequently, the stocks of pure resale carriers tanked and most were forced to declare bankruptcy. Carriers that had made some facilities-based infrastructure investments fared better.

What this experience suggests is that genuine head-to-head, facilities-based competition will not develop so long as regulators are proposing technology sharing or network sharing as the cure-all for America's communications woes. While the authors of the Telecom Act generally believed that open-access rules were to be transitional in character and were to be narrowly applied during the transition period, those sentiments were not explicitly written into law. As a result, the FCC, which was eager to produce numerical results to satisfy its competition mandate, decided to sacrifice long-term industry innovation and investment for increased short-term entry by resellers. The danger now is that this regulatory system will be extended to other industry sectors (such as cable networks) or applied to emerging technologies (such as broadband Internet access).

Although infrastructure sharing continues to have great appeal for regulators, it is hardly the path to true telecommunications freedom or competition. In fact, it is really just communications socialism: collective control of the underlying means of production. Worse yet, forced access demands the continuation of a regime of price controls within the communications sector since someone must set the interconnection or lease price and that someone will end up being regulatory officials.

If forced access has a future in the communications industry, then true industry competition, innovation, and investment do not. Congress must abandon the use of this insidious industrial policy technique by making sure it is not applied to emerging technologies and then taking steps to sunset forced-access provisions that cover the provision of local telephone service.

Ending Universal Service Entitlements

Universal service subsidies are relics of a bygone age that continue to distort market pricing and competitive entry. The system has been riddled with inefficient cross-subsidies, artificially inflated prices, geographic rate averaging, and hidden phone bill charges for average Americans. While some reform efforts have been entertained in recent years, they have been quite limited and mostly cosmetic in nature.

To make matters worse, section 254 of the Telecommunications Act mandated that the FCC take steps to expand the future definition of universal service. It did not take the agency long to follow up on this request. In May 1997 the agency created the "E-Rate" program (known among its critics as the "Gore tax" since it was heavily promoted by then–vice president Al Gore), which unilaterally established a new government bureaucracy to help wire schools and libraries to the Internet. The FCC then dictated that the American people would pick up the $2.25 billion per year tab for the program by imposing a hidden tax on everyone's phone bills.

Although the constitutionality of the E-Rate program was questioned initially, the program withstood court challenges and early legislative reform efforts. Consequently, the E-Rate threatens to become yet another entrenched Washington entitlement program and further set back needed reform efforts.

In addition, a new crop of federal spending initiatives is now creeping up that covers telecommunications services, the Internet, and the high-technology sector in general. Although not a formally unified effort, the combined effect of federal legislative activity on this front is tantamount to the creation of what might be called a "Digital New Deal." That is, just as policymakers proposed a litany of "New Deal" programs and spending initiatives during the Depression, lawmakers are today devising myriad new federal programs aimed at solving the many supposed emergencies or disasters that will befall industry or consumers without government assistance. The recent troubles of the dot-com and telecommunications sectors have only added fuel to the fire of interventionism.

These new communications-, cyberspace-, and Internet-related spending initiatives that policymakers are considering, or have already implemented, can basically be grouped into four general categories: (1) broadband deployment; (2) digital education, civic participation, and cultural initiatives; (3) cyber security; and (4) research and development. Dozens of new federal programs were proposed in these areas during the 107th Congress. And dozens of other promotional programs already exist.

The dangers of the rising cyber pork should be obvious. Washington subsidy and entitlement programs typically have a never-ending lifespan and often open the door to increased federal regulatory intervention. Political meddling of this variety could also displace private-sector investment efforts or result in technological favoritism by favoring or promoting one set of technologies or providers over another. Moreover, subsidy programs aren't really necessary in an environment characterized by proliferating consumer choices but uncertain market demand for new services. Finally, and most profound, perhaps the leading argument against the creation of a Digital New Deal is that, by inviting the feds to act as a market facilitator, the industry runs the risk of becoming more politicized over time.

Congress should abolish the current system of federal entitlements and devolve to the states responsibility for any subsidy programs that are deemed necessary in the future. A federal telecommunications welfare state is not justified. If schools desire specific technologies or communications connections, they can petition their state or local leaders for funding the same way they would for textbooks or chalkboards: through an accountable, on-budget state appropriation. There is nothing unique or special about communications or computing technologies that justifies a federal entitlement program paid for through hidden telephone taxes while other tools of learning are paid for through state and local budgets.

Spectrum Reform and Privatization

The Telecommunications Act largely ignored the wireless sector and spectrum reform in general. That was a highly unfortunate oversight by Congress, given the ongoing problems associated with centralized bureaucratic management of the electromagnetic spectrum. For more than seven decades, the FCC has treated the spectrum as a socialized public resource and the results have been predictable: gross misallocation, delayed innovation, and the creation of artificial scarcity.

In recent years, however, the FCC has gradually come to accept the logic of a free market in spectrum allocation and management. The shift to the use of auctions in the early 1990s was a major step forward in this regard. Previously, all spectrum allocations had been made through comparative hearings or random lotteries. While not all new spectrum allocations are made through auctions, many are, meaning that those who value the resource most highly are now obtaining the spectrum.

Moreover, the FCC has recently signaled its interest in allowing spectrum license holders greater flexibility in use to ensure that this valuable resource can be put to its most efficient use. While the agency has not yet followed through on this reform, recent FCC Spectrum Policy Task Force meetings and initiatives suggest that the agency is at least moving in the right direction.

But auctions and flexible use, while important steps, are not enough. The task of spectrum reform will only be complete once policymakers grant property rights in spectrum. Just as America has a full-fledged private property rights regime for real estate, so too should wireless spectrum properties be accorded the full protection of the law. As long as federal regulators parcel out spectrum under a licensing system, the process will be a politicized mess. The alternative—a pure free market for the ownership, control, and trade of spectrum properties—should be a top priority.

To begin this task, Congress should grant incumbent spectrum holders a property right in their existing or future allocation. This means spectrum holders would no longer lease their allocation from the federal government but instead would own it outright and be able to use it (or sell it) as they saw fit. This also means that all arbitrary federal regulatory oversight of the spectrum would end, including content or speech controls on broadcasters. Federal regulators would be responsible only for dealing with technical trespass (interference) violations and disputes that arose between holders of adjoining spectrum.

For all potential uses of scarce spectrum to which there are competing claims, auctions should be used to allocate the spectrum. Firms would file plans of their bidding proposals with the FCC and then post bonds proving they had enough capital to bid credibly for the given allocation. The commission also could establish competitive bidding rules (as it did

423

in previous auctions) to ensure that bidding collusion did not take place. These auctions would not be one-time events; they would be ongoing as spectrum claims developed and multiplied.

Policymakers should not rig these auctions in any way, either to favor certain demographic groups or to artificially boost the amount of money raised for the federal Treasury by such auctions. The primary goal of spectrum auctions is to allocate spectrum to its most highly valued use by offering it up for competitive bidding, not to funnel money into the federal coffers.

Under this new system, spectrum owners—better thought of as "band managers" for the bands of spectrum they will own and manage—would henceforth have complete freedom to use, sublease, combine, or sell spectrum in any way they saw fit.

Government agencies and public-sector users should purchase the spectrum they need at ongoing auctions. It should be noted that government agencies already control a significant portion of the spectrum, so under this scheme, they would be granted rights to their existing holdings. Congress or state governments should ensure that public-sector spectrum users have money in their budgets for ongoing spectrum acquisition.

Finally, as Table 41.1 shows, regarding spectrum "commons" areas— or portions of the electromagnetic spectrum that are less scarce and can be shared by many users without assigning specific rights—the government has three options. (1) It can directly allocate certain bands of spectrum for commons use, much as it purchases large portions of land for public parks, and then open those areas to common use. (2) At the opposite end of the spectrum, so to speak, government could simply rely on private band managers to contract with independent users to create commons areas within their allocation. Practically speaking, however, it might be very difficult for commons areas to develop under this model, given the need for coordination across many bands. The transaction costs would be enormous. (3) A final compromise between these two extremes would be for public officials to designate certain ceilings and floors above and below which certain noninterfering uses of the spectrum would be tolerated. In spectrum parlance, these ceilings and floors are known as "overlay" and "underlay" rights or areas. This is a quite practical solution, as such "easements" already exist today in some bands of the spectrum.

While all three of these options represent practical and legitimate solutions to the need for ongoing spectrum commons areas, one option that should be taken off the table is the adoption of a pure commons regime

Table 41.1
Property Rights vs. a Spectrum Commons: What Are the Options?

	Requires Ongoing Regulatory Oversight	Requires Little Continuing Oversight
Emphasis on Importance of Property Rights	**Ceilings and Floors— Easements Model**: Use auctions and property rights for mutually exclusive uses but impose federal ceiling-floor requirements ("easements") above or below which band managers have no control. So long as they do not meaningfully interfere, allow unlimited overlay or underlay across all private bands. Possible historical models: airline traffic above private property or subsoil mineral or oil drilling rights.	**Pure Property Rights Model**: Grant incumbent spectrum holders property rights in their allocations. Use auctions and property rights for new mutually exclusive uses of spectrum. Grant spectrum owners the absolute right of excludability and flexible use. Rely on private band managers to subdivide and sublease portions of their band to common uses.
Emphasis on Importance of Commons	**Public Parks Model**: Most of spectrum fully privatized but feds (perhaps states and localities or even private associations) purchase large swaths of spectrum and open it up for free use to create a spectrum commons. Or the FCC could just generously expand "Part 15" rules for unlicensed spectrum.	**Pure Commons-Homesteading Model**: No exclusive property rights. Let overlay and underlay users tap into spectrum as they wish and fight about the interference later in the courts or have faith that new devices ("agile radio," or software-defined radios) will allow everyone to work things out voluntarily.

for the spectrum. Some spectrum engineers and academics—infatuated with the exciting technologies emerging today that enable reuse and efficient sharing of the spectrum—have called for adoption of a pure spectrum commons model to govern ongoing spectrum allocations. Those theorists believe that new technologies such as software-defined radios and smart antennas can allow users to infinitely divide the spectrum and shatter the notion of spectrum scarcity in the process.

But that is a stretch. There will almost certainly be some scarcity at work within the spectrum, just as there is for all natural resources. If nothing else, the limits of the human imagination create scarcities within the spectrum. More practically, commons areas are likely to encourage overuse and congestion, which will force many parties to search out privately managed bands where they could pay a premium for uninterrupted use. And the commons crowd does not have a useful transitional solution to the issue of spectrum incumbency. Existing users, many of which have controlled a specific swath of spectrum for several decades, would not take lightly the idea of sharing their allocation with newcomers. And a good case can be made that they should not be forced to share that spectrum, given their long-standing control and use of the resource. It would be better to grandfather them into a property rights model by granting them complete ownership and flexible use rights to that spectrum.

Under the property rights regime envisioned above, the FCC would get out of the spectrum management business altogether. Residual regulatory functions, such as the adjudication of interference disputes or international coordination, could be left to some sort of "spectrum court," which would be a set of administrative law judges with particular expertise in resolving technical spectrum disputes.

Ending the HDTV Fiasco

America's 15-year high-definition television (HDTV) industrial policy experiment has been a failure. When industry and government officials began debating what the next generation of television signals would look like in the mid-1980s, prettier pictures and better sound appeared to be just around the corner. But the rollout of digital television (DTV) has stagnated, and many skeptics are wondering if the entire experiment should not be abandoned so that the spectrum allocated for over-the-air (OTA) digital television can be used for other important uses.

One reason for the sluggish pace of change in this sector can be traced back to the scandalous manner in which broadcasters received the spectrum over which digital television transition is supposed to take place. Each broadcaster in America already has a six megahertz (MHz) spectrum allocation that is used to provide consumers old-fashioned analog TV signals. But broadcasters argued that they would need the government to give them an additional 6 MHz of high-quality spectrum to simulcast digital signals alongside analog broadcasts until Americans made the complete transition to DTV sets. Moreover, the broadcasters didn't want to pay for this spectrum, which was quite valuable "beach front quality" spectrum. Amazingly, as part of the Telecom Act of 1996, they convinced policymakers to do exactly that—"loan" them an additional 6 MHz allocation free of charge even though many other spectrum users were salivating at the prospect of bidding billions to obtain that same spectrum for other uses. Broadcasters would continue to transmit analog signals on their old 6-MHz analog slice of spectrum until 2006, *or until 85 percent of Americans had made the migration to digital television*, and then return the old spectrum to the FCC for auction. Estimates of the value of the new digital spectrum given to the broadcasters to make the transition to DTV ran between $10 billion and $100 billion. The logic behind this giveaway was that local OTA broadcasting remained an important public service that should be continued in the digital age regardless of the cost of doing so.

The problem is, the opportunity costs associated with this giveaway are very high and get higher with each passing year. While Americans wait for the rollout of DTV to occur, countless other service providers are being denied the opportunity to use that same spectrum for alternative uses that the public might actually demand. Nonetheless, policymakers, egged on by the broadcast lobby, continue to go to great lengths to try to make the transition work. For example, in August 2002 the FCC mandated that television set manufacturers include digital tuners in all their new sets by 2006 to help speed the transition even though the tuners will add more than $200 to the cost of each new television. Likewise, Capitol Hill policymakers were rumored to be considering legislation mandating that cable companies carry all local digital TV broadcast signals on their systems without compensation. Cable firms are already strapped with analog "must carry" rules that eat up capacity and offer them no compensation in return. Under the so-called dual must carry rules now under consideration, cable operators would be forced to dedicate even more of their capacity to the retransmission of OTA broadcast signals, meaning less room for other cable channels or even Internet access.

These mandates are essentially an attempt to transfer responsibility for the failed transition to other parties. But until the broadcasters make more of their programming available in high definition, such mandates aren't really going to help anything. And, regrettably, very little is being shown in HDTV by broadcasters today and, consequently, only a very small percentage of American households has felt compelled to make the digital transition in their homes. So there is little to no chance that 85 percent

427

of American households will have made the DTV transition by 2006, meaning that broadcasters will not be able to return their old analog spectrum for auction on time.

So, what can Congress do now? Policymakers should consider taking back the valuable digital spectrum they lent to broadcasters and selling it to other companies that could put it to better use. Alternatively, Congress could just let the broadcasters sell it off themselves and then split the proceeds with the government. These aren't perfect solutions, but they are certainly better than continuing with the current failed industrial policy. The goal now should be to open this squandered broadcast spectrum to other uses as quickly as possible.

It should be noted that the end of this industry policy is not the end of HDTV altogether. Today, well over 80 percent of Americans opt to receive their television programming via satellite or cable systems, meaning broadcast stations have become just another set of channels in the universe of choices for consumers. The vast majority of this subscription-based programming is delivered digitally, and an increasing portion of it is high definition in nature. When consumers demand more HDTV services, they will be able to receive them through satellite and cable carriers. And many broadcasters will air a certain portion of their programming in HDTV or sell it to cable and satellite carriers to retransmit. HDTV can naturally evolve and become a viable option for many households, but it will be on a timetable determined by consumers, not bureaucrats or legislators.

The "Public Interest Standard" Charade

The HDTV fiasco is a fine example of a Washington industrial policy undertaken in the name of serving the "public interest." The history of communications and technology regulation is littered with countless other examples of such "public interest" crusades. Although it has spawned innumerable policy directives and spending initiatives over the past seven decades, this amorphous concept has managed to elude definition. Much as they "know" pornography, omniscient members of Congress and their brethren at the FCC always seem to know the "public interest" when they see it. But since the public interest is whatever they say it is, it's a splendidly convenient (if not a tad bit circular) concept by which to regulate one of the biggest sectors of the U.S. economy.

But what truly is "in the public interest"? It is whatever the public says it is. How is that determined? By the interaction of millions of diverse interests and actors in a free marketplace. Asking the FCC to define the public interest for the communications sector is akin to asking a hypothetical Federal Automobile Commission to define what types of cars consumers will demand next year and then determining which firms should be able to supply them and on what terms. Just as the forces of supply and demand are spontaneously calibrated by a free market in cars, computers, corn, or coffee, the public interest in communications can be discovered by the voluntary interaction of companies and consumers in a free market. The FCC's public interest standard should be abandoned immediately.

Cleaning Up the Telecom Industry Tax Mess

Finally, regulation is not the only thing holding back America's increasingly competitive communications and broadband sector. Burdensome and unique tax rules also remain a serious threat. That is largely due to the fact that policymakers at the state and local levels have long treated this sector as a cash cow from which they could draw substantial sums. They justified such heavy levies by arguing that the industry was a natural monopoly. But the telecommunications industry is no longer being treated as a regulated monopoly, so policymakers should stop taxing it as though it were. That is, as competition comes to communications in America, tax policies based on the regulated monopoly model of the past must be comprehensively reformed.

Some of these taxes are federal in nature and can be addressed by Congress or the FCC. A good example is the federal 3 percent excise tax on telecommunications put in place during the Spanish-American War of 1898. This anachronistic tax should be repealed immediately. And the hidden taxes associated with the E-Rate or "Gore Tax" program should also be repealed or at least devolved to a lower level of government for administration.

Regrettably, however, the more problematic tax policy issues arise from burdensome state and local mandates. For example, many states impose discriminatory ad valorem taxes on interstate communications services by taxing telecommunications business property at rates higher than other property, driving up costs for consumers. Federal protections against such taxes—already in effect for railroads, airlines, and trucking—should be extended to telecommunications. Many governments impose multiple and extremely high taxes on communications services. Such taxes should be slashed to a single tax per state and locality, and filing and auditing procedures should be radically streamlined. Finally, taxes and tolls on Internet access should be permanently banned since those charges represent a burdensome levy on the free flow of information and the construction of new interstate broadband networks.

Suggested Readings

Bell, Tom W., and Solveig Singleton. *Regulators' Revenge: The Future of Telecommunications Deregulation.* Washington: Cato Institute, 1998.

Crandall, Robert W."A Somewhat Better Connection." *Regulation* (Summer 2002): 22–28.

Gasman, Lawrence. *Telecompetition: The Free Market Road to the Information Superhighway.* Washington: Cato Institute, 1994.

_____. "Universal Service: The New Telecommunications Entitlements and Taxes." Cato Institute Policy Analysis no. 310, June 25, 1998, www.cato.org/pubs/pas/pa-310es.html.

Hazlett, Thomas W. "Economic and Political Consequences of the 1996 Telecommunications Act." *Regulation* 23, no. 3 (2000): 36–45, www.cato.org/pubs/regulation/regv23n3/hazlett.pdf.

Kahn, Alfred E. "How to Treat the Costs of Shared Voice and Video Networks in a Post-Regulatory Age." Cato Institute Policy Analysis no. 264, November 27, 1998, www.cato.org/pubs/pas/pa-264es.html.

Kwerel, Evan R., and John R. Williams. "Moving toward a Market for Spectrum." *Regulation,* no. 2 (1993): 53–62.

Lee, William E. "Open Access, Private Interests, and the Emerging Broadband Market." Cato Institute Policy Analysis no. 379, August 29, 2000, www.cato.org/pubs/pas/pa-379es.html.

Leighton, Wayne A. "Broadband Deployment and the Digital Divide: A Primer." Cato Institute Policy Analysis no. 410, August 7, 2001, www.cato.org/pubs/pas/pa-410es.html.

_____. "Prescriptive Regulations and Telecommunications: Old Lessons Not Learned." *Cato Journal* 20, no. 3 (Winter 2001), www.cato.org/pubs/journal/cj20n3/cj20n3-4.pdf.

Thierer, Adam D. "Forced Access Follies Continue: The Case of Special Access Services." Cato Institute TechKnowledge, no. 32, January 28, 2002, www.cato.org/tech/tk/020128-tk.html.

_____. "A 10-Point Agenda for Comprehensive Telecom Reform." Cato Institute Briefing Paper no. 63, May 8, 2001, www.cato.org/pubs/briefs/bp-063es.html.

—Prepared by Adam Thierer

ENERGY AND ENVIRONMENT

42. Electricity Policy

Congress should

- repeal the Federal Power Act of 1935 and abolish the Federal Energy Regulatory Commission (FERC);
- repeal the 1935 Public Utility Holding Company Act (PUHCA) and the 1978 Public Utility Regulatory Policy Act (PURPA);
- privatize federal power marketing authorities, the Tennessee Valley Authority, and all federal power generation facilities;
- eliminate all tax preferences applicable to municipal power companies and electricity cooperatives;
- eliminate all federal price subsidies, tax incentives, and regulatory preferences for renewable energy;
- declare that any state or municipal regulation of the generation, transmission, distribution, or retail sale of electricity interferes with interstate trade and is a violation of the U.S. Constitution's Commerce Clause; and
- require open, nondiscriminatory access to all federal public rights-of-way for electricity transmission and distribution services, except when such services present a public safety hazard.

The electricity regulatory system in the United States produced large discrepancies in costs between states in the 1970s and 1980s. By the early 1990s many states with a large nuclear or independent power component had high retail prices, and those that stuck with traditional coal-based facilities (and hydropower) had low-cost electricity.

Even though the regulatory system did not protect consumers from high-cost electricity, no one has proposed eliminating regulation. The response to the cost discrepancy has been initiation of a policy of mandatory open access to "restructure" regulation instead of eliminating it.

431

Under mandatory open access, competition is introduced into the generation sector, but transmission and distribution systems remain regulated monopolies to which generators have access at nondiscriminatory prices.

Transmission and Distribution: The Intellectual Discussion

The case for a competitive market in generation was accepted long ago by academics. Academic discussion now is about how large a role decentralized markets can play in the operation of the transmission system.

Some observers argue that, with the assistance of computer models, decentralized trade between buyers and sellers of electricity can occur and reach an efficient equilibrium without central direction as long as every sale is accompanied by transmission rights that reflect the physical ability of the transmission system to carry the flow.

Other observers believe the decentralized solution would entail enormous transaction costs because of the many agents required to facilitate the development and trading of transmission rights. Those people argue that the inability of transmission rights to reflect the true effects of generator output on the system would require central intervention anyway.

Another important issue in transmission policy is the identification and funding of new transmission investment. Again, there are two sides to the debate: one advocates centralized solutions and the other advocates decentralized solutions. According to the latter view, consortia of generators would fund new investment and, in turn, get rights (that reflect the physical ability of the transmission system to carry the flow according to computer simulations) to inject power into or take power from the system in proportion to their financial contributions.

Economist Paul Joskow offers the more traditional centralized view of transmission investment:

> Transmission investment decisions do not immediately strike me as being ideally suited to relying entirely on the invisible hand. Transmission investments are lumpy, characterized by economies of scale and can have physical impacts throughout the network. The combination of imperfectly defined property rights, economies of scale and long-lived sunk costs for transmission investments, and imperfect competition in the supply of generating services can lead to either underinvestment or overinvestment at particular points on the network if we rely entirely on market forces [Chao and Huntington, p. 24].

Even if the decentralized solution is imperfect, mandatory open access is probably worse. The experience we have had with mandatory open access in telecommunications since 1996 should make us very wary about going down the same road in electricity policy. Mandatory open access eliminates the incentive for new infrastructure. Under the regime that seems to be in place in the states that have restructured their electricity regulations, large commercial users and independent generators are going to demand that the transmission system serve their needs at rates determined by public service commissions. As economist Robert Crandall says:

> There is no limit to the ideas that I may have for using your property at prices that are as low as I could obtain by building the facilities myself. . . . Unfortunately, this [open access policy] is based in large part on assuming that sharing the infrastructure built under all of the distorted incentives created by regulation will somehow lead to efficient competition.

Thus the right question to ask is, not whether decentralized transmission investment would be optimal, but whether it would be good enough to work.

Transmission and Distribution: The Political Discussion

The political discussion at the state and federal levels has not reflected the intellectual discussion. Instead, it reflects conflicts that arise within the mandatory-open-access paradigm.

Half the states are not actively considering deregulation because their costs are low and stable because of extensive use of coal or hydropower sources. Such states have little interest in developing more extensive transmission systems to serve merchant power plants participating in the interstate market. People who advocate mandatory open access (merchant power producers and large industrial consumers) want an increased federal regulatory role in transmission service to prevent vertically integrated utilities from Balkanizing the national transmission market. But the mandatory-open-access lobby is not really on the side of the angels, despite their pro-competition rhetoric, because they want the costs of new transmission investment to be borne by all electricity ratepayers rather than by new merchant generators.

A central question under mandatory open access is, How can we prevent traditional utilities from favoring their own generators (to the extent they do not divest them) through manipulation of access to and pricing of transmission facilities that they also own? The predominant answer has been to hand the operation of the transmission network to nonprofit entities—independent system operators—organized by the old utilities. But those operators are political institutions whose structure invites inefficiency, inconsistency, and dominance by transmission owners.

An alternative organizational model for transmission is a for-profit transmission company regulated under "incentive regulation," rather than traditional command-and-control regulation, to promote dynamic efficiency. Many people object to private for-profit transmission companies because, until they face genuine rivalry, either from competing wires systems or distributed generation from decentralized natural-gas generators, for-profit transmission companies would have an incentive to restrict use of their lines and raise prices, as would any monopolist. Incentive regulation overcomes such objections because it allows the company to make more money by increasing than by decreasing throughput in the transmission system.

After a transition period of incentive regulation, transmission and distribution should be deregulated. Evidence does not suggest that regulation by commission, which has given us excessively costly nuclear-power and cogeneration contracts, has protected consumers in the ways that populist rhetoric suggests.

There are several reasons to believe that the market power of unregulated transmission and distribution companies would be less than conventional wisdom suggests.

- Competition might well arise from small turbines using natural gas to generate electricity. Electricity transmission owners have nothing to gain from alienating customers to the point where they switch to the natural-gas alternative.
- Before exclusive franchises were granted by governments, multiple entrepreneurs were quite willing to generate and distribute electricity.
- Mandatory open access to state and federally created rights-of-way is a much less mischievous policy than is mandatory open access to the wires themselves. The threat of such access may be sufficient to induce incumbent electricity transmission companies to price their services competitively.

Electricity Policy after California

No discussion of electricity policy would be complete without a discussion of the events in California during 2000–01. Large supply reductions (hydro shortage and natural gas shortage) and large weather-related demand increases (hot summer and very cold winter) simultaneously hit the state.

None of those shocks was triggered by state policy. However, the price increases resulting from decreased supply and increased demand were made more severe by several characteristics of state policy.

First, California adopted regulations in 1994 (known as the RECLAIM program) to control emissions of nitrogen oxides (NO_x) in southern California. In the winter of 1999, rights to emit NO_x were selling for about \$2 per pound. The widespread use of old, polluting, natural-gas turbines to replace the lost hydropower rapidly depleted the fixed quota of NO_x permits available. By the summer of 2000, they were selling for \$30 to \$40 per pound, a cost of 3 to 12 cents per kilowatt-hour, depending on the emissions of the generating unit. In January 2001, California regulators waived NO_x permit requirements for power generators for the next three years, but the damage had been done.

Second, a characteristic of the California electricity auction market also created incentives for high rather than low market-clearing prices. The rules of the auction allowed generators to offer different amounts of electricity at different prices rather than all of their output at one price. Under those rules, generators had the incentive to offer a small amount of their output at very high prices because, if the high bid were accepted, they would receive that price for all their output. And if the bid were not accepted, the generators would lose only the sale of a small fraction of their possible output. Normally such bidding behavior would be unprofitable because the probability of the high bid's being accepted would be small, but, in a very tight supply situation, the probability of the bid's being accepted rises considerably, and the opportunity cost of the unsold power falls.

Third, the operators of the California transmission grid placed an "infinite" value on keeping the grid operational. But retail price controls prevented consumers from seeing the price of doing so. That, in turn, induced generators to price high because they knew there would be no reduction in demand as a consequence of their pricing behavior.

Some economists argue that market power (the withholding of output from a low-cost facility to induce use of output from a high-cost facility) explains some of the price increase. Their evidence is the large amount of capacity offline in California in the winter of 2000–01. Other economists argue that the natural-gas units that were offline had never been intended to run as continuously as they did in the summer of 2000 to replace the hydro, and thus the maintenance rationale offered by the operators was legitimate.

Other explanations of the California debacle are not consistent with the evidence. Environmentalists' resistance to new plants is not the cause of too little supply. Supply did not increase at a rate greater than population growth anywhere in the West (except Montana) including Nevada and Arizona, which do not have strong consumer or environmental movements.

Some people have claimed that the state's reluctance to permit long-term contracts with generators and the state requirement that electricity be sold in a single price auction in which the highest bid sets the market price are responsible for the high prices. Both claims are incorrect. Single prices set by the producer with the highest costs are a feature of all commodities markets. Long-term contracts would have simply altered who suffered losses of wealth as the result of unanticipated supply and demand shocks; such contracts could not have prevented the supply and demand shocks from causing price increases for someone in the supply chain. Long-term contracts are simply spot prices plus an insurance contract, which cannot be less than spot prices alone.

Other states have not adopted better deregulation designs. They have not had crises because they do not rely on hydro, nor do they use natural gas for electricity production in the winter. Many have retail price controls combined with wholesale markets and thus are vulnerable to a California-style imbalance between the two rates although many have fuel-cost pass-through provisions.

An important lesson from California is that price matters. Demand would have been dramatically lower if some customers had faced the actual market price for electricity rather than fixed retail prices. Industry consultant Eric Hirst argues that if only 20 percent of the total retail demand faced actual market hourly prices, and as a response to those prices reduced demand by 20 percent, the resulting 4 percent drop in aggregate demand would have cut hourly prices by almost 50 percent. In California 8,000 megawatts of commercial and industrial load have "real-time" meters, which would allow hourly pricing, but they are not billed on that basis. The public utility commission could solve the problem by instituting real-time pricing.

The important lesson from California is that electricity markets should be fully deregulated. Wholesale deregulation with retail price controls is a recipe for disaster.

What Should Be Done?

The entire existing federal apparatus for regulating electricity should be repealed because the market failure rationales for its existence do not exist. The Federal Power Act, the Federal Energy Regulatory Commission (FERC), PURPA (a limited version of mandatory access, whose main function has been to force utilities to purchase power from third parties at nonmarket prices), and the archaic PUHCA (which strictly controls the ownership and management structures of electric utilities) all should go.

Congress should also ensure a level economic playing field by privatizing the federal power marketing authorities, the Tennessee Valley Authority, and all federal power generation facilities; and tax and fiscal preferences granted to municipal power companies and electricity cooperatives should be terminated.

All federal price subsidies, tax incentives, and regulatory preferences for renewable energy should also be eliminated. The environmental benefits of renewable energy are dramatically overstated. In fact, every single renewable energy source has drawn legitimate opposition from environmental organizations. If and when fossil fuels become more scarce, the electricity industry, without assistance, will turn to more abundant (i.e., cheaper) alternatives.

The price advantage currently enjoyed by fossil fuels cannot be attributed to present or past subsidies. Research suggests that, historically, the actions of government have kept petroleum prices above rather than below an unregulated market price. The only fuel that government has consistently subsidized is nuclear, but the effect of the subsidies has been to displace some coal and natural gas production of electricity and raise rather than lower the price of electricity.

The most damaging electricity regulations, however, emanate from state public utility commissions that restrict entry and set rates. Should states have the right to create restrictions on entry (franchises) in the electric utility market? May the federal government prevent states from harming consumers?

Investor-owned utilities and their trade association argue that the federal government may not prevent states from regulating utilities. But precedent exists for such intervention. Congress deregulated *interstate* trucking in 1980, but state regulation of *intrastate* trucking continued, and its main effect was to restrict entry by new firms and raise the price of shipping for consumers. In 1994 Congress prohibited states from regulating motor carriers, except household movers, and no constitutional questions have been raised.

While many legislators are (rightly) reluctant to interfere in state regulatory affairs, the Constitution's Commerce Clause gives Congress the power to remove barriers to interstate trade erected by state lawmakers. Congress should therefore preempt all state or municipal regulations that control the generation, transmission, distribution, or retail sale of electricity.

Suggested Readings

Awerbuch, Shimon, Leonard Hyman, and Andrew Vesey. *Unlocking the Benefits of Restructuring: A Blueprint for Transmission.* Vienna, Va.: Public Utilities Reports Incorporated, 1999.

Borenstein, Severin, and James Bushnell. "Electricity Restructuring: Deregulation or Reregulation?" *Regulation* 23, no. 2 (2000): 46–52.

Brennan, Tim. "Questioning the Conventional Wisdom." *Regulation* 24, no. 3 (2001): 63–69.

Chao, Hung-po, and Hillard Huntington, eds. *Designing Competitive Electricity Markets.* Boston: Kluwer, 1998.

Crandall, Robert W. "Managed Competition in U.S. Telecommunications." Washington: AEI-Brookings Joint Center for Regulatory Studies Working Paper no. 99-1, March 1999.

Hale, Douglas R, Thomas J. Overbye, and Thomas Leckey. "Competition Requires Transmission Capacity." *Regulation* 23, no. 2 (2000): 40–45.

Lenard, Thomas M. "FERC's New Regulatory Agenda." *Regulation* 25, no. 3 (2002).

Michaels, Robert J. "Can Non-profit Transmission Be Independent?" *Regulation* 23, no. 3 (2000): 61–66.

Rassenti, Stephen. "Turning Off the Lights." *Regulation* 24, no. 3 (2001): 70–76.

Taylor, Jerry, and Peter VanDoren. "California's Electricity Crisis: What's Going On, Who's to Blame, and What to Do." Cato Institute Policy Analysis no. 406, July 3, 2001.

VanDoren, Peter M. "The Deregulation of Electricity: A Primer." Cato Institute Policy Analysis no. 320, October 6, 1998.

—Prepared by Peter VanDoren

43. Environmental Protection

Congress should

- establish a mechanism by which states can apply for regulatory waivers from the Environmental Protection Agency in order to allow states some flexibility in establishing environmental priorities and to facilitate experiments in innovative regulatory approaches;
- replace the Federal Insecticide, Fungicide, and Rodenticide Act and the Toxic Substances Control Act with a consumer products labeling program under the auspices of the Food and Drug Administration;
- repeal the Comprehensive Environmental Response, Compensation, and Liability Act and privatize the cleanup of Superfund sites;
- replace the Resource Conservation and Recovery Act with minimal standards for discharge into groundwater aquifers;
- privatize federal lands by granting ownership rights to existing users and auctioning off the remaining lands;
- eliminate federal subsidies and programs that exacerbate environmental damage; and
- replace the Endangered Species Act and section 404 of the Clean Water Act with a federal biological trust fund.

Federal environmental policy is horribly off track, and the debate over what to do about it is characterized by a lack of rigorous thinking. Any discussion of how to reform this or that statute must begin with a discussion of why the statute is there in the first place. Only then can an informed discussion begin about the appropriate role of government in environmental protection. The details of that role must, of necessity, come last.

The Theory of Environmental Regulation

Air sheds, watersheds, groundwater, scenic lands, and ecologically important but sensitive ecosystems are widely considered "public goods." That is, in an unregulated marketplace, people who pay to "consume" environmental goods and services (say, those who purchase a conservation easement for an ecologically important wetland) are unable to keep those who *don't* pay from enjoying the benefits of that purchase. This leads to widespread "free riding" and less-than-efficient investments in environmental goods.

This "market failure" necessitates government intervention. While there are numerous ways that the government could intervene in environmental marketplaces to address market failure, the method employed by the federal government is public ownership of air, water, and subsurface resources as well as of some sensitive ecosystems. Congress exercises its power over those resources by delegating to executive agencies the authority to determine how resources can and can't be used—that is, by establishing pollution and public land use regulations—usually, but not always, on the basis of assessments of human health risk. The Environmental Protection Agency (EPA) is further empowered to determine the exact manner in which regulated entities are to go about meeting pollution standards—usually, but not always, dictating the installation of particular control devices or technologies.

Accurate, timely, and accessible information about environmental exposures is also considered by some to be a public good. Absent such laws as the Toxic Substances Control Act and the Federal Insecticide, Fungicide, and Rodenticide Act, individuals, some people think, would be unable to effectively police their exposures to dangerous chemicals. A variation of this argument contends that it is so costly and time-consuming for people to gain access to the environmental health information necessary for intelligent decisionmaking that government must act in the individual's stead and make those decisions for society as a whole.

Debates about the regulation of pollution generally begin with an acceptance of the above claims. The political arguments today are over the details:

- Do concentrations of chemical x in the environment truly pose a health risk to the public? If so, we regulate. If not, we don't.
- Should environmental regulations have to pass a cost/benefit test?
- Should government tell firms exactly how to go about meeting federal environmental standards, or should government simply dictate the

permissible concentration of pollutants in a given air shed or water-shed and allow firms some degree of flexibility in complying with those standards?

- How stringently should regulations be enforced, and who should do the enforcing—the EPA, state governments, environmental organizations through third-party lawsuits, or some combination of the three?

Debates over public land issues are less complicated but just as heated. Both the political left and the political right accept the idea that public ownership of scenic lands and sensitive ecosystems is necessary to address the inability to fully prevent free riders from enjoying the benefits of the conservation activity of others.

For example, many if not most Americans would pay some money to ensure that the Grand Canyon remains unexploited for commercial purposes. Yet only a subset of those Americans might contribute money for that purpose because they know that others will do so. Environmentalists thus worry that, without public ownership of land, the incentive to free ride on the activism of others will lead to a suboptimal provision of ecological preservation.

The Real Environmental Debate

Although environmental debates sound like they're arguments about science and public health (with a smattering of economics tossed in), they're really debates about preferences and *whose* preferences should be imposed on society. Although participants argue that "sound science" ought to determine whose preferences determine the standards (and that *their* science is better than their opponents'), science cannot referee the debate.

Consider the dispute about the regulation of potentially unhealthy pollutants, the central mission of the EPA. The agency examines toxicological and epidemiological data to ascertain the exposure level at which suspect substances impose measurable human health risks. Even assuming that such analyses are capable of providing the requisite information (a matter, incidentally, that is hotly debated within the scientific and public health community), who is to say whether one risk tolerance is preferable to another?

The amount of resources one is willing to spend on risk avoidance is ultimately subjective. Everyone's risk tolerance is different. Scientists can

441

help inform our decisions, but they cannot point us to the "correct" decision.

Should experts—acting on behalf of regulatory agencies—decide what sort of environmental quality people should or should not have a right to consume? In no other area of the economy do scientists have the power to rule in such a manner. After all, people are allowed to consume all kinds of things—power crystals, magnets, age-defying vitamins, and organic food—that scientists, doctors, and public health officials think are silly or even potentially counterproductive.

Many people, perhaps even a majority of voting Americans, want to secure cleaner air and cleaner water regardless of whether those improvements significantly reduce human health risks. Under the present political regime, however, no such improvements can occur without some alleged scientific justification. That is why people who wish to improve environmental quality are forced to embrace whatever science they can—no matter how dubious—to get what they want. They should not, however, have to engage in such scientific gymnastics to secure desired goods or services.

The debate over public land use is likewise garbed in the dubious cloth of science. How do we know whether public lands are more "valuable" if left wild than if developed in some way? While there are methods, such as contingent valuation surveys, to measure the "existence value" of any particular parcel of land, they yield highly dubious information for the simple reason that what people *say* they're willing to pay in surveys rarely comports with their actual behavior in the marketplace.

Likewise, there's no objectively correct way to measure the economic benefits provided by certain ecological services (such as water filtration services provided by wetlands) because so many of the resources affected are, at the moment, outside the marketplace. The debate, again, is more a battle of subjective preferences than a battle of ecological economics simply because the information necessary to inform the latter is unobtainable by government.

The Case for Preference Neutrality

A government that is fully respectful of the rights of individuals to live their lives as they wish (as long as they respect the rights of others to do likewise) would be neutral regarding the subjective preferences of its citizens. People who are more risk tolerant than others should have a right to exercise their preferences, and those who are less risk tolerant than others should have that same right. This reasonable premise has some striking policy implications because the present order is most definitely *not* neutral regarding environmental preferences.

Preference neutrality works well when it comes to the consumption of private goods, such as those regulated by the Federal Insecticide, Fungicide, and Rodenticide Act (FIFRA) and the Toxic Substances Control Act (TSCA). It does not work well, however, when it comes to the consumption of public environmental goods, which pose a far more difficult problem. Within the same city, for instance, one person cannot exercise his preference for cleaner air without infringing upon another's preference for air quality as it is at present. After all, nothing is free, and people vary (legitimately) in their willingness to trade off environmental goods and services for other goods and services.

A policy founded on preference neutrality requires that we do as little violence to minority preferences as possible. Since some majority will, of necessity, be imposing its preferences on some minority, the only way to provide safeguards for minority preferences is to require some sort of supermajority consensus before decisions about public goods are made.

Reform the Clean Air and Clean Water Acts

As noted earlier, within limits, there are no right or wrong air or water quality standards. Political leaders need not constantly war over those issues. Accepting public preferences for cleaner air and water—even without sufficient scientific justification—still leaves a great amount of room for productive reform.

The Problem with Command-and-Control Regulation

There is little reason for government to prescribe exactly how firms are to go about complying with pollution standards. Command-and-control regulations, which require regulators to determine exactly which technologies and what manufacturing methods are to be adopted for pollution control in every single facility in the nation, place on public officials informational requirements that are impossible to meet in the real world. This task is complicated by the fact that every air shed and watershed has different carrying capacities for different pollutants.

Individual plant managers have better incentives to discover the most efficient ways to control pollution at their facilities than do EPA technicians and consultants. That is the case, not only because those managers have more direct knowledge of their facilities and the technology of production, but because competition forces cost minimization, and even the most dedicated EPA official isn't going to lie awake nights searching for new solutions to pollution control problems.

Economist Tom Tietenberg reports that empirical studies show that "performance-based" standards—those that require regulators simply to decide how much pollution can be allowed from a facility and leave it to the facility to meet that standard in whatever way it desires—result in uniformly lower control costs. A 1990 joint Amoco-EPA study of a Yorktown, Virginia, oil refinery, for instance, found that federal environmental standards could be met at 20 percent of current costs if the refinery were allowed to adopt alternatives to EPA mandates.

The only real objection to performance-based regulation is that policing compliance is problematic. That's because regulatory flexibility requires credible monitoring data to ensure compliance. Yet comprehensive monitoring produces reams of data that are difficult for regulators to thoroughly assess. Monitoring can also be extremely expensive, which gives firms an additional incentive to circumvent the law. Environmentalists support the present command-and-control regime because technology-based standards are easier to police than are actual emissions.

Still, the excessive regulatory costs associated with technology-based standards and the rent-seeking mischief that naturally results from such regimes have persuaded most environmental economists that the economic gains promised by regulatory flexibility more than offset the increased difficulty of policing compliance. Experiments with such market-oriented reforms—for example, the sulfur emissions trading program instituted by the 1990 Clean Air Act amendments to address acid rain—have not resulted in any increase in regulatory noncompliance. The cost of beefing up the EPA compliance office is tiny compared with the gains produced by regulatory flexibility.

Provide for State Regulatory Waivers

Despite the well-known problems associated with command-and-control environmental regulation, it's unlikely that Congress will find the political capital necessary to reform thousands of pages of counterproductive rules and regulations found in more than a dozen sprawling environmental statutes, given the entrenched special interests that benefit politically and economically from their existence. Accordingly, Congress should take a page from the welfare reform experience and allow states to appeal for waivers from EPA in order to facilitate experiments in regulatory policy.

Case Western law professor Jonathan Adler proposes that Congress adopt a mechanism similar to section 160 of the 1996 Telecommunications Act to facilitate this reform. Section 160 allows telecommunication companies to submit a request for a regulatory waiver from the Federal Communications Commission. The FCC "shall forebear from applying any regulation or any provision" of the act to a company or class of service providers if the FCC determines upon review of the petition that

- "enforcement of such regulation or provision is not necessary" to ensure that rates "are just and reasonable and are not unreasonably discriminatory,"
- "enforcement of such regulation or provision is not necessary for the protection of consumers," or
- "forbearance from applying such provision or regulation is consistent with the public interest."

The FCC has one year to respond or the petition is deemed granted, and any decision to grant or deny forbearance is subject to judicial review under the Administrative Procedure Act.

Adapting a mechanism akin to section 160 of the 1996 Telecommunication Act to the environmental arena would mean allowing states to apply for forbearance from any standard or requirement administered by EPA. The state would be expected to submit supporting material detailing the basis for the request and explain why the waiver would serve the public interest. EPA would then provide public notice, seek comment from interested parties, and make a call one way or the other within one year pending judicial review under the aegis of the Administrative Procedure Act.

Some states may wish to experiment with market-oriented emissions trading programs or pollution taxes in lieu of the existing federally imposed command-and-control regimen. Other states might privatize some aspects of the environmental commons and allow civil courts to police accusations of pollution trespass. Others might adopt more limited performance-based regulatory reforms. A few states might even propose reallocation of regulatory efforts in order to concentrate on some relatively more important environmental issues instead of others. A policy of preference neutrality suggests tolerance regarding any such proposals.

Allowing "50 regulatory flowers to bloom" admittedly entails some degree of risk. Although some state experiments will likely bear economic and environmental fruit, others will probably fail to meet expectations. Such risks will certainly engender political opposition to the entire enterprise, but politicians should remember that useful innovations are virtually impossible without the risk of failure. In fact, the risks of failure underscore the value of decentralized policy experiments since localized policy failures would have far less damaging consequences than federal policy failures. Moreover, failed experiments provide useful information, cautioning reformers in other states about problems to avoid. Successful state experiments, on the other hand, could become models for reform elsewhere.

Repeal FIFRA and TSCA

A policy of preference neutrality would be most easily applicable to consumer preferences that do not directly affect the rights of others to exercise alternative preferences (so-called private goods). TSCA and FIFRA impose politically derived risk preferences (and their related costs) on individuals without respect for those who are more risk tolerant than the political majority. Accordingly, both statutes should be abolished.

Of course, some people argue that the cost of obtaining good risk information is too great. That's not altogether obvious (a plethora of private, third-party reporting organizations, such as Underwriters Laboratories, Consumer's Union, Green Seal, various kosher and halal food certification groups, the Better Business Bureau, and the Good Housekeeping Institute, are well-known and on the job today), and there are remedies available beyond the uniform imposition of politically derived risk tolerances. Mandatory labeling standards—perhaps accompanied by Food and Drug Administration advisories—would address the concern about this alleged market imperfection and do minimal violence to the marketplace and the rights of individual consumers (for a detailed discussion of this recommendation, see Chapter 39).

Repeal CERCLA

The Comprehensive Environmental Response, Compensation, and Liability Act (CERCLA), commonly known as "Superfund," addresses the potential risks posed by the past disposal of hazardous wastes. Most scientists and public health officials agree that the risks posed by sites not yet cleaned up under CERCLA are virtually nonexistent. Although those sites might pose a hazard if they were converted to different uses—say, if a school with a dirt playground were built on top of an old Superfund site—such concerns are easily addressed by not converting such sites to problematic uses.

In reality, CERCLA is an extremely expensive land reclamation project, dedicated to turning contaminated land, which at present poses little danger of harm to nearby residents, into land as pure and clean as the driven snow. Congress should acknowledge that some sites are simply not worth reclaiming; containment and isolation should be permitted as an alternative.

Accordingly, CERCLA should be abolished. Superfund sites and potential Superfund sites that have yet to be addressed should be privatized in a reverse Dutch auction in which government offers to *pay* potential bidders for assuming ownership of and responsibility for the land. The amount offered escalates until some private party is willing to accept the deal. Owners would then assume full liability for any future damage that might occur; that would set up the proper incentives for the private remediation or isolation of potentially dangerous environmental contaminants.

Repeal RCRA

The Resource Conservation and Recovery Act (RCRA) regulates the commercial use and disposal of potentially toxic chemicals primarily as a means of protecting groundwater aquifers from contamination. Yet RCRA is not necessary to remedy any traditional environmental market failure.

Groundwater aquifers are not a public good. Ownership is easily created through unitization, the same means employed by owners of oil wells to allocate property rights across geographically disperse fields. Owners of aquifers are quite capable of restricting consumption to people who pay for water and policing the integrity of their aquifers through the tort system.

But even if groundwater resources remain in government hands, there's little reason for such incredibly prescriptive and excessively costly regulations as the kind imposed by RCRA, a statute that stipulates detailed cradle-to-grave management standards for thousands of substances. Better to repeal RCRA and replace it with a minimal discharge standard. That is, prohibit significant discharges of pollutants (as defined by government) into groundwater and impose heavy fines and penalties—perhaps even shutdown orders—on firms discovered to be in violation of the standard.

A requirement that potential dischargers maintain special liability insurance further ensures that firms have strong incentives to minimize the chance of contamination (insurance companies would be reluctant to issue coverage to those whose practices put the insurance company at risk). Public groundwater monitoring costs would be borne by industry, preferably through a special tax levied on the purchase of liability coverage.

Privatize the Federal Lands

Fully 31 percent of all land in the United States—662 million acres—are owned by the federal government, and 95 percent of those acres are under the control of either the Department of the Interior or the Department of Agriculture. Those holdings are concentrated in 11 western states. For example, 88 percent of Nevada, 67 percent of Alaska, 68 percent of Utah, 63 percent of Idaho, 50 percent of California, 49 percent of Wyoming, and 48 percent of Oregon are owned by the federal government.

The federal government also owns a vast estate of commercially marketed resources: 50 percent of the nation's softwood timber, 12 percent of grazing lands, and 30 percent of all coal reserves. Approximately 30 percent of the nation's coal production; 6 to 7 percent of domestic gas and oil production; and 90 percent of copper, 80 percent of silver, and almost 100 percent of all nickel production are from federal lands.

That state of affairs is far more disturbing than most observers realize. First, as University of Colorado law professor Dale Oesterle observes, "The federal ownership of large amounts of land, much of it with significant commodity producing potential, puts the federal government at the core of our national market system, affecting the prices in nationally significant markets and myriad down-stream products." Indeed, the federal government owns a very large slice of the country's means of production, which fundamentally subverts the free-market system.

Second, the federal government is an extremely poor manager of resources. The cost of its grazing, timber, and water management programs greatly exceeds the commercial revenues. As virtually all ecologists concede, the federal government has been a horrible steward of environmental resources. Subsidies for both commercial and recreational industries have distorted markets (sometimes dramatically) and done great harm to the ecosystems of the western United States.

The most neutral way (from a wealth standpoint) to divest public lands is to recognize the implicit claims that different groups of citizens have on the federal estate. Lands at present devoted to the national parks and recreation would be simply given to nonprofit organizations representing such users. Lands now devoted to resource industries—such as the public grazing lands and forests traditionally devoted to timber operations—

would be given to present permit holders and users. Lands that are supporting mixed use or no use at all would be auctioned off over a set period of time. Every American would be issued an equal share of land scrip, which would be redeemable only in a public land auction. Individuals would be free to buy, sell, or donate their scrip as they pleased, but only the government-issued scrip would be accepted as currency during the land auction.

The virtue of this reform is that it minimizes conflict by accepting current political arrangements regarding public resource use, and it also allows those arrangements to change via postauction exchange. The benefits of privatization would be captured entirely by the American people.

End Subsidies for Resource Exploitation

The foremost engine of environmental destruction in America today is not the private sector but federal and state government. A great deal of environmental harm could be alleviated by eliminating the subsidized use of natural resources.

Five "Brownest" Programs in the Budget

- Agricultural subsidies are responsible for excessive pesticide, fungicide, and herbicide use with corresponding increases in non-point-source pollution.
- Sugar import quotas, tariffs, and price-support loans sustain a domestic sugar industry that might not otherwise exist; the destruction of the Everglades is the ecological result.
- Electricity subsidies via the power marketing administrations and the Tennessee Valley Authority artificially boost demand for energy and thereby are responsible for millions of tons of low-level radioactive waste and the disappearance of wild rivers in the West.
- Irrigation subsidies and socialized water services, which generally underwrite half of the cost of consumption, have done incalculable damage to western habitat while artificially promoting uneconomic agriculture with all the attendant environmental consequences. They also lead to tremendous overuse of water resources and worsen periodic shortages.
- Federal construction grant projects—such as the river maintenance, flood control, and agricultural reclamation undertakings of the Army Corps of Engineers—allow uneconomic projects to go forward and cause an array of serious environmental problems.

Repeal the Endangered Species Act

As Chapter 15 argues, compensating property owners for takings meant to secure public goods such as biological diversity is a simple matter of fairness and constitutional justice. But protecting property rights is also a necessary prerequisite for ecological protection. Property owners who expect to experience economic losses if their property is identified as ecologically important are tempted to destroy that habitat or species population before public officials become aware of its existence. Numerous analysts, from people at the National Wilderness Institute to ecological economist Randal O'Toole, conclude that the "shoot, shovel, and shut up" dynamic largely explains why the Endangered Species Act (ESA) has failed to either stabilize listed populations or return a single species to health.

The ESA, which prevents private property owners from making certain uses of their land in order to secure the "public good" of biological diversity, should thus be repealed since it provides no compensation to landowners for public takings. Instead, a federal biological trust should be established that would be funded out of general revenues at whatever level Congress found appropriate. The trust fund would be used to purchase conservation easements (in a voluntary and noncoercive fashion) from private landowners in order to protect the habitat of endangered species.

The virtue of such a reform is that landowners would have incentives rather than disincentives to protect species habitat. Moreover, the cost of biological preservation would become more transparent, which allows better-informed decisionmaking about the use of resources. Finally, such a reform would decriminalize the "ranching" of endangered species for commercial purposes. The ESA prohibits such practices out of a misguided belief that any commercial use of an endangered species inevitably contributes to its decline. Yet the experience of the African elephant and other threatened species belies that concern and strongly suggests that, if private parties are allowed to own and trade animals as commodities, commercial demand is a critical component of population protection.

Similarly, section 404 of the Clean Water Act—the provision that ostensibly empowers the EPA to regulate wetlands—should be repealed. Like the ESA, it takes private property out of otherwise inoffensive uses for a public purpose and provides disincentives for wetland conservation. Protection of wetlands habitat should be left to the federal biological trust fund.

The "Greenest" Political Agenda Is Economic Growth

There are a number of reasons why economic growth is perhaps the most important of all environmental policies. First, it takes a healthy, growing economy to afford the pollution control technologies necessitated by environmental protection. A poorer nation, for example, could scarcely have afforded the nearly $200 billion this nation has spent on sewage treatment plants over the past 30 years.

Second, growing consumer demand for environmental goods (parks; recreational facilities; land for hunting, fishing, and hiking; and urban air and water quality) is largely responsible for the improving quantity and quality of both public and private ecological resources. Virtually all analysts agree that, for the vast majority of consumers, environmental amenities are "luxury goods" that are in greatest demand in the wealthiest societies. Economic growth is thus indirectly responsible for improving environmental quality in that it creates the conditions necessary for increased demand for (and the corresponding increase in supply of) environmental quality.

Third, advances in technology, production methods, and manufacturing practices—both a cause and a consequence of economic growth—have historically resulted in less, not more, pollution. Even advances in nonenvironmental technologies and industries have indirectly resulted in more efficient resource consumption and less pollution.

Conclusion

Science can inform individual preferences but not resolve environmental conflicts. Environmental goods and services, to the greatest extent possible, should be treated like other goods and services in the marketplace. People should be free to secure their preferences about the consumption of environmental goods such as clean air or clean water regardless of whether some scientists think such preferences are legitimate or not. Likewise, people should be free, to the greatest extent possible, to make decisions consistent with their own risk tolerances regardless of scientific or even public opinion.

Policies that override individual preferences in favor of political preferences are incapable of pleasing a majority of people or resolving subjective disputes. No matter what environmental risk thresholds are set, only those at the political mean will be pleased. The best we can do when it comes to the governance of public goods is to establish mechanisms that allow people the right to secure their preferences to the greatest extent possible.

The way to efficiently accomplish that task is to establish markets that allow people to buy and sell the right to use what are now public resources. To whom those rights are initially distributed does not matter from an economic standpoint or from a philosophical standpoint because no one group has any better claim than another to exploit public goods. It does, however, matter from a wealth standpoint: some parties will win and some will lose depending on the method of divestiture chosen. The path of least political resistance is to acknowledge current resource use arrangements at the beginning of the reform process.

Suggested Readings

Adler, Jonathan. "Let Fifty Flowers Bloom: Transforming the States into Laboratories of Environmental Policy." Roundtable Paper Series, American Enterprise Institute Federalism Project, September 20, 2001.

Anderson, Terry, and Donald Leal. *Free Market Environmentalism: Revised Edition.* New York: Palgrave, 2001.

Anderson, Terry, et al. "How and Why to Privatize Federal Lands." Cato Institute Policy Analysis no. 363, December 9, 1999.

Beckerman, Wilfred. *Through Green-Colored Glasses: Environmentalism Reconsidered.* Washington: Cato Institute, 1996.

DeLong, James. *Out of Bounds, Out of Control: Regulatory Enforcement at the EPA.* Washington: Cato Institute, 2002.

————. "Privatizing Superfund: How to Clean Up Hazardous Waste." Cato Institute Policy Analysis no. 247, December 18, 1995.

Goklany, Indur. *Clearing the Air: The Real Story of the War on Air Pollution.* Washington: Cato Institute, 1999.

Stroup, Richard. *Eco-Nomics.* Washington: Cato Institute, 2003, forthcoming.

Tietenberg, Tom. *Environmental and Natural Resource Economics.* New York: Harper-Collins, 1992.

VanDoren, Peter. *Cancer, Chemicals, and Choices: Risk Reduction through Markets.* Washington: Cato Institute, 1999.

Yilmaz, Yesim. "Private Regulation: A Real Alternative for Regulatory Reform." Cato Institute Policy Analysis no. 303, April 20, 1998

—Prepared by Jerry Taylor

44. Environmental Health: Risks and Reality

Congress should

- take back the regulatory authority it has delegated to the Environmental Protection Agency;
- transfer responsibility for the safety of chemicals to industry;
- address the question, What is an acceptable level of risk?
- reexamine the acceptable risk level it set in the Food Quality Protection Act; and
- strip the EPA of its research functions.

Humans have always linked the environment to disease, and investigations of those links have led to important triumphs over infectious diseases. Investigations of possible links between chemicals in the environment and human diseases—cancer in particular—have been politically popular. They have also been costly and fruitless fiascoes. Congress faces a clear choice: It can continue funding the wasteful programs at the Environmental Protection Agency and elsewhere that are predicated on the belief that environmental chemicals are a health risk worth the expenditure of billions of dollars. Or it can find out, for itself and the public, what those programs accomplish and act on that information to restore some measure of sanity to environmental policy.

Triumph: The Environment and Infectious Diseases

Humans recognized that air and water harbored diseases long before there was any understanding of the mechanisms of disease transmission. The Italian *mala aria* ("bad air" or "miasma") came into English as "malaria." People learned to avoid damp places, but "bad air" wasn't to blame. The subsequent discovery that certain mosquitoes that breed in damp or wet places spread the microbes that cause the disease led to malaria control. In 1854 the physician John Snow determined that London residents who purchased water from a particular water company were likely to develop cholera. He inferred that a ''cholera poison'' was present in the water of the people who had become sick, and using water from other sources greatly reduced the incidence of cholera (the organism that causes cholera was not identified until 1883).

By mid-20th century, microorganisms—viruses, bacteria, amoebas, and so on—that are sometimes present in air, water, soil, and food had been identified as the causes of most diseases. Sanitation—the provision of clean drinking water and well-engineered sewage and waste disposal—along with immunization programs reduced the toll of diseases that had been the big killers of infants, children, and women in childbirth and had been responsible for more deaths in the world's soldiery than all the clubs, spears, bullets, bombs, and shells in history. Better surgery and medical care, especially the discovery and production of antibiotics, gave mankind the upper hand over formerly fatal or disabling traumatic injuries and infections.

To be sure, many diseases, although less common than before, persist, and the last few decades have seen some major unpleasant surprises such as AIDS and the emergence of antibiotic-resistant bacteria. By any measure, however, identification of disease agents that are transmitted through air, water, and soil has opened the door to controlling them.

Hubris and Political Expediency: Chemicals in the Environment and Cancer

The inevitable byproduct of control of infectious diseases was that more people lived to the ages at which they were likely to develop diseases that are common in the elderly. Nowhere was that clearer than in the soaring numbers of deaths caused by cancer. By the late 1960s, environmental activists, politicians, and scientists of various stripes loudly proclaimed that the country was caught in a terrifying and growing ''cancer epidemic'' and that chemicals in the environment were responsible.

The conjecture that environmental chemicals were causing cancer was based on two observations: workers in a few occupations, who had been exposed to very high concentrations of some chemicals, had increased risks of cancer, and greatly increased chemical production during and after World War II had resulted in more chemicals in the air, water, and soil. No causal link, however, was demonstrated between environmental chemicals and cancer.

The cry "The environment causes 90 [or 80 or 70] percent of cancer!" was frightening, but it carried a promise. Simply reducing exposures to environmental chemicals promised to eliminate much of the cancer that plagued the nation. The promise was very appealing to policymakers, who saw an opportunity to do something about a dreaded disease. The policies enacted when the promise shone brightest persist, and they need changing.

First of all, there was (and is) no cancer epidemic in the sense that the disease was (or is) becoming more common. As was well-known to scientists by 1981, the control of infectious diseases had resulted in more people reaching the ages at which cancer has always been common, but the frequency of cancer had not increased in any age group.

Even so, wasn't it possible that environmental chemicals were a major cause of cancer? The answer, again available in 1981, was no. At worst, chemical pollution of air, water, and soil was associated with 2 percent of cancers. In remarkable agreement, EPA scientists who examined the same question in 1986 estimated that chemical pollutants were associated with 1 to 3 percent of all cancers.

Before and during the time that science was deflating the myths of the "cancer epidemic" and the environmental causes of cancer, President Nixon established the EPA (in 1970) and Congress passed a number of laws (in the 1970s) that directed the EPA to regulate environmental chemicals that cause cancer. By 1981 there was no reason to expect that any action of the EPA could have much effect on cancer, but the agency, with congressional provision of funding, has established a great risk assessment enterprise.

EPA-funded scientists and, far more often, scientists who work for companies that must comply with EPA regulations, stuff laboratory rats and mice with near-lethal amounts of chemicals to see if the chemicals cause cancer. Regardless of the mismatch between the huge doses of chemicals administered to animals and human exposures, which are often thousands of times lower, risk assessors, again in accordance with EPA guidelines, estimate the cancer risk the chemicals pose to humans.

That procedure "identifies" plenty of carcinogens. About 50 percent of all tested chemicals, whether naturally occurring in fruits and vegetables and human metabolism or the products of the chemical industry, cause cancer in the tests. Although the EPA directs its attention to the synthetic chemicals because it can regulate those, exposures to naturally occurring carcinogens (as identified in animal tests) are far higher.

One of the foundations of the EPA's cancer risk assessments has been the assumption that any exposure to a carcinogenic chemical, no matter how small, increases the risk of cancer. As a result, one critical point of the EPA's policies has been the definition of an acceptable level of risk. The usual acceptable level is an estimated one additional cancer case in a million people.

It is unclear where the "one-in-a-million" number came from, and the suggestion that it's because no lover ever said, "you're one in a hundred thousand" seems as good as any. Whatever its origins, that level is a major determinant of the stringency, costs, and expected benefits of regulations. Regulatory costs are enormous and benefits are very uncertain and tiny, at best.

EPA regulations, most of them directed at carcinogens, cost about $8 million for each estimated year of life saved. That is 400 times more expensive than medical care, which saves a year of life for less than $20,000, on average. Although the Office of Management and Budget values a human life at $5.5 million, the EPA's regulations require the expenditure of about 1.5 times as much money to save one estimated year of life. Whether EPA regulations save anything at all is far from clear. Most EPA risk estimates are based on animal tests, and, to its credit, the EPA acknowledges that those tests may be completely misleading about human risk, in which case, human risk may be zero. If the risk is zero, spending a dollar to reduce it is a complete waste.

But haven't there been benefits? Experts on the causes, prevention, and treatment of cancer have provided the clearest answer. If there are any benefits, they are so tiny that they cannot be seen or measured. University and federal scientists have verified that the rates of new cancer cases and cancer deaths have been falling since about 1990 because of decreased smoking, increased standards of living, and, probably, better diets. Mortality has fallen because of improvements in diagnosis and treatment. Nowhere in the analysis of the decreases is there mention of environmental chemicals or their regulation.

The EPA can claim no successes in terms of lives saved or diseases prevented. It has produced no breakthroughs in understanding the causes and prevention of disease. It has reaped constantly increased funding and imposed huge and increasing regulatory costs by claiming it is protecting public health. It is not.

More Hubris and Political Expedience: Noncancer Health Risks from the Environment

Carcinogens are losing their regulatory luster. The announcement that chemical after chemical is a carcinogen has engendered a fatalistic "everything causes cancer'' attitude among the public. Many scientists question the value of the standard ''stuff the rat full of the chemical'' cancer test and the extrapolation of results from that test to predictions of human effects. Even worse for the EPA, an editorial, ''Our Contribution to the Public Fear of Cancer,'' in a magazine published by the National Institutes of Health reflects increasing disenchantment with the idea that regulation can affect cancer. ''A current view is that given a safe workplace, the remaining risk factors (sunlight, diet, smoking) are, for the most part, under our individual control.''

As the promise of regulatory control of cancer dims, other health risks are being propped up. ''Environmental estrogens''—a widely diverse group of chemicals that are blamed for adverse effects on reproduction, sexual development, and school performance; increasing hyperactivity in children; and just about every other malady in humans and animals—are the current favorite of environmental activists and regulatory agencies.

The diversity of the chemicals and the diversity of the purported effects are a gold mine for environmental activists and regulators. Accusing Chemical C of causing Effect E can cause the manufacturer or user or disposer of Chemical C to run tests to see if it really does. If, in fact, there is no evidence for any increase in Effect E, it's a simple thing to make a new accusation and blame Chemical C for causing Effect EE. The testing and risk assessment enterprise that was erected to feed the EPA's cancer regulation effort will be a tiny thing indeed compared with the one that will be necessary to chase every effect blamed on environmental estrogens.

Children are the other great shining hope for environmental activists and regulators. Surely children are at more risk than adults from whatever dangers lurk in the environment. After all, they eat more and drink more and breathe more in proportion to their body weight than do adults. Of course, the risks from many (probably most) environmental exposures are zero for adults, and they would be zero for children. But the emotional appeal of protecting children is a strong selling point for increasing regulations.

Environmental estrogens and risks to children came together in Congress's hasty passage of the Food Quality Protection Act (FQPA) in 1996. The new law imposes sweeping new testing requirements on manufacturers of pesticides and other chemicals that might end up in the food supply, no matter how trivial the amount, and it decreases the permitted exposures to such chemicals because the lower exposures are deemed necessary to protect children. Nowhere is there evidence that current levels of those chemicals in food are causing adverse effects in children, but the new testing and regulatory requirements may drive a major proportion of pesticides off the market.

An unintentional consequence of the disappearance of pesticides will be an increase in food prices, especially for fresh fruits and vegetables. As prices increase, consumption of fresh fruits and vegetables will decline. The National Cancer Institute says that eating five or more fresh fruits or vegetables every day reduces the risk of cancer. Some people will be priced out of that cancer prevention activity.

There is no limit to the risks that can be associated with chemicals in the environment. Risks can be manufactured out of, literally, thin air, and they find ready acceptance in the media and Congress and give rise to cries that the government should do something about them. Draconian steps such as banning a chemical are relatively rare. Flawed as it is, the regulatory process has checks and balances that allow commercial interests to oppose regulations. It's far easier for Congress to impose additional testing requirements as it did in FQPA. The tests take time, cost great amounts of money, heighten public awareness that "chemicals are bad," and divert attention from other activities that might improve health. They will not improve health, and they may make it worse by increasing the cost of food and other necessities.

Congressional Actions

The treadmill of pointing to potential environmental health risks, testing to see if the risks exist, extrapolating from the test results to expected effects on human health, and imposing more regulations and tests on the producers and consumers in the economy will continue until Congress asserts its responsibility and authority. That assertion can take several forms.

Congress Should Take Back the Regulatory Authority It Has Delegated to the EPA

Congress can eliminate the EPA and return its responsibilities to the agencies and states from which they were taken, but Congress is unlikely to do so. Short of that, Congress can impose its authority on the EPA and make the agency accountable to elected officials.

David Schoenbrod has described the process by which Congress delegates its legislative authority to executive branch agencies when it authorizes them to make regulations. To restore congressional responsibility in accord with the Constitution, he proposes executive branch agencies be required to submit a proposed regulation to an up-or-down vote in Congress before it can be promulgated. See Chapter 8 for a more complete discussion.

The Congressional Review Act approaches this problem by providing for congressional review of a regulation after it has been promulgated. As was vividly demonstrated by congressional response to the EPA's 1997 regulations under the Clean Air Act, the Congressional Review Act is toothless. By the time a regulation is promulgated, the administration, including the president, has signed off on it. Having committed himself to the regulation, the president can be expected to veto a congressional vote against the regulation, and he can expect members of his party to support the veto, and a two-thirds congressional vote to override the veto is unlikely.

Schoenbrod's proposal would require only a simple majority in Congress to stop a regulation. Adoption of his proposal would make Congress responsible for regulations, and make members of Congress responsible to the voters for regulations.

Congress Should Transfer Responsibility for the Safety of Chemicals to Industry

See Chapter 39 on third-party certification.

Congress Should Address the Question, What Is an Acceptable Level of Risk?

Congress should decide on the level of risk (or the range of levels) that is acceptable. It should immediately throw out the one-in-a-million risk number that the EPA has adopted as the dividing line between acceptable and unacceptable cancer risks and tell the EPA not to rely on it anymore.

Congress should then decide on an acceptable risk number based on real-world risks. For instance, the risk of a white-collar worker's dying from a job-related accident or from a job-related disease appears to be an acceptable risk—no one receives hazard pay for such a job, and insurance companies don't increase premiums to cover those risks. A risk of equal magnitude or 1/2 or 1/10 of some other fraction of that number might be set as acceptable. Congress can commission studies by executive branch agencies and independent organizations to produce estimates of and justifications for acceptable risks for exposures to carcinogens, hold hearings

459

to consider the suggested numbers, and decide on an acceptable number or range of numbers.

Congress Should Reexamine the Acceptable Risk Level It Set in the Food Quality Protection Act

Six years have passed since Congress passed and the president signed the FQPA, and its provisions are already driving a large number of pesticides off the market. The EPA, trade associations, agricultural organizations, and consumer and environmental groups are all involved in trying to implement the new law. While those efforts go ahead, there has been no attempt by Congress to understand (1) if the new provisions are necessary and (2) what the effects of those provisions will be on food production, distribution, and costs.

Congress should debate those questions. Unless it does, regulations based on the hastily passed FQPA will be promulgated, and the acceptable risk number for noncancer health risks that is incorporated in them will spread throughout the government. Health will not be improved, but costs—and prices of food and other commodities—will increase.

Congress Should Strip the EPA of Its Research Functions

Congress has ample evidence that the EPA cannot manage good scientific research, and Congress should strip the agency of any research capability and funding. Instead of good science, the EPA practices a form of political science that provides justification for the agency's regulatory agenda. In 1992 a committee of scientists who examined the EPA's research reached the following conclusions, among others:

- "EPA has not always ensured that contrasting, reputable scientific views are well-explored and well-documented. . . . [EPA's] legal process fosters the presentation of the extremes of scientific opinion."
- "EPA science is *perceived* by many people, both inside and outside the Agency, to be adjusted to fit policy [emphasis in original]."
- "Scientists at all levels throughout EPA believe the Agency does not use their science effectively."

In 1998 U.S. District Court Judge Thomas Osteen ruled that the EPA had wrongly declared secondhand smoke a human carcinogen and blasted the EPA's 1993 risk assessment about secondhand smoke. He said the EPA had "adjusted established procedure and scientific norms to validate the Agency's public conclusion . . . disregarded information and made findings on selective information; . . . failed to disclose important findings and reasoning; and left significant questions without answers.'' Even more bluntly, ''There is evidence in the record supporting the accusation that EPA 'cherry picked' its data.''

The EPA has demonstrated that it cannot collect and evaluate scientific data about environmental health risks honestly. Recognizing that fact, Congress needs to designate other organizations to collect and analyze the data. Or, if Congress elects to allow manufacturers to self-certify the safety of their products or to allow them to contract with third-party organizations for certification, Congress can place the costs and responsibilities for chemical safety on the organizations that will most benefit from ensuring the safety of chemicals in the environment.

Recommended Readings

Adams, John. ''Cars, Cholera, and Cows: The Management of Risk and Uncertainty.'' Cato Institute Policy Analysis no. 335, March 4, 1999.

Ames, Bruce. ''The Causes and Prevention of Cancer: Do Federal Regulations Help?'' Washington: Marshall Institute, March 28, 2002.

DeGregori, Thomas. *Bountiful Harvest: Technology, Food Safety, and the Environment.* Washington: Cato Institute, 2002.

Gough, Michael, and Steve Milloy. ''EPA's Cancer Risk Guidelines: Guidance to Nowhere.'' Cato Institute Policy Analysis no. 263, November 12, 1996.

Milloy, Steve. *Junk Science Judo.* Washington: Cato Institute, 2001.

Powell, Mark. *Science at EPA: Information in the Regulatory Process.* Washington: Resources for the Future, 1999.

VanDoren, Peter. *Chemicals, Cancer, and Choices.* Washington: Cato Institute, 1999.

—Prepared by Michael Gough

45. Global Warming

> **Congress should** vote on the ratification of the Kyoto Protocol on global warming, which requires a two-thirds majority in the Senate.

Background

The United Nations Framework Convention on Climate Change (FCCC) and the subsequent Kyoto Protocol require the United States to reduce the net emissions of carbon dioxide and other important greenhouse gases to 7 percent below 1990 levels, on average, for the five-year period beginning in 2008. The Framework Convention and the protocol are based on a naive interpretation of a science that now views reductions in carbon dioxide as a very inefficient way to influence climate change. As a result, the economic costs of the convention and protocol are enormous, and the benefits are undetectable. Even if all the world's nations met their commitments under the Kyoto Protocol, there would be no discernible effect on the globe's climate.

The Framework Convention was signed by the United States at the Rio de Janeiro Earth Summit in 1992. As originally conceived, the purpose of the convention was "to prevent dangerous human interference in the climate system." The original goal was to reduce emissions of carbon dioxide, the principal human "greenhouse" gas, to 1990 levels by the year 2000. Only two nations have met that goal, and they have done so because of historic changes unrelated to environmental concerns. In 1990 the reunification of Germany resulted in the absorption of the wildly polluting East, whose economic inefficiency was so great that much of its industry was simply shut down. Great Britain met the target because of privatization of the coal industry.

Carbon dioxide emissions in the United States have risen approximately 15 percent since 1990. But at Kyoto in December 1997 the Clinton

463

administration, under the leadership of Vice President Al Gore, agreed to a protocol to the FCCC that requires us to reduce our emissions 7 percent below 1990 levels over the averaging period, 2008–12. Because of recent increases in emissions, this constitutes a reduction of between 30 and 40 percent (depending on whether the increase since 1990 is assumed to be exponential or merely linear) beneath where they would be under a "business as usual" scenario. That "business as usual" has resulted in one of the greatest explosions in wealth creation in the history of the world.

As shown in the balance of this chapter, while global warming is likely to be modest, the Kyoto Protocol will have no detectable effect on that warming. These two arguments compelled the Bush administration to abandon the protocol. It is now up to the Senate to complete this work by voting on ratification, which requires a two-thirds majority.

The protocol currently enjoys very little support in the Senate, and in all likelihood it will fail to achieve the votes necessary for ratification by a large margin. There are several reasons for this lack of support: scientific, economic, and political. The ultimate elimination of the Kyoto Protocol will remove one of the greatest obstacles to technological progress on climate change and should result in a rational reexamination of the issue and, perhaps, an international agreement more grounded in facts than the current protocol.

Members of Congress should note that calls for dramatic emissions reductions are usually accompanied by lurid rhetoric about weather and climate disasters. The purpose of this chapter is to provide the facts that counter such emotional appeals.

No credible argument counters the notion that the planetary average surface temperature is warmer than it was 100 years ago. But what does that warming mean? If that warming were in the coldest air of winter, rather than in the heat of summer, the overall effect would clearly change from bad to good. Although most mathematical simulations of climate predict an overall increase in precipitation, is more precipitation really a bad thing? If there were a sudden and dramatic increase in the frequency of severe floods with no concomitant positive effects, then obviously the answer would be that global warming is a terrible disaster. But what if gentle spring rains increase while the severity of hurricanes declines?

Figure 45.1 details the surface temperature history of the Northern Hemisphere, 1900–2001. (Southern Hemisphere records are not as reliable because of the paucity of coverage over the vast Southern Ocean and Antarctica.) There are two distinct warmings of similar magnitude. The

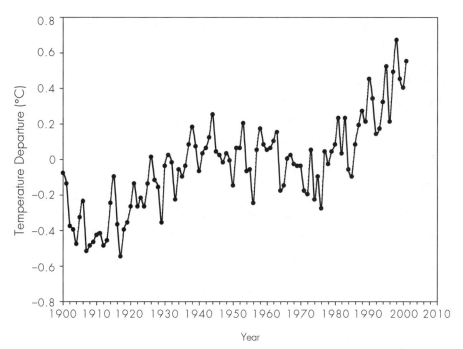

Figure 45.1
Northern Hemisphere annual temperature history, 1900–2001.

first occurred from 1910 to 1940 and likely had little if anything to do with changes in the earth's greenhouse effect, as three-quarters of the greenhouse emissions occurred in the postwar era. Federal scientists Judith Lean and David Rind and Harvard astrophysicist Sallie Baliunas argue persuasively that this early warming is largely a result of solar changes.

Warming Occurs Primarily in the Winter, Not the Summer

The Largest Warming Is in the Coldest, Deadliest Airmasses

The second warming, which began about 35 years ago, is much more interesting. Greenhouse-effect physics predicts that human-induced climate change should take place more in the winter than in the summer, and that it should further be concentrated in the coldest air of winter. The propensity for greenhouse warming to occur in frigid dry air has enormous implications that have largely been ignored in the raucous debate about climate change.

In fact, observed warming since World War II is twice as large in winter as it is in summer. In the winter, three-quarters of the total warming

465

is confined to the frigid airmasses that reside in Siberia and northwestern North America.

Summer warming has been, predictably, much less than winter warming. Less than one-third of the observed warming of the second half of the 20th century occurred in the summer, while two-thirds occurred in the winter.

An individual living in Siberia or northwestern North America has, for the last 50 years, experienced a winter half-year warming of nearly 1.1 degree Celsius. Cold airmasses that originate in these regions, on the "edges" of winter (April and October), are usually responsible for the last freeze in the spring and the first freeze in the fall in temperate latitudes. Reducing the inherent coldness lengthens the growing season. There are several lines of evidence in the scientific literature indicating that this is occurring.

Temperature Variability Is Declining, Not Increasing

One of the common arguments for emissions reductions is the notion that the weather has become more variable. The opposite is true.

Economic and ecological systems are adapted to both average conditions and expected variation. So, as the temperature warms, do annual and seasonal temperature swings become more erratic? In the last century, some years were warm and some cold. This natural variability allows us to examine whether the seasonal and monthly variability in those years is different from the variability in years with near-mean temperatures.

Figure 45.2 shows monthly variability in the last 100 years. Before 1940 (including the warming of 1910–40), there was little change. In the last third of the 20th century, there was a considerable decline. In other words, as the greenhouse enhancement has warmed the extremely cold air of Siberia and northwestern North America, the within-year variability has dropped. There is no evidence that the fluctuations in the earth's temperatures are greater now than they were at the beginning of the 20th century. Conversely, most evidence suggests that temperature has become less variable.

Precipitation, Droughts, and Floods Show No Ominous Changes

The standard measure of drought is known as the Palmer Drought Severity Index. Figure 45.3 shows the percentage of the lower 48 U.S. states experiencing severe Palmer drought back to the beginning of the record in 1895. Clearly, there is no overall trend; what's more, the drought

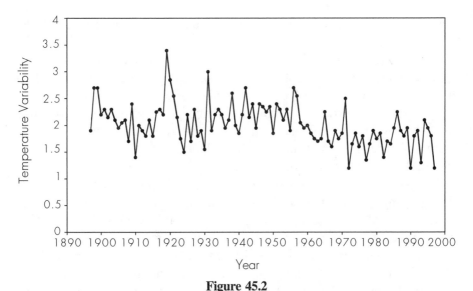

Figure 45.2
Intra-annual global temperature variability. Temperature variability has been declining
since greenhouse warming began.

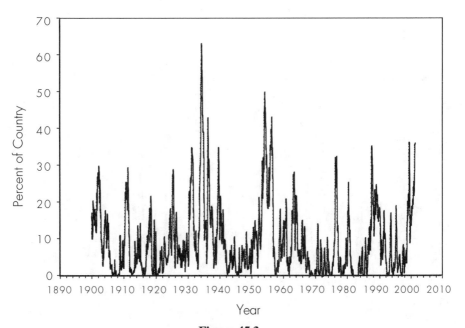

Figure 45.3
The percentage of the United States experiencing severe or extreme drought
conditions fluctuates from year to year but shows no long-term trend.

periods in the 1930s and 1950s dwarf anything we saw in the last quarter of the 20th century.

What about rainfall? The Palmer Index measures wetness as well as drought. Here we do see a slight but statistically significant increase. This is clearly a net benefit of climate change. Every summer most of the United States experiences a moisture deficit, as solar-driven evaporation dries the soil at a greater rate than rainfall can replenish moisture. So any increase in precipitation is likely to be welcomed by American agriculture. Figure 45.4 demonstrates this increase.

Even this salutary trend has been twisted in the service of climate doomsaying. In August 2002, Maryland governor Parris Glendening blamed the region's severe drought on global warming. In fact, U.S. precipitation has increased by about 10 percent in the last 100 years, or roughly three inches. Some scientists attribute that to other atmospheric changes accompanying warming. For warming to have increased the frequency of drought, then, this additional increment of rainfall, plus another large amount sufficient to provoke a major drought, must somehow be evaporated away by higher temperatures. This is simply not the case: The average change in U.S. temperature in the last 100 years has been a mere

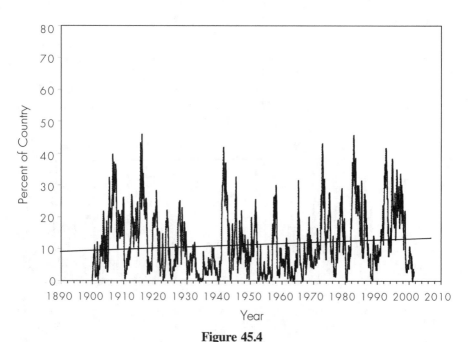

Figure 45.4
The percentage of the United States that is substantially wet shows a statistically significant increase. This is largely beneficial for American agriculture.

0.4°C, which increases evaporation a mere half-inch or so. So, if anything, global warming has added about 2.5 inches of water per year to U.S. soil.

We often hear that flooding rains are increasing from global warming. This originates from a study of U.S. rainfall by federal climatologist Tom Karl, who found that there is an increasing fraction of U.S. rainfall coming from storms of more than two inches per day.

The environmental lobby has seized upon this fact without actual analysis of the results. What Karl found is that the majority of the increase is in storms of between two and three inches per day. Those are not floods. With regard to storms capable of significant flooding, those producing five or more inches of rainfall a day, the increase is so slight as to be meaningless. On the average, a person will now experience two more days in his entire expected life span of 27,350 days in which it rains five or more inches.

Another way to look for precipitation extremes is to examine streamflow data in undammed basins. In 1999 U.S. Geological Survey scientist Harry Lins published a paper showing no increase in the frequency of flooding streamflow but a decrease in the frequency of the lowest (drought) flow categories. That is to say, streamflow records indicate decreased drought and no change in floods over the long historical perspective.

There Is No Increase in the Frequency or Severity of Hurricanes

The notion that global warming is making the most destructive storms worse or more frequent is one of the most compelling appeals for greenhouse emission reductions. It has absolutely no basis in fact.

Figure 45.5 shows the number of hurricanes striking the United States per decade. It is obvious that, if anything, recent decades are notable for their lack of storms. Of even more interest is the fact that the maximum wind velocity measured in Atlantic and Caribbean Basin storms has actually declined significantly in the last 50 years, as shown in data published by the United Nations Intergovernmental Panel on Climate Change (IPCC) (Figure 45.6).

Heat-Related Mortality Is Declining, Not Increasing

The popular perception is that heat-related deaths have increased, and will continue to increase, with global warming. The IPCC says, "[Based upon data from several North American cities], the annual number of heat-related deaths would approximately double by 2020 and would increase several fold by 2050."

Research shows that this is just plain wrong. Figure 45.7 shows the relation of death rates in Philadelphia, a typical urban core, to "effective

469

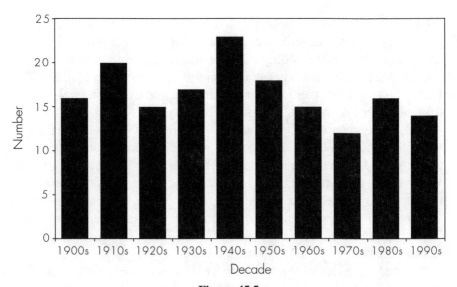

Figure 45.5
Number of hurricanes striking the United States per decade. If anything, recent
decades have had fewer storms than average.

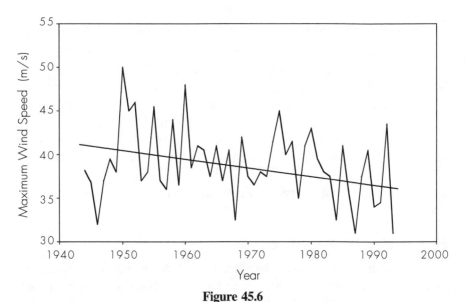

Figure 45.6
Maximum winds measured by aircraft in Atlantic and Caribbean storms show a
statistically significant decline (IPCC 1996), despite stories of increased severity.

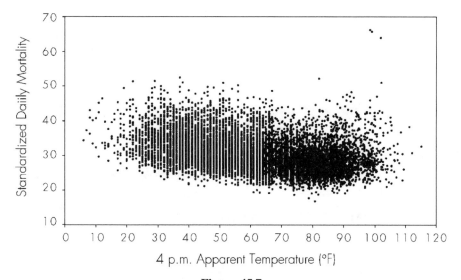

Figure 45.7
In Philadelphia, typical of most American cities, the daily mortality generally
decreases with temperature, with the exception of the very hottest days.

temperature,'' which is the combination of heat and humidity that makes
people uncomfortable. In general, heat-related deaths *decline* with effective
temperature, although there are a few days that show remarkable death
excursions at high temperature—the few dots that can be seen in the upper
right portion of the graph. These are death excursions similar to those of
Chicago's July 1995 heat wave, which was responsible for several hundred
excess deaths.

But, as Figure 45.8 shows, as we progressed through the last half of
the 20th century, the increase in the number of people who died at high
temperatures declined to near-zero values. This is a result of increased
use of air conditioning, effective medical care, and public education about
the dangers of excessive heat. In other words, over time, the same technology that slightly raises the surface temperature (fossil-fuel-driven electricity
production) saves lives. Proposals to make energy more expensive as a
means of fighting climate change will have the perverse effect of killing
those who can least afford expensive electricity, resulting in a return to
the heat-related death patterns of the past.

Future Warming Is Likely to Be Modest in Scale

By now, dozens of different computer simulations that estimate future
warming have been executed. How do we decide which, if any, is likely
to be correct?

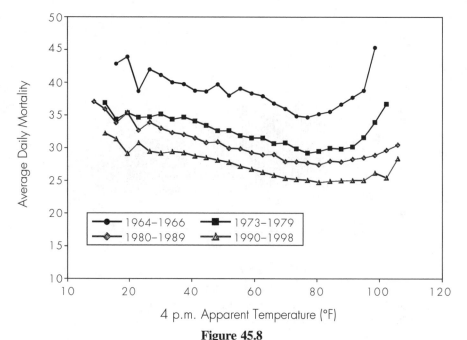

Figure 45.8

In a northern city, such as Philadelphia, where extremely hot conditions occur less frequently than in the South, the population exhibits a higher mortality rate on hot days. However, over time, the sensitivity of the population of Philadelphia to high temperatures has been declining.

The key to the future lies in the rather extended period during which humans have already altered the natural greenhouse effect—roughly from the start of the Industrial Revolution in the late 19th century to the present. The concentration of atmospheric carbon dioxide—the main greenhouse emission resulting from human activity—varied from 260 to 320 parts per million (ppm) between the end of the glacial stage, 10,800 years ago, and the Industrial Revolution. The average value during that period was near the low end of that range, about 280 ppm. The current concentration is 365 ppm, about a 30 percent increase.

But there are other emissions that increase the atmosphere's natural greenhouse effect. Methane emissions, for example, contribute a warming of another 20 percent beyond the enhanced carbon dioxide greenhouse effect. Another 15 percent increase comes from chlorofluorocarbons (CFCs), refrigerants whose atmospheric concentrations have yet to decline much, despite the Montreal Protocol against their manufacture because they might reduce stratospheric ozone. A host of other anthropogenic emissions contributes much smaller additional increments. When all is said and done, in toto the emissions produce a "carbon dioxide equivalent" concentration that is about 60 percent above the background levels recorded prior to the Industrial Revolution.

Nearly 20 years ago, a few climate scientists noted that the planet had not warmed as much as would be expected from early computer simulations of greenhouse warming. By 1996 the IPCC acknowledged that that observation had become the consensus of the broad scientific constituency. Although it has been fashionable to try to "explain" the lack of warming by the presence of sulfate aerosols, a product of combustion that was thought to cool the surface, that explanation has never withstood simple tests. The alternative explanation put forth by the IPCC is that the sensitivity of surface temperature was simply overestimated.

Evidence leads us to conclude that the warming we saw in the last third of the 20th century was largely from greenhouse changes. It is very linear (constant in rate) at about 0.15°C per decade at the surface. A small solar component is calculated to be around 0.02°C per decade. That leaves us with about 0.13°C per decade as a human greenhouse signal.

Figure 45.9 shows the warming since 1960 as well as output from a large suite of climate forecast models. The models' forecasts are also all

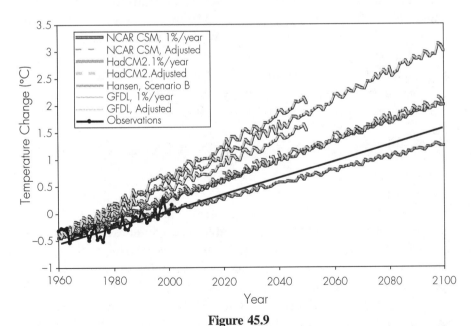

Figure 45.9
Observed warming of the last 35 years superimposed on typical climate model projections. The observed linear trend is near the lowest value that the climate models predict and considerably below the mean projected warming.

linear, but note that they differ in the slope of their projected warming. These differences result from internal model dynamics and assumptions, including the rate of increase of greenhouse changes. For example, the rate of greenhouse increase has been running at about 75 percent of the UN's "central" estimate for decades. Most computer models assume an even larger value than the UN's already high figure; indeed, several researchers have recently demonstrated that the true value is a mere 45 percent of the modeled assumption.

Nonetheless, with few exceptions, all the climate models predict warmings over the next century that are essentially linear. It seems logical to now let nature adjudicate what the proper rate for warming is; this is also shown in Figure 45.9. By the middle of this century, we are left with an additional surface warming of 0.65°C to 0.75°C, with 0.75°C to 0.85°C in the winter half year and 0.60°C to 0.65°C in the summer.

Interestingly, these 50-year figures are quite similar to the warming that occurred during the late 20th century.

What have we to show for a century of warming? In 1900 life expectancy at birth in the United States was 42 years. After 100 years of global warming, it was exactly twice that number, 84 years. Urban infrastructure in the United States has adapted so well to both average and warmed climates that heat-related deaths are disappearing. After a global warming of 0.6°C, U.S. crop yields quintupled. World food production per capita has increased by nearly 50 percent in the last half century. An untold story is that carbon dioxide itself makes most crops grow better: by the year 2050 that direct stimulation of planetary greening will feed an increment of 1.5 billion people the equivalent of today's diet.

The Kyoto Protocol Does Nothing about Global Warming

No known mechanism can stop global warming in the near term. International agreements, such as the Kyoto Protocol to the United Nations Framework Convention on Climate Change, will have no detectable effect on average temperature within any reasonable policy time frame of 50 years or so—even with full compliance. Climate modelers at the U.S. National Center for Atmospheric Research calculate that full compliance with the Kyoto Protocol by all signatory nations would reduce global surface temperature by 0.07°C by 2050, and 0.14°C by 2100. Congress should note the dangers of an expensive environmental accord with no benefit. The Senate should consider the Kyoto Protocol for ratification, with the resultant negative vote paving the way for more rational environmental regulation.

Recently, National Aeronautics and Space Administration scientist James Hansen, whose 1988 congressional testimony started the global warming furor, wrote that reducing carbon dioxide is a highly ineffective means of slowing global warming in the 50-year time horizon. Rather, he argues, concentrating on the other greenhouse gases, such as CFCs and methane (which has stopped increasing in the atmosphere for only partially known reasons), is much more effective and politically acceptable than the costly Kyoto Protocol, which, he wrote, "cast the developed and developing worlds as adversaries." Hansen is clearly stating that the Kyoto Protocol is scientifically ill-advised.

Rather, the more serious question the facts on global warming provoke is this: Is the way the planet warms something that we should even try to stop?

Suggested Readings

Balling, R. C. Jr., P. J. Michaels, and P. C. Knappenberger. "Analysis of Winter and Summer Warming Rates in Gridded Temperature Time Series." *Climate Research* 9 (1988): 175–81.

Davis, R. E., et al. "Decadal Changes in Summer Mortality in the United States." *Proceedings of the 12th Conference on Applied Climatology*, Asheville, N.C., 2000, pp. 184–87.

Hansen, J. E., et al. "A Common-Sense Climate Index: Is Our Climate Changing Noticeably?" *Proceedings of the National Academy of Sciences* 95 (2000): 4113–20.

———. "Global Warming in the Twenty-First Century: An Alternative Scenario." *Proceedings of the National Academy of Sciences* (2000), www.pnas.org.

Intergovernmental Panel on Climate Change. *Climate Change 1995: The Science of Climate Change: Contribution of Working Group I to the Second Assessment Report of the Intergovernmental Panel on Climate Change.* Edited by J. T. Houghton et al. Cambridge: Cambridge University Press, 1996.

Karl, T. R., R. W. Knight, and N. Plummer. "Trends in High-Frequency Climate Variability in the Twentieth Century." *Nature* 377 (1995): 217–20.

Lean, J., and D. Rind. "Climate Forcing by Changing Solar Radiation." *Journal of Climate* 11 (1998): 3069–94.

Lins, H. F., and J. R. Slack. "Streamflow Trends in the United States." *Geophysical Research Letters* 26 (1999): 277–330.

Michaels, P. J. "The Consequences of Kyoto." Cato Institute Policy Analysis no. 307, May 7, 1998.

———. "Long Hot Year: Latest Science Debunks Global Warming Hysteria." Cato Institute Policy Analysis no. 329, December 31, 1998.

Michaels, P. J., and R. C. Balling Jr. *The Satanic Gases.* Washington: Cato Institute, 2000.

Michaels, P. J., et al. "Analysis of Trends in the Variability of Daily and Monthly Historical Temperature Measurements." *Climate Research* 10 (1998): 27–33.

———. "Observed Warming in Cold Anticyclones." *Climate Research* 14 (2000): 1–6.

Wittwer, S. H. *Food, Climate, and Carbon Dioxide.* Boca Raton, Fla.: CRC Press, 1995.

—Prepared by Patrick J. Michaels

475

46. Department of Energy

Congress should

- eliminate the U.S. Department of Energy;
- transfer the National Nuclear Security Administration (NNSA), which is responsible for managing the DOE's nuclear-industrial complex, to the Department of Defense;
- renegotiate the DOE's nuclear weapons cleanup programs to reflect prioritization of containment and neutralization of risk rather than removal and return of sites to pristine conditions and transfer cleanup responsibilities to the NNSA;
- privatize all laboratories, except two of the three weapons laboratories, managed by the DOE;
- eliminate all research and development programs overseen by the DOE and replace them with a robust R&D tax credit;
- sell the assets held by the power marketing administrations to the highest bidders;
- sell the Strategic Petroleum Reserve; and
- spin off the Federal Energy Regulatory Commission, the Energy Information Administration, and the Office of Civilian Radioactive Waste Management (which is responsible for regulating the long-term disposal of high-level nuclear waste) as independent agencies within the executive branch.

The Department of Energy is a large department by any measure. It has a budget of $21.3 billion per year. Approximately 115,000 workers are employed in 35 states at the DOE's national laboratories, cleanup sites, and other facilities. Notwithstanding its name, the DOE's primary role is that of caretaker of America's nuclear-industrial complex. Nearly three-quarters of the department's budget is devoted to nuclear weapons safety and nuclear cleanup activities.

The DOE is a 1970s' dinosaur that has outlived its usefulness. Energy production, distribution, and consumption are better directed by market forces than by government planners and bureaucrats. Likewise, weapons maintenance and related nuclear activities are better directed by Defense than by Energy personnel. There is no more reason for a department of energy than for a department of automobiles.

First, Eliminate the Department

Even if few of the actual functions of the DOE were eliminated, eliminating the department and transferring its programs to other agencies would be a worthwhile undertaking. Maintaining a cabinet-level energy department is risky because it provides a ready structure for the reintroduction of direct federal interventions in the energy market—a perfect command post from which some future "Energy Czar" could once again punish energy producers and consumers in the event of some temporary energy "emergency." Elimination of the DOE would make it difficult for government to launch any future interventions in the energy marketplace.

Moreover, the DOE is demonstrably the most bureaucratically dysfunctional agency in government. Its inability to provide even the most basic security for our nuclear secrets is well-known. Its ability to protect workers and communities around its nuclear weapons facilities—such as those in Paducah, Kentucky—is seriously in doubt. Those problems, however, are simply well-publicized manifestations of a deeper problem: the department's inability to competently supervise the activities of the contractors who manage and operate its facilities and programs.

That failure is important because fully 90 percent of the department's budget is spent on contracts with third parties whose competence and integrity have been placed seriously in doubt by report after report and scandal after scandal. Despite repeated warnings by the U.S. General Accounting Office that the department's management and supervision of contractors have been ridiculously lax and grossly incompetent, the problems continue with no institutional remedy in sight.

There are two commonly marshaled rationales for the DOE: first, that the department is needed to discourage and ameliorate the occasional energy market dislocations that harm consumers and, second, that the department is needed to secure America's "energy independence" from OPEC. Both rationales are intellectually threadbare.

The occasional energy dislocations of the past two decades underscore the fact that the DOE is incapable of "smoothing out" the rough edges of world oil markets. It is an economic fact of life that small changes in global oil supply or demand have very large effects on prices in the short term. That leads to large transfers of wealth from consumers to firms in times of supply decreases and from firms to consumers in times of supply increases. There is absolutely nothing that the DOE can do about that. When the federal government *has* tried to shelter consumers from short-term price spikes (primarily by imposing price controls, instituting rationing, and levying windfall profit taxes), energy markets have been even further distorted and consumer welfare has gone from bad to worse.

Other energy markets of concern—primarily gasoline markets and electricity markets—are largely beyond the reach of the DOE. Antitrust law polices the former, and the independent Federal Energy Regulatory Commission somewhat polices the latter (state public utility commissions take the lead regulatory role in electricity markets).

The other main objective of the DOE—the promotion of energy independence—is practically unachievable. Changes in oil supplies anywhere in the world affect oil prices everywhere in the world as long as oil is freely traded in markets. International oil shocks also spill over into domestic coal and natural gas markets. The United States would have to isolate its entire domestic energy market from the world energy market in order to eliminate the price effects of supply shocks elsewhere in the world—an economically prohibitive exercise.

In the event of a new energy crisis, Congress would be best advised to ensure energy supplies and fuel diversity by allowing markets to work unimpeded by bureaucratic second-guessing. The existence of an energy department presents too strong a temptation for intervention, which is widely acknowledged to have been disastrous in the past.

Reorganize the Nuclear-Industrial Complex

The DOE might be better named the "Department of Nuclear Weaponry and Science."

Although stockpile maintenance and cleanup operations certainly need to be continued, the agency responsible for those activities hardly needs to be represented at the president's cabinet table. There is no compelling reason for those activities to be under the administrative umbrella of an "energy" department, since "energy" has virtually nothing to do with either administrative function.

It makes administrative sense for those activities to be assumed by the Department of Defense. As the National Defense Research Institute of the RAND Corporation recently pointed out, "It is questionable whether there remains any reason to continue the separation of nuclear responsibilities between DoD and DoE." Likewise, a 1995 GAO survey of 37 academic experts and former DOE officials found overwhelming support for removing the DOE from the business of nuclear weapons development, stockpile maintenance, and arms control verification.

The newly constituted National Nuclear Security Administration—which has been charged by Congress with oversight of the nuclear-industrial complex managed by the DOE—should thus be spun off from the department and placed under the organizational auspices of the Department of Defense. The weapons-related activities of Los Alamos, Lawrence Livermore, and Sandia should be reduced to reflect post–Cold War realities, consolidated within two of those national laboratories, and placed under the direction of the NNSA.

Reform Federal Environmental Cleanup Programs

The DOE's various cleanup programs—amounting to $6 billion annually—are necessitated by the environmental mismanagement of the nuclear weapons complex. Federal nuclear weapons facilities, such as Rocky Flats, Colorado, and Hanford, Washington, are expected to take 30 years or more to clean up. Current cleanup standards negotiated by the DOE with state and local communities establish rigorous protocols, based on the federal Superfund statute, that are aimed at returning sites to near-pristine conditions. Estimates of the ultimate cost of such cleanups vary dramatically, but even the most conservative estimate of $200 billion rivals the cost of the savings-and-loan bailout. Other estimates peg ultimate cleanup costs as high as $1 trillion.

While cleaning up those sites is certainly a federal responsibility, the cleanup standards adopted by the DOE are unachievable as well as inordinately costly. Although that is widely understood within the scientific community, the point was perhaps best made in a report issued in 1995 by an advisory board appointed by the DOE to study the national laboratories:

> Probably the most important reason behind the slow pace of assessment and cleanup is the low quality of science and technology that is being applied in the field. Many of the methods, such as "pump and treat" for contaminated groundwater remediation, cannot provide the claimed benefits. There is a lack of realization that many—and most experts believe most—existing remediation approaches are doomed to technical failure. Others would require unacceptable expenditures and much extended time to reach their stated objectives.

Current standards negotiated by the DOE for cleanup of nuclear sites are, even if desirable, untenable both economically and politically. Moving to a standard of risk neutralization allows far more sites to be cleaned up and correspondingly speedier health protection for the general public. Most environmental engineers believe that such a change in cleanup protocols on federal sites would cut total remediation costs by at least 50 percent.

If the NNSA is transferred to the Department of Defense, it makes sense to transfer cleanup operations there as well. RAND notes that "under the assumption that DOE continued to manage environmental cleanup, there would arise the issue of who was responsible for new environmental problems created by a DoD organization. It is not clear that bifurcating responsibility for nuclear waste cleanup—between old and new, or between that from weapons programs and that from other sources—would be prudent." Accordingly, it makes sense to also give the NNSA this authority. The aforementioned GAO survey of energy experts likewise found an overwhelming consensus for transferring civilian nuclear disposal; nuclear weapons waste management and cleanup; and all matters of environmental, safety, and health oversight out of the DOE.

Privatize the National Laboratories

The DOE maintains 9 multiprogram laboratories (which account for 70 percent of the department's total laboratory budget and 80 percent of all laboratory personnel) and 13 program-dedicated laboratories, all but 4 of which are managed and operated for the department by various university and corporate contractors. Because those laboratories have a total annual operating budget of about $10 billion and a combined payroll of approximately 60,000 people, the taxpayers' "investment" in those laboratories has been truly staggering.

The national laboratories today are no longer focused exclusively on weapons programming; they have branched out to include environmental, commercial, and various other research activities now that the Cold War is over.

More than 30 reports and audits over the last several decades—including those of seven internal advisory groups—have warned that the laboratories' missions are unfocused and questionable, that the DOE micromanages the laboratories, and that the laboratories do not operate in an integrated manner. Still, the GAO reported in September 1998 that the department had refused to implement most of the recommendations made in those audits and reports and that the actions that had been undertaken by the department were of dubious value.

Perhaps the most compelling recent analysis of the national laboratories is the February 1995 Galvin Report, the product of a corporate-academic task force appointed by the secretary of energy, that trumpeted "critical finding" as "so much more fundamental than we anticipated that we could not in good conscience ignore it. The principle behind that finding is: government ownership and operation of these laboratories does not work well." The prescription?

> The principal organizational recommendation of this Task Force is that the laboratories be as close to corporatized as is imaginable. We are convinced that simply fine-tuning a policy or a mission, a project, or certain administrative functions will produce minimal benefits at best.

Accordingly, Congress should float, for purchase by any interested party, stock in each separate laboratory save for two of the three main weapons laboratories (Lawrence Livermore, Sandia, and Los Alamos). If there is insufficient commercial interest in any particular facility, the federal government should turn operation of that facility over to the management agent currently under contract to the federal government. That agent would then retain full ownership rights to the laboratory and be free to operate it as it wished, contracting with public and private entities in the free market, or close it down. The federal government would retain full liability for past environmental contamination at all the privatized laboratories and would be responsible—through the NNSA—for remedying any environmental contamination that threatened public health.

Eliminate Energy Research and Development

The DOE spends $7 billion annually on research and development. About half of that sum is spent on basic scientific research. The emphasis on R&D is so great at the DOE that, in its 2001 budget request to Congress (titled "Strength through Science"), the department straightforwardly declared that "DoE is a Science Agency."

Over the past four decades, the federal government has poured nearly $100 billion into nondefense nuclear science and energy R&D, 70 percent of which since the mid-1980s has been devoted to applied energy R&D. Clearly, federal energy R&D expenditures have not been trivial.

There are two primary justifications for federally supported energy R&D. The main justification is that R&D is a "public good." No firm that discovers new technologies or production practices can fully exclude other firms from appropriating those discovers for their own commercial benefit. Private firms will thus underinvest in R&D and supplemental government investment is necessary to improve overall economic efficiency. The second justification is mercantilist: other nations subsidize the R&D programs of their domestic industries, and, if the United States did not do likewise, it would competitively disadvantage firms headquartered in the United States.

While the former argument is almost certainly true to some extent, it's worth noting that the United States became the richest nation in the world long before there was any significant American leadership in science and technology. Most federal programs to promote science and technology, moreover, were initiated after World War II. Subsequently, U.S. economic growth has been among the lowest of the major nations.

The historical and cross-national record reveals a strong relationship between real expenditures for R&D and the level of national output—but little relationship with the rate of economic growth. This record is more consistent with the hypothesis that R&D is an income-elastic consumption good, something that rich people and rich nations do, rather than an investment that will increase future economic growth.

The mercantilist justification is even weaker. The international character of science is such that discoveries made in one nation are available to scientists in all. The existence of the free rider problem at the international level suggests that the relative competitive position of an economy may not be improved by funding R&D. As noted by the late Harry Johnson, an economist at the University of Chicago, a position of leadership in basic science

> might benefit a nation almost exclusively in terms of intangible national prestige of scientific accomplishment, the concrete benefits of the application of scientific findings being reaped mainly by other nations. In that case, the expenditure of public money on the support of basic scientific research would serve mainly to save other countries the cost of basic research and enable them to concentrate on development and application.

Regardless of the theoretical debate, there is little evidence to suggest that the tens of billions of dollars poured into energy R&D have ever produced more net economic benefits than costs or that the energy economy today would be any different absent such R&D expenditures.

Perhaps the most serious examination of federal R&D programs—conducted for the Brookings Institution by economists Linda Cohen of the University of California at Irvine and Roger Noll of Stanford University—found that energy R&D has been an abject failure and a pork barrel for political gain. MIT's Thomas Lee, Ben Ball Jr., and Richard Tabors likewise observe that "the experience of the 1970s and 1980s taught us that if a technology is commercially viable, then government support is not needed; and if a technology is not commercially viable, no amount of government support will make it so."

Even the Galvin Report concluded that the DOE's laboratories—where most of the department's R&D takes place—"are not now, nor will they become, cornucopias of relevant technology for a broad range of industries."

Those conclusions were reached by Cato's chairman Bill Niskanen, who found in a regression analysis that a $100 increase in real federal R&D outlays per employee (which would increase current federal outlays by about $17 billion) might increase the annual productivity rate by about one-quarter of a percentage point within five years. All the near-term effects of R&D outlays on productivity growth, however, appear related entirely to defense R&D. Civilian and space R&D outlays appear to have no effect on near-term productivity growth. The long-term effects may be greater but cannot be ascertained from the statistical sample of 1956–95 used by Niskanen.

The reason that energy R&D has such a disappointing track record is that politicians and bureaucrats are charged with deciding which industries, technologies, and projects to support on the basis of political, not economic or scientific, considerations. As former senator William Proxmire once remarked: "Money will go where the political power is. Anyone who thinks government funds will be allocated to firms according to merit has not lived or served in Washington very long." Eric Reichl, former director of the Synthetic Fuel Corporation and long-time member of the DOE's Energy Research Advisory Board, agrees: "The more R&D dollars are available, the more of them will go to some marginal ideas. The high-merit ideas will always find support, even from—or particularly from—private industry. In general, then, government R&D dollars will tend to flow to marginal ideas. Exceptions always exist, but they are just that, exceptions."

Federal energy R&D expenditures should be immediately eliminated. The argument that they have provided a net social benefit to the economy is simply dogma masquerading as fact. The GAO audit of a recent DOE report of its R&D "Success Stories," for instance, revealed "basic math errors, problems in supporting economic analyses, and unsupported links between the benefits cited and DoE's role or the technology. These problems make DoE's estimates of the benefits of these cases questionable.'' In fact, no cost/benefit analysis of any kind has ever been produced to justify past or present DOE R&D programming.

The case for government support of civilian R&D is that the return to the economy is higher than the return to the firm, not that the government has better information on what R&D has the highest return. Government-sponsored R&D programs may increase the total level of investment, but allocation of the incremental expenditure is constrained by lack of information and is unduly influenced by vocal user and supplier interests.

Science policy would probably make a larger contribution to economic growth by merely augmenting private R&D expenditures, leaving the allocation decisions entirely to private organizations. The most effective instrument for supporting civilian R&D, then, is probably a tax credit for private R&D expenditures.

Unlike the present credit, however, an ideal credit would

- apply to total R&D expenditures by a firm, not merely to the increment above some base period, and
- be refundable to avoid a bias against start-up firms with no near-term tax liability.

Similarly, the most effective instrument to support basic research in universities would be a grant to match funds raised from private sources. University-based scientists would make their case to private firms rather than to some government-appointed peer-review committee.

Failing that, Congress should transfer DOE's R&D programs to the National Science Foundation. Energy programs would then compete with nonenergy programs for financial support.

Privatize the Power Marketing Administrations

The DOE sells about 19 percent of the nation's annual power production. The facilities that generate that power are mostly dams: Hoover, Grand Coulee, and 129 other smaller dams operated by the Army Corps of Engineers and the Bureau of Reclamation. The DOE's remaining power marketing administrations (PMAs)—the agencies that deliver public power wholesale (with the exception of the Bonneville Power Administration, which also sells power retail) to publicly owned utilities and rural power cooperatives—are, together, as large as major private power companies.

The PMAs were originally justified on two premises: first, that monopoly electricity corporations would not find enough profit in electrifying rural America and thus government must step in and provide the power and, second, that government could provide power to consumers at less cost than could private companies because it could do so "at cost" without worrying about capital costs or profit margins.

The first premise is now irrelevant. Rural America is thoroughly electrified and will remain so with or without the PMAs. Moreover, 60 percent of rural America is already served by investor-owned utilities.

The second premise—that federal power would be cheap—was a socialist chimera. Public electricity generation has proven to be far more costly than private generation.

All of the PMAs should be privatized by asset divestiture and sold to the highest bidders by an asset privatization working group under the management of the Department of the Treasury. The divested assets should include the right to market power produced at federal facilities (without any price constraint) and the generation equipment associated with energy production at those facilities (owned primarily by the Army Corps of Engineers and the Bureau of Reclamation). The privatization plan should grandfather in existing operating conditions at hydroelectric generating facilities, including minimum flows from the dams, and provide a "preference" to current customers that would relieve them from current contract requirements if they so desired. Sale of the four PMAs proposed by the Clinton administration in 1995 (but, alas, proposed no longer) was estimated to bring in between $3.4 billion and $9 billion to the federal treasury. Bonneville was likely to bring in approximately $9 billion.

Although there might not be a market for the largest federal dams, such as Hoover and Grand Coulee (although that remains to be seen), there are more than 100 smaller dams that would find ready buyers. More than 2,000 hydropower facilities are owned by the private sector (compared to 172 facilities owned by the public), and 56 percent of the nation's hydropower is generated by private companies. Those facilities are not necessarily small generators. The Conowingo Dam, a 500-megawatt facility on Maryland's Susquehanna River, and the Brownlee Dam, a 585-megawatt facility on the Snake River, are both owned by nonfederal power companies.

Sale of federally owned dams would also allow environmentalists and the recreational industry the option of buying and retiring those dams in the interest of riparian protection and, indirectly, the health of various fisheries. There is little merit to the idea that the federal government knows a priori the highest and best economic use for riparian resources. It may well be that society values the environmental benefits of untamed waterways more than it values the low-cost electricity that those waterways provide. If that is the case, the public should be afforded the opportunity to make those preferences known through the marketplace.

Most retail consumers of public power would experience no rate increases under privatization (assuming, that is, that environmentalists do not win bids to own privatized hydroelectric facilities). The reason is that, even though public power is sold to intermediary wholesale purchasers at from 1 to 3 cents per kilowatt-hour, those wholesalers (rural electric cooperatives and municipal utilities) typically resell that power to their customers at market rates—6 to 8 cents per kilowatt-hour. In other words, the retail customers of public power do not receive the public subsidy; the rural electric cooperatives and municipal utilities do.

Sell the Strategic Petroleum Reserve

The federal government maintains a 583-million-barrel Strategic Petroleum Reserve (SPR) of unrefined, generally high-sulfur crude oil in five caverns in Texas and Louisiana. The mission of the SPR, according to the DOE, is "to reduce U.S. vulnerability to economic, national security, and foreign policy consequences of petroleum supply disruptions." As the oil price spikes of 2000 clearly demonstrated, however, no petroleum reserve—no matter how large—can insulate the United States from the effects of international supply disruptions.

The military rationale for the SPR is dubious. Joshua Gotbaum, former assistant secretary for economic security at the Department of Defense, testified before the Senate in 1995 that the military could fight two major regional wars nearly simultaneously while using only one-eighth of America's current domestic oil production. And short of a seamless naval embargo, no oil boycott could prevent the United States from purchasing oil in the international marketplace. As noted by MIT economist Morris Adelman: "The danger is of a production cutback, not an 'embargo.' The world oil market is one big ocean, connected to every bay and inlet. For that reason the 'embargo' of 1973–74 was a sham. Diversion was not even necessary, it was simply a swap of customers and suppliers between Arab and non-Arab sources."

The idea that the government should buy oil when it is cheap and store it for future use when prices are high seems reasonable at first glance, but the maintenance of a federal reserve discourages private firms from maintaining stockpiles. That's because it's very costly to store oil over time. Private stockpiles make economic sense only if they can be sold at very high prices (which are necessary to recoup storage costs), but the threat that the federal government may flood the market during times of shortage makes firms far less certain that domestic prices would ever stay high enough to ensure a profit on stockpiled oil. In fact, a back-of-the-envelope calculation suggests that—after adjusting for inflation and figuring in the costs of storage and maintenance—the oil in the SPR has cost the treasury at least $60 a barrel. Yet no serious energy economist expects oil prices to ever equal the price of putting a barrel of oil in the SPR. If one thinks of the SPR as the functional equivalent of an insurance policy, then the premium on the policy exceeds the benefits of the policy.

Although hedging against the risk of supply disruption and temporary shortages may make sense, the maintenance of a physical stockpile is only one way—and a very expensive way—of doing so. Futures markets (for instance, the oil futures market on the New York Mercantile Exchange) provide an alternative to stockpiles by enabling consumers to lock in purchase prices for as long as six years into the future.

Selling the SPR would bring $16 billion in revenue to the treasury.

Conclusion

The remainder of the DOE's responsibilities could be easily parceled out to independent or semi-independent agencies. The Federal Energy Regulatory Commission and the Energy Information Administration—although nominally within the DOE management structure—are nearly autonomous now and could be made officially so. The DOE's Office of Civilian Radioactive Waste Management, which is responsible for regulating the long-term storage of high-level nuclear waste, could be transformed into an independent agency or placed under the authority of the Department of the Interior.

The views expressed here may be rare in Washington, but they are orthodox among serious economists. As noted by Richard Gordon, professor of mineral economics at Pennsylvania State University and recipient of the International Association of Energy Economists' Outstanding Contributions Award, "The dominant theme of academic writings is that governments have done more harm than good in energy," a view "almost universally supported by academic energy economists, whatever their political outlook."

Eliminating the Department of Energy and most of its nondefense functions would save taxpayers at least $10 billion annually and tens of billions more through the privatization of federal assets. Such a step would eliminate what is perhaps the largest slice of corporate welfare in the budget and improve the overall efficiency of the economy—which is burdened, not helped, by federal intervention in the energy market.

Suggested Readings

Adelman, M. A. *The Genie Out of the Bottle: World Oil since 1970.* Cambridge, Mass.: MIT Press, 1996.

Block, Michael, and John Shadegg. "Lights Out on Federal Power: Privatization for the 21st Century." Washington: Progress and Freedom Foundation, October 1996.

Bradley, Robert L. Jr. *Oil, Gas, and Government: The U.S. Experience.* Lanham, Md.: Rowman & Littlefield, 1996.

Lee, Thomas, Ben Ball Jr., and Richard Tabors. *Energy Aftermath.* Boston: Harvard Business School Press, 1990.

Niskanen, William A. "R&D and Economic Growth—Cautionary Thoughts." In *Science for the 21st Century.* Edited by Claude Barfeld. Washington: AEI Press, 1997.

Robinson, Colin. "Energy Economists and Economic Liberalism." *Energy Journal* 21, no. 2 (2000).

Stelzer, Irwin. *The Department of Energy: An Agency That Cannot Be Reinvented.* Washington: American Enterprise Institute Studies in Policy Reform, 1996.

Taylor, Jerry, and Peter VanDoren. "Evaluating the Case for Renewable Energy: Is Government Support Warranted?" Cato Institute Policy Analysis no. 422, January 10, 2002.

VanDoren, Peter. *Politics, Markets, and Congressional Policy Choices.* Ann Arbor: University of Michigan Press, 1991.

Wirl, Franz. *The Economics of Conservation Programs.* Boston: Kluwer, 1997.

—Prepared by Jerry Taylor

FOREIGN AND DEFENSE POLICY

47. U.S. Security Strategy

Congress should

- act as a much-needed check on the executive branch's reflexive tendency to expand the global political and military role of the United States under the guise of U.S. "global leadership" or the U.S. war on terrorism,
- initiate a comprehensive review of existing U.S. security commitments and jettison those that are not clearly linked to vital national security interests,
- review the defense budget and make the necessary reductions to bring it in line with a security strategy that is based on the defense of vital national security interests, and
- refuse to provide funding for military interventions except when such an intervention is a necessary response to a national security threat.

Since September 11, 2001, it has been easy and tempting to define U.S. national security strategy solely in terms of the terrorist threat. Some observers would fill the vacuum in the threat environment left by the demise of the Soviet Union by focusing on al-Qaeda and other terrorist organizations. But such thinking would simply be falling back on Cold War habits. Instead of focusing solely on terrorism, the United States needs to formulate a viable national security posture to address the greatly changed strategic environment, of which the terrorist threat is only one component.

In the 21st century, instead of devoting tremendous national resources—blood and treasure—to defending the entire world against all manner of threats, the United States should behave as a normal great power. Like any great power, the United States must vigorously protect its vital national security interests using many means, including force. Absent a hegemonic threat, such as the Soviet Union, however, the United States should be able to rise above most day-to-day turmoil around the globe.

Instead of curtailing Cold War–era overseas security commitments, the United States has assumed significant new ones under the mantle of U.S. "global leadership." Much of the Persian Gulf region has become a de facto U.S. military protectorate, and the enlarged NATO obligates the United States to defend 19 countries (up from 16) as if they were U.S. territory. Another round of NATO expansion, which makes the first look modest, is in the offing. The United States is also increasingly immersed in parochial regional conflicts, most notably in the Balkans—where Washington's preoccupation with Kosovo adds to the burden undertaken in Bosnia with the ill-conceived Dayton accords.

The war on terrorism is the most recent example of not focusing on the core threats to vital U.S. security interests. What started as a war against terrorists with global reach (i.e., the al-Qaeda terrorist network responsible for the September 11 attacks) has morphed into a larger war against terrorism in general (even terrorist groups that do not focus their attacks against the United States) and "rogue states" seeking to acquire weapons of mass destruction.

U.S. "Global Leadership" and Strategic Overextension

The United States cannot solve all the world's problems or rid the world of evil. It cannot act as the world's armed social worker—taking responsibility for rehabilitating the rest of world by redressing human rights violations, humanitarian disasters, and the absence of democracy wherever such blight offends American sensibilities. And the United States cannot exterminate terrorism.

Nor can the United States be the global cop. Washington is not the arbiter of law and order throughout the world, even when it comes to such matters as weapons proliferation or the activities of the "axis of evil" (Iraq, Iran, and North Korea) and other "rogue states."

Policymakers and politicians often call upon the United States to play each of those roles or, more ominously, both. Republicans and Democrats alike call upon the United States to show "global leadership"—suggesting that the United States is responsible to some degree for everyone, everywhere. Even the most ardent internationalists may not necessarily believe that. But basing U.S. national security strategy on a mission to lead the world clearly results in making all crises and conflicts important rather than deciding which situations demand Washington's attention and which can be left to run their course. It is a prescription for strategic overextension, inconsistency, and hypocrisy.

September 11 only further highlights the need for the United States to distance itself from problems that are not vital to U.S. national security. Much of the anti-American resentment around the world—particularly in the Islamic world—is the result of interventionist U.S. foreign policy. The more the United States meddles in the internal affairs of other countries and regions, the more likely such actions will be to fuel extreme hatred of the United States. Such hatred is a steppingstone to violence, including terrorism. The Bush administration even admits the relationship between American "global presence and engagement" and retaliatory acts of terrorism against the United States. Therefore, the United States would actually be more secure if it became less involved in other people's problems.

Making Promises Washington Cannot Keep

Put simply, the United States is incapable of keeping many of the commitments it has made. Moreover, there was no credible strategic rationale for assuming most of those obligations in the first place. That recklessness has been expensive, and the costs are sure to rise unless major adjustments are made.

The potential military implications of making empty promises (or threats) are obvious. When the United States intervened in Somalia, pledging to create stability amidst cruel urban warfare, it quickly became apparent that U.S. troops had undertaken a mission without adequate resources. American soldiers lacked both physical equipment suitable for such warfare and, perhaps even more serious, Washington's political backing to succeed in their mission. One of the more gruesome results was the ambush that killed 18 U.S. Army Rangers in the streets of Mogadishu. Pressure immediately built to withdraw U.S. forces. When the high costs—both financial and human—of such commitments become apparent, the American public is unwilling to support interventions that do not involve U.S. vital interests.

Even in the war on terrorism, the United States is flirting with involvement in situations that entail nonvital interests. The U.S. involvement in the Philippines and in the Republic of Georgia provides two examples. The U.S. military is aiding the Philippine government in dealing with the Abu Sayef guerrillas, who are not so much terrorists as financially motivated kidnappers. Even Philippine president Gloria Macapagal Arroyo admits that there ceased to be evidence of al-Qaeda in the Philippines after 1995. The U.S. plan to train and equip the Georgian military is based on the belief that al-Qaeda members and other Islamic extremists from Chechnya have taken refuge in the Pankisi Gorge region along the Georgia-Chechnya border. But such terrorists are Russia's problem more than America's. And clearly the Georgian government is using the pretext of terrorism to invite the U.S. military to protect the country against Russia (which supported the U.S.-led military effort in Afghanistan) and its influence over Georgian provinces seeking independence and closer ties to Russia.

Instead of focusing on mopping up the remnants of al-Qaeda and Taliban in Afghanistan, the U.S. military presence there has moved dangerously close to peacekeeping and nation-building operations. The military mission now seems to be focused on protecting Afghan president Hamid Karzai and keeping his government in power. That is a prescription for disaster. In the end, it is impossible for an intervening party's actions (no matter how well-intentioned) to not alter the power calculations of all the rival factions. Invariably, the outside party will do something that is seen as benefiting one side's interests at the expense of all others' interests. And the outside party then becomes a target for violence. The United States needs to learn from and not repeat what happened in Lebanon in the 1980s and Somalia in the 1990s.

Pursuing a policy of intervention anywhere and everywhere has concrete costs that the United States can ill afford. The budget for national defense—approximately $400 billion in fiscal year 2003—is one of the most obvious financial costs. In real terms, today's budget is greater than the average budget during the Cold War and costs about $1,400 per year for every American man, woman, and child. Much of that sum can be attributed to Washington's overambitious national security posture.

The human costs must also be considered. Impressive military spending is not always enough to maintain a stance of global military leadership—sometimes U.S. troops will have to be put at risk to prove U.S. prowess. Americans will die for purposes far less important than U.S. security.

Alleged Benefits of U.S. Political and Military Leadership

Proponents of the U.S. crusade to lead the world point to several purported benefits of that policy. One of the most persistent myths is that—by assuming responsibility for leading the world—the United States is able to persuade other countries to share the costs of initiatives that it would otherwise have to bear alone. The Gulf War is the preeminent example of such alleged burden sharing. Yet the United States offered concrete economic or political rewards to many key countries to encourage their participation in the coalition against Iraq. Moreover, Washington today continues to pay about $80 billion per year to defend Saudi Arabia and the other wealthy southern Persian Gulf states. The Europeans buy far more oil from this region than does the United States but do little to help defend it. The price tag for defending the region clearly eclipses any temporary burden sharing that occurred back in 1991. Washington's willingness to assume responsibility for security in many parts of the world—not only in the Persian Gulf region but in East Asia and Europe as well—encourages free riding, not burden sharing.

More important, the United States does not need to defend Persian Gulf oil at all. The oil market has changed dramatically since the 1970s. (Even then, oil shortages reduced the nation's gross domestic product by less than half of 1 percent.) New technology has allowed new sources of oil to be tapped and increased the efficiency of its usage. As a result, the Persian Gulf supplies less of the world's oil than it did during the 1970s. In addition, the U.S. economy is much less vulnerable to oil shocks than it was in the 1970s: the United States spent 9 percent of its gross domestic product on oil in the 1970s; today it spends only 3 percent, and the economy can more easily shift to other fuels. Even at the time of the Gulf War, prominent economists from across the political spectrum cautioned that defending oil was not a justification for war. That argument is even stronger today.

Another rationale for attempting to manage global security is that a world without U.S. hegemony would soon degenerate into a tangle of chaos and instability, in which weapons proliferation, genocide, terrorism, and other offensive activities would be rampant. Prophets of such a development hint that if the United States fails to exercise robust political and military leadership today, the world is condemned to repeat the biggest mistakes of the 20th century—or perhaps do something even worse.

Such thinking is seriously flawed. First, instability in the international system is nothing new, and most episodes do not affect U.S. vital interests. Furthermore, to assert that U.S. global leadership can stave off otherwise inevitable global chaos vastly overstates the power of any single country to influence world events. Indeed, many of the problems that plague the world today, such as civil wars and ethnic strife, are largely impervious to external solutions. There is little to back up an assertion that only Washington's management of international security can save the world from political, economic, or military conflagration.

A World without U.S. Intervention

If Washington renounces world political and military leadership, is the United States condemned to stand idly by while villains and irredentists around the world terrorize helpless populations? It is unfortunate but true that brutal civil or subregional conflicts are likely to mar the future—as they do the present and have the past. Furthermore, there are many parochial wars that simply cannot be settled by outside powers at an acceptable cost to those powers, whether or not the United States claims the mantle of global leadership.

A more critical issue is the evolution of the international system after the United States adopts a policy of strategic independence. Washington can exert considerable, though not complete, influence over how that system develops. A number of different systems may be acceptable to the United States, but two conditions are essential: First, power must be diffuse—that is, not concentrated in the hands of a single state or multinational organization. Second, the system must have a means of checking aspiring hegemons.

Such a system could take several forms. One possibility is to strengthen regional security organizations—both to keep order among member states and to take care of contingencies in their immediate areas. The European Union, with a more robust military capability, would likely be an appropriate organization for promoting security in Europe.

Spheres of influence would also be a possibility. Although that idea sometimes has a sinister connotation, there is nothing inherently wrong with the concept that major powers take an interest and play a major role in affairs in their regions. As long as dominant powers restrict their activities to normal great power behavior—which would generally mean shoring up prestige and security but not expanding their domains—spheres of influence are potentially a valuable means of keeping order in certain regions.

Yet another alternative is the establishment of regional balance-of-power arrangements. This approach would be appropriate in areas where there is no dominant power around which a sphere of influence is likely to develop—such as in the Middle East, where the locus of power tends to shift among the larger states and little enthusiasm exists for a regional security organization.

The United States as Balancer of Last Resort

As long as any international system possesses the two key features mentioned above—diffuse power and a means of checking would-be hegemons—the United States could tolerate a variety of regional arrange-ments. As long as no single power or group of powers emerges with the capability and intent of challenging American vital interests, the United States will be reasonably secure. In particular, as long as a hostile hegemon does not have the potential to overrun regions of high economic output—that is, Europe or East Asia—or does not try to interrupt U.S. trade, American vital interests will not be threatened.

To further enhance its security, the United States should always maintain sufficient military strength so that it could reestablish the balance of power if a serious imbalance were to develop. It should, however, act only as a balancer of last resort. The United States should allow smaller-scale shifts and civil strife to be addressed at the regional level. The risks and costs of serving as balancer of last resort are much more manageable than is a quixotic crusade to lead the world.

Suggested Readings

Carpenter, Ted Galen. *Peace and Freedom: Foreign Policy for a Constitutional Republic.* Washington: Cato Institute, 2002.

————. "Toward Strategic Independence: Protecting Vital American Interests." *Brown Journal of World Affairs* 2, no. 1 (Summer 1995).

Conry, Barbara. "U.S. Global Leadership: A Euphemism for World Policeman." Cato Institute Policy Analysis no. 267, February 5, 1997.

Eland, Ivan. *Putting "Defense" Back into U.S. Defense Policy.* Westport, Conn.: Praeger, 2001.

Layne, Christopher. "From Preponderance to Offshore Balancing: America's Future Grand Strategy." *International Security* 22, no. 2 (Summer 1997).

Mandelbaum, Michael. "Foreign Policy as Social Work." *Foreign Affairs* 75, no. 1 (January–February 1996).

Nordlinger, Eric. *Isolationism Reconsidered: American Foreign Policy for a New Century.* Princeton, N.J.: Princeton University Press, 1995.

Olsen, Edward A. *U.S. National Defense for the Twenty-First Century: The Grand Exit Strategy.* London: Frank Cass, 2002.

—Prepared by Barbara Conry and Charles V. Peña

48. The Defense Budget

Congress should

- reduce the budget for national defense from the current sum of about $400 billion to about $200 billion (in fiscal year 2004 dollars)—in increments over five years;
- add to the $200 billion total the $10 billion per year spent appropriately on military operations in the war on terrorism;
- make it clear that the reduced budget must be accompanied by a more restrained national military posture that requires enough forces to fight one major theater war instead of the current posture based on the need to fight in two theaters nearly simultaneously;
- restructure U.S. forces to reflect the American geostrategic advantage of virtual invulnerability to invasion by deeply cutting ground forces (Army and Marines) while retaining a larger percentage of the Navy and Air Force;
- authorize a force structure of 5 active-duty Army divisions (down from 10 now), 1 active Marine division (reduced from 3 now), 14 Air Force fighter wings (down from 20 now), 200 Navy ships (down from 316), and 6 carrier battle groups with 6 Navy air wings (reduced from 12 and 11, respectively);
- require that the armed services compensate for reduced active forces by relying more on the National Guard and the reserves in any major conflict;
- terminate force structure or weapons systems that are unneeded and use the savings to give taxpayers a break and to beef up neglected mission areas; and
- terminate all peacekeeping and overseas presence missions so that the armed services can concentrate on training to fight wars and to deploy from the U.S. homeland in an expeditionary mode should that become necessary.

The Context for Defense Policy

Paradoxically, the massive amount the United States spends on national defense each year, and the profligate military interventions conducted overseas with the forces generated by such spending, may actually make the United States less, rather than more, secure.

A nation's defense policy (including the defense budget) should reflect its security situation—that is, the geopolitical realities of its environment. U.S. defense policy fails to take such realities into account.

Advocates of higher military budgets regret that U.S. spending on national defense has declined to about 3 percent of the nation's gross domestic product, its lowest point since 1940. As a result, they argue that U.S. security is being severely compromised. Although defense spending as a percentage of GDP is a good indicator of what proportion of the national wealth is being appropriated for defense, it is not an indicator of what amount should be spent on a nation's defense. Such spending should be based on the nation's geostrategic situation and the threats to its vital interests (which have declined dramatically since the end of the Cold War). Besides, no nation ever fought another nation with a percentage of its GDP. Nations fight other nations with military forces that are purchased with finite quantities of resources.

When the U.S. annual budget for national defense is compared with those of other nations, the true magnitude of U.S. defense spending becomes clear. The United States alone accounts for more than one-third of the world's military spending. U.S. defense spending roughly equals the combined spending of the next 11 nations—8 of which are our wealthy friends and allies (only Russia and China fall outside this group). The United States spends more than all of its wealthy friends and allies combined and about double what all of its rich NATO allies combined spend. More important, the United States spends three times the combined amount spent by nations that are "potential threat states"—Russia, China, Iraq, Iran, Syria, Libya, Cuba, and North Korea.

The United States could probably spend less, not more, than other major nations and remain secure. The United States is blessed with one of the most secure geostrategic environments the world has ever seen. It is virtually invulnerable to an invasion. The United States has two great oceans separating it from other major powers and weak and friendly neighbors on its borders, and no major power exists in the Western Hemisphere to pose a challenge. Most important, any nation foolish enough to attack the United States would face the devastation of its homeland by the world's most formidable nuclear arsenal. In short, a large portion of the $400 billion spent annually on defense (almost $1,400 per American) has nothing to do with U.S. security and lots to do with the expensive, self-appointed role of "world leader."

Of course, the attacks on September 11 brought home the vulnerability of the United States to strikes by terrorists using conventional means. Even the Bush administration admits that a strategy of global presence and engagement causes retaliatory attacks on the United States. The huge U.S. military is much larger than needed to conduct the small brushfire wars required to fight terrorism (much of the war on terrorism will be conducted by U.S. intelligence and law enforcement agencies, not the military)—the only real major threat to U.S. security in the post–Cold War world. (The $10 billion per year spent appropriately on military operations in the war on terrorism is only a small portion of the $400 billion per year spent on national defense and would be added to Cato's proposed $200 billion budget for national defense.) In fact, the large military and the temptation to use it to intervene all over the world actually reduce the security of the U.S. homeland. Therefore, adopting a policy of military restraint and cutting the defense budget would actually enhance security at home.

New Criterion for Determining the Size of U.S. Forces Is Needed

The virtual invulnerability of the United States allows it to define its vital interests narrowly and intervene militarily only when they are threatened. There has always been—and will always be—instability in the world (although, since the Cold War ended, most indicators have shown that it is declining). In the vast majority of cases, however, instability will not threaten vital American interests. If the United States pursued a policy of military restraint, it could reduce its budget for national defense by half—from $400 billion to about $200 billion (fiscal 2004 dollars) per year—and still be, by far, the most capable military power in the world. (Japan—which comes in a distant second among nations with first-rate militaries on any scale of defense expenditures—spends only about $45 billion per year on defense.)

Adopting a policy of military restraint would allow the United States to size its forces to fight one major theater war instead of two concurrently, as envisioned by the Pentagon. Even that reduction in forces would provide some hedge against uncertainty. Acting as a "balancer of last resort," the

United States would assist other nations in shoring up a deteriorating balance of power only in such critical regions as Europe and East Asia (the areas of the world with large concentrations of economic and technological power). Like-minded nations in the affected region would provide most of the ground forces and some air forces; the United States would also provide air power—its comparative advantage. U.S. air power could quickly be dispatched to help friendly nations halt the offensive of a serious aggressor state. Some U.S. ground forces eventually might be needed to help retake lost territory, but that is a remote possibility that should not be considered a high-priority mission.

In a post–Cold War world, the goal of purchasing enough forces to fight in two theaters nearly simultaneously can be abandoned because it is now extremely unlikely that the United States would be required to balance against a regional hegemon in Europe and East Asia at the same time (a World War II scenario). The Bush administration has moved below the force posture needed to win two regional wars decisively, which was followed during the Clinton administration, but still wants enough forces to win decisively in one theater and to stop an enemy offensive in the other region. But if two regional aggressors arose simultaneously, there would be plenty of lead time to build up U.S. forces. It now takes much longer to develop and produce high-technology weapons than it did before World War II, and the United States would be in the lead rather than attempting to catch up with potential aggressors. In the unlikely event that two hegemons arose quickly, the United States could fight them sequentially rather than nearly simultaneously.

Optimal U.S. Force Structure

The Department of Defense's 1993 Bottom-Up Review (BUR) allocated a block of forces to conduct one major regional conflict. The block consisted of 4–5 Army divisions, 4–5 Marine brigades (between 1 and 2 divisions), 10 Air Force wings, 100 heavy bombers, and 4–5 aircraft carrier battle groups. Prudent military planning might require that this "one war" force structure be augmented to add even more cushion for unforeseen circumstances. Thus, an optimal force structure can be created that still saves money. That force structure would consist of 5 active Army divisions (down from 10 now), 1 active Marine division (reduced from 3 now), 14 Air Force air wings (down from 20 now), 187 heavy bombers (down only slightly from 208 now), 200 ships (down from 317), 6 aircraft carrier battle groups and 6 Navy air wings (reduced from 12 and 11, respectively), and 25 nuclear-powered attack submarines (down from the current force of 55 vessels).

Such a force structure would cut 5 active Army divisions, 2 active Marine divisions, 6 Air Force air wings, and more than 100 ships from existing forces. Thus, it would cut Army forces by 50 percent, Marine forces by 67 percent, tactical Air Force forces by 30 percent, and Navy forces by a little more than one-third (Table 48.1). (The optimal budget is roughly half the current level. Some of the savings accruing from reducing the forces are used to purchase high-technology items—such as electronic sensors and information systems and precision weapons—that are vital to winning future wars.)

In this alternative force structure, ground forces—the Army and the Marine Corps—have been reduced more than the Air Force and Navy. Such a shift of emphasis makes sense for a nation that faces no threat from an invading ground force. There are long distances between the United States and any potential adversary. With a small standing army, more reliance would need to be placed on the National Guard and the reserves. In the case of the rare, large-scale war in a foreign theater that requires substantial ground forces to win back lost territory, plenty of time will be available to mobilize the forces of the National Guard and the reserves.

Table 48.1
Proposed Cuts in U.S. Military Forces

Force Component	Planned Force	Optimal Force Structure	Percentage Reduction
Active Army divisions	10	5	50
Active Marine divisions	3	1	67
Air Force tactical fighter wings	20	14	30
Air Force heavy bombers	208	187	0
Total Navy ships	317	200	37
Navy aircraft carrier battle groups	12	6	50
Navy carrier air wings	11	6	45
Nuclear-powered attack submarines	55	25	55

SOURCE: Planned force structure from William Cohen, *Annual Report to the President and Congress* (Washington: U.S. Department of Defense, 2001).

A much smaller Marine Corps will also rely more heavily on the reserves. Although the BUR stated the need for more than one division to fight a major conflict, one existing reserve division can supplement the active division to meet that requirement. Only one Marine division needs to be active; there has been no large-scale amphibious assault since Inchon during the Korean War. In the post–World War II period, the Marines have most often been used in small-scale interventions in the Third World. Such interventions should be undertaken only rarely.

The Air Force would be cut the least of any service. Air power proved devastatingly effective during the wars in the Persian Gulf and Kosovo, and the United States has traditionally had a comparative advantage in air power. Air Force tactical aircraft should be favored over Navy tactical aircraft because land-based aircraft have a greater range and bomb-carrying capacity (that is, have greater efficiency) than aircraft that operate from carriers.

In any major war, friendly nations will more than likely provide land bases from which U.S. aircraft can operate. If such bases become more vulnerable to enemy missile attacks, the United States will need to buy theater missile defenses to protect the bases, purchase short-take-off aircraft that can be dispersed to unfinished airfields, or use long-range heavy bombers that can operate from distant bases in the region. Such measures would be better than relying more on expensive aircraft carriers and naval aircraft. For this reason, the U.S. heavy bomber fleet—which has great range and large bomb-carrying capacity—should be reduced only slightly.

Nonetheless, some aircraft carriers and naval aircraft are needed. Like the Marines, in the post–World War II period Navy carriers have been used primarily to provide forward presence in overseas theaters and for small-scale interventions in the Third World (so-called crisis response). If the United States observed a policy of military restraint, the need for such missions would be rare. Instead, carrier battle groups would sail from the United States and be used to control the seas, to protect American trade if it were threatened, and to provide air power in the rare instances when land bases were not available.

The elimination of the overseas military presence and crisis response missions would allow a substantial reduction in the number of carrier battle groups. Six carrier battle groups would suffice to control the seas and protect trade. The United States—with six carriers—would still have bone-crushing dominance over any other fleet in the world. Although the BUR suggested that four or five carriers would be needed to fight a regional conflict, there has always been a dispute about whether that number included the carrier at the dock undergoing extensive overhaul. To be conservative, another carrier was added, bringing the total to six.

After the Cold War, the Navy's increased emphasis on providing air support for Marine amphibious assaults made Marine air wings redundant; such air wings should be eliminated.

The demise of the Soviet nuclear attack submarine fleet would allow the United States to cut its attack submarine force by more than half, from 55 to 25.

Savings achieved through decommissioning some military units and their existing equipment could be supplemented by savings accruing from canceling new weapons systems, currently in development or production, that are either unneeded in principle or relics of the Cold War. Some of those savings could be returned to taxpayers through reductions in the defense budget and some could be reallocated to increase funding for previously neglected, but important, military missions.

Terminate All Peacekeeping and Overseas Presence Missions

Peacekeeping and overseas presence missions (U.S. troops stationed overseas and regular naval deployments in overseas theaters) have nothing to do with safeguarding vital U.S. interests. In the more benign security environment of the post–Cold War world, such missions only discourage wealthy U.S. allies from spending the resources needed to provide for their own security. Furthermore, those missions lower morale in U.S. forces and consume resources and time that should be used for training to fight wars and to deploy from the United States in the rare cases in which a foreign conflict threatens U.S. vital interests.

Benefits of Adopting the Alternative Defense Posture

Adopting a foreign policy of military restraint overseas, buying the forces needed to fight one regional war, and reducing the budget for national defense by more than a third would help to keep the United States out of unnecessary foreign wars. Such potential quagmires have little to do with vital American security interests and incur exorbitant costs—in both resources and American lives (those of both U.S. military personnel overseas and civilians at home, who will be the victims of terrorist attacks in retaliation for an interventionist American foreign policy). A smaller military would also help safeguard U.S. liberties at home.

Suggested Readings

Carpenter, Ted Galen. *A Search for Enemies: America's Alliances after the Cold War.* Washington: Cato Institute, 1992.

Conetta, Carl, and Charles Knight. "Inventing Threats." *Bulletin of Atomic Scientists,* March–April 1998.

Eland, Ivan. *Putting "Defense" Back in U.S. Defense Policy: Rethinking U.S. Security.* Westport, Conn.: Praeger, 2001.

———. "Subtract Unneeded Nuclear Attack Submarines from the Fleet." Cato Institute Foreign Policy Briefing no. 47, April 2, 1998.

———. "Tilting at Windmills: Post–Cold War Military Threats to U.S. Security." Cato Institute Policy Analysis no. 332, February 8, 1999.

Isenberg, David, and Ivan Eland. "Empty Promises: Why the Bush Administration's Half-Hearted Attempts at Defense Reform Have Failed." Cato Institute Policy Analysis no. 442, June 11, 2002.

Murray, Williamson. "Hard Choices: Fighter Procurement in the Next Century." Cato Institute Policy Analysis no. 334, February 26, 1999.

———. "The United States Should Begin Work on a New Bomber Program Now." Cato Institute Policy Analysis no. 368, March 16, 2000.

—Prepared by Ivan Eland

49. Cut Unneeded Weapon Systems

Congress should terminate or reduce procurement of the following unneeded weapon systems:

- the Air Force's F-22 fighter,
- the Navy's F/A-18E/F Super Hornet carrier-based fighter/ attack aircraft,
- the Navy's Virginia-class submarine,
- the Marine Corps' V-22 tiltrotor transport aircraft, and
- the Army's Comanche helicopter.

New Threat Environment Requires a Reallocation of Resources

The war in Afghanistan following the September 11, 2001, terrorist attacks confirmed what the Bush administration and many defense analysts had anticipated: the forces, weapons, and tactics of the Cold War are not optimal for fighting new adversaries in the post–Cold War era. The war in Afghanistan was won with unmanned aerial vehicles providing reconnaissance and surveillance and special forces on the ground supporting attacking aircraft (the most efficient of which were long-range bombers) by calling in targets. Previously, the paradigm had been to use manned fighter aircraft to support large ground forces engaged against the adversary, with unmanned aerial vehicles playing a marginal role. The terrorist attacks and subsequent war showed that President Bush's initiative to transform the military to fight future threats was more vital than ever before.

Both in his campaign and in his first months in office, the president spoke of transforming the military by modernizing weapons selectively and moving beyond marginal improvements to radically new technologies. He also advocated a military defined less by size and more by mobility and the ability to deploy more easily and project power over long distances.

The president has terminated the Army's Crusader mobile artillery gun, which was too heavy to deploy easily. Yet, for the most part, vested interests have resisted the president's call to transform the nation's armed forces.

Congress should help the president modernize weapons selectively and skip a generation of technology by cutting unneeded or Cold War–era arms programs and reallocating resources to more urgent needs and research programs for futuristic weapons.

Cut Unneeded and Cold War–Era Weapons

Many weapons the Pentagon is currently procuring were originally designed during the Cold War (for example, the Marine Corps' V-22 tiltrotor aircraft). Some weapons now in development entered that process during the Cold War and were to be used against a threat that is now gone or never came to fruition (for example, the Army's Comanche helicopter and the Air Force's F-22 fighter). In addition, the tradition-bound military services are buying successors to Cold War systems (for example, the Navy's Virginia-class submarine and F-18E/F aircraft). Some weapons are too costly (for example, the F-22). Finally, both the executive branch and Congress build unneeded weapons to dole out pork to inefficient defense industries and favored congressional districts. Thus, inertia, tradition, and pork undermine the rational development and procurement of weapon systems. Congress should terminate or reduce procurement of the following "white elephant" weapons:

F-22 Raptor and F/A-18E/F Tactical Fighters

The current generation of American aircraft (the Air Force's F-15 and F-16 and the Navy's F-14 and F-18C/D) will enjoy crushing air superiority over all other air forces for the foreseeable future. According to Eliot Cohen, director of the Strategic Studies Program at Johns Hopkins University and an acknowledged expert on air power, "There's not anybody who's going to be comparable to us for as long as you can see."

But the U.S. military services are currently developing or purchasing three new fighter aircraft (the Air Force's F-22, the Navy's F/A-18E/F, and the multiservice Joint Strike Fighter) at a cost of about $340 billion. The three new fighter aircraft alone will consume a quarter of the Pentagon's annual budget for procuring new weapons and "crowd out" the purchase of weapons that should have a higher priority—for example, a modestly priced replacement for aging U.S. bombers. Thus, two of the three aircraft—the F-22 and F/A-18E/F—should be terminated or purchased only in drastically reduced numbers.

The Air Force designed the stealthy F-22 aircraft primarily to fight futuristic Soviet fighters that were never built. The F-22 would replace the best air superiority fighter in the world today—the F-15C. The United States could maintain its current dominance of the skies well into the future using upgraded F-15Cs, superbly trained pilots, new munitions, and Airborne Warning and Control System aircraft (the best aircraft in the world for management of air battle and a potent force multiplier). No current or future threat to U.S. air superiority exists that would justify spending nearly $63 billion for 341 F-22 aircraft. As a result, the aircraft will probably be used mainly for air-to-ground attack, which it is not optimally designed to do. (Besides, the United States already has the F-117 and B-2 planes to perform stealthy ground attack missions.) At nearly $200 million for each aircraft, the F-22 is the most expensive, least needed fighter ever built.

Although the F/A-18E/F is an entirely different aircraft than the F/A-18C/D, it is not much of an improvement for about double the price ($86 million for each E/F model). For example, although the E/F has a longer range and greater payload than the C/D, it still has a shorter range and smaller payload than the retired A-6 attack aircraft at a time when the aircraft carrier is being pushed farther out to sea by enemy mines, cruise missiles, and diesel submarines. Because the air-to-air threat environment is so low, the C/D model will most likely suffice for future air defense of the fleet until the stealthy Navy version of the Joint Strike Fighter comes on line. If a ground attack aircraft with longer range and greater payload is needed before the stealthy Navy Joint Strike Fighter is ready, a special naval version of the F-117 Nighthawk might provide an interim capability.

Virginia-Class Submarines

With the demise of the Soviet Union and the Russian submarine fleet rusting in port, the existing U.S. force of Seawolf and 688 Los Angeles–class vessels is unquestionably the best in the world and will remain so for the foreseeable future. No other navy in the world even comes close to U.S. undersea power. But the Navy has already begun constructing 30 new Virginia-class submarines (at an average cost of $2.2 billion per ship) and decommissioning older 688 boats before their useful life is over. The Virginia-class submarines will, in most respects, be less capable than the Seawolf class—in size, speed, diving depth, and weapons capacity.

According to the U.S. General Accounting Office, the Navy could retain its goal of 55 submarines in the force by merely refueling the nuclear reactors of the older 688 boats. Moreover, the Navy justified hiking its force goal from 50 to 55 submarines on the basis of increased requirements for intelligence collection. During the Cold War the main target of intelligence gathering by U.S. submarines was the Soviet fleet. Because most of that fleet does not get out of port much anymore, the Pentagon has added more countries to the list of reconnaissance targets. Yet justifying the 55-boat goal on the basis of collecting intelligence is questionable. With the end of the Cold War, conventional threats to the U.S. Navy and the United States declined and so should have requirements for gathering intelligence on such threats; instead they have doubled since 1989. Although, in certain instances, the submarine can provide unique collection capabilities, the United States has many other more versatile assets for spying—for example, manned and unmanned aircraft and satellites—that can perform missions less expensively than $2 billion submarines and are not limited to collection in littoral areas. The United States should reduce its submarine goal and terminate the Virginia-class line.

The V-22 Tiltrotor Aircraft

The V-22—which takes off (and lands) like a helicopter, then tilts its rotors and flies as a fixed-wing aircraft—transports Marines and their light equipment from amphibious ships to shore. The aircraft can go faster and farther than a CH-53 heavy-lift helicopter but cannot carry the heavy equipment the CH-53 can.

The V-22 program has been troubled by crashes and is 10 years behind schedule and $15 billion over budget. In the 1980s and 1990s, senior officials from the Reagan, Bush, and Clinton administrations, including Secretary of Defense Dick Cheney, recommended that the aircraft be canceled. Because of the exorbitant cost of the aircraft, the first Bush administration tried to terminate the program, but Congress reinstated it. The V-22 is truly a vampire: despite the numerous crashes and the admission that the aircraft needs to be reengineered, the 2003 budget funds production at a low rate until a fix can be found.

At almost $80 million per V-22 aircraft, transporting Marines and equipment to shore by air could be done much more cheaply by buying new versions of existing CH-53 rotary aircraft or even smaller helicopters like the Blackhawk CH-60. Besides, against a capable opponent, if faster V-22s transport Marines and their light equipment inland behind enemy lines and if slower CH-53s carry their heavy equipment, the Marines may die before the heavy equipment reaches them.

Comanche Helicopter

The stealthy Comanche light reconnaissance (scout) and attack helicopter was originally designed to hunt Soviet tanks on the central plains of Europe. With the end of the Cold War and the demise of the threat of Soviet armored attack, the aircraft has been remarketed as the "quarterback of the digital battlefield"—that is, a disseminator of tactical reconnaissance information during battle. Suspicions naturally arise when the threat justifying a weapon collapses, but the system lives on and develops another mission.

The Comanche is supposed to replace the OH-58 Kiowa scout helicopter; the aircraft is also supposed to succeed the AH-1 Cobra light attack helicopter in Army divisions that do not have the Apache heavy attack helicopter. Even in the Gulf War against a Soviet-style armored force, the Apache killed tanks effectively, with no need for a scout helicopter. Besides, in the future, unmanned aerial vehicles (UAVs) and better information networks may render the manned reconnaissance helicopter obsolete. UAVs are in some ways better reconnaissance platforms than the Comanche. The unmanned aircraft are 15 percent faster, can loiter over an area five times longer without refueling, and do not expose pilots to enemy fire during usually dangerous reconnaissance missions. The AH-1 Cobra can be replaced by added purchases of an armed version of the OH-58 helicopter—the Kiowa Warrior—which performed well in the Gulf War.

At more than $30 million per helicopter, the Comanche is a very expensive aircraft that can operate at night and in all weather. Although the Comanche was originally touted as inexpensive, it is now more expensive than the heavier Apache that has similar capabilities. The Apache is being upgraded substantially with digital technology and augmented firepower. The addition of the Longbow millimeter-wave radar will allow the Apache to operate at night and in most weather conditions. An Army with upgraded Apaches supplemented by added purchases of Kiowa Warriors should be able to deal effectively with the less-threatening post–Cold War environment.

Some Savings from Cutting Unneeded Weapons Could Fund More Critical Needs

Some of the savings generated by cutting unneeded weapons could be used to fund research, development, and procurement in areas that the services usually neglect: special forces, long-range bombers, unmanned aerial vehicles, defenses against cruise missiles, technology to detect and neutralize sea mines, and equipment to protect against attacks with biological and chemical weapons (Table 49.1). The war in Afghanistan showed that long-range bombers were devastating when guided to their targets by information from unmanned aerial vehicles and special forces on the ground. Much has been invested in defending U.S. forces against ballistic missiles; less effort has been put into defending troops against attacks from cheaper and more effective cruise missiles. More and more terrorists and countries are working on weapons of mass destruction, so more should be invested in defending U.S. forces and civilians at home from biological

Table 49.1
Weapon Systems to Terminate or Cut and Missions and Weapons That Need Increased Funding

Weapon or Mission	Function	Service
Weapon Systems to Terminate or Cut		
F-22	Air superiority fighter	Air Force
F/A-18E/F	Carrier-based fighter attack aircraft	Navy
Virginia-class submarine	Attack submarine	Navy
V-22	Tiltrotor transport aircraft	Marine Corps
Comanche	Reconnaissance attack helicopter	Army
Neglected Missions and Weapons in Need of Increased Funding		
Unmanned aerial vehicles	Reconnaissance, strike, etc.	All
Heavy bomber (R&D)	High-capacity, long-range bomb delivery	Air Force
Special forces	Intelligence gathering, commando attacks, designation of targets	Army, Navy, Air Force
Cruise missile defenses	Defend U.S. forces against cruise missiles	Army, Marine Corps
Mine countermeasures	Detect and neutralize sea mines	Navy, Marine Corps
Chemical and biological defense	Defend forces and civilian population	All

and chemical weapons. The Navy has neglected capabilities that can detect and neutralize sea mines, which can be devastating to naval operations. Because great advancements can be achieved for small amounts of funding in most of those areas, the remainder of the savings from cuts could be returned to the taxpayer.

Suggested Readings

Center for Defense Information. *Weekly Defense Monitor.* Various issues.

Cohen, William S. *Annual Report to the President and Congress.* Washington: U.S. Department of Defense, 2001.

Eland, Ivan. *Putting "Defense" Back in U.S. Defense Policy: Rethinking U.S. Security in the Post–Cold War World.* Westport, Conn.: Praeger, 2001.

———. "Subtract Unneeded Nuclear Attack Submarines from the Fleet." Cato Institute Foreign Policy Briefing no. 47, April 2, 1998.

Murray, Williamson. "Hard Choices: Fighter Procurement in the Next Century." Cato Institute Policy Analysis no. 334, February 26, 1999.

———. "The United States Should Begin Work on a New Bomber Now." Cato Institute Policy Analysis no. 368, March 16, 2000.

—Prepared by Ivan Eland

50. Strategic Nuclear Forces and Missile Defense

Congress should

- endorse a truly "national" limited land-based missile defense;
- eschew grandiose sea- and space-based missile defenses—which are unnecessary, expensive "international" systems designed to protect wealthy U.S. allies and friends and provide a robust shield for unneeded U.S. interventions overseas;
- pressure the administration not to rush development and deployment of land-based missile defense so that the system can be thoroughly tested under realistic conditions before a decision is made to deploy it;
- encourage the administration to destroy—rather than put in storage—warheads as part of the arms reduction agreement to reduce operationally deployed forces to 1,700–2,200 warheads within the next 10 years;
- encourage the administration to propose even deeper cuts in offensive strategic nuclear forces—down to a maximum of 1,500 warheads; and
- reduce the triad of U.S. nuclear forces—nuclear-capable bombers, intercontinental ballistic missiles (ICBMs), and sea-launched ballistic missiles (SLBMs)—to a dyad.

The administration withdrew from the ABM Treaty to eliminate constraints on its goal of pursuing a robust ballistic missile defense program. Although the administration envisions a global, layered missile defense system (incorporating land-, sea-, and space-based weapons), the reality is that a limited land-based system designed to protect the U.S. homeland against the potential threat of long-range missiles from "rogue" states is the most mature (though still not thoroughly tested and proven) and closest to fruition. Rather than be rushed to deployment, a limited missile defense system should be developed at a measured pace because an excessively rapid development program could waste taxpayer dollars on an ineffective system. Missile defense should remain a research and development (R&D) program until it has been thoroughly tested under realistic operational conditions. Only then should a decision be made about its deployment.

Any defense expenditures—including those on missile defense—must be commensurate with the threat. More robust missile defenses are not justified by the present limited threat. Also, sinking large amounts of money into more comprehensive missile defenses—when even the limited land-based system might fail because of technical problems or lack of adequate testing—is questionable.

A Limited Missile Defense Is Needed for a Limited Threat

Although it is not certain that North Korea or any other rogue state will be capable of launching a missile attack against the United States by 2005, the R&D program for missile defense is being rushed to have a system deployed by that date. Even if the threat from North Korea did materialize by that date, the United States would probably be able to use its offensive nuclear force to deter a missile attack from North Korea, another rogue state, or any other state. Thus, missile defense would be a backup system against a missile attack from a pariah state. Rushing development to deploy a system without thorough and realistic operational testing increases the probability that the system will ultimately be delayed, will experience escalating costs, or will simply not work.

More important, rogue states have or will have options for striking the United States other than long-range ballistic missiles. Such countries already possess short- and medium-range ballistic missiles that could be launched from ships operating in international waters off the U.S. coasts. And a missile defense designed for use against long-range ICBMs will not have the capability to intercept these shorter-range missiles. Moreover, the kinds of missile defense systems designed to counter these threats (commonly referred to as theater missile defense) would be extremely expensive to deploy to protect the entire nation or even the coastlines (the limited areas such systems can protect would require greater numbers of systems) and are not part of the administration's plan for a missile defense system to protect the United States.

Rogue nations also may possess or could acquire cruise missiles that could be launched from ships or, possibly, aircraft. Again, a missile defense against long-range ICBMs will not be able to counter these threats, which would require deploying an extensive (and likely expensive) air defense system.

Finally, September 11, 2001, clearly demonstrated that the United States is vulnerable to terrorist attack.

Such threats to the American homeland may be more inexpensive, accurate, reliable, and thus more probable than that posed by ICBMs launched from rogue states. Even the most hostile pariah state is likely to hesitate to launch from its territory an ICBM against the United States. U.S. satellites can detect the origin of such long-range missile launches, and the world's most powerful nuclear force would almost certainly retaliate against the attacking nation. In contrast, the origin of terrorist attacks or missile launches from ships or aircraft may be harder to determine, which makes U.S. retaliation—and therefore deterrence—more difficult. The existence of the other threats does not, of course, refute the argument that long-range ballistic missiles also pose a threat and that the U.S. government should combat the threats that can be defeated. But we must understand that long-range ballistic missiles will be just one of several possible threats.

None of the proposed missile defense systems to protect the United States will have a defensive capability against either short-range ballistic missiles or cruise missiles—delivery systems that rogue states and others already possess. The best reason to have a limited missile defense may be the possibility of accidental—rather than intentional—launches from such states and limited accidental launches from established nuclear powers. Pariah states with newly acquired long-range missiles and nuclear warheads may have poor early warning systems, only rudimentary command and control over such forces, nonexistent nuclear doctrine, and insufficient safeguards against an accidental launch. In addition, in the past, Russia's decrepit early warning systems have almost led to accidental launches.

Nevertheless, the primary threat from accidental or intentional launches from rogue states is likely to be relatively modest (a few ICBMs) and unsophisticated (their missiles are unlikely to have multiple warheads or sophisticated decoys), requiring an equally modest response. A limited ground-based missile defense system of 100 or so interceptors could provide sufficient defensive capability against such threats.

The Limited Threat Does Not Warrant "International" Defenses

Although it is portrayed to the American public as a "national" missile defense, the global, layered system consisting of land-, sea-, and space-based weapons favored by the administration is really an "international" missile defense system that would also defend U.S. allies and "friends," even though they are wealthy enough to build their own missile defenses.

The main objective of observers who support more comprehensive, robust, and layered missile defense systems does not seem to be defense of the U.S. homeland. Instead, their aim seems to be to create a stronger shield behind which the United States can intervene against potential regional adversaries possessing weapons of mass destruction and the long-range missiles to deliver them. According to that reasoning, if such adversaries cannot threaten the United States or its allies with catastrophic retaliation, U.S. policymakers will feel more confident about intervening militarily. But because no missile defense system can guarantee that all incoming warheads will be destroyed, such an increase in U.S. military activism could actually undermine U.S. security in a catastrophic way. Thus, deployment of a missile defense should be confined to a more limited land-based "national" system, which is the most technologically mature system.

Some proponents of missile defense argue that a sea-based system can be deployed more quickly and will be less expensive than the limited land-based system. They contend that the Navy Theater Wide system (a system that is currently being designed to provide midcourse intercept capability against slower, shorter-range theater ballistic missiles) can be upgraded to destroy long-range ICBMs in their boost phase (when under powered flight at the beginning of their trajectories). To intercept faster, longer-range missiles in the boost phase, a new, faster interceptor would need to be developed. That interceptor would probably not be compatible with the vertical launchers of Navy ships. Forward-deployed sea-based missile defense against ICBMs might also experience operational difficulties, including greater vulnerability to attack, and detract from the Navy's other missions, or require expensive new dedicated ships for missile defense.

Some proponents have also advocated a sea-based midcourse system as an alternative to a land-based system. But this would require dedicated Aegis ships deployed near Alaska (where the proposed limited land-based system would be deployed), necessitating an investment in additional ships and crews. And such ships would still be dependent on land-based radars—the Aegis SPY-1B radar system is designed to track shorter-range and slower ballistic and cruise missiles, and an X-band radar for ICBMs is too large to be fitted aboard an Aegis ship. So it is puzzling how such a system would be an improvement over a land-based deployment.

Even if a sea-based missile defense could be developed faster and more inexpensively than the more mature land-based system (a dubious proposition since the sea-based system would depend on sensor, communication, and kill vehicle technology being developed for the land-based system), critical gaps in coverage would necessitate supplementing the sea-based system with expensive space-based weapons. Unlike land-based missile defense against ICBMs, a sea-based system is not a stand-alone system.

Also, many advocates of sea- and space-based weapons want to protect U.S. friends and allies. But the United States should refuse to cover those wealthy nations—which spend too little on their own defense and already benefit from significant U.S. security guarantees—with a missile defense. A layered international missile defense that adds sea- and space-based weapons will escalate the costs of the system dramatically. In addition, an international defense is not warranted by the limited threat and should not be used to defend rich allies who can afford to build their own missile defenses.

A limited land-based system (for example, a hundred or more ground-based interceptors designed to defend against tens of warheads from rogue states) would not enable the United States to undermine nuclear stability by threatening Russia's surviving offensive nuclear forces (even at reduced levels, numbering in the hundreds or thousands of warheads), but more robust defenses might do so. In addition, deploying robust defenses might cause an "action-reaction" cycle with China. As China modernizes and builds up its small nuclear forces (which will probably happen whether or not U.S. defenses are deployed), robust defenses are much more likely to cause a larger Chinese buildup than is a limited system. Congress needs to encourage the administration to pursue a limited missile defense to signal to both powers that the United States is not trying to achieve strategic advantage.

Combine Limited Missile Defense with Deeper Cuts in Offensive Strategic Weapons

The most prudent course of action is to pursue development of a limited missile defense system to defend the United States against rogue state threats and accidental launches and negotiate even deeper cuts in strategic offensive forces.

In the much milder nuclear threat environment of a post–Cold War world, if the United States changed its nuclear doctrine from war fighting to deterrence, deep mutual reductions in offensive forces to levels below the 1,700 to 2,200 operationally deployed warheads of the Bush-Putin arms reduction agreement (perhaps a ceiling as low as 1,500 warheads) would still allow the United States to deter Russia and smaller or emerging nuclear powers (Figure 50.1). Also, with much lower numbers of warheads in that more benign environment, it would be more efficient and cost-effective to reduce the triad of nuclear forces—nuclear-capable bombers, ICBMs, and SLBMs—to a dyad (possibly ICBMs and bombers or SLBMs and bombers). The reduced threat of nuclear war would require less redundancy among U.S. forces to complicate the attack plans of the adversary.

Figure 50.1
Proposed Limits on Warheads in Each of the U.S. and Russian Arsenals

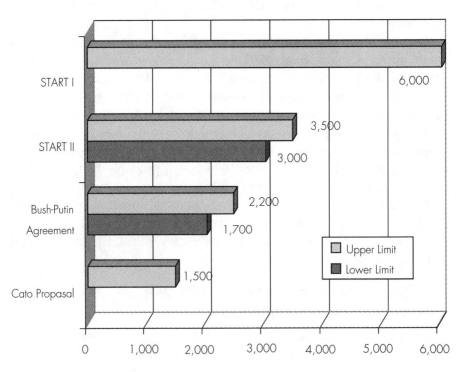

Perhaps most important, the United States should destroy rather than put in reserve the warheads taken off operational deployment. The primary rationale for retaining more weapons in reserve is as a hedge against some unforeseen future threat. The perceived need for a reserve seems to reflect the thinking of many conservatives and military officials that Russia could one day again become a nuclear rival or that China could pose a future nuclear threat. If the United States and Russia have truly entered a new stage in their relationship, then actions should match the rhetoric. Furthermore, the "hedging" logic becomes a self-fulfilling prophecy. If the United States retains more weapons, so will Russia. And the Chinese will likely view the entire U.S. strategic arsenal—not just deployed weapons—as a threat and react accordingly. Counting rules that allow the United States to retain more weapons create an incentive for Russia, China, and others to do the same.

Lower numbers of warheads in the inventories of Russia and the United States would probably mean lower numbers of warheads on alert status, and lower numbers of warheads on alert status would substantially reduce the risk of an accidental nuclear launch. The lower inventory levels would also mean that fewer nuclear warheads would be available to be stolen or sold to rogue states or terrorist groups (that possibility is a particular concern for the aging and insecure Russian nuclear stockpile).

Concerns about the safety and security of nuclear warheads put into reserve status further highlight the need to destroy rather than store warheads. If the Russians decide to retain more weapons in storage, there are legitimate concerns about the safety and security of those weapons. By definition, they will be less secure than deployed weapons guarded regularly by military personnel. Their relative lack of security makes them attractive targets for terrorists seeking to acquire weapons of mass destruction. So taking the weapons off operational deployment without destroying them could possibly lessen U.S. security rather than enhance it.

Recommended Readings

Coyle, Phillip. "Rhetoric or Reality? Missile Defense under Bush." *Arms Control Today* 32, no. 4 (May 2002).

Eland, Ivan. "Let's Make National Missile Defense Truly 'National.'" Cato Institute Foreign Policy Briefing no. 58, June 27, 2000.

Grahman, Bradley. *Hit to Kill: The New Battle over Shielding America from Missile Attack.* New York: Public Affairs, 2001.

Holum, John. "Assessing the New U.S.-Russian Pact." *Arms Control Today* 32, no. 5 (June 2002).

Jones, Rodney. "Taking National Missile Defense to Sea: A Critique of Sea-Based and Boost-Phase Proposals." Council for a Livable World Education Fund, October 2000.

Krepon, Michael. "Defusing Today's Doomsday Machines." *New Democrat Blueprint* (Winter 2000): 20–24.

Newhouse, John. "The Missile Defense Debate." *Foreign Affairs* 80, no. 4 (July–August 2001).

O'Harlon, Michael E., James M. Lindsay, and Michael H. Armacost. "Defending America: The Case for Limited National Missile Defense." Brookings Institution, 2001.

Peña, Charles V. "Arms Control and Missile Defense: Not Mutually Exclusive." Cato Institute Policy Analysis no. 376, July 26, 2000.

———. "From the Sea: National Missile Defense Is Neither Cheap Nor Easy." Cato Institute Foreign Policy Briefing no. 60, September 6, 2000.

Peña, Charles V., and Barbara Conry. "National Missile Defense: Examining the Options." Cato Policy Analysis no. 337, March 16, 1999.

Slocombe, Walter B. "Stability Effects of Limited Missile Defenses: The Case for the Affirmative." *The Global Politics and Strategy of Missile Defense*, Pugwash Occasional Papers 3, no. 1 (March 2002).

Tanks, David. "National Missile Defense: Policy Issues and Technological Capabilities." Institute for Foreign Policy Analysis, April 2000.

—Prepared by Charles V. Peña

51. Policy toward NATO

Congress should

- refuse to appropriate funds for any "out-of-area" NATO military missions;
- oppose any further expansion of the alliance;
- recognize that the growing gap between the military capabilities of U.S. forces and those of the European members makes NATO increasingly less useful for significant military operations;
- recognize that NATO has little relevance in the war against America's terrorist adversaries;
- pass a joint resolution endorsing the new European Security and Defense Policy;
- pass legislation requiring the withdrawal of all U.S. forces stationed in Europe by 2005; and
- conduct a comprehensive debate about whether continued U.S. membership in NATO serves American interests—especially in light of the alliance's change of focus from territorial defense to murky peacekeeping and humanitarian intervention missions.

Ever since the end of its Cold War mission in the early 1990s, NATO has sought to reinvent itself and remain relevant to Europe's new security environment. The latest effort has been to take on the mission against terrorism. That is likely to work no better than the previous campaign to turn the alliance into a crisis-management organization to deal with turmoil in the Balkans and other turbulent regions. Try as they may, NATO partisans cannot escape the reality that the alliance is a Cold War institution that is not well suited to address the security problems of the 21st century.

The admission of Poland, Hungary, and the Czech Republic to NATO in 1999 was a watershed event. It wasn't merely that the alliance was enlarged; that had occurred before. But for the first time NATO undertook security responsibilities in Central and Eastern Europe. There also appear to be no discernible limits to the potential enlargement of the alliance. Indeed, NATO is now poised to invite the Baltic republics and other East European nations to join.

While NATO contemplates enlarging its membership even further, another equally momentous change has taken place in the alliance. When NATO was first established in 1949, it was explicitly an alliance to defend the territorial integrity of its member states. Indeed, the North Atlantic Treaty contained a provision describing the region to be covered, lest there be any implication that the United States was undertaking the protection of the colonial holdings of its new West European allies.

NATO forces never fired a shot in anger during the Cold War, and the alliance's first military operation did not involve the defense of a member from attack. Instead, that initial mission took place in Bosnia, with NATO aircraft bombing Bosnian Serb positions and the alliance trying to prop up the Muslim-dominated government in Sarajevo. Later, NATO took responsibility for implementing the Dayton Accords by deploying a peace-keeping contingent in Bosnia, where it remains to this day. Then, in 1999, the alliance launched an attack on Yugoslavia for Belgrade's conduct in one of its own provinces: Kosovo.

Surprisingly few people in the United States or Western Europe pointed out that the Bosnia and Kosovo missions were a stark departure from NATO's original purpose or questioned whether they were authorized under the provisions of the North Atlantic Treaty. Yet the Serbs never attacked or even threatened to attack a NATO member. Sending NATO troops on such "out-of-area" missions was a dramatic transformation of the alliance's rationale. But the treaty has never been amended, nor has such a change been debated by Congress or the parliaments of the other NATO members.

Some thoughtful members of Congress and experts in the foreign policy community have raised questions about the implications of the expansion of NATO's membership and the transformation of NATO's purpose, however. The two innovations are closely linked, and there are ample reasons to be worried about both of them.

Many proponents of enlargement insist that a new NATO—something more akin to a Euro-Atlantic collective security organization than to a traditional military alliance—is evolving. U.S. policymakers are apparently attempting to create a weird hybrid entity—part traditional alliance and part collective security organization.

The American people are likely to end up with the worst of both worlds: a NATO that periodically becomes entangled in messy, Bosnia-style peace-keeping missions and Kosovo-style military interventions involving disputes that have little, if any, relevance to vital American interests and a NATO that is obligated to protect the alliance's new members in Central and Eastern Europe if a threat by one of their neighbors—including their great-power neighbor, Russia—ever emerges.

Both scenarios are worrisome. There is little doubt that many NATO supporters see the Bosnia and Kosovo interventions as a model for future NATO enterprises. Indeed, the transformation of NATO's focus has been both breathtaking and alarming. It was once an alliance to keep Western Europe—a major strategic and economic prize—out of the orbit of an aggressively expansionist superpower, the Soviet Union. It has now become the babysitter of the Balkans.

The Dangers of the "New Nato"

As the leader of the "new NATO," the United States is incurring expensive and thankless responsibilities. The Bosnia mission has already cost American taxpayers nearly $20 billion, and the meter is still running. The ongoing intervention in Kosovo is running another $3 billion a year, and the lives of American military personnel will be at risk there for years to come. Yet even the out-of-area adventures in the Balkans do not fully satisfy the ambitions of some "new NATO" enthusiasts. Former secretary of state Warren Christopher and former secretary of defense William Perry suggest that the alliance become an instrument for the projection of force anywhere in the world "Western interests" are threatened. In a moment of exuberance, then–secretary of state Madeleine Albright stated that NATO should be prepared to deal with unpleasant developments "from the Middle East to Central Africa." NATO officials have shown increasing interest in the security problems of the Caucasus and Central Asia.

The prospect of U.S. and other NATO troops being used as armed social workers in vague out-of-area crusades is bad enough, but the other scenario is equally troubling. For all the propaganda about the "new NATO" and its more political orientation, NATO remains a military alliance that is obliged to protect its members from armed attack from any source. As NATO incorporates the nations of Central and Eastern Europe, that obligation could entangle the United States in parochial disputes involving a new member and one of its neighbors. Alliance obligations might even put the United States in the middle of a conflict between two NATO members—something that Washington already frets about because of the bad blood between Greece and Turkey.

Most ominous of all, Russia has important strategic, economic, and cultural interests throughout much of Eastern Europe going back generations and, in some cases, centuries. Extending security commitments to nations in what Moscow regards as its geopolitical "back yard" virtually invites a challenge at some point. True, that is not an immediate problem. The danger of an open breach between Russia and the West has receded, given Russian president Vladimir Putin's surprisingly accommodationist policies and the creation of the new Russia-NATO council as a sop to Russia. The complete disarray of the Russian military also makes a challenge in the next decade or so highly improbable.

Nevertheless, the long-term danger remains. One cannot assume that Russia will remain militarily weak and politically compliant forever. Yet NATO's (and America's) security obligations to the alliance's new members go on indefinitely. All that would be needed for a major crisis is for one of Putin's successors to decide that a NATO presence on Russia's doorstep is intolerable. It ought to be a firm rule of American foreign policy not to extend security commitments that would be disastrous for the United States to honor. In dealing with the "new, improved NATO," American officials are violating that cardinal rule.

Any Russian challenge in the future would create a horrific dilemma for the United States. Washington would have to renege on treaty obligations to its new allies or risk war with a nuclear-armed great power. The former option would leave American credibility in ruins; the latter option might leave America itself in ruins.

Congress needs to take immediate steps to limit the risks arising from America's involvement in the new version of NATO. At the very least, Congress should explicitly repudiate attempts to convert the alliance into a force to police the Balkans and other troubled regions. That means passing legislation to terminate the missions in Bosnia and Kosovo. More generally, Congress should pass a joint resolution barring funding for out-of-area NATO missions and affirming that the alliance's only legitimate mission, as authorized in the North Atlantic Treaty, is to protect the territories of member states. Finally, Congress ought to express clear opposition to any further expansion of the alliance's membership.

The Need for a Broader Debate

Those measures, however, are only interim, damage-limitation steps. There is an urgent need for Congress to reassess America's entire commitment to NATO. That debate would end NATO supporters' habit of regarding the preservation of the alliance as a goal in itself. The proper goal is the protection of vital American security interests. NATO (or any other institution) is merely a means to that end and ought to be retained only if the benefits of preservation decisively outweigh the potential costs and risks. It is not at all clear that the "new NATO" passes that test.

A comprehensive congressional debate on NATO's purpose might lead to long-overdue changes in Washington's European policy. For example, a continued U.S. troop presence in Europe is an issue that is separable from U.S. membership in the alliance. When NATO was founded, Washington did not contemplate stationing U.S. forces on the Continent as part of the U.S. commitment. Indeed, the Truman administration assured the Senate that the United States would not provide a troop presence. The administration later sent troops to Europe because of the tense global environment caused by the Korean War, but even then assurances were given that it was merely a temporary step until the West Europeans achieved full recovery from the devastation of World War II.

If a U.S. troop presence was not deemed an indispensable corollary to America's NATO membership in 1949—during one of the most dangerous periods of the Cold War—it should certainly not be viewed as such in the far more benign European security environment of the 21st century. The 108th Congress should finally fulfill President Truman's promise and bring home the troops "temporarily" deployed to Europe in 1951. That step is even more urgent since the September 11, 2001, attacks. The United States does not have the luxury of allowing military personnel to sit uselessly in Western Europe when there is a war to be waged elsewhere against terrorist adversaries.

Such a decision would also signal a willingness to examine the ultimate foreign policy sacred cow: continued U.S. membership in NATO. Despite the concerted efforts of U.S. and European leaders to create a new NATO and make it relevant to the post–Cold War era, the alliance is intrinsically a Cold War relic. It was designed to provide a U.S. security shield for a demoralized, war-ravaged Western Europe facing an aggressively expansionist totalitarian adversary. That situation bears no resemblance to the current security environment. It was one thing to suggest that a weak Western Europe could not defend itself against a military superpower. It is something quite different to argue that a prosperous Western Europe cannot be a strategic counterweight to a Russia shorn of its empire and East European satellite buffer states or deal with the security problems caused by ethnic fanatics in the Balkans.

The U.S.-European Military Gap

Congress ought to view with skepticism the effort of NATO partisans to make the alliance relevant to the war against terrorism. Even though NATO invoked Article 5 of the North Atlantic Treaty (which declares that an attack on one member is an attack on all) in response to the events of September 11, the alliance played no meaningful military role in the U.S. campaign in Afghanistan. The assistance that NATO members have provided to the United States against al-Qaeda has been bilateral and largely nonmilitary. That type of assistance could be provided even if NATO did not exist.

The lack of NATO's military relevance to the war against terrorism is not surprising. There are many reasons for that lack of relevance, but an especially important one is the growing gap in military capabilities between the forces of the United States and those of other NATO members. That gap first became evident in the 1991 Persian Gulf War when U.S. military leaders discovered that the military units of even major NATO allies such as Britain and France were not all that useful. The gap had grown enormously by the time of the Kosovo war in 1999 when U.S. planes flew the overwhelming majority of combat missions. In the period since that conflict, even NATO secretary general George Robertson and other staunch defenders of the alliance have warned that the gap in capabilities has grown so large that, if it is not reversed, joint operations of U.S. forces and those of other members of NATO will become difficult or even impossible. Since military interoperability has long been one of the chief selling points for retaining NATO, that is no small admission.

The gap is the result of the perennial underinvestment in defense by the European members of the alliance. That underinvestment is made possible because the Europeans know that they can continue to free ride on the U.S. security guarantee through NATO. The result is that the forces of the European members of NATO are not terribly useful for the war against terrorism or any other large-scale, significant military operation. They are adequate for peacekeeping missions in places such as the Balkans, but that is about the extent of their current or prospective capabilities. Only if the United States changes the incentive structure by ending the security subsidy it provides through NATO is the European underinvestment in defense likely to change.

An Alternative to NATO

Congress should consider whether it is time to insist that the Europeans provide for their own defense and take responsibility for maintaining security and stability in their own region instead of clinging to the American security blanket. At least one institutional mechanism, the European Security and Defense Policy under the auspices of the European Union, has the potential to be a successor to NATO. The nations of the European Union collectively have a greater population than the United States as well as a larger economy. All that has been lacking is the will to build a credible military force and develop a coordinated EU foreign policy. Those steps are more likely to be taken if the United States stops insisting on a NATO-centric policy merely to preserve Washington's dominant position in the transatlantic relationship.

The United States would have the option of establishing a limited security relationship with the EU—as a hedge against developments in Europe that might have a serious effect on important American interests. Under such a system, however, Europeans would finally have primary responsibility for the security of Europe, and America's risk exposure would be appropriately limited.

Suggested Readings

Art, Robert J. "Creating a Disaster: NATO's Open Door Policy." *Political Science Quarterly* 113, no. 3 (Fall 1998).

Carpenter, Ted Galen. *Beyond NATO: Staying Out of Europe's Wars*. Washington: Cato Institute, 1994.

Carpenter, Ted Galen, ed. *NATO's Empty Victory: A Postmortem on the Balkan War*. Washington: Cato Institute, 2000.

_____. *NATO Enters the 21st Century*. London: Frank Cass, 2001.

Carpenter, Ted Galen, and Barbara Conry, eds. *NATO Enlargement: Illusions and Reality*. Washington: Cato Institute, 1998.

Danner, Mark. "Marooned in the Cold War: America, the Alliance, and the Quest for a Vanished World." *World Policy Journal* 14, no. 3 (Fall 1997).

Layne, Christopher. "Death Knell for NATO? The Bush Administration Confronts the European Security and Defense Policy." Cato Institute Policy Analysis no. 394, April 4, 2001.

Mandelbaum, Michael. *The Dawn of Peace in Europe*. New York: Twentieth Century Fund, 1996.

_____. "NATO Expansion: A Bridge to the Nineteenth Century." Washington: Center for Political and Strategic Studies, June 1997.

Mearsheimer, John J. *The Tragedy of Great Power Politics*. New York: W.W. Norton, 2001.

Perlmutter, Amos, and Ted Galen Carpenter. "NATO's Expensive Trip East." *Foreign Affairs* 77, no. 1 (January–February 1998).

Schake, Kori, Amaya Bloch-Lainé, and Charles Grant. "Building a European Defense Capability." *Survival* 41, no. 1 (Spring 1999).

Yost, David S. "The NATO Capabilities Gap and the European Union." *Survival* 42, no. 4 (Winter 2000–01).

—Prepared by Ted Galen Carpenter

52. Moving on in the Balkans

Congress should

- support the transfer of peacekeeping responsibility in Bosnia and Kosovo to America's European allies;
- insist on the withdrawal of all U.S. ground troops from the Balkans by 2004;
- wean the futile nation-building schemes in Bosnia and Kosovo from American aid by reducing government funding to zero over the next few years;
- oppose any new U.S. nation-building or peacekeeping missions in the Balkans, particularly in Macedonia;
- resist the urge to tell the Europeans, and the Balkan peoples themselves, how to govern the region;
- avoid using (or threatening) trade sanctions to force Serbia and Montenegro to accept Washington's views in the future; and
- encourage political and economic liberalization in the Balkan States.

The Balkans have been a major focus of U.S. foreign policy since 1992. In the last 10 years, the United States has spent billions of dollars and a sizable diplomatic and military effort trying to establish peace and build new nation-states in the region. However, in view of America's negligible interests in the Balkans, the region's position on Washington's agenda has been disproportionate to its importance.

Equally troubling, America's Balkan policy has largely been a disappointment. Although an uneasy peace has been achieved, Washington's wards in Bosnia and Kosovo are hardly closer to becoming lasting, stable multiethnic democracies than they were when they were created. Indeed, the region as a whole is still roiled by ethnic strife that threatens to unravel what little has been accomplished and entangle the United States in further difficulties down the road. Unfortunately, at a time when America's focus and resources are needed elsewhere, there appears to be no end in sight to the quagmire our Balkan policy has become.

Considering American interests and the security environment since September 11, 2001, the United States needs to fundamentally overhaul its Balkan policy. This should include a removal of U.S. peacekeeping troops, an end to Washington's nation-building activities, and a more honest approach to the realities of the region. Fortunately, Washington can safely rely on its rich and powerful European allies to pick up the slack and maintain peace and stability as the United States withdraws from the Balkans.

NATO Peacekeeping

The United States should end its participation in NATO's peacekeeping missions in the Balkans. With few interests in the region, considerable responsibilities around the globe, and threats to its homeland security, the United States needs to stop using its military forces as well-armed babysitters. Although the Bush administration made a campaign promise to terminate this overlong intervention and several thousand troops have been pulled out over the last two years, a sizable number of U.S. soldiers remain in Bosnia and Kosovo. Yet President Bush continues to assert that the U.S. military presence should not be "indefinite." Congress should insist that the administration translate its promises and rhetoric into action that leads to a final exit of U.S. troops.

The United States can start the departure process by redefining the mission. Because Europe has significantly greater interests in the region, the seven-year-old peacekeeping mission in Bosnia and three-and-a-half-year-old peacekeeping mission in Kosovo should both be reframed as European operations. This will allow the 2,500 U.S. troops in Bosnia and roughly 5,300 in Kosovo to depart at a sensible but certain pace.

The departure of American forces will have significant benefits for all parties involved. For the United States, one important benefit would be to distance itself from the region's ethnic disputes—troubles that are unlikely to end any time soon and only stand to worsen in the decade ahead. If these conflicts do escalate, the United States would be well advised to stay out the next time and allow the Europeans to handle them. Indeed, a more realistic and potentially longer-lasting approach would allow the parties to the conflict to resolve it themselves. At most, the

United States should provide diplomatic support for solutions that do not require its military arm.

Another benefit of a U.S. pullout will be significant savings, allowing resources currently allocated for peacekeeping to be used for more pressing tasks at home and abroad. Not only will the United States save the nearly $2 billion annually that now supports Balkan peacekeeping, but it will free thousands of U.S. troops to focus on more important missions such as the war on al-Qaeda. This will be especially welcome considering that military leaders have complained about the lack of available troops.

The departure of U.S. troops will also stop the drastic readiness slide suffered by units tasked with peacekeeping. No longer would units be so strained by their peacekeeping duties that they are deemed practically unfit for war fighting, as recently was the case with the Army's Third Infantry Division.

The United States will benefit in less obvious ways as well. First, American soldiers and statesmen will no longer be distracted by these nonvital missions. Second, military morale and retention will likely improve since peacekeeping missions have contributed to declines in both since the Balkan intervention began. Third, less pressure will be placed on National Guard and reserve units, freeing these citizen-soldiers for a return to civilian life or for other, more pressing military needs.

However, the United States will not be the sole beneficiary of an end to U.S. peacekeeping in Bosnia and Kosovo. Europe will reap rewards as well. In carrying out the Balkan operations itself, Europe would take a long overdue step in building a common security and defense identity, one that does not depend psychologically and militarily on transatlantic participation of the United States. That would not only make those with more at stake in (and closest to) Bosnia and Kosovo responsible for maintaining regional stability, it would also strengthen the credibility of European security institutions and improve the quality, impact, and visibility of their operations. A peacekeeping mission will be an ideal way for Europe to exercise its security muscles and for the European states to reemerge as responsible security actors. As former U.S. ambassador to NATO Robert E. Hunter noted, "The Balkans is the place to test the possibilities that now exist for a true European security and defense identity."

Lest Congress fear that Europe cannot effectively replace the U.S. presence in the Balkans, it should take heart from several recent positive developments. Foremost among these are NATO efforts to facilitate the development of European security institutions. For example, the European Security and Defense Policy and the Combined Joint Task Force have been created to allow Europe to act without engaging the full apparatus of the transatlantic alliance (i.e., the United States). The development of these NATO-friendly institutions also negates the argument that an American pullback will adversely affect the credibility of the alliance.

Congress can derive further confidence from the Europeans' relatively positive peacekeeping performances in their sectors of Bosnia and Kosovo. Even more promising was their execution of Operation Alba in which Italy, Greece, and others intervened militarily in Albania in 1997 in order to restore order and deliver humanitarian assistance. Indeed, a European takeover of the Balkan missions could help build a foundation for longer-term benefits: the normalization of international politics in Eurasia and the end of the U.S. burden of providing security for Europe. In short, an end to the U.S. peacekeeping missions would be a positive step for both the United States and Europe.

Bosnia

The 1995 Dayton Agreement ended more than three years of ethnic war and called for the creation of a unitary, multiethnic Bosnian state. Despite great efforts to build a stable, well-functioning, and democratic nation-state comprising Bosnian Muslims, Croats, and Serbs, the international community is scarcely closer to meeting that goal than it was at the end of the war. Instead, nation building in Bosnia has primarily squandered resources, created imperious international rulers, and served as a bad example of democracy in action for the Balkan people. Indeed, Bosnia is little more than a protectorate of the West that has become dangerously dependent on the international community running the country.

Despite billions of dollars in assistance, Bosnia remains an economic basket case. Of course, nation builders will argue that the new country has experienced positive growth. However, most of that so-called growth reflects the influx of international aid, not an expanding national economy. An official in the Office of the High Representative, the de facto international ruler of Bosnia, even admitted: ''There's really no economic growth. . . . There's no job creation.''

The truth is, Bosnia is not improving economically. State-owned businesses are struggling to stay open or are dormant, while a majority of Bosnians are out of work. Those who are working are dependents of the international organizations that employ them—a recipe unlikely to produce long-term economic growth and stability. Fraud and corruption are also rampant. Numerous other drags on economic growth exist, including onerous taxes and regulations that stifle business activity and deter investment. The situation is such that the Organization for Security and Cooperation in Europe's Robert Barry concluded, "You've got to be crazy to invest in this country where it is a given that if you obey the laws you're going to lose money."

Unfortunately, there is little hope for change. Privatization moves at a snail's pace, despite the pro-market rhetoric of eager Bosnian aid recipients. Instead, the socialist economy of the past lives on and is staunchly defended by those who benefit from it. Change is hindered by Bosnian officials resistant to relinquishing the communist era's bureaucratic system of jobs and privileges, and equally determined to avoid ceding control to their ethnic rivals. This reticence is especially difficult to overcome since, in most cases, the leaders of Bosnia's major state-owned enterprises are also members of the local ruling political parties—themselves divided along ethnic lines—who use these enterprises to further their financial and political interests. Ironically, the international community in Bosnia pays large amounts of rent to these state-owned businesses, thus effectively funneling money into nationalist parties that are considered the principal obstacles to peace. In short, despite Western efforts, Bosnia's economy has not seen the radical overhaul it needs, and the outlook is bleak. A recent economic study ranked Bosnia as one of the "most unfree" economies in the world, not exactly an international success.

Bosnia's troubles are unfortunately not simply economic. The political situation is unresolved and ripe for failure. The country is essentially divided into three ethnic regions dominated by nationalist parties. The fall 2002 elections underlined this fact. Moreover, the hoped-for reintegration of society has not occurred. Displaced persons have rationally not returned to areas where they would be in the minority. The fact is, Bosnia's rival ethnic groups do not want to live with each other—or fear that they cannot.

More troubling, and perhaps fatal to the nation builders' hopes, is that the Dayton Agreement contains the seeds of Bosnia's self-destruction. Essentially, this political framework creates incentives for group-oriented behavior since it generates an internal security dilemma: any increase in the power of one group is a potential threat to individuals belonging to other groups. In such a situation, it is strategically rational for individuals and groups to behave in ways that threaten the long-term viability of a multiethnic Bosnia. Although peacekeepers can prevent widespread kill-ings, they can do little more than mitigate the effects of the deep-seated ethnic animosity and suspicion that are rampant throughout Bosnia.

Another problematic feature of the current political arrangement is that Western officials running the country are treating Bosnians to an ineffective political education. The Office of the High Representative is giving the Bosnians a good lesson in colonial rule rather than democracy. It regularly flouts democratic norms, rules by decree, shows utter disrespect for the electoral process, and violates any semblance of media freedom. Indeed, former high representative Wolfgang Petritsch virtually imposed a new constitution on Bosnia—one neither tenable nor endorsed by the country's people. This same man recently bragged that he had "powers that would make a 19th century viceroy envious" and "did not hesitate to use my authority to impose legislation and dismiss domestic officials." Rather than helping the situation, autocratic Western nation builders are running roughshod over Bosnians, imposing their social engineering projects on people who are ignored if they complain. This effectively creates depen-dents who will not be able to act on their own when given the chance and sours them on what they are told is democratic rule. Thus, any short-term gains and the appearance of progress are coming at a serious future cost.

The United States has sunk billions of dollars in a country that seems to have little hope of surviving on its own as presently structured. That money has been put to ineffective and illiberal uses and subsidized the institutional remnants of a defunct communist state. Congress should stop funding this Western experiment in social engineering and neocolonialism.

Kosovo

In 1999, NATO defeated Yugoslavia (Serbia and Montenegro) in a short air war that centered on the political situation and ethnic conflict in Serbia's southern province of Kosovo. After that "victory," the United States joined a Western nation-building project in Kosovo fleshed out in UN Security Council Resolution 1244. That resolution essentially commit-ted the United States to an effort to develop democratic structures that will "ensure conditions for a peaceful and normal life for all inhabitants of Kosovo" and pave the way for a "substantial autonomy." In other words, the West was agreeing to create another Bosnia—a multiethnic democracy comprising former combatants. This time, the constituent groups were Kosovar Serbs and Kosovar Albanians, and somehow the province was expected to remain part of Serbia but enjoy significant autonomy.

Clearly, the international community has had its hands full accomplishing such a difficult task. Nearly 40,000 foreign troops, including 6,000 Americans, occupied Kosovo as part of the NATO-led Kosovo Force (KFOR). Accompanying these troops under the UN Interim Administration Mission in Kosovo (UNMIK) were thousands of administrators and police who were tasked with running the province (assisted by a small army of aid workers sent by nongovernmental organizations).

Since the end of the war, Kosovo has become nothing less than a Western protectorate. Of course, this does not seem to bother Balkan nation builders. Carlos Westendorp, former high representative in Bosnia, declared that ''a full international protectorate is required'' for Kosovo. He deflected criticism by arguing, ''This is not the moment for post-colonial sensitivities.'' Apparently it is not, at least among the UNMIKistas.

Spurred on by UN regulations giving it ''all legislative and executive authority . . . including the administration of the judiciary,'' UNMIK (and its top official, the Special Representative of the United Nations) has taken responsibility for nearly every facet of life. It has overseen everything from Kosovo's health care to garbage collection. It has also declared the German mark the local currency; paid the wages of teachers, doctors, and civil servants; and decided on matters as picayune as the cost of vending licenses to sell ice cream on Kosovo's street corners. Few things have been left to the Kosovars. The Special Representative's Office has even moved to shape election outcomes and shutter independent media outlets that publish controversial material and opinions. Fortunately, devolution of some of these responsibilities is on the horizon, but the fact is, the special representative has been a colonial autocrat in all but name.

Unfortunately, there is no apparent end in sight for this mission. After years of peacekeeping and billions of dollars expended, the stated goals of Resolution 1244 are barely closer to fulfillment than they were when they were crafted. Kosovo is still rent by ethnic strife, and interethnic violence remains an all-too-regular phenomenon. Indeed, most of Kosovo's non-Albanian population has been driven out by Kosovar Albanians, fled the province in fear, or settled in NATO-protected enclaves. In the summer of 2001, Serbs were victimized by home bombings in northern Kosovo. The reintegration of society necessary to meet the UN's goal of a multieth-nic Kosovo has also failed to materialize. Only a few hundred of the more than 200,000 non-Albanian residents of Kosovo driven out during and after the war have returned home. Furthermore, the Kosovo economy remains a shambles, the province is awash in crime (including organized crime revolving around drug and even human trafficking), corruption is rampant, and minority rights are practically nonexistent. Michael Steiner, the current special representative, admits that the international community's mission will be a long one requiring significant commitments of arms and other resources.

Yet even as this nation-building project continues to falter, a more troubling problem is at the heart of the mission. To wit, a fatal and fundamental difference exists between the purported goal of the international community—an autonomous, multiethnic Kosovo within Serbia—and the aspirations of the Kosovar Albanians, especially the former members of the Kosovo Liberation Army. Moderates and extremists alike in this community have not given up on their wartime goal of full independence. Therefore, even though the international effort has provided some element of peace, it is a false peace under the current arrangement. Today's Kosovo is in a state of political limbo that serves only to perpetuate local fears. This is particularly true for Kosovo's ethnic Serbs. It also energizes independence-minded Kosovar Albanians who are working toward severing the few remaining ties to Serbia. This means that Washington's attempt to build a peaceful multiethnic democracy will certainly fail. But it could be worse. Should Kosovar Albanian militants decide NATO forces are in the way of their plans for an independent Kosovo, U.S. forces could end up fighting their former de facto allies. Congress should, therefore, immediately stop funding this expensive and futile mission.

Macedonia

Macedonia has been and continues to be plagued by the same problem Serbia faced in Kosovo before 1999. In both situations, ethnic Albanian militants committed terrorist acts and incited violence to further their irredentist aims. In Serbia, the Kosovo Liberation Army played the West like a fine instrument to advance its goal of a Greater Albania. Emboldened by their success in Kosovo, Albanian irredentists have attempted to run the same game plan in Macedonia. In response to the resulting violence, the West was able to broker a deal between Albanian rebels and the Macedonian government in 2001. However, that agreement largely served to again reward the perpetrators of violence. NATO also sent several thousand peacekeepers to Macedonia, though U.S. forces already there have fortunately been restricted to support activities. Despite these efforts (or perhaps even because of them), the situation is likely to get worse. Indeed, a recent U.S. State Department report notes that "worsening relations between ethnic Macedonians and Albanians calls into question whether the framework agreement will be able to foster long-term coexistence." Considering the difficulties and inherent flaws in its Kosovo experience, the United States should avoid involvement in a Macedonian ethnic quarrel frighteningly similar to the one that ultimately led to war and a seemingly endless nation-building project in Kosovo.

Serbia and Montenegro

The two remaining republics of the former Yugoslavia have recently agreed to remain together in a newly named federal state of Serbia and Montenegro. This is a good sign for the region and for the post-Milosevic democratic regime in Belgrade. Although many Montenegrans still harbor a desire for independence, the new arrangement devolves significant amounts of power to the two republics so that a destabilizing schism does not appear on the horizon. However, if the peaceful reconciliation proves only temporary, Congress should firmly object to any plans that will entail a significant role for the United States. It should also insist that the administration avoid giving Montenegro any security guarantees—explicit or implicit. Such guarantees would be a sure recipe for abetting the types of destabilizing forces that tore Kosovo apart.

Meanwhile, the United States should encourage trade liberalization and privatization in Serbia and Montenegro. It should also avoid using trade sanctions as a way to whip Belgrade into line on Bosnia and Kosovo or to micromanage political developments inside the country. Such attempts to dictate from afar will only undermine the state's new democratic rulers and hurt the economic foundations of this struggling country. Should Milosevic's cronies return to power in Serbia, Congress should remain committed to trade with the republic. Trade barriers will only injure the country's private sector and stunt an emerging middle class, thus hurting those who would naturally form an opposition that supports democracy and liberalization.

Future U.S. Policy

America's extensive involvement in the Balkans has been a near total failure that needs to end. Congress should commence efforts to bring home the remaining U.S. troops and stop its financial support for the international community's dubious nation-building efforts. However, this does not mean that the United States should ignore the region.

The United States should certainly maintain an intelligence operation in the area to provide early warning of any anti-American terrorist operations based there. Furthermore, a U.S. pullback does not rule out using military force to strike and destroy any terrorist organizations that are using the Balkans as platforms for attacks against U.S. interests.

The United States should play a role in pressing for further liberalization in the region. It can also offer its good offices to help parties there peacefully reconcile their differences. Indeed, without the necessity of rhetorically supporting its wards and its intervention, the United States would be freer to act as an honest broker in any negotiations. It would also be better able to criticize any illiberal policies adopted by Balkan regimes. The United States would also be well advised to immediately begin educating the international community about the current underlying conditions in these countries. This may awaken nation builders who try to build their castles on shifting sands and head off any potential criticism if the situation eventually gets worse under the Europeans.

Once it turns over Balkan policy to the European Union (and to the Balkan peoples themselves), the United States should firmly avoid trying to control the situation as back-seat drivers. That is true for both Congress and the executive. Instead, the United States should allow the Europeans to pursue their own agenda as long as those measures do not jeopardize American security or economic interests. In other words, the Europeans should be given a free hand, unfettered by American desires to micromanage the future of the region. Indeed, the United States should not stand in the way if Europe somehow decides that the partition of Bosnia, Kosovo, or Macedonia, or all three, is the best long-range solution. However, the Europeans should also fully realize that, no matter what course they pursue, the United States will not bail them out militarily if the going gets rough. In short, the watchword of American policy toward the Balkans should be restraint.

Suggested Readings

Carpenter, Ted Galen. ''Waist Deep in the Balkans and Sinking: Washington Confronts the Crisis in Macedonia.'' Cato Institute Policy Analysis no. 397, April 30, 2001.

Carpenter, Ted Galen, ed. *NATO's Empty Victory: A Postmortem on the Balkan War.* Washington: Cato Institute, 2002.

Chandler, David. *Bosnia: Faking Democracy after Dayton.* 2d ed. London: Pluto Press, 2000.

Corwin, Phillip. *Dubious Mandate: A Memoir of the UN in Bosnia, Summer 1995.* Durham, N.C.: Duke University Press, 1999.

Dempsey, Gary T, ed. *Exiting the Balkan Thicket.* Washington: Cato Institute, 2002.

Dempsey, Gary T., with Roger W. Fontaine. *Fool's Errands: America's Recent Encounters with Nation Building.* Washington: Cato Institute, 2001.

Judah, Tim. *Kosovo: War and Revenge.* New Haven, Conn.: Yale University Press, 2000.

Langewiesche, William. "Peace Is Hell." *Atlantic Monthly,* October 2001.

Layne, Christopher. "Blunder in the Balkans: The Clinton Administration's Bungled War against Serbia." Cato Institute Policy Analysis no. 345, May 20, 1999.

———. "Faulty Justifications and Ominous Prospects: NATO's 'Victory' in Kosovo." Cato Institute Policy Analysis no. 357, October 25, 1999.

Layne, Christopher, and Benjamin Schwarz. "Dubious Anniversary: Kosovo One Year Later." Cato Institute Policy Analysis no. 373, June 10, 2000.

—Prepared by William Ruger

53. The U.S. Alliance with Saudi Arabia

> **The U.S. Government should**
> - forcefully press Riyadh to aid American efforts to investigate terrorist activities and cut off private funding for terrorist groups, even at the cost of today's cozy relationship;
> - use visa and transportation rules to encourage release of captive American citizens by, for instance, denying U.S. visas to men who have abused their power under Saudi law to prevent wives and children from leaving the country;
> - put greater official distance between itself and the Saudi Arabian regime, thereby reducing Washington's identification with a corrupt kleptocracy;
> - end training of the Saudi national guard, a force directed at suppressing domestic unrest rather than guarding against external enemies;
> - withdraw U.S. military forces from Saudi Arabia; and
> - recognize that the feared Saudi "oil weapon" is a myth.

In early 2002 rumors circulated that Saudi Arabia was considering asking the United States to withdraw its troops from the gulf kingdom. Outraged denials arose in both Washington and Riyadh. But even before the September 11, 2001, terrorist assaults, Saudi Arabia was among Washington's more dubious allies. Washington should take the initiative in refashioning a relationship that has far more negatives than positives for the United States. The House of Saud has long leaned toward the West. King Abdul Al Aziz Al Saud, who fathered 44 sons, is the font of today's royal family, including King Fahd. The latter suffered a series of strokes beginning in 1995, however, and his half-brother Crown Prince Abdullah largely runs the government.

Saudi Arabia would be unimportant but for the massive oil deposits sitting beneath its seemingly endless deserts. There have been tensions with the West, especially during the oil boycott against the West in 1973 and 1974. However, most attention has focused on defending the Persian Gulf region from other potential invaders.

To contain Saddam Hussein's Iraq, America augments its military units in Turkey and carrier forces in the Persian Gulf with about 5,000 Air Force personnel in Saudi Arabia as part of the Southern Watch command, comprising aircraft ranging from F-15s and F-16s to C-130s and KC-135s. Another 1,300 military personnel and civilian contractors have worked with the Saudi national guard. No temporary response to Saddam's aggression, America's presence has a "permanent feel," as Howard Schneider of the *Washington Post* put it.

Although the relationship between Riyadh and Washington is close, it has rarely been easy. For American administrations that loudly promote democracy in nations as diverse as China, Iraq, and Zimbabwe, the alliance with Saudi Arabia has been a deep embarrassment.

Saudi Arabia is an absolute monarchy, an almost medieval theocracy, with power concentrated in the hands of senior royalty and wealth spread among some 7,000 Al Saud princes (some analysts estimate that the number of royals is as high as 30,000). Political opposition (even mild criticism) is forbidden. In practice, there are few procedural protections for anyone arrested or charged by the government; the semiautonomous religious police, or *Mutawaa'in*, intimidate and detain citizens and foreigners alike. The government may invade homes and violate privacy whenever it chooses; travel is limited. Women are covered, cloistered, and confined, much as they were in Afghanistan under the Taliban.

It is perhaps no surprise that such a regime has an unenviable reputation for corruption. Most ugly, though, is the religious totalitarianism enforced by Riyadh. Non-Muslim worship as well as proselytizing is prohibited for citizens and foreigners alike. Conversion means apostasy, which is punishable by death.

Moreover, up to 100 American women and children are essentially held captive in Saudi Arabia, having been denied a husband's or father's permission to travel. Some of the victims have been kidnapped despite valid U.S. custody orders granted while both parents were residing in America. Yet Washington's efforts to aid them have been sporadic at best, dependent on the initiative of individual ambassadors, and ultimately ineffective.

Such pervasive thuggish behavior alone is rarely enough to preclude Washington's maintaining diplomatic relations, but it should discourage the United States from affirmatively embracing the Saudi regime, even in the name of stability. Moreover, U.S. policies have identified Washington with the Saudi kleptocracy. Americans are now paying for that association, which has made the United States a target for terrorists. Ending America's support for the corrupt regime in Riyadh and expelling U.S. forces from the gulf appear to be one of Osama bin Laden's main goals. The Saudi ruling elite is also paying with increased domestic unrest for its repression and links to Washington. Moreover, the long-term drop in energy prices has caused economic pain in Saudi Arabia; unemployment is now estimated at 15 percent overall and at 20 percent for those under 30. That has helped generate unrest, but the discontented feel helpless to promote political change.

Soaring dissatisfaction with the regime due to slumping revenues and a slowing economy has merged with criticism of America. Many Saudis are angry at U.S. support for the House of Saud. Additional irritants are Washington's support of Israel and attacks on Iraq, and more recently the air strikes in Afghanistan. Admiration for Saudi terrorist bin Laden is evident even among those who dislike his austere Islamic vision. Worries Richard Murphy, a one-time U.S. ambassador to Saudi Arabia now with the Council on Foreign Relations, "After 11 years, we've worn out our welcome on the popular level, though not with the leadership."

Enabling Terrorism

Criticism tends to be expressed through religious leaders. Radical free-lancers have developed a widespread following: 15 of the 19 hijackers of September 11 were from Saudi Arabia. One Saudi businessman told the *Wall Street Journal,* "Many young people are disgruntled and disenchanted with our society's openness to the West and U.S. foreign policy." But the Saudi leadership has proved wary of aiding the United States despite direct attacks on Americans. The 1996 bomb attack on the Khobar Towers barracks in Dharan killed 19 Americans and wounded another 372. However, U.S. efforts to investigate the bombing were hamstrung by the Saudis, who refused to turn over relevant information and to extradite any of the 13 Saudis indicted by an American grand jury.

In the same year, the Saudis refused, despite U.S. urging, to take custody of bin Laden from Sudan. In 1998 bin Laden and several other extremist Muslim leaders issued a manifesto calling for a holy war to drive the United States from Islamic lands. Even so, U.S. officials were unable "to get anything at all from King Fahd" to challenge bin Laden's financial

network, charged John O'Neill, a former FBI official involved with counterterrorism who died in the attack on the World Trade Center, where he
was security chief.

Riyadh's reluctance to risk popular displeasure by identifying with
Washington continues even after the deaths of 3,000 Americans on September 11, 2001. Despite public protestations that all is well between the two
governments, Bush administration officials privately acknowledge that
Saudi officials were not as cooperative as had been hoped. True, the
Saudis allowed Washington to use the operations center at Prince Sultan
Air Base, near Riyadh. Nevertheless, Saudi Arabia joined its neighbors
in attempting to keep its distance, ostentatiously announcing that no foreign
troops would use Saudi facilities to stage attacks.

Unfortunately, the refusal to aggressively defend cooperation with the
West encourages the growth of extremist sentiments. Still, the lack of a
public endorsement pales in comparison with Riyadh's support for the
very Islamic fundamentalism that threatens to consume the regime in
Riyadh as well as to murder more Americans in future terrorist attacks.

Riyadh's strategy is to buy off everyone. It long subsidized Arab governments and guerrilla movements at war with Israel, and it opposed the
1979 peace treaty between Egypt and Israel. The regime was, along with
Pakistan, the primary financial backer of the Taliban in Afghanistan, which
provided sanctuary for bin Laden and his training camps. It is widely
believed that Saudi businessmen have made contributions to bin Laden
in an attempt to purchase protection. There are serious charges of financial
support from some of the Saudi royal family for bin Laden's al-Qaeda
network.

The problem runs even deeper. The Saudi state, run by royals who
often flaunt their libertinism, enforces the extreme Wahhabi form of Islam
at home and subsidizes its practice abroad.

Wahhabism is thought to dominate as many as 80 percent of the mosques
in America. Within this sect, hostile to modernity and the West, political
extremism and support for terrorism have flourished in Saudi Arabia itself.
Moreover, the threat now reaches beyond the Middle East to Indonesia,
Malaysia, and even the Philippines.

The Oil Issue

By any normal assessment, Americans should care little if the House
of Saud fell, as have other illegitimate monarchies, such as Iran's Peacock
throne. Except for one thing: Saudi Arabia has oil. Washington frets about

a fundamentalist revolution. Worries Saudi oil expert Nawaf Obaid, such a government would be "ten times more powerful [than] Iraq or Iran." Contrary to the conventional wisdom, however, the Saudis' trump hand is surprisingly weak. True, with 262 billion barrels of oil in proven reserves, Saudi Arabia has about one-quarter of the world's resources and 8.7 times America's supplies. Riyadh is not only the world's leading supplier, but as a low-cost producer, it can easily augment its daily exports, which were 9.1 million barrels a day in 2000.

However, the reserves figure vastly overstates the importance of Middle Eastern oil to the U.S. (and Western) economy. Saudi Arabia accounted for about 10 percent of production in 2001. Were the Saudi regime to fall, prices would rise substantially only if the conqueror, whether internal or external, held the oil off the market. The result then would be significant economic pain in the short term, though the Strategic Petroleum Reserve, which the president has vowed to fill, would help moderate prices.

A policy of withholding oil would, however, defeat the very purpose of conquest, even for a fundamentalist regime. After all, the Iranian revolution did not cause Iran to stop exporting oil; in fact, production increased steadily in the 1990s. If a new Saudi regime did halt sales, the primary beneficiaries would be other oil producers, who would likely increase exports in response to the higher prices. A targeted boycott against only the United States would be ineffective, since oil is a uniform product available around the world. In fact, the embargo of 1973–74 had little impact on production; the global recession of 1975 caused a far more noticeable drop.

A new government might decide to pump less oil in order to raise prices. Such a strategy would require international cooperation, yet the oil producers have long found it difficult to coordinate price hikes and limit cheating on agreed-upon quotas. Even if effective, restricting sales would have only a limited impact. A decade ago, when oil was selling for about $20 a barrel, energy economist David R. Henderson, a professor at the Naval Postgraduate School, figured that the worst case result of an Iraqi seizure of the Saudi oil fields would be about a 50 percent price increase, costing the U.S. economy about one-half of 1 percent of GDP. The real price hike as a result of losing Saudi oil likely would be even less today and would fall on an economy more than one-quarter larger. In any case, the economic impact would decline over time.

Countries such as Kuwait, Iran, Nigeria, Russia, and the United Arab Emirates have the ability to pump significantly more oil. A resolution of the Iraq issue would bring substantial new supplies online; Baghdad pumped 2.2 million barrels a day in 1990, before becoming subject to sanctions after the end of the Gulf War. As economist Susan Lee puts it, should Riyadh turn off the pumps, "the U.S. would find itself plenty of new best friends."

Sharply higher prices would bring forth new energy supplies elsewhere. Total proven world oil reserves were 660 billion barrels in 1980, 1,009 billion in 1990, and 1,046 billion at the end of 2000. Yet in the last decade alone the world's people consumed 250 billion barrels of oil. How could that be? A combination of new discoveries and technological advances increased the amount of economically recoverable oil. Reserves rose even as oil prices dropped.

America is dotted with high-cost wells that could be unplugged. The nation's outer continental shelf alone is thought to contain more than our current proven reserves. Barely 15,000 acres of the 19.6 million acre Arctic National Wildlife Reserve could contain a similar amount of oil (as well as supplies of natural gas).

Moreover, energy companies are looking for new oil deposits around the world, including the Caspian Basin, Russia, and West Africa. Estimates of as yet undiscovered potentially recoverable oil range from 1 trillion to 6 trillion barrels. Higher prices would further stimulate exploration, as well as production of alternative fuels and conservation, reducing oil consumption. In short, an unfriendly Saudi Arabia might hurt America's pocketbook; it would not threaten America's survival. Although in an unlikely worst case, the loss of most Persian Gulf oil, the cost hike might be significant, that risk must be balanced against the annual expense of maintaining forces directed at protecting Saudi oil, estimated at $50 billion by Georgetown University's Earl Ravenal. On top come the costs of fighting terrorism, inflamed by America's presence in Saudi Arabia.

To mention Saudi Arabia's shortcomings or suggest that the regime's survival is not vital to America makes policymakers in Washington and Riyadh nervous. The House of Saud doesn't take criticism well.

Divorcing Saudi Arabia

The United States should reassess the current Washington-Riyadh axis. The American commitment to the Saudi royal family is a moral blemish and a practical danger. It has already drawn the United States into one conventional war and has helped to make Americans targets for terrorism, which generated far more casualties in one day than did the Gulf War, the Kosovo conflict, and the Afghanistan campaign (so far) combined.

Stability in the Persian Gulf is of value, but it is not even clear that America's presence increases Saudi stability. Certainly the royal family will do whatever it takes to maintain its power and privileges against internal opposition. If its ruthlessness is insufficient, the American presence is not likely to help, unless the United States is prepared to commit ground forces—in addition to those presently on station—to prop up the monarchy, creating the prospect of a lengthy occupation and increased terrorist activity.

Of greater concern is the possibility of renewed external aggression, most obviously by Iraq, though that country remains in greatly weakened condition. But even before September 11 the Gulf States were working to resolve conflicts and improve their ability to defend themselves without Washington's help. The prospect of American disengagement would, like the prospect of a hanging, help greatly concentrate the mind. Such a prospect would also increase pressure on the Gulf States to forge defensive relationships with surrounding powers, most notably Iran, Syria, and Turkey, and to inaugurate serious political reform to generate a popular willingness to defend the incumbent regimes.

If the Gulf States fail to act, however, the United States shouldn't worry unduly about the future of the Saudi regime. Expanding America's military, going to war, and risking civilian casualties as a result of more terrorism in order to defend Riyadh costs far more than stability in the Persian Gulf is worth. Should the House of Saud fall, or be overrun, Washington would finally be relieved of the moral deadweight of defending that regime. And consumers would almost certainly continue to purchase oil, if not directly from a hostile Saudi regime, then from other producers in a marketplace that would remain global. Americans would adjust to any higher prices by finding new supplies, developing alternative energy forms, and reducing consumption.

There were many causes of September 11. Some, such as America's status as a free society whose influence permeates the globe, reflect the country's very being and cannot and should not be changed. But some U.S. actions would be of dubious benefit even if they did not put Americans at risk. Washington's willingness to make common cause with the morally decrepit, theocratic monarchy in Riyadh is an example. The United States must not retreat from the world, but it should stop intervening militarily and supporting illegitimate and unpopular regimes where its vital interests are not involved—as in Saudi Arabia.

Suggested Readings

Aburish, K. Said. *The Rise, Corruption and Coming Fall of the House of Saud.* New York: St. Martins, 1996.

Adelman, M. A. *The Genie Out of the Bottle: World Oil since 1970.* Cambridge, Mass.: MIT Press, 1996.

Amnesty International. "Saudi Arabia: A Secret State of Suffering," March 27, 2001, www.amnesty.org.

Amnesty International. "Saudi Arabia." Report 2001, December 2000, www.amnesty.org.

Bandow, Doug. "Befriending Saudi Princes: A High Price for a Dubious Alliance." Cato Institute Policy Analysis no. 428, March 20, 2002.

Bohi, Douglas, and Michael Toman. *The Economics of Energy.* Boston: Kluwer Academic Publishers, 1996.

Bradley, Robert. *The Mirage of Oil Protection.* Lanham, Md.: University Press of America, 1989.

Carpenter, Ted Galen. "Postwar Strategy: An Alternative View." *Joint Force Quarterly,* no. 27 (Winter 2000–01).

Conry, Barbara. "America's Misguided Policy of Dual Containment in the Persian Gulf." Cato Institute Foreign Policy Briefing no. 33, November 10, 1994.

Fandy, Mamoun. *Saudi Arabia and the Politics of Dissent.* New York: St. Martins, 2001.

Hadar, Leon. *Quagmire: America in the Middle East.* Washington: Cato Institute, 1992.

Hersh, Seymour. "King's Ransom: How Vulnerable Are the Saudi Royals?" *New Yorker,* October 22, 2001.

Lee, Susan. "We Can Live without Saudi Oil." *Wall Street Journal,* November 13, 2001.

Richman, Sheldon. "'Ancient History': U.S. Conduct in the Middle East since World War II and the Folly of Intervention." Cato Institute Policy Analysis no. 159, August 16, 1991.

—Prepared by Doug Bandow

54. East Asian Defense Commitments

The U.S. government should

- withdraw American military forces from South Korea over the next two years and terminate the mutual defense treaty at the end of that period;
- begin a four-year phased pullout of American troops from Japan, beginning with forces on Okinawa;
- replace the bilateral U.S.-Japanese defense treaty with an agreement that allows emergency base and port access and maintains joint military exercises and intelligence cooperation;
- drop proposals for enhanced defense ties with Singapore, eliminate the AUSMIN agreement with Australia, and make clear to the Philippine government and people that the Visiting Forces Agreement and anti-terrorist assistance do not commit the United States to military action on behalf of the Philippines, especially in any territorial disagreement involving the South China Sea;
- promote regional security cooperation through the Association of Southeast Asian Nations (ASEAN) and other appropriate institutions;
- expand economic and limited security ties with China while pressing Beijing to accelerate democratic, human rights, and market reforms and to resolve international disputes peacefully; and
- drop Washington's implicit defense guarantee to Taiwan but sell Taipei any weapons it deems necessary for its defense.

After the end of World War II the United States established an extensive forward military presence and fought two wars in East Asia as part of its strategy to contain communism. The Cold War ended a decade ago, but America's defense posture has changed little. The administration is committed to keeping at least 100,000 military personnel in East Asia and the western Pacific, apparently forever. The Pentagon's infamous 1995 assessment of security policy in East Asia (the so-called Nye Report) made the astonishing assertion that "the end of the Cold War has not diminished" the importance of any of America's regional security commitments.

Indeed, Washington has been *increasing* U.S. military ties, approving a new security treaty with the Philippines and involving special forces in Manila's fight against Abu Sayyaf guerrillas, for instance, and offering an implicit defense guarantee to Taiwan against China. Rather than expand America's military presence in East Asia at a time when credible security threats against the United States are diminishing, Congress should use its budgetary and legislative authority to initiate a phased withdrawal of American forces from South Korea and Japan and prepare to center Washington's reduced military presence in the central Pacific rather than East Asia.

Changed Threat Environment

American policy in the Far East has succeeded. For five decades Washington provided a defense shield behind which noncommunist governments throughout East Asia were able to grow economically (despite their recent setbacks) and democratically. Japan is the world's second-ranked economic power; Taiwan's dramatic jump from poverty to prosperity forced the leaders of the communist mainland to undertake fundamental economic reforms. South Korea now outstrips North Korea by virtually every measure of national power. After years of failure, the Philippines seems to be on the path of prosperity, while countries like Thailand have grown dramatically and will eventually recover from their temporary economic travails.

Serious threats to America's allies and interests have essentially disappeared. There is no more Soviet Union; a much weaker Russia has neither the capability nor the will for Asian adventurism.

Elsewhere real, tough-minded communism has dissolved into a cynical excuse for incumbent officeholders to maintain power. More than a decade after the Tiananmen Square massacre, China is combining support for greater economic liberty with respect for greater individual autonomy. So far Beijing's military renewal has been modest, and China has been assertive rather than aggressive, though its saber rattling at Taiwan remains of concern.

Southeast Asia remains roiled by economic and political instability, but such problems threaten no one outside the immediate region. Only North Korea remains a potential threat, but it is no replacement for the Soviet Union. Pyongyang is bankrupt and starving, essentially friendless, and, despite its willingness to wave the threat of an atomic bomb to gain respect, will only fall further behind the South. Moreover, sporadically warmer relations between the two Koreas after the summit between the South's Kim Dae Jung and the North's Jim Jong Il offer the hope, though obviously not the guarantee, of growing détente between the two states.

Some analysts privately, and a few publicly, say that Japan poses a potential threat to regional peace. However, Tokyo has gained all of the influence and wealth through peace that it had hoped to attain through war and the Greater East Asia Co-Prosperity Sphere in the 1930s.

Moreover, the lesson of World War II remains vivid to most Japanese: in recent years the nation has been convulsed by political debates over such modest actions as sending medical personnel to the Gulf War, providing peacekeeping troops to the UN operation in Cambodia, and authorizing military participation in civilian rescues.

Even mainstream politicians committed to a somewhat more assertive posture—which has become increasingly respectable—have routinely sacrificed military spending to budget concerns. The Koizumi government has moved to modestly expand Tokyo's defense responsibilities, but they remain far below both Japan's economic resources and its strategic interests.

Rethinking American Strategy

So far neither the Bush administration nor Congress seems to have noticed the many dramatic changes. Indeed, the Bush administration's proposed $46 billion increase in military spending for 2003 is more than any other country spends on defense. U.S. taxpayers spent roughly $13 trillion (in current dollars) and sacrificed 92,000 lives to win the Cold War. With the dramatic diminution of security threats and the equally dramatic growth of allied capabilities, the American people should no longer be expected to surrender more dollars and risk more lives to police East Asia for as long as friendly states believe it to be convenient. However much it might be in the interest of other nations for Washington to defend them—and what country would not naturally desire that the world's remaining superpower subsidize its defense?—it is not in America's interest to do so.

Unless the administration acts, Congress should take the lead in adjusting U.S. overseas deployments. Legislators should reduce the defense budget as well as overall force levels and foreign deployments; Washington should develop a comprehensive plan for the phased withdrawal of all forces currently stationed in East Asia and the termination of U.S. defense guarantees to allied nations.

The starting point for a new East Asian strategy is disengagement from the Korean peninsula, the international flashpoint that could most easily involve the United States in war. Although North Korea remains unpredictable and potentially dangerous, the 2000 summit and intermittent diplomatic steps since then suggest that Pyongyang has decided on a more pacific course, probably out of economic desperation. In any case, the South should be able to defend itself. It now possesses twice the population of, around 40 times the gross domestic product of, and a vast technological lead over the North. Especially after having rebounded from the Asian economic crisis the South is well able to spend whatever is necessary to make up for the withdrawal of 37,000 American troops. The North could then choose to engage in meaningful arms control or lose an inter-Korean arms race.

The potential for a North Korean nuclear bomb is unnerving. Pyongyang's recent admission that it has covertly pursued a uranium enrichment program has significantly raised tensions. That program is a violation of the commitments North Korea made in the 1994 framework agreement. Washington should work with China, Japan, and Russia to get North Korea to end its violation. More generally, the United States should work to reduce tensions on the peninsula. Washington should allow Seoul to take the lead in dealing with the North, supporting rather than undercutting South Korean efforts to draw the DPRK into a more responsible international role. At the same time, Washington should not only lift trade sanctions against the North but also normalize diplomatic relations—modest concessions that would offer the North ongoing benefits in return for maintaining a peaceful course.

Although we should remain cautious about any promises by Pyongyang, engagement offers greater prospects of success than does plunging the peninsula into a new cold, or possibly hot, war. There are no good options if Pyongyang persists in attempting to develop an atomic bomb, and a continued American conventional military presence is certainly not one.

U.S. ground forces in the South would become nuclear hostages, enhancing the North's leverage over America.

Time for a Setting Sun

Washington should follow a similar strategy in Japan, which no longer faces a serious threat. Whatever dangers to Japan remain or might arise in the future, from, say, an aggressive China, could be met by a modest Japanese military buildup. Of course, many of Japan's neighbors have long viewed Washington's presence more as an occupation force to contain Tokyo than as a force to contain Moscow. But the Japanese do not possess a double dose of original sin; their nation, along with the rest of the world, has changed dramatically over the last half century. The Japanese people have neither the desire to start another conflict nor the incentive to do so, having come to economically dominate East Asia peacefully.

Moreover, Tokyo is unlikely to accept a permanent foreign watchdog, and tensions will grow as the lack of other missions for the U.S. forces becomes increasingly obvious. Popular anger is already evident in Okinawa, where American military facilities occupy one-fifth of the island's landmass. Washington should develop a six-year program for the withdrawal of all U.S. forces from Japan, starting with those in Okinawa. At the end of that period Washington and Tokyo should replace their mutual defense treaty with a more limited agreement providing for emergency base and port access, joint military exercises, and intelligence sharing.

The United States need not expand base access elsewhere in the region. Washington should drop proposals to increase defense cooperation with Singapore and tightly circumscribe the scope of its Visiting Forces Agreement with the Philippines, which was promoted by former president Joseph Estrada and other Filipino supporters as a mechanism for drawing the United States into any confrontation with China. The United States needs also to limit any future military training missions, sharply insulating American forces from involvement in domestic conflicts, such as that involving the Abu Sayyaf, essentially a gang of bandits. The United States has suffered no damage attributable to the closing of its bases in the Philippines, which had become expensive anachronisms, in 1992. Instead of upgrading U.S. military ties, Washington should be transferring security responsibilities to its allies and friends.

Even less relevant is the Australia–New Zealand–United States (ANZUS) accord, which went into deep-freeze in 1984 after New Zealand blocked port access by nuclear-armed and nuclear-powered American ships, and the annual Australia–United States Ministerial Consultations (AUSMIN). ANZUS, created in the aftermath of World War II, was directed less at containing the Soviet Union, which had no military presence in the South Pacific, than at preventing a new round of Japanese aggression. But since Tokyo had been decisively defeated and completely disarmed, later to be fully integrated into the Western alliance, ANZUS was outmoded the day it was signed.

Which leaves AUSMIN. But Australia faces no meaningful threats to its security. An attack by a serious military power—China, India, Vietnam—is a paranoid fantasy. An Indonesian implosion might flood Australia with refugees, but not hostile troops. Anyway, Australia, blessed with splendid isolation and economic prosperity, can easily provide whatever forces it deems necessary to defend itself.

Washington should simply discard AUSMIN. Australia and America should maintain mutually beneficial military cooperation, such as intelligence sharing and emergency port access, and ink a free-trade agreement. At the same time, Canberra should enhance its own military role in the region.

Regional Security Cooperation

Indeed, the United States should encourage expanded regional security discussions. Through either ASEAN or another organization, smaller countries throughout East Asia should develop a cooperative defense relationship with Australia, New Zealand, South Korea, and especially Japan.

Fear of the latter ignores five decades of dramatic changes. Tokyo could do much to improve regional security. A measured military buildup, focused on defensive weapons and conducted in consultation with Japan's neighbors, would help prevent the creation of a dangerous vacuum following the departure of American forces, as feared by proponents of continuing U.S. dominance. Washington's position should be that of a distant balancer, leaving its friends to handle their own affairs but poised to act if a hegemonic threat arises that allied states cannot contain.

The United States could aid in the creation of a more effective regional security framework by encouraging the peaceful resolution of various boundary and territorial disputes. None presently seems likely to lead to war, but all impede better bilateral and multilateral cooperation. To help dissipate international tensions, Washington should offer its good offices to help mediate the Japanese–South Korean squabble over the Takeshima/ Tokdu islands, the Japanese-Russian quarrel over the "northern territories"

(Sakhalin island), and the multifaceted dispute involving China and several other countries that claim the Paracel and Spratly islands. Most important, the United States should make clear that resolution of those (and other similar) controversies is up to the interested parties, not America. Such a "tough love" policy forced Australia to assume the lead role in establishing a UN peacekeeping force in East Timor in the aftermath of that territory's messy divorce from Indonesia.

The end of Cold War rivalry between the United States and the Soviet Union allows Washington to take a more balanced position vis-à-vis the People's Republic of China (PRC). Washington should continue to promote good political relations, expand the military dialogue, and encourage additional economic reform.

However, the United States need not fear bruising the PRC's sensitivities when discussing China's foreign arms sales, human rights abuses, attempted bullying of Taiwan, and interference with America's internal affairs by seeking to block even private visits to the United States by Taiwanese officials. America should speak frankly on those issues, though Congress should resist pressure to limit trade with and investment in China. While nothing is inevitable, extensive economic ties offer what is probably the most powerful tool for weakening central communist control in the PRC.

Congress also needs to take the lead in repairing flawed administration policy toward the Republic of China (ROC). Relocated to Taiwan after the communist victory on the mainland in 1949, the ROC still claimed to be the legitimate government of all China until the late 1980s. Seven years after Richard Nixon made his historic trip to the PRC in 1972, the United States dropped diplomatic recognition of the ROC. Many other nations followed suit. Since then Taiwan has existed uneasily at the periphery of global politics—an economic powerhouse but a diplomatic midget.

The ROC's behaving increasingly like a sovereign state caused the PRC to rattle its sabers—or, more accurately, test its missiles—in early 1996. Beijing's threats led Washington to respond with a warning of "grave consequences," meaning military intervention, should hostilities erupt. The election in March 2000 of Chen Shui-bian of the Democratic Progressive Party, which has long championed Taiwanese independence, further increased tensions across the Taiwan Strait.

The United States does not have sufficient interests at stake to risk war with nuclear-armed China over Taiwan. However, Washington, after making clear that it believes the status of Taiwan, whether reunified with the mainland or independent, is up to the people of Taiwan to decide, should sell the ROC whatever weapons, such as attack submarines, Taipei desires to purchase for its own defense.

Conclusion

Asia, particularly East Asia, is likely to grow more important to the United States in coming years. That makes it essential that Washington simultaneously reduce the military burden on the American economy and force its trading competitors to bear the full cost of their own defense. Otherwise, U.S. firms will be less able to take advantage of expanding regional economic opportunities. More important, the United States will be more secure if friendly powers in the region, rather than relying on America, are able and willing to contain nearby conflicts.

Jettisoning antiquated alliances and commitments and reducing a bloated force structure does not mean the United States would no longer be an Asian-Pacific power. After bringing its forces home from South Korea and Japan, America should center a reduced defense presence around Wake Island, Guam, and Hawaii. The United States would remain the globe's strongest military power, with the ability to intervene throughout East Asia if necessary. However, American policy would be dictated by the interests of the American people, not those of the populous and prosperous security dependents that Washington has accumulated through-out the region.

Suggested Readings

Bandow, Doug. "America's Obsolete Korean Commitment." *Orbis* (Fall 1998): 605–17.
_____. "Free Rider: South Korea's Dual Dependence on America." Cato Institute Policy Analysis no. 308, May 19, 1998.
_____. "Korean Détente: A Threat to Washington's Anachronistic Military Presence?" Cato Institute Foreign Policy Briefing no. 59, August 17, 2000.
_____. "Okinawa: Liberating Washington's East Asian Military Colony." Cato Institute Policy Analysis no. 314, September 1, 1998.
_____. "Old Wine in New Bottles: The Pentagon's East Asian Security Report." Cato Institute Policy Analysis no. 344, May 18, 1999.
_____. *Tripwire: Korea and U.S. Foreign Policy in a Changed World.* Washington: Cato Institute, 1996.
Carpenter, Ted Galen. "Going Too Far: Bush's Pledge to Defend Taiwan." Cato Institute Foreign Policy Briefing no. 66, May 30, 2001.
_____. "Let Taiwan Defend Itself." Cato Institute Policy Analysis no. 313, August 24, 1998.
_____. "Managing a Great Power Relationship: The United States, China and East Asian Security." *Journal of Strategic Studies* 21, no. 1 (March 1998).

_____. "Washington's Smothering Strategy: American Interests in East Asia." *World Policy Journal* 14, no. 4 (Winter 1997–98).

Harrison, Selig S. *Korean Endgame: A Strategy for Reunification and U.S. Disengagement*. Princeton, N.J.: Princeton University Press, 2002.

Johnson, Chalmers, and E. B. Keehn. "The Pentagon's Ossified Strategy." *Foreign Affairs* 74, no. 4 (July–August 1995).

Layne, Christopher. "Less Is More: Minimal Realism in East Asia." *National Journal* 43 (Spring 1996).

Olsen, Edward A. "A Northeast Asian Peace Dividend." *Strategic Review* (Summer 1998).

_____. *U.S. National Defense for the Twenty-First Century: The Grand Exit Strategy*. London: Frank Cass, 2002.

Zich, Arthur. "Okinawa, Seoul: Are the Bases Needed?" *Impact* 12 (March 1997).

—Prepared by Doug Bandow

55. Policy toward India and Pakistan

> **The U.S. government should**
>
> - focus on democratic India as a leading diplomatic and economic partner of the United States in South Asia and as a strategic counterbalance to China,
> - reassess economic and military ties with Pakistan as part of a policy of U.S. "constructive disengagement" from that unstable military dictatorship,
> - reject plans to establish a long-term military presence in Pakistan,
> - treat India as a central player in the U.S.-led campaign against terrorism and the radical Islamic forces in South Asia,
> - refrain from pressing India not to use its military force against terrorism emanating from Pakistan, and
> - resist calls for an activist U.S. diplomatic role in mediating the dispute between India and Pakistan over Kashmir.

The easing in June 2002 of the tensions between India and Pakistan, South Asia's two nuclear-armed countries, was portrayed as a major success for U.S. diplomacy. According to the State Department's spin, Deputy Secretary Richard Armitage helped to prevent an Indo-Pakistani war, including the possible use of nuclear arms, after winning a pledge from President Pervez Musharraf of Pakistan to halt terrorism in the disputed state of Kashmir. In response, New Delhi permitted Pakistani commercial aircraft to again use Indian airspace and withdrew its naval forces from the Arabian Sea.

Building on this modest reduction in regional tension, Secretary of State Colin Powell visited South Asia in July 2002 and described both governments as America's "allies" in the war on terrorism, projecting an even-handed U.S. diplomatic approach. Yet other statements by Powell seemed to reflect a vague diplomatic tilt toward Pakistan. He accepted the Pakistani position that the infiltration of Muslim terrorists from Pakistan into Indian-controlled Kashmir had declined, despite the skepticism expressed by Indian officials. Moreover, by proposing to place the issue of Kashmir on "the international agenda," Powell was siding with Pakistan, which wants Washington to play a more active role in future negotiations aimed at resolving that dispute. India has supported the idea of bilateral Indo-Pakistani talks about Kashmir but refuses to hold them until there is clear evidence that Islamabad has put an end to its sponsorship of terrorism in Kashmir.

It's not surprising, therefore, that New Delhi regards the American view articulated by Powell as running contrary to India's national interests as well as reflecting a distorted analysis of the current Indo-Pakistani tensions and the balance of power in South Asia. What the Bush administration has done through its attempt at mediation has been to help a weak Pakistan to strengthen its diplomatic hand in the confrontation with a more militarily powerful India. Musharraf, like Soviet leader Nikita Khrushchev during the 1962 Cuban missile crisis with the United States, recognized that the conventional and nuclear military balance of power favored the other side. And, like Khrushchev, he had no choice but to submit to the ultimatum imposed on him and bring an end to the terrorist infiltration into Indian-held Kashmir (in the same way that Khrushchev had to withdraw the nuclear missiles from Cuba).

The Bush administration's diplomacy involved more than just helping Musharraf save face. It helped reduce the pressure on the Pakistani leader by hailing his public commitments to prevent terrorists from slipping into India. But Musharraf's anti-terrorist measures proved to be temporary, enabling him to preserve U.S. support without actually ending the backing for Muslim militants in Kashmir. Pakistan continues to tolerate the presence of terrorist camps on its side of the line of control in Kashmir, allowing the anti-Indian militant groups to maintain their communication networks and logistical backup in Pakistan. And while the infiltration of terrorists did slow initially after Musharraf's pledges were given to Washington, it has resumed at a level almost as high as before June 2002.

Equally important, the Indians resent what they consider the double standard that Washington applies in its war on terrorism in South Asia and the Middle East. India's position on talks with Pakistan has not been very different from that of the Israeli government, which has refused to restart negotiations with the Palestinian Authority until the latter takes concrete steps to end terrorism. The Bush administration has regarded Israel as a partner in the war on terrorism, accused the PA of supporting anti-Israeli terrorism, and refrained from treating those two entities even-handedly. Indeed, unlike in the case of India and Pakistan, Washington has not only expressed total support for Israel's preconditions for talks with the PA but has also called for the removal from power of PA president Yasser Arafat. President Bush, who has refused to meet with Arafat, has also linked any U.S. support for the Palestinians to their adoption of an ambitious agenda of political and economic reform. But Musharraf, a dictator whose military coup brought an end to Pakistan's democratic political system and whose main base of power is the political axis between Pakistan's leading anti-democratic forces (the military and the religious establishments), was invited to the White House and was showered with military and economic assistance. Indian leaders have noticed that inconsistency.

Pakistan under Musharraf has had even more ties with terrorism and anti-American groups and policies than the PA has had under Arafat. In fact, when President Bush declared that the next phase of the anti-terrorism campaign would be aimed at pressing the members of the so-called axis of evil not to develop chemical, biological, and nuclear weapons and stressed that the war against terrorism would be grounded in a set of universal values, including the rule of law, religious freedom, and respect for women, he could legitimately have included Pakistan in that axis. After all, Pakistan's leaders have maintained close ties to radical Muslim terrorist groups and have pursued successful efforts to acquire weapons of mass destruction (WMD). And they have either supported or tolerated policies with clear anti-Western and pro-militant Islamic orientations that are the antithesis of the universal values that the Bush administration is supposedly promoting.

Instead of being placed on President Bush's list of "evil" states, or at least being condemned and isolated diplomatically like Arafat's PA, Musharraf's Pakistan is now topping America's "A List" of the anti-terrorism coalition. Ironically, the September 11, 2001, attacks on New York and Washington and the ensuing U.S.-led war on terrorism have given Musharraf an opportunity to improve the relationship between Washington and Islamabad. That relationship had experienced a steep decline in the 1990s, as the end of both the Cold War and the common struggle against the Soviet occupation of Afghanistan eroded the perception of shared strategic interests.

563

But since September 11, General Musharraf, whose regime had been the main source of diplomatic and military support for the terrorist Taliban in neighboring Afghanistan, has portrayed his regime as an ally of Washington in its counterterrorism campaign. Despite his record—heading a military clique that assisted radical Islamic terrorist groups in Afghanistan and Kashmir, pressing for a war with India, advancing Pakistan's nuclear weapons program, presiding over a corrupt and mismanaged economy— Musharraf is being hailed by the Bush administration as a "courageous" and "visionary" leader who is ready to reorient his country toward a pro-American position and adopt major political and economic reforms. In exchange for his belated support, Musharraf has been rewarded with U.S. diplomatic backing and substantial economic aid.

There is no doubt that Musharraf's decision to join the U.S. war on terrorism did not reflect a structural transformation in Pakistan's policy. It was a result of tactical considerations aimed at limiting the losses that Islamabad would suffer because of the collapse of the friendly Taliban regime in Kabul. Rejecting cooperation with Washington would have provoked American wrath and placed at risk Pakistan's strategic and economic interests in South Asia. But while some cooperation between the United States and Pakistan is necessary to wage the war against terrorism, it must not evolve into a new long-term strategic alliance. Washington should view Pakistan, with its dictatorship, failed economy, and insecure nuclear arsenal, as a reluctant supporter of U.S. goals at best and as a potential long-term problem at worst. If anything, the Bush administration's concern with nuclear proliferation and with the possible transfer of WMD to terrorist groups should make Pakistan—a nuclear military power whose military leaders and scientists are committed to the notion of an "Islamic Bomb" and have maintained ties to the international network of radical Islamic groups, including al-Qaeda—a focus of U.S. anti-proliferation and anti-terrorism policies.

Indeed, changing international realities and developments in Asia provide the Bush administration and Congress with an opportunity to consider "constructive disengagement" from Pakistan. That nation has little strategic value to Washington over the long term. Indeed, it is likely to become more of a burden than an asset as far as long-term U.S. interests and values are concerned. Hence, U.S. policymakers and lawmakers should reject the idea of establishing permanent military bases in the hostile political environment of Pakistan. They should also recognize that any effort to prop up the Pakistani military involves long-term risks, including the possibility that the powerful military machine of Pakistan will fall one day into the hands of a radical Islamic regime.

Conversely, Washington should recognize that Westernized and secular India is a more reliable and important partner than Pakistan in the war on terrorism. Moreover, India, some seven times more populous than Pakistan, should be the focus of U.S. strategic and economic interests in South Asia. Such a policy would reflect genuine American national interests at the end of the Cold War and in the aftermath of September 11. The United States has a clear interest in establishing strong ties with India, one of the rising political, economic, and military powers in Asia and a potential strategic counterbalance to an increasingly assertive and difficult China. India is also the world's largest democracy as well as an important emerging economy and an expanding market for U.S. goods and investment.

The strengthening of U.S. ties with India should not, however, be construed as unconditional support for India's position on Kashmir in a way that could increase the power of the more hawkish nationalist forces in New Delhi. Washington should remain committed to a peaceful, negotiated settlement of the Kashmir dispute leading (it is to be hoped) to an outcome that will give that province more political autonomy. But the United States should not get directly involved in trying to mediate that conflict and should recognize that American interests would be preserved if the resolution of the conflict reflected the balance of power in the region—which clearly favors India. On the other hand, a solution that tilts in the direction of the radical Muslim terrorists in Kashmir would amount to a defeat of the U.S. goals in the war on terrorism. Hence, pressing the Indians not to respond to terrorist acts directed from Pakistan and resisting calls by Indian leaders for the United States to condemn anti-Indian terrorism in Kashmir project more than morally dubious double standards. Such a policy runs contrary to U.S. national interests.

Suggested Readings

Ganguly, Sumit. *Conflict Unending: India-Pakistan Tensions since 1947.* New York: Columbia University Press, 2002.

Gobarev, Victor M. "India as a World Power: Changing Washington's Myopic Policy." Cato Institute Policy Analysis no. 381, September 11, 2002.

Gurcharan, Das. *India Unbound.* New York: Knopf, 2001.

Hadar, Leon T. "Pakistan in America's War against Terrorism: Strategic Ally or Unreliable Client?" Cato Institute Policy Analysis no. 436, May 8, 2002.

Kux, Dennis. *The United States and Pakistan, 1947–2000.* Baltimore: Johns Hopkins University Press, 2001.

Perkovich, George. *India's Nuclear Bomb: The Impact on Global Proliferation.* Berkeley: University of California Press, 1999.
Rashid, Ahmed. *Taliban.* New Haven, Conn.: Yale University Press, 2000.

—Prepared by Leon T. Hadar

56. The International War on Drugs

Congress should

- repeal the Anti-Drug Abuse Acts of 1986 and 1988 and all legislation requiring the United States to certify drug-source countries' cooperation in counternarcotics efforts,
- declare an end to the international war on drugs, and
- remove U.S. trade barriers to the products of developing countries.

Washington's international drug control campaign exhibits every flaw inherent in central planning. The war on drugs—a program whose budget has more than quadrupled over the past 15 years—has failed remarkably in all aspects of its overseas mission. Most telling, illicit drugs continue to flow across U.S. borders, unaffected by the more than $35 billion Washington has spent since 1981 in its supply-side campaign. The purity of cocaine and heroin, moreover, has increased, while the prices of those drugs have fallen dramatically during the same period.

The U.S. government has not only federalized the social problem of drug abuse by treating narcotics use as a criminal offense; it has intruded into the complex social settings of dozens of countries around the globe by pressuring foreign governments to adopt laws and policies of its liking. In the process, the U.S.-led war on drugs has severely aggravated the political and economic problems of drug-source nations and increased financing for terrorist groups. Counternarcotics strategy thus conflicts with sound foreign policy goals, namely the encouragement of free markets, democracy, and peace. For countless reasons, the international drug war is both undesirable and unwinnable.

Failure on Three Fronts

One component of the supply-side campaign has been interdiction of drug traffic coming into the United States. That approach has been ineffective at reducing the availability of cocaine and heroin because authorities seize only 5 to 15 percent of drug imports and because traffickers easily adapt to such disruptions by using new smuggling innovations and routes. In an implicit recognition of the failure of interdiction efforts, the Clinton administration began favoring strategies that focus on drug-producing countries. Yet there was little reason to believe that an approach that emphasized eradication, crop-substitution, and interdiction efforts in drug-source countries would be more successful than interdiction of drugs along transit routes. A principal reason that supply reduction efforts cannot be expected to affect the use of cocaine, for example, lies in the price structure of the illicit drug industry. Smuggling costs make up only 10 percent of the final value of cocaine in the United States. Those costs, combined with all other production costs outside the United States, account for only 13 percent of cocaine's retail price. Drug traffickers thus have every incentive to continue bringing their product to market; they view eradication and interdiction as a mere cost of doing business. Moreover, even if such efforts were successful at raising the price of coca paste or cocaine in drug-source countries, their effect on the final price of cocaine in the United States would be negligible. As analyst Kevin Jack Riley has observed, "Using source country price increases to create domestic scarcities is similar to attempting to raise glass prices by pushing sand back into the sea."

The efforts of international drug warriors are also routinely frustrated by drug traffickers' dynamic responses to counternarcotics policies. Already expecting interference in their business, traffickers build redundant processing facilities in case current ones are destroyed, for example, or stockpile their product inside the United States in case of smuggling interruptions. The massive resources available to the $300 billion global illicit drug industry also enable it to react to counternarcotics strategies with ease. At best, drug war "victories" are ephemeral as the industry accommodates itself to new conditions. That situation has reduced U.S. officials to citing drug seizure figures or expressions of political will by foreign governments as important gains in the U.S.-orchestrated war on drugs.

The evidence from the field is less compelling. According to the State Department's annual *International Narcotics Control Strategy Report*, the total area planted in coca from 1987 to 1995 grew from 176,000 hectares to 214,000 hectares, dropping subsequently to 190,000 in 2001. The area planted in opium poppy, mostly in South Asia, more than doubled from 112,585 hectares to 249,610 hectares from 1987 to 1996 and fell to 143,918 hectares in 2001. The decreases in recent years have resulted from a combination of oversupply, the Taliban's crackdown on opium production in Afghanistan, intensified crackdowns on coca-growing regions in Peru and Bolivia, and a fungus that has attacked the coca plant. However, since those figures do not reveal important qualitative information, they can be misleading. For example, the destruction of less productive older plants and the cultivation of new, more productive plants are not captured by those data.

Indeed, the State Department's estimates of net production of illicit drug crops illustrate the futility of its overseas campaign. From 1987 to 2000, opium production increased from 2,242 metric tons to 5,010 metric tons, dropping to 1,236 metric tons in 2001, a fall due almost entirely to the Taliban's ruthless enforcement policies in Afghanistan, a country where Washington has no influence. Yet as the State Department itself concedes, although ''total potential world-wide opium production in 1999 was at its lowest point in a decade and a half, the approximately three thousand metric tons potentially available were more than enough to supply global heroin demand many times over.'' And despite increased eradication efforts—the U.S. government pressures source-country governments to eliminate drug crops by spraying pesticides, slashing illegal plants, or burning peasants' fields—coca leaf production increased from 291,100 metric tons in 1987 to 655,800 metric tons in 2001 (see Figure 56.1). Peasant farmers still view illegal drug cultivation as advantageous despite coercive drug control measures.

Figure 56.1
Potential Coca Leaf Production, 1993–2001
(Bolivia, Colombia, Ecuador, Peru)

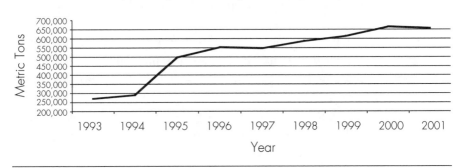

SOURCE: U.S. Department of State, Bureau for International Narcotics and Law Enforcement Affairs, *International Narcotics Control Strategy Report*, 2002.

Less coercive schemes have also been tried. Crop-substitution and alternative development programs, for example, seek to encourage peasants to join the legal market in agriculture or other sectors. U.S. aid finances infrastructure projects, such as roads and bridges, and subsidizes the cultivation of legal agricultural goods, such as coffee and corn.

Here, too, serious obstacles and unintended consequences undermine the best-laid plans of Washington and the governments of drug-source countries. Coca plants, for example, grow in areas and under conditions that are thoroughly inhospitable to legal crops, making a switch to legal alternatives unrealistic. (Only 5 to 10 percent of the major coca-growing regions in Peru and Bolivia may be suitable for legal crops.)

Farmers can also earn far higher returns from illicit plants than from the alternatives. For that reason, even when they enter crop-substitution programs, peasants often continue to grow drug plants in other areas. Ironically, in such cases, the U.S. government subsidizes the production of illegal drugs.

Indeed, programs that pay peasants not to produce coca can have other effects policymakers did not anticipate, as analysts Patrick Clawson and Rensselaer Lee point out: "The voluntary programs are similar to the crop acreage reduction program that the U.S. government uses to raise the income of wheat farmers. It is not clear why Washington thinks that a crop reduction program raises the income of Midwest wheat farmers but lowers the income of Andean coca farmers. In fact, in both cases, the crop reduction program really is a price support program that can raise farmer income."

The drug industry also benefits from improved infrastructure. One World Bank report reviewed road projects, funded by the World Bank, the U.S. Agency for International Development, and the Inter-American Development Bank, in coca-growing regions in Peru. "While the roads were useful in expanding coca production, they have severely hampered the development of legal activities." It is interesting to note that the major coca-growing regions in Peru and Bolivia—the Upper Huallaga Valley and the Chapare, respectively—were sites of major U.S.-funded development projects in previous decades.

Finally, even if alternative development programs were able to raise the prices of legal crops so that they exceeded or were at least competitive with the price paid for illegal crops, that situation could not last. The cost of growing coca, for example, represents such a small fraction of the final value of cocaine—less than 1 percent—that the illicit drug industry will always be able to pay farmers more than the subsidized alternatives could command.

Coerced Cooperation

The main components of the international narcotics control campaign have produced dismal results and hold little promise of improvement. Although that reality may be well recognized by drug-source nations, U.S. law ensures that most of those countries' governments comply, however reluctantly, with U.S. demands. The Anti-Drug Abuse Acts of 1986 and 1988 condition foreign aid and access to the U.S. market on the adoption of narcotics control initiatives in foreign countries.

That legislation directs the president to determine annually whether drug-producing and drug-transit countries are fully cooperating in the U.S.-led drug war. The certification procedure employs a series of trade and aid sanctions and rewards intended to gain that cooperation. If the president decertifies a country, or if Congress rejects the president's certification, the United States imposes mandatory sanctions that include the suspension of 50 percent of U.S. aid and some trade benefits. Discretionary sanctions may include the end of preferential tariff treatment, limits on air traffic between the United States and the decertified country, and increased duties on the country's exports to the United States.

U.S. Policy Is Not Just Ineffective

Efforts to "get tough" on drug-producing nations have caused an increase in violence and corruption, distorted economies, and undermined fragile democratic governments and the institutions of civil society. As long as drugs remain outside the legal framework of the market and U.S. demand continues, the enormous profit potential that results not only makes eliminating the industry impossible but makes the attempts to do so thoroughly destructive.

It is Washington's prohibitionist strategy—and not the narcotics trade per se—that is responsible for the problems usually associated with drug trafficking. Colombia, the principal target of Washington's international drug control campaign, has over the years seen its judicial, legislative, and executive branches become steadily corrupted by the drug trade. Crackdowns on leading trafficking organizations have produced widespread violence and even dismantled cartels, but they have not affected the country's illicit export performance.

571

The pervasive influence of the illegal drug industry in Colombian society, and the Colombian government's apparently insufficient efforts to escalate the war against traffickers, led to Clinton's 1996 and 1997 decertifications of that country. In 1998 Colombian journalist Andrés Cavelier complained that the decertifications had caused the private sector to suffer: "Because of threats of economic sanctions, legitimate sectors such as the flower industry have been obliged to hire expensive public relations firms to lobby official Washington against the imposition of sanctions."

Colombia's efforts to convince the United States that it wishes to cooperate in the fight against narcotics led Bogotá to undertake coca eradication and other counternarcotic initiatives. Those initiatives have created resentment among peasant populations, who have consequently increased their support of major guerrilla groups, and have reinforced the business relationship between drug traffickers and the rebels who protect illicit drug operations. Indeed, Colombia's various guerrilla organizations earn anywhere from $100 million to $150 million a year from drug-related activities.

Furthermore, the escalation of the drug war has provoked a wave of guerrilla violence that has destabilized Colombia and successfully displaced government authority in large parts of the country. "If you can single out one act that has played a decisive role," Defense Minister Juan Carlos Esguerra explained as far back as 1996, "I have no doubt that it is our frontal offensive against narco-trafficking in the southeast of the country."

The United States has responded by massively increasing, in 2000, aid to Colombia to $1.3 billion, most of which has gone to the military, and by subsequently expanding the counterdrug initiative in the Andean region. Washington has also sent to Colombia U.S. personnel, including Special Forces trainers and hundreds of advisers from the Central Intelligence Agency, the Drug Enforcement Agency, the Defense Intelligence Agency, and other U.S. agencies. Because the drug war has helped blur the line between the illicit drug industry and various insurgent groups, U.S. anti-narcotics aid is increasingly being used to fight the long-standing guerrilla movement—a use that is dragging the United States into Colombia's messy political and social setting.

The U.S.-orchestrated drug war in Colombia and elsewhere has thus weakened the rule of law and the institutions of civil society and financed terrorism. In Peru, for example, the Maoist Shining Path guerrillas received up to $100 million per year during the 1980s from their marriage of convenience with drug traffickers. That situation prompted Harvard econo-mist Robert Barro to suggest that "the U.S. government could achieve pretty much the same results if it gave the aid money directly to the terrorists."

The crippling of the Shining Path came only after the Peruvian govern-ment suspended coca plant eradication programs and concentrated its efforts on anti-terrorist activities and market liberalization. Unfortunately, the administration of President Alberto Fujimori abrogated the constitution in 1992 in a move intended to fight the rebel groups and institutional corruption, problems nourished by the drug war. Peru later reintroduced democratic rule and initiated further market reforms. Renewed U.S. efforts to get tough on Peru (the country did not receive full certification in 1994 or 1995), however, may compromise those successes. The resumption of coca eradication and other traditional anti-narcotics measures is worrisome in a country that has recently experienced economic stagnation, the return of populist rhetoric, and outbursts of terrorist violence.

Washington's heavy-handed ways have recently been evident in Bolivia as well. The livelihood of thousands of coca growers in the Chapare region has been wiped out by years of a vigorous, U.S.-backed coca eradication campaign that has not managed to provide the farmers with alternative sources of income. The result has been not only an increase in social unrest; the eradication program has also led to the rise of Evo Morales, an anti-American, anti–free market political leader representing the griev-ances of the dispossessed farmers. In the presidential elections of June 2002, Morales came in a close second to the market-liberal candidate, Gonzalo Sánchez de Lozada. The populist candidate received a further boost from Washington shortly before the elections when the U.S. ambassa-dor warned Bolivians not to vote for Morales, a message that had the opposite effect. The prospects that the president will be able to advance market-oriented policies have been diminished by the new political promi-nence of Morales, whose party now controls the largest bloc in the congress.

Latin American societies are not the only ones threatened by the global prohibitionist model. Illegal opium production takes place in Pakistan, Afghanistan, China, India, Thailand, Vietnam, Burma, and other countries in South and Central Asia. Many of those nations are struggling to become more market oriented and establish the foundations of civil society. U.S. supply-reduction efforts are increasingly focusing on countries that produce those drugs. Yet, if aggressive prosecution of the drug war has managed to undermine relatively well rooted democracies such as Colombia's, there is every reason to believe that U.S. drug policy in Asia may be even more reckless.

Mexico provides perhaps the most urgent warning to leaders of Washington's anti-narcotics crusade. Major Mexican drug cartels gained strength and influence as the U.S.-led interdiction campaign in the Caribbean, which began in the mid-1980s, rerouted narcotics traffic through Mexico. Unfortunately, the result has been a sort of "Colombianization" of Mexico, where drug-related violence has since increased. The 1993 killing of Cardinal Juan Jesús Posadas in Guadalajara, the assassinations of top ruling party officials, and the discovery of hundreds of millions of dollars in the overseas bank accounts of former president Carlos Salinas's brother all appear to be connected to the illicit drug business. The 1997 arrest and subsequent conviction of Mexican "drug czar" Gen. Jesús Gutiérrez Rebollo for protecting drug traffickers, the later indictment of the governor of the state of Quintana Roo, and President Vincente Fox's arrest of hundreds of police officers on drug-related charges only confirmed that the illicit industry has managed to corrupt government officials at all levels.

The destabilization of Mexico is especially unfortunate because of the country's efforts at economic and political liberalization. Unlike its treatment of Colombia, however, Washington has consistently granted Mexico full certification despite evidence of narcocorruption throughout the Mexican government. The inconsistency of U.S. drug policy toward the region is plain, but the internal contradictions of U.S. foreign policy would probably become too conspicuous were Washington to threaten sanctions against a partner in the North American Free Trade Agreement. An increasingly unstable Mexico also has serious implications for the United States. If Mexico experienced the level of social violence and volatility seen in Colombia or Peru, for instance, the United States would be directly affected—a development that would almost certainly provoke Washington's increased involvement in Mexico's complex domestic affairs.

The uneven standard by which Washington certifies nations is even more obvious when one looks outside Latin America. Where Washington has little or no influence, it is not hesitant to decertify a country—as has consistently been the case for Iran, Burma, and Syria. Yet, as the Council on Foreign Relations points out: "Iran pursues a vigorous drug control effort, forcibly eradicating opium crops, seizing large stocks of drugs, arresting users, and executing traffickers. By contrast, Russia is both a substantial opium producer as well as a transit country and money laundering center of growing importance but it is not included on the list of countries requiring annual certification.'' U.S. officials have fortunately, though far too slowly, recognized that the certification process is not serving U.S. interests and have deemphasized that aspect of the drug war in recent years.

Finally, Washington has not only created severe difficulties for drug-producing nations, its drug control efforts have helped disperse the narcotics industry to countries that might otherwise have avoided such penetration. Venezuela, Argentina, and Brazil, for example, have seen an upsurge in drug-related activity. Similarly, international disruptions in the various stages of illicit drug production have encouraged local traffickers to be self-sufficient in all stages of production. For example, the crackdown on Colombia's Cali cartel, which temporarily depressed coca prices in Peru in the 1990s, prompted the Peruvian industry to enter more advanced stages of cocaine production. More dramatic, while supply reduction initiatives have temporarily reduced coca production in Peru and Bolivia, in recent years those efforts have resulted in a more than 150 percent increase in coca cultivation in Colombia, making it the world's largest producer of the crop.

Toward a Constructive Approach

Washington's international drug war has failed by every measure. Production of drugs in foreign countries has increased, and the flow of drugs to the United States has continued. The Council on Foreign Relations notes, ''For twenty years, these programs have done little more than rearrange the map of drug production and trafficking.'' In fact, the impact of U.S. narcotics control policies is even worse, severely aggravating political, economic, and social problems in developing countries. Attempts to escalate the drug war, even in a dramatic way, will do little to change those realities.

Similarly, a more multilateral approach to fighting the drug war—through the United Nations or the Organization of American States, for example—will not work. Involving more governments and bureaucracies may marginally deflect political criticism away from the United States, but that approach cannot solve the fundamental problems created by prohibition: corruption, political violence, the destruction of civil society, the distortion of economic activity, and increased financing of terrorism. The multilateral strategy will have especially low credibility if international organizations present wildly unrealistic solutions, such as the UN's 1998 plan to eliminate global drug production in 10 years.

Washington should instead encourage the worldwide shift away from statism toward the creation of markets and civil society by ending its international crusade against drugs and opening its markets to drug-source countries' legal goods. Doing so will hardly affect U.S. drug consumption, but it would at least be a recognition that narcotics abuse is a domestic social problem that foreign policy cannot solve.

Suggested Readings

Clawson, Patrick L., and Rensselaer Lee III. *The Andean Cocaine Industry*. New York: St. Martin's, 1996.

Carpenter, Ted Galen. *Bad Neighbor Policy: Washington's Futile War on Drugs in Latin America*. New York: Palgrave, 2003.

———. "Ending the International Drug War." In *How to Legalize Drugs*. Edited by Jefferson M. Fish. Northvale, N.J.: Jason Aronson, 1998.

Council on Foreign Relations. *Rethinking International Drug Control: New Directions for U.S. Policy*. New York: Council on Foreign Relations, 1997.

Riley, Kevin Jack. *Snow Job? The War against International Cocaine Trafficking*. New Brunswick, N.J.: Transaction, 1996.

Thoumi, Francisco. *Political Economy and Illegal Drugs in Colombia*. Boulder, Colo.: Lynne Reinner, 1995.

—Prepared by Ian Vásquez

57. Relations with China

Congress should

- treat China as a normal great power, not as a "strategic partner" or a probable adversary;
- continue to liberalize U.S.-Chinese relations and hold China to its World Trade Organization commitments;
- avoid imposing economic sanctions against China even for narrowly defined objectives, since such measures will undermine permanent normal trade relations (PNTR);
- reject the proposed Taiwan Security Enhancement Act but support Taiwan's requests to purchase defensive weapons systems; and
- recognize that advancing economic freedom in China has had positive effects on civil society and personal freedom for the Chinese people.

Constructive Partner or Emerging Threat?

U.S.-Chinese relations have become increasingly unpredictable. Only a short time ago, both governments spoke of a "strategic partnership" and sought ways to enhance already substantial economic and political ties. The bombing of the Chinese embassy in Belgrade, the release of the Cox report alleging systematic nuclear espionage by the People's Republic of China, and the forced landing of a U.S. spy plane on Hainan Island produced a new round of tensions. Those have been offset, somewhat, by China's accession to the World Trade Organization and by cooperation between Beijing and Washington in the war against terrorism. But, as the 2002 reports by the U.S.-China Security Review Commission and the

Pentagon illustrate, there is deep concern that China will be an increasing threat to U.S. global economic and military power.

It would be a major mistake, however, to backslide from a policy of engagement into one of containment and to treat China as an adversary rather than as a normal great power. Managing relations with China and avoiding the extremes of confrontation or wishful thinking will be one of the key challenges facing U.S. policymakers in the next decade.

China's economy has grown precisely because Beijing has allowed greater economic freedom. The rapid growth of trade has increased per capita incomes in China and provided the Chinese people with new opportunities. In 1978 the total value of Chinese imports and exports amounted to only $20.6 billion. By the end of 2001, their value had increased to $509.8 billion (Figure 57.1). China's desire to compete in world markets is good for consumers and poses no threat to U.S. security.

Protectionists in the United States who point to large and growing trade deficits with China and to increased U.S. investment in China should not be allowed to block trade liberalization by injudicious use of national security and human rights arguments. Further liberalization of U.S.-

Figure 57.1
China's Opening to the Outside World

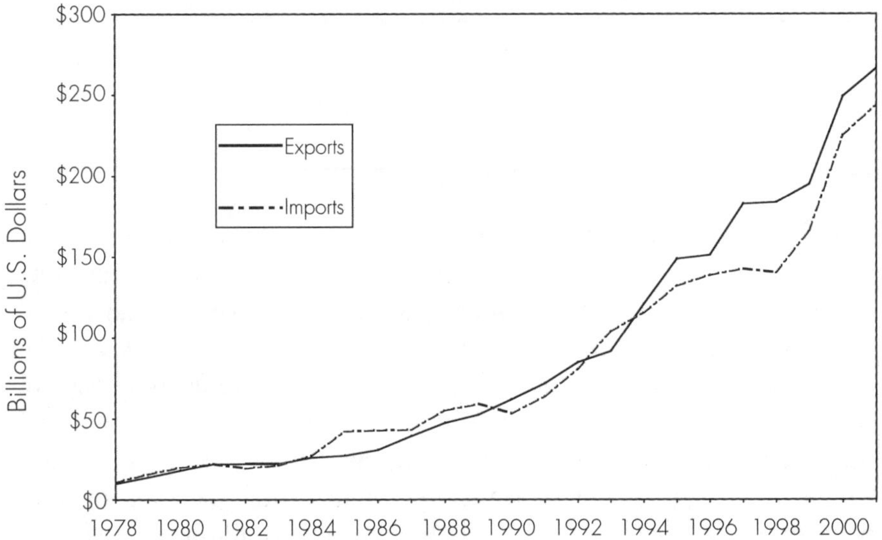

SOURCE: PRC General Administration of Customs, *China's Customs Statistics.*

Chinese trade is a win-win strategy and can play an important role in promoting peace and prosperity. Containment would do the opposite.

The U.S.-China Commission report "The National Security Implications of the Economic Relationship between the United States and China" offered more than 40 recommendations, many of which implicitly assume that China is a threat to U.S. economic and military power. Congress should not enact any recommendation that would endanger our policy of engagement. In particular, Congress should strongly oppose the creation of a "federally mandated corporate reporting system." That system is designed to force U.S. firms doing business in China to provide extensive data on all their business activities, even those that have no significant impact on national security.

U.S. firms investing in China would be strictly monitored and have to account for their investments in China and how those might affect jobs in the United States. Enactment of such a recommendation would impose a heavy burden on U.S. firms and put them at a competitive disadvantage in the Chinese market. Reduced investment in that market would have a negative impact on the U.S. market, because subsidiaries in China would import fewer U.S.-made components.

The USCC report also calls for Congress to "renew the Super 301 provision of U.S. trade law and request the Administration to identify and report on other tools that would be most effective in opening China's market to U.S. exports if China fails to comply with its WTO commitments." Such a step would be unwise. China should be given ample time to meet its obligations to the WTO and to the United States under the 1999 bilateral market access agreement. The United States should work through the WTO dispute resolution mechanism and target specific cases that are *significant* rather than try to prosecute *every* infraction of the trade agreement. It is in the interests of both Washington and Beijing to open China's markets. China will be undergoing important changes in its leadership, and the reformers need to have congressional support.

Likewise, Congress should not follow the commission's advice to "amend the CVD [countervailing duty] law to specifically state that it applies to NMEs [nonmarket economies]." The purpose of that recommendation is "to protect U.S. industries from unfair competition from the imports of these economies." In fact, China is unfairly treated by the use of NME methodology in determining production costs in antidumping cases. The methodology is grossly defective and prevents China from realizing its comparative cost advantage. Moreover, China has a higher economic freedom rating than Russia, yet the European Union has dropped the NME label for Russia. The United States should do the same for China. U.S. consumers would gain as a result.

Congress should not let protectionist interests dominate future U.S.-Chinese relations. The USCC report sends the wrong signal to Congress and to China. Instead of seeing China as a threat, Congress needs to cooperate with China in ways that are mutually beneficial. As Joseph Borich, executive director of the Washington State China Relations Council, noted in his July 2002 *CRC Update:*

> The draconian system the commission would create will do little or nothing to promote the long-term security of the U.S. Conversely, it would undermine shared Sino-U.S. interests, create a whole new layer of federal bureaucracy and bureaucratic requirements to bedevil U.S. business, and lay the basis for a self-fulfilling prophecy that could actually diminish our security.

Continued trade liberalization and engagement on a number of fronts, including a more liberal visa policy that permits Chinese students to study in the United States, especially law, economics, and the humanities, will have positive long-term benefits. Visa procedures should be reexamined. So long as individuals pose no threat to our national security, they should be encouraged to learn about our free society firsthand. Free trade can help normalize China and transform it into a modern economy and a civil society under the rule of law. Backsliding into protectionism cannot.

Both the USCC and Pentagon reports imply that as China grows wealthier its military spending will increase to the detriment of the United States and our Asian allies. That danger cannot be overlooked, but the probability is small compared with the likelihood that, as the nonstate sector in China grows, the Chinese Communist Party will lose power and political reform will ensue.

China is a normal, albeit sometimes difficult, rising great power. China's behavior can sometimes pose challenges, but the country is not a dangerous threat to U.S. security. China's military spending is a tiny fraction of U.S. defense spending. It will take decades before China can even come close to *current* U.S. spending levels. (China officially spends $19 billion on defense, but the actual figure is somewhere between $40 billion and $60 billion. In contrast, U.S. defense spending for fiscal year 2003 is $397 billion.) China's weapons systems are no match for those of the United States—although China is making a serious effort to modernize its armed forces.

The Taiwan Question

The most serious potential flashpoint in relations between the United States and China involves the status of Taiwan. China is primarily concerned with its domestic stability and with Taiwan's ultimate return to the motherland. The United States should insist that China use peaceful means to settle the Taiwan question. Despite Beijing's objections, the United States should be more willing to sell Taiwan the weapons it needs for its own defense. However, Congress should reject the proposed Taiwan Security Enhancement Act, which would create extensive military ties between Washington and Taipei and put the United States in the middle of the dangerous PRC-Taiwan dispute. The best way to bring about a peaceful resolution to the Taiwan issue is to further liberalize trade relations between the mainland and Taiwan.

During the past 10 years, Taiwanese investors have committed more than $70 billion to Chinese projects. Those investors have a strong incentive to maintain peace in order to increase their own prosperity. Likewise, they have an incentive to have direct trade, transport, and postal links with the mainland. The sooner those links are established, the better the chance for a cooperative solution to the Taiwan question. Congress should recognize that reality.

As a free country, Taiwan obviously has no incentive to become part of the PRC at this time. But if liberal economic policies on both sides of the strait continue, then China may undergo the quiet revolution that has occurred on the island. In that case, a peaceful solution to the Taiwan question could be realized. Congress should foster that process. Taiwan's recent accession to the WTO, following in China's footsteps, is a positive development that offers hope for the future.

Forging a Constructive Relationship

The dark side of the Chinese communist state is disturbing and must not be ignored. But that unsavory record should not be allowed to hide the progress that the Chinese people have made since economic reforms began in 1978. Increased trade has promoted the growth of markets relative to state planning, given millions of people new opportunities, and substantially raised living standards, especially in the coastal cities where economic liberalization has advanced the most. The primary goal of U.S. foreign policy should be to further the liberalization trend in China by maintaining a cooperative, constructive relationship. The most direct means of achieving that goal is through closer trade ties.

China has benefited most not from Western aid but from trade. As Ma Yu, a senior research fellow of the Chinese Academy of International Trade and Economic Cooperation, recently wrote in China Daily's *Business Weekly*, "The root cause of China's high-speed economic growth . . . is the policy of reform and opening-up." Congress should not take any actions that would stall that process.

The challenge for the United States is to exploit opportunities for further gains from trade and move closer to a constructive partnership with the PRC—but at the same time protect vital U.S. interests. Unfortunately, U.S. policy is drifting toward confrontation, as witnessed, in particular, by the USCC and Pentagon reports. That strategy risks creating a self-fulfilling prophecy that China will become an enemy. Indeed, a growing chorus in Congress and the U.S. foreign policy community argues that the PRC is a belligerent dictatorship and an implacable future enemy of the United States.

Painting China as an economic and military adversary is dangerous and misguided. Free trade is mutually beneficial—both China and other countries gain from trade liberalization. There is no doubt that, as the Chinese economy grows, so will the Chinese military budget. But that is not unusual for a large nation-state, and thus far China's military spending and its military modernization effort have been relatively modest.

It is true that no one can be certain how the PRC will behave on security issues in the future. Unlike Nazi Germany or the Soviet Union, however, the PRC is not a messianic, expansionist power; it is a normal rising (or reawakening) great power. At times, that can be difficult for other countries to deal with, but such a country does not pose a malignant security threat.

Proceed with Caution

The best course is to treat China as a normal (albeit sometimes repressive and prickly) great power and avoid the extremes of viewing the PRC as either an enemy or a strategic partner. The United States would also be wise to encourage other major countries in Asia to think more seriously about how they intend to deal with a rising China. A collection of diffident, militarily weak neighbors, wholly dependent on the United States for protection, is not likely to cause Beijing to behave cautiously.

Beijing's behavior toward regional neighbors has been a curious amalgam of conciliation and abrasiveness. Examples of conciliation include efforts to dampen the border disputes with such important land neighbors as India, Vietnam, Russia, and Kazakhstan and a campaign to build close political and economic ties with South Korea. The PRC has also been helpful in trying to discourage the North Korean regime from pursuing nuclear weapons and ballistic missile programs and has facilitated the recent détente between the two Koreas. At the same time, China's relations with Japan, the Philippines, and some other oceanic neighbors are noticeably more confrontational, and Beijing still aggressively pushes its territorial claims in the South China Sea.

Taiwan remains an especially dangerous flashpoint. Any move toward formal independence by Taipei would surely provoke military action by Beijing. Yet China's economic future depends strongly on Taiwan's prosperity, so military action is likely seen as a last resort. The increasing popularity of Taiwanese president Chen Shui-bian may eventually cause Beijing to open a serious dialogue with the island's leaders.

China's Changing Tide

The domestic tension created by Beijing's strategy of opening China's economy to the outside world while preventing meaningful political change has to be released sooner or later. The question is, How far and how fast will China go toward creating a fully open society based on private property and limited government? Gradualism appears to have worked reasonably well so far, but the inefficiency of China's state sector is apparent and corruption is rampant.

Yet it is undeniable that a significant transformation has occurred in the post-Mao era. Slowly but surely China is moving toward a stronger civil society, with the driving force being the market-oriented reforms initiated by Deng Xiaoping. Chinese intellectuals are now largely free to travel and lecture outside the mainland, and they are more interested in the works of Hayek and Friedman than those of Marx and Engels. Whether China will go all the way to a true free-market system, though, remains highly uncertain.

That uncertainty is why the United States needs a clear, realistic, and prudent foreign policy toward the PRC. Instead of painting China as a serious threat one day and as a de facto strategic ally the next, the United States needs to formulate a balanced view consistent with our own principles—a view that recognizes our long-term interest in engaging China while at the same time protecting our national security. The PRC's claims to the South China Sea islands and its relations with Japan and Taiwan must be viewed from that perspective.

It is also important to consider the future of economic, political, and social reform in China and how that future may be shaped by the liberal influence of Hong Kong and Taiwan. Will freedom spill over from those more open societies to the mainland, or will Chinese communism slowly corrupt the rule of law and weaken the free market in Hong Kong and seek to absorb and subordinate Taiwan? It seems clear that, unless it privatizes state-owned enterprises, China faces continuing problems of corruption and inefficiency. But wholesale privatization would undermine the last vestiges of party power. So the challenge for China's leadership is stark.

Ultimately, the creation of real as opposed to pseudo markets in China will require the full recognition of private property rights. The recent amendment to Article 11 of the PRC constitution, which places the nonstate sector and private enterprise on a par with state-owned enterprises, is a step in that direction. But without further constitutional and political reform that places rights to life, liberty, and property above the party, and allows for both economic and political freedom, there can be no certainty of ownership.

Article 11 of the PRC Constitution, as Amended March 15, 1999

"Individual, private and other non-public economies that exist within the limits prescribed by law are *major components* of the socialist market economy. The state protects the lawful rights and interests of individual and private economies . . ." (emphasis added).

That is why it is so important for China to face foreign economic competition and to be exposed to new ideas. Every step in the direction of greater economic freedom will provide further opportunities for the Chinese people to enlarge their private space and shrink the relative size of the state. Pressures will then build for greater social and political freedom.

An independent scholar in Beijing gave the best concise answer to the question of whether China will be a constructive partner or an emerging threat in the early 21st century. In his view, the answer will "depend, to a very great extent, on the fate of liberalism in China: a liberal China will be a constructive partner; a nationalistic and authoritarian China will be an emerging threat." America must prepare for both possibilities, but its policies should avoid needless snubs and provocations that would undermine the prospect for the emergence of a democratic, peaceful China.

Recommended Readings

Carpenter, Ted Galen. "Going Too Far: Bush's Pledge to Defend Taiwan." Cato Institute Foreign Policy Briefing no. 66, May 30, 2001.

———. "Let Taiwan Defend Itself." Cato Institute Policy Analysis no. 313, August 24, 1998.

———. "Managing a Great Power Relationship: The United States, China and East Asian Security." *Journal of Strategic Studies* 21, no. 1 (March 1998).

———. "Roiling Asia: U.S. Coziness with China Upsets the Neighbors." *Foreign Affairs* 77, no. 6 (November–December 1998).

Carpenter, Ted Galen, and James A. Dorn, eds. *China's Future: Constructive Partner or Emerging Threat?* Washington: Cato Institute, 2000.

Dorn, James A. "China's Future: Market Socialism or Market Taoism?" *Cato Journal* 18, no. 1 (Spring–Summer 1998): 131–46.

———. "Trade and Human Rights: The Case of China." *Cato Journal* 16 (Spring–Summer 1996).

Dorn, James A., ed. *China in the New Millennium: Market Reforms and Social Development.* Washington: Cato Institute, 1998.

Kristof, Nicholas D., and Sheryl Wudunn. *China Wakes: The Struggle for the Soul of a Rising Power.* New York: Times Books, 1994.

Lampton, David M., ed. *The Making of Chinese Foreign and Security Policy in the Era of Reform, 1978–2000.* Stanford, Calif.: Stanford University Press, 2001.

Vogel, Ezra F., ed. *Living with China: U.S.-China Relations in the Twenty-First Century.* New York: Norton, 1997.

—Prepared by Ted Galen Carpenter and James A. Dorn

58. The Israeli-Palestinian Conflict

Congress should

- resist calls for increased U.S. diplomatic efforts to resolve the Israeli-Palestinian conflict;
- oppose U.S. "nation-building" undertakings in the Palestinian territories;
- reject proposals to dispatch U.S. troops as part of international peacekeeping forces in the Palestinian territories;
- support efforts by Arab states and the European Union to help resolve the Israeli-Palestinian conflict;
- phase out all U.S. military and economic aid programs for Israel, while forgiving repayment of past military loans;
- terminate all financial assistance to the Palestinian Authority; and
- consider replacing the current interventionist policy in the Middle East with a policy of "constructive disengagement."

President Bush's June 24, 2002, address on the Middle East situation disappointed critics at home and abroad who chastise the White House for failing to "do something" to bring an end to the conflict between Israelis and Palestinians. Those critics have accused the Bush administration of being disengaged from that conflict and suggested that the administration's low-key approach helped to produce the current violence and brought about an erosion in U.S. "leadership." Washington, they argue, should adopt an activist role aimed at forcing Israel to withdraw from the West Bank and Gaza and creating the conditions for the establishment of an independent Palestinian state.

Although President Bush did promise in the address to work with other players to create a Palestinian state within three years, he refrained from committing Washington to a step-by-step peacemaking process and resisted calls to pressure Israel. Instead, he suggested that it was the bankrupt Palestinian leadership and its support for terrorism that were responsible for the failure to establish an independent state.

The president's address fell short of the expectations of observers who wanted Washington to help restart Israeli-Palestinian negotiations. It did, however, propose a combined strategy of nation building and peacemaking, drawing Washington into new commitments to reform the Palestinian Authority and to select a Palestinian leadership that would make peace with Israel under American supervision.

A formal effort to create a Westernized Palestine living in peace with Israel is expected to follow military action in Iraq by the United States and seems to be part of an ambitious undertaking to bring peace and stability to the Middle East and make it safe for democracy. The central problem with the Bush plan is the incompatibility of its drive to establish democracy in the Palestinian territories and its goal of maintaining U.S. strategic interests in the Middle East by making peace between Israelis and Palestinians. Free elections in the Palestinian territories are likely to elevate to power forces that would be opposed to peace with Israel, even given the more moderate positions of the Israel Labor Party. An American crusade for democracy in a new Palestinian state would only help to erode the fragile foundations of Washington's realpolitik goals of a U.S.-backed Palestinian-Israeli agreement.

Instead of trying to implement impractical Wilsonian goals in the Holy Land and the entire Middle East, which would force the United States to assume imperial commitments in that region, officials and lawmakers should consider an alternative policy of "constructive disengagement," which might include incentives for the creation of regional military and economic arrangements in which the European Union played an expanded role. Washington should reject demands to internationalize the conflict between Israelis and Palestinians, which assume that the United States should and would be responsible for resolving it and paying the costs involved. Instead, the Bush administration and Congress should encourage the process of "localizing" what is in essence a civil war. Such a policy fits with U.S. national security interests and would also be more conducive to resolving the conflict.

This argument for gradual U.S. disengagement from the Middle East and "localizing" the Palestinian-Israeli conflict runs contrary to the conventional wisdom in Washington. The bloody images of Palestinian terrorism and Israeli reprisals that are being constantly broadcast by the television networks create pressure on the White House to project American leadership and help end the horrific violence. The *New York Times* and other leading U.S. publications quote Middle East experts lashing out at President Bush for failing to come up with a peacemaking strategy and warn of the dire consequences of American inaction. Some of them even propose sending U.S. troops to guarantee a border between Israel and a new Palestinian state. But those pundits have yet to come up with a rationale for placing the Israeli-Palestinian conflict at the top of U.S. foreign policy priorities. Or, to put it differently, they should explain to the American people why benign neglect of that conflict would have an adverse effect on core U.S. national interests.

Hyperactive U.S. diplomacy toward Arab-Israeli conflicts could arguably have been justified in the context of the Cold War, as a way of containing Soviet expansionism in the region and securing Western access to its oil resources. But today there is no global ideological and military power threatening to exploit Arab-Israeli tensions as part of a strategy to dominate the Middle East, and the global energy supply is determined mostly by market considerations. Israel has made peace and established diplomatic relations with its former Arab enemies, Egypt and Jordan, and has the military capability, including a nuclear arsenal, to deter Syria, Iraq, and Iran. The Arab-Israeli conflict thus has been ''deinternationalized'' and transformed into a civil war between Jews and Arabs over the control of the territory of Israel and Palestine, including Jerusalem. The war, with its national, ethnic, and religious dimensions, is clearly a human tragedy, but—like the conflicts between Azeris and Armenians and Serbs and Albanians—it must be solved by the groups involved. The United States can and should express diplomatic support for the peaceful resolution of such conflicts and for the creation of strong civil societies, but we must be aware of the limits of our influence.

Americans who contend that the United States has a moral obligation to bring an end to the bloodshed should recognize that pro-peace factions in Israel and the Palestinian territories are rather weak. Both sides are willing to pay the costs of what they regard as a fight for survival, and there is no reason why the Americans should save them from themselves. Not unlike other civil wars, this one will end when—and only when— the sides are exhausted and conclude that their interests would be served more effectively around the negotiating table than on the battlefield.

In the meantime, there are no indications that the war in the Holy Land will spill over into a regional Arab-Israeli war and affect U.S. interests,

since, unlike the situation during the 1973 Mideast War, the Arab governments lack both the military power to defeat Israel and the diplomatic
and economic ability to threaten American interests. Thus, like that of
most other ethnic and religious conflicts, the impact of the Israeli-Palestinian dispute on U.S. national interests is limited. Arab governments, including those of Egypt and Jordan, which have embassies in Tel-Aviv, may
sympathize with the Palestinian cause, but they lack the power to militarily
challenge Israel. Low energy prices make it impossible for them to reapply
the so-called oil weapon. And without the aid of any new geostrategic
great power interested in checkmating Washington, they are now playing
a weak diplomatic hand as they try to help the Palestinians reinternational-
ize the conflict with Israel.

The Arab "allies" of the United States, including Saudi Arabia and
Egypt, argue that Washington is obligated to come to the rescue of the
Palestinians. But they should not expect the United States to "deliver"
Israel. Instead of complaining about the failure of the United States to make
peace in the Holy Land, and warning Americans of the dire consequences of
a low diplomatic profile, Egypt, Jordan, and Saudi Arabia should recognize
that it is in their national interests and that of the long-term stability of
the region to do something to resolve the Israeli-Palestinian conflict in a
regional context.

After all, it was a process of direct negotiations between Israelis and
Palestinians, without any direct U.S. involvement, that led to the signing
of the Oslo Agreement (and later the peace accord between Jordan and
Israel). Conversely, it was the attempt by the Clinton administration to
interject itself into the Palestinian-Israeli negotiations, leading to the 2001
Camp David talks, that helped create the conditions for the outbreak of
the current intifada (uprising). By rushing into the Camp David summit,
determined to resolve in a few days what are profound and long-standing
differences, President Clinton created unrealistic expectations and found
himself siding with Israel on the issue of Jerusalem, where no U.S. national
interest is at stake. All Clinton accomplished was to provoke an anti-
American backlash in the Arab world.

If anything, the growing conflict in Israel and rising anti-American
sentiment in the Arab world suggest that it is time to turn Washington's
traditional diplomatic strategy on its head. As demonstrated by the outcome
of recent U.S. efforts in the region, U.S. diplomatic activism doesn't
secure regional stability. Rather, it tends to intensify ethnic and religious
animosities and harden opposition to the United States. Even during the

Cold War, when Washington attempted to help mediate the conflict between Arabs and Israelis, its efforts proved successful during the 1979 Egyptian-Israeli peace talks only when the two sides agreed in advance to resolve their differences. Conversely, when the United States tried to intervene diplomatically and militarily in the Israeli-Palestinian war in Lebanon in the early 1980s, the move produced devastating effects on U.S. interests, including a dramatic increase in anti-American terrorism.

But a policy of "localizing" the Palestinian-Israeli conflict should not be equated with a U.S. "green light" to Israel to continue with its occupation and colonization of the Palestinian territories. A process of U.S. disengagement from the Middle East should set the stage for the United States to reassess its relationship with Israel and, in particular, to reconsider whether the huge military and economic aid that Washington is providing Israel serves U.S. strategic interests. U.S. military assistance for Israel not only provides it with incentives to adopt policies that ignite anti-American sentiments among Arabs but also runs contrary to Israel's own interest of integrating itself into the Middle East. And the annual economic aid package to Israel only helps to subsidize that country's statist economy. In the short run, Washington should at least cut economic aid to Israel by the amount of money Israel spends on building settlements in the occupied territories and condition military aid on Israel's agreement to stop using American-made weapons against civilians. At the same time, Washington should terminate financial assistance to the Palestinian Authority. In the long run, a normalization of the U.S relationship with Israel should include the elimination of aid to that country. That step would create an incentive for Israel to reform its sluggish economy and integrate itself politically into the region.

Israel could play an active role in regional military and economic arrangements and strengthen ties with the European Union. In fact, the United States should not resist but welcome the EU's playing a more activist diplomatic, military, and economic role in the Middle East— especially EU initiatives to help mediate the Palestinian-Israeli conflict. With its geographical proximity to the Middle East, its dependence on energy supplies from the Persian Gulf, and its close economic and demographic ties to the region, including a large community of Arab immigrants, the EU should be expected to replace the United States as the leading global military player in the region. If it extracted itself from diplomatic entanglements and military commitments in the Middle East and normalized its relationship with Israel, the United States might be welcomed into the region as a trustworthy friend and economic partner.

Suggested Readings

Friedman, Thomas. *From Beirut to Jerusalem.* New York: Anchor, 1990.

Fromkin, David. *A Peace to End All Peace: The Fall of the Ottoman Empire and the Creation of the Modern Middle East.* New York: Owl Books, 2001.

Hadar, Leon T. "Extricating America from Its Middle Eastern Entanglement." Cato Institute Policy Analysis no. 154, June 12, 1991.

_____. "The Green Peril: Creating the Islamic Fundamentalist Threat." Cato Institute Policy Analysis no. 177, August 27, 1992.

_____. *Quagmire: America in the Middle East.* Washington: Cato Institute, 1992.

_____. "The Real Lesson of the Oslo Accord: Localize the Arab-Israeli Conflict." Cato Institute Foreign Briefing no. 31, May 9, 1994.

Morris, Benny. *Righteous Victims: A History of the Zionist-Arab Conflict, 1881–1999.* New York: Knopf, 2001.

Richman, Sheldon L. "Ancient History: U.S. Conduct in the Middle East since World War II and the Folly of Intervention." Cato Institute Policy Analysis no. 159, August 16, 1991.

Segev, Tom. *One Palestine, Complete: Jews and Arabs under the British Mandate.* New York: Owl Books, 2001.

Shlaim, Avi. *The Iron Wall: Israel and the Arab World.* New York: W.W. Norton, 2001.

—Prepared by Leon T. Hadar

59. U.S.-Russian Relations

Congress should

- monitor closely the growing strategic ties between Russia and China,
- insist on a strong legislative role in U.S.-Russian diplomacy to set a good example for a fragile Russian democracy,
- urge the president not to base U.S.-Russian relations on personal ties with Russian president Vladimir Putin,
- insist that no commitments affecting U.S. security in regions near Russia are undertaken by the president without congressional approval,
- ensure that the United States not make security promises to the nations of Eastern Europe or Central Asia that it might not be able to fulfill,
- urge the president to proceed cautiously on the issue of Kaliningrad, and
- oppose any action that suggests that the United States believes Russia belongs to a different civilization.

When the Bush administration took office, it was very suspicious of Russian president Vladimir Putin. "Anyone who tells you they have Putin figured out is blowing smoke," President Bush told *Time* magazine during the presidential campaign. But after a few months in office, his view changed. "I want to look him in the eye," Bush said shortly before their first meeting, "and see if I can see his soul."

President Bush liked what he saw, and the two leaders have developed what appears to be a remarkably close personal relationship that seems to be based on absolute trust. "I looked the man in the eye and shook his hand," Bush said with regard to a strategic arms agreement. "And if we need to write it down on a piece of paper, I'll be glad to do that."

Unquestionably, good relations between leaders are to be preferred to bad relations. In addition, the support the Russian government has given to the United States since the terrorist attack in September 2001 has been extremely helpful and a marked change from the hostility that characterized relations during the Cold War. Yet Putin is not the first Russian leader to turn toward the West. It may be significant that Putin has a portrait of Peter the Great in his office. Peter also thought that Russia should learn from the West, but Peter was an autocrat whose reform effort, observes historian Bernard Pares, "grew out of the needs of his army."

Russia is no longer a superpower, but it still controls a vast landmass in the center of Eurasia. Although Russia no longer has a global reach, it still exercises considerable influence along its periphery. And it is along that periphery that we must look to understand Russian foreign policy.

Shifting Alliances

With the end of the Cold War, the putative object of both East and West was to heal the division of Europe and, indeed, of the world. Former Soviet president Mikhail Gorbachev spoke of a "common European home," while Western officials spoke of a "Europe whole and free." But disagreements about how that objective was to be achieved and about the future role of NATO soon emerged. For most observers, the abolition of NATO at the moment of its triumph was unthinkable. Leaving it as it was similarly appeared unthinkable, because that would simply preserve the division of Europe that characterized the Cold War. By default, then, the only remaining option was expansion.

Expansion, however, raised the question of Russia's potential membership. The Clinton administration left this possibility open, but others foreclosed it. Writing in the *Washington Post* in May 2002, Czech president Vaclav Havel stressed that "it would make no sense to consider Russia for membership in NATO, even though its location and civilization are not far distant from the West." But to say that Russia is not eligible for NATO membership because its civilization is not quite close enough to ours is to risk a dangerous reaction. "Ukraine is not a western country but belongs to Slavic civilization and Orthodox culture," argues Victor Chernomyrdin, the former Russian prime minister who is now ambassador to Ukraine. "Nobody awaits either Russia or Ukraine in the West. They'll try to be friends with us, they'll promise a lot to us, but they'll never declare us as their natural partners."

The danger is not just to the reunification of Europe. A true Russian-NATO partnership, Havel has insisted, "can be built only when each of the parties knows its true identity and when neither attempts to dictate how the other should define itself, or whom the other may or may not accept as allies." But if we tell the Russians they cannot be our allies, we are in effect telling them to find allies elsewhere. In 2002, at the same time Russia was being admitted as a "junior partner" in NATO, it was also consolidating relations with its other big neighbors. On June 5 at a summit in St. Petersburg, Russia, China, and four Central Asian countries (Kazakhstan, Kyrgyzstan, Tajikistan, and Uzbekistan) signed the Charter of the Shanghai Cooperation Organization, solidifying its formal international legal status. In addition, the Indian ambassador to Russia indicated that his country was interested in joining the SCO, an overture that Putin said was "positively viewed" by Russia.

When the idea of a Russian-Chinese-Indian triangle was broached several years ago, it was widely ridiculed as unrealistic. Now that assessment might have to be reexamined. Besides expanding the role of the SCO, Putin was also a principal force behind the creation of a new Eurasian security organization, the Conference on Interaction and Confidence-Building Measures in Asia, which had its inaugural meeting in Kazakhstan in June 2002.

Thus, at the same time Putin was convincing most experts of his tilt toward the West, he was quietly expanding Russia's diplomatic clout in other directions. Significantly, only Russia has a seat at the table of all three organizations: NATO, SCO, and CICA. Given the limited resources he has to work with, Putin has demonstrated remarkable diplomatic skill.

Russia and China

An example of that skill can be found in the Sino-Russian relationship, especially in the aftermath of President Bush's decision in December 2001 to withdraw from the ABM Treaty. At the time, the absence of any thunderous denunciations from Moscow or Beijing was taken as proof that they were "yielding to pressure." At the end of the month, however, the Itar-Tass news agency reported that Russia had agreed to sell China two *Sovremenny* destroyers, which are armed with cruise missiles designed to counter the U.S. Navy's Aegis air defense systems. "The US withdrawal from the ABM treaty made the mainland feel even more vulnerable. Beijing was forced to move closer to Russia," wrote Lau Nai-keung, a delegate to China's People's Political Consultative Conference.

Since then, Russia's arms sales to China have continued. Last June Russian sources reported the sale of eight Kilo-class diesel submarines, which will be armed with long-range anti-ship cruise missiles. Even more significant is the sale of the naval variant of 30 advanced Sukhoi fighters. "The Americans won't be roaming in the Taiwan Strait [after this deal]," observed Konstantin Makiyenko, deputy head of the Center for Analysis of Strategies and Technologies. People who would argue that Russia has made a decisive turn toward the West and abandoned the idea of an Eastern counterweight to NATO and the United States must explain these arms sales and the statements justifying them.

Central Asia and the Caucasus

Central Asia and the Caucasus is a region in which the interests of Russia, China, India, and the United States intersect, especially after September 11. Although many observers were surprised by Putin's acceptance of the U.S. presence in the region, he evidently viewed the American war against terrorism as support for Russian strategic objectives, since Russia had been supporting the Northern Alliance against the Taliban. Even so, Russia (and China as well) has indicated that it would be less willing to accept a permanent U.S. military presence in the area.

One major concern here is the struggle for oil routes. The United States has pushed for a pipeline from Baku, Azerbaijan, to Ceyhan, Turkey, in order to bypass both Russia and Iran. This initiative has provoked some irritation in Moscow, which may view the U.S. presence with more suspicion if it becomes extended. According to Alexei Arbatov, deputy head of the Russian parliament's defense affairs committee, "if relations develop toward struggle for influence and control over oil and natural gas pipelines in the region, the U.S. presence would be very bothersome."

A special problem exists in Georgia, which Russia accuses of sheltering terrorists from Chechnya. It is unclear how much authority the Georgian government exercises in the border region, and the U.S. government has provided some military assistance to Georgia to help it cope. Russian-Georgian relations have been exceptionally strained since the breakup of the Soviet Union, and the United States needs to tread carefully here. Russia and Georgia will be neighbors forever, while the United States is far away with a lot of other issues demanding attention and resources. Since it is unlikely that the United States will be in Georgia forever, Washington should be careful about making promises it will not be able to keep.

Kaliningrad

If the triangular diplomacy among Russia, China, and India bears watching, so does a growing problem in the West: Kaliningrad. In the aftermath of World War II, East Prussia was divided between Poland and the Soviet Union. Although that arrangement was supposed to be temporary, over time it became effectively permanent. With the disintegration of the Soviet Union, Kaliningrad became separated from the rest of Russia, much as Alaska is separated from the contiguous 48 states.

So far this situation has not presented any particular obstacles. The expansion of NATO and the European Union to include the Baltic States presents a problem, however, because Kaliningrad would then be effectively cut off from the rest of Russia. "What we hear today is worse than the cold war, because it divides the sovereignty of Russia," President Putin declared last June with regard to the visa requirements the EU would impose on Russian citizens wishing to cross EU territory to travel from Kaliningrad to the rest of Russia. "We will never agree to the division of Russia's sovereignty." Similarly, Russian defense minister Sergei Ivanov told a Finnish newspaper that if the Baltic States join NATO, "Russia will then be forced to review not only its own military positions but also the entire spectrum of international relations, both with the alliance as a whole and with the mentioned Baltic States."

Such statements should be viewed in the context of the strategic triangle already discussed. Moreover, the emotional content of the Kaliningrad issue should not be dismissed. In this regard, the EU visa requirement seems to resonate even more than NATO expansion, at least for the moment. "We are not savages here. We are part of European civilization," exclaims Vitaly P. Zhdanov, director of Kaliningrad's economic department. Although there is little the United States can do about the EU's attitude, it should be mindful that Putin can use these issues to drive wedges among the Western countries: indeed, last summer Putin won a more accommodating stance during a meeting with French president Jacques Chirac. Given the growing number of issues dividing the United States from its European allies, such a policy could prove very attractive.

Public Diplomacy

In a speech to the Foreign Ministry on January 26, 2001, Putin expressed dissatisfaction with its efforts in the area of public diplomacy. A campaign of public diplomacy is designed to go over the heads of political leaders

and reach the people themselves. The Bush administration itself has emphasized the need for public diplomacy, establishing an Office of Global
Communications in the White House to coordinate U.S. efforts. But
whereas the American effort seems designed primarily to affect public
opinion in Arab countries, the intent of the Russian effort appears to be
to influence Western public opinion.

A good example of this approach occurred immediately after President
Bush announced that the United States would withdraw from the ABM
Treaty. On December 15, 2001, the *Financial Times* published an interview
with Putin, in which he indicated he would have been willing to renegotiate
the treaty but the United States refused. Putin stressed that the United
States was within its rights and that Bush never misled him, but he indicated
that the issue was not a bilateral one between the United States and Russia.
"I believe the US-Russian bilateral relationship is of major importance
for our two nations. But it is also of great importance, taking into account
that these are two leading nuclear powers in the world, for overall international security," he stressed. "If relations between Russia and the West,
Russia and NATO, Russia and the US continue to develop in the spirit
of partnership and even of alliance, then no harm will be done."

Or put it another way, if the other countries of the West do not correct
the American tendency toward unilateralism, then harm could be done.
In phrasing the issue in this way, Putin exploits the unease already evident
in some European circles. "Tension and distrust now are the most important factors in America's relations with its European allies," William Pfaff
stressed in the *International Herald Tribune* last July. "Sooner or later
the European powers will have to deal with the consequences of U.S.
unilateralism." Perhaps Putin's remarks were not meant to take advantage
of this situation, but given his knowledge of European politics—he lived
in East Germany during the Cold War and speaks fluent German—some
thought should be given to the possibility that his policy is more calculating.

Russia and Western Civilization

If some of the trends mentioned here are troubling, others are more
reassuring. For example, Putin has vigorously denounced the rise of right-
wing nationalist and anti-Semitic movements in Russia. He has pointed
out that nationalism and intolerance also affect "so-called developed
democracies," and in using that language he put forth a challenge to the
United States to be true to our democratic principles. It is a challenge the
Congress needs to take up, not only because it is fair, but because it

resonates with the history of the 20th century. In the interwar years, the Western democracies did not pay sufficient attention to the erosion of democracy in Germany. We should not make that mistake again, and to the extent our example establishes a model to be emulated, we should be conscious of the example we set.

In this regard, particular attention should be paid to the tendency to divide Europe along civilizational lines. "Europe ends where Western Christianity ends and Islam and Orthodoxy begin," writes Samuel P. Huntington in *The Clash of Civilizations and the Remaking of World Order*. "The identification of Europe with Western Christendom provides a clear criterion for the admission of new members to Western organizations." As we have seen, this argument is being used to justify the division of Europe. Such a division would be nothing short of a tragedy, a betrayal of the hope generated by the end of the Cold War after a century of bloody conflict. Americans, in particular, should be aware of the danger. We should recognize from our own history the hypocrisy of asserting that there are two parts to Europe's bus, that Russia and other Orthodox countries belong in the back of the bus—which, of course, is just as good as the front, only different. No people with any dignity or intelligence will accept this argument, and although no American administration has adopted this position, Congress should be aware that it is influencing the debate over NATO expansion with potentially catastrophic consequences.

First, for most Russians it would signify a betrayal. As far as they are concerned, they ended the Cold War not because they were defeated militarily but because they realized communism was inherently flawed. The Warsaw Pact was abolished and they withdrew their military forces to their own territory, expecting their actions would be met with goodwill. For NATO to reciprocate by expanding to Russia's borders—especially if it excludes Russia from equal status because it supposedly belongs to a different (read inferior) civilization—is bound to enrage ordinary Russians. Congress, if it is asked to approve further NATO expansion, should be aware of this issue and take it into consideration in its deliberations.

Second, Congress should be aware that alliances provoke the formation of counteralliances; that, after all, is the logic of the balance of power. The SCO and the CICA have not received the attention they deserve. To be sure, they are not alliances like NATO, but they could form the basis of something more if Russia feels alienated.

Perhaps most important of all, however, Congress has to make it clear that diplomacy is not the exclusive domain of the executive branch. As

Alexander Hamilton wrote in *Federalist* no. 75, "The history of human conduct does not warrant that exalted opinion of human virtue which would make it wise in a nation to commit interests of so delicate and momentous a kind, as those which concern its intercourse with the rest of the world, to the sole disposal of a magistrate created and circumstanced as would be a President of the United States." And history has continued to vindicate Hamilton's argument. "I got the impression that here was a man who could be relied upon when he had given his word," British prime minister Neville Chamberlain wrote his sister after meeting Adolf Hitler in September 1938. It did not take long for Chamberlain to be disabused of his optimism.

We can hope that President Bush has more insight into the human soul than Chamberlain did, but as Hamilton pointed out, the security and safety of the United States cannot be left to the discretion of a single individual. In addition, personal diplomacy raises the question of what endures after the persons leave the scene. Agreements between countries should have some institutional arrangements binding the countries, and agreements between individuals, even if well meant, do not meet that standard. Even worse, they risk recreating the era in which the state was identified with a single individual, or sovereign.

"In republican government, the legislative authority necessarily predominates" over the executive, James Madison wrote in *Federalist* no. 51. One of the most disturbing elements in Russia now is the effective sidelining of the legislature. Russian history resonates with tragedies flowing from the excessive concentration of power in the hands of a single individual, and it is in the fundamental American interest to ensure that this situation is not repeated. Consequently, it is critical that Congress set an example for Russia—and, indeed, for the rest of the world's aspiring democracies— of how a republican government operates. It is no exaggeration to say that the future of democracy itself hangs in the balance here. Congress, therefore, must insist that the executive be accountable to the legislature for its activities and, above all, that any agreement affecting the security of the American people be submitted publicly for its approval.

Suggested Readings

Haass, Richard N. "U.S.-Russian Relations in the Post-Post-Cold War World." June 1, 2002, www.state.gov/s/p/rem/10643.htm.

Kober, Stanley. "The Great Game, Round 2: Washington's Misguided Support for the Baku-Ceyhan Oil Pipeline." Cato Institute Foreign Policy Briefing no. 63, October 31, 2000.

————. "NATO Expansion Flashpoint No. 3: Kaliningrad." Cato Institute Foreign Policy Briefing no. 46, February 11, 1998.

Lieven, Anatol. *Ukraine & Russia.* Washington: U.S. Institute of Peace, 1999.

Putin, Vladimir. Speech by President of the Russian Federation V. V. Putin at the Russian Federation Ministry of Foreign Affairs, January 26, 2001, http://president.kremlin.ru/withflash/appears/2001/01/26.shtml (in Russian).

Sagdeev, Roald, and Susan Eisenhower, eds. *Islam and Central Asia.* Washington: Center for Political and Strategic Studies, 2000.

Trenin, Dmitri. *The End of Eurasia.* Washington: Carnegie Endowment for International Peace, 2001.

Tishkov, Valery. *Ethnicity, Nationalism and Conflict in and after the Soviet Union.* London: Sage, 1997.

—Prepared by Stanley Kober

60. Relations with Cuba

Congress should

- repeal the Cuban Liberty and Democratic Solidarity (Libertad, or Helms-Burton) Act of 1996;
- repeal the Cuban Democracy (Torricelli) Act of 1992;
- restore the policy of granting Cuban refugees political asylum in the United States;
- eliminate or privatize Radio and TV Marti;
- end all trade sanctions on Cuba and allow U.S. citizens and companies to visit and establish businesses in Cuba as they see fit; and
- move toward the normalization of diplomatic relations with Cuba.

In 1970, 17 of 26 countries in Latin America and the Caribbean had authoritarian regimes. Today, only Cuba has a dictatorial regime. To be sure, the transition to market-oriented democracies, which protect individual liberty and property rights under the rule of law, is far from complete in any of the region's countries and has suffered setbacks in some of them. Economic sanctions have not been responsible for the general shift toward liberalization, however. They have, in fact, failed to bring about democratic regimes anywhere in the hemisphere, and Cuba has been no exception. Indeed, Cuba is the one country in the hemisphere against which the U.S. government has persistently and actively used a full economic embargo as its main policy tool in an attempt to compel a democratic transformation.

The failure of sanctions against Cuba should come as no surprise since sanctions are notorious for their unintended consequences—harming those they are meant to help. In Cuba, Fidel Castro is the last person to feel the pain caused by the U.S. measures. If sanctions failed to dislodge the military regime in Haiti, the poorest and most vulnerable country in the region, it is difficult to believe that they could be successful in Cuba.

A Cold War Relic

Sanctions against Cuba were first authorized under the Foreign Assistance Act of 1961, passed by the 87th Congress. In 1962 President John F. Kennedy issued an executive order implementing the trade embargo as a response to Castro's expropriation of American assets and his decision to offer the Soviet Union a permanent military base and an intelligence post just 90 miles off the coast of Florida at the height of the Cold War. Castro's decision confirmed Cuba as the Soviet Union's main ally in the Western Hemisphere.

For three decades, Cuba was a threat to U.S. national security. Not only did Cuba export Marxist-Leninist revolutions to Third World countries (most notably, Angola and Nicaragua), but, more important, it served as a base for Soviet intelligence operations and allowed Soviet naval vessels port access rights. However, with the collapse of the Soviet Union and the subsequent end of Soviet subsidies to Cuba in the early 1990s, that threat virtually ceased to exist. (There is always the possibility that Castro will do something reckless.) With the demise of the security threat posed by Cuba, all valid justifications for the embargo also disappeared.

Trade sanctions against Cuba, however, were not lifted. The embargo was instead tightened in 1992 with the passage of the Cuban Democracy (Torricelli) Act, a bill that former president George Bush signed into law. The justification for it was not national security interests but the Castro regime's form of government and human rights abuses. That change of focus was reflected in the language of the act, the first finding of which was Castro's "consistent disregard for internationally accepted standards of human rights and for democratic values."

In 1996 Congress passed the Cuban Liberty and Democratic Solidarity (Libertad) Act, a bill that President Clinton had threatened to veto but signed into law in the aftermath of the downing of two U.S. civilian planes by Cuban fighter jets in international airspace.

The Unintended Consequences of a Flawed Policy

The Libertad Act, better known as the Helms-Burton Act, named after its sponsors Sen. Jesse Helms (R-N.C.) and Rep. Dan Burton (R-Ind.), is an ill-conceived law. It grants U.S. citizens whose property was expropriated by Castro the right to sue in U.S. courts foreign companies and citizens "trafficking" in that property (Title III). That right—not granted to U.S. citizens who may have lost property in other countries—is problematic because it essentially extends U.S. jurisdiction to the results of events that occurred on foreign territory.

By imposing sanctions on foreign companies profiting from property confiscated by the Castro regime, the Helms-Burton Act seeks to discourage investment in Cuba. But fears that foreign investment there, which is much lower than official figures claim, will save the communist system from its inherent flaws are unfounded; significant capital flows to Cuba will not occur unless and until market reforms are introduced. While Helms-Burton may have slowed investment in Cuba, U.S. allies (in particular, Canada, Mexico, and members of the European Union) have not welcomed that attempt to influence their foreign policy by threat of U.S. sanctions. Consequently, they have repeatedly threatened to impose retaliatory sanctions and to take the United States to the World Trade Organization.

In May 1998 the Clinton administration and the European Union reached a tentative agreement that would exclude citizens of EU countries from Titles III and IV (denying entry visas to the executives of companies "trafficking" in confiscated property) of the Helms-Burton Act in exchange for guarantees from the EU not to subsidize investments in expropriated properties. President Bush has continued the policy of repeatedly waiving Title III of the act. But because only the Congress can repeal Titles III and IV, U.S.-EU trade relations remain uncertain, and the possibility that the EU will impose retaliatory sanctions or take the United States to the WTO remains. That confrontation has risked poisoning U.S. relations with otherwise friendly countries that are far more important than Cuba to the economic well-being and security of the United States. It also serves to divert attention, both inside and outside Cuba, from the island's internal crisis.

Moreover, any increase in Washington's hostility would only benefit the hard-liners within the Cuban government. Indeed, the embargo continues to be the best—and now the only—excuse that Castro has for his failed policies. As a Hoover Institution report on Cuba stated, Castro knows that "the embargo to some degree keeps him from becoming just another in a centuries-long string of failed Latin American dictators. . . . Nothing would come so close to 'killing' him while he is still alive as lifting the embargo."

Although the Soviet Union provided Cuba with more than $100 billion in subsidies and credits during their three-decade relationship, Cuban officials, who have estimated the cumulative cost of the embargo at more than $40 billion, incessantly condemn U.S. policies for causing the meager existence of the Cuban people. Elizardo Sánchez Santa Cruz, a leading dissident in Cuba, has aptly summed up that strategy: "[Castro] wants to continue exaggerating the image of the external enemy which has been vital for the Cuban Government during decades, an external enemy which can be blamed for the failure of the totalitarian model implanted here." The more supporters of the embargo stress the importance of sanctions in bringing Castro down, the more credible becomes Castro's claim that the United States is responsible for Cuba's misery.

As long as Castro can point to the United States as an external enemy, he will be successful in barring dissent, justifying control over the economy and the flow of information, and stirring up nationalist and anti-U.S. sentiments in Cuba.

Cuba Must Determine Its Own Destiny

Perhaps the biggest shortcoming of U.S. policy toward Cuba is its false assumption that democratic capitalism can somehow be forcibly exported from Washington to Havana. That assumption is explicitly stated in the Helms-Burton Act, the first purpose of which is "to assist the Cuban people in regaining their freedom and prosperity, as well as in joining the community of democratic countries that are flourishing in the Western Hemisphere."

But the shift toward democratic capitalism that began in the Western Hemisphere two decades ago has little to do with Washington's efforts to export democracy. Rather, it has to do with Latin America's realization that previous policies and regimes had failed to provide self-sustaining growth and increasing prosperity. The region's ability to benefit from a market system will depend in large part on its success in sustaining market reforms, which, again, will depend entirely on Latin American countries, not on the United States.

Now that the Cold War has ended, Cuba no longer poses a credible threat to the United States. Whether Cuba has a totalitarian or a democratic regime, though important, is not a vital U.S. national security concern. The transformation of Cuban society, as difficult as that may be, should be left to the Cuban people, not to the U.S. government. As William F. Buckley Jr. has stated, "If the Cuban people overthrow Mr. Castro, that is the end for which devoutly we pray. But if they do not, he is their problem."

Furthermore, there is little historical evidence, in Cuba or elsewhere, that tightening the screws on Cuba will produce an anti-Castro rebellion. Cato scholar James Dorn has observed that "the threat of using trade restrictions to advance human rights is fraught with danger . . . [because] it undermines the market dynamic that in the end is the best instrument for creating wealth and preserving freedom."

Even though Cuba—unlike other communist countries, such as China or Vietnam, with which the United States actively trades—has not undertaken meaningful market reforms, an open U.S. trade policy is likely to be more subversive of its system than is an embargo. Proponents of the Cuban embargo vastly underestimate the extent to which increased foreign trade and investment can undermine Cuban communism even if that business is conducted with state entities.

Cuban officialdom appears to be well aware of that danger. For example, Cuba's opening of its tourism industry to foreign investment has been accompanied by measures that restrict ordinary Cubans from visiting foreign hotels and tourist facilities. As a result, Cubans have come to resent their government for what is known as "tourism apartheid." In recent years, Cuban officials have also issued increasing warnings against corruption, indicating the regime's fear that unofficial business dealings, especially with foreigners, may weaken allegiance to the government and even create vested interests that favor more extensive market openings. As the Hoover Institution study concluded, "In time, increasing amounts [of expanded tourism, trade, and investment] would go beyond the state, and although economics will not single-handedly liberate Cuba, it may contribute some to that end. This is so, in part, because the repressive Cubans within the state apparatus are subject to influences that can tilt their allegiances in positive ways."

Further undercutting the regime's authority is the widespread dollar economy that has emerged as a consequence of foreign presence and remittances from abroad, estimated at $800 million annually, which the Helms-Burton Act had banned until the spring of 1998. Today about 50 percent of the Cuban population has access to dollars. The dollarization of the Cuban economy—a phenomenon now legalized by the Cuban regime as a result of its inability to control it—has essentially eliminated the regime's authority to dictate the country's monetary policy.

Replacing the all-encompassing state with one that allows greater space for voluntary interaction requires strengthening elements of civil society, that is, groups not dependent on the state. That development is more likely to come about in an environment of increased interaction with outside groups than in an environment of increased isolation and state control.

At present, there are signs that civil society is slowly emerging in Cuba, despite Castro's attempts to suppress it. For example, the Catholic Church, the main recipient of humanitarian aid from international nongovernmental organizations, has experienced a resurgence since the Archbishop of Havana was made a Cardinal. And, since the visit by Pope John Paul II in January 1998, which clearly established the Church as the only nationwide nongovernmental institution, it has pressed to expand its role in education and social work.

Finally, there are the small-business owners who are able to earn a living in the small but growing nonstate sector. The 160,000 *cuentapropistas*, or "workers on their own account," are approximately 4 percent of the total workforce; half of them are working with government-approved licenses and the other half in the informal sector. According to Philip Peters, vice president of the Lexington Institute, those workers "are dramatically improving their standard of living and supplying goods and services while learning the habits of independent actors in competitive markets." For instance, private farmers bring 85 percent of the produce sold in markets although they cultivate only 15 percent of the arable land. And, because most independent workers are in the service industries (mostly restaurant and food service), they would greatly benefit from the presence of Americans visiting for business or pleasure.

Cuban exiles should also be allowed to participate in the transformation of Cuban society. However, their participation need not require active involvement of the U.S. government. Thus, Radio and TV Marti, government entities that broadcast to Cuba, should be privatized or closed down. If the exile community believes that those stations are a useful resource in their struggle against the Castro regime, they have the means—there are no legal impediments—to finance such an operation.

A New Cuba Policy Based on American Principles

Washington's policies toward Cuba should be consistent with traditional American principles. First, the United States should restore the practice of granting political asylum to Cuban refugees. The 1994 and 1995 immigration accords between the Clinton administration and the Cuban government have turned the United States into Castro's de jure partner in oppressing those Cubans who risk their lives to escape repression. The "wet feet, dry feet" policy, which grants political asylum to Cuban refugees who make it to the U.S. shore on their own and forces the U.S. Coast Guard to return to Cuba those refugees that it picks up at sea, should be eliminated. Instead, the U.S. government should grant political asylum to all Cubans who escape the island.

There is no reason to believe that Cuban refugees would not continue to help the U.S. economy as they always have. The 1980 boatlift, in which 120,000 Cuban refugees reached U.S. shores, proved a boon to the economy of South Florida. In addition, since the Cuban-American community has repeatedly demonstrated its ability and desire to provide for refugees until they can provide for themselves, such a policy need not cost U.S. taxpayers.

Second, the U.S. government should protect its own citizens' inalienable rights and recognize that free trade is itself a human right. As Dorn says: "The supposed dichotomy between the right to trade and human rights is a false one. . . . As moral agents, individuals necessarily claim the rights to liberty and property in order to live fully and to pursue their interests in a responsible manner." In the case of Cuba, U.S. citizens and companies should be allowed to decide for themselves—as they are in the case of dozens of countries around the world whose political and human rights records are less than admirable—whether and how they should trade with it.

Third, U.S. policy toward Cuba should focus on national security interests, not on transforming Cuban society or micromanaging the affairs of a transitional government as current law obliges Washington to do. That means lifting the embargo and establishing with Cuba the types of diplomatic ties that the United States maintains with other states, even dictatorial ones, that do not threaten its national security. Those measures, especially the ending of current sanctions, will ensure a more peaceful and smooth transition in Cuba. After all, as former Reagan National Security Council member Roger Fontaine explains, "It is not in our interest to acquire another economic basket case in the Caribbean."

Unfortunately, strengthening the economic embargo has left the United States in a very uncomfortable position. Washington has depleted its policy options for dealing with future crises in Cuba or provocations from Castro.

Given the absence of other options and with the prospect of chaos on America's doorstep, U.S. officials will be under tremendous pressure to intervene militarily. Some people claim that a relaxation of the embargo would deprive the United States of its most effective tool for effecting change in Cuba, but tightening the embargo has left the United States with only its most reckless one.

The Tide Is Turning

Since the Pope's visit to Cuba in early 1998 and the Elián González incident—the shipwrecked six-year-old lost his mother at sea and was rescued by Florida fishermen during Thanksgiving weekend of 1999—U.S. businesspeople, policymakers, and the U.S. population at large have shown a growing interest in Cuba. For instance, in early 1998 the U.S. Chamber of Commerce joined religious and humanitarian groups to create a coalition to support the end of restrictions on the sale of food and medicine to Cuba. In the fall of 1998, 24 senators, led by Sen. John Warner (R-Va.), and several foreign policy experts, including former secretaries of state Henry Kissinger, Lawrence Eagleburger, and George Shultz, unsuccessfully asked President Clinton to appoint a bipartisan congressional commission to reevaluate U.S. policy toward Cuba. More than 3,400 U.S. business leaders visited the country in 2000.

In the closing days of its second session, the 106th Congress passed a measure as part of its agricultural funding bill that allows cash sales of food and medicine to Cuba but prohibits private-sector financing from the United States. It is doubtful that the measure will create a significant new market for U.S. farmers, as proponents of the bill desire, because Cuba is both broke and uncreditworthy.

The 106th Congress also turned the travel ban to Cuba, which had been implemented by executive order, into law. Turning that ban into law makes it more difficult to revoke the restrictions that deny the majority of Americans their right to travel freely. Already, about 200,000 Americans per year travel to Cuba, including 80,000 who do so without the explicit authorization of the U.S. government. If the travel restrictions were to be lifted completely, the number of American citizens traveling to Cuba would certainly increase, as would their contacts with Cuban citizens who work outside the state sector.

Indeed, in 2001 and 2002, respectively, the House of Representatives voted 240–186 and 262–167 to overturn the ban on traveling to Cuba. During that time, an increasing number of politicians, including governors and U.S. senators, visited the island. In May 2002 former president Jimmy Carter traveled to Havana and called for an end to the trade and travel embargo. Underlining the liberalizing potential of U.S. travel to Cuba, Carter used his visit to draw Cuba's national attention to the Varela project, a Cuban democratization initiative that had thus far received no play in the official media. Signs of increasing political dissatisfaction with the embargo show that the tide of opinion is clearly changing.

Conclusion

Sen. Robert G. Torricelli (D-N.J.) offered the following justification for U.S. policy after Helms-Burton was passed by Congress: "Different policies might have worked, might have been taken. But the die has been cast. Years ago we decided on this strategy and we are in the end game now. It is too late to change strategy." But even many people who may agree with Torricelli's position recognize, as Cuban exile Carlos Alberto Montaner does, that "the embargo, at this stage of the game, is probably a strategic error, political clumsiness from Washington which provides Castro with an alibi." In fact, it is not too late to change strategy and the "endgame" may yet take years to complete. U.S. clumsiness, unfortunately, increases the likelihood of a violent Cuban transition into which the United States would unnecessarily be drawn.

A better policy would recognize that, while Castro may be a clever political manipulator, his economic forecasting and planning have been dismal. Supporters of the embargo casually assume that Castro wants an end to the embargo because he believes that step would solve his economic problems. More likely, Castro fears the lifting of the U.S. sanctions. It is difficult to believe, for example, that he did not calculate a strong U.S. response when he ordered the attack on two U.S. planes in early 1996. It is time for Washington to stop playing into Castro's hands and instead pull the rug out from under him by ending the embargo.

Suggested Readings

Clarke, Jonathan G., and William Ratliff. "Report from Havana: Time for a Reality Check on U.S. Policy toward Cuba." Cato Institute Policy Analysis no. 418, October 31, 2001.

Council on Foreign Relations. "U.S.-Cuban Relations in the 21st Century." Report of an Independent Task Force Sponsored by the Council on Foreign Relations. New York: Council on Foreign Relations, 1999.

Flake, Jeff. "Will U.S. Trade with Cuba Promote Freedom or Subsidize Tyranny?" Remarks at Cato Policy Forum, July 25, 2002, www.cato.org–events–020725pf.html.

Glassman, James K. "No Sanctions, No Castro." *Washington Post,* January 20, 1998.

Human Rights Watch. "Cuba's Repressive Machinery: Human Rights Forty Years after the Revolution." New York: Human Rights Watch, 1999.

Montaner, Carlos A. "Cuba Today: The Slow Demise of Castroism." In *Essays in English Language.* Madrid: Fundación para el análisis y los estudios sociales, 1996.

Peters, Philip. "Islands of Enterprise: Cuba's Emerging Small Business Sector." Arlington, Va.: Alexis de Tocqueville Institution, 1997.

_____. "A Policy toward Cuba That Serves U.S. Interests." Cato Institute Policy Analysis no. 384, November 2, 2000.

Ratliff, William, and Roger Fontaine. "A Strategic Flip-Flop on the Caribbean: Lift the Embargo on Cuba." Hoover Institution *Essays in Public Policy,* no. 100 (2000).

Vásquez, Ian. "Washington's Dubious Crusade for Hemispheric Democracy." Cato Institute Policy Analysis no. 201, January 12, 1994.

—Prepared by L. Jacobo Rodríguez and Ian Vásquez

INTERNATIONAL ECONOMIC POLICY

61. Trade

Congress should

- recognize that the relative openness of American markets is an important source of our economic vitality and that remaining trade barriers are a drag on growth and prosperity;
- move the focus of U.S. trade policy away from "reciprocity" and "level playing fields" toward commitment here and abroad to free-trade principles;
- take unilateral action to reform U.S. protectionist policies;
- refrain from exerting protectionist pressure on U.S. negotiators in trade negotiations, especially with respect to (1) labor and environmental standards and (2) antidumping and other trade remedy laws;
- enact implementing legislation for market-opening trade agreements;
- maintain support for the World Trade Organization as a body for settling disputes;
- avoid using trade deficits as an excuse for trade restrictions; and
- adjust export control laws to the reality of today's international marketplace.

Free Trade Means Free Markets

Its opponents like to portray free trade as an ivory-tower theory, but in fact the case for knocking down trade barriers rests on common sense. It is now widely recognized that free markets are indispensable to our prosperity: when people are free to buy, sell, and invest with each other as they choose, they are able to achieve far more than when governments attempt to control economic decisions. Given that fact, isn't it obvious that free markets work even better when we widen the circle of people with whom we can buy, sell, and invest? Free trade is nothing more than the extension of free markets across political boundaries. The benefits of free trade are the benefits of *larger* free markets: by multiplying our potential business partners, we multiply the opportunities for wealth creation.

From this perspective, it becomes clear that Americans gain from open U.S. markets even when other countries' markets are relatively closed. The fact that people in other countries are not as free as they should be is no reason to restrict the freedom of Americans. When goods, services, and capital can flow over U.S. borders without interference, Americans are able to take full advantage of the opportunities of the international marketplace. They can buy the best and cheapest goods and services the world has to offer; they can sell to the most promising markets; they can choose among the best investment opportunities; and they can tap into the worldwide pool of capital.

Unfortunately, supporters of open markets seldom put their case in those straightforward terms. Instead, trade liberalization in this country is identified almost exclusively with international negotiations in which the removal of U.S. trade barriers is contingent upon the removal of barriers abroad. Such negotiations convey the impression that exports are the primary benefit that accrues from international trade and that open markets at home are the price we pay for greater export opportunities. That impression is misleading—and ultimately harmful to prospects for continued liberalization.

The idea that exports are good and imports are harmful is the essence of the mercantilist fallacy that lies at the root of most protectionist thinking. That fallacy turns truth on its head: imports are in fact the primary benefit of trade. Imports give us goods that are cheaper or better than those we can produce ourselves; exports, which represent production that Americans do not get to consume, are actually the price we pay for the imports we enjoy. To the extent that free traders perpetuate the mercantilist fallacy by endorsing the dogmas of "reciprocity" and "level playing fields," they are helping to foster a political culture that is hostile to open markets.

Opinion polls show that many Americans believe that U.S. openness to the rest of the world is destroying jobs and eroding living standards. That such "globalphobia" could be so widespread demonstrates that free traders are doing something wrong. To combat the current intellectual confusion, supporters of trade liberalization should return to their free-market roots. They need to meet mercantilist misconceptions head-on and to make the case that free trade is its own reward.

Alternatives to Reciprocity

Adopting a principled free-market approach to trade policy means more than a change in rhetoric—it means programmatic change as well. Free traders should expand beyond their traditionally exclusive reliance on negotiated liberalization and launch a campaign for the unilateral reduction or outright elimination of U.S. trade barriers—including the antidumping law, still-high tariffs on many products, import restrictions linked to agricultural price support programs, the Jones Act ban on foreign shipping between U.S. ports, the similar denial of cabotage rights to foreign airlines, and foreign ownership limits for air transport and broadcasting.

Top 10 Most Costly U.S. Trade Barriers

Quota, tariff, and licensing barriers to imported

- Textiles and apparel
- Domestic maritime transport (Jones Act)
- Sugar
- Dairy products
- Footwear
- Frozen fruits, fruit juices, and vegetables
- Ball and roller bearings
- Watches, clocks, watch cases and parts
- Table and kitchenware
- Costume jewelry

SOURCE: U.S. International Trade Commission.

Advocating unilateral reform would enable free traders to frame the trade debate in terms that give them the natural advantage. Instead of always defending free trade, they could attack its alternative: protectionism in actual practice. The beneficiaries of protection would be forced to explain why they deserve their special privileges and why the welfare of other American businesses and their workers, not to mention consumers, should be sacrificed on their account. The U.S. sugar protection program, for example, forces domestic consumers to pay double the world price for

615

sugar and costs American sugar-using industries and consumers an estimated $1.9 billion a year. Meanwhile, removal of quotas and tariffs on imported textiles and apparel would result in a welfare gain to the U.S. economy of $13 billion, according to the U.S. International Trade Commission.

Free traders need to reclaim their populist roots. Today trade liberalization is often characterized as elitist—padding the bottom lines of Fortune 500 multinationals and confirming the cosmopolitan prejudices of highly educated professionals. The stereotype is only confirmed by free trade's reliance on secretive negotiations and international bureaucracies. Unilateralism would combat that stereotype by stressing those aspects of the free-trade cause with the greatest populist appeal: cutting taxes and eliminating corporate welfare.

Furthermore, unilateral U.S. reforms would do more to encourage liberalization abroad than any trade negotiations ever could. The most sweeping and dramatic moves toward freer trade in recent years—in countries as diverse as Australia, New Zealand, Chile, Mexico, and India—have occurred not at the bargaining table but unilaterally. The leaders of those countries finally realized that isolation from the world economy was a recipe for economic stagnation, and therefore they sought to emulate the relatively open-market policies of more prosperous countries. History shows, therefore, that the most effective form of international economic leadership is leadership by example.

Still, pursuing unilateral reform would not mean an end to trade negotiations. International agreements can facilitate the liberalization process by recruiting export interests to support free trade at home; also, such agreements provide a useful institutional constraint against protectionist backsliding. But a new U.S. negotiating posture is needed, one that replaces demands for reciprocity with commitment to free-trade principles.

Instead of seeking to "win" at the negotiating table by "getting" more than it "gives," the United States could define some liberalization objectives—for example, tariff reductions, reforms of antidumping laws, rules on treatment of foreign investment, rules against protectionist misuse of health and safety standards, and so on—and offer to elevate its own unilaterally adopted free-trade policies into binding international commitments, provided that some "critical mass" of other countries agreed to exceed a defined minimum threshold of liberalization.

The United States does not need protectionist policies as "bargaining chips" to exert significant leverage. For example, other countries signed on to the 1997 multilateral agreements on telecommunications and financial services even though the only major U.S. "concession" was to lock in current levels of openness. Also, U.S. involvement in international agreements is desirable apart from any consideration of "concessions," since U.S. participation lends legitimacy to an agreement, thereby increasing other countries' confidence in the integrity of each others' commitments.

Thus, by taking a principled free-market approach, free traders can revitalize their cause both here and abroad. In particular, they can enjoy the best of both the unilateral and the multilateral worlds.

Oversight during Trade Negotiations

If Congress were to adopt a policy of unilateral trade liberalization, the need for the highly contentious "trade promotion authority" (TPA) legislation would disappear. Trade barriers would be eliminated by domestic legislation; afterwards, if the United States were to enter into international agreements, no changes in U.S. laws would be necessary.

Until the United States embraces unilateral liberalization, however, traditional trade negotiations represent the best available vehicle for reforming protectionist policies here and abroad. In such negotiations, the White House, not Congress, controls the agenda. Under the TPA legislation signed into law in August 2002, Congress retains the power to vote up or down on trade agreements presented to it, but the negotiations themselves are the responsibility of the executive branch.

Nevertheless, Congress still can exert considerable influence on the course of trade negotiations. Formally and informally, it consults with the administration while negotiations are pending and can pressure the administration to take this or that negotiating position. That pressure can have either a positive or a negative impact on the prospects for open trade.

Unfortunately, congressional input far too often undermines trade negotiations by pushing the United States to adopt anti-trade negotiating positions. Congressional pressure has been particularly misdirected in two areas: (1) labor and environmental standards and (2) U.S. trade remedy laws.

Many members of Congress have strongly urged the inclusion of agreements on international labor and environmental standards in any new trade agreements. The whole purpose of trade negotiations, however, is to reduce governmental interference in cross-border flows of goods and services; international regulatory mandates on labor and environmental matters would threaten to increase government interference in those flows and thus subvert the basic mission of negotiations. Meanwhile, labor and environmental standards are implacably opposed by developing countries, and a U.S. negotiating position that insisted upon such standards could end up dooming negotiations to fail.

The U.S. trade remedy laws—the antidumping, countervailing duty, and Section 201 "safeguard" laws—and their counterparts in other countries are badly in need of reform. In particular, the antidumping law, which purports to focus on "unfair trade," frequently penalizes healthy foreign competition for business practices routinely engaged in by American companies. While the U.S. antidumping law victimizes American import-using industries and consumers, foreign copycat laws now target U.S. exporters with depressing frequency. Indeed, the United States was the third leading victim of worldwide antidumping actions during the second half of the 1990s.

The prospects for reform here and abroad, however, are dimmed by vehement congressional opposition to any trade negotiations that might "weaken" U.S. trade laws. That opposition threatens, not just to block improvements in trade laws, but to prevent market-opening agreements more generally. Many of our trade partners are demanding changes to antidumping rules as a condition of any new agreements. If congressional pressure forces the administration into adopting an obstructionist position on antidumping, the United States could ultimately pay a grievously heavy price in lost opportunities to open markets around the world.

Implement Market-Opening Agreements

The 108th Congress should have the opportunity to reduce trade barriers here and abroad by passing the legislation needed to implement bilateral free-trade agreements. In particular, agreements with Chile and Singapore are nearing completion. Those countries are minor trading partners of the United States, and thus free-trade agreements with them would mark only modest steps toward more open trade. But they are steps in the right direction, and Congress should take them as soon as it has the opportunity. Meanwhile, Congress should encourage the negotiation of free-trade agreements with other, more important trade partners—including, for example, Australia, New Zealand, and South Korea. In addition, Congress should support the Bush administration's efforts to negotiate a Free Trade Area of the Americas.

Trade Deficits

America's trade deficit is not an economic problem. It is the benign consequence of a persistent surplus of foreign capital flowing into the United States. That additional capital has helped to make U.S. workers more productive, raising living standards above what they would be without it and building the foundation for future growth.

The underlying cause of the U.S. trade deficit is the fact that domestic savings in the United States are insufficient to fund all the available domestic investment opportunities. Any savings gap is filled by a net inflow of foreign investment. Those foreign funds allow Americans to buy more than we sell in the international market for goods and services, resulting in a trade deficit. As long as the pool of domestic savings available for investment is smaller than the actual level of investment, the United States will run a trade deficit.

The trade deficit is not the cause of alleged and real problems in the U.S. economy; rather, it is but a reflection of America's relative attractiveness as a home for global investment. As a result, the trade deficit tends to expand and contract along with the overall economy. By virtually every measure, U.S. economic performance is superior during years in which the trade deficit rises compared to years in which it shrinks. In contrast to conventional wisdom, rising trade deficits are associated with faster growth, falling unemployment, and accelerating manufacturing output. That explains why the U.S. trade deficit rose during the decade-long economic expansion of the 1990s but then actually shrank somewhat during the recession year of 2001.

Specifically, there is no credible evidence that expanded trade and bilateral deficits with such trading partners as Mexico and China cause a net loss of jobs. In fact, manufacturing output and the volume of imported goods tend to rise and fall together because both are stimulated by overall economic growth. During the late 1990s manufacturing output and import volume rose strongly, while in 2001 a slumping economy caused manufacturing output and the volume of imported goods to both plunge. The U.S. economy actually added a net 707,000 manufacturing jobs during the first four years of the North American Free Trade Agreement, from 1994 through 1997. Recent job losses, meanwhile, have been caused by slumping demand, first abroad and more recently at home, not by rising imports or trade agreements.

The only real sense in which the trade deficit is a threat to the U.S. economy is its potential effect on public policy. Persistent worries about the trade deficit could prompt policymakers to implement a "cure" for the trade deficit, such as higher tariff barriers, that itself could impose serious damage on the economy. Members of the 108th Congress should reject the idea of "balanced trade" as a policy goal. The best policy response would be to ignore the U.S. trade deficit and concentrate on maintaining a strong and open domestic economy that welcomes trade and foreign investment.

World Trade Organization

The World Trade Organization is at present the primary institutional support for an open world trading order. In addition to serving as a forum for ongoing trade negotiations, the WTO and its dispute settlement procedures uphold a limited but real rule of law in international commerce. The WTO strongly advances the U.S. national interest in free markets here and abroad and therefore deserves strong U.S. support.

Congress should support the new Doha Round of WTO negotiations. If successfully concluded, those talks could open vast new markets for American exports, raise global welfare by hundreds of billions of dollars, and help protect American consumers from trade-distorting barriers here at home.

Complaints that the WTO impinges on U.S. sovereignty are groundless. The WTO cannot overturn U.S. laws; at most, it can declare that U.S. laws are inconsistent with international obligations. Whether we honor those obligations is up to us.

But honor them we should. The principles of market access and nondiscrimination incorporated in WTO agreements are ones that ought to be reflected in U.S. policy. When U.S. laws violate those principles, they ought to be changed. It is a mistake to complain simply because the United States "loses" a case in the WTO; when the dispute settlement process leads the U.S. government to reform protectionist policies, that is a victory, not a defeat, for the American people. Furthermore, by heeding "adverse" WTO decisions, the United States sets an example for the rest of the world. We stand to gain when other countries follow the WTO's free-trade rules. Consequently, we have a large stake in the legitimacy and credibility of the dispute settlement process, which cannot be sustained if we selectively disregard WTO rulings.

Congress should show its support for the WTO process by passing legislation to implement all outstanding adverse WTO rulings as soon as possible. In particular, Congress should reform U.S. tax laws to eliminate the WTO-inconsistent preference for exports under what was formerly known as the "foreign sales corporation" provision. Meanwhile, there are a large and growing number of outstanding rulings against various aspects of the U.S. trade laws. To the extent that legislation is needed to implement those rulings, Congress should move immediately to make the necessary changes to U.S. law.

In addition, Congress should urge the administration to negotiate improvements in the WTO dispute settlement process—specifically, by deemphasizing trade sanctions, or "retaliation," as a tool for enforcing WTO rulings. Sanctions are a perverse and ineffective method of encouraging other nations to open their markets. By withdrawing "concessions," sanctions reinforce the faulty notion that our market-opening commitments are a favor we do other countries contingent on good behavior. In reality, sanctions punish our own consumers and producers by making the target list of import goods more expensive or even inaccessible. Meanwhile, sanctions make the global economy less free and tend to arouse resentment in our trading partners.

Instead, alternatives to sanctions should be explored. WTO members found to be out of conformity with agreed-upon rules could instead offer market-opening "compensation" by lowering barriers on other goods, or they could face suspension of the privilege of using the dispute settlement mechanism. Such alternative enforcement mechanisms would encourage compliance with WTO rulings without the perverse side effects of sanctions.

Export Barriers

Although we complain about other countries' barriers to our exports, the fact is that many barriers are homegrown. In particular, America's export control policies remain detached from the realities of the global marketplace. U.S. companies should be allowed to sell technologies that are being sold freely elsewhere in the world by their foreign competitors and the sale of which fails to present a clear danger to U.S. citizens or world peace. That is not the case today for many products, and much bureaucratic wrangling is needed before others can be exported.

Sales and investments abroad by U.S. companies are also hindered by ill-considered foreign policy trade sanctions against Cuba, Burma, and other countries. The Cuban embargo is discussed in Chapter 60. It should be noted here, though, that trade sanctions rarely accomplish their foreign policy objectives. Instead, they end up hurting the very people they are designed to help—the unfortunate subjects of despotic regimes. Absent compelling national security considerations, trade sanctions are almost always a bad idea. Trade and investment, on the other hand, can improve the lot of despotism's victims while sowing the seeds of political change.

Suggested Readings

Bailey, Ronald. "The Looming Trade War over Plant Biotechnology." Cato Institute Trade Policy Analysis no. 18, August 1, 2002.

Griswold, Daniel T. "America's Record Trade Deficit: A Symbol of Economic Strength." Cato Institute Trade Policy Analysis no. 13, February 9, 2001.

———. "Trade, Labor and the Environment: How Blue and Green Sanctions Threaten Higher Standards." Cato Institute Trade Policy Analysis no. 15, August 2, 2001.

Groombridge, Mark. "America's Bittersweet Sugar Policy." Cato Institute Trade Policy Briefing Paper no. 13, December 4, 2001.

Irwin, Douglas. A. *Free Trade under Fire*. Princeton, N.J.: Princeton University Press, 2002.

Lash, William H. III, and Daniel T. Griswold. "WTO Report Card II: An Exercise or Surrender of U.S. Sovereignty?" Cato Institute Trade Policy Briefing Paper no. 9, May 4, 2000.

Lindsey, Brink. *Against the Dead Hand: The Uncertain Struggle for Global Capitalism*. New York: John Wiley & Sons, 2002.

———. "The U.S. Antidumping Law: Rhetoric versus Reality." Cato Institute Trade Policy Analysis no. 7, August 16, 1999.

Lindsey, Brink, and Dan Ikenson. "Coming Home to Roost: Proliferating Antidumping Laws and the Growing Threat to U.S. Exports." Cato Institute Trade Policy Analysis no. 14, July 30, 2001.

U.S. International Trade Commission. "The Economic Effects of Significant U.S. Import Restraints." June 2002.

All Cato Institute trade studies are available online at www.freetrade.org.

—Prepared by Brink Lindsey

62. International Tax Competition

Congress should

- protect American fiscal sovereignty from foreign tax harmonization initiatives;
- require the withdrawal of the proposed IRS regulation that would mandate the reporting of foreign investors' interest earned in the United States;
- oppose anti-competitive legislation that would restrict companies from reincorporating abroad; and
- pursue fundamental tax reform, including substantially cutting the high federal corporate income tax rate and adopting a territorial tax system.

Individual citizens choose where to work, invest, and shop. Businesses choose where to locate research, production, and headquarters functions. In making those choices, individuals and businesses consider a range of economic factors, including the attractiveness of tax regimes. Tax competition occurs when governments respond to tax changes that occur in neighboring jurisdictions that affect their ability to attract individuals, businesses, and investment. Competition can take place between governments at the national, state, and local levels.

With more open international borders, it is easier for individuals and businesses to avoid high-tax countries, which makes it more difficult for governments to enforce oppressive tax burdens. In the past decade, cross-border investment flows have soared. As a result, U.S. policymakers need to exercise budget discipline and reduce tax rates in order to attract and retain investment.

When there is tax competition, countries have a strong incentive to move away from excessive taxes on capital, including taxes on business profits, dividends, interest, and capital gains. Businesses and investors can quickly respond to differences in capital taxes by reallocating mobile capital income to lower-tax countries. That phenomenon occurs, for example, when U.S. companies consider moving their headquarters abroad to escape from the high U.S. corporate income tax rate and the complex "worldwide" tax system imposed by the federal government. Tax competition is a positive force because it creates pressure to reduce economically damaging taxes, such as the corporate income tax. Reductions in the corporate tax are also beneficial because it is a hidden tax that ultimately falls on individuals. Thus reducing the corporate tax moves the tax system toward more transparency and helps taxpayers to better measure the size and the cost of government.

Tax competition provides incentives to policymakers to implement more efficient budget policies and eliminate unneeded spending programs. Tax competition pushes tax rates down, allows citizens to enjoy more of their earnings, and creates a business environment more conducive to entrepreneurship and economic growth.

Tax competition is illustrated by the substantial reductions in personal and corporate income tax rates in nearly every industrial country since the U.S. tax cuts of the 1980s. The average top individual income tax rate for members of the Organization for Economic Cooperation and Development fell from 55 percent in 1986 to 41 percent by 2000, and the average top corporate tax rate for members fell from 41 percent in 1986 to 32 percent by 2000.

Also, capital gains taxes, withholding taxes, and wealth taxes have been cut in numerous countries. While politicians in many countries have become more pro-market in recent decades, they have also been pushed to reduce tax rates because investors and entrepreneurs were shifting their activities to lower-tax countries.

Although recent tax reductions have been very beneficial to the U.S. and foreign economies, tax competition has not yet reduced overall tax burdens (tax revenues measured as a percentage of gross domestic product) in most countries. Part of the reason overall burdens have remained high is that governments have taken heavy-handed measures to try to protect their tax bases. Such measures have included enactment of complex tax rules on foreign business income, efforts to limit tax competition through international pressure on low-tax nations, attacks on financial privacy, and protectionist legislation to restrict companies and taxpayers from relocating in more attractive tax jurisdictions. Congress needs to oppose such anti-competitive measures because they undermine U.S. economic strength.

Protect American Fiscal Sovereignty from Foreign Tax Harmonization Initiatives

Tax competition and lower tax rates are very good for stimulating long-term economic growth. However, many policymakers favor income redistribution over growth and, as a result, seek to undermine and halt the process of tax competition.

The European Union and OECD have been at the forefront of global efforts to stifle tax competition. In recent years, there have been a number of efforts to harmonize tax systems across countries to limit competition in the manner of a cartel. The EU has led that effort by pushing its member countries to harmonize their tax systems. The most far-reaching EU harmonization initiative has been the imposition of a minimum standard value-added tax rate of 15 percent in 1992. The EU has also tried to get member countries to harmonize income tax rates and has tried to get the United States to impose taxes on Internet sales.

At the international level, the EU and OECD have focused on indirect methods of nullifying tax competition, such as information sharing between governments. The EU is promoting a scheme known as the EU Savings Tax Directive. The OECD has pursued a policy against what it calls "harmful tax competition." OECD reports in 1998, 2000, and 2001 identified "harmful" tax practices by OECD member countries and listed 41 low-tax jurisdictions of which the OECD disapproves.

The EU and OECD initiatives aim to give tax collectors in each country access to information about the economic activities of their citizens abroad with the aim of reducing the attractiveness of low-tax countries. Many countries tax individual residents on some portion of their income on a worldwide basis, so gaining access to foreign information helps high-tax countries sustain their high rates. However, unconditional information exchanges raise serious issues of financial privacy and national sovereignty and undermine beneficial tax competition.

Another threat is the United Nations, which has come out in favor of restricting international tax competition. A high-level UN panel in 2001 suggested creating an International Tax Organization that would harmonize tax policy, engage in surveillance of tax systems, and push countries to "desist from harmful tax competition." Such a new bureaucracy surely would have a strong bias toward tax increases. The UN report suggests creation of a "global source of funds" from a "high yielding tax source." It also suggests study of a "Tobin tax" on foreign exchange transactions to finance "global public goods." And it says that an ITO

625

"could take a lead role in restraining the tax competition designed to attract multinationals."

Some observers think that an ITO might be like the World Trade Organization, which handles trade disputes. But while most economists agree on the benchmark of free trade, there is no such benchmark in the tax world. Proponents of broad-based income taxes and proponents of consumption-based taxes would come to vastly different conclusions about what an ITO should enforce. Fortunately, the UN has not yet acted on its proposals.

Congress should be very concerned that the OECD or other international bodies do not start creating international "standards" that lock in high-rate income tax systems that preclude pro-growth tax reforms very much needed in America.

Require the Withdrawal of the Proposed IRS Regulation That Would Mandate Reporting of Bank Deposit Information on Foreign Investors

In July 2002, the IRS commissioner issued a regulation (REG 133254-02) to help foreign governments tax income earned in America. The proposal is based on a scheme that was proposed by former president Clinton three days before he left office. The IRS regulation would force U.S. banks to report the deposit interest they pay to account holders from other countries. It would target residents of 15 European nations and a few other countries such as New Zealand and Australia.

The IRS regulation is bad economic policy and disregards the intent of Congress regarding current tax policies. Interest earned on bank deposits paid to individual foreign investors has been tax-free for many years. On several occasions, Congress has debated whether or not to retain this tax exemption, and it has determined to keep it because it helps draw inflows of investment to the U.S. economy.

Note that this proposed regulation is designed, not to help the U.S. government collect taxes, but to help foreign governments collect their taxes. The IRS has not completed a required cost/benefit analysis of the proposal. Such as analysis would probably find that the regulation would have a damaging effect on the economy as foreign investors withdrew funds from U.S. banks. Figures from the U.S. Department of Commerce show that the market value of private foreign investment in the United States at the end of 2000 was about $9 trillion, with about $1.8 trillion held in bank deposits that would be vulnerable to flowing out of the country if the regulation was imposed. Investment would be shifted to lower-tax jurisdictions that have greater privacy. It makes no sense to inflict such damage on the American economy. The IRS should withdraw this regulation.

Oppose Anti-Competitive Legislation That Would Restrict U.S. Companies from Reincorporating Abroad

Because the U.S. tax code burdens U.S. firms with high tax rates and complex and uncompetitive rules, a growing number of companies are moving their place of incorporation to foreign jurisdictions. In a transaction, referred to as an inversion, a U.S. company is placed under a newly created foreign parent company formed in a low-tax jurisdiction. That allows companies to reduce taxes paid to the U.S. government on their foreign operations. They do not typically change their actual business structure, and they continue to pay taxes on U.S.-source income to the U.S. government.

Corporate inversions are part of the broader dynamic of rising global tax competition. A 2002 U.S. Treasury report recognizes that inversions raise broad issues of business tax burdens and calls for a comprehensive reexamination of U.S. international tax rules. Yet, rather than tackle the underlying problems of an uncompetitive corporate income tax, many members of Congress are trying to hinder competitive relocations with laws that represent narrow-minded fiscal protectionism. The political quick-fix proposals introduced during the 107th Congress generally aimed to tax foreign parent companies created for an inversion as if they were U.S. companies, if they retain basically the same structure they had before inversion. Various tests would be created to determine whether particular firms should be treated as foreign or domestic.

Sponsors of those proposals claimed that companies are currently exploiting a ''loophole'' that needs to be closed. But the tax advantage that foreign companies have over U.S. companies in world markets is not a loophole. It is a systematic problem with the U.S. tax code. Indeed, the tax savings that U.S. firms gain by incorporating abroad are one measure of the excessive U.S. business tax burden.

Even if anti–corporate inversion legislation passes, the basic tax advantage of foreign firms would remain. As a result, foreign firms will continue to acquire U.S. firms at a rapid pace. U.S. firms will continue to be at a cost disadvantage in world markets and will have less cash available to hire U.S. workers and pay U.S. shareholders. Also, a growing number of

627

forward-looking U.S. start-up firms may decide to incorporate abroad to enjoy long-term tax savings without having to go through the complex and costly process of inversion.

Anti-inversion legislation offers no economic benefits; it simply raises tax costs for U.S. companies and complicates the tax code. Congress should reject protectionist anti-inversion legislation and stop putting off long-overdue business tax reforms.

Engage in Fundamental Tax Reform by Substantially Cutting the Corporate Income Tax Rate and Adopting a Territorial Tax System

Secretary of the Treasury Paul O'Neill has noted, "If the tax code disadvantages U.S. companies competing in the global markets, then we should address the anti-competitive provisions of the code." Policymakers can begin right away with two basic steps:

Cut the Corporate Tax Rate

The recent rise in corporate inversions is a warning that the U.S. corporate tax has become dangerously uncompetitive. When the United States led the world in 1986 by cutting the corporate rate from 46 to 34 percent, most major countries followed suit and some surpassed us by cutting even further. But the United States then raised its rate to 35 percent and piled ever more complex tax rules on international businesses. At 40 percent (federal plus the state average), the U.S. corporate income tax rate is the fourth highest in the 30-country OECD (Figure 62.1).

A substantial cut in the corporate tax rate would greatly reduce the inversion problem and other corporate tax avoidance problems that have concerned policymakers. For example, there has been concern about "earnings stripping," which occurs when foreign parent firms lend excessively to their U.S. subsidiaries in order to reduce U.S. taxable income with large interest deductions. Lowering the statutory tax rate would reduce the incentive for earnings stripping.

In a global economy with 60,000 multinational corporations and trillions of dollars of investment funds searching for good returns, the high U.S. corporate tax rate is not sustainable. Unless the United States substantially cuts its tax rates, wasteful tax avoidance will increase, complex and uncompetitive legislative responses will ensue, and the performance of the U.S. economic engine will suffer.

Figure 62.1
Average Top Corporate Income Tax Rate in the OECD

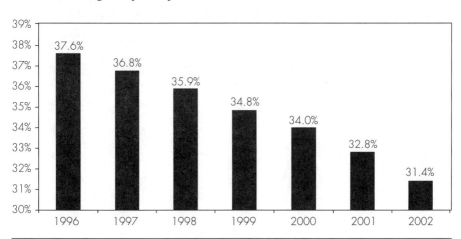

Source: Cato calculations based on KPMG data. Unweighted averages.

Adopt a Territorial Tax System

Along with a lower rate, the United States should adopt a territorial tax system. That would eliminate the need for corporate inversions and allow U.S. firms to compete on a level playing field in foreign markets.

A territorial system would be much simpler than the complex worldwide system that has been built piecemeal over decades without a consistent foundation. As the Treasury study notes, ''The U.S. rules for the taxation of foreign-source income are unique in their breadth of reach and degree of complexity.'' Many of those rules would be done away with under a territorial system. The ultimate solution is to replace our income-based tax system with a low-rate territorial system that has a consumption base. That way, global corporations will be encouraged to move their operations and profits into the United States rather than flee to lower-tax climates.

Suggested Readings

De Rugy, Veronique. ''President Bush Should Withdraw Clinton Era IRS Regulation.'' Cato Institute Daily Commentary, December 21, 2001.

———. ''Repel the Tax Cartel.'' Cato Institute Daily Commentary, June 7, 2002.

———. ''Runaway Corporations: Political Band-Aids vs. Long-Term Solutions.'' Cato Institute Tax & Budget Bulletin no. 9, July 2002.

Edwards, Chris. ''New Data Show U.S. Has Fourth Highest Corporate Tax Rate.'' Cato Institute Tax & Budget Bulletin no. 3, April 2002.

Edwards, Chris, and Veronique de Rugy. ''International Tax Competition: A 21st-Century Restraint on the Government.'' Cato Institute Policy Analysis no. 431, April 12, 2002.

Langer, Marshall. "Harmful Tax Competition: Who Are the Real Tax Havens?" *Tax Notes*, January 29, 2001.

Mitchell, Daniel. "The Adverse Impact of Tax Harmonization and Information Exchange on the U.S. Economy." *Prosperitas* 1, no. 4 (November 2001), www.freedomandprosperity.org.

OECD. "Harmful Tax Competition: An Emerging Global Issue." April 1998, www.oecd.org.

_____. "Tax Rates Are Falling." *OECD in Washington,* no. 25, March–April 2001, www.oecdwash.org.

U.S. Department of the Treasury. "Corporate Inversion Transactions: Tax Policy Implications." May 2002.

—Prepared by Veronique de Rugy

63. Immigration

Congress should

- expand, or at least maintain, current legal immigration quotas;
- focus border-control resources on efforts to keep terrorists out of the country;
- create a temporary worker visa for less-skilled immigrants from Mexico to work in the United States to meet labor shortages and reduce incentives for illegal immigration;
- repeal the arbitrary cap on H1-B visas for highly skilled workers;
- reinstate and make permanent the 245(i) provision to allow foreign-born residents who are legally qualified to live in the United States to remain in the country while they readjust their status; and
- reverse the recent decline in the number of refugees accepted by the United States.

America was founded, shaped, and built in large measure by immigrants seeking freedom and opportunity. Since 1820, 66 million immigrants have entered the United States legally, and each new wave stirred controversy in its day. In the mid-1800s, Irish immigrants were scorned as lazy drunks too beholden to the pope in Rome. At the turn of the century, a wave of "New Immigrants"—Poles, Italians, Austro-Hungarians, and Russian Jews—was believed to be too different to ever assimilate into American life. Today the same fears arise about immigrants from Latin America and Asia, but current critics of immigration are as wrong as their counterparts were in previous eras.

Immigration is not undermining the American experiment; it is an integral part of it. We are a nation of immigrants. Successive waves of immigrants have kept our country demographically young, enriched our culture, and added to our productive capacity as a nation, enhancing our influence in the world.

Immigration gives America an economic edge in the global economy. Immigrants bring innovative ideas and entrepreneurial spirit to the United States, most notably in Silicon Valley and other high-technology centers. They provide business contacts with other markets, enhancing America's ability to trade and invest profitably abroad. They keep our economy flexible, allowing American producers to keep prices down and meet changing consumer demands. An authoritative 1997 study by the National Academy of Sciences concluded that immigration delivers a ''significant positive gain'' to native Americans of as much as $10 billion each year.

Contrary to popular myth, immigrants do not push Americans out of jobs. Immigrants tend to fill jobs that Americans cannot or will not fill in sufficient numbers to meet demand, mostly at the high and low ends of the skill spectrum. Immigrants are disproportionately represented in such high-skilled fields as medicine, physics, and computer science but also in lower-skilled sectors such as hotels and restaurants, domestic service, construction, and light manufacturing. Immigrants also raise demand for goods as well as the supply. During the long boom of the 1990s, and especially in the second half of the decade, the national unemployment rate fell below 4 percent and real wages rose up and down the income scale during a time of relatively high immigration.

Immigrants are not a drain on government finances. The NAS study also found that the typical immigrant and his or her offspring will pay a net $80,000 more in taxes during their lifetimes than they collect in government services. For immigrants with college degrees, the net fiscal return is $198,000. It is true that low-skilled immigrants and refugees tend to use welfare more than the typical ''native'' household, but welfare and immigration reform legislation in 1996 made it much more difficult for new immigrants to collect welfare. As a result, immigrant use of welfare has plunged even more steeply than use among the general population.

Immigration actually improves the finances of the two largest federal income-transfer programs, Social Security and Medicare. In a 1998 report, the Social Security Administration concluded, ''The cost of the system decreases with increasing rates of immigration because immigration occurs at relatively young ages, thereby increasing the numbers of covered workers earlier than the numbers of beneficiaries.''

Despite the claims of opponents of immigration, today's flow is not out of proportion to historical levels. Legal immigration in the last decade averaged about 900,000 people per year, historically high in absolute numbers, but the rate of 4.3 immigrants per year per 1,000 U.S. residents is less than half the rate during the Great Migration at the turn of the last century. (See Figure 63.1.) Today, slightly more than 10 percent of U.S. residents are foreign born, an increase from 4.7 percent in 1970 but still well below the 14.7 percent who were foreign born in 1910.

Immigrants cannot be fairly blamed for causing "overpopulation" or "urban sprawl." America's annual population growth of 1 percent is below the average growth rate of the last century. According to the most recent census, 22 percent of U.S. counties lost population between 1990 and 2000. Immigrants have kept major metropolitan areas vibrant and are revitalizing demographically declining areas of the country.

Border Control and the War on Terrorism

In the wake of the terrorist attacks of September 11, 2001, long-time critics of immigration tried to exploit legitimate concerns about security to argue for drastic cuts in immigration. But "border security" and immigration are two separate matters. Immigrants are only a small subset of the total number of foreigners who enter the United States every year. Of the more than 30 million foreigners who entered legally in fiscal year 2000, fewer than 1 million were would-be immigrants. The vast majority

Figure 63.1
American Immigration in Perspective, by Decade, 1820–2000

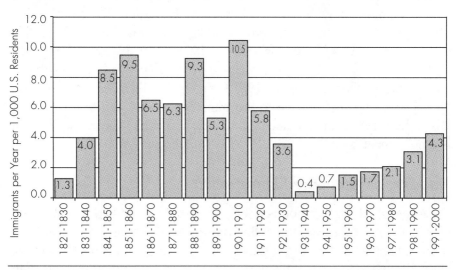

SOURCES: 2000 *Statistical Yearbook of the Immigration and Naturalization Service*; and 2001 *Statistical Abstract of the United States.*

came as tourists, business travelers, and students or were Mexicans and Canadians who crossed the border for a few days to shop or visit family and then returned home with no intention of settling permanently in the United States.

None of the 19 terrorists who attacked America on September 11, 2001, came as immigrants. They did not apply to the Immigration and Naturalization Service for permanent status. Like most aliens who enter the United States, they were here on temporary tourist and student visas. We could reduce the number of immigrants to zero and still not stop terrorists from slipping into the country on nonimmigrant visas.

The Enhanced Border Security and Visa Entry Reform Act of 2002 represents the right kind of policy response to terrorism. The legislation, signed by President Bush in May 2002, focuses directly on identifying terrorist suspects abroad and keeping them out of the country. Among its provisions, it requires tamper-resistant, machine-readable entry documents and restricts visas from countries that sponsor terrorism. Notably absent from the bill were any provisions rolling back levels of legal immigration or bolstering efforts to curb undocumented migration from Mexico. Most members of the 107th Congress rightly understood that immigrants who come to America to work are not a threat to national security.

America's Legal Immigration System

The United States maintained an essentially unrestricted immigration policy for most of its history. The Chinese Exclusion Act of 1882 and some qualitative restrictions were the only exceptions. But in the 1920s Congress responded to growing xenophobia and fear that new immigrants were racially "inferior" by establishing strict quotas that favored immigrants from northern Europe. In 1965 Congress finally repealed race-based quotas and, in effect, increased the numerical limits. In 1990 Congress raised the numbers and included more visas for people whose immigration is employment based.

Non-Employment-Based Immigration

Current legal immigration is tightly regulated and limited by numerical quotas and per country ceilings that prevent people from a few countries from obtaining all the visas. Legal immigration is limited to refugees, close family members of citizens and legal residents, and individuals with a company to sponsor them. A limited number of "diversity" visas are also distributed to immigrants from "underrepresented" countries. All categories are numerically restricted, except for the "immediate relatives" of U.S. citizens, whose totals have not shown a long-term, upward trend.

Family Reunification

Under U.S. law, an American citizen can sponsor (1) a spouse or minor child, (2) a parent, (3) a married child or a child 21 or older, or (4) a brother or sister. A lawful permanent resident (green card holder) can sponsor only a spouse or child. No "extended family" immigration categories exist for aunts, uncles, or cousins. In 2000, 78 percent of all family-sponsored immigration visas went to spouses and children. The other 22 percent went to the parents and siblings of U.S. citizens.

Refugees

Congress should reject any rigid "cap" on the admission of refugees. Such a cap is designed to slash the number of refugees admitted and would prevent flexible responses to emerging world situations. The annual number of refugees is set each year by consultations between the president and Congress. The number of refugees admitted has been dropping steadily in recent years, from an average of 121,000 per year under the first President Bush, to 82,000 per year under President Clinton, to fewer than 70,000 under the current President Bush. In fact, the number admitted in FY02 fell well below the 70,000 that the president and Congress had agreed upon in 2001. Although security concerns were cited, refugees are among the most thoroughly screened of visa categories. The U.S. Committee for Refugees estimates that 15 million people have been displaced from their homes by war, persecution, or natural disaster. To promote a more stable and humane world, Congress should keep the door open to refugees from other nations by raising the number of refugees allowed to its more traditional level of 100,000 or more.

Asylum

Unlike refugees, who are accepted for admission while still outside the United States, people seeking political asylum must first enter the country and then request permission to stay. Contrary to the popular impression, gaining political asylum is not automatic. According to the INS, less than half of the claims considered in fiscal year 2000 were approved. INS administrative reforms corrected the system's key problems (asylum applicants can no longer receive work papers and disappear into the workforce).

The number of first-time claims has dropped dramatically, and almost all new cases are completed within 180 days of filing.

The legislative changes contained in the 1996 immigration law were thus unnecessary and have created a new set of problems. There was no need to require individuals to file for asylum within one year of arriving in the United States, as Congress did in the 1996 immigration bill. Many victims of torture and persecution need time for their emotional wounds to heal and view asylum as an inevitable break with their families and followers back home.

Another problem is the "expedited removal" provision of the 1996 law, which allows low-level INS officials to prevent those arriving without valid documents from receiving a full hearing of their asylum claims. It is not difficult to understand why people fleeing torture or other forms of persecution often cannot obtain valid travel documents from their own governments. The "extraordinary circumstances" exception to the one-year time limit and the summary proceedings established to screen those entering without valid documents do not ensure a high enough standard of procedural protection for people with legitimate claims.

It is a human rights as well as an economic imperative that both the one-year time limit and the expedited removal provisions be changed.

Employment-Based Immigration: The H-1B Debate

Foreign-born workers have filled an important role in the American economy. Nowhere is the contribution of immigrants more apparent than in the high-technology and other knowledge-based sectors. Silicon Valley and other high-tech sectors would cease to function if we were to foolishly close our door to skilled and educated immigrants. These immigrants represent human capital that can make our entire economy more productive. Immigrants have founded companies and developed new products that have created employment opportunities for millions of Americans.

The primary means of hiring highly skilled foreign-born workers is the H-1B visa. Though overly bureaucratic, the system works reasonably well. It allows U.S. companies to hire in a timely manner foreign nationals with the right skills for the job. H-1B visas are generally approved within 60 days. They are valid for six years but must be renewed after three years. The company granted the visa must agree to pay the new employee at least the "prevailing wage" for that area and industry. H-1B visa holders are not immigrants or permanent residents, and they cannot progress toward citizenship.

A visa system for highly skilled foreign-born workers existed for decades without a cap, but in 1990 Congress imposed an arbitrary annual quota of 65,000 H-1B visas. As America's information economy gained steam in the second half of the 1990s, the quota proved to be too restrictive. In 2000 Congress raised the annual cap to 195,000 for three years. Under the law, the quota will revert to the old level of 65,000 in FY04, which could cripple the ability of America's most dynamic companies to remain ahead of global competition.

Despite the charge of critics, H-1B professionals do not depress wages, create unemployment, or cost taxpayers money. H-1B workers are generally among the best-paid workers in U.S. industry. Among the more than half a million H-1B visas issued from 1991 through September 1999, the Department of Labor found only seven cases of willful underpayment by an employer. The sharp downturn in the high-tech and information technology sectors that began in 2000 has cut the number of H1-B visa requests in half, demonstrating that visa requests are driven by demand, not by firms' desire to replace U.S. workers with lower-paid foreign workers.

Congress should act immediately to keep the cap at a high enough level to meet demand or, preferably, repeal the cap altogether to allow U.S. companies to hire the workers they need when they need them to stay competitive in the global economy. At the very least, Congress should permanently raise the cap to a minimum of 200,000 annually, with automatic annual increases of 10 percent thereafter. Department of Labor certifications should not place uneconomic regulatory burdens on U.S. firms that are already under market pressure to offer competitive wages and benefits to their workers.

Legal Immigration Reform: What Congress Should Do

Congress has followed a policy of "immigrants yes, welfare no" by overwhelmingly rejecting cuts in legal immigration while at the same time passing a welfare bill that makes immigrants ineligible for public assistance. Immigrant welfare use, often overstated, is now a dead issue in the immigration policy debate. Since illegal immigration is the main concern, and legal immigration is not a problem, it is not clear why Congress needs to make more than modest reforms to the current legal immigration system.

Congress should continue to keep the issues of legal and illegal immigration separate. For legal immigrants, Congress should at least maintain current family categories and quotas. Ideally, Congress should raise the current numbers by, among other things, setting aside separate visas for the one-third of spouses and children of lawful permanent residents in the immigration backlog who are physically separated from their sponsors. It should do so without tearing apart the current family immigration system, as the U.S. Commission on Immigration Reform recommended.

Illegal Immigration: What Congress Should Do

To better defend ourselves against terrorism and promote economic growth, America's border-control system requires a reorientation of mission. For the last two decades, U.S. immigration policy has been obsessed with nabbing mostly Mexican-born workers whose only "crime" is their desire to work, save, and build a better life for their families. Those workers pose no threat to national security.

The federal government's 15-year war against Mexican migration has failed by any objective measure. Employer sanctions and border blockades have not stopped the inflow of Mexican workers drawn by persistent demand for their labor. Coercive efforts to keep willing workers out have spawned an underground culture of fraud and smuggling, caused hundreds of unnecessary deaths in the desert, and diverted attention and resources away from real matters of border security. Those efforts have disrupted the traditional circular flow of Mexican migration, perversely increasing the stock of illegal Mexican workers and family members in the United States.

Important sectors of the U.S. economy have turned to low-skilled immigrant workers, documented and undocumented, to fill persistent job vacancies. Hotels and motels, restaurants, construction, light manufacturing, health care, retailing, and other services are major employers of low-skilled immigrant labor. The demand for less-skilled labor will continue to grow in the years ahead. According to the Department of Labor, occupations with the largest growth in absolute numbers will be in those categories that require only "short-term on-the-job training" of one month or less. Those categories include food preparation and service (including fast food); waiters and waitresses; retail salespersons; cashiers; nursing aides, orderlies and attendants; janitors and cleaners; home health aides; manual laborers; freight, stock, and materials movers; landscaping and groundskeeping workers; and manual packers and packagers—all occupations where low-skilled immigrants from Mexico can be expected to help meet the rising demand for workers. Across the U.S. economy, the Labor Department estimates that the total number of jobs requiring only short-term training will increase from 53.2 million in 2000 to 60.9 million by 2010, a net increase of 7.7 million jobs.

Meanwhile, the supply of American workers suitable for such work continues to fall because of an aging workforce and rising education levels. The median age of American workers continues to increase as the large cohort of Baby Boomers begins to near retirement age. Younger and older workers alike are now more educated as the share of adult native men without a high school diploma has plunged, from 53.6 percent in 1960 to 9.0 percent in 1998. Yet U.S. immigration law provides no legal channels through which low-skilled foreign-born workers can enter the United States to fill the growing gap between demand and supply on the lower rungs of the labor ladder.

Repeal Employer Sanctions

Congress should begin by repealing employer sanctions. Passed in 1986 and widely viewed as a failure, employer sanctions have made it a crime to "knowingly" hire an illegal immigrant. It should be the job of the federal government, not private business owners, to keep out of the country people who are not supposed to be here. The U.S. General Accounting Office found that employer sanctions have created a nationwide pattern of discrimination. The nation's largest labor organization, the AFL-CIO, has joined major business organizations such as the U.S. Chamber of Commerce in formally opposing employer sanctions as a tool of enforcement.

Congress must oppose any related expansion of INS "pilot projects" to a full-fledged national computerized employment ID system. It should also prohibit any requirement that government-issued documents, such as birth certificates and Social Security cards, become de facto national ID cards, as was the intention of the 1996 immigration bill. If such a law were enacted, one of our most basic rights, the right to earn a living, would be at the mercy of an unreliable government computer system. Computer verification would also compromise the right to privacy and invite abuse by government officials.

Reinstate Section 245(i)

Section 245(i) of U.S. immigration law is a humane provision that allows people who are residing in the United States and who are legally qualified to stay here to pay a fee to remain in the country while they apply for permanent residency. These are people who are typically married to American citizens or other legal residents, who are working, and who have become productive members of their communities. Although they are in technical violation of U.S. law, they pose no threat to our national security. They can be checked and processed by U.S. authorities more thoroughly here than at our overworked consulates abroad, all without disrupting their work and family life. During the 107th Congress, the House voted by a 2-to-1 margin to extend the provision, but it was blocked procedurally in the Senate.

Legalize and Regularize Mexican Immigration

The best long-term solution to illegal immigration from Mexico is sustained growth south of the border to create sufficient opportunities and security at home for Mexican workers. Meanwhile, the United States and Mexico should take steps toward an immigration system that recognizes the reality and the benefits of Mexican migration to the United States.

One element of a more open border policy could be a temporary visa system under which Mexicans would be allowed to work in the United States for a fixed time before returning to Mexico. Visa holders would be allowed to work in any job in which there was demand for their labor, including those occupations in which illegal immigrants commonly find work today. Such a program would allow Americans to enjoy the many benefits of employing Mexican-born workers in sectors where demand for labor is especially high.

At the same time, an expanded and orderly visa program would drastically reduce the disorderly and dangerous flow of illegal immigrants across sparsely populated areas of America's 2,000-mile border with Mexico. It would enhance our national security by draining a large section of the underground swamp of smuggling and document fraud that facilitates illegal immigration. It would encourage millions of currently undocumented workers to make themselves known to authorities by registering with the government, reducing cover for terrorists who manage to enter the country and overstay their visas.

Legalization would allow the government to devote more of its resources to keeping terrorists out of the country. Before September 11, 2001, the U.S. government had stationed more than four times as many border enforcement agents on the Mexican border as along the Canadian border, even though the Canadian border is more than twice as long and has been the preferred border of entry for Middle Easterners trying to enter the United States illegally. A system that allows Mexican workers to enter the United States legally would free thousands of government personnel and save an estimated $3 billion a year—resources that would then be available to fight terrorism.

Suggested Readings

Griswold, Daniel T. "Willing Workers: Fixing the Problem of Illegal Mexican Migration to the United States." Cato Institute Trade Policy Analysis no. 19, October 15, 2002.

Handlin, Oscar. *The Uprooted: The Epic Story of the Great Migrations That Made the American People.* New York: Little Brown, 1973.

Massey, Douglas S., Jorge Durand, and Nolan J. Malone. *Beyond Smoke and Mirrors: Mexican Immigration in an Era of Economic Integration.* New York: Russell Sage Foundation, 2002.

Masters, Suzette Brooks, and Ted Ruthizer. "The H-1B Straitjacket: Why Congress Should Repeal the Cap on Foreign-Born Highly Skilled Workers." Cato Institute Trade Briefing Paper no. 7, March 3, 2000.

Micklethwait, John. "The New Americans." *The Economist,* March 11, 2000.

Moore, Stephen. *A Fiscal Portrait of the Newest Americans.* Washington: Cato Institute and National Immigration Forum, 1998.

National Research Council. *The New Americans: Economic, Demographic, and Fiscal Effects of Immigration.* Washington: National Academy Press, 1997.

Pistone, Michele R. "New Asylum Laws: Undermining an American Ideal." Cato Institute Policy Analysis no. 299, March 24, 1998.

Simon, Julian L. *Immigration: The Demographic and Economic Facts.* Washington: Cato Institute and National Immigration Forum, 1995.

—Prepared by Daniel T. Griswold

64. International Financial Crises and the IMF

Congress should

- reject additional funding requests for the International Monetary Fund;
- close down the Exchange Stabilization Fund at the U.S. Department of the Treasury;
- avoid giving the IMF new missions, including that of overseeing sovereign debt restructuring or becoming a bankruptcy court for countries; and
- withdraw the United States from the IMF.

Since the $30 billion bailout of Mexico in 1995, national-currency and financial crises in developing countries have increased, as has the incidence of IMF-led bailout packages. Since 1997 those packages have totaled some $280 billion for Latin America, Asia, Russia, and Turkey. Many of those bailouts and the turmoil in international financial markets resulted in the United States contributing $18 billion to massively increase the IMF's resources in 1998. U.S. Treasury officials disingenuously claimed it did not cost U.S. taxpayers a dime, but Cato Institute chairman William Niskanen put the U.S. relationship with the IMF more accurately: "U.S. government membership in the IMF is like being a limited partner in a financial firm that makes high-risk loans, pays dividends at a rate lower than that on Treasury bills, and makes large periodic cash calls for additional funds."

But the monetary costs of supporting the IMF were not the most important reasons to have opposed more funding. The costs to the global economy are high, and the people who are most directly affected by IMF interventions—the world's poor—are those who can least afford it. If the goal is to help developing countries progress economically and to promote a liberal global economy, then, at the very least, rich countries should seek to reduce the IMF's resources and activities.

Free-market economists have long been critical of the IMF. International financial crises may have brought much attention to the fund in recent years, but the lending agency's record over the past 50 years has been dismal, as numerous books and studies have documented. The IMF does not appear to have helped countries either to achieve self-sustaining growth or to implement market reforms.

Despite its poor performance, the IMF has proven to be a remarkably resilient institution. When the system of fixed exchange rates ended in the early 1970s, so did the agency's original mission of maintaining exchange-rate stability by lending to countries experiencing balance-of-payments problems. Instead of closing down, however, the fund has created new missions for itself with each new crisis, each time expanding its economic influence or resources, or both. On average, the IMF has requested and received an increase in resources every five years.

Although the IMF in theory makes short-term loans in exchange for policy changes in recipient countries, it has not helped countries move to the free market. Instead, the fund has created loan addicts. More than 70 nations have depended on IMF aid for 20 or more years; 24 countries have received IMF credit for 30 or more years. Once a country receives IMF credit, it is likely to depend on IMF aid for most, if not all, of the following years. That is not evidence of either the success of the fund's so-called conditionality or the temporary nature of the fund's short-term loans.

The fund has thus moved away from its original mission of providing short-term balance-of-payment assistance and has instead fostered dependence on aid. Because of that, a congressional commission on international financial institutions, known as the Meltzer Commission, has advised that the fund should stop providing long-term loans, a recommendation endorsed by former U.S. treasury secretary Lawrence Summers. There has also been more of a consensus about the detrimental effects of bailouts, including strong statements to that effect by Treasury Secretary Paul O'Neill. However, neither the IMF nor the U.S. Treasury has discontinued that IMF function. Using the IMF to bail out a country experiencing a currency or debt crisis is a bad idea for three reasons.

Moral Hazard

The first reason is that it creates moral hazard. That is, the more the IMF bails out countries, the more we can expect countries to slip into crises in the future because governments and investors will engage in risky behavior in the expectation that, if anything goes wrong, the IMF will come to their rescue.

Moral hazard at the international level is not new. During each election cycle from 1976 to 1994, for example, Mexico experienced a currency crisis caused by irresponsible monetary and fiscal policy. Each episode was accompanied by U.S. Treasury and IMF bailouts, each time in increasing amounts. And although IMF and U.S. officials claimed that the 1995 Mexican bailout was a success, its legacy was the Asian crisis of 1997— at least in its severity. Indeed, the bailout of Mexico was a signal to the world that, if anything went wrong in emerging economies, the IMF would come to investors' rescue. Moral hazard helps explain the near doubling of capital flows to East Asia in 1995 alone.

Governments in Asia were not discouraged from maintaining flawed policies as long as lenders kept the capital flowing. Lenders, for their part, behaved imprudently with the knowledge that government money would be used in case of financial troubles. That knowledge by no means meant that investors did not care if a crisis erupted, but it led to the mispricing of risk and a change in the investment calculations of lenders. Thailand, Indonesia, and South Korea, after all, shared some common factors that should have led to more investor caution but did not. Those factors included borrowing in foreign currencies and lending in domestic currency under pegged exchange rates, extensively borrowing in the short term while lending in the long term, lack of supervision of borrowers' balance sheets by foreign lenders, government-directed credit, and shaky financial systems. The financial crisis in Asia was created in Asia, but the aggravating effect of moral hazard was extensive. As Michael Prowse of the *Financial Times* commented after the Mexican bailout, "Rubin and Co. wanted to make global capitalism safe for the mutual fund investor. They actually made it far riskier."

The facts that governments would never choose to lead their countries into crises and that national leaders have been replaced after such crises are often cited as evidence that moral hazard is not a problem. In fact, "moral hazard is not all-or-nothing but operates at the margin," explains economist Lawrence H. White. "Any IMF policy that allows finance ministers to delay the day of reckoning reduces their caution, especially so where political instability makes their planning horizons short."

Moral hazard also exists at the national level, where governments explicitly or implicitly guarantee that they will rescue domestic banks, thus encouraging risky bank behavior. The proliferation of government-subsi-dized risk since 1982 has led to at least 90 severe banking crises in the developing world, and the bailout costs in 20 of those cases have ranged between 10 and 25 percent of gross domestic product. In a world of increasingly liberal capital flows, IMF bailouts only encourage govern-ments to maintain flawed arrangements and foreign lenders to keep lending to those governments. Thus, even in countries whose monetary and fiscal policies appear conservative, crises can break out as malinvestment and the need to pay for bailouts become evident. The claim that markets react irrationally in countries whose macroeconomic fundamentals are sound ignores the liabilities governments face under those conditions—a factor markets take into account.

Still, advocates of the IMF argue that it must lend to prevent a "contagion effect" in other countries. The fund has thus provided bailouts to countries after economic crises have occurred (e.g., Mexico and Thailand) and before potential crises (e.g., Argentina, Brazil, and Russia). Neither timing has successfully prevented future financial turmoil. Countries that have succumbed to financial crises have done so because of poor domestic policies; countries that do not maintain poor policies have not suffered from so-called contagion. The real contagion effect is not what IMF proponents typically have in mind, but rather that of future crises encour-aged by the bailouts themselves.

An Expensive, Unjust Solution

IMF bailouts are expensive, bureaucratic, and fundamentally unjust solutions to economic crises. In the first place, the financial aid cuts investors' losses rather than allowing them to bear the full responsibility for their decisions. Just as profits should not be socialized when times are good, neither should losses be socialized during difficult times. "The $57 billion committed to Korea," Harvard economist Jeffrey Sachs observed, "didn't help anybody but the banks." Unfortunately, ordinary Asian citi-zens who had nothing to do with creating the crisis are being forced to pay the added debt burden imposed by IMF loans.

IMF bailouts pose another burden on ordinary citizens because the bailouts don't work very well. The fund's money goes to the governments that have created the crises to begin with and that have shown themselves to be unwilling or reluctant to introduce necessary reforms. Giving money to such governments does not tend to promote market reforms; it tends to delay them because it takes the pressure off governments to change their policies. Suspension of loans will tend to concentrate the minds of policymakers in the various troubled countries. To the extent that the IMF steps in and provides money, reform will be less forthcoming. Indeed, despite a postcrisis recovery in some Asian countries (caused principally by lower exchange and interest rates), fundamental structural reform has not taken place in any of the Asian countries. Thus, the citizens of recipient Asian nations suffer the added burden of IMF intervention. Not only do they have to pay a greater debt, they also have to suffer prolonged economic agony that is produced by the fund's bailouts.

But what about the fund's "strong conditionality"? Don't the strict conditions of IMF lending ensure that important policy changes will be made? Again, the record of long-term dependence of countries shows that conditionality has not worked well in the past. The Meltzer Commission, for example, surveyed the research on conditionality, including that of the IMF and the World Bank, and found "no evidence of systematic, predictable effects from most of the conditions." In addition to the fund's poor record, there is another good reason why IMF conditions have little credibility. As we have seen with Russia over the past several years, a country—especially a highly visible one—that does not stick to IMF conditions risks having its loans suspended. When loans are cut off, recipient governments tend to become more serious about reform. Note that the IMF encourages misbehaving governments to introduce reforms by cutting loans off; it is the *cutoff* of credit that induces policy change.

Unfortunately, when policy changes are forthcoming, the IMF resumes lending. Indeed, the IMF has a bureaucratic incentive to lend. It simply cannot afford to watch countries reform on their own because that would risk making the IMF appear irrelevant. The resumption of financial aid starts the process over again and prolongs the period of reform. The fund's pressure to lend money in order to keep borrowers current on previous loans and to be able to ask for more money is well documented. The IMF's bureaucratic incentive to lend is also well known to both recipient governments and the IMF itself, which makes the fund's conditionality that much less credible. It is telling that the conditions of the IMF's $11.2 billion loan to Russia, approved in July 1998 (weeks before the collapse of the ruble), were virtually identical to those of previous loan packages totaling more than $20 billion in 1992, 1993, 1994, 1995, and 1996. It is also telling that, since Russia's debt default in 1998, its economic and reform performance without IMF aid and advice has been superior to that of previous years.

Undermining Better Solutions

Third, IMF bailouts undermine superior, less-expensive market solutions. In the absence of an IMF, creditors and debtors would do what creditors and debtors always do in cases of illiquidity or insolvency: renegotiate debt or enter into bankruptcy procedures. In a world without the IMF, both parties would have an incentive to do so because the alternative, to do nothing, would mean a complete loss. Direct negotiations between private parties and bankruptcy procedures are essential if capitalism is to work. As James Glassman has stated, capitalism without bankruptcy is like Christianity without Hell. IMF bailouts, unfortunately, undermine one of the most important underpinnings of a free economy by overriding the market mechanism. As the Meltzer Commission noted: "The IMF creates disincentives for debt resolution when it lends to insolvent sovereign borrowers. This is contrary to an early hope that IMF lending to insolvent countries would facilitate debt renegotiation. The opposite often seems to transpire; the provision of an apparently unlimited external supply of funds forestalls creditors and debtors from offering concessions." There is simply no reason why international creditors and borrowers should be treated any differently than are lenders and debtors in the domestic market.

Governments would also react differently if no IMF interventions were forthcoming. There would be little alternative to widespread and rapid reforms if policymakers were not shielded from economic reality. Lawrence Lindsey, chief economic adviser to President Bush, who has opposed bailouts, has noted, for example, "All of the 'conditions' supposedly negotiated by the IMF will be forced on South Korea by the market." Of course, there is always the possibility that a government would be reluctant to change its ways under any circumstances; but that is a possibility that is larger, and indeed has become a reality, under IMF programs. "Perhaps, the IMF's assistance cushions the decline in income and living standards," reflected the Meltzer Commission. But it found that "neither the IMF, nor others, has produced much evidence that its policies and actions have this beneficial effect."

The IMF as Bankruptcy Court for Countries?

Recognizing the dysfunctional relationship between international creditors and debtors, and in an effort to "minimize moral hazard," in the words of IMF managing director Horst Kohler, the IMF has proposed a new way of dealing with sovereign debt and default. The fund's Sovereign Debt Restructuring Mechanism would turn the IMF into a sort of bankruptcy court for countries. Although the IMF has not abandoned the use of bailouts, the international bankruptcy proposal would fundamentally change the mission of the IMF. The spectacular collapse of the highly indebted Argentine economy in 2002, after having received IMF bailout packages of more than $40 billion, indisputably revealed the need for a new approach to debt problems that did not shield lenders and borrowers from economic reality at all costs.

Yet the bankruptcy approach proposed by the fund is fraught with problems. The changes called for require the IMF's charter to be amended, a procedure that would take years to complete if accepted by its members. The fund would play a central role in determining what countries would qualify for default and why, including countries holding IMF debt. IMF financing would still be used during debt negotiations. In practice, that would encourage creditors to prolong the workout process in an effort to extract more IMF financing; debtors could also use the IMF money to game the system and delay needed reforms. The result of putting the fund at the center of debt renegotiations would likely be unpredictability, financial volatility, and higher borrowing costs to emerging markets across the board regardless of whether some countries merit such an outcome or not.

Better approaches involve direct negotiations between creditors and debtors without the IMF's cumbersome, third-party interventions. For example, Undersecretary of the Treasury for International Affairs John Taylor has proposed that creditors begin relying on collective action clauses, which would allow a majority of creditors to negotiate in the name of all creditors in the event of a default, thus eliminating the problem of "holdout" creditors. Carnegie Mellon University economists Adam Lerrick and Allan Meltzer point out that all of the protections offered by a formal bankruptcy court can be incorporated into new debt issues. Lerrick and Meltzer also show how market mechanisms already exist to renegotiate outstanding debt in a short period of time without the aid of the IMF. Such well-established capital market tools as exchange offers and exit consent amendments can be used to voluntarily convert old debt into new debt with majority action clauses and to change the nonpayment terms of the old debt. Those tools, and Argentina's experience with a well-organized creditors' committee formed before the country defaulted, undermine the argument that coordination among creditors would be too difficult to achieve absent an IMF-backed bankruptcy procedure.

The IMF as a Lender of Last Resort and Surveillance Agency?

Many people who recognize the practical problems of IMF bailouts, including moral hazard, questionable policy advice, and the difficulty of enforcing conditions, still believe that the IMF is needed as an international lender of last resort. Yet the IMF does not perform that function now, nor can it. A true lender of last resort provides funds at a penalty rate to solvent banks that are temporarily threatened by panic, thereby containing financial turmoil. By contrast, the IMF provides subsidized funds that bail out insolvent financial institutions, thereby discouraging much-needed bankruptcy proceedings and corporate restructuring. The IMF cannot act quickly or create money as can true lenders of last resort. Countries that experience threats to their financial systems can rely on their own central banks as lenders of last resort. That includes the United States, where the Federal Reserve is charged with such a mission. The Fed's failure to perform that mission earlier this century—not the absence of an international lender of last resort—led to the Great Depression. It is highly improbable that the Fed would repeat the same monumental policy mistakes today.

Others have recommended that the IMF strengthen its role as a watchdog agency that provides an "early warning" of potential financial troubles. Yet it is unclear how a warning mechanism would work. As economist Raymond Mikesell asks, "Who would be warned and when? As soon as the financial community receives a warning that a country is facing financial difficulty, a massive capital outflow is likely to occur, in which case crisis prevention would be out of the question."

On the other hand, if the IMF perceives serious financial difficulties in a country and does not disclose that information, then it undermines its credibility as a credit-rating agency for countries. That appears to have been the case in Thailand, where the IMF claimed, postcrisis, that it issued warnings about the economy before the crisis erupted but kept those concerns confidential. The fund's credibility is further undercut by inherent conflicts of interest: in many cases, it would be evaluating countries in which it has its own money at stake; in all cases, it would be evaluating countries that, as member-owners of the IMF, have contributed to the fund's pool of resources. Only by ceasing to lend could the agency increase its integrity. At that point, however, its evaluations would merely replicate a service already available.

The Exchange Stabilization Fund

The executive branch has also used a little-known account, the Exchange Stabilization Fund, at the Treasury Department to circumvent Congress in providing foreign aid. Originally set up in 1934 to stabilize the value of the dollar, the ESF has since been used to prop up foreign currencies and economies. Most recently, it has been used as a bailout fund for countries in crisis. In 1995 the ESF made a $12 billion loan, its largest, to Mexico; it has since made available billions of dollars more to South Korea, Thailand, Indonesia, and other countries.

The ESF should be closed down because its bailout function suffers from the same defects that afflict the IMF: it creates moral hazard, delays reforms, and precludes superior market solutions to financial crises. Moreover, the ESF is an undemocratic institution since it is exempt from legislative oversight and its transactions, under the sole discretion of the executive branch, are secretive. Economist Anna Schwartz finds that the ESF failed even in its original mission, having "always been wasteful and ineffective at controlling the relative price of the U.S. dollar."

Conclusion

Crises in Latin America, Asia, and elsewhere have occurred because of flawed domestic policies. Bailouts by the IMF or the U.S. Treasury only encourage further crises and aggravate current ones. At a time when the world is moving toward the market, the bureaucratic response to government-induced financial turmoil makes matters worse. The market is far more effective in enforcing conditions, promoting reform, and minimizing the risk of a crisis spreading in the near term or far into the future. It is also more effective at dealing with sovereign debt and default. The United States and other major donors should reject further funding for the IMF or schemes that would turn the IMF into a bankruptcy court for countries. That would send a signal to the world that the fund's resources are not, in fact, unlimited and that lenders and borrowers should be held accountable for their actions. Beyond that, the United States should help the world's poor by withdrawing from the IMF.

Suggested Readings

Calomiris, Charles W. "The IMF's Imprudent Role as Lender of Last Resort." *Cato Journal* 17, no. 3 (Winter 1998).

DeRosa, David. *In Defense of Free Capital Markets: The Case against the New International Financial Architecture*. Princeton, N.J.: Bloomberg, 2001.

Hoskins, W. Lee, and James W. Coons. "Mexico: Policy Failure, Moral Hazard, and Market Solutions." Cato Institute Policy Analysis no. 243, October 10, 1995.

International Financial Institution Advisory Commission (Meltzer Commission). "Report to the U.S. Congress and the U.S. Department of the Treasury." March 8, 2000. www.house.gov/jec/imf/meltzer.htm.

Lerrick, Adam, and Allan H. Meltzer. "Sovereign Default: The Private Sector Can Resolve Bankruptcy without a Formal Court." Carnegie Mellon Gailliot Center for Public Policy, *Quarterly International Economics Report*, April 2002.

Meltzer, Allan H. "Asian Problems and the IMF." *Cato Journal* 17, no. 3 (Winter 1998).

Schwartz, Anna J. "Time to Terminate the ESF and the IMF." Cato Institute Foreign Policy Briefing no. 48, August 26, 1998.

Shultz, George, William Simon, and Walter Wriston. "Who Needs the IMF?" *Wall Street Journal*, February 3, 1998.

Vásquez, Ian. "The Asian Crisis: Why the IMF Should Not Intervene." *Vital Speeches*, April 15, 1998.

_____. "The Brady Plan and Market-Based Solutions to Debt Crises." *Cato Journal* 16, no. 2 (Fall 1996).

_____. "Repairing the Lender-Borrower Relationship in International Finance." Cato Institute Foreign Policy Briefing no. 54, September 27, 1999.

_____. "A Retrospective on the Mexican Bailout." *Cato Journal* 21, no. 3 (Winter 2002).

Vásquez, Ian, ed. *Global Fortune: The Stumble and Rise of World Capitalism.* Washington: Cato Institute, 2000.

—Prepared by Ian Vásquez

65. U.S. Policy toward Latin America

Congress should

- unilaterally open the U.S. market to goods from Latin America,
- support a free-trade agreement with Chile,
- support the Free Trade Area of the Americas, and
- facilitate dollarization for any country that wishes to adopt the dollar as its national currency.

In limited but important ways, Washington can positively influence economic policy in Latin America. At a time when much of the region is experiencing economic and political instability, the rise of neopopulism, and a general backlash against free-market reforms that were partially implemented in the 1990s, the United States should exercise its influence by opening its market to the region's goods and by encouraging market reforms.

Since the passage of the North American Free Trade Agreement with Mexico and Canada in 1993, however, the United States has shown no such leadership. Instead, Washington promised to create a hemispheric free-trade zone, known as the Free Trade Area of the Americas, but made little effort to promote the idea.

The result was unfortunate and a window of opportunity was lost. Latin American countries that were eager to enter into an FTAA gradually became disillusioned with years of U.S. inaction, and many have now turned decidedly against the idea of free trade. Worse, as economist Sebastian Edwards points out, Washington's promise of promoting the FTAA had the perverse effect of actually halting unilateral trade barrier reductions in Latin America as those countries waited to negotiate reductions with the United States, an expectation that went unfulfilled. Moreover, since the Mexican peso crisis of 1994–95, Washington has supported massive International Monetary Fund bailouts that have encouraged irresponsible behavior by investors and policymakers and have surely increased the severity of economic crises in the region.

President Bush has recently emphasized the FTAA as a policy priority. But his administration's support for increased steel tariffs and farm subsidies has undermined Washington's credibility in a region already wary of U.S. intentions. The United States can take steps to regain the initiative. To do so, it must first understand where the region stands.

Latin America since the 1990s

The early 1990s saw the introduction of far-reaching market reforms in many, but not all, Latin American countries, especially in the areas of monetary policy, trade and investment liberalization, and privatization of state-owned enterprises. Countries in the region ended hyperinflation, reduced their tariffs unilaterally, and eventually sold more than $150 billion of state assets. The initial results were high growth and the widespread popularity of the reforms in the countries that did the most to reform. Mexican president Carlos Salinas was the most popular outgoing president in Mexican history in 1994, and Presidents Alberto Fujimori of Peru and Carlos Menem of Argentina were reelected by wide margins in the mid-1990s.

By the end of the decade and the beginning of the next one, however, a number of countries had experienced years of recession, political instability, and economic crises. Even countries that had introduced only timid reforms had that experience. The IMF bailed out Mexico, Argentina, Brazil, and Uruguay, some more than once. Most spectacular was the collapse of the Argentine economy in early 2002. That country's default and devaluation sent it into a deep depression, calling into question market reforms in the minds of many Argentineans. Latin America's disappointing per capita growth of 1.5 percent per year in the 1990s was still better than that of the "lost decade" of the 1980s (-0.68 percent), but it certainly did not live up to expectations and was too often accompanied by economic turmoil. It is within that context of disillusionment that politicians using populist or demagogic rhetoric have risen to power in Argentina, Brazil, Venezuela, Peru, and elsewhere, vilifying the free market as the source of their countries' troubles.

But to blame the market is hopelessly wrongheaded. It is important to remember that the regionwide shift to the market occurred because of the failure of past policies, not because governments were committed to free-market principles. For example, the left-leaning ruling party in Mexico, the Peronist party in Argentina, and Fujimori's upstart party, which campaigned against radical market reforms in Peru, introduced liberalization. By the mid-1990s, with the success of the early reforms, governments lost interest in liberalization. The unfinished reform agenda was extensive and brought diminishing returns in the form of slower growth and negative economic indicators. Argentina, for example, suffered from chronically high unemployment throughout the 1990s because it never reformed its rigid labor laws. Latin America had only begun to embrace economic freedom.

Indeed, a whole range of institutions and policies has been left untouched. The pervasiveness of a vast informal economy in most Latin American countries attests to that fact. The region's citizens have long responded to the high costs of the formal legal and regulatory system by simply operating outside it. They have found the formal system of rules to be prohibitively expensive. The private property rights of the poor in urban and rural areas, for example, are typically not recognized or protected by the state since property titling is complicated or impossible. Yet private property lies at the heart of a market system, and the absence of property titles severely restrains the creation of wealth. Bureaucratic red tape also pushes people into the informal sector. Opening a small business in Latin America legally can cost thousands of dollars in licensing fees and take months or years for approval—a procedure that costs less and takes days in rich countries. The rule of law, another institution essential to the functioning of a market economy, is severely defective or nonexistent in the region. Latin America has been given low scores on both the rule of law and business regulation in *Economic Freedom of the World.*

Other sectors, including health care, education, and public security, have seen virtually no reform although they have continued to deteriorate, often despite increases in spending. That situation has led Argentinean economist Ricardo López Murphy to complain that Argentineans pay Swedish-level tax rates for public services of African quality.

Thus, Latin America in the 1990s moved partially down the path of economic freedom, but it still has a long way to travel if it is to sustain growth and avoid financial turmoil. Indeed, the continued adherence to old policy practices in large part explains the region's economic crises of the past decade. The crash of the Mexican peso, for example, resulted from a government-managed exchange rate and expansionary monetary and fiscal policies during an election year, policies thoroughly inconsistent with market economics. Likewise, Argentina's default resulted from a 90 percent increase in both public spending and debt from 1991 to 2000, far outstripping the 50 percent growth in gross domestic product of that period.

Chile and Mexico Teach the Real Lessons from Latin America

Despite such disappointments, the most important lessons coming out of Latin America are encouraging. As Jackson Diehl of the *Washington Post* notes, "The latest debt crisis is serving to underline not just the failures of those countries that embraced liberal economics in the 1990s but the breakthrough success of the two nations that did it right: Chile and Mexico." Those two countries, and some Central American nations including El Salvador and Costa Rica, are increasingly setting themselves apart from the rest of Latin America in terms of economic and political performance.

The sharpest contrast is provided by Chile, the country that has applied and maintained the most far-reaching and coherent set of market-liberal policies for the longest time. The resulting high growth has enabled the country to more than double its per capita income in the last 15 years and to achieve impressive advances in a range of human development indicators. According to the Santiago-based Institute for Liberty and Development, for example, Chilean growth of about 7 percent from 1987 to 1998 reduced the poverty rate from 45 to 22 percent during that period.

Mexico has likewise maintained economic stability and a growth rate notably higher than the regional average since the peso crisis of 1994–95. Like Chile, it has accomplished much within the context of democratic transfers of power. Mexican growth has raised per capita income above precrisis levels and has done so relatively rapidly. The key to Mexico's performance has been NAFTA. Free trade with the United States enabled Mexico to begin recovering from its crisis within a year. It took Mexico six years to recover from its economic crisis of 1982, at a time when its economy was fairly closed.

The divergence in performance between the free-trade countries of Chile and Mexico and the more protectionist countries in most of the rest of the region will become even clearer in coming years, especially if neopopulism holds sway in the latter countries. The United States can buttress that demonstration effect by signing on to a free-trade agreement with Chile, a treaty for which negotiations were completed at the end of 2002. A free-trade agreement with Chile would not only benefit the United States and Chile; it would also send a signal to the region that the United States is willing to reward countries that implement free-market policies.

Washington should follow suit with El Salvador and other Latin American countries that have liberalized their economies and are eager to sign a trade treaty with the United States. Indeed, Congress should also support efforts to promote a Free Trade Area of the Americas, although that initiative looks increasingly difficult to realize, given the region's political outlook.

Independent of free-trade negotiations, the United States should immediately reduce its barriers to Latin America's exports, especially textiles and agricultural products. At a time when U.S. credibility on trade is at a low point, such a move would restore some goodwill toward Washington and might help persuade reluctant countries to reduce some of their own trade barriers. At the very least, the United States could then not be blamed for hypocrisy, and the welfare of both the United States and Latin America would improve. Such a unilateral policy of reducing trade barriers, moreover, would not be in conflict with the goal of negotiating free-trade agreements. As Cato Institute scholar Brink Lindsey points out, the United States has successfully negotiated trade agreements affecting sectors in the U.S. economy that enjoy virtually no protectionism (e.g., telecommunications and financial services). For countries that are interested in free trade with the United States, such agreements offer the advantage of "locking in" free trade both at home and abroad. Indeed, the certainty provided by free-trade treaties is one of their greatest benefits and explains why they tend to result in increases of both trade and investment.

Dollarization

The United States should support another positive trend in the hemisphere: dollarization. In an effort to eliminate currency risk, including sudden and large devaluations and other manifestations of irresponsible monetary policy, Ecuador and El Salvador have joined Panama as countries that use the U.S. dollar as their national currency. Because most of the region's central banks have a poor record of maintaining the value of their currencies, Latin Americans already use the dollar widely, and it has become the currency of choice in many countries, including Cuba. Other countries, such as Argentina, may wish to replace their currencies with the dollar as well.

The United States should neither discourage nor encourage those moves but should facilitate official dollarization where it occurs. That may mean sharing the dollar's seigniorage—or the profit that derives from printing currency—with countries that decide to dollarize. In that way, the United

States would neither gain nor lose money as a result of another country's decision to dollarize, but the dollarizing country might more easily dollarize if it could still earn seigniorage from the currency it uses. Dollarization alone cannot solve a country's economic problems, but for countries with poor monetary policies, dollarization would end currency risk, reduce interest rates, and help stimulate investment and growth.

Time for a U.S. Policy toward Latin America

The United States can play a strategic role in promoting economic freedom, stability, and growth in Latin America—something it has not done for nearly a decade. That means reversing the current policy characterized by bailouts, protectionist measures, and mixed messages to the region. It also means that Washington must end its destructive war on drugs in the region, which works at cross-purposes with important U.S. policy priorities (see Chapter 56 on the international war on drugs). In drug-source countries such as Colombia, the drug war is fueling corruption and violence, financing terrorism, undermining the rule of law, and otherwise debilitating the institutions of civil society. The impact of the U.S.-led war on drugs south of the border has been imperceptible in the United States, but its consequences in Latin America are completely at odds with Washington's stated goal of encouraging free markets.

The rhetoric of free trade must be followed by policy actions consistent with such language. Congress should support a unilateral reduction of trade barriers to the region's goods and negotiate free-trade agreements with countries eager to do so, beginning with Chile. The United States would thus highlight the success of market reformers in the region by rewarding them without penalizing others. The diverging performances of the countries that embrace economic freedom and the rest can have a powerful effect on the policy direction that Latin American countries subsequently take.

Suggested Readings

Carpenter, Ted Galen. *Bad Neighbor Policy: Washington's Futile War on Drugs in Latin America.* New York: Palgrave, 2003.

Falcoff, Mark. "Colombia: A Questionable Choice of Objectives." AEI Latin American Outlook, March 2002.

Haber, Stephen. *Crony Capitalism and Economic Growth in Latin America: Theory and Evidence.* Stanford, Calif.: Hoover Institution Press, 2002.

Mendoza, Plinio Apuleyo, Carlos Alberto Montaner, and Alvaro Vargas Llosa. *Guide to the Perfect Latin American Idiot.* New York: Madison Books, 2001.

Montaner, Carlos Alberto. *Las Raices Torcidas de América Latina.* Barcelona: Plaza & Janes, 2001.

Schuler, Kurt. "Fixing Argentina." Cato Institute Policy Analysis no. 445, July 16, 2002.

Váliz, Claudio. *The New World of the Gothic Fox: Culture and Economy in English and Spanish America.* Berkeley: University of California Press, 1994.

Vargas Llosa, Mario. Foreword to *The Other Path,* by Hernando de Soto. New York: Harper and Row, 1989.

Vásquez, Ian. "A Retrospective on the Mexican Bailout." *Cato Journal* 21, no. 3 (Winter 2002).

—Prepared by Ian Vásquez

66. Foreign Aid and Economic Development

Congress should

- abolish the U.S. Agency for International Development and end government-to-government aid programs;
- withdraw from the World Bank and the five regional multilateral development banks;
- not use foreign aid to encourage or reward market reforms in the developing world;
- eliminate programs, such as enterprise funds, that provide loans to the private sector in developing countries and oppose schemes that guarantee private-sector investments abroad;
- privatize or abolish the Export-Import Bank, the Overseas Private Investment Corporation, the U.S. Trade and Development Agency, and other sources of international corporate welfare;
- forgive the debts of heavily indebted countries on the condition that they not receive any further foreign aid; and
- end government support of microenterprise lending and non-governmental organizations.

President Bush has called for increasing U.S. bilateral development assistance by about 50 percent by fiscal year 2006, gradually raising the aid above the current level of roughly $10 billion. The new Millennium Challenge Account would direct the additional funds to poor countries that have sound policy environments. Likewise, the World Bank is advocating a doubling of the current $50 billion official development assistance worldwide.

Those calls for significant increases in foreign aid are based on the argument that aid agencies have learned from the failure of past foreign

661

aid programs and that overseas assistance can now be generally effective in promoting growth. But what we know about aid and development provides little reason for such enthusiasm:

- There is no correlation between aid and growth.
- Aid that goes into a poor policy environment doesn't work and contributes to debt.
- Aid conditioned on market reforms has been a failure.
- Countries that have adapted market-oriented policies have done so because of factors unrelated to aid.
- There is a strong relationship between economic freedom and growth.

A widespread consensus has formed about the above points, even among development experts. As developing countries began introducing market reforms in the late 1980s and early 1990s, the most successful reformers also experienced noticeably better economic performance. As would be expected, the improvement among the successful reformers also improved the apparent performance of foreign aid in those countries—thus the new emphasis on giving aid to countries that have already adopted good policies. The new approach to aid is dubious for many reasons, not the least of which is the fact that countries with sound policies will already be rewarded with economic growth and do not need foreign aid. In any event, much, if not most, foreign assistance will continue to follow traditional practice.

The Dismal Record of Foreign Aid

By the 1990s the failure of conventional government-to-government aid schemes had been widely recognized and brought the entire foreign assistance process under scrutiny. For example, a Clinton administration task force conceded that, "despite decades of foreign assistance, most of Africa and parts of Latin America, Asia and the Middle East are economically worse off today than they were 20 years ago." As early as 1989 a bipartisan task force of the House Foreign Affairs Committee concluded that U.S. aid programs "no longer either advance U.S. interests abroad or promote economic development."

Multilateral aid has also played a prominent role in the post–World War II period. The World Bank, to which the United States is the major contributor, was created in 1944 to provide aid mostly for infrastructure projects in countries that could not attract private capital on their own. The World Bank has since expanded its lending functions, as have the five regional development banks that have subsequently been created on the World Bank's model: the Inter-American Development Bank, the Asian Development Bank, the African Development Bank, the European Bank for Reconstruction and Development, and the Middle East Development Bank.

Despite record levels of lending, however, the multilateral development banks have not achieved more success at promoting economic growth than has U.S. AID. Numerous self-evaluations of World Bank performance over the years, for example, have uncovered high failure rates of bank-financed projects. In 2000, the bipartisan Meltzer Commission of the U.S. Congress found a 55 to 60 percent failure rate of World Bank projects based on the bank's own evaluations. A 1998 World Bank report concluded that aid agencies "saw themselves as being primarily in the business of dishing out money, so it is not surprising that much [aid] went into poorly managed economies—with little result." The report also said that foreign aid had often been "an unmitigated failure." "No one who has seen the evidence on aid effectiveness," commented Oxford University economist Paul Collier in 1997, "can honestly say that aid is currently achieving its objective."

Although a small group of countries in the developing world (some of which received aid at some point) has achieved self-sustaining economic growth, most recipients of aid have not. Rather, as a 1989 U.S. AID report suggested, aid has tended to create dependence on the part of borrower countries.

There are several reasons why massive transfers from the developed to the developing world have not led to a corresponding transfer of prosperity. Aid has traditionally been lent to governments, has supported central planning, and has been based on a fundamentally flawed vision of development.

By lending to governments, U.S. AID and the multilateral development agencies supported by Washington have helped expand the state sector at the expense of the private sector in poor countries. U.S. aid to India from 1961 to 1989, for example, amounted to well over $2 billion, almost all of which went to the Indian state. Ghanaian-born economist George Ayittey complained that, as late as 1989, 90 percent of U.S. aid to sub-Saharan Africa went directly to governments.

Foreign aid has thus financed governments, both authoritarian and democratic, whose policies have been the principal cause of their countries' impoverishment. Trade protectionism, byzantine licensing schemes, inflationary monetary policy, price and wage controls, nationalization of industries, exchange-rate controls, state-run agricultural marketing boards, and restrictions on foreign and domestic investment, for example, have all been supported explicitly or implicitly by U.S. foreign aid programs.

Not only has lack of economic freedom kept literally billions of people in poverty; development planning has thoroughly politicized the economies of developing countries. Centralization of economic decisionmaking in the hands of political authorities has meant that a substantial amount of poor countries' otherwise useful resources has been diverted to unproductive activities such as rent seeking by private interests or politically motivated spending by the state.

Research by economist Peter Boone of the London School of Economics confirms the dismal record of foreign aid to the developing world. After reviewing aid flows to more than 95 countries, Boone found that "virtually all aid goes to consumption" and that "aid does not increase investment and growth, nor benefit the poor as measured by improvements in human development indicators, but it does increase the size of government."

It has become abundantly clear that as long as the conditions for economic growth do not exist in developing countries, no amount of foreign aid will be able to produce economic growth. Moreover, economic growth in poor countries does not depend on official transfers from outside sources. Indeed, were that not so, no country on earth could ever have escaped from initial poverty. The long-held premise of foreign assistance—that poor countries were poor because they lacked capital—not only ignored thousands of years of economic development history; it also was contradicted by contemporary events in the developing world, which saw the accumulation of massive debt, not development.

Promoting Market Reforms

Even aid intended to advance market liberalization can produce undesirable results. Such aid takes the pressure off recipient governments and allows them to postpone, rather than promote, necessary but politically difficult reforms. Ernest Preeg, former chief economist at U.S. AID, for instance, noted that problem in the Philippines after the collapse of the Marcos dictatorship: "As large amounts of aid flowed to the Aquino government from the United States and other donors, the urgency for reform dissipated. Economic aid became a cushion for postponing difficult internal decisions on reform. A central policy focus of the Aquino government became that of obtaining more and more aid rather than prompt implementation of the reform program."

A similar outcome is evident in the Middle East, which receives about one-third of U.S. economic aid, most of which is received by the governments of Egypt and Israel. It should not be surprising, then, that the region is notable for its low levels of economic freedom and almost complete lack of economic reform. In 1996 the Institute for Advanced Strategic and Political Studies, an Israeli think tank, complained: "Almost one-seventh of the GDP comes to Israel as charity. This has proven to be economically disastrous. It prevents reform, causes inflation, fosters waste, ruins our competitiveness and efficiency, and increases the future tax burden on our children who will have to repay the part of the aid that comes as loans." In 1998 the institute again complained that foreign aid "is the single greatest obstacle to economic freedom in Israel."

Far more effective at promoting market reforms is the suspension or elimination of aid. Although U.S. AID lists South Korea and Taiwan as success stories of U.S. economic assistance, those countries began to take off economically only after massive U.S. aid was cut off. As even the World Bank has conceded, "Reform is more likely to be preceded by a decline in aid than an increase in aid." When India faced Western sanctions in 1998 in response to nuclear tests there, the *International Herald Tribune* reported that "India approved at least 50 foreign-investment projects to compensate for the loss of aid from Japan and the United States" and that it would take additional measures to attract capital. In the end, the countries that have done the most to reform economically have made changes despite foreign aid, not because of it.

Still, much aid is delivered on the condition that recipient countries implement market-oriented economic policies. Such conditionality is the basis for the World Bank's structural adjustment lending, which it began in the early 1980s after it realized that pouring money into unsound economies would not lead to self-sustaining growth. But aid conditioned on reform has not been effective at inducing reform. One 1997 World Bank study noted that there "is no systematic effect of aid on policy." A 2002 World Bank study admitted that "too often, governments receiving aid were not truly committed to reforms" and that "the Bank has often been overly optimistic about the prospects for reform, thereby contributing to misallocation of aid." Oxford's Paul Collier explains: "Some governments have chosen to reform, others to regress, but these choices appear to have been largely independent of the aid relationship. The micro-evidence of this result has been accumulating for some years. It has been suppressed by an unholy alliance of the donors and their critics. Obviously, the donors did not wish to admit that their conditionality was a charade."

Lending agencies have an institutional bias toward continued lending even if market reforms are not adequately introduced. Yale University economist Gustav Ranis explains that within some lending agencies, "ultimately the need to lend will overcome the need to ensure that those [loan] conditions are indeed met." In the worst cases, of course, lending agencies do suspend loans in an effort to encourage reforms. When those reforms begin or are promised, however, the agencies predictably respond by resuming the loans—a process Ranis has referred to as a "time-consuming and expensive ritual dance."

In sum, aiding reforming nations, however superficially appealing, does not produce rapid and widespread liberalization. Just as Congress should reject funding regimes that are uninterested in reform, it should reject schemes that call for funding countries on the basis of their records of reform. This includes the Bush administration's Millennium Account. The most obvious problem with that program is that it is based on a conceptual flaw: countries that are implementing the right policies for growth, and therefore do not need foreign aid, will be receiving aid. The practical problems are also formidable. The Millennium Account and other programs of its kind will require that U.S. AID and other aid agencies—all of which have a poor record in determining when and where to disburse foreign aid—make complex judgment calls about what countries deserve the aid and when. Moreover, it is difficult to believe that bureaucratic self-interest, micromanagement by Congress, and other political considerations will not continue to play a role in the disbursement of this kind of foreign aid. Indeed, had they received substantial foreign assistance as a reward for implementing far-reaching liberalization measures, it is unlikely that countries such as Chile or the Czech Republic would be as economically sound as they are today.

Helping the Private Sector

Enterprise funds are another initiative intended to help market economies. Under this approach, U.S. AID and the Overseas Private Investment Corporation have established and financed venture funds throughout the developing world. Their purpose is to promote economic progress and "jump-start" the market by investing in the private sector.

It was always unclear exactly how such government-supported funds find profitable private ventures in which the private sector is unwilling to invest. Numerous evaluations have now found that most enterprise funds are losing money, and many have simply displaced private investment that otherwise would have taken place. Moreover, there is no evidence that the funds have generated additional private investment, had a positive impact on development, or helped create a better investment environment in poor countries.

Similar efforts to underwrite private entrepreneurs are evident at the World Bank (through its expanding program to guarantee private-sector investment) and at U.S. agencies such as the Export-Import Bank, OPIC, and the Trade and Development Agency, which provide comparable services.

U.S. officials justify those programs on the grounds that they help promote development and benefit the U.S. economy. Yet the provision of loan guarantees and subsidized insurance to the private sector relieves the governments of underdeveloped countries from creating an investment environment that would attract foreign capital on its own. To attract much-needed investment, countries should establish secure property rights and clear economic policies, rather than rely on Washington-backed schemes that allow avoidance of those reforms.

Moreover, while some corporations clearly benefit from the array of foreign assistance schemes, the U.S. economy and American taxpayers do not. Subsidized loans and insurance programs merely amount to corporate welfare. Macroeconomic policies and conditions, not corporate welfare programs, affect factors such as the unemployment rate and the size of the trade deficit. Programs that benefit specific interest groups manage only to rearrange resources within the U.S. economy and do so in a very wasteful manner. Indeed, the United States did not achieve and does not maintain its status as the world's largest exporter because of agencies like the Export-Import Bank, which finances about 1 percent of U.S. exports.

Even U.S. AID claims that the main beneficiary of its lending is the United States because close to 80 percent of its contracts and grants go to American firms. That argument is also fallacious. "To argue that aid helps the domestic economy," renowned economist Peter Bauer explains, "is like saying that a shop-keeper benefits from having his cash register burgled so long as the burglar spends part of the proceeds in his shop."

Debt Relief

Some 42 poor countries today suffer from inordinately high foreign debt levels. Thus, the World Bank and the IMF have devised a $37.2 billion debt-relief initiative for the world's heavily indebted poor countries (HIPCs). To fund the HIPC program, the aid agencies are requesting about half of that money from the United States and other donors. The initiative, of course, is an implicit recognition of the failure of past lending to produce self-sustaining growth, especially since an overwhelming percentage of eligible countries' public foreign debt is owed to bilateral and multilateral lending agencies. Indeed, 96 percent of those countries' long-term debt is public or publically guaranteed (Table 66.1).

Forgiving poor nations' debt, of course, is a sound idea, on the condition that no other aid is forthcoming. Unfortunately, the multilateral debt initiative promises to keep poor countries on a borrowing treadmill, since they will be eligible for future multilateral loans based on conditionality. There is no reason, however, to believe that conditionality will work any better in the future than it has in the past. Again, as a recent World Bank study emphasized, "A conditioned loan is no guarantee that reforms will be carried out—or last once they are."

Nor is there reason to believe that debt relief will work better now than in the past. As former World Bank economist William Easterly has documented, donor nations have been forgiving poor countries' debts since the late 1970s, and the result has simply been more debt. From 1989 to 1997, 41 highly indebted countries saw some $33 billion of debt forgiveness, yet they still find themselves in an untenable position. Indeed, they have been borrowing ever-larger amounts from aid agencies. Easterly notes, moreover, that private credit to the HIPCs has been virtually replaced by foreign aid and that foreign aid itself has been lent on increasingly easier terms. Thus, when the World Bank and IMF call for debt forgiveness, it is the latest in a series of failed attempts by rich countries to resolve poor countries' debts.

At the same time, it has become increasingly evident that the debt-relief scheme is a financial shell game that allows the multilaterals to repay their previous loans without having to write-down bad debt and thus without negatively affecting their financial status. If official donors wished to forgive debt, they could do so easily. Contributing money to the multilateral debt-relief initiative, however, will do little to promote reform or self-sustaining growth.

Other Initiatives

The inadequacy of government-to-government aid programs has prompted an increased reliance on nongovernmental organizations (NGOs). NGOs, or private voluntary organizations (PVOs), are said to be more effective at delivering aid and accomplishing development objectives

Table 66.1
Heavily Indebted Poor Countries:
Amount of Debt Attributable to Official Aid and Other
Government-Backed Schemes, 2000

	Total Long-Term Debt (billion dollars)	Total Public and Publicly Guaranteed Debt (billion dollars)	Total Public and Publicly Guaranteed Debt as a Percentage of Long-Term Debt
Angola	8.76	8.76	100.00
Benin	1.44	1.44	100.00
Bolivia	5.14	4.12	80.15
Burkina Faso	1.14	1.14	100.00
Burundi	1.03	1.03	100.00
Cameroon	7.67	7.36	95.87
Central African Rep.	0.81	0.81	100.00
Chad	1.01	1.01	100.00
Comoros	0.20	0.20	100.00
Congo, Dem. Rep.	7.84	7.84	100.00
Congo, Rep.	3.76	3.76	100.00
Cote d'Ivoire	10.55	9.06	85.94
Ethiopia	5.32	5.32	100.00
Gambia, The	0.43	0.43	100.00
Ghana	5.79	5.53	95.56
Guinea	2.94	2.94	100.00
Guinea-Bissau	0.82	0.82	100.00
Guyana	1.21	1.21	99.67
Honduras	4.90	4.34	88.56
Kenya	5.36	5.18	96.73
Lao PDR	2.45	2.45	100.00
Liberia	1.04	1.04	100.00
Madagascar	4.30	4.30	100.00
Malawi	2.56	2.56	100.00
Mali	2.64	2.64	100.00
Mauritania	2.15	2.15	100.00
Mozambique	6.35	4.60	72.47
Myanmar	5.36	5.36	100.00
Nicaragua	5.86	5.60	95.60
Niger	1.48	1.41	95.41

(continued)

Table 66.1
(continued)

	Total Long-Term Debt (billion dollars)	Total Public and Publicly Guaranteed Debt (billion dollars)	Total Public and Publicly Guaranteed Debt as a Percentage of Long-Term Debt
Rwanda	1.15	1.15	100.00
Sao Tome and Principe	0.29	0.29	100.00
Senegal	2.97	2.96	99.57
Sierra Leone	0.97	0.97	100.00
Somalia	1.83	1.83	100.00
Sudan	9.14	8.65	94.57
Tanzania	6.35	6.33	99.56
Togo	1.23	1.23	100.00
Uganda	3.00	3.00	100.00
Vietnam	11.55	11.55	100.00
Yemen, Rep.	4.52	4.52	100.00
Zambia	4.51	4.45	98.57
Total	157.80	151.31	95.89

SOURCE: World Bank, *World Development Indicators Online*, September 2002, http://publications.worldbank.org/WDI.

because they are less bureaucratic and more in touch with the on-the-ground realities of their clients.

Although channeling official aid monies through PVOs has been referred to as a ''privatized'' form of foreign assistance, it is often difficult to make a sharp distinction between government agencies and PVOs beyond the fact that the latter are subject to less oversight and are less accountable. Michael Maren, a former employee at Catholic Relief Services and U.S. AID, notes that most PVOs receive most of their funds from government sources.

Given that relationship—PVO dependence on government hardly makes them private or voluntary—Maren and others have described how the charitable goals on which PVOs are founded have been undermined. The nonprofit organization Development GAP, for example, observed that U.S. AID's ''overfunding of a number of groups has taxed their management capabilities, changed their institutional style, and made them more bureaucratic and unresponsive to the expressed needs of the poor overseas.''

''When aid bureaucracies evaluate the work of NGOs,'' Maren adds, ''they have no incentive to criticize them.'' For their part, NGOs naturally have an incentive to keep official funds flowing. In the final analysis, government provision of foreign assistance through PVOs instead of traditional channels does not produce dramatically different results.

Microenterprise lending, another increasingly popular program among advocates of aid, is designed to provide small amounts of credit to the world's poorest people. The loans are used by the poor to establish livestock, manufacturing, and trade enterprises, for example.

Many microloan programs, such as the one run by the Grameen Bank in Bangladesh, appear to be highly successful. Grameen has disbursed more than $1.5 billion since the 1970s and achieved a repayment rate of about 98 percent. Microenterprise lending institutions, moreover, are intended to be economically viable, able to achieve financial self-sufficiency within three to seven years. Given those qualities, it is not clear why microlending organizations would require subsidies. Indeed, microenterprise banks typically refer to themselves as profitable enterprises. For those and other reasons, Princeton University's Jonathan Morduch concluded in a 1999 study that ''the greatest promise of microfinance is so far unmet, and the boldest claims do not withstand close scrutiny.'' He added that, according to some estimates, ''if subsidies are pulled and costs cannot be reduced, as many as 95 percent of current programs will eventually have to close shop.''

Furthermore, microenterprise programs alleviate the conditions of the poor, but they do not address the causes of the lack of credit faced by the poor. In developing countries, for example, about 70 percent of poor people's property is not recognized by the state. Without secure private property rights, most of the world's poor cannot use collateral to obtain a loan. The Institute for Liberty and Democracy, a Peruvian think tank, found that where poor people's property in Peru was registered, new businesses were created, production increased, asset values rose by 200 percent, and credit became available. Of course, the scarcity of credit is also caused by a host of other policy measures, such as financial regulation that makes it prohibitively expensive to provide banking services for the poor.

In sum, microenterprise programs can be beneficial, but successful programs need not receive aid subsidies. The success of microenterprise programs, moreover, will depend on specific conditions, which vary greatly from country to country. For that reason, microenterprise projects should be financed privately by people who have their own money at stake rather than by international aid bureaucracies that appear intent on replicating such projects throughout the developing world.

Conclusion

Numerous studies have found that economic growth is strongly related to the level of economic freedom. Put simply, the greater a country's economic freedom, the greater its level of prosperity over time. Likewise, the greater a country's economic freedom, the faster it will grow (Figure 66.1). Economic freedom, which includes not only policies, such as free trade and stable money, but also institutions, such as the rule of law and the security of private property rights, does not only increase income. It is also strongly related to improvements in other development indicators such as longevity, access to safe drinking water, lower corruption, and lower poverty rates (Figure 66.2).

Figure 66.1
Economic Freedom and Economic Growth during the 1990s

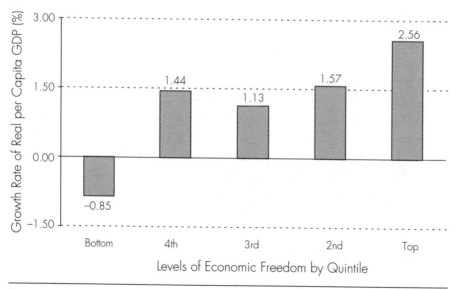

SOURCE: James Gwartney and Robert Lawson, *Economic Freedom of the World: 2002 Annual Report* (Vancouver: Fraser Institute, 2002).

Figure 66.2
Economic Freedom and the Income Level of the Poorest 10%

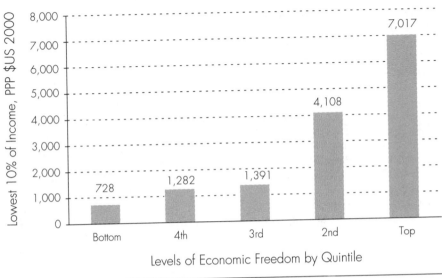

SOURCE: James Gwartney and Robert Lawson, *Economic Freedom of the World: 2002 Annual Report* (Vancouver: Fraser Institute, 2002).

NOTE: PPP = purchasing power parity.

Those developing countries, such as Chile and Taiwan, that have most liberalized their economies and achieved high levels of growth have done far more to reduce poverty and improve their citizens' standards of living than have foreign aid programs.

In the end, a country's progress depends almost entirely on its domestic policies and institutions, not on outside factors such as foreign aid. Congress should recognize that foreign aid has not caused the worldwide shift toward the market and that appeals for more foreign aid, even when intended to promote the market, will continue to do more harm than good.

Suggested Readings

Bhalla, Surjit. *Imagine There Is No Country: Poverty, Inequality and Growth in the Era of Globalization.* Washington: Institute for International Economics, 2002.

Bandow, Doug, and Ian Vásquez, eds. *Perpetuating Poverty: The World Bank, the IMF, and the Developing World.* Washington: Cato Institute, 1994.

Bauer, P. T. *Dissent on Development.* Cambridge, Mass.: Harvard University Press, 1972.

De Soto, Hernando. *The Mystery of Capital: Why Capitalism Triumphs in the West and Fails Everywhere Else.* New York: Basic Books, 2000.

Dollar, David, and Aart Kraay. "Trade, Growth and Poverty." World Bank research paper, March 2001.

Dorn, James A., Steve H. Hanke, and Alan A. Walters, eds. *The Revolution in Development Economics*. Washington: Cato Institute, 1998.

Easterly, William. *The Elusive Quest for Growth: Economists' Adventures and Misadventures in the Topics*. Cambridge, Mass.: MIT Press, 2001.

Gwartney, James, and Robert Lawson. *Economic Freedom of the World 2002*. Vancouver: Fraser Institute, 2002.

International Financial Institution Advisory Commission (Meltzer Commission). "Report to the U.S. Congress and the Department of the Treasury." March 8, 2000. www.house.gov/jec/imf/meltyzer.htm.

Lal, Deepak. *The Poverty of "Development Economics."* London: Institute of Economic Affairs, 1983, 1997.

Lindsey, Brink. *Against the Dead Hand: The Uncertain Struggle for Global Capitalism*. New York: John Wiley & Sons, 2002.

Lukas, Aaron, and Ian Vásquez. "Rethinking the Export-Import Bank." Cato Institute Trade Briefing Paper no. 15, March 12, 2002.

Maren, Michael. *The Road to Hell: Foreign Aid and International Charity*. New York: Free Press, 1997.

Vásquez, Ian. "Ending Mass Poverty." *Economic Perspectives*, U.S. Department of State electronic journal, September 2001, http://usinfo.state.gov/journals/ites/0901/ijee/toc.htm.

———. "Official Assistance, Economic Freedom, and Policy Change: Is Foreign Aid Like Champagne?" *Cato Journal* 18, no. 2 (Fall 1998).

Walters, Alan. "Do We Need the IMF and the World Bank?" Institute of Economic Affairs Current Controversies no. 10, September 1994.

World Bank. *Assessing Aid: What Works, What Doesn't, And Why*. New York: Oxford University Press, 1998.

—Prepared by Ian Vásquez

Contributors

Charles W. Baird is professor of economics at California State University at Hayward.

Doug Bandow is a senior fellow at the Cato Institute and author of *Tripwire: Korea and U. S. Foreign Policy in a Changed World.*

Patrick Basham is a senior fellow in the Cato Institute's Center for Representative Government.

David Boaz is executive vice president of the Cato Institute.

Ted Galen Carpenter is vice president for defense and foreign policy studies at the Cato Institute and author of *Peace and Freedom: Foreign Policy for a Constitutional Republic.*

Barbara Conry is an associate policy analyst with the Cato Institute and coeditor of *NATO Enlargement: Illusions and Reality.*

Edward H. Crane is president of the Cato Institute.

Clyde Wayne Crews Jr. is director of technology studies at the Cato Institute.

Tad DeHaven is a research assistant in fiscal policy studies at the Cato Institute.

Veronique de Rugy is a fiscal policy analyst at the Cato Institute.

James A. Dorn is vice president for academic affairs at the Cato Institute and coeditor of *China's Future: Constructive Partner or Emerging Threat?*

Chris Edwards is director of fiscal policy studies at the Cato Institute.

Ivan Eland is director of defense policy studies at the Cato Institute and author of *Putting "Defense" Back in Defense Policy: Rethinking U. S. Security in the Post–Cold War World.*

Michael Gough is an adjunct scholar of the Cato Institute and coauthor of *Silencing Science.*

Daniel T. Griswold is associate director of the Cato Institute's Center for Trade Policy Studies and coeditor of *Economic Casualties: How U.S. Foreign Policy Undermines Trade, Growth, and Liberty.*

Marie E. Gryphon is an education policy analyst at the Cato Institute.

Leon T. Hadar is a research fellow in foreign policy studies at the Cato Institute.

Scott E. Harrington is professor of insurance and finance and Francis M. Hipp Distinguished Faculty Fellow in the Darla Moore College of Business Administration, University of South Carolina.

Gene Healy is senior editor at the Cato Institute.

Stanley Kober is a research fellow in foreign policy studies at the Cato Institute.

Robert A. Levy is senior fellow in constitutional studies at the Cato Institute.

Brink Lindsey is director of the Cato Institute's Center for Trade Policy Studies and author of *Against the Dead Hand: The Uncertain Struggle for Global Capitalism.*

Timothy Lynch is director of the Cato Institute's Project on Criminal Justice and editor of *After Prohibition: An Adult Approach to Drug Policies in the 21st Century.*

Patrick J. Michaels is professor of environmental sciences at the University of Virginia, senior fellow in environmental studies at the Cato Institute, and author of *Satanic Gases: Clearing the Air about Global Warming.*

Tom Miller is director of health policy studies at the Cato Institute.

William A. Niskanen is chairman of the Cato Institute and author of *Policy Analysis and Public Choice.*

Tom G. Palmer is senior fellow at the Cato Institute.

Charles V. Peña is senior defense policy analyst at the Cato Institute.

Roger Pilon is vice president for legal affairs at the Cato Institute where he holds the B. Kenneth Simon Chair in Constitutional Studies and is director of Cato's Center for Constitutional Studies. He is also editor of *The Rule of Law in the Wake of Clinton.*

Sheldon Richman is editor of *Ideas on Liberty.*

L. Jacobo Rodríguez is financial services analyst at the Cato Institute.

William Ruger is a research fellow in foreign policy studies at the Cato Institute.

David Salisbury is director of the Center for Educational Freedom at the Cato Institute.

John Samples is director of the Center for Representative Government at the Cato Institute.

David Schoenbrod, a former senior attorney and cofounder of the Natural Resources Defense Council and now a professor at New York Law School, is an adjunct scholar of the Cato Institute and author of *Power without Responsibility: How Congress Abuses the People through Delegation.*

Geoffrey F. Segal is director of privatization and government reform at the Reason Foundation.

Michael Tanner is director of health and welfare studies at the Cato Institute, author of *The End of Welfare: Fighting Poverty in the Civil Society,* and coauthor of *A New Deal for Social Security.*

Jerry Taylor is director of natural resource studies at the Cato Institute.

Adam Thierer is director of telecommunications studies at the Cato Institute.

Peter VanDoren is editor of *Regulation* magazine and author of *Chemicals, Cancer, and Choices: Risk Reduction through Markets.*

Ian Vásquez is director of the Project on Global Economic Liberty at the Cato Institute and editor of *Global Fortune: The Stumble and Rise of World Capitalism.*